Debt, Stabilization and Development

Debt, Stabilization and Development

Essays in Memory of Carlos Díaz-Alejandro

Edited by
Guillermo Calvo,
Ronald Findlay,
Pentti Kouri and
Jorge Braga de Macedo

Basil Blackwell
World Institute for Development Economics Research
of
The United Nations University

First published 1989

Basil Blackwell Ltd
108 Cowley Road, Oxford, OX4 1JF, UK

Basil Blackwell Inc.
3 Cambridge Center
Cambridge, Massachusetts 02142, USA

and

World Institute for Development Economics Research (WIDER) –
The United Nations University
Annankatu 42 C, 00100 Helsinki, Finland

British Library Cataloguing in Publication Data

A CIP catalogue record for this book is available from the British Library.

Library of Congress Cataloging in Publication Data

Debt, stabilization, and development: essays in memory of Carlos Díaz-Alejandro / edited by Guillermo Calvo, et al.
p. cm.
Papers from a conference held at WIDER in 1986.
Bibliography: p.
Includes index.
ISBN 0–631–15685–2
1. Debts, External—Developing countries—Congresses. 2. Debts, External—Latin America—Congresses. 3. Economic stabilization—Congresses. 4. Economic policy—Congresses. 5. International trade—Congresses. 6. Díaz-Alejandro, Carlos Federico—Congresses. I. Díaz-Alejandro, Carlos Federico. II. Calvo, Guillermo. III. World Institute for Development Economics Research.
HJ8899.D45 1986
338.9′009172′4—dc19 88–19135
CIP

Typeset in 10 on 11½ pt. Times
by Vera-Reyes. Inc.
Printed in Great Britain by
The Camelot Press Ltd, Southampton

Contents

List of Contributors

Albert Berry	University of Toronto
William H. Branson	Princeton University
Richard A. Brecher	Carleton University
Edward P. Buffie	Vanderbilt University
Guillermo A. Calvo	University of Pennsylvania
Eliana Cardoso	Boston University
Vittorio Corbo	The World Bank
W. Max Corden	School of Advanced International Studies, Johns Hopkins University
Jonathan Eaton	University of Virginia
Sebastian Edwards	University of California, Los Angeles
Barry Eichengreen	University of California, Berkeley
Ronald Findlay	Columbia University
Albert Fishlow	University of California, Berkeley
Ricardo Ffrench-Davis	CIEPLAN, Santiago, Chile
Mark Gersovitz	Princeton University
G. K. Helleiner	University of Toronto
Ronald W. Jones	Rochester University
Vijay Joshi	Oxford University
Louka T. Katseli	University of Athens
Mohsin Khan	International Monetary Fund
Charles Kindleberger	Massachusetts Institute of Technology
Pentti J. K. Kouri	New York University
Anne O. Krueger	Duke University
Paul Krugman	Massachusetts Institute of Technology
I. M. D. Little	Oxford University
Pedro Malan	The World Bank
Jorge Braga de Macedo	University of Lisbon
Carlos Massad	ECLA, Santiago, Chile
Jaime de Melo	The World Bank
Maurice Obstfeld	University of Pennsylvania
José Antonio Ocampo	FEDESARROLLO, Bogota, Columbia
Göran Ohlin	United Nations, New York
Juan Carlos de Pablo	CEMA, Buenos Aires, Argentina
George Perry	The Brookings Institution
Edmund S. Phelps	Columbia University

Gustav Ranis	Yale University
Jeffrey Sachs	Harvard University
Raaj Kumar Sah	Yale University
T. N. Srinivasan	Yale University
Frances Stewart	Oxford University
Joseph E. Stiglitz	Stanford University
Francisco Thoumi	Inter-American Development Bank
John Williamson	Institute for International Economics, Washington, DC

The research conference held at The World Institute of Development Economics Research (WIDER) in the summer of 1986 in memory of Carlos Díaz-Alejandro brought together many of his colleagues and professional associates. To convey the atmosphere of that occasion and introduce this volume, we publish the speech of Dr Lal Jayawardena, Director of WIDER, welcoming participants. The speech touches on his personal recollections of Díaz-Alejandro and their planned research work at WIDER.

WIDER was established as the first research and training centre of The United Nations University in 1984, and started work in Helsinki in 1985. The principal purpose of the institute is to help identify and meet the need for policy-oriented socio-economic research on pressing global and development problems as well as common domestic problems and their interrelationships.

The Editors

Foreword

All of us are so exposed to daily visual assaults in newspapers and on the television screen about incidents of violence and human distress that it is easy to lose the meaning of a truly tragic event. For Shakespeare the fact of death was no tragedy. A tragedy is the plucking away of someone we admire with his life's promise unfulfilled. This was sadly and tragically the case with our friend Carlos, whose memory we honour by this conference.

Perhaps the only people you get to know really well, and who know you, warts and all, are your teachers, student friends of long standing and professional colleagues. In this sense many of you knew Carlos in a way I was never privileged to know him. The detailed reminiscences provided by his teacher, Professor Kindleberger, supplemented by the views of his two oldest student friends, Gerry Helleiner who is here, and Edmar Bacha, who has had to bow out at the last moment, and those on the faculty of Columbia, who together with Pentti Kouri helped me to organize this conference, are a great deal more authoritative than anything I can say.

I missed an opportunity of getting to know Carlos in 1971 when he was due to visit Sri Lanka as a member of the International Labour Organisation (ILO) Employment Strategy Mission that Dudley Seers led in that year, and where I functioned as the local Sri Lankan counterpart to Dudley. Carlos was supposed to handle external sector policy issues for the Mission but at the last minute his visit fell through and I am sure we are the poorer for that.

I met him subsequently in a United Nations setting later in the 1970s and remember calling him up when my compatriot, Gamani Corea, then Secretary General of the United Nations Commission for Trade and Development (UNCTAD), wanted to recruit Carlos to head a research institute he was then thinking of setting up within UNCTAD. Carlos unfortunately was unable to accept.

We met twice afterwards, once in London when we were planning a conference under the auspices of the Third World Foundation, and finally in Toronto a few months before his death, along with Gerry Helleiner. I had then just taken on my appointment in WIDER and was seeking to pick the brains of academic friends about what directions I might most usefully take. Gerry Helleiner was one of the first I reached out to and it was at his suggestion that Carlos came up to Toronto to spend a day with us. Out of that meeting came a visit by Gerry to Helsinki, and ideas about WIDER's work programme in the area of money, finance and trade. We had also planned to collaborate on the range of country studies concerning the adjustment process on which we have just completed a conference that Carlos would have joined Gerry Helleiner and Lance Taylor in directing.[1] Had things gone on course he would have visited us last summer and we would have developed a work programme on capital flight from Latin America which we finalized on the taxi ride we took together to Toronto airport. We also finalized a list of Latin Americans – pupils and colleagues of Carlos – who might usefully be involved in WIDER, and several of them I have since been able to reach out to.

We talked on that last taxi ride also about our friend Pentti Kouri, who took the key initiative in bringing this conference together, and I recall Carlos saying 'Oh yes, Pentti, the great Gatsby' – a remark made with great affection and whimsical good humour in the kind of tone I believe that is true to Charlie Kindleberger's memory of several of Carlos's notes to him.

That just about exhausts my set of personal reminiscences about Carlos.

There was another quality of Carlos's about which a former colleague wrote in notes he made for me; I quote:

> 'Consulted and advised everyone, i.e. Bernstein, Council of Foreign Relations, Ford, ODC, UNCTAD, G24, CEPAL, World Bank.'

This symbolized for me his capacity to relate professionally and personally to a wide variety of people without getting involved in their own personal political or professional differences. As a result Carlos had friends throughout the spectrum of the professional world, ranging from those of a neoclassical and monetarist persuasion, to structuralists, radical Latin American economists and those working in the neo-Marxian and post-Keynesian tradition. I can think of very few others with a similarly wide range of professional contacts who would, if he were asked to declare himself, place himself somewhere in the middle of the left spectrum.

A paper written for us recently on re-thinking the issues concerning liberalization as a policy recommendation for developing countries, has this to say:

> The last reconnaissance was by the late Carlos Díaz-Alejandro (1978) – it amply reflected his scholarly breadth. He concluded that a case can be made for partial severing of an economy's international links, with the ones subject to the knife to be selected as much for political as economic reasons. On more narrowly technical grounds, partial delinking is also the recommendation here – criteria are suggested to single out connections bringing the least benefits or exacting the greatest costs. Creation of new links is also considered, especially in trade and finance between economies of the South.
>
> Thinking about openness involves several levels of abstraction – empirical, theoretical in the sense of bourgeoise economics, political, and ideological. Díaz-Alejandro walked tightropes across them all.

I have since read Carlos's article and I think I know what this means.

Carlos had the capacity to see the several facets of a complex issue, but unlike the two-handed economist who is the bane of policymakers he had no difficulty in converting himself into a one-handed economist when it was necessary to come down on one side or another of a question.

Carlos was what I would like to think of as the quintessential WIDER man, always seeking to bridge ideological and disciplinary divides, which I see as one of WIDER's key roles. WIDER should be open, just as Carlos was, to the major intellectual currents of the profession. It should also, like Carlos, following in a well-known tradition going back to my own mentor, Raul Prebisch, challenge orthodoxy when it can be done with vigour and rigour.

It should finally help support lines of professional enquiry outside the professional mainstream where the simple fact of getting together a critical mass of people who normally work in isolation can often accomplish professional breakthroughs. But it should also insist that all its work be transparent and available for the critical scrutiny of the profession as a whole. It is, I suspect, precisely because Carlos symbolized in his own person the role I have described for WIDER that Gerry Helleiner suggested that we should reach out to him at the beginning of our venture.

I am profoundly sorry that he was unable to take part in our endeavour, but the fact that economists holding the variety of viewpoints represented in this room have made the pilgrimage to Helsinki to honour Carlos is itself a vindication of the approach he would have encouraged me to follow had he been able to join us in the adventure we are engaged in.

Lal Jayawardena

NOTE

1 The country studies have since been published and are available from WIDER; the summary volume by Lance Taylor, entitled 'Varieties of Stabilization Experience' is published by Oxford University Press.

Carlos Díaz-Alejandro: An Appreciation

In June of 1985 I went to two funerals within one week, that of Simon Kuznets and that of Carlos Díaz-Alejandro. While the death of colleagues and friends is always a tragedy, Simon was 84 and Carlos was 48 and that rendered the latter an infinitely sadder occasion.

But there were other links between these two men which are worth recalling. When Carlos first came to Yale in the early 1960s the Growth Center was organizing its so-called Country Analysis Program – Carlos chose Argentina – and we had bi-monthly seminars to figure out how to approach the problem, how much standardization to impose and how much to leave to individual initiative. Simon used to come down from Harvard for these meetings and Carlos soon became his favorite, an economist who respected history, used data carefully, and theory selectively. I well remember those grey winter afternoons at 52 Hillhouse Avenue or at the Ruggles' home when we discussed developing country typologies, development theory and the content of projected data collections.

Carlos later left us for Minnesota, but happily there was to be a second coming and this time as a fully baked senior member of the group, a change which Carlos noted and enjoyed. He came into his own, moved into a bigger office, and the famous flourish of his signature became more pronounced. It was a joy to see that full flowering of the man and his intellect, yet he never lost his common touch, his complete approachability, his concern with the underdogs of the world, most of all his wonderful sense of humor. Increasingly one could see him assume the role of irreplaceable bridge-builder across Hillhouse Avenue, across the generations within the faculty, and as the honest broker between North and South on a larger stage. He was interested in the truth, forever looking for positive sum policy games, never closed or doctrinaire in his approach. In his later years he turned increasingly to history as his inspiration, threatening to withdraw from the beckoning world of policy advisor, consultant, and general savant and to retreat into his scholarly garret. But too many people wanted a piece of him and the best he could manage in his lifetime was to assume the role of 'flying monk'. One can only guess what would have happened if his life cycle had been allowed to play itself out.

Carlos held many causes dear, but prime among these was his passion for maximum intellectual interchange between Latin Americans and Northerners at all levels of educational experience and at all stages of life. In his own low-key and jokey fashion he believed that there was a better world out there and that, working together, with mutual tolerance and open-mindedness, analysts from North and South could overcome vested ideas as well as vested interests and bring us closer to it. If there is one lasting memorial to be built in his name it is to demonstrate our willingness to eschew religious views, whether main-street or side-street, to be open to one another, and to give each other the benefit of the doubt.

This presumably is also the goal to which WIDER is addressed and I would like to thank Lal Jayawardena, its head, and the organizers of this meeting, for helping us take this first step.

Gustav Ranis

1

Introduction

This volume of essays is offered as a tribute to the memory of Carlos Díaz-Alejandro. It is based on the proceedings of a conference held in Helsinki, under the sponsorship of WIDER, in August 1986. All those who attended that conference, dedicated to his memory, were his friends, whose professional work, and to an even greater extent their personal lives, were enriched by contact with the vivifying mind and spirit of this remarkable human being. His unique contribution to the profession consisted not only in the depth and originality of his scholarship, as displayed in numerous books and articles, but in the way he served as a personal clearing house for ideas and anecdotes, theories and problems, between the 'two cultures' of economics in North and Latin America. His personal warmth and charm were irresistible to people of all nationalities, ages and political persuasions, making his death on 17 July 1985, one day short of his 48th birthday, a shattering loss. Readers who did not have the good fortune to meet and know this man can perhaps get some inkling of what he was like from the brief eulogy by Gustav Ranis and the introductory essay (chapter 2) by Charles Kindleberger, whose disciple Carlos remained throughout his career. Professor Kindleberger has often spoken with pride of his many students at MIT, but his favorite was undoubtedly Díaz-Alejandro, who came closest in his own work to the style of the master himself, in the weaving together of history and theory, fact and idea.

The rest of the papers are organized around the related themes of 'Debt, Stabilization and Development', which reflect Díaz-Alejandro's own interests and contributions. What he shared with his mentors – Kindleberger, Albert Hirschman and Arthur Lewis – was the practice of embedding economic problems in their historical context, thus avoiding the sterility of pure logic-chopping that characterizes so much of the economics of his own generation and the next. It is therefore salutary to begin with two explicitly historical essays, one by Albert Fishlow, an almost exact contemporary, and another by one of Díaz-Alejandro's own students at Yale, Barry Eichengreen. Fishlow succeeds magnificently in invoking the spirit and style of Díaz-Alejandro not only by the very choice of the title of his paper, but in substance as well, by his insightful comparison of two historical episodes – the Argentine and Brazilian experiences during the 'Baring Crisis' of the 1890s – which throws light on the related problems of those same countries in the 1980s.

In an era when economists based in North America are liberally giving advice to South America, it is helpful to have available Barry Eichengreen's perceptive evaluation of a pioneer in this sort of endeavor, the 'money doctor' Edward Kemmerer. After these historical perspectives on 'International Lending and the Debt Crisis' we close this opening section with a paper by Jeffrey Sachs that looks at possible solutions to the LDC debt problem in the light of imaginatively drawn analogies with the literature on contract law and industrial organization.

The next section is on 'The Theory and Measurement of International Capital Movements'. Jonathan Eaton and Mark Gersovitz continue their pioneering line of research into the sovereign debt problem in the light of the new approaches to credit rationing and bankruptcy in models with moral hazard and asymmetric information. Díaz-Alejandro had himself used their earlier papers extensively in his own work, finding this approach a refreshing and realistic departure from the more traditional neoclassical framework. In the next paper, Maurice Obstfeld presents some ingenious and sophisticated new econometric tests to assess the extent to which the world capital market is integrated.

The effects of controls on trade and payment regimes and the difficulties involved in removing them without dislocations to the economy are the subject of the next two papers on 'Liberalization of Trade and Exchange Controls'. Sebastian Edwards extends the existing theory on the relationships between controls, the terms of trade and the real exchange rate and gives a comparative analysis of the experience with liberalization of several Latin American countries. William Branson and Jorge Braga de Macedo look at the role of smuggling and other illegal activities in frustrating attempts at reform of the payments system in the Sudan.

The experiences of Argentina, Uruguay and Chile in attempting to stabilize their economies through a pre-announced path for the nominal exchange rate, the famous *tablita*, have stimulated an extensive theoretical and empirical literature. Much of this literature was inspired by Díaz-Alejandro's paper on 'Southern Cone Stabilization Plans', with its prescient warnings on the underlying lack of viability of this approach and on the extent to which governments might be driven to contractionary measures to validate these exchange rate targets.[1] Guillermo Calvo analyzes these issues of credibility problems in the context of some stylized models in his paper on 'Incredible Reforms'. Vittorio Corbo and Jaime de Melo examine thoroughly the relative importance of policy errors and adverse external shocks in the experience of the Southern Cone countries in the other paper in this section on 'Stabilization and Economic Reform'.

The next two papers on 'Macroeconomic Theory and Policy in Developing Countries' are connected with a project that Díaz-Alejandro was planning to engage in together with Max Corden and Ian Little, in which the three of them would supervise a series of studies on the comparative study of macroeconomic stabilization plans in developing countries on behalf of the World Bank. Max Corden's survey, in this volume, of the relevance to developing countries of recent contributions to macroeconomic theory, particularly the 'rational expectations' approach, grew out of this project, as does the paper by Ian Little and Vijay Joshi which examines Indian experience with macroeconomic policy.

The last six papers in the volume are mainly theoretical in character, but all derive their inspiration from policy problems with which Díaz-Alejandro was intimately concerned. First we have two papers on 'New Developments in Open Economy Macroeconomics', by Edmund Phelps and Pentti Kouri. Phelps' paper is concerned with extending the familiar 'workhorse' in this field, the Mundell-Fleming model, to explicitly incorporate a distinct capital-goods sector and an endogenously determined mark-up of selling price over marginal cost, which is shown to have interesting implications for the international transmission of fiscal and other shocks originating in one country. Kouri develops a new dynamic model of the real exchange rate and its effects on the capital account.

The final section is on 'International Trade, Factor Mobility and Development'. Paul Krugman examines the implications for the developing countries of the 'new' trade theory, which involves increasing returns and monopolistic competition, an area in which he has been one of the pioneers. Richard Brecher, co-author with Díaz-Alejandro of a famous paper on the adverse effects of foreign investment in a tariff-distorted economy, discusses a related problem, the welfare effects of foreign investment in an economy characterized by unemployment resulting from a rigid real wage.[2] Ronald Findlay examines the evolving patterns of interdependence between the developed and the developing countries by means of some stylized 'North–South' models. Díaz-Alejandro's characteristically cool and dispassionate analysis of the 'delinking' issue in the North–South dialogue was an inspiration to this and other modelling efforts in this area.[3] Finally Raaj Kumar Sah and Joseph Stiglitz present an ambitious attempt to incorporate such key social variables as trust and honesty in the development process within the framework of a stochastic model.

We would like to express our deepest gratitude to all the authors and discussants for responding so magnificently to our invitation to honor the memory of our dear friend. Special thanks are also due to Dr Lal Jayawardena and his staff at WIDER for their warm hospitality at the Helsinki conference. Mr Ray Fleming handled the arrangements with exemplary thoroughness. We hope that this volume goes some way to compensating all these kind people for their efforts.

NOTES

1 See chapter 13 of A. Velasco (ed.) *Trade, Development and the World Economy: Selected Essays of Carlos Díaz-Alejandro*, Basil Blackwell, Oxford, 1988.
2 'Tariffs, foreign capital and immiserizing growth', chapter 4 of Velasco (ed.).
3 'Delinking North and South: unshackled or unhinged?', chapter 6 of Velasco (ed.).

2

From Graduate Student to Professional Peer: An Appreciation of Carlos F. Díaz-Alejandro

Charles P. Kindleberger

On several occasions when I have been on the same platform with a former student I have found it impossible to resist telling a story I first heard in a class in Logic at the University of Pennsylvania in the spring of 1929. In Ancient Greece a young man wanted to learn sophistry and went to the agora, asked a renowned sophist to give him lessons, cautioning, however, that he had no money for tuition. The older man said that was not a problem and that the two could draw up a contract providing that when the young man won his first case he would pay his teacher. The lessons were duly delivered and absorbed. Years went by, however, and the young man did not practice sophistry. In due course the old teacher needed money, as old teachers will, and took the young man to court. He said, 'Learned judge, you decide. If you decide in my favor the young man must pay me. If, on the other hand, you decide in his favor, he will have won his first case and by the terms of the contract, he must pay.' But the young man had been an assiduous student and countered with the following: 'Learned judge, if you say I won I don't have to pay, and if you say I lose I shall have lost my first case and don't have to pay.'

I do not recall how a logician would solve this case, and perhaps never learned. Its use, of course, is to protect me in the case that a student outshines me. That only shows what a good teacher I am.

The story goes deeper, however, as it illustrates how the hierarchical relationship between teacher and student evolves into one of the equality of professional peers. This metamorphosis seems to me to be a good scaffolding within which to build my memorial of my dear student, advisee, thesis writer, colleague, critic and friend, Carlos F. Díaz-Alejandro, with whom I have had an active interchange at the personal and professional level for twenty-nine and a half years. The attempt runs the risk of excessive intrusion into the account by me. I shall do my best to limit this. I do not claim the pattern is general. I have been and am warm friends with many of my graduate students, but with few to the same extent as with Carlos. Fortunately I am of Anglo-Saxon and not of Latin origin and can keep this account unemotional at least to some degree. But I apologize in advance for any offense on either score.

The first item in the 'file' is a letter from Carlos dated 12 December 1956, asking for an application form for admission to graduate school. The file is one kept on all graduate students so long as they are being closely followed and includes a mass of material: correspondence dealing with admissions and fellowship aid, records of courses taken, grades, general examinations and orals, copies of correspondence about the dissertation and job hunting, letters of recommendation for jobs, fellowships and the like. Some instructors dealing with a student, current or past, turn the correspondence over to the central file. Others do not. When correspondence is kept in a personal file, or discarded in an occasional effort to slim one's accumulation of paper, the graduate file stops. The last item is a letter from Minnesota dated 23 October 1967, addressing me as Professor Kindleberger. The few letters retained in my personal file pick up in 1981 where I am addressed by nickname. I am certain that an abundant exchange took place meanwhile. In addition, I have on my shelves volumes of *Festschriften* and symposia to which we both contributed, and two of Carlos's contributions to symposia at MIT with which I was associated. My last contacts with him in the spring of 1985 were at the March meeting of the American Economic Association Executive Committee which he attended as a member of the Committee on Honors and Awards, at a meeting at the Council on Foreign Relations on 28 April when I spoke and he introduced me, and at the memorial service in Boston for Paul N. Rosenstein-Rodan on 10 May 1985, at which he gave one of the eulogies.

The early entries in the graduate student file are of interest. His home address is given as Havana, Cuba, where he was born on 18 July 1937, forty-eight years less one day before his death in New York City. He spent one year of college at Leicester Junior College, Leicester, Massachusetts, before transferring for three years to Miami University in Oxford, Ohio. The letters from Miami University were fulsome in their praise: 'One of the best minds of all the students that I have taught' (Delbert Snider); 'the best student I have seen at Miami University in seventeen years' (George W. P. Thatcher); 'one of our best economics majors – ever' (Paul M. Vaile). All emphasized his agreeable quality: 'very personable,' 'modest,' 'completely honest with himself and others,' 'mature concerns,' and the like. At the time the admissions procedure of the department required a statement of the purposes that the applicant hoped to serve if admitted for the doctorate program in economics. Carlos's statement, received with his application dated 21 January 1957, included the following excerpts, some prescient, others geographically wide of the mark:

> . . . For the last three years my main interest could be best referred to as 'Political Economy.' I am very hopeful that sound and dynamic economic policies could do a great deal toward improving the general standard of

> living of my country Cuba. This fact has weighed heavily in my decision to select Economics as my career. Furthermore, I am quite interested in government and politics in general . . .
>
> I would like to . . . have a general knowledge in all fields of Economics and mastery of the principles governing economic development and growth, and the governmental policies which would be appropriate to facilitate them . . .
>
> After receiving my Ph.D. degree, I hope to find employment in the Department of Economic Research of the Cuban National Bank. Later on, I would like to formulate, or help to formulate, the policies of that institution and those of the government . . .

Later, on the MIT departmental admissions committee, I was disposed to mark down candidates who wished to do good in the world, below those who were primarily curious as to how the economy worked. Had that standard been applied in the case of Carlos Díaz-Alejandro, it would have resulted in a misallocation.

The MIT program in economics started out connected with industry and was called 'Industrial Economics', a term that startles one today when looking at old forms. Carlos's career as a student of economics got off to a fast start with A's in micro and macro, A−'s in international economics and mathematics for economists and an A+ in economic history. In the second term he recorded two A+'s (a grade that most of the faculty did not mete out), one in economic history from W. W. Rostow who was new, and one in fiscal policy, I believe from Richard Musgrave who was filling in; he was given A's in the second part of micro and in mathematics for economists and another A− in international. Having written off most of his minor in management on the basis of business courses at Miami University, he had time in his second year to take more theory, statistical theory, reading courses in economics, and mathematics in the math department, both in the spring of 1959 and in the spring of 1960 when he was working on the thesis. In graduate courses in linear algebra, methods of applied mathematics, and probability, competing against graduate students in mathematics, he received C's.

The general examinations were taken in May 1959. Grades on these are not communicated to students, except in the vaguest terms, so that professors record what they really think, the better to evaluate students later for letters of recommendation when MIT's reputation is at stake. The average grade has been somewhere between Fair + and Good −. Carlos received Excellent on the international written, Excellent − in theory and in 'fluctuations' (macro) and Good + in development. On the oral he had Excellent in international, and Excellent − to Good + in theory and in development, for an overall grade of Excellent −. A typed comment on the form, that sounds like me, reads:

> Good flow of language. Occasionally too much. No facts on international trade, but handles those supplied very well. Flubbed external economies.

Consensus is that he will make an excellent economist and that with some experience to check the poor ideas the flow will stand him in good stead.

On 11 June 1959, a letter to Professor Snider at Miami University said that MIT was trying to institute a policy of writing people who had recommended students to give an account of their progress. 'It is very easy to do this about Carlos F. Díaz.' His grades in courses and the general examination were detailed, as was his having won a Ford Foundation fellowship to write his dissertation on Brazilian (sic) experience with devaluation, a topic suggested by Alexanda Kafka that would 'make an important contribution to a subject that has just about been exhausted theoretically and where empirical research is very much needed. In short, Mr Díaz stands out at MIT in an outstanding class of graduate students, and we predict a successful career for him in economics.' Knowledgeable economists will be aware that the dissertation in the end dealt with Argentine experience. How the Brazil reference crept in, by error or if the topic was later changed, is lost to me.

At this stage the file turns to two topics: job search and dissertation writing. An attempt to wheedle a fellowship in Demography out of the Population Council for the second year goes back to February 1958 and is too honest to have been effective, saying that his interest in demography was secondary. In December 1959, a note to Carlos talks of a luncheon with J. J. Polak of the International Monetary Fund (IMF) who both had an interest in recruiting Carlos and a suggestion about the relevance of Mexican experience for the absorption doctrines that Carlos was studying in Argentina. In 1960–1 I was on sabbatical, from which I brought back exchanges of letters of May and July discussing firstly the content of the thesis, but secondly and more important, whether Yale University would regard the thesis as finished as deemed necessary for him to start there as an assistant professor. In October 1961 a letter to him discussed how he could get portions of the thesis published. Perhaps the topic was too narrow for publication in the series that the MIT department was trying to get started for outstanding theses. I suggested sending it to the DiTella Foundation in Buenos Aires to see if they would be interested, or to the International Finance Section at Princeton where Professor Machlup might be interested in it for the support it gave him against Sidney Alexander (not much) in the clash between the elasticity and the absorption approaches. It appears from correspondence of July 1962 that he had shortened it too much for the Princeton series which seems to have turned it down, and now needed to loosen it up for the MIT series that accepted it in principle. Some correspondence in the file expresses the doubt of one professor that the thesis was of broad enough interest to merit subsidized publication, but apparently the commitment had already been made.

The program that Carlos joined at Yale was that of the Growth Center, headed originally by Lloyd G. Reynolds and later by Gustav Ranis. The idea was to work out a set of statistics to be collected by different researchers on a comparable basis, with each then writing a monograph on a separate country. Carlos was assigned to Argentina, and after a year of preliminary research in New Haven, went off thence. He had not finished the revision of the dissertation, but thought that this could be better done after his year in Buenos Aires.

The flight of Batista and the takeover by Fidel Castro in 1959 had given him both anguish and notoriety. After his first year at MIT he had gone to Havana, on 11 August 1958.

> I am enjoying a pleasant summer, dividing working hours almost equally between the beach and my father's business. I have managed to do some reading, but the heat has taken all ambition out of me.

A letter from him dated 13 May 1961, when I was on sabbatical, largely about the thesis, remarked: 'I have retired from my public life as a speechmaker. As a matter of fact I loathe to discuss politics, especially Cuban politics. Now I am against Castro, but with little hope.' A letter recommending him to a department of economics as late as 30 November 1964, sums up his Cuban connection in these terms:

> He is a native Cuban, and he took the Castro Bay-of-Pigs business seriously and hard, disturbed over the policies of the two governments and unhappy at seeing his country torn up.

Ten days later a letter to another university adds slightly to this picture:

> A Cuban, he was pro-Castro for some time, changed at about the same time as Pazos, who had a strong and good influence on him.

That letter goes on to make an economic point, '. . . He is likely to be underpriced now, as contrasted with three years from now. And he is very good indeed, one of the stars of the best class we have had at MIT in my sixteen years. ______ is after him, but he tells me that he might stay another year or two at Yale. First class, or as we used to say at O.S.S., *Erste Klasse*.'

These letters of November and December 1965 were a prelude to a flurry of letter-writing in 1966. On 1 February I wrote to Professor Powell who had asked for an appraisal as Yale contemplated a reappointment after a three-year stint.

> Professor Díaz-Alejandro is a very much sought-after young man. For one thing, he is clearly the top young man in the Latin American field. I understand that he has this year, at the completion of his first appointment from Yale, received seven offers of appointment. But Díaz-Alejandro is more than a Latin American economist: he is a distinguished theorist generally in the fields of international trade and economic development. I know nothing about his teaching ability, but judging by his interest, enthusiasm, energy and friendliness, I confidently estimate that it is of a high order. He is perhaps less dedicated to theory than B______, J______, M______ and V______ of my students, but in his own way he is every bit their equal in excellence.

(This last was offered in response to a specific request for comparisons.)

A month later Professor Powell asked for and received another letter as Carlos had received a good offer from another university, and Yale was preparing to appoint him an associate professor for a five-year term. The file has letters to Professor O. N. Brownlee at Minnesota, including perceptive remarks by Robert Solow:

> During his years here, Díaz was one of our best and liveliest students. . . . The characteristic thing about Díaz is that his primary orientation is always toward policy, but unlike so many people with that interest he has a good analytical mind and uses it on policy problems. . . . You can be sure that Díaz will never turn out soft-headed stuff, nor will he turn out work that is remote from real life issues.
>
> Combined with all this, he is an extraordinarily pleasant, alert and civilized person . . .

In the end, Carlos decided to go to Minnesota where he stayed until 1969, at which time he returned to Yale as a full professor. In 1983 he moved to Columbia. In the spring of 1985 I wrote more letters for him for Harvard and Princeton. When he died he had accepted an appointment to Harvard but had not moved to Cambridge. I leave to his curriculum vitae the many consultantships, members of commissions, boards, advisory committees and the like with which he was associated, both in Latin America and in the United States.

Graduate students of course teach each other, but occasionally a teacher contributes to the process as catalyst. The file has a letter of 12 July 1961, addressed to Carlos that says in part:

> You will be interested to learn that I left your two chapters with Egon Sohmen who returned them to me with the following characteristically slashing remarks:
>
> 'I enclose the two chapters (II and III) by Díaz. He is obviously a very competent man. Where I do not agree, of course, is his unquestioning acceptance of the view that devaluation must always increase the price level, hence lower the standard of living of the majority. I thought this had been disproved in the meantime. He lacks an understanding (so widespread, alas, a short-coming) of resource allocation and its consequences.'

The last exchange in the file starts with a letter from me on 10 February 1967, saying:

> I got in a bit of a dispute with a student over your thesis. His paper, my comment and a letter from him are appended. I think it was OK of you to assume that there would be hoarding in the short run and that the substitution effect in the short run was unimportant. He does not. Would you judge whether this paper should have received an A? How do you like the thought that students are working away at your writings while you take your ease?

His reply to the last point on 14 March read:

> The thought of students working away at my writings makes me feel old and bloated.

On 23 March, he wrote a long and thoughtful letter to the student on the substance of the argument.

The paths from studentship to professional equality are many and varied, and my association with Carlos included acknowledgements in prefaces, inscriptions in presentation copies of books, conferences, his participation in my projects, mine in his, papers together in conference volumes and *Festschriften*, citations of him by me, my serving as a critic of volumes in which he was represented and so forth, too many forms to summarize in orderly fashion. Some parts of the transition are observable in the material in my files and on my shelves.

When does a student call his professor by his first name? It depends, of course, on the brashness of the student and the warmth of the professor. Carlos seems to me to have been unusually shy. No letter in the graduate student file (up to 1967) uses my Christian name. One to the graduate student in 1967 refers to me as CPK which is an efficient compromise. Because of the gap between the graduate student file and the 1982 letters, I cannot tell exactly when he shifted. But evidence from the inscriptions puts it before March 1977.

This transitional progress in intimacy is mirrored with a lead in the inscriptions in the three volumes he gave me. *Exchange-Rate Devaluation* is mockingly presented:

> To the Chief Presbyterian
> from one of his apprentices,
> with respect and affection.
> Carlos F. Díaz-A.
> Minneapolis, April 13, 1966

The mockery is stepped up in the inscription in *Essays on the Economic History*:

> Tibi Professori Carolo Kindleberger
> exemplare magistro, magnanimo duci, viro honesto, anglosaxoni
> cultivato et cultivatori,
> Carolus Díaz-Alejandro
> maxima salutem dici tibique hoc donum praesentat.
> Datum ad Novum Portun
> X, MCMLXX A.D.

For *Colombia*, the teasing is less formal:

> To Sarah and Charlie,
> from their populist step-son
> Carlos F.
> Princeton, March 5, 1977

and for the reprint of 'Latin American debt: I don't think we are in Kansas any more' (*Brookings Papers*, 1984):

To the Master CPK
Abrazos
Carlos 'F'

with the 'F' circled and an arrow pointing to it to remind me that I had more than once addressed him with the wrong middle initial.

I suspect that teasing is a means of effecting the transition from the structured hierarchical relationship to one of equality. In particular I recall an episode when Carlos and Ronald Findlay cooperatively worked me over. I was giving a dinner seminar at Columbia, in some year I could perhaps reconstruct but it would be trouble, perhaps 1969, and was seated by Carlos, who had come down from New Haven. Memory does not suffice to indicate which took what role. One, say Carlos, took a piece of paper and wrote out an enormous mathematical expression, laden with integrals, complex fractions, exponentials, etc., concluding 'Therefore CPK is right.' In reply, Ron Findlay drew a three-dimensional diagram replete with surfaces of various shapes tangent to one another, and curves, some through axes, others asymptotic, and so on, adding 'Therefore CPK is right.' On occasion the mockery went public: his puff for the jacket of a book that he calls 'a collection of Kindlebergeriana' reads in part 'Aficionados of multinationals, scholars, teachers and other Kindleberger groupies. . . .'

To watch the maturing friendship of students is a lagniappe for the teacher, or caviar for the general. Jaroslav Vanek and the late Egon Sohmen roomed together in the mid-1950s at MIT and kept up a long friendship until Sohmen died in 1976. Ronald Findlay and Carlos Díaz-Alejandro saw a lot of each other in New York even before Carlos left Yale for Columbia.

They both came to Boston on 12 July 1971 and sat together I judge from the fact that their signatures on the flyleaf of a presentation volume are one under the other. But I especially envied my friend Max Corden who had them both at Nuffield College in the same term in 1977, if I remember correctly, when Corden, Findlay and Díaz-Alejandro produced geometric international trade theory by the ream, month after month. A typical externality of this period is contained in a letter from Corden to me: 'He was such a wonderful companion – we got to know him really well when he was at Nuffield College with Ronald – Dorothy felt he was like a brother. And then, a really civilised economist. . . .' Many teachers, but especially I, have difficulty with depth perception among students, knowing who were contemporaries and knew each other and how well. With Carlos, the problem was not troublesome.

CPK as impresario: In the spring of 1969 I spent half the time in the Economics Department and half the time in the Sloan School of Management at MIT, in the latter capacity organizing a series of lectures on the multinational corporation that later appeared as a book (*The International Corporation*, MIT Press, Cambridge, Massachusetts, 1971). Carlos contributed a lecture that appeared as 'Direct foreign investment in Latin America.' My preface states about Carlos:

> He brings to the troubled question of US investment in Latin America wide experience for a young man, a knowledge of history, and a well-honed kit of economic tools. But the heart of the matter is political. A long history of cavalier treatment of Latin American individuals, traditions, governments, and business by American businessmen corrupts attempts to keep the discussion on an economic level, and even then such legislation as the Hickenlooper amendment leads Latin Americans to believe that the United States turns economic disputes into political shows of strength.

Seven years later, a weekend conference at MIT's Sloan School on multinational firms emanating from small countries, – to eliminate some part of the political element, – resulted in Tamir Agmon and me editing *Multinationals from Small Countries* (MIT Press, Cambridge, Massachusetts, 1977). Carlos looked through the telescope from the other end, writing on 'Foreign direct investment by Latin Americans.'

CFDA as impresario: In 1982, Rosemary Thorp and Carlos planned the session on Latin American economic history during the 1930s at the 44th International Congress of Americanists, held in Manchester, England, and I was asked to sum up the various papers at the conclusion after Carlos had set the keynote in a paper entitled 'Latin America in the 1930s.' The papers appeared in Rosemary Thorp (ed.) *Latin America in the 1930s: The Role of the Periphery in World Crisis* (Macmillan, London, 1984). By this time I was teasing him. His paper for the *Festschrift* in honor of Sir Arthur Lewis [Mark Gersovitz, Carlos F. Díaz-Alejandro, Gustav Ranis and Mark R. Rosenzweig (eds.) *The Theory and Experience of Economic Development*, George Allen & Unwin, London, 1982] had been on 'Latin America in the Depression, 1919–39,' and another article was entitled 'Latin America in the 1940s.' I asked whether he was planning to do the economic history of Latin America decade by decade, with the more interesting decades assigned two papers each.

What I found especially flattering was that Carlos's interests seemed to evolve in the same direction as mine have done, though of course in a different region. He worked on trade and foreign exchange, on economic history and ultimately on financial history, including financial crises. We moved in the same circles, and found ourselves writing for the same *Festschriften* – for Paul N. Rosenstein-Rodan, for Arthur Lewis and for Robert Triffin. My records show that we attended four conferences together: on the frontiers for research in international economics in Princeton, on economic information in Kiel, on small open economies in Dublin (1979) and, as already mentioned, on Latin America in the 1930s, when Carlos gave the opening paper and I the closing one. My paper for Kiel was sent to Carlos for comment before the event as evidenced by its embellishment in footnote 33 by a reference to Jorges Luis Borges' short story, 'The

Library of Babel' (in *Ficciones*, Grove Press, New York, 1962), provided by Carlos. The Dublin conference was difficult to place in time because there was no single conference volume and such papers as were published appeared separately. I pinned the date down by consulting my family photograph album which has several pictures of Carlos with me and Ronald Jones, and with Professor and Mrs Dermot McAleese. In the course of the search I found two other snapshots of Carlos, one of him and me (and Jürg Niehans) at a party given by Rudiger Dornbusch on 8 January 1976, and another showing him with very long hair at some party in Budapest dated 29 January 1976 (the picture is cropped and some of the message on the reverse side is lost).

However, my greatest profit and pleasure came not from public occasions but from exchanging papers in draft, or reprints, and commenting freely in correspondence. It is regrettable that in retiring from MIT and taking papers home I disposed of most of these files.

A 1981 letter was kept as a personal treasure.

> Dear Charlie,
>
> What a good 'Life'!
>
> Again I was amazed by how many of what I thought were my insights (in grad. school one learns more from fellow students than from faculty, etc.) came from you.
>
> Also blushingly enjoyed pp. 243–244. [This passage refers to the distinction of MIT graduates in international economics and mentions Carlos along with Bhagwati, Branson, Chacholiades, Findlay, Jones, Hymer, Magee, Mundell, Sohmen and Vanek.]
>
> When I grow up I want a Life like that!

The 1982 correspondence between Stockholm and New Haven covered the 1930s in Latin America, financial integration, financial repression. The letter of 15 November 1982 gives reasons for leaving Yale for Columbia, including pull factors: Findlay, Calvo, Bhagwati, Manhattan, and push factors: New Haven. My letter of 10 November starts,

> Dear Carlos,
>
> You really believe in international multilateral balancing. I ask for comments on my paper. You provide them not. You ask for comments on yours, assuming, I guess, that you will comment on papers of others and they will do so for me . . .

The letter of 22 November 1982, commenting on the Edmar Lisboa Bacha and Carlos paper 'International financial intermediation: A long and tropical view' (Princeton *Essays in International Finance*, no. 147, May 1982), which was not sent, starts out:

> Dear Carlos,
>
> I have finally caught up with your (with Bacha) Princeton essay which I like a lot. I cannot resist, however, one or two pot shots.

Typed across the head of the letter is 'Not sent. But the essay is far too optimistic.' I assume the reason for suppressing it was that there were too many niggling pot shots and that the total gave the wrong impression. In February 1983 there was a letter from him on my draft Zahid Hussain lecture, largely on French and British financial integration, which is all I know, in which he listed five criticisms from the point of view of a Moslem Punjabi. Point (e) starts, 'Last but not least (remember my application to enter MIT in 1957!).' I did not, and did not have the application handy. Now that I do I cannot see what he meant. Nonetheless the remark suggests that inside every professional peer there is a student who sometimes reacts to a teacher.

After 1983 there is a gap until 1985. I had sent him for comment some draft lectures on international capital movements. He wrote or said hastily when we met in New York on 28 April, that it needed more on financial intermediation in the Third World lending instance. I asked what was meant, but there was not time in the larger group to explain. On 6 May 1985 came the last written communication from him in which he regressed for a minute to the role of student again:

> Dear Charlie,
> I was very impressed by your CFR session, and even awed. I worked during the morning on an eloquent and witty introduction, but so many of your old buddies unnerved me, and I ended up feeling and acting like a callow youth.

Then the professional friend takes over, answering my question:

> In the old days, Argentines bought Argentine bonds in London at arm's length. Today, Chase Manhattan lends to Argentina, and private Argentines have bank accounts with Chase . . .

The letter ends:

> Jerry Green [head of the Harvard Department of Economics] called to inform me that Bok approved my appointment. I await a call from Mike Spence [Dean of Arts and Sciences] to make sure they're not planning to ask me to teach Spanish five days a week. One never knows with that Imperial university.
>
> Abrazos
> Carlos F

Sometimes the complimentary ending was spelled 'Abracos' instead of with a 'z,' and sometimes it was accompanied by 'Venceremos.' In all that he wrote by holograph his liveliness and warmth shone.

It would be good to have a broad view of Carlos from *his* students. I was lucky enough to run into one, Michael Klein, who worked as his research assistant at Columbia when he was writing 'Latin American debt: Not in Kansas any more.' I asked him to write me a letter. He writes of Carlos's keen insights, wide-ranging knowledge and his entertaining wit, 'the enthusiasm, skill and joy that Carlos brought to the problem'. But he referred to Carlos only as 'Professor Díaz-Alejandro.' José Antonio Ocampo wrote a dissertation under Carlos at Yale and became his peer, writing a paper on Colombia in the 1930s for the Rosemary Thorp symposium. Alas, too few can share that rite of passage.

His draft paper of April 1983, 'Goodbye financial repression, hello financial crash,' says on p. 7 'the financial history of Latin America remains to be written. . . .' I believe he would have written it. We are the poorer for our lack of such a history. Far more we are impoverished in spirit by the loss of the man.

The theme of the transition from graduate student to professional peer is, of course, only a peg on which to hang my appreciation of Carlos as an economist and as a person. Solow is right in emphasizing his concern for policy, rarely combined so effectively with strong analytical talent, a sense of history and empathy for those left behind in the distribution of income and wealth. He and Corden are both right in pointing to his civilized nature. I had intended to call attention to the imaginative illustrations by his artist brother Ramon Alejandro for the frontispiece of *Colombia* and *Essays on the Economic History*, – a brother he frequently visited in Paris. Michael Klein reminds us of his wit, and I should add, ability to turn an arresting phrase. I have left no room in this account for his courage as a Dissenting Member of the Kissinger Commission on Central America, on which he spoke eloquently and wittily in an interview in *The New Journal*, published at Yale (vol. 16, no. 4, 3 February 1984), an assignment representing still another facet of his complex personality, a sense of duty. Carlos was the paragon of Latin American economists and of economists generally, as student, colleague, collaborator and friend.

In my drawer of stationery supplies is a mailing label for adhering to a large manila envelope addressed to Carlos at Columbia. I must have planned to mail him a paper, and then delivered it by hand. Its presence, now useless, is a poignant reminder of our present emptiness.

NOTES

I acknowledge with thanks the comments on an earlier draft by Ronald Findlay and Barbara Solow.

Part I

INTERNATIONAL LENDING AND THE DEBT CRISIS: HISTORICAL PERSPECTIVES AND CONTEMPORARY SOLUTIONS

3

Lessons of the 1890s for the 1980s

Albert Fishlow

Introduction

The developing country debt problem of the 1980s has led to a resurgent interest in past episodes of financial crisis. This search for illumination is highly appropriate. What is a novelty in the post-1945 experience, because of smaller and largely public flows to developing countries until the 1970s, has ample precedent earlier.

Indeed, the principal locus of the current problem, Latin America, has been the scene of recurrent episodes of financial expansion and subsequent contraction: the 1820s, the 1870s, the 1890s and the 1930s stand out. The 1830s and 1850s are missing both because of the concentration of inflows to the United States in those decades, and because of reaction to the defaults of the 1820s. In a regular fashion, inversely associated with long swings of domestic investment in Great Britain, foreign capital flowed to peripheral countries to finance infrastructure construction and there then followed a crisis of overextension and a period of quiescence.[1]

The comparison of the current decline in incomes in Latin America with the Great Depression experience is an obvious one, a discussion to which Carlos Díaz was an early and prominent contributor. His sympathies were clear as was his penchant (albeit sometimes qualified) for the indigenous policy responses then, and again more recently, adopted by many of the Latin American countries confronting an adverse international environment: 'In a world of erratic changes of terms of trade, unpredictable protectionism, and high capital mobility, commitment to fixed exchange rates, unlimited convertibility, and gold-standard-type monetary rules seems rash and risky.'[2]

The decade of the 1890s, and its possible lessons, has received less scrutiny. Charles Kindleberger's recent treatment helps rectify that imbalance. His conclusion that 'of all the crises in the last hundred years or so, [the crisis of 1890–3] most closely resembles the difficulties the world is passing through in 1983,' justifies at least one more look.[3] My perspective, moreover, will be another. I intend to focus only upon the comparative experiences of Argentina and Brazil during the period as a basis for concluding observations about the relevance of the 1890s for the 1980s.

Section 1 provides a highly condensed story of the economic fluctuations of the two countries at the end of the nineteenth century. Both Argentina and Brazil, but with important differences, experienced booms in the 1880s followed by debt crises and significant downturns in the 1890s. Section 2 analyzes the relative contribution of internal policies and changes in the external environment, in particular, commodity prices and access to capital markets, to the adjustments that became necessary. Section 3 examines the behavior of capital markets more closely. A special interest is shown in the valuation of Argentine and Brazilian securities on the London market, and the implications of market opinion for new capital inflows. Section 4 turns to the internal adjustment in the two countries, and the role of real income and wage decline in facilitating increased production of exports and import substitutes and reduction in demand for imports. Section 5 examines parallels with the present situation.

1. Stylized History

1.1 Upturn and Crisis

The last quarter of the nineteenth century saw a progressive integration of peripheral producers of raw materials into the international economy. British capital was a central ingredient in this process. It financed construction of railways that brought new land into production and permitted recipient countries to live beyond their means through import surpluses. High incomes attracted the immigrant labor that was needed to populate resource-rich countries and extend the world economic frontier. That combination yielded a subsequent growing supply of primary exports that justified the initial investments and established the basis for continuing economic growth in the peripheral countries and for rapid expansion of global trade.

Migration and capital flows were, however, uneven. Infrastructure investment required long gestation periods before it began to pay. Commodity prices were subject to fluctuation. The supply of foreign capital was susceptible to wild enthusiasms, and thus not surprisingly, to their disappointment. This long swing was particularly pronounced in the 1880s and 1890s in Latin America. Between 1886 and 1890 some £130 million of calls for portfolio investment in the region were recorded in the London market; in 1891–5, the comparable total is £26 million.[4]

Argentina and Brazil were active participants in this process of peripheral development. They were the largest recipients of foreign investment in the region. Estimates suggest that £63 million of issues in 1886–90 were destined for Argentina, and £24 million for Brazil.[5] In the words of a prominent historian of Argentina, 'the British investment during the 1880s expanded at a rate astonishing by the standards of that age and greater than during any subsequent decade.'[6] There was, in addition, direct investment not recorded in the conventional financial operations. There was even purchase of local securities. In particular, a considerable proportion of the Argentine *cedulas* denominated in domestic currency and issued by mortgage banks to provide credit to rural producers circulated abroad.

The most salient results of this substantial inflow of capital show up directly in physical indexes of railroad construction: the Argentine network about doubled from 5800 km in 1886 to 12 500 km in 1891; for Brazil, the corresponding increase was from 7600 km to 10 600 km.[7] The corollary to internal transport improvement was an expansion of international trade. Argentine exports grew in volume at an annual rate of 9 per cent between 1886 and 1890, but confronted weak prices. In Brazil, nominal receipts rose at a comparable rate, but because of rising prices rather than quantities. Increased coffee production from the new frontier was to come, but with a lag owing to the time required for trees to mature and bear.[8]

External trade was not the only measure of heightened economic activity. Immigration was another. Net immigration into Argentina reached a peak of 220 000 in 1889, a pre-1914 maximum, after averaging more than 100 000 in the four previous years. Gross Brazilian immigration, where there was a lesser seasonal offset, peaked at 217 000 in 1891, and averaged 90 000 in the preceding four years.[9] Contemporary accounts also corroborate rising domestic investment and proclaim a period of economic progress.

Yet, despite these signs of prosperity, the second half of the 1880s was not entirely tranquil in the two countries. Paradoxically, the favorable external environment lent itself to domestic economic experimentation and sharp political discord.

In Argentina, economic policy was frankly expansionary to the verge of excess. The country had abandoned the gold standard in 1884 in favor of an inconvertible monetary standard. That removed the responsibility for equilibrating the balance of payments from the money supply to the exchange rate. In the absence of that discipline, easy credit prevailed. Note issue increased from 75 million paper pesos in 1885 to 245 million in 1890, in part the consequence of provincial banks that were opened in response to new, less stringent requirements. Public expenditure contributed in the same direction; central government deficits increased from 30 per cent of receipts in 1886 to almost 50 per cent in 1888 and 1889. In response to such expansionary impulses, foreign exchange moved to a premium, first sharply upward to 37 per cent in 1885 and thereafter in a narrower range until upward pressures in 1889 and 1890. The progressively higher gold premiums themselves contributed to increased government outlays. External debt service, already almost 40 per cent of expenditures in the late 1880s, was obligated in gold while revenues, until 1891, were received in paper.[10]

The Baring Crisis in November 1890 thus had been preceded by what John Williams, in an uncharacteristic flourish, termed a 'financial and monetary debauch.' London observers, and the market, had taken notice of Argentine inflation and exchange rate depreciation. Holders of peso cedulas experienced capital losses, and could not help but do so. Yet there was little need for domestic restraint so long as capital flows continued to underwrite rising expenditure. Ferns characterizes the government of President Juarez Celman as 'the least qualified imaginable to undertake measures of the severity required and the Argentine community of 1888–9 the least likely to endure them.' The choice was not entirely theirs. Efforts by the government to obtain increased financial support abroad as the situation deteriorated in 1889 were conditioned by foreign bankers upon adoption of an orthodox stabilization program. Contraction, and at foreign behest, was unacceptable to a political leadership that had already broached the possibility of paying the 1872 loan in paper pesos as a means of unilaterally imposed debt relief. Domestic opposition to the Celman presidency mounted, as stories of corruption and private gain from external borrowing circulated. A belated Argentine austerity proposal started a new round of international negotiations that again failed because of government inability to follow through. In July an insurgency occurred, and Celman resigned on 6 August, ushering in a new government committed to more responsible domestic economic policies.[11]

The Baring Crisis broke in November 1890 before these could take effect. Baring Brothers was the victim of an excessive faith in uninterrupted Argentine expansion. The firm underwrote and continued to hold an 1888 Buenos Aires waterworks issue that the market was unprepared to absorb in view of mounting doubts about the Argentine situation. Barings was eased into an orderly insolvency through timely intervention of the British government, the Bank of England and the London banking community. That solution, though it averted a major international financial crisis, did nothing for the continuing flow of resources to Latin America, which henceforth virtually ceased. Argentina at the end of 1890 was faced with the specter of a drastic balance of payments adjustment without the assistance of finance. The country soon was forced to suspend external debt service, and began negotiations on its debt obligations.

The Brazilian route to its eventual Funding Loan in 1898 that staved off default was similar in respect of contributing domestic expansion, but different in the severity and timing of the reduction in capital inflows. Internal economic policy in the 1880s began from a conspicuously and consciously conservative basis. Fiscal deficits, and they were incurred, especially between 1882 and 1886, were financed by internal and external debt in preference to monetary issue. The underlying philosophy was bullionist; the proximate objective was restoration of exchange convertibility at the official 1846 parity of 27 pence per milreis. So long as the exchange rate remained below that point, as it did, gold standard rules called for domestic monetary contraction.[12]

Quickening economic expansion in the second half of the decade gave rise to demands for increased credit. An internal debate ensued between the bullionists and those seeking a more elastic supply of money to attend the needs of commerce. To this impulse was joined another, and powerful, current. Abolition of slavery, finally voted for in 1888, gave rise to new pressures from powerful agricultural interests. They sought monetary accommodation not merely to sustain a new wage-based labor market, but also to permit cheap credit in order to compensate for the capital losses from emancipation. Those concerns were given increased weight by the rising political uncertainty that threatened the continuity of the Empire: conservatives suddenly had an enhanced voice. On the other side, the strong balance of payments, because of favorable coffee prices and capital inflows, translated into accumulating reserves and a strengthening exchange rate that began to approximate par. Matters were ripe for a more expansive monetary policy.

It awaited the proclamation of the Republic in November 1889 for the definitive conversion to monetary heterodoxy. Exchange rate convertibility was no longer the principal objective of domestic policy. Developmental necessities would determine the money supply. The domestic interest rate would be the measure of its adequacy. The exchange rate, linked to the balance of payments, would take care of itself as export potential grew. Under the guidance, and defense, of Finance Minister Rui Barbosa, the supply of money expanded by 94 per cent in 1890, and by a further 42 per cent in 1891. Special financial provisions were extended to industry. A boom took shape, one in which real growth and speculative activity merged in what has come to be known as the Encilhamento.[13]

The milreis underwent a rapid devaluation in 1890 and 1891, and continued its descent until 1898. External confidence was shaken not only by these expansionary policies of the new Republic but also by a succession of political uncertainties that led to the resignation of the first Republican president, Marshall Deodoro. This is not to mention the negative effects of the Baring Crisis upon evaluations of creditworthiness in Latin America and elsewhere. Not long thereafter came the Frank rebellion and its military repression in 1893 and 1894. The surprise is that despite such a cumulation of internal and external problems, Brazil avoided a decisive default.

Until 1897, through a combination of increased internal taxes, higher tariff collections and continued, if limited, access to foreign loans, the government met its obligations. It did so despite increasing debt service due to exchange rate depreciation. Government requirements for sterling to make its external payments more than doubled between 1892 and 1894, and amounted to more than 100 per cent of the 1894 trade surplus. A new external loan in 1895 staved off disaster, but did not prevent debt service charges from absorbing a fourth of total federal government receipts in 1897. The government sought another loan, but was not encouraged by its London bankers. Brazil eased into its virtual default with a whimper rather than a bang.

1.2 Crisis Resolution and Adjustment

The Argentine problem, because of its direct link with the Baring crisis, was an object of immediate attention from the London bankers. Baring's ability to liquidate its Argentine holdings in an orderly fashion rested upon restoration of confidence in the Argentine economy and in the prospects for responsible governance. In addition, the continued profitability of the extensive British foreign investment in the railways depended upon reversing the accelerating gold premium that reduced sterling profits. An international bankers' committee was immediately put together, chaired by Lord Rothschild. In the absence of French and German concurrence, whose representatives preferred a less generous new loan, a settlement was reached in March 1891.

The agreement provided for a loan of £15 million to enable the federal government to continue to meet its debt service for a period of three years. The domestic counterpart of these resources was to be used partially by the Argentine government to reduce the volume of currency in circulation. The understood rationale for such external support was that the Argentine default was primarily developmental: a temporary embarrassment that would later easily be made good by economic growth. Sound internal policies would hasten the end of the liquidity problem.[14]

Despite the Rothschild loan, prices of Argentine securities continued to slide, and the economy did not evince signs of real recovery. There were two reasons for this. One was that Argentina's domestic policy continued to be unsettled and the other was that political uncertainties intruded. Landowners favored an inflationary environment, for their mortgage debts were fixed for the most part in national pesos, and thus had diminished with rising domestic prices. Devaluation also provided gains from increased export profits to the extent that domestic wages did not fully keep pace with higher export prices. In the midst of output decline, and with a presidential election ahead, domestic deflation was not a popular course.

But even the £15 million loan, although viewed as generous by creditors, was inadequate after the much larger voluntary capital inflows before the crisis. In 1888–9, those had averaged £40 million annually, and in 1890, £15 million for the single year. The Rothschild solution corresponded only to the interest due from the federal government, excluding the foreign exchange needs of provincial governments and private foreign investors. Relative to total debt service, the loan amounted only to about a third of Argentine obligations. It thus could not prevent the dramatic decline in imports of more than 50 per cent in 1891, and a corresponding fall in real income. Rather, the loan alleviated immediate pressures on the federal government to increase its share of domestic income on the basis of increased taxes and/or lower expenditures. The Rothschild agreement therefore did not avert a surge of anti-British sentiment, the British being blamed for the internal economic depression.

Many, and not only Argentines, felt that a more traditional default would have been preferable. The American consul wrote from Buenos Aires:

> I do not think the government has, or will have for several years to come, the available resources to meet the service of its obligations, with all the

> economies it may practice and with all the surplus it may be able to accumulate from increased tariff and heavy internal taxation. I do not believe it will find itself in much better condition at the end of the three years' *moritorium* to resume the payment of interest on its bonded and *cedula* indebtedness than it is now. The *moritorium*, which seems to have been primarily intended to help the fallen house of Baring Brothers & Co., or rather the creditors of that house, has, so far as the Argentine Republic is concerned, only postponed pay day and ultimate liquidation and quite uselessly increased the bonded debt of the nation. It would have been a public relief for the Government to have defaulted outright and thus to have at once placed itself in a position to receive overtures from its creditors, leaving the house of Baring Brothers & Co. to have gone into bankruptcy in the usual way. For, in my opinion, the only hope of the Argentine Republic is in a scaling of the amount of its indebtedness or a refunding of it at a lower rate of interest.[15]

That certainly was the view of the new Finance Minister in the Saenz Pena government elected in 1892. New debt was not viewed as appropriate for repaying old, the more so since the new funding loan sold at a significant discount. Minister Romero's determination to end the earlier agreement soon bore fruit with a new accord in 1893, the *Arreglo Romero*. It substituted a set period of reduced debt service for the capitalization of interest of the 1891 arrangements. For five years interest payments were to be reduced by an average of 30 per cent and amortization suspended until 1901. Further, the defaulted provincial debt was to be eventually consolidated in the hands of the national government, at a discount as it turned out, and the railroad guarantees phased out. Although the *Arreglo* received an initially cool reception in both Buenos Aires and London, the settlement held, and was the basis for the subsequent service of the debt.

Debt relief was perhaps as significant from a political as from an economic perspective. The arrangement did not save all that much. Full debt service, including the railway guarantees and internal gold bonds, might have come to $10 million gold pesos, or £2 million, more. Thus the *Arreglo* was less generous than the funding loan. The former Finance Minister, Vicente Lopez, attacked the plan, commenting, 'Analysis . . . demonstrate[s] that, in reality, there is no motive for continuing to hold up the nation as bankrupt before our foreign creditors.' The response emphasized a slightly larger gain, but more importantly, the need for such relief to equilibrate the federal government accounts.[16] Even in conditions of developmental default, public sector financial capacity was central. And if the foreigners could pay, rather than Argentines having to borrow, so much the better.

The creditors agreed because the market rejected the borrowing solution: the 6 per cent funding loan sold at discounts of up to 50 per cent at various times. The interest cost of borrowing thus greatly exceeded the rate of increase of government revenues, leading to a rising fiscal burden that Romero rejected. Indeed, the Argentine government did not use fully the funding bonds. While eventual economic improvement might have altered the key relationships between the effective interest rate and the expansion of economic activity, at the depth of the depression in 1893 it was better to keep Argentina engaged than risk overt default. Creditors hoped for settlement of the provincial debts. These amounted to about 70 per cent of the national debt, and their lack of service was a major source of balance of payments relief obtained by Argentina through the 1890s. Between 1897 and 1900 the national government assumed the provincial debt in 4 per cent bonds valued at less than 60 per cent of their face value. That gain, formally recognized well after the immediate crisis, was worth considerably more than the *Arreglo*.[17]

The eventual economic recovery that restored Argentine creditworthiness was fueled by rising exports and a large positive trade balance. After 1893 a surplus was achieved every year through the end of the 1890s, culminating in the more than 50 per cent excess over imports in 1899. Rapid volume increases were supplemented by rising export prices that increased by between 7 and 10 per cent a year, as estimated by different sources. Such was the improved state of the merchandise accounts that interest payments were resumed in full in 1897, a year prior to the stipulated date of the *Arreglo*. Foreign borrowing recovered as well, but was never sufficient to offset debt service for the remainder of the decade. Not until the beginning of the twentieth century did another boom, with its positive resource transfers through import surpluses, resume.

Complementary domestic policy was appropriately conservative in restraining aggregate demand and imports. The volume of the monetary issue remained virtually constant after 1893. Public finance was brought under control, as deficits became smaller relative to revenues. Internal sources of taxation increased. Where at the end of the 1880s import and export duties had accounted for more than 70 per cent of receipts, in 1899 the proportion had been reduced to one-half, despite growing trade.[18]

By 1900 Argentina was on a sound enough footing to rejoin the gold standard. It did so not at the previous par, but at one which reflected the then prevailing foreign exchange rate. Indeed, convertibility was now favored to prevent continuing appreciation of the peso to the disadvantage of agricultural export interests.

The Brazilian debt problem, as we have seen, lagged much behind that of Argentina. Its resolution was less dramatic, and more dependent upon internal measures. Debt service was maintained without interruption through the critical years of the early 1890s after the Baring Crisis. When the possibility of a moratorium was broached in 1897, Brazil's bankers, the Rothschilds, as they had for Argentina, favored a new funding loan to cover continuing interest payments rather than debt relief. The funding loan of 1898 amounted to more than £8 million, and covered prospective government interest expenses on the external debt for three years. Amortization of outstanding loans was also suspended for 13 years, further reducing needed payments. On its side, Brazil agreed to undertake no new borrowing, internal or external. Such was the improved state of financial markets in the late 1890s, and the sanguine response to the Brazilian problem, that the bonds sold at par, 'a financial success equalled only once before in the history of the country.'[19]

The domestic counterpart of the agreement, as in the 1891 Argentine plan, was a Brazilian commitment to withdraw from circulation Treasury notes in proportion to the issue of the funding bonds. These were to be deposited with three foreign banks in Rio and destroyed, unless the exchange rate had risen in the interim to validate their conversion. Revenues that otherwise would have been applied to the service of the public debt, in other words, would be used to diminish the money supply that was seen to underlie the parlous state of the foreign exchange . The loan was intended to compensate for a foreign exchange constraint, but not to underwrite a public sector deficit. Increased revenues were thus a central policy objective. Internal taxes were raised and extended to new products. Federal railroads were rented to private enterprises to operate. New gold surcharges on customs duties were voted.

This deflationary program was presided over by Finance Minister Joaquim Murtinho. An account by a sympathetic contemporary praises him for 'not having yielded even an instant and [having] challenged the unpopularity [of the measures], which reached to rebellion, in order to present Brazil in conditions to present itself with unbowed head in front of its creditors.'[20] Murtinho's contractionary monetary and fiscal policies were a coherent reflection of his strongly held Spencerian philosophy. He was fully committed to *laissez-faire*, and its welcome destruction of unnatural, protected activity. Free competition would lead, 'through business failures to natural selection, revealed by the disappearance of the inferior and the permanence of the superior.'[21] The crisis should be in proportion to the excesses that made the cure necessary. Murtinho's views were strongly influenced by the Englishman, J.P. Wileman, whose book, *Brazilian Exchange*, had been published in 1896 criticizing Brazilian heterodoxy and advocating instead: '*No more loans, or guarantees. No more Deficits. More Stability of exchange*.'[22]

This policy direction, in conjunction with large trade balances that began to appear in 1900, was successful in firming the exchange rate. But there was also a cost in slackened domestic activity, punctuated by a severe banking crisis in 1900. The abolition of additional note issuance facilities by the Bank of the Republic in 1899 exposed it to suspension of payments only a year later when anxious depositors sought to withdraw their funds. As in Argentina, the appreciation of the exchange rate affected exporters adversely and stimulated resistance. Convertibility was restored in 1906 to limit deflationary excess. A favorable balance of payments attracted a new surge of foreign investment in the last great expansion of capital export before the First World War.

Both Argentina and Brazil thus emerged from the crisis of the 1890s to gold standard orthodoxy in the first decade of the twentieth century. From threatened default in each case, averted by responsive aid from British investment banks, they came full circle to renewed creditworthiness and capital inflow. Rapid economic growth prior to the First World War completes the tale.

2. The Role of Internal and External Factors in Provoking Crisis

The prior condensed historical account sets the stage for this section's quantitative analysis of the comparative influence of domestic policy and external circumstances in leading Argentina and Brazil to the brink of default. Both are relevant. One cannot simply point to evidence of expansive domestic policy as proof of its importance. Large capital inflows necessarily imply an import surplus and spending beyond one's means. To blame countries indiscriminately for increased demand that absorbs larger supply is to miss the connection between internal and external equilibrium. That does not mean, of course, that demand can never be excessive and spill over to unsustainable borrowing.

Ideally, the focus should be the origins of current account deficits and the allocation of foreign saving. Data limitations preclude such an analysis, but the issue can be meaningfully recast by assessing the relative contribution of internal and external factors to the determination of the variable exchange rates in the two countries. That was the way, moreover, in which John Williams first posed the question for Argentina in his classic treatment many years ago, and which Mario Teijeiro has recently reviewed. It is also the issue that Gustavo Henrique Barroso Franco has examined for Brazil in a new treatment of the period. The exchange rate stands as the decisive element linking together the balance of payments and the internal economy, and is a measure of the consistency of domestic policy.

Williams' assessment of the role of monetary policy was decidedly anti-bullionist, and thus against the weight of contemporaneous Argentine opinion: 'It is not intended, in any case, to deny that excessive issues of paper were an important cause of its depreciation, but merely to insist that it was by no means the sole cause, and that, contrary to the opinion of many Argentine writers, the balance of payments was also an important cause of currency depreciation – in my judgement the most important single cause.'[23] Teijeiro contests this conclusion, asserting that ' . . . the phenomenon of the exchange rate is essentially a monetary matter . . . a fall in external finance would have reflected itself essentially in the level of the imports which were being financed until then. . . .'[24] Franco's view for Brazil is the same as Williams', 'that the principal determinant of exchange devaluation was the succession of large deficits in the balance of payments, beginning in 1890, whose origin traces, principally, to the retraction of capital movements to Brazil.'[25]

A resolution of the matter depends upon specification and econometric estimation of the underlying set of relationships. The money supply, through its effects on domestic expenditure, interest rates and inflation, obviously cannot be neglected. But on the side of the balance of payments, apart from the variation in capital flows, there is also the fluctuation of export quantities and international prices. In the appendix, a simple macroeconomic model is used to formalize these interrelationships. It makes clear how these variables influence nominal exchange rates. It is more difficult, except as a residual, to introduce the effects of sheer speculation that also entered, at least in the short term, to determine market exchange rates. And there are potential simultaneity problems emanating from reciprocal influence of the exchange rate on the independent variables that I subsequently discuss.

Table 3.1 presents the statistical results achieved from a reduced form specification relating exchange rates in the two countries to the money supply, estimates of the net capital account less debt service, export earnings (or the terms of trade), and British wholesale prices. I focus first on the least squares estimates. The findings are quite encouraging. Signs are correct, and the elasticities fall into an expected range; note in particular that the response to foreign prices is approximately unitary. Not only are the R^2 high, but the individual coefficients are significant. In the case of Brazil, the coefficient values are not very sensitive whether exports or the terms of trade are used to measure exogenous effects on foreign exchange receipts; for Argentina, the coefficient on foreign prices becomes insignificant. Nor is there much to be gained from substituting alternative Brazilian trade series.[26]

With these estimates as a basis, several important substantive conclusions can be drawn. In the first place, there is a clear difference in the explanation of foreign exchange rates in the two countries. In Argentina, the variation in the net resources available as a result of foreign indebtedness enters as a significant variable; in Brazil it does not. In both, the domestic money supply is highly significant, albeit in Argentina with an elasticity significantly less than one. Even in Brazil, with its higher elasticity in the export receipts formulation, the bullionist story is incomplete: as in Argentina, variation in real export earnings is a significant additional factor.

These results confirm Williams' emphasis upon the balance of payments as a contributing factor to Argentine depreciation. Teijeiro's revisionism derives from the assumption that the exchange rate is determined exclusively by monetary policy. Changes in the capital account are argued to reflect themselves solely in changes in imports on a one-to-one basis. Accordingly, his estimated regression derives from a pure monetary approach without a consideration of the alternative hypotheses. Although it achieves statistical significance, such a test is inadequate for the purpose of examining the role of fluctuations in the capital account.

Specifically, as applied to the Argentine situation in 1888–91, when the gold premium rose from 48 per cent to 287 per cent, the coefficients from equation 1 of table 3.1 allocate less than 60 per cent of the depreciation to the influence of the money supply and more than 40 per cent to the sharp

Table 3.1 Regression results

	Dependent variables	Real export receipts[a]	Terms of trade[a]	Money supply[a]	Capital inflow minus debt service	Foreign price[a]	$\bar{R}^2$	D−W
		Independent variables						
Argentina	Gold premium[a] 1884=100							
Least squares								
1884–1900		−0.54		0.64	−0.0018	−1.18	0.95	2.49
		(5.34)		(11.28)	(3.84)	(2.64)		
1884–99			−0.50	0.51	−0.0013	−0.18	0.91	1.89
			(2.18)	(5.70)	(2.07)	(0.23)		
Instrumental variables[b]								
1885–1900		−0.62		0.73	−0.0011	−1.22	0.91	2.01
		(3.84)		(2.21)	(0.25)	(1.71)		
Brazil	Milreis per pound[a]							
Least squares								
1877–97[c]		−0.63		0.87	0.0051	−0.86	0.92	1.95
		(3.00)		(8.13)	(0.91)	(2.33)		
1877–97[c,d]			0.16	0.60	−0.0029	−1.20	0.96	1.77
			(1.75)	(6.33)	(0.93)	(2.41)		
Instrumental variables[b]								
1877–97		−1.31		1.03	−0.0134	−1.67	0.78	1.57
		(1.38)		(1.80)	(0.29)	(1.77)		

[a] Expressed in logarithms.
[b] Instruments: time, lagged real exports, lagged money supply, foreign prices.
[c] Residuals corrected by a first-order moving averages process.
[d] Residuals corrected by a one-period autogressive process.

Sources:

Argentina

Gold premium: Ford, *Gold Standard*, p. 139

Value and price of exports: Diéguez, 'Crecimiento e Inestabilidad'

Import price: British export price deflator from Albert H. Imlah, *Economic Elements in the Pax Britannica*, New York, 1969, pp. 94 ff

Money supply: *Extracto Estadistico, 1915* (average of preceding and current year)

Capital account: Williams, *Argentine International Trade*, pp. 45, 101, 136 and 154

Foreign price: B.R. Mitchell, *Abstract of British Historical Statistics*, Cambridge, 1962, pp. 474–5. The Sauerbeck-Statist wholesale price index was used

Brazil

Milreis per pence: *Anuário Estatístico, 1939–40*, pp. 1353–4
Value of exports: *Anuário*, p. 1358
Price of coffee: *Anuário*, p. 1378
Import price: as above

(Fiscal year averaged until calendar year series begins in 1888)

Money supply: Carlos M. Palaez and Wilson Suzigan, *História Monetária do Brasil*, Rio de Janeiro, 1976, Table A.3, pp. 442 ff. (end of June values)
Capital account: Franco, *Reforma Monetária*, pp. 47–8. (Debt service was calculated from Table A-3, p. 47)
Foreign price: as above

reduction in capital inflow; increased real exports in that same period move the results only modestly in the other direction. Of course, within that time interval, a different causal structure may have prevailed, possibly giving even more significance to the dislocations imposed by the sudden decline in foreign exchange availability. Contemporary preoccupation with monetary excess is not misplaced, the more so since the policy was under domestic control in a way that capital flows were not, but that explanation is far from the whole story.

The pattern of residuals tells us more. The actual level of the gold premium in 1890, before the Baring Crisis, is much lower than predicted; in 1891, much higher (by more than a standard error in both years). Once the news was out, the market overreacted relative to its earlier excess optimism. The Rothschild agreement of 1891 did little to tranquilize speculators in foreign exchange. Nor for that matter is there a discernible influence of the *Arreglo Romero* in 1893. The predominant cause of the eventual appreciation was the steady improvement in export receipts and a stable money supply. Net cash flows from foreign investment remained negative starting in 1890.

In the Brazilian case, the level of net flow on capital account is statistically insignificant in influencing fluctuations of the exchange rate. Contrary to Franco's generalization from the Argentine experience, the Baring Crisis is not a decisive factor. On reflection, the result is not surprising. While Brazil received a large capital inflow in 1888 and 1889, the local peak is not as pronounced as for Argentina; 1883 is as important as the latter year, for example. Correspondingly, the extent of change in the capital account in the 1888–91 period is less severe than it was for an Argentina much more dependent upon capital imports. The Argentine net balance on capital account goes from 150 per cent of recorded imports to minus a third. In Brazil, the variation is about half as great; the net balance moves from less than 100 per cent to minus 15 per cent. At the same time, the Brazilian quantity of money more than triples as against the Argentine doubling.

On the other side, external loans continued to be contracted in the 1890s, during 1893 and 1895–7. Indeed, capital flows remained positive on the eve of the refunding. The balance of payments counts in the Brazilian case through trade rather than through irregular capital flow. That is again consistent with the timing of the Brazilian default, brought on in the later 1890s by continuously falling coffee prices rather than slowing foreign investment in 1890–1 as in Argentina.

The Brazilian external crisis in the early 1890s was much less severe. The exchange rate depreciated but economic activity persisted, and even accelerated.

While net immigration to Argentina was negative in 1891, as imports declined by more than 50 per cent, population inflows to Brazil more than doubled, possibly reflecting exits from Argentina. In subsequent years, until 1898, Brazil attracted much higher levels of immigration than it had earlier, and record proportions of total movement to the United States, Argentina and Brazil. A machinery and equipment export series to Brazil from the industrialized countries shows higher sales in the period 1891–6 than in previous or subsequent periods. The fall-off from peak purchases in 1890–1 was only 15 per cent.[27]

When Brazil was forced finally to resort to a funding loan in 1898, it was after the international crisis was already over. Rather, the crisis was particular, one of diminishing coffee prices due to oversupply. Brazil was a prominent contributor to the problem: its exports had expanded by 1897 to the 9 million sack level from the earlier capacity of 5 to 6 million sacks. Its sterling receipts fell over the same period by almost a third. That is the reason for continuing depreciation after the effects of smaller foreign investment and the large increase in the money supply had worked themselves out by the mid-1890s. Brazil specialized in a commodity that failed to share the general price upturn associated with cyclical revival. Brazil was not able to grow into its debt until the coffee price stabilized after 1900 and then began to ascend after 1909. That, and the rubber boom, assured a rising trend in export receipts prior to the First World War.

The structure of residuals from the exchange rate equation corroborates the limited contagion effects from the Baring Crisis. There is a substantial – more than a standard error – *undershooting* of the actual exchange rate relative to its predicted value in 1890 and 1891. The actual rate remains slightly below its predicted value in 1892. The very large increase in the money supply sanctioned by the Republic ought to have driven the milreis down more than it did. Despite the political uncertainties surrounding the establishment of the Republic, markets did not speculate against Brazil as long as there was a continuing capacity to service debt, as there was. This lag, moreover, helped to keep imports of capital goods cheaper just at a time when domestic policy was expansive, and contributed to the more import-substitution-intensive style of Brazilian adjustment that will be further explored in part 4.

These regressions take the money supply as exogenous. Yet, as I have emphasized in part 1, there was a reciprocal influence exercised by the exchange rate upon the note issue through government need to cover the increased debt service measured in domestic currency. There were pressures as well from the local business community for more credit to compensate for depreciation of the exchange rate. These reasons help to explain the inability of governments in either country to shift easily, or early, to more restrictive monetary policies in response to balance of payments constraints. The Argentine promise to destroy paper money as the counterpart of the Rothschild Loan in 1891 was not kept. In Brazil, those draconian measures were not applied until the exchange rate began to appreciate again after 1898. Still, the responsiveness of the money supply to the exchange rate was

Table 3.2 Causality tests, money and exchange rates, Brazil

	F test on future coefficients	
Regression equation	1882.3–1905.4	1888.1–1902.4
Money on exchange rates	6.46[a]	1.23
Exchange rates on money	1.34	0.93

Data were in logarithms and prefiltered by a two-period autogressive process. The equations included a constant, seasonal dummy variables and a time trend in addition to current, eight lagged, and four future values of the independent variable.

[a] Significant at 0.01 level.

hardly regular or assured. Governments did seek to increase their sources of revenue, both by surtaxes on imports as well as by new internal levies. And Brazil was able to contract new external loans.

Quarterly series on the exchange rate and money supply for Brazil permit a closer examination of this causality question. Table 3.2 reports the results of Sims causality tests on the two-way relationship between money and the exchange rate. (Although the embedded relationship within a larger model would ideally call for a multivariate test, the requisite quarterly information is not available.) For the long period, from 1882 to 1905, the tests are consistent with a causal structure of one-way influence of the money supply on the exchange rate. Further values of exchange rates make a statistically significant contribution to the explanation of nominal money. That contribution is conspicuously absent in the reverse regression.

Note, however, that the explanatory influence of the money supply on exchange rates in these equations is modest; R^2 reaches only 0.13.[28] The signs of the effects are consistent in the lag structure, with the exception of a statistically significant reverse effect in the third lagged quarter, and a reverse effect again in the eighth. The sum of the elasticities is, however, implausibly high. These quarterly results corroborate the view that the relationship of the exchange rate to the money supply was not the simple bi-variate one proposed by the bullionists, but was also strongly influenced by the evolution of capital flows and export earnings.

For the shorter interval from 1888 to 1902, encompassing the period of greatest interest, the conclusion, moreover, is indeterminate. In neither case is there a significant future influence on the other variable. This mixed result confirms the possibility of a more complex interaction during at least some part of the 1890s, but it is difficult to introduce such endogeneity into the model in a meaningful way, given the limited available data and degrees of freedom.

Beyond the simultaneity of the money supply, there is the further question of the influence of exchange rate changes on capital flows as well as on export receipts. Foreign investment in the two countries, while influenced by local circumstances, also was affected by British conditions and response to general international opportunities for capital flow. Moreover, the obvious persistence of investment in both Argentina and Brazil, despite depreciation, argues against a straightforward reciprocal relationship. The supply effect of the exchange rate for Argentine exports, and the fact that Brazil was not a price taker in the coffee market, introduce other sources of potential bias.

An instrumental variable solution to the problem, such as applied by Cardoso in her analysis of Brazilian exchange rates, is one way to deal with such simultaneity.[29] It should be recognized, however, that the lack of an obvious and available broader set of exogenous variables deriving from a complete model does make the results somewhat arbitrary. Different instruments yield different estimates. Using as instruments lagged values of some of the suspect variables it is possible to approximate the coefficients of the least squares results, albeit with much less statistical significance. These equations are also presented in table 3.1. Unfortunately they fail to replicate the least squares finding of a significant difference in the role of net financial flows in the two countries. I am not inclined to exaggerate this lapse. Additional evidence corroborates the distinction between the Brazilian and Argentine experiences.

3. Stock Market Evaluations

This differentiation shows up vividly in the London stock exchange evaluation of the prospects of the two countries during this period. Figures 3.1 and 3.2 plot the quarterly prices of Argentine and Brazilian government bonds, railway debentures and railway shares between the end of 1883 and 1900.

The Argentine collapse in all categories is dramatic. Note in particular the decline in prices of government bonds beginning at the end of 1889. A revision of confidence does not simply await the Baring Crisis; rather, prior price softness of government issues made Baring Brothers unable to sell off its large holdings of a new Buenos Aires waterworks issue and it became increasingly illiquid. A small recovery is apparent in 1891, related to the Rothschild Agreement, but that gives way to a further decline. Most series do not reach bottom until 1893.

Brazilian performance is far less cyclical as prices move within a much narrower range. The price decline of the early 1890s awaits the fall-out from the Baring Crisis in 1890, and lasts until 1893. Thereafter only the price series of government bonds betrays the later Brazilian refunding in 1898. Evaluation of railroad prospects, especially in the case of the debentures, was for the most part independent of the country's foreign exchange and fiscal difficulties.

Table 3.3 presents the results of a more formal analysis of the comparative price variability of shares of Argentine and Brazil railways. Three well-established private lines were chosen. Their earnings and dividends were independent of the government guarantees that other newer and riskier projects continued to require. Their prices would therefore be expected to be less affected by concerns about inadequate public receipts and to provide

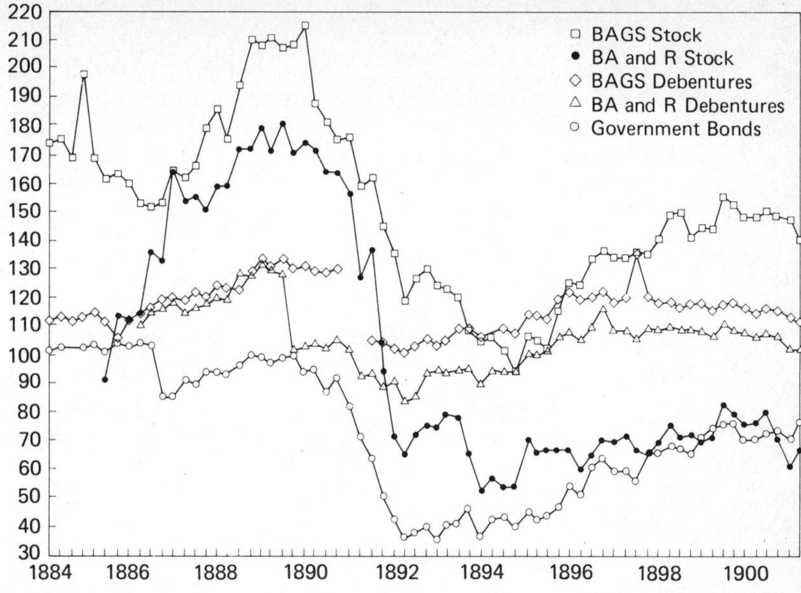

Figure 3.1 Argentine securities prices. Quarterly data, 1883.IV–1900.IV

a better measure of differential investor reaction to returns in the two countries. I use a Shiller excess volatility test to describe market evaluation. The first column shows the standard deviation of actual market price, P. The second shows the standard deviation of the price, P^*, calculated with perfect foresight from the stream of real future dividends, discounted to present value.[30]

Efficient markets, where the expected actual price is equal to the *ex post* rational price, P^*, should correspond to a smaller variance of the actual price series than the constructed series because of forecast error. In fact, here, as in other applications, the reverse is true. The values in column 1 regularly and substantially exceed those in column 2. My interest is not in definitively testing the formal efficiency of the London Stock Exchange at the end of the nineteenth century; there are problems associated with a simple application of the method, particularly in small sample periods such as I have used here.[31] Rather, I wish to emphasize how these specific observed prices over the course of the last nineteenth-century long swing in foreign investment were much more variable than their relatively stable stream of dividends would give reason to expect. The implication is that something else is at work other than continuously accurate assessment of potential profits.

Commentators on historical cyclical processes have long insisted on

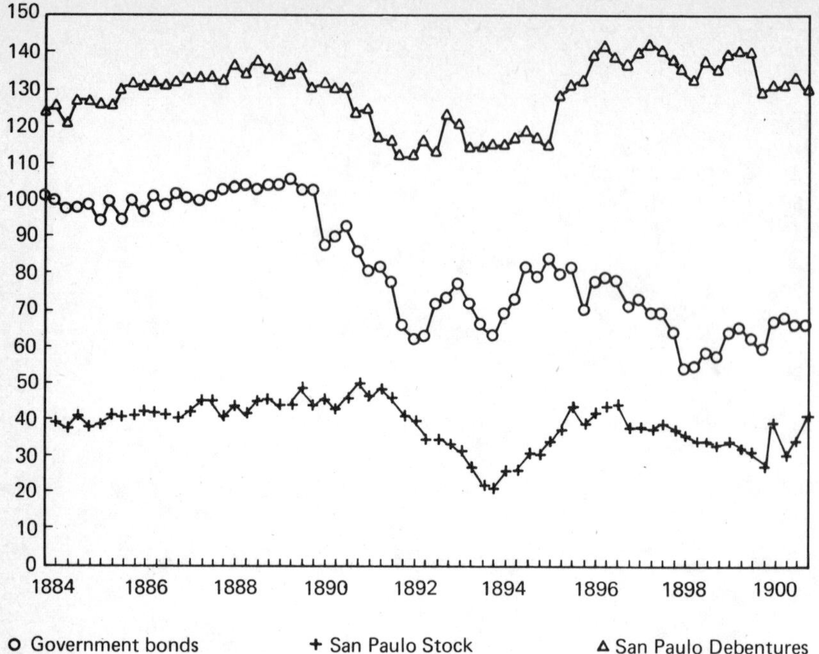

Figure 3.2 Brazilian securities prices. Quarterly data, 1883.IV–1900.IV

cumulative excesses and faulty expectations. The statistical results are more consistent with Charles Kindleberger's story of *Manias*, *Panics*, *and Crashes*, than with assumptions that markets accurately use all the information available to them all the time. German investors, when they stopped subscribing to Argentine loans in 1888, may have been able to form rational expectations, but their less fortunate British counterparts evidently did not.[32]

Foreign securities posed a special informational problem. There was a large difference between information available to insiders and to outsiders. It was the insiders who not only manipulated what outside investors learned about the real state of affairs, especially in an era in which the financial press was not always independent, but who also influenced outcomes by their own decisions. When investment banks made available additional resources to stave off Brazilian default, they preserved their own reputations and boosted the values of Brazilian securities. Baring Brothers, when it extended credit to Argentina from 1888 to 1890, did so in the hope of being able subsequently to benefit directly from a better market evaluation.

This overreaction of markets, whether through fads or self-justifying bubbles, was not confined to Argentine securities, although that shift of enthusiasm is evident in the high price volatility recorded in table 3.3. For the Sao Paulo Railway, as for the Pennsylvania Railroad, the cyclical swing

Table 3.3 Variance bounds test, 1883 IV–1900 I[a]

	$\sigma(P_t)$	$\sigma(P_t^*)$
Argentina		
Buenos Aires Great Southern	31.3	7.7
Buenos Aires & Rosario	47.0	7.0
Brazil		
Sao Paulo RR	7.2	1.7
United States		
Pennsylvania RR	7.8	1.4
Pennsylvania RR (detrended)[b]	0.08	0.008

[a] Dividend data were used for the period until 1914 to calculate P^*.
[b] Detrended by dividing estimated exponential values for price and dividends into actual values. Detrending was unnecessary for other series.

Sources:
Nominal prices: *The Economist*
Argentine railway dividends: C. Lewis, *British Railways in Argentina, 1857–1914*
Brazilian railway dividends: R. Graham, *Britain and Modernization*
Pennsylvania railway dividends: *Poor's Manual of Railroads*
British wholesale price deflator: B.R. Mitchell, *European Historical Statistics*

in share prices also greatly exceeded the real variation in earnings. Foreign issues underwent a generalized reduction after 1890, without a fine discrimination of underlying values. Distinctions were not altogether lacking. How the reallocation of portfolios came out, however, is not altogether clear. On the one hand, S. F. Van Oss noted the strength of European securities after the Baring Crisis: 'The alternating *rage* for South American and European Securities and its result upon their quotations has been one of the most interesting phenomena of the Stock markets during recent years.' On the other, there is reference to British sale of good US securities in order to able to carry 'bad Latin American loans,' with attendant price pressure.[33]

Of particular importance here, the calculations of table 3.3 provide no indication of a stronger unwarranted reaction in the share prices of the Brazilian Sao Paulo Railway than of the American Pennsylvania Railroad. Despite much contemporary comment, the contagion effect arising from Brazilian proximity to Argentina does not seem to have been especially severe. The statistical result is consistent with the continuing ability of the Brazilian government to call upon its foreign bankers in the early 1890s. Brazil's problem was not the Baring Crisis but adverse export earnings.

A final observation relates to the much greater calculated variability of the *ex post* rational Argentine share prices compared to other railroads. The real cycle was in fact more severe in that country, as I comment in part 4. The market was not wrong to be more cyclical than with respect to other securities; it seems, however, to have far surpassed what was justified.

Table 3.4 Standard deviations of spot interest returns, 1883 IV–1900 I

Security	*Standard deviation*	
UK Consols	0.00148	
Argentina		
Government bonds[a]	0.0232	
Buenos Aires Great Southern	0.00828	(to 1890.2)
	0.00219	(1891.1 to 1900.1)
Buenos Aires & Rosario	0.00337	
Brazil		
Government bonds	0.00976	
Sao Paulo RR	0.00293	
United States		
Government bonds	0.00170	
Pennsylvania RR	0.00090	

[a] Adjusted for temporary reduction in interest rates in accordance with *Arreglo Romero* of 1893.

Source: Nominal prices: *The Economist*

Table 3.4 elaborates another comparative measure of the volatility of the London market response. It presents the standard deviations of the spot returns on two debt instruments, government bonds and private railway debentures, for Argentina, Brazil and the United States, all against the benchmark British Consols. Rankings are as expected. The greatest variability attaches to Argentine government bonds, followed by Brazilian, and then, close together and much smaller, the American and British public securities. All of the differences between these variances, except for the narrow American and British difference, are statistically significant using a conventional F-test at the 0.01 level. The variation among private bonds is much smaller than for public issues, and there is little to choose between the Argentine and Brazilian issues, both of which are much greater than that of the Pennsylvania Railroad.

These large fluctuations in security prices were not completely dysfunctional. They served an important signalling function. The sharp decline in prices of Argentine bonds set in motion external relief, first the Funding Loan of 1891, and when that failed to serve, the *Arreglo Romero* in 1893. Faced with the *fait accompli* of capital losses, investors had an incentive to accept settlements that might improve their situation. Debt relief, if it could serve improved market evaluation, was worth trying. Investment banks, with limited direct exposure, could and did serve as intermediaries to allocate the losses emanating from investment mistakes between countries and bondholders. They thereby minimized sacrifice to the dead hand of the past. Sometimes, however, they enforced past obligations. When renegotiations were unsuccessful, the banks were instrumental in reducing country access to capital markets.

The market itself stood as a decisive arbiter of the success of those policies. Its failure in 1891 and 1892 to validate the preferred Rothschild expedient of capitalizing interest contributed to a willingness to consider a more favorable settlement for Argentina. In contrary fashion, the more enthusiastic reception of the Brazilian Funding Loan of 1898 at par value, in part because of the severely deflationary domestic policies that improved balance of payments prospects, precluded resort to more generous efforts.

This discussion of market evaluation of Argentine and Brazilian issues supports two basic conclusions. First is the mixed rationality and irrationality of market performance. While markets were hardly perfectly efficient, as their overreactions demonstrate, they nonetheless made important distinctions among borrowers and among different classes of securities. The Baring Crisis hit Argentina hardest, and government bonds far the worst. Second is the important relationship between the barometer of the market and investment banker intervention. Overt valuations facilitated concessions from creditors to debtors and helped to align relief more closely to capacity to pay. This institutional mechanism operated in the 1890s, without a formal governmental structure, to ease the internal adjustment required of Argentina and Brazil in response to deteriorating external circumstances.

4. Internal Adjustment

Adjustment could not be evaded. After the flow of capital slowed, it was incumbent upon Argentina and Brazil to improve their trade balances. In the Argentine case, the first phase was a dramatic reduction of imports in 1891 to virtually half the previous year's level. Not until 1904 would the 1890 import level be surpassed. Almost certainly that decline was associated with a large fall in income; the immigration data are certainly consistent with an unusually large reversal in economic activity. Thereafter, as the beneficient effects of earlier investment were realized, gradually increasing exports played the role of easing the foreign exchange constraint. The depreciation of the exchange rate was not a central factor in evoking this new export supply; it largely compensated for the decline in food and raw material prices worldwide.

Import substitution, however, was unambiguously favored by the new structure of relative prices. Domestic prices of imports rose in accordance with the gold premium, moderated only a little by modestly declining British export prices of manufactures. In addition, as the expanded need for governmental revenue was felt, tariffs were raised, adding a further margin of profit for local industrial activity. Crucial to the result was the failure of nominal wages to keep pace. Calculations of Argentine real wages confirm a large difference depending upon whether the nominal series is deflated by the exchange rate or a cost of living index. Recent research by Roberto Cortes Conde emphasizes the latter, and hence an improvement in the standard of living, in contrast to the conventional wisdom of significant deterioration.[34] But from the standpoint of the firm, what counts is the product wage. Cheap food prices kept nominal wages low, despite slowing immigration, and favored industry.

That there was significant progress in the industrial sector in Argentina from 1890 to 1895 seems clear. Exactly how much is still a question. As one Argentine chronicler of the industrial sector puts it: 'Unfortunately, for lack of [data], we cannot express in numbers the notable advance registered in the quinquennium 1890–95.'[35] The return of prosperity to the rural sector at the end of the decade reduced the momentum towards industrialization created by the foreign exchange crisis. Argentina followed comparative advantage by specializing in primary exports. Sectoral production accounts after 1900 show the share of manufacturing in that year to be about what it was in 1910, and for that matter, only slightly lower than it was at the end of the 1920s.[36]

It took more than a decade of large trade surpluses in the 1890s for Argentina to come into favor again in world capital markets. That was still in time to participate in the last British surge of foreign investment before the First World War. External capital made up a large share once more of total investment, though undoubtedly smaller than it had been before. There was less excess on this occasion, and no repetition of the earlier debacle. Debt export ratios had been reduced to serviceable proportions by economic growth.

The Brazilian adjustment, like the crisis itself, was different in character. It did not have to be as restrictive in the early 1890s. Indeed, for a time – as had been true earlier in Argentina – an expansive domestic policy coincided with continuing imports of machinery and equipment. While the Argentine share of British exports of equipment and railroad material more than halved from 1886–90 to 1891–5, the Brazilian share more than doubled.[37] The significant increase in import of capital goods in the early 1890s was applied to domestic production of manufactures, especially textiles, in substitution for their import.[38] Tariffs were increased in 1890 and 1891 by imposing gold quotas, but thereafter they fell as a percentage of import value despite imposition of surcharges for fiscal needs; exchange depreciation more than compensated. Murtinho would have been less exercised on the subject of 'unnatural industrialization' when he assumed office in 1898, had so much expansion not occurred in the early part of the decade.

At first appearance this industrial surge seems to have occurred with a relative price structure that was less favorable than the Argentine. The ratio between domestic prices, as given by the Lobo cost of living index, and the price of imports does not register a large increase.[39] The close correspondence between the two indexes is not definitive evidence. The Lobo index includes relatively few products, nine, of which three were imports, and does not accurately reflect either prices of manufactured products or domestic wages. J. P. Wileman's contemporary observation, and his illustrative data, are more convincing: "There is always a considerable interval between the rise in the price of bullion and exports and that of labour and local values, such as rent, food staples, &c; and it is, unquestionably, this differential rise in prices that confers such great and positive advantages on production and exports, by reducing their real cost and raising profits . . . To take an example we find that the price of labour in the factories of the Co. Union Fabril of Rio Grande has risen from the year 1889 to 1893 from 1$500 to Rs. 2$358, equivalent to 53.1 per cent; whilst the prices of exports and bullion have risen 151 per cent."[40] Note that wages were likely to be held down, despite economic expansion, by a continuing flow of immigrants. With continued opportunities for imports of capital goods and reduced imports of consumption goods, this created a very favorable climate for Brazilian business investment.

The later balance of payments crisis in Brazil reinforced this industrialization although Murtinho's policy rhetoric would hardly have suggested it. The requisite trade surpluses after the Funding Loan of 1898 were achieved not only through export growth but through import restraint: between 1898 and 1902 imports (in deflated £ sterling) fell by more than 10 per cent and were much below their level in the early 1890s. Deflationary policies soon came to depend for their success upon increased tariff revenue, which provided a cushion of greater protection that partially offset an eventually appreciating exchange rate. Between 1900 and 1902, total import collections, aided by a gold quota surcharge, rose by 20 per cent while the new internal consumption taxes responsible for significant revenue gains after 1898 fell by almost 10 per cent.[41]

In the last analysis, Brazil was better able to sustain its surge of industrial activity begun in the 1890s because coffee was a less favorable export opportunity than Argentine wheat and meat. By the beginning of the twentieth century there was a widening consensus that coffee was in oversupply, leading by 1906 to active Brazilian efforts to support its international price. Sao Paulo coffee wealth, which earlier had diversified already into industrial and other investments, was increasingly attracted into manufacturing as a profitable long-run application. With the rise of industrial investment after 1902, the state soon established itself as the leading center of Brazilian, and Latin American, industrial production. In 1907, an early and incomplete industrial census showed the state of Sao Paulo trailing the city of Rio de Janeiro; by 1919, the census showed Sao Paulo as the principal industrial center, responsible for more than a third of national value added.[42]

Unlike Argentina, which could reliably depend upon vigorous export growth for renewed prosperity, Brazil found itself in balance of payments difficulty again on the eve of the First World War. It took another funding loan in 1914 to avert a formal default. This recurrence of the foreign exchange constraint was not to be the last. In these conditions, it is not surprising that import substitution found a more comfortable setting in Brazil than Argentina.

5. Lessons from the Past

The Argentine and Brazilian experiences of the 1890s suggest four conclusions that relate to the present debt problem of developing countries.

First, the difference between the Argentine and Brazilian crises in the 1890s emphasizes the importance of attention to the specifics within the commonality of the external environment. Although both countries participated in the same international cycle, their pattern of response was nonetheless quite individual. The path to the debt problem, as well as efforts to resolve it, were distinct. Such subtlety is often lacking in present discussions. All sorts of countries are thrown together under the same rubric: Latin American and African, oil exporters and oil importers, diversified exporters and commodity producers. More troubling, while the current debt policy heralds its case-by-case approach, the analysis is typically excessively universal. Excess demand is invariably at fault for external disequilibrium and extensive balance of payments adjustment via the same set of policy instruments must be accomplished within a short span, whatever the cost in domestic output and income. Only now, after several years of painful lost growth, is there beginning to be greater sensitivity to the different structural conditions in debtor countries. Indeed, the problem with the case-by-case approach that is presumably current policy is that the analysis proceeds universally: balance of payments adjustment comes first, and at whatever expense.

A second, and related, lesson derives from the historical response to imminent default. Late nineteenth-century international financial institutions responded both speedily and flexibly. Two elements were central. In the first instance, investment banks recognized the importance of debtor country capacity to pay in devising their debt rescheduling arrangements. Market evaluations assisted in persuading creditors of the need to make adequate concessions. In the second place, debtor countries had strong incentives to cooperate in reaching an agreement. Peripheral countries like Argentina and Brazil were integrated into a growing international economy and could anticipate a return to capital markets under the auspices of the same investment banks. Countries today do not receive the same recognition of the gravity of their debt problem – it is always about to be resolved by OECD growth and a little more austerity – and at the same time face a lack of new capital inflows as commercial banks curtail their commitments. Private arrangements seemed to have operated in the past more effectively than our more formal multilateral debt regime. They assured a pragmatism and practicality that would be welcome now.

A third conclusion is the apparent greater ease of historical adjustment of Argentina and Brazil. Trends were favorable for immigration and utilization of new land. Regular developmental growth permitted a continuing expansion of export capacity in Argentina that produced the export surpluses required before a return to new capital inflow. In Brazil, much larger coffee output coincided with favorable prices in the upswing in the first decade of the twentieth century. Austerity was more temporary. In part for that reason, it was also politically easier to sustain the required reverse transfer of resources. Expectations about continuing rises in real income were more limited in a world that was profoundly cyclical; prosperity never lasted, but, on the other hand, reasonably could be expected to return. Adjustment was measured over the course of the decadal downswing of the Kuznets cycle, not in a matter of a few years. Debtor countries now are rightly less confident about the regularity of recovery of the global economy, and face more impatient societies that demand higher standards of economic performance.

I conclude with a final observation derived from this examination of the 1890s. Developmental strategies began to diverge for Argentina and Brazil at that time, as the latter began to opt for greater industrialization while the former pursued its considerable absolute and comparative advantages in agriculture. Conventional wisdom, and high Argentine real income, scorned the Brazilian attempt at import substitution. Looking back, the Brazilian choice does not now seem quite so unreasonable. There is something to be said, as Carlos Díaz-Alejandro would have, for national innovation, intervention and experiment when simple orthodoxy fails to provide satisfactory answers in the face of large changes in the economic environment.

NOTES

I am indebted to Menzie Chinn for much appreciated research assistance and valuable observations, and to Eliana Cardoso and two anonymous Brazilian referees for helpful comments on an earlier draft.

1 For a discussion of this process over a longer span, see my 'Lessons from the past: capital markets during the nineteenth century and the interwar period,' *International Organization*, 39 (1985), pp. 383–440.

2 Carlos F. Díaz-Alejandro, 'Stories of the 1930's for the 1980's,' in *Financial Policies and the World Capital Market: The Problem of the Latin American Countries*, eds Pedro Aspe Armella et al. (National Bureau of Economic Research, Chicago, 1983), p. 32.

3 Charles P. Kindleberger, 'International propagation of financial crises: the experience of 1888–93,' in *International Capital Movements, Debt and Monetary System*, eds Wolfram Engels et al. p. 217.

4 These estimates follow Matthew Simon's estimates of calls on the London market, republished in *The Export of Capital from Britain 1870–1914*, ed. A. R. Hall (London, 1968), p. 40.

5 Estimates that are crudely comparable with Simon's calls are derived, for Argentina, from A. G. Ford, *The Gold Standard 1880–1914: Britain and Argentina* (Oxford, 1962), p. 195; for Brazil, from Gustavo Henrique Barroso Franco, *Reforma Monetária e Inestabilidade durante a Transição Republicana* (Rio de Janeiro, 1983), p. 41.

6 H.S. Ferns, *Britain and Argentina in the Nineteenth Century* (Oxford, 1960), p. 397.

7 For Argentina, Ernesto Tornquist et al., *The Economic Development of the Argentine Republic in the Last Fifty Years* (Buenos Aires, 1919), p. 117; for Brazil, IBGE, *Anuário Estatístico do Brasil, 1939–40*, Appendix, p. 1336.

8 Direct measures of production do not exist for this period. Argentine national accounts, as estimated by the Economic Commission of Latin America, begin in

1900. (See Carlos F. Díaz-Alejandro, *Essays on the Economic History of the Argentine Republic*, New Haven, 1970, Appendix table 19, pp. 418ff.) The estimates of Contador and Haddad for Brazil, although sometimes used, are quite inappropriate. They are simply the nominal value of imports and exports deflated by an index of purchasing power parity. As such they do not correspond to real trade quantities, and largely mirror movements in the exchange rate. No wonder, then, that the early 1890s show decline while a period of later deflationary policy produces a large increase in 'output.' Note as well the extraordinarily large changes in prices, measured by the index of purchasing power parity. ('Produto Real, Moeda e Preços: A Experiencia Brasileira no Período 1861–1970,' *Revista Brasileira de Estatística*, 36, no. 143 (July/Sept. 1975), pp. 407–40.)

These Argentine export data are the revised estimates based on market rather than official prices. (Hector Diéguez, 'Crecimiento e Inestabilidad del Valor y el Volumen Físico de las Exportaciones Argentinas en el Período 1864–1963,' *Desarollo Económico*, 12, no. 46 (July/Sept. 1972), pp. 333–49.) The Brazilian data are from *Anuário Estatística, 1939–40*, Appendix, pp. 1353ff.

9 Argentine migration data are in Tornqist, *Economic Development*, p. 15. For Brazil, see Douglas H. Graham, 'Migração Estrangeira e a Questão da Oferta de Mão-de-Obra no Crescimento Econômico Brasileiro – 1880–1930,' *Estudos Economicos*, 3, no. 1 (1973), p. 33.

10 For information on public finances see Tornquist, *Economic Development*, ch. XII, pp. 276ff. For note issue, Ford, *Gold Standard*, p. 195.

11 John H. Williams, *Argentine International Trade under Inconvertible Paper Money: 1880–1900* (reprinted, New York, 1971), p. 114. H.S. Ferns, *Britain and Argentina*, p. 441.

12 For this discussion, I follow Franco's recent analysis of monetary reform in the 1880s, *Reforma Monetária*. See also the still useful contemporary view in J.P. Calógeras, *A Política Monetária do Brasil* (translated and reprinted, Sao Paulo, 1960).

13 I have emphasized the important real consequences of the Encilhamento in my 'Origins and consequences of import substitution in Brazil,' in *International Trade and Economic Development: Essays in Honor of Raul Prebisch*, ed. Luis Di Marco (New York, 1982). For a more recent analysis, see Maria Barbara Levy, 'O Encilhamento,' in *Economia Brasileira: Uma Visão Histórica*, ed. Paulo Neuhaus (Rio de Janeiro, 1980), pp. 191–256.

14 See the discussion in Williams, *Argentine International Trade*, pp. 123ff.

15 *Reports from the Consuls of the United States*, vol. XXXVIII (Washington, 1892), p. 453.

16 See the discussion in the *Review of the River Plate*, Sept. 16, 1893, pp. 11ff.

17 The national government exchanged $86 million gold pesos in 4 per cent bonds for $151.8 million gold pesos of provincial bonds according to the 1899 Report of the Finance Ministry cited by Harold E. Peters, *The Foreign Debt of the Argentine Republic* (Baltimore, 1934), p. 47.

18 Data on the distribution of revenues at the end of the 1880s come from Laura Randall, *A Comparative Economic History of Latin America, 1500–1914* (Ann Arbor, 1977), vol. 2, p. 221; for 1899, from Tornquist, *Economic Development*, pp. 288–9.

19 J.P. Calógeras, *A History of Brazil* (Chapel Hill, 1939), p. 303, translator's footnote. The information on external loans published in the supplement to the

1939–40 *Anuário Estatístico*, p. 1423, indicates two previous sales at par, in 1825 and 1859.

20 Calógeras, *A Política Monetária*, p. 329.

21 Richard Graham, *Britain and the Onset of Modernization in Brazil, 1850–1914* (Cambridge, 1968), p. 246.

22 J.P. Wileman, *Brazilian Exchange* (Buenos Aires, 1896), p. 266. In his espousal of orthodoxy, Wileman caustically criticizes Ruy Barbosa and others for the 'dangerous tendency to regard Brazil as an exceptionally favoured community to which ordinary rules do not apply . . .' (p. 163).

23 Williams, *Argentine International Trade*, p. 137.

24 Mario O. Teijeiro, 'Inversion Britanica en Argentina: Causas y Consecuencias del Panico Baring,' (Buenos Aires, 1979), p. 10. I am indebted to Juan Carlos de Pablo for having called this unpublished piece to my attention.

25 Franco, *Reforma Monetária*, p. 142.

26 There is some question about the accuracy of Brazilian trade data during this period. J.F. Normano, *Brazil: A Study of Economic Types* (Chapel Hill, 1935), pp. 194–5, and Calógeras, p. 325, present estimates that diverge from those of the *Anuário Estatístico* that were used. (Beginning in 1901, there is coincidence between all three sources.) The *Anuário* estimates typically are intermediate. They themselves are defective by virtue of their apparent inclusion of precious metals in the merchandise accounts. See Luiz Aranha Correa do Lago, 'Balança comercial, balanço de pagamentos e meio circulante no Brasil no Segundo Imperio: uma nota para uma revisão,' *Revista Brasileira de Economia*, 36(4) (out./dez. 1982), pp. 489–508, who makes corrections only for an earlier period.

I have re-estimated the equations using the two alternative export series for the years that they are available. The key result, the insignificance of net capital inflows, is unaffected; indeed, in both instances, the coefficient is less significant.

27 For the series of industrial machinery exports to Brazil, in constant £ sterling, see Wilson Suzigan, *Indústria Brasileira*, (Sao Paulo, 1986), pp. 354–78.

28 This limited explanation of the variance contrasts with the R^2 of 0.8 Sims obtains between money and nominal income in the original article setting forth his method. Christopher Sims, 'Money, income, and causality,' *American Economic Review*, 62, no. 4 (September 1972), pp. 540–52.

29 'Exchange rates in nineteenth century Brazil: an econometric model,' *Journal of Development Studies*, 19, no. 2, (Jan. 1983), pp. 170–8.

30 The original exposition of the variance bounds test is in Robert Shiller, 'Do stock prices move too much to be justified by subsequent changes in dividends?' *American Economic Review*, 71, no. 3 (June 1981), pp. 421–36.

31 For a recent critique of Shiller's article, with references to others, and Shiller's reply, see Terry A. Marsh and Robert C. Merton, 'Dividend variability and variance bounds tests for the rationality of stock market prices,' *American Economic Review*, 76, no. 3 (June 1986), pp. 483ff.

32 This is the title, of course, of Kindleberger's recent history of financial crises, published in 1978. The reference to German foresight can be found on p. 109.

33 S.F. Van Oss, *Stock Exchange Values: A Decade of Finance, 1885 to 1895* (London, 1895), p. lxxvi; Kindleberger, *Manias*, p. 133, citing Sprague's *History of Crises Under the National Banking System* (reprinted New York, 1968), p. 132.

34 Roberto Cortés Conde, *El Progreso Argentino, 1880–1914* (Buenos Aires, 1979), ch. 4, pp. 211ff.

35 Adolfo Dorfman, *História de la Indústria Argentina* (Buenos Aires, 1942), p. 201.
36 Laura Randall calculates the percentages in her *Comparative Economic History*, p. 240.
37 These data are based upon British trade statistics as presented by Eduardo A. Zalduendo, *Libras y Rieles* (Buenos Aires, 1974), p. 89.
38 For a detailed review of Brazilian industrialization, and its interpretation, during this period, see Suzigan, *Indústria Brasileira*, from which the imports of machinery have been used.
39 The index is described in Eulália Maria Lahmeyer Lobo et al., 'Evolução dos Preços e do Padrão de Vida no Rio de Janeiro, 1820–1930 – Resultados Preliminares,' *Revista Brasileira de Economia*, 5, no. 4 (out./dez/ 1971), pp. 235–66. Eliana Cardoso plots a relative price series based on that index which trends downward during the 1890s. See her 'Exchange rates in nineteenth-century Brazil,' *Journal of Development Studies*, 19, no. 2 (January 1983), p. 171. Suzigan, *Indústria Brasileira*, appendix 2, also uses it to measure relative prices of imports.
40 J. P. Wileman, *Brazilian Exchange*, pp. 166–7. Wileman calculates that in 1893, a third of the gross profit of the firm can be attributed to decline of real wages. (p. 173)
41 For deflating the sterling imports, I have used the import price index (British wholesale prices until 1901) reported in Wilson Suzigan, *Indústria Brasileira*, p. 381. Information on government revenue comes from Annibal Villela and Wilson Suzigan, *Política do Governo e Crescimento da Economia Brasileira, 1889–1945* (Rio de Janeiro, 1975), p. 404.
42 Suzigan, *Indústria Brasileira*, has an extensive discussion on the origins of industrial capital, in which immigrant commercial profits also played an important role. For the rapid advance of Sao Paulo to industrial prominence, see also Villela and Suzigan, *Política do Governo e Crescimento da Economia Brasileira*, pp. 339–44.

APPENDIX

A simple macroeconomic model of simultaneous internal and external equilibrium can be used to relate exchange rates, income, domestic prices and interest rates to a set of exogenous determinants.[1]

I start with a conventional internal equilibrium relationship between the level of real income and real exchange rates, measured in domestic currency per unit of foreign currency, and real interest rates:

$$Y = f(ExR \,/\, P, r) \qquad (3A.1)$$

Y is positively related to a higher (i.e. depreciated) exchange rate since the net export surplus increases, and also inversely related to higher interest rates through sensitivity of investment expenditures.

The next equation is a standard demand for money equation relating real demand for money balances to real income and to the opportunity cost of holding money, the nominal interest rate: the sum of inflation and the real interest rate:

$$\frac{\text{Mon}}{P} = g(Y, r + \dot{P}/P) \tag{3A.2}$$

Equation (3A.3) is the balance of payments identity:

$$P_x X - P_m M(Y, ExR/P) + F - iD = 0 \tag{3A.3}$$

Exports are taken here as exogenous. Where there is relatively little substitutability in production, and long lags in response to past price signals as with coffee, this simplification is justifiable. Imports increase with income and decline with a depreciated exchange rate. F is net foreign lending, while iD is interest on past debt.

Equation (3A.4) sets up a relationship of domestic prices to the exchange rate, foreign prices and income:

$$P = h(P^*, ExR, Y) \tag{3A.4}$$

Purchasing power parity does not always hold owing to divergent non-traded price movements that are dependent upon the size of real income relative to capacity. This provides scope for the real exchange rate changes necessary to assure joint internal and external equilibrium.

This model determines the four endogenous variables Y, ExR, r and P for given values of Mon, $P_x X/P_m$, P^* and $(F - iD)$.(Export earnings are here deflated by an import price index and thereby converted to a measure of import capacity.)

Because of data limitations, the only dependent variable available for test, but a relevant one for our purposes, is the nominal exchange rate. Its relationship to the exogenous variables is clear. An increased supply of money leads to increased real expenditure and/or domestic prices which in turn contribute to a balance of payments deficit; hence the relationship with nominal exchange rates is positive. Larger import capacity leads to a lower (appreciated) exchange rate since it produces an excess supply of foreign exchange. Nominal exchange rates are inversely related to foreign prices through the change in domestic competitiveness and hence import demand. Finally, an increase in loans net of debt service operates exactly like an expansion of exports.

NOTE

1 This model differs in two respects from a related one of Eliana Cardoso, which she used as the basis for analyzing Brazilian exchange rates over the period 1862–1906. Unlike her, I do not reduce import demand back to domestic supply, and hence do not require a domestic wage variable. The data are at best precarious (a questionable cost of living index must be used), and nominal wages are regarded dubiously as exogenous. On the other hand, this version places the capital account in a place of prominence, which seems more appropriate in a late-nineteenth-century context. See her 'Exchange rates in nineteenth-century Brazil: an econometric model,' *Journal of Development Studies*, 19, no. 2 (January 1983), pp. 170–8.

COMMENT 1

Eliana A. Cardoso

> '¿Que dia es hoy?' Aureliano le contestó que era martes. 'Eso mismo pensaba yo', dijo José Arcadio Buendia. 'pero de pronto me he dado cuenta de que sigue siendo lunes, como ayer. Mira el cielo, mira las paredes, mira las bigonias. También hoy es lunes'. Acostumbrado a sus manias, Aureliano no le hizo caso. Al dia seguiente, miércoles, José Arcadio Buendia volvió al taller. 'Eso es un desastre – dijo. Mira el aire, oye el zumbido del sol, igual que ayer y antier. También hoy es lunes.'
>
> Gabriel Garcia Marquez

Fishlow's 'Lessons' is an accomplished and interesting paper. I concentrate my comments on the comparisons between then and now, retaining the flavor of my oral remarks.

Terms of trade deterioration and a cessation of capital inflows make for a deadly combination. That was the case in the 1890s and again is the case in the 1980s. Those are issues identified by Fishlow. I would add that budget deficits and their links to debt and money should not be left aside. In the presence of budget deficits financed by external borrowing, a capital halt forces money creation and inflation. Terms of trade deterioration, followed almost inevitably by depreciation, increases the real cost of servicing the external debt, further worsening the budget. That has been the case in Brazil both in 1891 and in 1983.

But let me start with Argentina. Argentinians

> are always in trouble about their currency. Either it is too good for home use, or as frequently happens it is too bad for foreign exchange. Generally they have too much of it, but their own idea is that they do not have enough. The Argentinians alter their currency almost as frequently as they change their finance ministers. No people on earth has a keener interest in currency experiments than the Argentinians.

One might think of this as a comment on recent experience, but in fact it was written one hundred years ago. When W.R. Lawson wrote this para-

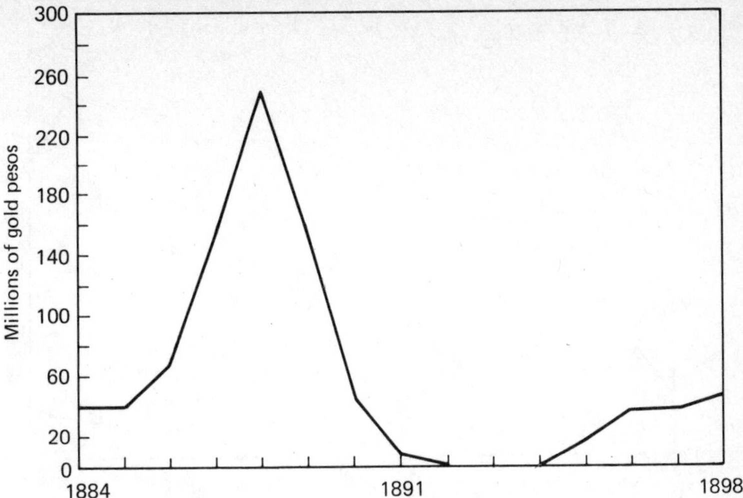

Figure 3C.1 Argentina: foreign borrowing (millions of gold pesos) *Source*: J. H. Williams, *Argentinian International Trade under Inconvertible Paper Money* (Harvard, 1920)

graph in the *Bankers' Magazine* in 1889, he held rational expectations about the Austral Plan and Brodersohn's frustrated attempts at controlling the budget deficit and inflation. Last year the currency was again too good to be true.

As figure 3C.1 shows in a dramatic way, and as Fishlow convincingly argued, the 1890's disaster followed the stoppage of capital inflows in 1889 and the Argentinian terms of trade deterioration.

Then a miracle happened. The invention of the refrigeration process made it possible for Argentina to become a supplier of frozen meat in the world market. From practically zero tons in 1896, chilled beef exports rose to nearly 400 000 tons in 1913, as the new technology was used to ship meat to Europe. For many years Argentina grew happily on the backs of its cows.

If there is a lesson to be learnt from the past, it is that technology innovation is just great. But since it cannot be picked up from trees, economic prospects for Argentina in 1986 looked bleak. Specially if one believes that freezing prices does not work as well as freezing meat.

I turn now to the Brazilian case. Let me first spend a moment on some remarks about Fishlow's equation for the exchange rate behavior in the second half of the nineteenth century.

Fishlow's equations diverge from previous estimates for the Brazilian case,[1] mainly because he has chosen to place the capital account on the right-hand side of his equation. Nonetheless, fundamentals, like real exports and the budget deficit, as well as expectations about their behavior, jointly

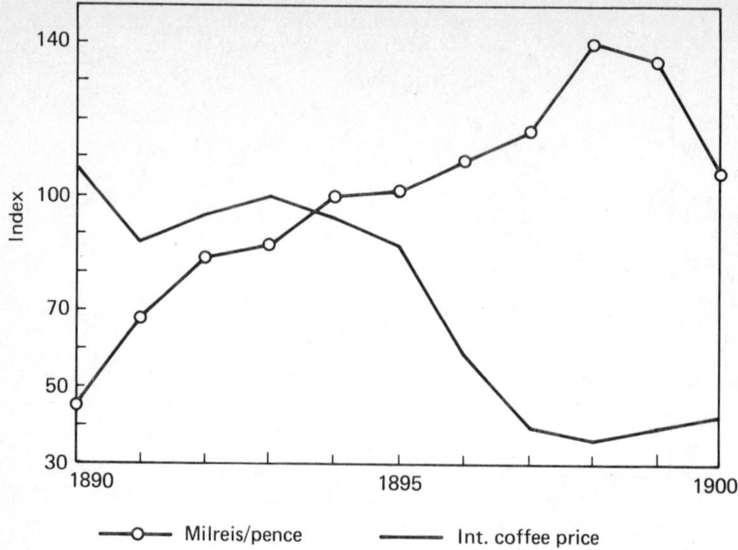

Figure 3C.2 Brazil: exchange rate and coffee prices (indices) *Source*: IBGE, Anuário Estatístico 1939–1940

determine both the exchange rate and capital flows. It is difficult to justify the inclusion of the capital account as an exogenous right-hand side variable in the exchange rate equation.

One should also note another important problem of simultaneity. Export revenues in the nineteenth century were in large part determined by the international price of coffee, which was determined simultaneously with the exchange rate, because of the Brazilian monopoly. Figure 3C.2 shows the remarkable inverse relationship between the two. This problem of simultaneity can be circumvented by the use of bags of coffee and tons of rubber as instruments for real exports.

The problem of the capital inflows simultaneity is a more difficult one. As a consequence one is not surprised by the fact that the coefficient of the variable representing capital inflows minus debt service is not significant. From this finding, Fishlow concludes that 'Brazil's problems were not the Baring Crisis but adverse export earnings' and that there is a 'significant difference in the role of net financial flows in Brazil and Argentina.' One feels skeptical about this conclusion after comparing figures 3C.1 and 3C.3 and observing that in the equations for Argentina the coefficient of the variable representing capital inflows net of debt service also is not significant when instrumental variables are used as the method of estimation.

And since we are at it, let me put in a word of caution concerning data. Difficulties concerning the data for the capital account in Brazil are large since detailed data only exist for central government borrowing, even

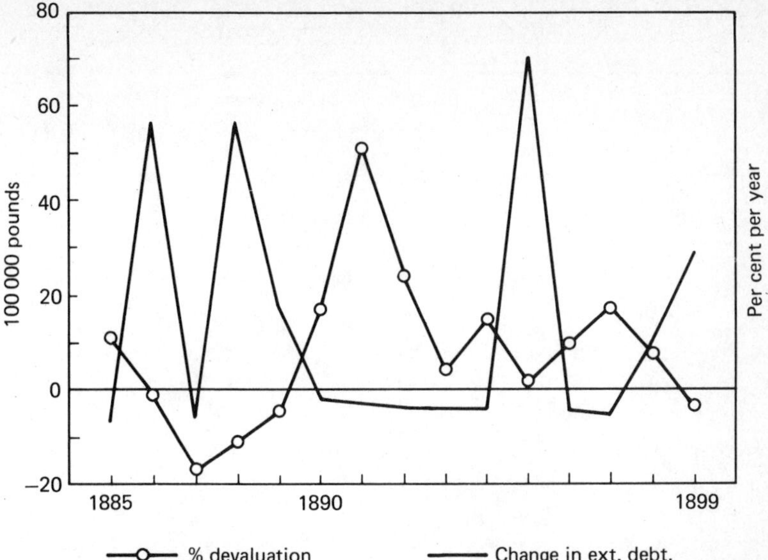

Figure 3C.3 Brazil: exchange rates and external borrowing, 1886–1899 (external borrowing = change in the external debt of the central government *Source*: Bouças, *História da Dıvida Externa* (Rio, 1950)

though it is known that borrowing by local governments and private capital flows were also important at the time. Fishlow's equation indicates that there is still work to be done to identify the issues he has raised.

I turn now to history. Table 3C.1 illustrates how years of decrease in government borrowing net of debt service coincide with the increase in the money base, and how the base could decrease in years where the external debt increased.

The story which underlies this relationship may be told as follows. As long as external credit is available, the government can easily finance its budget deficit, until rising credit requirements collide with credit rationing. The balance of payments crisis results and the exchange rate collapses. Deprived of capital inflows and faced with insufficient taxes, the government is then forced to extract from the private sector, either by money creation or increased domestic debt, the foreign exchange resources it needs. Besides that, the devaluation increases the debt service measured in domestic currency and thus the budget deficit measured in that currency also increases, increasing the required money creation.

Table 3C.2 shows data for the budget. The history of the Brazilian Empire was a history of budget deficits financed by external and domestic borrowing. The Minister Ouro Preto's report of the situation of the budget at the time of the proclamation of the Republic shows that taxes and other

Table 3C.1 Changes in the external debt, money growth and depreciation rates, Brazil, 1888–1902

	Year	*External debt Central Govt (millions of pounds)*	*Money base growth rate (%)*	*Rate of depreciation of milreis/pound (%)*
Abolition of slavery	1888			
Inauguration of the Republic	1889	1.78	12.4	–4.5
	1890	0	63.1	17.2
	1891	–0.31	42.5	51.3
Banking reform	1892	–0.39	5.3	23.9
Civil war	1893	–0.39	9.2	3.8
	1894	–0.40	10.6	14.9
	1895	7.05	–0.1	1.5
	1896	–0.45	5.2	9.7
	1897	–0.56	5.5	17.4
Funding loan	1898	1.03	1.3	7.4
	1899	2.91	–4.9	–3.4
Banking crisis	1900	2.37	–9.3	–21.7
	1901	1.42	–6.4	–16.4
	1902	0	–2.5	–5.0

Sources: Bouças, *História da Dívida Externa* (Ediçoes Financeiras, Rio, 1950); and Pelaéz and Wilson Suzigan, *História Monetária do Brasil* (IPEA, Rio, 1970).

Table 3C.2 Accumulated budget deficit, Brazil, 1824 to 1889 (millions of contos)

Expenditures	
Wars and debt service	664
Infrastructure	425
Calamities	87
Public health	30
Others	24
Total	12340
Revenues	360

Source: Bouças, *História*, 1950

revenues during the time of the Empire covered only 30 per cent of total expenditures. The Republic inherited the debt. The cessation of capital flows in 1889 meant that the deficit had to be financed by money creation. And money did increase.

As long as there is money in Brazil, there is always a feast, and a carnival there was until 1892. Those were the years of the *Encilhamento*. With large inflation rates, financial instability and deterioration of the terms of trade, the situation could not persist for very long. The whole affair culminated with the 1898 Funding Loan, whose conditionality terms were not better than the ones imposed by an IMF standby agreement. Taxes were increased and Murtinho rapidly proceeded to destroy paper currency.

Not having found a refrigeration process, like Argentina, Brazilians had a hard time, at least for a while. Adjustment took place via a dramatic drop in investment.

That adjustment resembles the current one: the other face of the current trade surpluses of 1984 and 1985 was a huge cut in investment expenditures. The current situation further reminds us of former times. Like then, inflation has been high and we had a monetary reform. Notwithstanding the inertialists, large budget deficits have been around for a long time and the cruzado plan could not succeed without a fiscal consolidation. With prices frozen by decree and fast monetization, the economy lived through a consumption boom, until a debt moratorium turned out to be unavoidable. We can only hope that we will not end up in the arms of the IMF, with a program comparable to the Funding Loan of 1889.

Fishlow's paper is in the fine tradition of Carlos's work. It brings extraordinary stories about extraordinary countries, fun enough to make one happy getting one's hands dirty with old books and moving back into economics.

NOTE

1 Eliana Cardoso, 'Exchange rates in nineteenth-century Brazil: an econometric model,' *Journal of Development Studies*, 19(2) (January 1983), pp. 170–8.

COMMENT 2

Ricardo Ffrench-Davis

I will comment on two of the issues that emerge from the interesting paper presented by Fishlow.

The British Government and the Bank of England played in the 1890s a somewhat similar role to that played by the US government, the FED and the IMF in the 1980s. In both cases their respective actions contributed to avert a financial crisis in the creditor center, but action was not enough to avoid an abrupt drop in the volume of capital flows. In the case of Argentina, there was a sharp change from large positive to large negative transfers. The arrangement of 1891, organized by the Bank of England with a group of banks headed by Rothschild, resembles the framework of the 1980s. The agreement involved a bond loan to finance part of interest payments. Bond coupons could be used in maturity to pay custom duties. It was one component of conditionality and guarantees of that time.

As in the present crisis, Argentina tried to expand exports, but there was a general fall of commodity prices. Exporters kept on expanding exports because the international price fall was compensated for by large domestic exchange-rate devaluations. As a consequence, the performance of export value was inferior to that of export quantum. Then, as is the case now, it was imports that contributed the bulk of external adjustment – they halved in 1891. Argentinian imports of machinery and equipment from Great Britain, as Fishlow reports, also halved as a share of British exports between 1886–90 and 1891–95; a striking similarity with the 1980s.

What are some of the outstanding differences? A larger share of borrowing by Argentina went to raise investment before 1890 than it did in the 1970s. Associated with it was the absence in the former period of the huge capital flight that prevailed in the more recent episode. The difference in behavior may be associated, presumably, with institutional factors: the largely unrestricted lending by creditor banks in the 1970s and the larger internationalization of capital markets and communication that has made capital flight easier in recent years.

The more limited internationalization of capital markets is also probably behind the heterogeneous changes faced by debtors in the earlier episode. As Fishlow concludes, both Argentina and Brazil were part of the same international cycle of the 1890s, but Brazil retained a continued, though limited, access to capital, and was able to maintain higher investment rates. Brazil's share of capital goods imports from Great Britain increased *pari passu* with the drop of Argentine imports from that source. The same heterogeneity emerges when analyzing other countries. For instance, Chile had limited access to lending in the 1880s, while in the 1890s could borrow more intensively, duplicating the foreign debt per capita during the decade (Sanfuentes, 1987). Other developing nations such as Australia and South Africa experienced financial shocks some time between 1888 and 1891 (Kindleberger, 1986). However, the similarity between the two episodes breaks in this respect. In fact, there has been a generalized concomitant end to voluntary lending and an across-the-board fall in imports of capital goods from the main creditor center (the USA) during the 1980s.

In brief, both the expansive and the contractive financial shocks appear to have been more generalized in the recent case, with finance playing a stronger role vis-à-vis other variables influencing economic events.

That introduces the second point that I want to consider: the relative weight of the financial dimension and its implications for stability. Pronounced swings and overshooting tend to be closely associated with finance. The title of one insightful paper by Carlos Díaz-Alejandro (1984) is illustrative of the role that finance can play: 'Good-bye financial repression, hello financial crash.'

The 1950s and 1960s and the early 1970s, despite several 'mini-manias' (Kindleberger, 1978), were decades of fast growth and increasing stability in the terms of trade. For instance, growth per capita in 1950–73 was in both developed and in developing countries roughly three times as large as it had been in the long periods of significant development in Great Britain (1700–1881) and the USA (late nineteenth century to mid-twentieth century) as measured by Kuznets (1956). One characteristic feature of the post-war decades was a moderate regulation of financial markets, which played a role subordinated to the 'real' sectors. The 1970s saw the liberalization of financial markets: international markets and domestic markets in less developed countries alike. Finance became, in the second half of the 1970s, the leading determinant of exchange rates in LDCs, debt-led appreciation giving way to large disequilibria in goods markets and paving the road to the crisis of the 1980s: it pushed domestic economies to accommodate large capital inflows that were not sustainable in the medium term. As Díaz-Alejandro (1984) asserted, some historical memory of past crisis would have helped to raise consciousness about the dangers of a permissive liberalization of financial markets.

Fishlow rightly ends his excellent paper with a note: he states that his historical comparison reveals that 'there is something to be said, as Carlos Díaz-Alejandro would have, for national innovation, intervention and experiment'. The role of finance in development strategies is one research area much in need of theoretical and policy design innovation.

REFERENCES

Díaz-Alejandro, C. (1984), 'Goodbye financial repression, hello financial crash.' The Hellen Kellogg Institute for International Studies Working Papers No. 24, University of Notre Dame, Indiana.

Kindleberger, C.P. (1978), *Manias, Panics and Crashes*, New York: Basic Books.

Kindleberger, C.P. (1986), *Keynesianism vs. Monetarism and Other Essays in Financial History*, London: George Allen & Unwin.

Kuznets, S. (1956), 'Quantitative aspects of the economic growth of nations: levels and variability of rates of growth'. *Economic Development and Cultural Change*, 5, no. 1, October.

Sanfuentes, A. (1987), 'La deuda pública externa de Chile entre 1818 y 1935,' *Notas Técnicas*, no. 96, Cieplan, Santiago, March.

4

House Calls of the Money Doctor: The Kemmerer Missions to Latin America, 1917–1931

Barry Eichengreen

> Once upon a time foreign money doctors roamed Latin America prescribing fixed exchange rates and passive gold exchange standard monetary rules. Bankers followed in their footsteps, from the halls of Montezuma to the shores of Daiquiri.
>
> Díaz-Alejandro (1982, p. 5)

Between 1917 and 1930 Professor Edwin Walter Kemmerer of Princeton University served as economic advisor or headed financial missions to seven Latin American countries. After diagnosing the financial condition of his patient (sometimes only under cover of night and with the protection of firearms), Dr Kemmerer prescribed the standard remedies and engaged in the physician's favorite recreation: a round of golf with his colleagues. If the patient swallowed his medicine and responded to treatment, he was favored with bedside visits from long lost friends such as Dillon, Reed.

Dr Kemmerer's house calls were not limited to Latin America. Shortly after receiving his PhD in 1903, he served as financial adviser to the United States Philippines Commission and as chief of the division of currency of the treasury of the Philippine Islands. He headed financial commissions to South Africa in 1924–5, Poland in 1926, and China in 1929, served as a consultant to the Dawes Commission in 1925, and co-chaired an economic survey of Turkey in 1934. Nor did Latin American governments rely exclusively on the most eminent of the money doctors: Kemmerer shared the practice with William Wilson Cumberland, a Princeton PhD; Arthur Young, a research associate at the University of California and Economic Advisor to the US State Department; Arthur's brother John Parke Young, prize pupil of Kemmerer's and student of Central American monetary affairs; and a number of other figures. Some countries such as Brazil preferred British practitioners like Otto Niemeyer or even Swiss and German specialists over American experts. But American money doctors dominated the practice through most of Latin America, and Kemmerer's name soon became synonymous with American financial missions to the region.

It is not hard to understand why Kemmerer involved himself in this practice. Not only was consulting for foreign governments heady stuff, it was lucrative as well. But why should Latin American governments solicit the advice of foreign financial experts in general and North Americans in particular? Insofar as the financial reforms of this era entailed certain common steps – establishing a central bank, regulating the financial sector, reforming the fiscal system, and securing access to foreign capital – foreign experts could offer familiarity and even hands-on experience with previous plans. Their assessment of the economic situation was, for better or worse, detached from domestic political considerations.[1] As for why American experts were preferred, Kemmerer himself offered three reasons. The first was a presumption that the United States was not looking for political aggrandizement. But with the expansion of US activities in Panama, Cuba, the Dominican Republic, Haiti, and Nicaragua, this notion came under increased scrutiny during the 1920s and better explained missions of American experts to China, Persia, Poland, South Africa, and Turkey than it did their employment in the Western Hemisphere.[2]

Kemmerer's second explanation was the rapid expansion and prosperity of the American economy. From a predominantly agricultural nation, seemingly an Argentina of North America, buffeted as recently as 1893 by Latin-American-style convertibility crises, the United States had transformed itself into the world's leading industrial power and the only large country with finances sufficiently sound to maintain its gold standard parity through the tumultuous post-First World War era. Until the Great Depression disabused them of any such notion, observers attributed this prosperity and financial stability to the reforms of central and commercial banking entailed in the Federal Reserve Act of 1914. Who better, therefore, than American financial experts to advise on the establishment of Federal Reserve Systems for Chile or Colombia?[3]

Kemmerer's third explanation for the preference for US advisers was the desire to attract American capital. The employment of American financial experts facilitated government bond flotations on the New York market and encouraged US direct foreign investment. According to Kemmerer,

> A country that appoints American financial advisers and follows their advice in reorganizing its finances, along what American investors consider to be the most successful modern lines, increases its chances of appealing to the American investor and of obtaining from him capital on favorable terms.[4]

In their relationship to the international capital market, the Kemmerer Missions bear a resemblance to IMF conditionality. In recent years commercial banks, when considering whether to extend loans, have been swayed by – indeed, often set as a precondition – the successful conclusion of negotiations with the IMF resulting in access to Fund resources in the upper credit tranches. In the 1920s, arranging the visit of a Kemmerer Commission and implementing its recommendations seemed to exert a similarly reassuring influence over capital markets and to have a catalytic impact on foreign lending. In each case the visit by foreign financial experts served as a market signal. Acceptance of the provisions of an IMF stabilization plan or a Kemmerer Report signaled to the market the government's acknowledgement of the desirability of policies consistent with the priorities of the lenders. Credible promises to balance the budget, stabilize the exchange rate, eliminate subsidies, and encourage wage moderation, all of which were recommendations of Kemmerer and IMF Missions alike, while short of guarantees and not enforceable by lenders, still reveal information about the preferences of the government and thereby influence bankers' assessments of credit and country risk.

Admittedly, the analogy between IMF and Kemmerer Missions is imperfect. The two differed in motives, circumstances, and provisions. IMF missions are typically initiated in response to an inflationary crisis entailing rapid exchange-rate depreciation and monetization of government budget deficits. In contrast, the Kemmerer Missions of the 1920s were not a response to financial crisis. Although exchange rates were oscillating and many government budgets were in deficit, inflation remained at single-digit levels and no spiral of rapid depreciation was underway. Yet from the viewpoint of foreign investors, if not domestic officials, there was some danger that the situation might lapse into crisis. In the final decades of the nineteenth century, many of the countries of Latin America had experienced persistent inflation and exchange-rate depreciation, culminating in debt default. Only at the turn of the century had they taken tentative steps toward joining the gold standard – the single arrangement, in the view of the markets, capable of eliminating financial instability. But with the gold standard's worldwide suspension during the First World War, inflation had been rekindled and exchange rates unpegged. Without exchange-rate stabilization in the form of a gold standard peg, market participants feared that the situation might soon deteriorate to the point where it resembled late-nineteenth-century conditions.

Moreover, the motives for inviting missions of foreign financial experts were not entirely the same in the 1920s as in the 1980s. In addition to its impact on international capital markets, Latin American governments desired the advice of foreign financial experts out of an interest in institutional reform. In many countries, efforts at domestic financial reform initiated some 25 years earlier had been hampered by the absence of a central bank to manage the gold standard and a regulatory apparatus to control the domestic banking system. In others, antiquated domestic tax systems and profligate bureaucracies fed the expansionary bias of fiscal policy, threatening to undermine any attempt to sustain the gold standard peg. The Kemmerer Missions, and the reforms with which they were associated, represented the culmination of a longstanding Latin American interest in fiscal and financial reform. In a sense, the Kemmerer Missions were a combination of the World Bank Missions of the 1960s, concerned with institutional reform, and

IMF Missions of the 1980s, concerned primarily with stabilization and external borrowing.

Finally, Kemmerer and IMF Missions differed in a critical provision. A notable feature of IMF stabilization programs, not shared by Kemmerer Missions, is that countries now receive additional liquidity from a multilateral source outside the commercial banking system, funds which can be used for debt service or for investment projects likely to generate export receipts.[5]

Despite these differences, the analogy between Kemmerer and IMF Missions raises a number of questions. One concerns the importance of the signaling function of a foreign mission compared to any catalytic impact on foreign lending of the injection of IMF liquidity. Another concerns the comparative advantage of purely private agents and supranational organizations in providing market signals. The Kemmerer Commissions were, after all, nothing more than groups of foreign academics hired as consultants by Latin American governments, in part because of the reassuring influence of their seal of approval on potential foreign lenders. Purely private agents also figure in the market-signaling process today. Large money center banks, which engage in significant external lending, have devised practices broadly similar to the conditionality also practiced by supranational organizations and by Kemmerer Commissions in the 1920s. Smaller banks often do not have sufficient information to make credit and country risk judgments and rely on the conditionality and lending decisions – in other words, on signals – transmitted by their larger, externally oriented counterparts.[6] In the 1920s, the thousands of small savers who purchased foreign bonds, and indeed some of the banks and issue houses that endorsed the prospectuses, found themselves in a similar situation and relied on the progress of a Kemmerer Mission when assessing a country's creditworthiness. To put both questions baldly, if it is primarily signals that matter and if private agents can provide them, why not dispense with the IMF?

1. The Structure of Kemmerer Reforms

Although their precise details might differ, the central recommendations of the Kemmerer Missions remained remarkably constant over time. Each commission submitted a series of memoranda centering on three recommendations: currency stabilization through restoration or establishment of the gold standard; legislation restricting the right of note issue to a central bank and regulating the activities of others in much the same manner that member banks were regulated by the US Federal Reserve System; and reform of the tax structure and fiscal system so as to increase revenues and enhance economic efficiency.[7]

Kemmerer's advocacy of the gold standard stemmed not just from his belief that governments could not be entrusted with financial discretion, although he spoke repeatedly of the inability of government authorities to resist the temptation of inflationary finance, quoting proverbs to the effect that 'We have gold because we cannot trust Governments.'[8] He emphasized, in addition, the positive externalities of international money: its tendency to promote international trade, international finance, international migration, and international flows of information.[9] He viewed monetary instability as a source of uncertainty which everywhere depressed business activity but nowhere so much as in the international sphere, paraphrasing Napoleon to the effect that what the world most needs is 'a common law, a common measure, and a common currency.'[10] Failing monetary union, participation in the gold standard was the next best thing, 'the gold standard . . . [being] the only standard which offers an early hope of becoming an international standard.'[11]

The second set of recommendations concerned reform of the banking structure. The right of note issue and responsibility for managing the gold standard were to be entrusted to a central bank. Other banks should be regulated to insure that through reckless credit expansion they did not undermine the gold standard's stability. Kemmerer was involved in the establishment of the Banco de la Reserva del Peru in 1922, the Banco de la Republica in Colombia in 1923, the Banco Central de Chile in 1925, the Banco Central del Ecuador in 1927, and the Banco Central de Bolivia in 1929.[12] In Chile, the recommendations of the experts were embodied in the Monetary Law of 1925. By eliminating all restrictions on the import and export of gold and opening the mint to its free coinage, Chile was placed on the gold standard. The central bank was granted a 50-year monopoly of note issue, and government agencies were prohibited from issuing 'such money or documents that may circulate as money during the period of the Bank's concession.'[13] In Ecuador, 24 new laws propounded by the commission provided the basis for reform. A new central bank, modeled on the US Federal Reserve, was to serve as fiscal agent of the government, made the sole depository of public funds, granted a 50-year monopoly of note issue, and obliged to peg the gold sucre to 20 US cents.[14] Limiting the right of note issue to the central bank, going onto the gold standard, and precluding the monetization of budget deficits were seen as necessary to insure effective control of note circulation and maintenance of monetary stability.

The third strand of the typical Kemmerer Report concerned budgetary reform. In Kemmerer's view, only a balanced budget was consistent with the maintenance of a fixed gold standard peg. He typically recommended adoption of a new budget law, entailing 'modern and scientific' procedures for the imposition, collection, and disbursement of taxes and the accumulation of a reserve of surplus funds. To coordinate budgetary control, responsibility for the public finances was to be centralized in a single ministry. Special subsidies granted to railways, highways, and commercial enterprises were to be eliminated as expensive, inefficient, and regressive. The organic budget law might include statutory limitations on the ability of the authorities to finance one year's expenditures out of the next year's revenues, accounting procedures to permit the consistent estimation of total revenues and outlays, and Gramm-Rudman-like powers for the Minister of Finance to apportion revenues to ministries as they accrued and 'order a reduction in the financial program of the Government if such reduction is deemed necessary for the financial stability of the Government.'[15]

It is easy to see why the standard Kemmerer Commission recommendations appealed to foreign investors. Going onto the gold standard and establishing an independent central bank precluded the financial excesses that the capital markets associated with a managed currency. Insuring that government expenditures, inclusive of interest payments, did not consistently outrun receipts protected a nation's debt-servicing capacity. Reforming the mechanisms through which funds were dispensed reduced the danger that borrowed funds would be dissipated by graft or squandered in nonproductive investment.

Anticipating the government's desire to turn to the international capital market, most Kemmerer Commissions submitted a plan for the public credit. The shallowness of domestic capital markets and foreign ignorance of domestic firms, particularly in smaller countries, dictated that capital be both foreign and 'be obtained in large part through government loans.'[16] While the beneficent effects of foreign capital were never questioned, governments were instructed to exercise care that the rate of return on investments financed with foreign funds exceeded their interest cost. Borrowing to finance current expenditure was justifiable only under extraordinary circumstances such as war or national disaster. Ordinarily, borrowing should be resorted to, the commissioners recommended, only for permanent public improvements. In most Latin American countries, this meant public works such as railways, toll roads, and irrigation projects.

The commissioners were at pains to distinguish public works which would pay their way from those which would not. Borrowing for non-self-supporting public works such as schools, public buildings, and toll-free roads was justifiable only insofar as the public was able and willing to bear the taxation needed to service the loan.[17] Typically, the experts proceeded on the assumption that the contribution of general revenues would be minimal. For example, in 1927 the Kemmerer Commission to Bolivia was requested to pass on the advisability of a proposal to construct a railroad from Cochabamba to Santa Cruz.[18] The Commissioners first noted that the Government had available little more than $6 million to fund a project whose estimated cost was between $21 million and $37 million. They then cited the opinion of 'high engineering authority' that the line could not be expected to pay its running expenses and fixed charges for many years following completion. After observing that 75 per cent of national revenue was already pledged to guarantee existing debt and that 37 per cent of the estimated national government budget was devoted to interest and amortization, they questioned whether the government could succeed in securing a commitment from a reputable banking house, and argued that even if it proved possible to obtain foreign money, doing so would be unwise because of the heavy burden of existing debt and the non-self-financing character of the investment project. These criteria sound strikingly modern but for the absence of a distinction between private and social returns.[19]

The experts recommended that the political authorities create a central agency empowered to determine the character and priority of public works and to oversee their completion. Insuring that funds were devoted to those projects with the highest rates of return and that borrowing only proceeded to the point where returns equaled the interest cost required that the national government control the issue of funded debt by departments and municipalities; projects of law to this effect were submitted. The negative externalities experienced by many national and departmental governments due to overborrowing by the few were duly noted by the experts.[20]

Other recommendations mainly concerned strategies to minimize the cost of foreign borrowing. Countries were urged to plan carefully the distribution of maturities and amortization payments to avoid driving the price of bonds down when issued and up when repurchased for amortization. Diversification was also deemed desirable to minimize the risk that refunding activities would be concentrated at moments when the loan market was disturbed. Governments were instructed to insist on prepayment rights to permit them to capitalize on unanticipated declines in interest rates. Sinking fund provisions, which required amortized bonds, instead of being cancelled, to be held by the bankers until maturity of the entire issue, were viewed as undesirable because of the additional expense of the commission involved and the danger that sequestered bonds might find their way back into the market. Governments were warned against provisions in some loan contracts binding the borrowing country to use loan proceeds for purchases of supplies from the country providing the funds or from specific concerns. The commissioners noted that such provisions proliferated in periods when the New York and London markets were disinclined to lend at favorable interest rates. Rather than representing a way to circumvent the capital market's hesitation, these provisions often entailed substantial hidden charges which the lenders might recoup many times over.[21]

Finally, borrowing nations were urged to establish strong connections with a reputable banking house. The commissioners noted that certain Latin American countries, like Colombia in 1923, had shopped around, using an offer from one banking house as a lever to obtain better terms from another. In the long run, they argued, this was inefficacious. Through a long-term relationship, a banking house can acquire a reputation as a source of information on economic conditions in the borrowing country. Since ignorance was seen as one of the principal impediments to borrowing, cultivation of what the commissioners described as a strong center of propaganda would rebound favorably on the borrowing country. A banking house which anticipated additional financing, they argued further, had an interest in maintaining an orderly market in the securities of the indebted country, which would lead it to intervene in support of that country's bonds if the market was disturbed by nearby revolution or default. Finally, a strong connection with a leading banking house was seen as useful in times of emergency. A temporary budget deficit could be tided over by short-term external borrowing only if the government possessed a firm connection with a foreign banker willing to incur the risks and expenses of such a loan in anticipation of future commissions.[22]

For countries in default, regaining access to the international capital market required adjustment of the existing debt and resumption of service. Ecuadorian debt service, at the time of the Kemmerer Commission's visit, was up to date on only one of four issues recognized by the national government, and interest on the First Mortgage Bonds, which accounted for 95 per cent of the total foreign debt, was 14 years in arrears. These interest arrears amounted to nearly two-thirds of the total principal outstanding.[23] In its negotiations with the Corporation of Foreign Bondholders, the Kemmerer Commission suggested that Ecuador press for a substantial reduction of the obligation. Most of the paper was held by speculators who had purchased it for 20 to 30 per cent of par and who would reap generous returns were the bonds redeemed at 35. Ecuador might obtain more favorable terms, he noted, if it paid cash rather than issued refunding bonds. While careful to note that the specific terms of the settlement were outside the province of the financial commission, the experts nonetheless suggested general lines that negotiations might follow. In the Ecuadorian case, the principal and interest arrears would cost the country $7 million if paid off at 35; Kemmerer envisaged a loan of $9 million, leaving $2 million for other productive uses.[24]

A problem faced by new Latin American regimes attempting to gain access to the US capital market was lack of diplomatic recognition. The State Department received letters from bondholders urging them not to recognize the new Ecuadorian regime until an acceptable debt settlement had been reached.[25] But as Kemmerer pointed out, this created a 'Catch 22' situation: Ecuador was unable to settle with the bondholders until it contracted a foreign loan, but it could not float a loan in New York before securing recognition. Thus, Kemmerer urged upon the State Department the more farsighted policy of according recognition.

2. Kemmerer Missions and US Lending

To analyze the capital market response to the Kemmerer Missions, I employ data on the value of US foreign lending through 1929 assembled by Lewis (1938). Lewis's tabulations have two advantages: first, she attempted to include all foreign securities purchased in the United States, not just publicly issued bonds and shares but also those privately taken; second, she sought to exclude any portion sold in foreign markets and securities of American-controlled enterprises. For each country and year, the total face value of issues is provided separately for short- and long-term debt and for national and provincial government, municipal and corporate issues.

A first test of the hypothesis that Kemmerer Missions initiated a rise in US

Table 4.1 Aggregate face value of foreign dollar loans issued to countries hosting Kemmerer Missions (millions of US dollars)

Year	*Colombia (1923)*	*Guatemala (1924)*	*Chile (1925)*	*Poland (1926)*	*Bolivia (1927)*
1921	—	—	44.0	—	9.3
1922	6.8	—	18.0	—	25.0
1923	—	—	—	—	—
1924	9.0	—	18.3	5.0	5.1
1925	4.0	—	55.2	44.4	—
1926	43.5	—	75.2	2.8	—
1927	68.4	—	22.5	47.0	12.3
1928	71.4	0.6	79.9	17.0	19.7
1929	1.8	—	42.4	—	—
1930	0.5	—	21.4	—	—

Source: Lewis (1938)

lending is to compute the *t*-statistic for the difference in mean levels of lending between the two years immediately preceding and immediately following each mission. The power of the tests is not high, since Lewis's period encompasses only five Kemmerer Missions: Colombia in 1923, Guatemala in 1924, Chile in 1925, Poland in 1926, and Bolivia in 1927 (see table 4.1). The *t*-statistic is 1.40 for long-term national loans and 1.74 for long-term municipal loans, with a critical 90 per cent value of 1.40 (one-tail test). In contrast, the *t*-statistics of 0.45 for short-term national loans, 1.00 for short-term municipal loans, and 0.15 for long-term corporate loans indicate insignificant increases in lending. (No short-term corporate loans to these countries are reported.) When the three years preceding and following each Kemmerer Mission are compared, Bolivia must be dropped for lack of data for 1930, but the *t*-statistic for long-term national loans rises to 1.55 and for long-term municipal loans to 1.87, compared to a critical value of 1.44. Again, there is no evidence that either short-term loans or loans to non-governmental entities were affected significantly by the Kemmerer Missions.

One approach to increasing the power of the test is to pool the five types of loans. The *t*-statistics are 1.46 for two-year periods and 1.47 for three-year periods, both compared to a critical value of 1.30; these are little different from those reported above. Another approach assumes that the impact of Kemmerer Missions is the same across categories of borrowers but recognizes that average levels of lending to each category differed. Lending can be regressed on dummy variables for type of borrower and for periods after Kemmerer's visits. Results appear in the first two columns of table 4.2. For three-year periods, the coefficient capturing the effects of Kemmerer's visits is statistically significant at the 95 per cent level (one-tail test); for two-year periods it approaches significance at that level.

Since the previous paragraph suggests that the impact of Kemmerer Missions on long-term national and municipal borrowing differed from their

Table 4.2 US lending and Kemmerer Missions (dependent variable is value of lending over two- or three-year period in millions of US dollars)

Variable	*Two year*	*Three year*	*Two year*	*Three year*
Constant	–2454.5	–4414.0	–728.4	–910.5
	(0.64)	(0.65)	(0.19)	(0.13)
Long-term national	17 179.0	26 995.0	8031.6	11 814.0
	(3.46)	(3.24)	(1.31)	(1.18)
Short-term national	1785.1	2231.4	1785.1	2231.4
	(0.36)	(0.25)	(0.38)	(0.27)
Long-term municipal	3404.4	4005.5	3671.2	4589.0
	(0.65)	(0.45)	(0.60)	(0.43)
Short-term municipal	1400.0	1750.0	1400.0	1750.0
	(0.28)	(0.20)	(0.29)	(0.21)
Period following mission	5129.0	9078.0	1656.7	2070.9
	(1.63)	(1.68)	(0.43)	(0.31)
Period following mission* long-term national			18 295.0	30 363.0
			(2.36)	(2.44)
Period following mission* long-term municipal			–933.5	–1166.9
			(0.12)	(0.09)
R^2	0.30	0.32	0.43	0.45
n	50	42	50	42

t-statistics in parentheses.

Source: See text

impact on short-term borrowing and borrowing by corporations, the dummy variables for long-term national or long-term municipal loans were interacted with the Kemmerer Mission dummy. These results appear in the final two columns of table 4.2. Only long-term loans to national governments appear to have been significantly affected by the Kemmerer Missions. The coefficient on such loans interacted with periods succeeding a Kemmerer Mission significantly exceeds zero at the 99 per cent level when three-year periods are compared, and approaches significance at that level for two-year periods.

Since the recommendations of the experts pertained principally to central government financial and fiscal affairs, it is plausible that loans to national governments were affected mainly. Moreover, since some reforms affected state and local public finance and brought under centralized control borrowing by other levels of government (this was not uniformly the case), it is plausible that the results should suggest some, albeit weaker, influence over lending to municipalities. The impact of reform of public finance on lending to corporations, a relationship emphasized by those who believed that financial stability was critical for commercial and industrial prosperity, is not evident in the data.

It can be objected that these effects are properly attributable to the fact of stabilization and going onto the gold standard rather than to the intervention of financial experts. If so, then the same rise of lending between the periods immediately preceding and following stabilization should be observed in other countries. Evidence for 22 other countries to which the US lent during the 1920s does not bear out this contention, however. Again, the two- and three-year periods preceding and following stabilization, chosen as the year in which that country returned to the gold standard *de facto*, may be compared. In every case the *t*-statistic for the difference in means is considerably smaller than the comparable *t*-statistic for countries with Kemmerer Missions. In no case is the difference in means statistically significant at the 90 per cent level.

The results of this section confirm that gold standard stabilizations which took place in conjunction with Kemmerer Missions were unusually conducive to foreign lending. To understand how and why this was so, it is necessary to examine individual country experiences.

3. The Success of Kemmerer Reforms

Whether judged according to Kemmerer's priorities, which attached special importance to maintaining price stability, restoring the gold standard, and balancing the government budget, or according to the favorable reaction of the international capital market as reflected in the enthusiasm with which it responded to subsequent attempts to float a loan, the Kemmerer Missions of the mid to late 1920s were more successful than those which came before or after. The explanation cannot lie in any improvement in procedures and recommendations since, as already noted, those procedures and recommendations changed little over time. Rather, the explanation must lie in the circumstances. Hence the contrast between the earlier and later missions sheds light on the circumstances under which Kemmerer-style conditionality is most likely to have a catalytic effect on international loan negotiations. That contrast suggests that changes in the domestic political and international economic environments, including the extent of political stability, trends in primary commodity prices, and conditions in the New York capital market, together account for the catalytic effect of the Kemmerer Missions of the later 1920s.

The role of these three determinants of the outcome of the Kemmerer Missions is illustrated by the contrasting cases of Mexico and Chile. The overarching importance of political stability is evident in the Mexican case. For most of the second decade of the twentieth century, Mexico had been racked by revolutionary and counter-revolutionary campaigns culminating in civil war. Service on the $600 million external debt was suspended in early 1914, and by 1915 political, economic, and fiscal institutions were nearing collapse. Following adoption of the Queretaro Constitution in 1917 and the restoration of some stability, Kemmerer was approached to organize a financial mission to the country. He and his associates recommended that the authorities balance the budget, stabilize the currency, and implement a program of fiscal reform designed to enhance the efficiency of tax collection and increase the progressivity of its incidence.[26]

No sooner had the commission begun to formulate these proposals than attempts to execute the land reform provisions suggested by the new Constitution and to limit the power of the Church began to 'unsettle confidence, reduce productivity, and make for unrest, with results involving both decreases in revenues and increases in expenditures.'[27] Article 27 of the new Constitution, which declared all subsoil resources the patrimony of the nation and raised the specter of nationalization of the petroleum industry, placed a cap on foreign investment. With the resurgence of unrest, railway lines were severed, agricultural output declined, and mining centers were overrun by bandits. The major banks were forced to close their doors and the nation was rendered dependent for money balances on the circulation of gold and silver coin and US dollars.[28] Political turmoil, in conjunction with newly progressive taxation, provided a double inducement for capital flight which defeated attempts to place the budget on a stable footing.

These disruptions rendered irrelevant Kemmerer's recommendation that Mexico adopt the gold standard immediately upon achieving a minimum specie backing of 40 per cent of note circulation, by ruling out any attempt to acquire the needed gold and threatening a run on reserves if the authorities were so reckless as to institute convertibility.[29] While provision for a central bank was incorporated into the new Constitution, that bank was only established in 1925. Thus, the Mexican authorities had no opportunity to demonstrate either their commitment to, or the efficacy of, Kemmerer's newly designed financial arrangements. While the budget avoided collapse, it did not move into balance in the manner the Commission recommended. The semblance of balance it retained was due to the tendency of the First World War and the postwar boom to stimulate oil revenues and inflate the prices of other mineral products. With the collapse of commodity prices after 1921 and the heavy expenditures incurred in suppressing the Huerta revolt of 1923–4, fiscal conditions disintegrated.

Not surprisingly, the capital market's response was not up to Kemmerer Commission standards. The Mexican authorities sought to capitalize on Kemmerer's visit and on the commodity-price boom of 1920–1 by securing US loans for use in stabilizing the currency, establishing the central bank, and financing reconstruction and development projects. But the Department of State, in collaboration with the International Committee of Bankers on Mexico, embargoed loans to the new government.[30] Not only did the State Department discourage lending directly, but it withheld diplomatic recognition, effectively blockading access to the New York market. The officials and the bankers were united by the former's interest in securing Mexico's signature on a treaty which would nullify the provisions of Article 27 and the latter's desire to see debt service resumed.

After convoluted negotiations and continued State Department pressure, in 1922 President Obregon announced Mexico's intention to resume payment on the external debt, subject only to agreement with the bankers on the size and schedule of payments and the disposition of back interest. Initially, discussions proceeded on the assumption that Mexico was not seeking new money. Just when the two parties seemed to have an agreement in hand, however, a loan to finance the establishment of the central bank was proposed by the Minister of Finance. This the American bankers refused. Mexico went ahead with the agreement nonetheless, recognizing an external debt of more than $500 million and interest arrearages of $280 million. However, the outbreak of the Huerta Rebellion made it impossible to transfer interest on schedule, and in June 1924 Obregon suspended the agreement with the bankers. As late as 1928, a committee of American financial experts reminded the bankers that 'internal dissensions and strained international relations have repeatedly shaken confidence in such a way as to cause exports of capital and discourage investment in Mexico'.[31]

Thus, the Mexican experience indicates that favorable commodity prices like those which prevailed in 1920–1 were, at best, a necessary condition for the successful implementation of the Kemmerer Commission recommendations. Fiscal reform, however well conceived, was likely to be ineffective if it was not accompanied by domestic political stability, in whose absence the capital market was unwilling to respond.

In contrast to the Mexican experience, Kemmerer's 1925 mission to Chile epitomized the work of the successful financial commission. Nearly four decades of inflation provided the backdrop to Kemmerer's visit.[32] In Chile, the pressure for monetization had traditionally emanated, not from government budget deficits, but from loans by the agricultural mortgage banks to the landed interests. When inflation accelerated, wages lagged behind prices, savings were eroded, and commerce was disrupted, while the mortgage burden of the large landowners was lightened.[33] In response to this situation, the mercantile middle class, miners, and agricultural laborers all pressed for economic and social reform.

The election of Arturo Alessandri in 1920 reflected these pressures, and Alessandri's new regime was successful in stabilizing the exchange rate and in nearly bringing inflation to a halt. His attempts to reform the public finances and obtain a mission of American financial experts were frustrated, however, by continued Congressional dominance of the landed interests. The deadlock led to Alessandri's replacement by a military junta in 1924, his recall to power following a counter-coup in 1925, and then his replacement by Colonel Carlos Ibanez and a semi-dictatorial regime before the end of the same year. There was then some resurgence of inflation. But however disturbing this political turmoil, it never involved the violence and disorder experienced in Mexico; if anything it strengthened the hand of those pressing for monetary reform. The 1924 revolution freed the government from the dominance of the landed interests, and until the adoption of a new constitution, the president was empowered to pass decree laws with only the approval of his Cabinet. These powers greatly expedited the process of financial reform. The military group backing the new regime unanimously supported monetary stabilization, pressured the government to implement a program, and turned out en masse to greet Kemmerer on his midnight arrival in Santiago.

External stability, the second necessary condition, was also present in the Chilean case. In the mid-1920s conditions in world markets for nitrates and copper were relatively favorable, stimulating export earnings. These earnings remained respectable even though real wages had reversed most of the erosion previously caused by inflation. There was no structural deficit in the public sector accounts contributing to a trade deficit. The exchange rate had remained relatively stable for four years and even moved upwards in anticipation of the visit of financial experts. The government's reserve position was strong: its gold reserves and nitrate pledges would have been sufficient to retire all the paper money in circulation.

Optimism in international capital markets regarding the developing world, a third condition favoring the success of Kemmerer-style reforms, was also present in the Chilean case. American bondholders invested $187 million in Chilean public institutions between June 1925 and August 1929, more than three times the 1919–25 total. It might be argued that the creditors' willingness to underwrite Chilean loans merely reflected the favorable political and economic developments described above. But in addition, the timing of Chile's stabilization was fortuitous: coming in 1925 it coincided with a boom in foreign lending by New York and London, which surely improved the terms and increased the availability of the loans that the Chileans secured. These loans permitted the monetary orthodoxy of the gold standard to coexist with loose domestic credit conditions and a highly expansionary program of public works.

Unlike those in Mexico, the authorities in Chile had an early opportunity to demonstrate the efficacy of, and their commitment to, these new arrangements. In the summer of 1926, the breakdown of Tacna-Arica negotiations with Peru created a war scare and a run on the central bank. In ten days the bank furnished $5 million in foreign exchange in a successful defence of the gold standard. Later, when the onset of the Great Depression forced other Latin American countries to depreciate their currencies in 1929, Chile remained on the gold standard through Britain's departure in September 1931.

While the roles of political stability, commodity prices, and capital-market conditions are somewhat less transparent in the Colombian case, the negotiations surrounding the Kemmerer Missions to Bogota in 1923 and 1930 shed special light on bank conditionality in the 1920s and on the role of American financial experts. As in other Latin American countries, labor, and the mercantile and industrial middle classes, challenged entrenched Conservative–Church leadership in the 1920s. The Colombian regime accommodated these pressures by passing legislation empowering the government to intervene in capital-labor disputes, to regulate health and safety, and to construct houses for the working class. But the post-First World War administration of Pedro Nel Ospina inherited a budgetary problem attributable, in part, to generous subsidies paid to the Church and Society of Jesus, and an inconvertible currency resulting from paper money issued during the European war.[34] Once Colombia's dispute with the United States over the separation of Panama was finally settled by the Tomson-Urrutia Treaty of 1921–2, Ospina turned to the US for financial assistance. The 1923 Kemmerer Mission offered the usual formula: establishment of a central bank, regulation of branch banking, reorganization of the customs system, adherence to the gold standard, maintenance of a balanced budget, and securing an arrangement with an exclusive fiscal agent.

The Commission's recommendations were implemented with some difficulty only over the objections of domestic bankers who opposed regulation, government employees who opposed fiscal austerity, residents of outlying regions who opposed economic centralization, coffee-growers who preferred the creation of an agricultural mortgage bank capable of providing liberal credit, and those who feared the undue influence of the United States. The capital market's response remained subdued until it became apparent that the new institutional arrangements would take.

As in Chile, an early demonstration of the efficacy of the new institutions, and of the authorities' commitment to them, proved critical. Not long after their adoption, the failure of one of the nation's largest importing and merchandising houses undermined the solvency of a major bank. As panic spread, the government declared a two-day bank holiday and took the opportunity to import bank notes by airplane. Through their free provision, the crisis was surmounted. Following this demonstration, Colombia's search for a fiscal agent initiated a competitive scramble between London and New York. The government had previously borrowed in Europe, and Lazards stood ready to act as its exclusive agent. Britain's presence had been reinforced by establishment of a Bogota office of the London and River Plate Bank in 1920, and of branch offices in subsequent years.[35] But Thomas Russell Lill, a member of the Kemmerer Commission who remained under contract to Colombia as Technical Advisor to the Government, used his influence to encourage the selection of an American banking firm. Recognizing the existence of a 'unique financial opening . . . [an] entering wedge . . .,' the State Department's legation in Bogota urged officials in Washington to arrange a cooperative offer from the principal American competitors, Blair and Morgan.[36]

Only $9 million of Colombian government bonds were floated in New York in 1924, and $8 million in 1925. But their value rose to $34 million in 1926, $67 million in 1927, and $79 million in the first half of 1928.[37] About this time observers grew alarmed over the nature and volume of Colombian borrowing. In 1928, the US Commerce Department warned that Colombian credit may have been endangered.[38] In 1929, Jefferson Caffery of the American legation in Bogota advised Washington that information provided by the Municipality of Bogota exaggerated the progress of public works, contained unduly optimistic revenue estimates, and was 'highly misleading and obviously designed for bond market propaganda.'[39] But it is unclear what role these fears, as opposed to the 1928 boom on Wall Street, and concomitant decline in US foreign lending, or the 1929 slump in coffee prices and deterioration in the government's budgetary position, played in the drop in American lending to Colombia after the first semester of 1928.

Another influence over American lending to Colombia was the dispute over oil concessions. At the end of 1927 and beginning of 1928, Colombia imposed new controls on the US-dominated oil industry, requiring firms to obtain drilling permits and pay a doubled tax on production on private lands. Members of the British legation suggested that New York issue houses, with the encouragement of the State and Commerce Departments, were refusing loans to Colombia and driving down the market prices of bonds to extract concessions on the oil question.[40]

The natural way to remedy the situation was to arrange a mission of foreign experts. First a petroleum commission was appointed to prepare new legislation clarifying the position of foreign companies, but with the approach of the 1930 presidential election, the Colombian Congress adjourned before it could be adopted. The election brought to power the Liberal Enrique Olaya Herrera, formerly the Colombian representative at Washington, who was well respected in the United States, and had campaigned on the promise to offer Kemmerer a return engagement. Following conferences at the Federal Reserve Bank of New York, he announced his intention to obtain a foreign loan and arranged a second Kemmerer Mission. This time, however, Kemmerer recommended against foreign borrowing. While he suggested that defending the gold standard, reducing expenditures, and reforming the administration of the customs and railroads might do much to reassure foreign bankers, Kemmerer suggested that recession in Latin America and the depressed state of the New York market made it 'extremely difficult to sell a large enough issue to fund the present deficit.'[41] Instead, the government was urged to sell bonds domestically.

The market's response to the 1930 Kemmerer Mission sheds light on which deterrents to foreign lending were binding. Contrary to Kemmerer's expectations, in 1930 Colombia successfully obtained $20 million in credit in New York, although Kemmerer's skepticism of Colombia's general ability to borrow in the Depression was subsequently proven correct. A syndicate headed by National City Bank advanced $3 million and turned over the residual in installments ending in June 1931. Obviously, recovery from the Depression was not a precondition for obtaining foreign money. The progress of petroleum legislation may have been more important, since Olaya's support for it was well known. Nonetheless, 60 per cent of the proceeds of the dollar loan was transferred to Colombia before any legislation was drafted, much less before it was signed by the President in March 1931.

The principal determinant of Colombian creditworthiness was the conditionality practiced by the American banks in conjunction with Kemmerer's activities. In some respects, the National City Bank conditionality and the Kemmerer conditionality were complementary. National City required, as a condition of the loan, that Colombia balance its budget but for that portion which would be financed by an internal loan of 6 million pesos, and that it revise its financial and customs systems. The government's invitation to Kemmerer signaled its willingness to do so, and its possession of a plan of action. 'Kemmerer's reforms substituted for more direct banker supervision of government . . . [and] appeared "scientifically" sound and less insulting to national pride.'[42] But in other respects the two forms of conditionality did not complement one another. National City wished Colombia to adopt, in addition to other measures, a debt ceiling law. Kemmerer objected to any such clause in the loan contract on the grounds that it was not enforceable if a future legislature wished to repeal it and that it would threaten the central bank's ability to lend freely in time of crisis. While favoring an exclusive arrangement with a fiscal agent, Kemmerer chided the bankers for their last-minute efforts to impose such conditions on Colombia in its time of need.[43]

By the end of 1930, Kemmerer's task was complete, whereas the bankers had yet to turn over the final installments of the loan. Before making the third payment in March 1931, the bankers demanded and secured the debt ceiling which limited interest and amortization to 30 per cent of government revenues.[44] They attempted to withhold the final payment on the grounds that the government budget deficit exceeded agreed limits. Olaya responded that the bankers' objections were mere technicalities. Unlike Kemmerer, the Colombian President retained some leverage: he conferred with the American Minister, who called the State Department, which encouraged National City Bank to turn over the remaining tranche.[45]

4. Conclusion

The resemblance of the Kemmerer Missions of the 1920s to IMF conditionality as practiced in recent years has been noted previously, both by Latin American historians, and by critics of the current international financial arrangements. Three questions are raised by the extent of the parallels. First, under what conditions is outside intervention needed to signal creditworthiness to the international capital market? Second, must the signal be provided by an international agency, or can the essential functions be carried out by the indebted government in conjunction with banks and experts from the private sector? Third, are there conditions under which the international capital markets fail to respond to signals of a country's fiscal and monetary orthodoxy, however convincing, creating an efficiency rationale for a transnational agency which can inject financial resources from a reserve outside the capital markets?

The Kemmerer Missions shed light on the manner in which this market-signaling process works. In the 1920s, creditworthiness meant that the government had taken steps to balance its budget, create an autonomous central bank, limit money and credit creation to levels consistent with maintenance of the gold standard, and allocate borrowed funds to projects yielding, at least, the market rate of return. Together these measures increased the likelihood that the nation would retain the capacity to service its debt. An invitation to Kemmerer signaled the authorities' willingness to contemplate these measures. Successful completion of his mission indicated that the government possessed a plan of action, and legislation implementing its recommendations signaled that it was taking concrete steps toward implementation.

But if the Kemmerer Commissions, despite their purely private status, were highly efficient providers of market signals, signals alone proved adequate only under favorable conditions. They worked well in the mid- to late 1920s, where working is defined as helping a country secure access to the international capital market, only because the industrialized countries were growing rapidly, export markets were buoyant, and financial centers were favorably inclined toward lending to developing regions. When these conditions disappeared, the response of the capital markets was disappointing; once trade collapsed and the fashion for foreign lending passed, Kemmerer's intervention was insufficient to restore access to foreign funds. The implication is that IMF conditionality — which differs by virtue of the Fund's own financial resources and by the leverage it can bring to bear on other lenders — is crucial precisely when access to external funds is most valuable.

NOTES

For permission to cite materials from the Kemmerer papers, I thank the Princeton University Library. For permission to cite materials in the Public Record Office, I thank the Controller of HM Stationery Office. Gustavo Franco, Jeffrey Williamson and especially José O'Campo provided helpful comments.

1 As the Colombian President told his Congress in 1923, reforms were more likely to be implemented if recommended by foreigners 'whose prestige would not be haggled away as would happen with our own professionals in a backward environment like ours, in which nothing and no one escape the objections and pettiness of politics.' Cited in Drake (1979, p. 22).
2 Angell (1933, pp. 4–41).
3 Kemmerer himself was a leading expert on the operation of the Federal Reserve System; see Kemmerer (1918a).
4 Kemmerer (1927, p. 4).
5 In this the Kemmerer Missions contrast with the League of Nations' European stabilization loans in the early 1920s. For details, see Nurkse (1946).
6 Friedman (1984, pp. 109–10).
7 Prototypical is the 1926–7 Ecuadorian mission described below and, in more detail, by Perez (1928).
8 Kemmerer (1944, p. 181).
9 Kemmerer (1944, ch. VII). See also Seidel (1972, p. 523).
10 Kemmerer (1916, p. 66).
11 Kemmerer (1934, p. 13).

12 Kemmerer (1926, p. 271).
13 Collins (1929, p. 476).
14 Perez (1928, p. 82).
15 'Report in support of a project of an organic budget law,' Kemmerer Papers, Princeton University (hereafter EWK), Box 432 (Colombia, 1930).
16 'Report on public credit' (submitted to the President of the Republic and the Ministers of Finance, on 15 March 1927, by the Commission of Financial Advisers), EWK, Box 216 (Ecuador, 1927), p. 1.
17 A clear statement of these rules appears in 'Republic of Bolivia: report on public credit' (as submitted to the President of the Republic and the Minister of Finance, on 2 July 1927 by the Commission of Financial Advisers), EWK, Box 66 (Bolivia, 1927).
18 'To His Excellency the President of the Republic of Bolivia' (La Paz, 24 June 1927), EWK, Box 137 (Bolivia, 1927). Other cost estimates are cited in the skeptical discussion of this project by Marsh (1928, pp. 83–6).
19 The absence of this distinction is notable in a 1930 Colombian report, in which the 2.1 per cent rate of return before depreciation and interest charges on Government investments in national railways is contrasted with the 12 per cent cost of borrowed funds, without any mention of indirect benefits to the nation or to the government budget. 'A plan of public credit,' EWK, Box 122 (Colombia, 1930), section IX, p. 5. But this distinction was alluded to in a 1923 memorandum to Colombian officials. 'Report on public credit,' EWK, Box 95 (Colombia, 1923).
20 'A plan of public credit,' EWK, Box 122 (Colombia, 1930), section III.
21 'Republic of Bolivia: report on public credit' (as submitted to the President and the Minister of Finance on 2 July 1927 by the Commission of Financial Advisors), EWK, Box 66 (Bolivia, 1927), pp. 20–1.
22 'Report on public credit,' EWK, Box 95 (Colombia, 1923), p. 3; 'Report on public credit' (submitted to the President of the Republic and the Ministers of Finance, on 15 March 1927, by the Commission of Financial Advisers), EWK, Box 216 (Ecuador, 1927), pp. 30–4; 'Republic of Bolivia: report on public credit' (as submitted to the President of the Republic and the Minister of Finance, on 2 July 1927 by the Commission of Financial Advisers), Box 66 (Bolivia, 1927), pp. 23–7.
23 'Report on public credit' (submitted to the President of the Republic and the Ministers of Finance, on 15 March 1927, by the Commission of Financial Advisers), EWK, Box 216 (Ecuador, 1927), p. 12.
24 'The financial situation in Ecuador' (Conversation with E.W. Kemmerer), Department of State, Division of Latin American Affairs, 29 December 1927, National Archives M 1294 822.57a/59, p. 1
25 'The financial situation in Ecuador' (Conversation with E.W. Kemmerer), Department of State, Division of Latin American Affairs, 29 December 1927, National Archives M 1294 822.57a/59, pp. 1–2.
26 Kemmerer's invitation was an outgrowth of consultations between representatives of the Mexican and American governments designed to paper over strains caused by the recently promulgated export tax on minerals and the impact of domestic unrest on the operations of foreign enterprises. Other members of the mission included Arthur Young and H.A. Chandler of Columbia University. The tax reform plan was sufficiently well received to provide the basis of the Mexican revenue system for a period of decades. Curti and Birr (1954, pp. 160–1).

27 'Report on the fiscal and economic condition of Mexico,' prepared for the International Committee of Bankers on Mexico, Thomas W. Lamont, Chairman, by Joseph Edmund Sterrett and Joseph Stancliffe Davis, New York, 25 May 1928, EWK, Box 107 (Mexico, 1928), p. 4.
28 Kemmerer (1918b, pp. 261–2).
29 The Commission's monetary proposals are described in Kemmerer (1918b).
30 On the origins of the International Bankers Committee, see Smith (1963). Further information on the Mexican episode may be found in Kane (1973).
31 'Report on the fiscal and economic condition of Mexico,' prepared for the International Committee of Bankers on Mexico, Thomas W. Lamont, Chairman, by Joseph Edmund Sterrett and Joseph Stancliffe Davis, New York, 25 May 1928, EWK, Box 107 (Mexico, 1928), p. 28.
32 For discussion, see Fetter (1931) or Davis (1963).
33 Kemmerer (1926, pp. 269–70).
34 Bernstein (1964, pp. 120–1).
35 Joslin (1963, pp. 239–41).
36 'To the Honorable Secretary of State, Washington, from Samuel H. Piles, Legation of the United States of America, Bogota, Colombia,' No. 337, 12 January 1924, National Archives M 1294 821.51/251, pp. 2–3.
37 For these and related statistics, see Young (1930).
38 Rippy (1931, pp. 166–73); Parks (1935, p. 473).
39 'To the Honorable Secretary of State, Washington, from Jefferson Caffery, Legation of the United States of America, Bogota, Colombia,' No. 665, 31 October 1929, National Archives, M 1294 821.51a, p. 2. See also letter No. 669, dated 4 November from the same file.
40 On Commerce Department actions, see Bureau of Foreign and Domestic Commerce, Special Circular No. 305, reprinted in US Senate (1931–2), pp. 730–8. On British interpretations, see 'To the Right Honourable Arthur Henderson, Esq. M.P., Department of Overseas Trade from the British Legation Bogota,' British Public Record Office 371/13478, 19 November 1929.
41 'A plan of public credit,' EWK, Box 122 (Colombia, 1930), section 6.
42 Drake (1979, p. 53).
43 Kemmerer Diary (transcript), EWK, 1930–175 (24 June 1930), 1930–262 (19 September 1930).
44 *New York Times*, 5 January 1931.
45 *New York Times*, 13 January 1932.

REFERENCES

Angell, James W. (1933), *Financial Foreign Policy of the United States*, New York: Council on Foreign Relations.

Bernstein, Harry (1964), *Venezuela and Colombia*, Englewood Cliffs, New Jersey: Prentice-Hall.

Collins, Harry T. (1927), 'Currency reforms in South America,' *Current History*, pp. 475–7.

Curti, Merle and Birr, Kendall (1954), *Prelude to Point Four: American Technical Missions Overseas, 1838–1938*, Madison: University of Wisconsin Press.

Davis, Tom E. (1963), 'Eight decades of inflation in Chile, 1879–1959: a political interpretation,' *Journal of Political Economy*, LXXI, 389–97.

Díaz-Alejandro, Carlos (1983), 'Stories of the 1930s for the 1980s,' In Pedro Aspe Armella, Rudiger Dornbusch and Maurice Obstfeld (eds.), *Financial Policies and the World Capital Market: The Problem of Latin American Countries*, Chicago: University of Chicago Press, pp. 5–35.

Drake, Paul W. (1979), 'The Origins of United States Economic Supremacy in South America: Colombia's Dance of the Millions, 1923–33,' Woodrow Wilson Center Latin American Program Working Paper no. 40.

Fetter, Frank W. (1931), *Monetary Inflation in Chile*, Princeton: Princeton University Press.

Friedman, Irving S. (1984), 'Private bank conditionality: comparisons with the IMF and the World Bank,' In John Williamson (ed.), *IMF Conditionality*, Cambridge: MIT Press, pp. 109–24.

Joslin, David (1963), *A Century of Banking in Latin America*, London: Oxford University Press.

Kane, N. Stephen (1973), 'Bankers and diplomats: the diplomacy of the dollar in Mexico, 1921–24.' *Business History Review*, XLVII, 335–52.

Kemmerer, E.W. (1916), 'A proposal for Pan-American monetary unity,' *Political Science Quarterly*, XXXI, 66–80.

Kemmerer, E.W. (1918a), *The ABC of the Federal Reserve System*, Princeton: Princeton University Press.

Kemmerer, E.W. (1918b), 'Money and prices: discussion,' *American Economic Review*, 8, 259–64.

Kemmerer, E.W. (1926), 'Chile returns to the gold standard,' *Journal of Political Economy*, 34, 265–73.

Kemmerer, E.W. (1927), 'Economic advisory work for governments,' *American Economic Review*, XVII, 1–12.

Kemmerer, E.W. (1934), *Kemmerer on Money*, Chicago: John C. Winston Company.

Kemmerer, E.W. (1944), *Gold and the Gold Standard*, New York: McGraw-Hill.

Lewis, Cleona (1938), *America's Stake in International Investments*, Washington, DC: The Brookings Institution.

Marsh, Magaret Alexander (1928), *The Bankers in Bolivia*, New York: Vanguard Press.

Nurkse, Ragnar (1946), *The Course and Control of Inflation*, Geneva: League of Nations.

Parks, E. Taylor (1935), *Colombia and the United States, 1765–1934*, Durham, North Carolina: Duke University Press.

Perez, Jorge Luis (1928), 'Ecuador and its economic rehabilitation: financial reforms of the Kemmerer Commission,' *Pan Pacific Progress*, p. 82.

Rippy, J. Fred (1931), *The Capitalists in Colombia*, New York: Vanguard Press.

Seidel, Robert N. (1972), 'American reformers abroad: The Kemmerer Missions in South America, 1923–1931,' *Journal of Economic History*, XXXII, 520–45.

Smith, Robert Freeman (1963), 'The formation and development of the International Bankers Committee on Mexico,' *Journal of Economic History*, 23, 574–86.

Young, Ralph (1930), *Handbook on American Underwriting of Foreign Securities*, United States Department of Commerce, Trade Promotion Series, No. 104, Washington, DC, USGPO.

COMMENT

Göran Ohlin

There is a lot of controversy about the role of the IMF these days but not very much discussion of how the international financial system would work without it. Perhaps it is a counterfactual that seems to fanciful too explore. But the issues of the day are not new as Carlos Díaz-Alejandro did so much to remind us, and the history of international finance is attracting a new interest as the power and influence of governments and the IMF diminishes.

The two papers in this session have focussed on different aspects of the financial history of Latin America. Fishlow has brought back the debt crises, adjustment problems, and refinancing needs of the 1890s and made them seem all too familiar. Eichengreen takes us back to the 1920s when a money doctor from Princeton dispensed advice in Latin America in ways that may seem comparable to what the IMF does today.

The parallel is not as compelling as it might seem. Kemmerer was invited by Latin American governments to help them enhance their credibility and credit. IMF missions, on the other hand, tend to arrive rather later, when the market has been exhausted and the IMF seems the only recourse. So there was an element of complicity in the Kemmerer missions while there is sometimes a stronger element of antagonism and political conflict in IMF missions. The IMF has some financial clout of its own, whereas Kemmerer came only to discuss and play golf.

Eichengreen has little to say about whether Kemmerer's advice was good or bad. He focusses on the effect of capital flows, which is ingenious although the methodology seems perilously close to econometric overkill. As to the quality of the advice, he notes that it was remarkably similar regardless of the country or the time. This is a familiar criticism of IMF prescriptions; it seems to imply that the advice was too uniform to be really serious, or that at least it was not adapted to specific needs.

One wonders about that. If the general tenor of the advice was fairly constant, was it surprising that Kemmerer harped on the same themes? Did he not have good reason to tell Latin American countries to get themselves a central monetary authority and to do something about their tax systems? The third theme that Eichengreen identifies was the need to go back on the gold standard, which may seem more controversial today, not least in the light of Carlos's analyses. But to many it undoubtedly seemed like a good idea at the time, and even today it could certainly be argued that it was a good idea at the time.

Eichengreen mentions some of the other money doctors and one would like to know what they were saying – I suspect it was pretty much the same thing.

But the Kemmerer Missions did not just promulgate general principles: as Eichengreen makes clear, they produced a whole series of memoranda with concrete suggestions on a number of different aspects of individual situations. These were not sewed up in a comprehensive agreement as IMF deals tend to be, and this might be a good idea to escape the rigidities, real or perceived, of IMF arrangements today.

As for the impact of the missions, Eichengreen seems to argue two opposite positions at the same time. Yes, they were influential because some countries did better with Kemmerer missions than others without them, in the sense that they were able to increase their borrowing. But no, it was all a matter of the times. When the going was good, commodities were doing well, and the markets were in favor of a country, things went well, but at other times he was not able to raise capital inflows, and when he tried to discourage the market from lending to Colombia he failed even at that.

In his conclusion Eichengreen suggests that the IMF is different precisely because it has the funds that Kemmerer lacked. But today the IMF does not really have enough money to turn things around and to make money flow uphill. Not even the Baker plan seems able to get banks to lend where they do not want to go. So on this concluding point Eichengreen does not convince me that we are much better off today than in the days of Kemmerer.

5

The Debt Overhang of Developing Countries

Jeffrey Sachs

1. Introduction

Carlos F. Díaz-Alejandro excelled at the writing of economic history, and nowhere were his findings more fascinating or pertinent than his descriptions of the Latin American economies in the 1930s. As Díaz-Alejandro stressed, the 1930s were years of great economic crisis, but also of great vitality and change. The Latin American debt crisis of that era ushered in a period of heterodox policies and, after the initial jolt of the Great Depression, surprisingly strong economic growth in most countries in the hemisphere. Until his untimely death, Díaz-Alejandro remained perplexed by the largely unsuccessful response of the Latin American countries to the debt crisis of the 1980s, in comparison to their successful adjustment in the 1930s.

This paper does not attempt a historical analysis of the difference in performance in the two eras, but it does suggest one of the factors that may explain partly the contrast. In the 1930s, almost all of the Latin American countries met the debt crisis with a unilateral moratorium on debt repayments, and these moratoria were only resolved after the Second World War. In the 1980s, almost all of the debtor countries have continued to service their debts, under rules of the game written and directed by the creditor governments. This continued debt servicing has helped the world to avert an international banking crisis, a prospect that was widely feared in the early 1980s. On the other hand, the debt strategy has not yet generated an economic recovery in the debtor economies, as was forecasted by the IMF and the creditor governments when the crisis began in 1982. The declining per capita income levels of the largest Latin American debtor countries are shown in table 5.1: we see that per capita income declined in all of the countries during the whole period 1981–5 and was continuing to fall in most of the countries last year. Brazil is the only case of a country that suffered a debt crisis being able to recover with significant growth rates.

Of course some of the continuing low growth must be attributed to policy mistakes in the debtor countries, and some must be attributed to the

Table 5.1 Change in per capita GDP, major Latin American debtors, 1981–5

	Cumulative change, 1981–5	*1985*[a]
Argentina	–18.5	–5.5
Bolivia	–28.4	–4.7
Brazil	–2.0	5.8
Chile	–8.7	0.8
Colombia	–0.1	0.5
Ecuador	–3.9	–0.2
Mexico	–4.3	n.a.
Peru	–14.8	–0.6
Uruguay	–18.6	–0.3
Venezuela	–21.6	–3.8

[a] Provisional estimates, subject to revision.

Source: *The Economic Crisis: Policies for Adjustment, Stabilization and Growth*, United Nations Economic Commission for Latin America and the Caribbean, April 1986

continuing decline in the terms of trade of most of the debtor countries. However, these countries have enjoyed some unexpectedly favorable developments as well (e.g. the fall in world interest rates in the past two years) and it is not clear whether on balance the world economic environment has been more or less harsh than the 'optimists' predicted in 1982. It is the theme of this paper that another reason for the absence of recovery in the debtor countries lies in the way that the debt crisis has been managed by the creditor governments and by the international organizations. The strategy errs by relying exclusively on debt rescheduling and new lending to get the debtor countries out of the crisis, rather than on a selective use of debt forgiveness.

Before explaining the case for partial debt forgiveness, it is important to stress that the debt issue should continue to be handled on a case-by-case basis. The debtor countries differ in important ways, in the reasons for their indebtedness, in their resiliency in the face of external shocks, and in their capacity to grow with high levels of debt. Certainly, there is no reason to consider writing off the debt of the Korean economy, nor would the Koreans choose to risk their international reputation by seeking debt forgiveness. Similarly, Brazil has demonstrated over the past decade the capacity to maintain high growth in the presence of high levels of indebtedness. The theme of this paper therefore is not directed at these countries, but rather at the ones that continue to stagnate under the burden of the foreign debt.

The most heavily indebted sovereign governments are like insolvent corporations, with their creditors being the international banks, multinational firms, the multilateral organizations, foreign governments, and the various domestic claimants on the budget. In the domestic context, insolvent firms can rely on the bankruptcy code, which tries to bring order among a firm's creditors, so that their individual actions do not undermine the efficient use of the firm's assets. For example, the creditors are (generally) enjoined from liquidating a firm by their individual actions if the firm is worth more as a going enterprise than in liquidation. In the international arena, however, a bankruptcy code for sovereign borrowers does not exist, and many debtor countries are being 'liquidated' via capital flight, low domestic investment, and squabbling among the creditors.

Of course, as in a bankruptcy proceeding, there has been significant cooperation among some of the creditors of the debtor countries. The commercial banks have held together to the extent of making several 'nonspontaneous' loans to the debtor countries, usually under the auspices of IMF programs. Lipson (1985) offers a convincing and interesting account of this cooperative behavior. Looking back on four years of experience, however, we can see that the extent of cooperation has not been enough, and perhaps inherently so. Despite the policy of concerted lending by the banks, banking exposure in Latin America is falling overall, not rising. Many banks and other creditors are able to opt out of the agreements, or are able to decrease exposures in the private sectors of the countries at the same time that their exposures to governments continue to build. Furthermore, many claimants on the debtor economies, including the multinational corporations, foreign suppliers, and domestic capitalists, are not even at the bargaining table, and thus have opted unilaterally to reduce their exposures.

The main result of the remaining noncooperative behavior in the system is the utter collapse of investment in the region, and the flight of much of the foreign capital that is in fact pumped in. The fall in investment rates in Latin America is the remarkable and disturbing backdrop of the rest of the paper. The drop in investment is illustrated in figure 5.1, which shows the rates of fixed capital formation during 1982–4 relative to 1980–1.

This paper sketches the case for a debt strategy that utilizes debt forgiveness in addition to debt rescheduling. It is necessarily schematic, as it does not go into detail for any particular country. Nor does it present a specific 'plan' for the debt. The purpose is rather to start a conceptual analysis of the issue of debt forgiveness, which to my knowledge has not yet been done. The paper is divided as follows. In section 2, we discuss the current strategy of debt management in very general terms, arguing that a strategy of debt forgiveness is not unthinkable, and would not do great damage to the international financial system. In section 3, the analytical case for debt forgiveness of highly overburdened debtors is presented. In section 4, some examples of previous sovereign defaults are explored to see what lessons they have for current debt management, and some preliminary ideas are put forward for new approaches to managing the debt crisis.

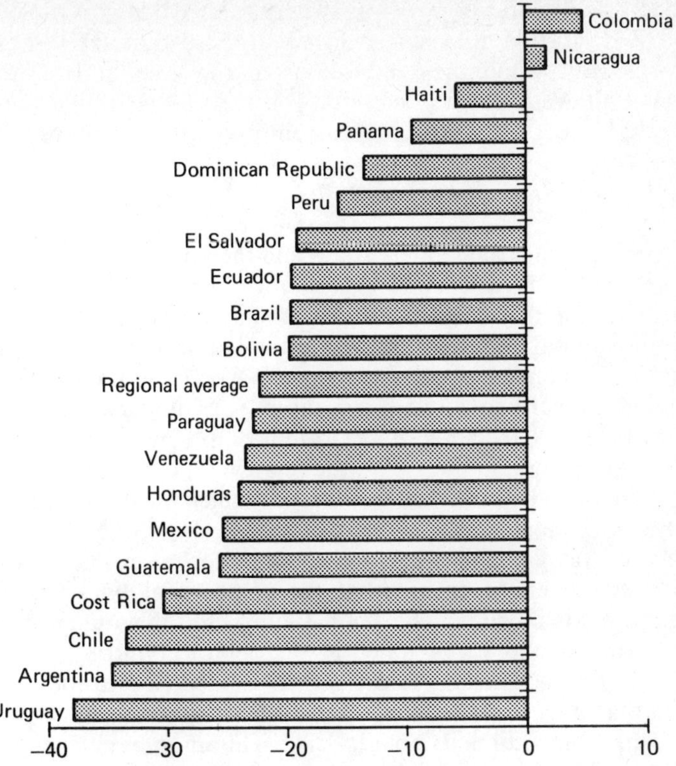

Figure 5.1 Latin America and the Caribbean: gross domestic fixed capital formation (percentage variation, 1982 1984 average/1980–1981 average). *Source*: ECLAC, on the basis of official data

2. The Present Strategy for Management of the Debt Crisis

It would take us far afield to examine why the Latin American economies have chosen to maintain debt repayments in the 1980s, even in the depths of economic depression, when these same countries chose to suspend debt repayments in the 1930s (though see Díaz-Alejandro 1984 and Fishlow 1985 for some interesting observations). I am confident that historical analysis would show that the room for unilateral action was much greater in the 1930s than it was in the 1980s. In the earlier episode, the world was without a clear 'hegemonic power,' to use Kindleberger's term, so that the policing of international agreements was lax. The industrial economies were in the midst of their own profound economic crisis, which left the creditor governments without the resources or ability to defend the interests of their citizens who held the bonds of the developing countries. Only in some special cases did major creditor nations have such close and deep historical ties with debtor countries that they chose to wield their power to enforce debt repayments. But when they did so, as in the case of Britain *vis-à-vis* Argentina and Australia, the creditor government generally prevailed. In most cases, however, creditor government pressure was not applied.

2.1 The Current Rules of the Game

In the past five years, the United States and the international organizations, mainly the IMF, have worked closely together to enforce the financial agreements of the debtor countries, and to maintain the ongoing operation of the international financial system. Certainly one of the main interests of the creditors in managing this crisis has been to protect the capital structure of the international banks, who own the bulk of the claims on the debtor countries. In the 1930s, a debt moratorium simply meant that bondholders suffered a capital loss; in the 1980s, the fear is that a moratorium could lead to the failure of some large banks, with unpredictable consequences on the international economy.

The basic strategy of the IMF and the creditor governments since 1982, therefore, has been to ensure that the commercial banks receive their interest payments on time. The US has supported this outcome through a variety of carrots and sticks aimed at the debtor countries. Most importantly, the IMF has signed agreements with the debtor countries only on the condition that the countries have a satisfactory arrangement with the commercial banks for continued debt servicing. This imposes enormous pressure on the countries to maintain debt servicing, since an agreement with the IMF has been the virtual *sine qua non* for triggering all of the other forms of official creditor assistance, including Paris Club reschedulings and loans from the World Bank and multilateral development banks.

No matter how deep has been the economic crisis in a debtor country, the US has never accepted the need for debt forgiveness. This has been true in Africa as well as Latin America. If necessary, the United States has been willing to engineer official credits for a debtor government in order to tide it over a debt payment to the commercial banks, but it has not yet contemplated allowing a country to skip a debt payment, or even to negotiate a debt payment below market cost. Thus, in recent months, the US Treasury has been organizing a credit line to Mexico of $1.6 billion for the purpose of allowing the Mexican government to make its commercial bank interest payments at the end of 1986. Moreover, the $12 billion loan package to Mexico now under discussion includes enough new official money to pay for most of Mexico's interest payments due to the bank for the next 18 months.

In general, the commercial banks have enjoyed a large resource transfer in their direction in recent years, while official creditors have been making a significant transfer to developing countries. If the official creditors are not 'bailing out' the banks, they are at least greatly facilitating the payment of interest to the banks. Some data on net resource transfers are shown in table

Table 5.2 Net resource transfers to major borrowing LDCs ($ billion)

	1981	*1982*	*1983*	*1984*
Private creditors				
Net debt flows	19.4	18.8	15.3	11.0
Interest payments	14.6	17.8	17.1	21.0
Net resource transfer	4.8	1.0	–1.8	–10.0
Official creditors				
Net debt flows	9.3	9.7	6.3	9.9
Interest payments	3.6	4.3	4.8	5.3
Net resource transfer	5.7	5.4	1.5	4.6

Source: World Bank, *World Debt Tables*, 1985–6 edition

5.2. The net transfer of resources to the debtor country is defined as the receipt of new loans, net of payments of principal and interest. A negative net transfer signifies that real resources are being transferred away from the debtor to the creditors. Note that the net transfer will be negative even if the creditors are increasing their exposure to the debtor country as long as the increase in loan exposure is smaller than interest payments made in the period.

As can be seen from the data in table 5.2, large positive net transfers of resources from the private creditors (mainly banks) came to a quick halt during 1982, and the transfers were negative during 1983 and significantly negative during 1984. At the same time, resource transfers from the official creditors continued to be positive during 1981–4. Unfortunately, comprehensive data are not yet available for 1985, but it seems on the basis of partial data that the trend of negative transfers from the banks and positive transfers from the official creditors continued. I report data in table 5.2 indicating that in 1985 the US commercial banks actually reduced in absolute terms the levels of their loan exposure to the major Latin American debtors, while of course they continued to receive large interest payments.

In sum, the banks have been able to maintain their interest income because the creditor governments have defended their claims. Where necessary, the official creditors have even committed public monies to ensure that the debtor countries punctually service the interest on their commercial bank debts. Of course, the creditor governments have also leaned on the commercial banks to accept half a loaf: the major banks have been required to join in concerted lending to the debtor countries as the price for receiving full interest payments. The bank regulators in the US have underwritten this agreement by allowing the banks to carry most of their loan exposure vis-à-vis the debtor countries at par, and to declare their interest receipts from the debtor countries as income, even though part of the interest receipts are received only as the result of new lending.

2.2 *Sanctity of Contracts*

The creditor governments have stressed that the punctual servicing of bank debt is crucial to preserve the 'sanctity of contract.' Simply put, the debtor countries voluntarily undertook the debt, and so should repay it. The simplest retort to this view is that the banks also voluntarily loaned the money, and at interest rate premia that compensated them for commercial risk. It therefore seems to be stretching the case to insist on full servicing of the commercial bank debt when that is possible only with official credits to help make the payments. A more satisfactory answer is that the 'sanctity of contract' argument can be overdone. Legal systems generally provide for the discharge (i.e. forgiveness) from contractual obligations under extenuating circumstances. The same principles should apply internationally, as several historical examples make clear.

Under common law and under the US Uniform Commercial Code, contracts may be discharged if performance of the contract would lead to a 'commercial impracticability.' Generally, this means that a contract will not be enforced if, after the signing of a contract, intervening events have rendered the contract highly uneconomical and if the following additional conditions hold: (a) the event could not have been reasonably foreseen by either party; (b) the costs of performing the contract have become 'extreme and unreasonable'; and (c) the party seeking discharge must not have created the situation leading to the impracticability of performance.

The basic motivation of the doctrine of 'commercial impracticability' is that it is highly expensive for the parties to a contract to prepare contractual agreements that cover all possible contingencies, even those of low probability. Instead of forcing contract writers to bear the high costs of specifying all contingencies, the law provides for the discharge of contracts if certain well-circumscribed and low-probability events make fulfillment of the contract too expensive to one of the parties. As Posner and Rosenfield (1977) note, 'the purpose of an economically based discharge doctrine is to supply those contract terms that the parties would have adopted if they had negotiated expressly over them.'

A recent example where this doctrine was invoked is the case of Westinghouse, which contracted in the 1970s to provide processed uranium to several power companies at a fixed price (see Joskow 1977 for a full discussion of the background of this case, and the applicability of the 'commercial impracticability' doctrine). After the contracts were signed, the spot market price of uranium tripled, and Westinghouse unilaterally announced that it would not honor its supply contracts, for to do so would cost the company several billion dollars. In fact, Westinghouse's plea of 'commercial impracticability' was not fully supported by the trial judge in the law suits brought by the nuclear power companies against Westinghouse, but crucially, the judge refused to enforce 'strict performance' of the contracts (i.e. requiring Westinghouse to deliver the uranium at the contract price). Rather, the judge pressed Westinghouse and the power companies to split the difference in out of court settlements. In the end, it appears that Westinghouse saved several billion dollars by seeking discharge from its contractual obligations.

While no legal analysis can be made here to demonstrate the applicability of the commercial impracticability doctrine to the case of developing country debt, the broad relevance is easily established. When the debt contracts with the banks were undertaken in the 1970s, real interest rates were low, and the terms of trade for the debtor countries were high. In the 1980s, real interest rates reached historically unprecedented peaks for the postwar period, while the terms of trade reached unprecedented lows. Díaz-Alejandro (1983) showed convincingly that the accumulation of Brazilian debt up until 1981 made good sense from an ex ante point of view. It was the unforseen, and essentially unforseeable shifts in the world macroeconomy that ultimately undermined Brazil's strategy of debt accumulation.

The 1920s and 1930s provide several clear illustrations of the risks that arise when creditor governments do not release fragile countries from their international obligations. Most economic historians would agree that the failure of the US to release its First World War allies from their war debts during the 1920s and early 1930s was a major destabilizing factor in the world economy, and a profound policy mistake. President Calvin Coolidge's incomprehension of the need to relieve the United States allies of their debts was immortalized in his famous remark on the debt, 'But they hired the money, didn't they?' In the event, the United States kept pressing for full servicing of the debts, even into the depths of the Great Depression. Hoover's pressure on the French to make payments in 1932, after a year's moratorium on servicing, led to the fall of the Herriot government. By 1933, payments of inter-allied war debts finally ceased, but only after the world economy and the US allies had suffered greatly.

The defaults by Latin American countries in the 1930s and 1940s on their international bonds are still more relevant to our discussion, and will be considered in greater detail later. Suffice it to note here that observers as astute as Henry Wallich (1943) had little doubt in the 1940s that the overhang of Latin American debt should be relieved through debt forgiveness. Rather than arguing that debt forgiveness would debilitate the private capital markets, Wallich argued the opposite, that 'a satisfactory settlement of the defaults would greatly improve the prospects of private foreign lending after the war.' He applauded the fact that the US government did not apply pressures to get full servicing of the debt, and noted, as an example, that 'apparently no attempt has been made [by the US government] to tie up the liberal [official] loans which began to be made in 1940 with demands for resumption of service to the defaulted bonds.'

As is well known, Argentina is the rare case in Latin America of a country that did not default on its loans in the 1930s. British political influence was able to keep the Argentine government on track in servicing its foreign debt, and was also able to impose on the country an onerous set of trade concessions in the notorious Roca-Runciman Treaty of 1933. Argentina did not exactly benefit from its continued debt servicing. As Mallon and Sourrouille (1975, p. 7) point out, the external economic pressures and related events, 'were at the same time symptoms and additional causes of xenophobic antagonisms toward the very visible control that foreigners held over vital segments of the national economy.' These antagonisms, they note, were crucial in the subsequent rise of Peron.

Certainly the most disastrous case of creditors failing to forgive a debt is that of the German reparations payments after the First World War. As is well known, German payments of reparations in the 1920s were largely financed by the back-to-back Dawes Loan and Young Loan. When foreign credit to Germany dried up in 1929, the German government resolved to continue paying its debts through intense deflation. As Kindleberger puts it:

> Deflation produced by the cutoff in American lending was enhanced by the brutal policies, beginning in March 1930, of Heinrich Bruning, German Prime Minister, who was determined to show the Allies that it was impossible for Germany to pay, even if he had to destroy the economy and the political system to do so.

He succeeded, as we know too well.

For good or bad, repudiations of international economic agreements are much more common than is widely believed, though usually the repudiation is by powerful creditor countries rather than weak debtor countries. Perhaps the most notorious violation of an international economic agreement in the postwar years was the 1971 repudiation by the United States of its obligation to maintain the parity value of the dollar under the International Monetary Fund Articles of Agreement. Under that agreement, the United States was obligated to maintain a fixed parity of the dollar, within a 10 per cent range, either by converting dollars into gold or by some other mechanism. In fact, when balance of payments pressures became too severe, the US unilaterally abandoned this obligation. President Nixon unilaterally suspended gold convertibility and devalued the exchange rate by 15 per cent. This action substantially and unilaterally reduced the real value of foreign claims on the United States, in contravention of treaty obligations.

Other cases of unilateral repudiation of international obligations abound. After signing long-term price agreements for natural gas sales to Europe, the Netherlands unilaterally abrogated those accords and demanded (and achieved) higher prices after the OPEC price increases in 1973–4. Similarly, Australia unilaterally abrogated long-term coal contracts with Japan after the rise in world oil prices. Most recently, members of the International Tin Agreement, comprised of both producer and consumer nations (including most European countries), have repudiated their debts to various private financial firms. From the early 1980s, the International Tin Council supported the price of tin by buying extensive stocks, and financed the purchases with loans from private financial institutions, collateralized with the tin stocks. When credit lines dried up, the Tin Council ceased purchasing tin.

The price of tin plummetted, and the Tin Council defaulted on its credit lines. Several lawsuits are now pending.

The examples of contract discharge and of unilateral contract repudiations are not arguments per se in favor of forgiving some of the developing country debt payments, but they do show that the 'unthinkable' of violating international contracts is not so unthinkable after all. The ultimate arguments for partial debt forgiveness should be based primarily on the equity and increased economic efficiency that would result from a partial discharge of the debtor countries' obligations. The demonstration of the efficiency gains is the task of the next section.

3. When Governments are Insolvent

The theme of this section is that debt rescheduling is an inadequate response to situations in which debts will eventually have to be forgiven. For many countries, the external obligations are so vast that the countries and their creditors both believe that eventually some of the debt will have to be forgiven. Under the current rules of the game, however, the need for eventual debt forgiveness is hidden by the process of debt rescheduling and new official credits. This is 'window dressing,' as many bankers acknowledge, but it is viewed as harmless. If the debts are to be written down, why not postpone that event as long as possible?

3.1 Analogy to Bankruptcy Law

The fundamental reason for bankruptcy law is that there are indeed costs to postponing the inevitable. Assuming that a firm or individual is insolvent, it is best to handle that fact expeditiously, in a collective proceeding of the creditors that involves some discharge of the debtor's obligations. Otherwise, three kinds of costs are likely to arise. First, the creditors will engage in a costly 'grab race,' in which they battle each other for the limited spoils of the debtor. Second, new creditors will withhold loans from the firm (or individual), for fear of getting entangled in the overhang of debt. Thus, good investment opportunities are likely to be passed up. Third, the debtor will face the wrong incentives on investment decisions. The firm or individual will pass up good investment opportunities (when judged by the market cost of capital) and will choose overly risky investment projects.

In a recent study of the US bankruptcy code, Jackson (1986) outlines many of the costs that are likely to arise in a grab race between the creditors. First, if individual creditors attempt to pursue separate remedies to collect their claims, they are likely to force the piecemeal liquidation of the firm, even if the firm is worth more as a going concern. Secured creditors will cash in on their collateral regardless of the value of the collateral to future operations of the firm. Creditors will spend inordinate resources to beat out the other creditors, in legal costs, monitoring the debtor, and so forth, thus expending resources that from the collective point of view of the creditors are not productive. Since there will be uncertainty among the creditors as to which creditors will win the race of debt collection, the expected utility of risk-averse creditors will decline. Compulsory and collective bankruptcy proceedings are necessary to avoid these costs.

Next, consider the problems that arise if the firm (or country) has new investment opportunities that are worthwhile when evaluated at the market cost of capital. Such projects can, in principle, be financed in three ways: by a new capital infusion from the existing creditors, by new capital from new creditors, or by self-financing by the equity holders of the firm (or country). With a large overhang of debt, each of these ways is likely to be problematic. Existing creditors will not put in new capital unless it is part of a collective arrangement. Because of the likely asymmetry in the position of the various existing creditors, and the problem of holdouts in a collective agreement, it is generally very difficult to arrive at a consensual agreement other than through a compulsory proceeding. The problem of arriving at an agreement is made considerably more complicated by the fact that the existing equity holders (or the government of a debtor country) are likely to face inappropriate incentives for managing the new capital.

The incentive problems are twofold. First, if the firm is insolvent, it is the creditors and not the equity holders (who are the firm's residual claimants) who stand to gain from the returns to a new investment. Indeed, the shareholders can benefit only if an investment has a very high rate of return that re-establishes the firm's solvency. Thus, the shareholders will prefer highly risky investments that offer at least a small chance of a very large payoff. By undertaking a risky investment, the shareholders gain a small chance at re-establishing the value of their claims, while they impose a high expected cost on the creditors, who will suffer in the likely event that the risky investment flops. For these reasons, it is unlikely that existing creditors will be willing to make new loans to an insolvent debtor, unless the creditors are able to achieve some management control over the choice of investment projects.

A new creditor is even less likely to offer a new loan than are the existing creditors, unless the new creditor can obtain some form of security for the loan, or unless the new creditor is inherently in a privileged class (e.g. a multilateral lending institution such as the IMF or World Bank). Without security, the new lender will get tangled up in the collection difficulties of the old debt. And in any event, potential new creditors understand that insolvent debtors are unlikely to have the incentive to manage the new funds with care.

The provision of security (e.g. collateral) for a new loan is itself extremely problematic. If a new loan is collateralized, but the money is used for 'consumption' purposes (e.g. a dividend distribution) or for a substandard investment, then the new loan will be repaid at the expense of the old creditors. In essence, the equity holders will gain by pocketing some of the new loan (in the form of dividends or increased managerial slack), while the original creditors will suffer a reduction in the value of their claims. Existing creditors will be very chary of allowing new secured creditors to enter the scene, even to finance ostensibly favorable investments. For this reason, commercial bank creditors generally favor the borrowing limits that the IMF imposes on overextended debtors. And in the context of bankruptcy, the pre-existing creditors generally take control of the firm's management before they permit the entry of new creditors.

Most of the inefficiencies of a debt overhang can be relieved by partial debt forgiveness. Importantly, since debt forgiveness overcomes economic inefficiencies that hamper the growth of the debtor, it is not surprising that debt forgiveness can be designed in such a way as to improve the position of both the creditors and the debtors. In the context of developing country debt, partial debt forgiveness can be the spur to growth in an overextended debtor country and can actually increase the eventual payments received by the creditors.

A Formal Model

The proposition that collective debt relief can help both the debtor country and the creditors can be illustrated in a simple two-period model. We will assume that the behavior of the debtor country is determined by a social planner, maximizing a two-period objective function for the country:

$$U = U(C1) + bU(C2) \tag{1}$$

To begin the discussion, let us start with the 'end game,' in the second period, in which claims against the debtor are being collected. Suppose that in total, the creditors are owed a sum T, which is to be divided among n creditors, where n is large. The debtor can voluntarily make a payment S, or can be forced to make a payment P through collection actions undertaken by the creditors. These actions could include lawsuits that tie up the property of the debtor government, lobbying actions to get embargoes and penalties imposed on the defaulting country, actions to hinder international commerce, etc. These collection actions are generally inefficient, in that they tend to impose costs on the debtor that are much greater than the net resources actually collected by the creditors.

Suppose that the debt is so high that it exceeds the maximum amount of the cost that can be imposed on the debtor by the collection actions of the creditors. In that case, it will pay for the debtor to partially default. It is also likely that it will be in the individual interest of each of the creditors to pursue collection actions, especially if the other creditors do so as well, in order that each creditor protect his share of the repayments. Even if the debtor makes a voluntary partial payment of the debt, this is unlikely to deter the collection actions of the individual creditors unless a common agreement can be reached among the creditors to stop the collection actions. In the resulting noncooperative equilibrium (not explicitly shown here) the creditors as a whole would undertake excessive collection actions, say with total cost C, and would receive gross benefits B for their efforts. The costs to the debtor would be P. Presumably, these values would have the following relative magnitude: $C < B < P < D$.

Now, if a collective settlement can be reached instead, it is clear that both the creditors and the debtor will be better off. The creditors should agree to stop all collection actions in return for a partial payment of the debt S, such that $B - C < S < P$. The exact amount S that is agreed to will of course depend on the relative bargaining power of the creditors and the debtor, which in turn will depend on the nature of the collection actions. Lipson (1985) points out that syndicated loan agreements are now written to facilitate this kind of collective agreement. For example, some loan agreements require that the syndicate must vote by a two-thirds majority (with bank votes weighted by loan exposure) before the syndicate declares a default and opens the way for collection actions.

In what follows, I assume that a voluntary agreement to forgive part of the debt is indeed reached in the end game, and that the bargaining power of the debtor and creditors is such that the debtor always agrees to service the debt in an amount at most equal to a fraction z of the second-period gross domestic product, $Q2$. If the debt due is less than $z\,Q2$, then the debt is fully repaid. If the debt due exceeds $z\,Q2$, then $z\,Q2$ is paid. In this notation, if T is the total amount of debt legally due, and S is the amount actually paid, I assume:

$$\begin{aligned} S &= T && \text{for } T \leqslant z\,Q2 \\ &= zQ2 && \text{for } T > z\,Q2 \end{aligned} \tag{2}$$

Finally, I assume that the repayment S is divided among the various creditors in proportion to their loan exposure (i.e. their share of the total principal due).

Now let us turn to the behavior of the creditors and debtor before the end game. To study this behavior in the simplest possible way, we assume a two-period set-up, in which the debtor enters the first period with an amount of debt due in the second period equal to D (there is no debt due in the first period). The holders of this claim D will be termed the 'original creditors,' to distinguish them from new creditors who may make one-period loans between the first and the second periods. The original creditors may decide, in the first period, to forgive some of the debt due in the second period. If they do so, they collectively set a new level of debt due R, which is less than D.

The economy's production technology is given simply as:

$$\begin{aligned} Q1 &= F(K1) \\ Q2 &= F(K2) \\ K2 &= K1 + I1 \end{aligned} \tag{3}$$

with the usual assumptions that $F' > 0$, $F'' < 0$.

The country may be able to attract new one-period loans in period 1. The principal due on such loans will be denoted $D1$. Such loans will be forthcoming from new creditors only if they will be repaid fully, with world interest rate r, in the second period (in other words, with total payment $(1 + r)D1$). Since the total debt T due in the second period will be $D1(1 + r)$ plus the amount R due from the original creditors, we can use equation (1) to see that the lending from the new creditors will be limited by the following condition:

$$D1(1+r) < zQ2 - R \qquad (4)$$

As long as equation (4) holds, then the new creditors will be fully repaid. Note that in order to implement equation (4), the lenders must calculate $Q2$, which equals $F(K2)$. The safe lending limit thus depends on the amount of investment that the debtor government will undertake in the first period. In particular, to implement condition (3), the new lenders must derive the debtor's investment function $I1 = I1(D1, R)$, and then rewrite (4) as (4′):

$$D1(1+r) < zQ2[K1 + I1(D1, R)] - R \qquad (4')$$

Implicitly, equation (4′) defines a lending limit for $D1$ in terms of the overhang of long-term debt R. Equation (4′) can be solved to yield a simple credit-rationing rule of the form:

$$D1 \leqslant h(R) \qquad (5)$$

It is easy to show that there exists an R^*, such that for $R > R^*$, $D1 = 0$. For R strictly greater than R^*, the country will not fully service its original debt, and so cannot find new lenders.

The original creditors, with claim D, have a single choice in the first period: whether to forgive part of the debt that will come due in the second period. If they jointly agree to do so, they change D to some amount $R < D$. If they take no action, then the debt due in period 2 remains D. The goal of the creditors is to maximize their ultimate repayment, which is given by $S - (1 + r)D1$. Remember that S denotes the debtor's full repayment in period 2, of which $(1 + r)D1$ goes to the first-period lenders. The creditors' problem can be stated as follows:

$$\max_{R}\; S - (1+r)D1 \qquad \text{subject to } R < D \qquad (6)$$

We shall see that the original creditors indeed sometimes have the incentive to forgive part of the debt even before it comes due in the second period.

The debtor has the choice of investment, consumption, and perhaps new borrowing, in the first period. The balance of payments constraint is simply:

$$D1 = I1 + C1 - Q1 \qquad (7)$$

Once the level of second-period debt R is selected by the original creditors, the debtor maximizes utility in equation (1) subject to equations (2), (3), (5), and (7).

We will now focus on the case in which the original debt D exceeds R^*. Assume first that the creditors do not forgive any of this debt. In this case, there will be no loans forthcoming in period 1, and part of the debt D will be defaulted in period 2. To choose the optimal level of investment $I1$, and the amount of debt repayment, the debtor solves the following two-period problem:

$$\max U(C1) + bU(C2) \tag{8}$$

$$\text{such that } C1 = F(K1) - I1$$

$$C2 = F(K1 + I1) - S$$

Note that since $S = zQ2$, we can also write $C2 = (1 - z)F(K1 + I1)$. The interior solution is obtained where:

$$U'(C1) = (1 - z)F'(K1 + I1)bU'(C2) \tag{9}$$

Note that total debt repayments equal $z\ F(K1 + I1)$, which by assumption, are less than D. The actual level of debt repayments are denoted as $S\hat{}$.

The key point can now be demonstrated. Suppose that the original creditors forgive part of the debt, so that the remaining debt is reduced to a level that will indeed be repaid. We can show with a partial writedown that the creditors can receive as much in actual repayments while the debtor is left better off. Alternatively, a new debt level can be selected that leaves both the creditors and the debtor better off. To show this, suppose that the debt is written down to $S\hat{}$ itself (that is, to the amount actually repaid in the previous problem). Then the debtor would face a maximization problem as in equation (8), but with $S\hat{}$ replacing S. Actual repayments would no longer be fixed as a fraction $zQ2$, since the debt would now be low enough to be fully repaid. Thus, the first-order condition in equation (9) would become:

$$U'(C1) = F'(K1 + I1)bU'(C2) \tag{10}$$

Comparing equations (10) and (9), it is easy to show that investment will be higher in (10), since the equations differ only by the presence of z in (9). Since $I1$ is higher, $Q2$ is higher as well in the case with the debt writedown, though the actual repayment to the creditors is the same in both cases: $S\hat{}$. It is simple to show that by writing down the original D to a level slightly above $S\hat{}$, both the creditors and the debtor are left better off.

What is happening here? When a debt overhang exists, the debt acts like a distortionary tax, with a corresponding deadweight burden. Since the debtor pays a fraction of income z to its creditors, any increase in output is taxed at the marginal rate z when viewed from the debtor's perspective. Given this tax rate, the levels of output and investment are chosen according to equation (8). Now, by writing down the debt to a level that will actually be paid, the debt becomes a lump-sum burden, rather than a marginal tax. It thus becomes profitable to invest more.

In words, when the debt overhang is large, part of each dollar of investment ends up working for Citibank, rather than for the country itself. When the debt is written down to manageable levels, the marginal returns to investment stay within the debtor country.

Another way to see these results is to write the investment function as $I1 = I1(R)$. For low levels of debt due in the second period, it is easy to show that $I1$ is a *rising* function of R. As the debt increases, the government chooses to invest more in order to maintain second-period consumption levels in the presence of rising repayment burden. However, once R rises to R^*, and the country plans to default partially, $I1$ falls discretely and discontinuously to the level solved for in equation (9). As R rises above R^*, $I1$ remains constant at the level in equation (9). Thus, $I1$ is a discontinuous function of R. Once the point of debt overhang is reached, investment is inefficiently reduced.

4. Insolvent Governments: The Practice

The theoretical analysis suggests that if countries are likely to default on their external debt, there are good reasons to forgive that debt now rather than later. In this section, I discuss some of the empirical evidence suggesting that for many countries, eventual default seems a good prediction. Furthermore, many of the risks of postponing debt forgiveness are evident in these countries: investment is very low, banks are reducing rather than increasing their exposures, and domestic capital is leaving the country via capital flight.

4.1 Market Evidence on Debtor Country Prospects

The most direct evidence on eventual prospects for the external debt is the market value of the debt itself. The market value of claims on the developing countries can be inferred from at least three sources. Most directly, an active secondary market in bank claims on the debtor countries has arisen in the past year, and by most accounts, there is a substantial amount of business now taking place in this market. The second source of information is from trading in the bonds of these countries. During the 1970s, the largest debtor countries were able to float bonds in both the European and US bond markets. Daily market quotations are available on these bonds. Third, it is possible to infer the market valuation of the bank claims by examining the overall stock market valuation of the commercial banks, as a function of the amount of their exposure in the developing countries. Assuming that the debt of the developing countries is priced by the market at a discount, we should expect to see that heavily exposed banks sell at a discount relative to lightly exposed banks.

All three sources of information point in the same direction: that the market places a varying, but reasonably high, probability of partial default on the debts of the major debtor countries. In November 1985, *The Economist* (16 November 1985) reported the following price ranges of bank debt in the secondary market:

Brazil	75–83 per cent of par value
Mexico	78–82 per cent of par value
Peru	32–6 per cent of par value

More recently, *Euromoney* (August 1986) presented the following data:

Brazil	76 per cent
Mexico	56 per cent
Ecuador	65 per cent
Argentina	66 per cent

The most hopelessly indebted country in Latin America, Bolivia, has been quoted during May–July 1986 at an amazing price of 6–11 per cent of par value.

Discounts of approximately this magnitude have also been found in studies of bonds and bank stock valuations. Steven Kyle made a detailed study of the prices of foreign bonds of Brazil, Argentina, and Mexico, and showed discounts of a similar magnitude. In a joint study with Kyle of bank stock prices I demonstrated that as of mid-1983, the commercial bank stocks were discounted by about 20 cents per dollar of exposure in Argentina, Brazil, and Mexico, the only countries for which detailed exposure data are available.

The worry over eventual default is also showing up increasingly in the behavior of bank regulators in several countries. According to a recent study by the Peat Marwick accounting firm, reported in the *Financial Times* (24 June 1986), eight creditor countries have introduced guidelines for provisioning for sovereign debt. The countries have all required that loss reserves be set aside in varying percentages for several debtor countries, with the extent of provisioning depending on the perceived riskiness of the debtor. Current provisioning regulations are as shown in table 5.3. Unfortunately, precise information on the required provisioning for each debtor country is not publicly available.

Note that these regulatory rules, while helpful from the point of view of banking supervision, tend to further shut the most highly indebted countries off from the possibility of any new credit. In the United States, for example, under the so-called ATRR provisions (allocated transfer risk reserve), when a country is assigned the classification of 'value impaired,' and the banks are required to provision for a proportion of their exposure, any new loans by US banks must immediately be provisioned in the same proportion. This rule effectively blocks new lending (except short-term trade credits) by American banks to the countries on the ATRR list, which as of the beginning of 1986 included Bolivia, Nicaragua, Peru, Poland, Sudan, and Zaire.

Table 5.3 Current provisioning regulations

Creditor country	*Range for loan loss provisioning (% of exposure that must be provisioned)*
Canada	10–15
Japan	1–5
Netherlands	5–100
Spain	1.5–100
Sweden	30–100
Switzerland	10–50
United States	15–80

Only a detailed country-by-country study will provide enough evidence on the need for explicit debt forgiveness. As I noted at the outset, the countries of Latin America differ greatly in their capacity to handle the external debt. Nonetheless, some rough indicators suggest that the discounting of the bank debts and the tightening of the banking regulations are having the effect that we might expect: new bank lending in Latin America is falling significantly, as is foreign direct investment, with the result that overall investment levels remain remarkably depressed. Latin American residents are following the international commercial banks in exporting capital at a rapid rate. Some recent data on these variables are included in table 5.4. Unfortunately, the data on foreign direct investment for Latin America stop in 1983, but a sharp slowdown in this form of capital inflow is evident from the data in table 5.5.

According to a study by Keefe, Bruyette & Woods, Inc. (1985), the banks are also changing the nature of their exposure in Latin America, by shifting their portfolios away from the private sector and toward government-guaranteed debt. What is happening, it appears, is that the banks are being required, in concerted lending exercises, to increase their loans to Latin American governments, but they are compensating for this increased risk by sharply withdrawing credits to private-sector firms. In this way, the heralded return of the Latin American economies to private market investment is being frustrated. In total, bank exposure to 'non-guaranteed, non-bank' borrowers (basically the non-bank private sector) in the Latin American countries dropped from approximately \$22.5 billion in June 1982 to \$15.4 billion in September 1984. Data depicting the overall shift in exposure toward the public sector are shown in table 5.6.

4.2 Impact of Debt Forgiveness on the Commercial Banks

With the regulators bearing down on the risky portfolios of the international banks, and with the stock market and secondary markets already valuing the LDC claims at far less than par, we have a somewhat perplexing situation. The debt overhang has already been discounted by the markets, but none of the debt has been forgiven. Since the markets have already written off some

Table 5.4 Variables affecting investment levels in Latin America

Country	*Change in US bank exposure mid-1984 to end 1985 ($billion)*	*Capital flight 1983–5 ($billion)*
Argentina	0.1	1
Brazil	–0.3	–3
Mexico	–1.7	–17
Venezuela	–3.9	–6
10 Latin debtors	–7.5	–30

Sources: US bank exposure from Statistical Release of the Financial Institutions Examination Council, 15 October 1984 and 15 April 1986; capital flight estimates from Morgan Guaranty World Financial Markets, March 1986. The 10 Latin American countries are: Argentina, Bolivia, Brazil, Chile, Colombia, Ecuador, Mexico, Peru, Uruguay, and Venezuela

Table 5.5 Capital inflow to Latin America, 1980–3

	Net inflow	*Direct investment ($billion) profit remittances*	*Balance*
1980	5.5	–4.0	1.5
1981	7.2	–4.9	2.3
1982	5.7	–4.9	0.8
1983	3.1	–3.2	–1.0

Table 5.6 US bank cross-border exposure to major Latin debtors: per cent of exposure owed by the public sector ($billion)

	June 1982	*June 1983*	*September 1984*
Argentina	31.1	38.7	49.5
Brazil	29.1	37.5	47.0
Chile	18.2	20.6	37.9
Mexico	35.2	39.1	50.3
Venezuela	42.4	46.6	49.0

Source: Keefe Nationwide Bankscan, 'US banks cushion their exposure to Latin America,' 19 February 1985

of the LDC debt, it is likely that a good part of the debt of many countries could be forgiven without further affecting the market valuation of the banks. In fact, according to the main theoretical result of the last section, explicit forgiveness could actually raise the bank's valuation, by increasing the expected value of eventual repayments by the debtor countries!

Since 1982, there has also been a significant rise in the money-center

Table 5.7 Debt exposure to Mexico (as a percentage of capital) of some of the leading banks

	Exposure as % of capital		*Loss of earnings from nonaccrual of Mexican interest in 1986 (%)*
	1982	*1986*	
Manufacturers Hanover	59	36	18
Bankers Trust	48	39	13
Chemical NY Corp	62	36	14
First Chicago	52	31	16
BankAmerica	48	37	43
WellsFargo	45	24	12
ChaseManhattan	46	28	11
MellonBank	34	26	11
J. P. Morgan	33	19	5
Citicorp	59	25	11
Average	49	30	15

Source: Keefe, Bruyette & Woods, Inc., Keefe Nationwide Bankscan, 'Mexican cliffhanger: The latest episode,' 17 June 1986

banks' capital-to-asset ratios and a drop in the share of bank assets in the developing countries. The result is a significant drop in the ratio of developing country debt exposure to primary bank capital, meaning that a reduction in bank values via a debt writeoff could now be more easily accommodated than just a few years ago. Consider, as an illustration, the drop in exposure to Mexico of some of the leading banks, as shown in table 5.7.

We see from table 5.7 that average exposure to Mexico of the leading money-center banks has declined from 49 per cent of capital in 1982 to only 30 per cent of capital in 1986. The final column shows the percentage drop of pretax earnings that these banks would suffer if Mexico were to pay no interest at all in 1986. Such a drop would cause an earnings drop of less than 20 per cent for all banks except for BankAmerica, whose earnings are suffering in 1986 because of other balance sheet losses.

Consider the Baker Plan proposal for bank lending in the context of debt forgiveness. The Baker Plan calls for bank lending to the largest 15 debtor countries to rise by $20 billion over three years. Suppose that instead of new lending, the $20 billion were to be granted in the form of debt forgiveness. Since the $20 billion represents an annual increase in exposure of about 2.2 per cent, or 6.6 per cent over three years, and since the exposure to capital ratio is on the order of 1.0, granting the entire Baker Plan money in the form of forgiveness would represent only about 6.6 per cent of bank capital. The evidence cited before suggested that this amount of capital has already been discounted by the markets.

4.3 Moving Toward a System of Debt Forgiveness

For many debtor countries, the current set of institutional arrangements are adequate. The problem lies with the subset of countries, mostly in Latin America and Africa, that are currently retrogressing under the weight of the debt burden. Up until now, the current approach has held forth few safety valves. To the extent that a country (e.g. Peru) has gotten deeper and deeper into trouble, it has not found an easing of credit terms, but the reverse. The debt overhang tends to intensify, bank regulators redline the country, and the commercial banks do their best to reduce exposure, especially on debt owed by the private sector. Only recently have some new approaches, based on repurchases of debt, started to appear. I will described these new directions below.

The experience of the 1930s and 1940s is instructive in thinking about a shift in strategy to include partial debt forgiveness. After the collapse of commodities prices in the early 1930s, most of the Latin American debtor countries suspended debt servicing on foreign bonds that they had floated in the US and the UK during the 1920s. The debt-servicing moratorium was unilateral, with little negotiation between creditors and debtors until after the Second World War. In the late 1940s, the debtor countries came up with revised debt servicing plans so that they could qualify for the loans of the newly created World Bank, which was requiring from each country an agreement between the government and its creditors as a precondition for disbursements. The World Bank did not, however, take a hard line in the type of agreements that could be reached.

The terms of the agreement were generally very favorable. The unpaid interest during the period of default was generally summed without capitalization, and added to the total stock of principal due. Thus, a $100 coupon due in 1932 and unpaid for the next fifteen years, was charged to the country at $100, rather than at $100 compounded at market interest rates. The resulting 'total debt due' was then refinanced with a new bond issue, usually at maturities of 30 to 50 years, at very low interest rates. In reality, the debt burden was reduced below even this low amount. One reason is that the debtor countries secretly entered the bond market in a big way in the late 1930s and early 1940s, in order to buy back their debt at prices of 10 to 15 cents on the dollar. A second crucial reason for the reduction of the debt burden was the rise in commodities prices during the Second World War.

In a forthcoming study, Jorgensen and I have calculated the extent of forgiveness implicit in the sequence of debt moratorium, buyback of debt, and eventual renegotiation of the bond contracts. We have calculated the net present value of the money raised by dollar-denominated external government bonds of several economies, and the net present value of repayments. These income and repayment streams are discounted to the year 1922, using the annual yield of US treasury bills. The ratio of repayments to debt flotations can exceed 1.0 if the debt is mostly repaid, and at coupon rates in excess of the T-bill rate. The ratio will be less than 1.0 if the

Table 5.8 Ratio of net present value (NPV) of repayments to NPV of government bond flotations for five Latin American economies

	Ratio of NPV of repayments to NPV of government bond flotations
Argentina	1.47
Bolivia	0.65
Chile	0.74
Colombia	1.09
Peru	0.62

risk premium on the coupon rates was insufficient to compensate for the nonpayments of interest and principal and for the buybacks at discounted prices. The preliminary results for five economies are shown in table 5.8. Note that Bolivia, Chile, and Peru achieved effective forgiveness in the range of 30 per cent. Argentina, on the contrary, both serviced the debt and paid high-risk premia at the same time.

The predominance of bond debt after the Second World War, rather than bank debt, provided a safety valve that does not now exist. Because of the extensive second-hand market in bonds, the debtor governments were able to buy back their own obligations, albeit discretely. Of course the low market quotations proved that the countries were not creditworthy, so that they could not borrow much again until the debt situation was resolved, but at least they could steadily reduce the outstanding burden without enormous public fanfare.

The current situation has so far produced no equivalent safety valve. The second-hand market was thin until recently, though it seems that increasing sales are now taking place. From a legal point of view, the market has had limited utility for the debtor countries, since most syndicated loan agreements enjoin the countries from direct buybacks of their own debt. Moreover, the banks have been reluctant to sell their syndicated loans for cash, since bank regulators have suggested that if a market discount is firmly established for a country's debt, they might require the banks to write down the book value of their remaining exposure in the country. The main implication of this accounting rule is that the banks have used the secondary market much more for swaps than for direct sales of their claims.

A recent innovation that is still a small part of the market is the so-called 'capitalization' of bank debt. The process, which has been used by Mexico, Chile, and some other debtor countries, works as follows. An international firm, with a subsidiary in the debtor country, buys the bank debt at a discount in the secondary market. It then delivers the debt to the central bank of the debtor country, at a somewhat higher price, payable in domestic currency and usable only for an increase in foreign direct investment in the country. Nissan, for example, recently purchased several million dollars of Mexican debt at 55 per cent of par, and sold the debt to the Bank of Mexico for 70 per cent. The proceeds, in Mexican pesos, were used for the recapitalization of the Nissan subsidiary in Mexico. Mexico achieved a buyback of debt at a discount (70 per cent), and Nissan obtained an effective subsidization on new investment in the country.

The thrust of this paper is that developments such as this should be fostered by the official creditors and the multilateral agencies. The World Bank and InterAmerican Development Bank should use their resources, for example, to lend the debtor countries money to buy back their debt. This would provide a cheap way to reduce exposure of the debtor countries, while at the same time providing a major stimulus to private-sector investment. There are several legal and regulatory problems that will have to be overcome in order to expand this kind of activity, but overcoming such impediments should be a major policy goal (see Buchheit 1986 for a discussion of the legal and regulatory aspects of debt capitalization schemes).

REFERENCES

Buchheit, Lee C. August 1986: Converting sovereign debt in equity investments. Law Firm of Cleary, Gottlieb, Steen & Hamilton, New York.

Díaz-Alejandro, Carlos F. 1984: Latin America in the 1930s. In Rosemary Thorp (ed.), *Latin America in the 1930s*, New York: St. Martin's Press.

Euromoney 1986: The debt swappers, 67–75.

Fishlow, A. 1985: Lessons from the past: capital markets during the 19th century and the interwar period. In M. Kahler (ed.), *The Politics of International Debt*, Ithaca: Cornell University Press.

Jackson, T. 1986: *The Logic and Limits of Bankruptcy Law*, Cambridge: Harvard University Press (forthcoming).

Joskow, P. 1977: Commercial impossibility, the uranium market and the Westinghouse case. *Journal of Legal Studies*, 119–76.

Lipson, C. 1985: International debt and international institutions. In Kahler, M. (ed.), *The Politics of International Debt*, Ithaca: Cornell University Press.

Mallon, R. D. and Sourrouille, J. V. 1975: *Economic Policymaking in a Conflict Society*, Cambridge Mass: Harvard University Press.

Posner, R. A. and Rosenfield, A. M. 1977: Impossibility and related doctrines in contract law: an economic analysis. *Journal of Legal Studies*, 83–118.

Sachs, J. 1983: Theoretical issues in international borrowing. Princeton Studies in International Finance, No. 54.

United Nations Economic Commission for Latin America and the Caribbean, 1986: *The Economic Crisis: Policies for Adjustment, Stabilization, and Growth*.

Wallich, H. 1943: The future of Latin American bonds. *American Economic Review*.

World Bank, *World Debt Tables*, 1985–6 edition.

COMMENT

George L. Perry

The system for foreign lending that Jeff Sachs analyzes takes a bankers' view that carries over from models of commercial lending. On that view, debts must be fully serviced and repaid because that is the condition that maintains creditworthiness for the borrower. The issue raised by Sachs' paper is whether that commercial lending model needs to be modified for dealing with the LDC crisis.

Certainly some features of the present LDC debt have no good parallels in commercial debt. Countries have ended up responsible for what was initially private debt, often under pressure from their creditors. Furthermore, capital flight has drained countries of funds that otherwise would have been available to service debt. Finally, the debt burden has been increased sharply by the loose fiscal–high interest rate policy mix of the chief creditor nation, the United States.

In addition to these special features of the debt, the LDC crisis has macroeconomic dimensions that ought to concern policymakers. During the past few years, many debtor nations have been pushed into depression, private capital has left the region, and investment spending has dried up. The laws and customs surrounding commercial lending should not automatically be accepted as the proper guide for events that have such macroeconomic consequences.

Finally, Sachs reminds us of some of the bad political outcomes, in Germany and elsewhere, that have followed from single-minded insistence on country debt repayment in the past. This history ought to inform the policymakers about the present. If the US State Department rather than the US Treasury had the main say in handling the LDC debt problem, policy might be more concerned about the consequences for debtors and more flexible in its search for solutions to the present crisis.

In arguing for the need to do something, Sachs does not resort to these political considerations that might be important in a broader view of the problem. Rather, he provides a model for thinking about the conditions under which partial debt forgiveness – or partial default, depending on whose perspective you take – would be the rational answer even within the commercial lending model that gives primacy to the banks' perspective on LDC loans. His evidence on the valuation of bank equities and the valuation of debt itself shows that partial default or some probability of total default, is already anticipated by markets. He argues that we are already at a point, in the case of many countries, where the rational strategy calls for partial debt forgiveness in exchange for policy reforms by the debtor nations.

What stands in the way of translating these market realities into a compromise on the debt burden itself? One issue, addressed below, is whether the market price of the debt can be relied on in the way Sachs proposes. Leaving that aside, there are some more general problems. Banks, understandably, want to recover as much as possible from their lending. Thus there may be a number of reasons why they may be unwilling to accept only present market values for some of their debt. They may want to maintain a tough bargaining stance in the belief that, eventually, debts will not default and the present market valuations will be proved wrong. They are concerned that by permitting favorable terms to some borrowers who are in particular need, they will encourage other borrowers to demand similar concessions. And they have no assurance that, if some of a country's debt is partially forgiven, the balance of the debt will, in fact, be a better risk for them than it was before.

Policymakers who might want to implement Sachs' ideas would see problems too, some of which correspond to the banks'. How can policymakers assure that debt forgiveness when and where it is appropriate does not lead countries that do not need it to demand it? And how can they assure that providing forgiveness now does not reduce the ability of countries to borrow in the future?

The key to the Sachs strategy lies in the proposition that the debtors will be both more willing and more able to meet future obligations if they get debt relief now. To make this outcome likely, it is probably essential that economic reforms accompany debt relief. One could ask why these reforms are not undertaken anyhow, independent of debt relief. The answer is that it is politically impossible to impose further hardships on the population simply to pay more interest to foreign banks. Thus debt forgiveness becomes the prize that makes it politically possible to impose needed economic reforms aimed, among other things, at enhancing debt service.

All this is a plausible story that has got all the signs right. I congratulate Jeff Sachs on devising a scheme that makes sense and that brings the issue down to market values for debt that are readily understandable and quantifiable. But although Jeff's plan gains in neatness as a result of depending on market values, that dependence may also be a drawback. The market value of a country's debt reflects both its fundamental ability to service that debt and its bargaining strategy with the banks as reflected in its willingness to service the debt. Without knowing how important the latter is, the market value of debt cannot be taken as an indication of the need for debt relief. And so long as debt relief may be tied to that market value, either because a Sachs plan is actually in place or even if it is simply being contemplated, it will pay countries to act so as to minimize the market value of their debt. This moral hazard includes not only how they conduct their economic affairs but also how they conduct their bargaining strategy with the banks and international agencies.

I am not certain whether these concerns about market value of debt are just a quibble or are more than that. I would like to be convinced that there is a way around the moral hazard problem, because Sachs' plan does have a neatness that makes it attractive and that could help make it workable. But if the essential element in the plan is getting the incentives right, that could be preserved even if the market value formula was dropped. In the present situation countries in debt trouble cannot be expected to undertake painful economic reforms because the benefits of reforms would accrue mainly to the foreign banks. The Sachs plan reduces that disincentive. An alternative formula for granting debt relief would be just as good, and perhaps more equitable, so long as it too reduced the disincentive to reform.

What about the future of international lending? If we get past the present hurdle and devise a practical way to implement solutions such as those that Sachs outlines – and for that matter even if we do not – the present crisis should force some rethinking about the system. For one thing, the assumption of private debts by governments, under pressure from creditors and from domestic political forces, is one unsavory characteristic of the present experience that international agencies should be concerned to avoid in the future. For another, the problem of discouraging capital flight at all the wrong times should be another item on their agenda. There ought to be ways to do that without discouraging capital inflows under normal conditions. Flexible exchange rates are one of the economists' favorite remedies for the kinds of capital flight problems that have plagued Latin America in the past. However the example of Pacific basin countries suggests that a flexible rate system may not be the only answer and that successful capital controls can be imposed if there is a political will to do so.

In the future, foreign equity investment will probably have to play a larger role in financing LDC growth than it has in the recent past. Furthermore, converting some of present debt into equity is likely to be one way present debt is reduced. But extensive foreign ownership has raised political problems in the past, and may again. For this and other reasons, equity finance cannot substitute entirely for lending, and the problem of how to restore net lending to troubled LDCs will remain.

Although they do not want to grant major concessions to the borrowers on their present debt, the banks could end up hanging tough for too long. The banks that hold most of today's loans are no longer the only sources of finance in the world. If, confronted with no feasible alternative, countries unilaterally renounce some of the present debt, they may find they can borrow elsewhere starting with a clean slate. Thus whatever their current bargaining, stance, banks are hardly immune from pressures for a cooperative settlement, perhaps along the lines Sachs outlines.

Part II

INTERNATIONAL CAPITAL MOVEMENTS: THEORY AND MEASUREMENT

6

Country Risk and the Organization of International Capital Transfer

Jonathan Eaton and Mark Gersovitz

1. Introduction

Carlos Díaz-Alejandro analyzed many aspects of the international transfer of capital. Among the factors that he stressed, perhaps none was given more emphasis than the way the transfer of capital is organized. It is in this cluster of issues that we find the themes for our paper.

On the side of suppliers of capital, the questions that arise most prominently in Díaz-Alejandro's writings are: (a) whether the cohesion among creditors that allows them to enforce contracts will also lead to other sorts of collusive behavior, perhaps reflected in returns to the providers of capital above their opportunity costs of funds (Bacha and Díaz-Alejandro 1982; Díaz-Alejandro 1984); and (b) whether there is sufficient flexibility in the contract under which capital is provided, given the contingencies that may arise (Díaz-Alejandro 1984). This latter topic subsumes some important aspects of the differences between lenders and direct investors.

As for the recipients of capital, one issue is whether the public sector obtains capital and compensates its owners in a centralized fashion, or whether private entities play this role atomistically (Díaz-Alejandro 1984). In the second case, the issue arises as to what actions the public sector takes if private agents do not fulfil their contractual obligations (Díaz-Alejandro 1985). Another related question concerns the role of capital transfers abroad by private agents (so-called capital flight), especially when the public sector may be responsible for recompensing foreign suppliers of capital (Díaz-Alejandro 1984).

All these considerations bear on the central issue of how much a country should borrow in an environment of country risk and the dual problem of assessing the cost of capital in such circumstances. Quoting Harberger twice:

> The 'risk premium' charged on loans should not be considered as part of the cost of borrowing, so long as that premium truly reflects the probability of default, and so long as that probability, in turn, is accurately perceived by both borrowers and lenders. . . . In short, the default premium reflects

> that part of the stated interest rate that is (on average) not expected to be paid. And if it is not expected to be paid, it is not part of the cost. . . . The above statement holds even when the probability of default is a function of the size of the debt of the individual borrower. (Harberger 1976: 1)

and later,

> [D]eveloping countries typically face an upward-rising supply curve of capital funds. The marginal cost *to the country* of borrowing exceeds the average cost. This is a genuine negative externality that in principle justifies a tax on foreign borrowing (that is, each additional foreign loan tends to increase the country risk premium to be paid as other foreign loans are renewed or new ones made). (Harberger 1985: 236)

In section 2 we characterize optimal borrowing in the presence of default risk, and discuss the relationships between the world interest rate, the interest rate charged to the borrower, and the social cost of capital to the national economy. Our results indicate that almost any relative ordering of these magnitudes is possible.

Whether market imperfections arise when borrowing is decentralized among individual firms is a question that has been addressed by Kahn (1984). In order to compare the implications of alternative organizational forms of capital transfer, section 3 summarizes some of his results.

A third issue that we address (in section 4) is the capacity of direct foreign investment, relative to the social optimum and to portfolio investment, to transfer capital to developing countries. Even when the penalty for expropriation is equivalent to that for default, different amounts of capital will be transferred. There is no necessary ordering, but we find a presumption that under laissez-faire direct investment cannot sustain as much movement of capital as portfolio investment.[1]

In these sections we also examine the optimal taxation of foreign investment with sovereign risk.[2] Portfolio and direct investments have different tax implications, and either a tax or a subsidy can be the better policy.

In section 5 we turn to the simultaneous interaction of public debt and private investment. One result is that even in a very simple framework there may be several equilibria. One is a Pareto optimum which satisfies all the standard marginal conditions and in which debt is repaid. The presence of large public debt-service obligations (and the tax obligations they foretell) implies a second, less favorable equilibrium characterized by a flight of private capital to foreign countries and nonrepayment of public debt.

2. Optimal Indebtedness

We consider a country with n potential domestic projects. Each project produces an output q (inclusive of remaining capital) determined by the production relationship

$$q_i = f_i(k_i) \qquad f_i' > 0, f_i'' < 0$$

where k_i is the amount invested.

The national capital stock is $\bar{K}$. There is also an international capital market in which the gross safe interest rate is given exogenously to this country at r. The government automatically enforces all loan contracts among nationals. If it fails to enforce a loan contract with a foreign lender then the country experiences a penalty equivalent to a loss of income of $P(x)$.[3] We introduce uncertainty by assuming that the penalty is stochastic: x is a random variable distributed uniformly on the interval [0, 1] and $P'(x) \geqslant 0$. The parties to the loan do not know what x will be when the loans are made, but they learn about it before repayment is to be made. Upon learning x, the government chooses to enforce existing debt contracts with foreigners, or not, depending upon the consequence for national income.

If the government sees to it that loans are repaid, national income is Y^N where

$$Y^N = Q - sK^f \tag{2.1}$$

Here s is the gross interest rate charged by foreign lenders,

$$Q \equiv \sum_{i=1}^{n} f_i(k_i)$$

the domestic output exclusive of any penalty, and

$$K^f \equiv \sum_{i=1}^{n} k_i - \bar{K}$$

the foreign debt. If the government chooses not to enforce contracts then national income is

$$Y^E(x) = Q - P(x) \tag{2.2}$$

The decision consequently depends upon whether

$$P(x) \lesseqgtr sK^f \tag{2.3}$$

The probability of default is x^* where $P(x^*) = sK^f$. If $x \geqslant x^*$ then the government defaults while if $x \geqslant x^*$ it repays.[4] We define the function

$$h(sK^f) \equiv 1 - x^* = 1 - P^{-1}(sK^f)$$

as the probability of repaying given that an amount sK^f is owed.

International loan markets determine an interest rate s, given the loan amount K^f, that satisfies the zero expected profit condition.[5]

$$s\,h(sK^f) = r \tag{2.4}$$

A possibility, of course, is that for some levels of K^f *no* value of s satisfies this relationship. These amounts will simply not be available.

At the time borrowing decisions are made, the penalty is unknown. We assume (a) that the government's objective, at this stage, is to maximize the expectation of a function U of national income and (b) that the government directly controls the amount invested in each project, the k_i's. Substituting (2.1) and (2.2), the objective function is:

$$W = \int_0^{1-h(sK^f)} U[Q - P(x)]\,dx + h(sK^f)\,U(Q - sK^f) \tag{2.5}$$

with K^f as defined above and condition (2.4) relating s and K^f.

The first-order condition for a maximum is:

$$\frac{dW}{dk_L} = \int_0^{1-h(s^f)} U'\,[Q - P(x)]\,f_i'(k_i)dx + h(sK^f)\,U'(Q - sK^f)\,[f_i'(k_i) - s - \frac{ds}{dK^f}K^f] = 0.\ i = 1, \ldots, n \tag{2.6}$$

From the zero expected profit condition (2.4):

$$\frac{ds}{dK^f} = \frac{-s/K^f}{1 + 1/\varepsilon} \tag{2.7}$$

where

$$\varepsilon \equiv \frac{h'(sK^f)sK^f}{h(sK^f)}$$

the (negative) elasticity of the repayment probability with respect to what is owed.

Using the expression for ε, condition (2.6) becomes

$$f_i'(k_i) = [r/(1 + \varepsilon)]\phi \tag{2.8}$$

where

$$\phi \equiv \{h(sK^f) + \int_0^{1-h(sKf)} U'[Y^E(x)]\,dx/U'(Y^N)\}^{-1}$$

Note first that the right-hand side of expression (2.8) is independent of i. Not surprisingly, optimality requires equating the marginal product of capital across projects.

In the case of constant marginal utility $\phi = 1$, while risk aversion implies that $\phi > 1$. Risk-averse borrowers should borrow less than risk-neutral borrowers. The reason is that, at the optimum, an increase in borrowing raises income by $f_i'(k_i)$ in the (high-income) default state and therefore must lower it in the (low-income) no-default state. An increase in risk aversion pushes the borrowing country toward doing just the opposite.[6]

At the optimum an increase in borrowing can never *lower* total debt-service obligations. Otherwise an increase in K^f would raise income in all states of the world. This condition insures that $1 + \varepsilon > 0$. Since $\varepsilon \leqslant 0$, condition (2.8) implies that, for $\varepsilon < 0$, even risk-neutral borrowers should borrow less than what equates the marginal product of capital to the world interest rate. The reason is that borrowing more raises the probability that the country will suffer the penalty.

Three special cases illustrate various possibilities in the relationships among the nominal interest rate, the cost of capital, and the amount borrowed at the optimum.

First, if the penalty is nonstochastic then credit will be available up to an amount P/r at rate r. No more is available above that amount regardless of the nominal rate. For $K^f < P/r$, $\varepsilon = 0$ and the standard equating of the marginal product of capital to the world *safe* interest rate is optimal. At $[K^f = P/r]$ credit is rationed, but competition keeps the rate charged at r.

Second, if the penalty is discretely distributed, as, for example, if $P(x) = P_1$ for x in $[0, \pi]$ and $P(x) = P_2$ for x in $[\pi, 1]$ then for $[P_1/r < K^f < P_2(1 - \pi)/r, \varepsilon = 0]$. Equating the marginal product to the safe world interest rate is optimal for a risk-neutral country. Even though there is the possibility of default, a marginal increase in the amount borrowed does not increase the likelihood of default, and therefore the marginal cost of borrowing is constant.

Third, if $P(x) = x/(1 - x)$, so that an infinite penalty is possible, then the probability of repayment is $1/(1 + sK^f)$. The zero profit condition (2.6) implies an inverse loan supply function:

$$s = r/(1 - rK^f) \tag{2.9}$$

with no capital available at a level above $1/r$. With risk neutrality optimal borrowing implies that

$$f_i'(k_i) = r/(1 - rK^f) = s \tag{2.10}$$

In general, there is no ordering of the marginal product of capital and s, the nominal interest rate, at the optimum. In the nonstochastic case $r = s$ but if credit is rationed then the marginal product of capital exceeds both r and s. In the case of the binomial distribution of the penalty and an interior value of K^f, $s = r/(1 - \pi) > r$, but with risk neutrality the marginal product of capital should equal r. Finally, in the third special case we considered, optimality happens to involve *equating* the marginal product of capital to s, contrary to the first quotation from Harberger.

Note also that the marginal cost of capital does not necessarily increase monotonically with the amount borrowed. In the case of the binomial distribution of the penalty the marginal cost is r both for K^f in $[0, P_1/r]$ and for K^f in $[P_1/r, (1 - \pi)P_2/r]$, but at $K^f = P_1/r$ the marginal cost is infinite since an infinitesimal increase in K^f raises interest costs by $\pi P_1/(1 - \pi)$.

3. Decentralized Borrowing

We now turn to the case in which each investment project is managed by a private national who borrows and invests in order to maximize his utility from the profit generated by the project.[7] This is the case considered by Kahn (1984), and our analysis largely follows his. The government's failure to enforce the loan obligations of *any* borrower provokes the implementation of the same penalty, and its severity is independent of the amount owed. The choice to enforce foreign debt contracts or not thus remains an all-or-nothing decision for the borrowing country. It suffers the same penalty regardless of how much is not repaid, so if it does not enforce one debt contract, there is no point in enforcing any other.

One reason for foreign lenders to adopt this attitude is their reliance on the government of the borrowing country to enforce even private contracts. Díaz-Alejandro's (1985) account of the 1982 financial crisis in Chile indicates that foreign lenders took exactly this stance when several private banks with large debts to US banks declared bankruptcy. As part of its free-market orientation the Chilean government had explicitly *not* guaranteed these debts, but the US banks threatened to embargo loans to the Chilean government anyway if these debts were cancelled. The government chose to assume them.

The amount borrowed in a decentralized allocation depends, among other things, on how the government distributes the cost of default, if it should occur, among borrowers. In general, in the event of default an individual borrower suffers an additional cost $\tau^i(k_i^f, x)$.[8] If the burden is distributed among borrowers according to their share of total borrowing, for example, then

$$\tau^i (k_i^f, x) = (k_i^f/K^f)\, P(x)$$

Let $u_i(\pi_i)$ denote the utility of the owner of the firm as a function of firm profit, π_i. He chooses k_i^d and k_i^f to maximize an objective function:

$$w_i \equiv \int_0^{1-h(sK^f)} u_i[f_i(k_i) - \tilde{r}k_i^d - \tau^i (k_i^f, x)]\, dx + h(sK^f)\, u_i\, [f_i(k_i) - \tilde{r}k_i^d - sk_i^f] \tag{3.1}$$

where $\tilde{r}$ is the interest rate on domestic capital and $k_i = k_i^d + K_i^f$.

The two first-order conditions for a maximum are

$$f_i'(k_i) = \tilde{r} + \frac{d\tilde{r}}{d_{k_i^d}}\, k_i^d \tag{3.2}$$

and

$$f_i'(k_i) = \{r \left[\frac{1+\varepsilon(k_i^f/K^f)}{1+\varepsilon} \right] + \int_0^{1-h(sK^f)} u_i'(x)\, \tau_k^i (k_i^f, x)\, dx/\bar{u}_i' - \frac{h(sK^f)}{K_f}\, \frac{\varepsilon}{1+\varepsilon}\, \frac{\bar{u}_i^r - \bar{u}_i^d}{\bar{u}_i'} \}\, \phi_i \tag{3.3}$$

where

$$\phi_i \equiv [h(sk^f) + \int_0^{1-h(sK^f)} u_i'(x)\, dx/\bar{u}_i']^{-1}$$

$$u'_i(x) \equiv u'_i[f_i(k_i) - \tilde{r}k^d_i - \tau^i(k^f_i, x)]$$

$$\bar{u}'_i \equiv u'[f_i(k_i) - \tilde{r}k^d_i - sk^f_i]$$

$$\bar{u}^d_i \equiv u_i[f_i(k_i) - \tilde{r}k^d_i - \tau^i(k^f_i, sK^f)]$$

$$\bar{u}^r_i \equiv u_i[f_i(k_i) - \tilde{r}k^d_i - sk^f_i]$$

and

$$\bar{k}^f_i \equiv \sum_{j \neq i} k^f_j$$

(foreign borrowing by other firms). The conditions that $1 + \varepsilon > 0$, that ε not increase as K^f rises, and that $\tau_{kk} \geqslant 0$ ensure that the second-order conditions for a maximum are satisfied.

Whether there is too much or too little borrowing under *laissez-faire*, in comparison with the social optimum, depends on four factors:[9]

1 *Risk*. If the tax system distributes the burden of the penalty in proportion to income, and private and public attitudes toward risk coincide, then $\phi_i = \phi$. Greater risk aversion on the part of private individuals than on the part of the public sector leads to less borrowing than is socially optimal. If the government is more risk averse then there is too much borrowing.[10]

2 *The 'commons' nature of interest costs*. An increase in the foreign debt of any single borrower reduces the probability of repayment (if $\varepsilon < 0$), raising the likelihood that others will experience the penalty. This cost is not internalized by any single borrower. This effect acts to raise borrowing above the socially optimal level. It is more important the larger ε, the elasticity of the repayment probability with respect to debt-service obligations, and the smaller k^f_i/K^f, the firm's share of total borrowing.

3 *The redistribution of the penalty*. If $\tau_k > 0$ then an individual borrower increases his share of the total burden of the penalty by borrowing more. This effect acts to discourage borrowing. This disincentive to borrow may outweigh the effect of additional borrowing on the cost of capital to other borrowers. In this case, relative to the social optimum, there is *under*-borrowing as long as private borrowers are at least as risk averse as the public.

4 *The incidence of the penalty*. Whether an individual borrower benefits or loses from a decision to default depends upon whether $sk^f_i \gtrless \tau^i(k^f_i, sK^f)$. To the extent that private borrowers as a group bear less than the full penalty of default, more will be borrowed than is socially optimal. The opposite is the case if private borrowers suffer more from default than the nation as a whole.

Note that under *laissez-faire*, borrowing does not typically equate the marginal product of capital across sectors. It is relatively lower in projects that contribute only a small share to total foreign borrowing, since here the external effect associated with borrowing is greater. It will also be lower in projects whose owners bear less of the burden of the penalty of default. A tendency may emerge, for example, for more to be invested in production of import substitutes or nontraded goods (see Gersovitz 1983; Khan 1984; Alexander 1985).

In summary, decentralization of borrowing decisions can lead either to under- or to overborrowing. The effect on different projects can vary. Either taxation or subsidization of borrowing may be optimal. In one particular case (if $\phi_i = \phi$, $\varepsilon = 0$ or $k_i^f/K^f = 0$, $\tau^i(k_i^f, sK^f) = sk_i^f$, and $\tau_k^i = 0$) the *laissez-faire* allocation corresponds to the social optimum.

4. Direct Foreign Investment

We now turn to the case in which foreigners invest directly in domestic projects. Foreign investors can borrow in the world capital market at the safe interest rate, r, and always repay their loans in this market. In the absence of expropriation foreign investors earn the after-tax profit on their investment, π_i, net of interest payments to foreign lenders. National income equals total output, less payments to foreign investors (equal to profits plus loans from abroad). As with default, expropriation imposes a cost $P(x)$ on the country where again $P'(x) \geqslant 0$ and x is perceived as uniformly distributed on $[0,1]$ at the time investments are made. Its exact value is known at the time of the expropriation decision, however.

For purposes of comparison with our analysis of default, we treat expropriation here as an all-or-nothing event. This assumption may be less appropriate for expropriation, since it is more likely to occur on a selective basis, with expropriation of each project provoking a separate penalty.[11]

If expropriated, foreign investors receive nothing from their investment in this country. They do not pay any local factors of production, but do repay loans from abroad.[12] In the absence of expropriation the investor remits an amount

$$s_i = \pi_i + rk_i^f \tag{4.1}$$

profit plus the payment on foreign loans. In contrast, portfolio investors providing an amount k_i^f would receive sk_i^f in the absence of default. The fact that remittances of direct investors depend directly upon output, while those of portfolio investors do not, is the basic difference between these contractual forms.

Defining total remittances with no expropriation as

$$S \equiv \sum_{i=1}^{n} s_i$$

and total domestic output (less any penalty) as

$$Q \equiv \sum_{i=1}^{n} f_i(k_i),$$

national income without expropriation is

$$Y^N = Q - S \tag{4.2}$$

while in the event of expropriation it is

$$Y^E(x) = Q - P(x) \tag{4.3}$$

The government will choose to expropriate or not as

$$S \gtrless P(x) \tag{4.4}$$

4.1 Laissez-faire Investment

The expected profit from an investment in project i is

$$\pi_i^e = -rk_i^f + h(S)\,[f_i(k_i) - y_i] \tag{4.5}$$

Here, as before, $h(S) \equiv 1 - P^{-1}(S)$; y_i is payment to local factors of production. A risk-neutral foreign investor will choose a k_i^f that satisfies the first-order condition

$$f_i'(k_i) = \{r - h'(S)\,\frac{\mathrm{d}S}{\mathrm{d}k_i^f}\,[f_i(k_i) - y_i]\} \,/\, h(S) \tag{4.6}$$

Competition among potential risk-neutral foreign investors will bid y_i up to the point at which $\pi_i^e = 0$, so that

$$y_i = f_i(k_i) - rk_i^f \,/\, h(S) \tag{4.7}$$

If there is no expropriation then the foreign investor remits

$$s_i = f_i(k_i) - y_i = rk_i^f \,/\, h(S) \tag{4.8}$$

Summing across potential investments,

$$S = rK^f \,/\, h(S) \tag{4.9}$$

which implicitly defines S as a function of K^f. Differentiating this relationship with respect to k_i^f indicates that

$$\frac{\mathrm{d}S}{\mathrm{d}k_i^f} = \frac{r}{h'(S)\,S + h(S)} = \frac{r/h(S)}{1+\varepsilon} \tag{4.10}$$

where, parallel to the case of portfolio investment

$$\varepsilon \equiv h'(S)\, S/\, h(S)$$

the (negative) elasticity of the probability of nonexpropriation with respect to remittances.

Substituting these relationships back into the first-order condition

$$f_i'(k_i) = r\left[\frac{1 + \varepsilon\,(\bar{k}_i^f/K^f)}{1+\varepsilon}\right] / \, h(S) \tag{4.11}$$

where

$$\bar{k}_i^f \equiv \sum_{j \neq i} k_i^f$$

foreign borrowing by other foreign investors.[13]

A comparison of the marginal products of capital under laissez-faire direct foreign investment and under laissez-faire foreign borrowing (for the risk-neutral case), *assuming that default and expropriation provoke equivalent penalties*, indicates no necessary ordering. Two effects operate in different directions:

1 If the marginal unit of foreign borrowing raises the share of the penalty of default borne by the individual borrower then the flow of capital under direct investment tends to exceed that under portfolio investment. *To the extent that the penalty of default is borne by those making the borrowing decision, while those making the investment decision avoid the penalty of expropriation, more capital is transferred under direct investment.*

2 The term

$$\varrho_i \equiv r\,[1 + \varepsilon(\bar{k}_i^f/K^f)] \,/\, (1 + \varepsilon)$$

is the expected marginal cost of an additional unit of foreign borrowing both for a domestic firm (less any penalty assessment) and for a foreign investor. Domestic firms earn a return $f_i'(k_i)$ *regardless of whether or not there is default*, but foreign investors earn this return *only if there is no expropriation*. Consequently, with risk neutrality, no marginal penalty assessment, and $\tau^i\,(k_i^f,\, sK^f) = sk_i^f$,

$$f_i'(k^i) = \varrho_i$$

with borrowing, but

$$h(S)\, f_i'(k^i) = \varrho_i$$

with direct investment. To the extent that this effect is relevant, portfolio investment can sustain more movement of capital.

4.2 Taxing Foreign Investment

We now introduce taxes on income remitted by foreign investors. To simplify things we assume that all projects are identical [that is, that $f_i(k) = f(k)$ for all i] and that there is no national capital ($K = 0$). In addition, we assume that ε is constant, implying that

$$P(x) = c\,(1 - x)^{1/\varepsilon},\ c > 0$$

The expected profit to a foreign investor who invests k in a typical project is now

$$\pi^e = -rk + h(S)\,(1 - t)\,[f(k) - y] \qquad (4.4')$$

where t is the tax rate on income remitted. The first-order condition for a maximum is

$$(1-t)h(S)f'(k) - r + h'(S)\frac{\mathrm{d}S}{\mathrm{d}K}(1-t)[f(k) - y] = 0 \qquad (4.6')$$

and the zero-profit condition is

$$y = f(k) - rk\,/\,h(S)(1-t) \qquad (4.7')$$

Expressions (4.9) and (4.10) continue to apply; taxing foreign investment does not affect the relationship between investment and after-tax remittances. Substituting (4.10) into (4.6′) and invoking symmetry, the first-order condition becomes

$$(1-t)\,h(S)f'(k) = r[1 + \varepsilon(n-1)/n]\,/\,(1+\varepsilon) \qquad (4.6'')$$

This condition, along with the aggregate zero-expected profit condition

$$rnk = h(S)S \qquad (4.9')$$

determine k and S.

An increase in the tax rate t affects k and S as follows:

$$\frac{\mathrm{d}k}{\mathrm{d}t} = \frac{h(S)k(1+\varepsilon)}{\Delta} \qquad (4.12)$$

$$\frac{\mathrm{d}S}{\mathrm{d}t} = \frac{rnk}{\Delta} \qquad (4.13)$$

where

$$\Delta \equiv (1-t)\, h(S)\, [\eta(1+\varepsilon) + \varepsilon]$$

and

$$\eta \equiv f''(k)\, k/f'(k)$$

As long as $1+\varepsilon > 0$, so that increasing remittances in the no-expropriation state raises expected remittances overall, $\Delta < 0$. Under this condition, an increase in the tax on remittances reduces both foreign investment and after-tax remittances if expropriation does not happen.

4.3 Optimal Taxation

We posit, as in section 2, a government that seeks to maximize the expectation of a function U of national income. The objective function may be written

$$W = \int_0^{1-h(s)} U[nf(k) - P(x)]\mathrm{d}x + h(S)\, U[nf(k) - S] \tag{4.14}$$

Differentiation of this expression with respect to t gives

$$\frac{\mathrm{d}W}{\mathrm{d}t} = [\phi^{-1}\, nf'(k)\, \frac{\mathrm{d}k}{\mathrm{d}t} - h(S)\, \frac{\mathrm{d}S}{\mathrm{d}t}\,] \cdot \overline{U'} \tag{4.15}$$

where, as in section 2,

$$\phi \equiv \{h(S) + \int_0^{1-h(S)} U'\, [Y^E(x)]\mathrm{d}x \,/\, U'\, (Y^N)\}^{-1}$$

The incorporation of (4.12) and (4.13) into (4.15), and use of (4.6″), yields

$$\frac{\mathrm{d}W}{\mathrm{d}t} = \frac{rnk}{\Delta}\{\phi^{-1}[1+\varepsilon(n-1)/n] - h(S)\} \tag{4.15′}$$

With $\Delta < 0$, from an initial situation in which $t = 0$, an increase in t raises or lowers expected welfare depending upon whether

$$h(S) \gtrless \phi 1 + \varepsilon(n-1)/n \tag{4.16}$$

If a firm's investment has a negligible spillover onto other firms ($\varepsilon = 0$ or $n = 1$) and if the government is risk neutral (so that $\phi = 1$) then a *subsidy* on direct foreign investment is optimal. The reason is simply that the country benefits from an additional unit of capital if it should expropriate, and this benefit is not captured by the firm that undertakes the investment.

To the extent that investment by a single borrower raises the expected cost of capital for other firms, more investment takes place under laissez-faire, given the underlying probability of expropriation.

If the country is risk neutral then condition (4.16) becomes

$$-\ \varepsilon\,(n-1)/n \gtrless 1 - h(S)$$

with the 'commons effect' in the left-hand side and the probability of expropriation on the right-hand side. To the extent that the externality effect is large, too much capital is invested. If the probability of expropriation is low, then the likelihood of the country's benefitting from an increase in its capital stock in the event of expropriation is low. In this case a tax on foreign investment is appropriate. If expropriation is likely, however, but externalities are small, then a subsidy is optimal. Risk aversion tilts the argument in favor of a tax. A tax shifts income from the high endowment states (expropriation) toward the low endowment state (protecting property rights). A subsidy does the opposite.[14]

To summarize the results of the last two sections, decentralized investment, whether it takes the form of borrowing by domestic firms or direct investment by foreigners, may generate an externality by raising the interest costs of other firms. This is Kahn's 'commons effect,' and it leads to overborrowing relative to the social optimum.

Both decentralized borrowing and decentralized investment, however, are subject to forces that could lead to underborrowing. An increase in a borrower's share of the burden of the default penalty, should default occur, is a disincentive to borrow that does not reflect a social cost of borrowing. The possibility of expropriation is a disincentive to invest that does not reflect a lower social return on an investment.

If loans to individual firms or individual investment projects stand alone in terms of the penalties that default or expropriation provoke, then there is no externality across projects. The commons problem disappears. If, in addition, borrowers suffer the full penalty of default on their own loans then, with risk neutrality, the private and socially optimal levels of portfolio borrowing coincide. The amount of direct foreign investment that takes place will be too low, relative to the optimum, however, since investors lose their return in the event of expropriation.

As argued above, investors seem more likely to adopt a stand-alone principle in the case of direct foreign investment. This is an additional reason why decentralized direct foreign investment can sustain less capital movement than portfolio investment under laissez-faire.

5. Public Borrowing and Private Investment: The Capital Flight Phenomenon

A number of countries with large public debts to foreign banks seem also to have large amounts of private capital invested abroad, a phenomenon referred to as capital flight. Cuddington (1986) and Dooley et al. (1986) provide alternative estimates of these flows for several countries. To some extent standard portfolio diversification motives can explain these two-way flows. What is peculiar about capital flight from large debtors is that capital *inflows* largely take the form of public and publicly guaranteed debt while outflows are private.

Khan and Haque (1985) explain this phenomenon on the basis of an asymmetric risk of expropriation. Nationals investing domestically face a risk of expropriation by their own government that exceeds the risk of default on foreign loans. This risk is avoided by investing abroad. Their analysis does not relate the government's expropriation decision to outstanding debt. In fact, prospective external debt-service obligations may contribute to the private sector's fear of expropriation, or of other forms of taxation, as a means for the government to raise funds to service debt. If capital located abroad escapes taxation and is free of expropriation risk, then capital flight can emerge as a *consequence* of heavy foreign borrowing.

The same phenomenon may explain the hesitation of foreign private investors to invest directly in the country. Investors can negotiate *ex ante* with the borrowing government a promised return on publicly guaranteed portfolio loans. Failure to pay the promised return constitutes default, and investors can invoke the associated penalty straightforwardly. In contrast, the host-country government can affect the return on direct private investment through myriad tax, exchange control, minimum wage, and other types of policy. It is difficult to draft and to adjudicate a binding contract that specifies contingencies under which a government may or may not adopt various policies that affect the return on a direct investment. Investors consequently would find it difficult to demonstrate that a host-country government has reneged on any *ex ante* guarantee. Informational asymmetries between the host-country government and the foreign firm might expose one side or the other to severe moral hazard problems if a contract were entered into and enforced.

In this section we explicitly introduce two forms of capital, public and private, into the production process. Total domestic output is a function of the domestic supplies of public capital P, private capital K, and L, other factors of production that are internationally immobile and in fixed supply domestically. These are called labor here. Output Q is determined by the relationship

$$Q = F(P, K, L) \tag{5.1}$$

Production is at constant returns to scale.

Marginal productivity conditions do *not* determine factor rewards, however. Payments to *private* factors (K and L) exhaust output. The government cannot capture the contribution of public investment to output by charging directly for the use of its capital. The (pre-tax) returns to private capital, $\tilde{r}$, and labor $\tilde{w}$, are homogeneous-of-degree-zero functions

$$\tilde{r} = g^K(P, K, L), g^K_K < 0 \tag{5.2}$$

$$\tilde{w} = g^L(P, K, L), g^L_L < 0 \tag{5.3}$$

that satisfy the relationship

$$g^K(P, K, L)\, K + g^L(P, K, L)\, L = F(P, K, L) \tag{5.4}$$

Hence payments to *private* factors alone exhaust output. The safe world interest rate is r and the national supply of capital is $\bar{K}$. At this point we assume that the penalty for default on public debt is too large to make this option attractive.

5.1 The Centralized Solution

Standard marginal productivity conditions dictate the centralized optimum; optimal values of P and K, denoted P^* and K^*, satisfy

$$F_P(P^*, K^*, L) = F_K(P^*, K^*, L) = r \tag{5.5}$$

Total external indebtedness D is

$$D = P^* + K^* - \bar{K}$$

5.2 Decentralized Solutions

We now assume that the government cannot allocate private capital directly, and must borrow to finance public investment. It can tax income from labor and from capital invested *domestically*. It cannot tax the wealth of its nationals directly, but only the income that this wealth generates after it is invested. Hence $\bar{K}$ is not directly available as a tax base to finance P.

The optimal allocation can be supported by choosing proportional tax rates t^*_K for capital and t^*_L for labor that satisfy

$$r = F_K(P^*, K^*, L) = (1-t^*_K)\, g^K(P, K, L) = (1-t^*_K)\, \tilde{r} \tag{5.6}$$

$$w = F_L(P^*, K^*, L) = (1-t^*_L)\, g^L(P, K, L) = (1-t^*_L)\, \tilde{w} \tag{5.7}$$

in which w is the after-tax wage. Multiplying (5.6) by K^* and (5.7) by L, adding the results, and invoking homogeneity ensures that

$$Q - wL - rK^* = F_P P^* = rP^* \tag{5.8}$$

The tax revenue exactly pays for the debt-service obligation on public debt.

This equilibrium is compatible with competitive behavior of private investors since the after-tax return on private investment equals the world interest rate.

5.3 Capital Flight and Country Runs

A difficulty arises with the sequencing of decisions. We assume that the government cannot undertake public investment subsequent to private investment. If it attempts to implement the optimal allocation it must first borrow and invest P^*, generating a debt-service obligation rP^*.

We assume that there is a limit on the revenue that can be raised from taxing labor income. We specify the limit as a function T^L (P, K, L), and assume here that

$$T^L(P^*, K^*, L) \geqslant t_L^* g^L(P^*, K^*, L)\, L \tag{5.9}$$

the optimal tax rate is feasible. In the extreme, all labor income is taxed, meaning that $T^L = g^L L$.

We impose two restrictions on this function. We assume that T^L is continuous. The first is that revenue extracted from labor income can never repay fully the public debt if the optimal amount is borrowed, i.e.,

$$T^L(P^*, K, L) < rP^* \tag{5.10}$$

The second is that an increase in the capital stock cannot generate a more than proportional increase in T^L, i.e.

$$T_K^L K/T^L \leqslant 1 \tag{5.11}$$

Given P^*, K and L, if the government services its debt then the tax burden on private investors will equal at least

$$T^K(P^*, K, L) = rP^* - T^L(P^*, K, L) \tag{5.12}$$

The maximum after-tax return on capital as a function K is

$$\Psi(K) = g^K(P^*, K, L) = [rP^* - T^L(P^*, K, L)]/K, \tag{5.13}$$

which we assume exceeds r for some values of K.

We now demonstrate the potential for multiple equilibria. One equilibrium is the social optimum just derived, in which $K = K^*$, $t_K = t_K^*$, and $(1-t_K^*)\, g^K = r$. Tax revenue covers debt-service obligations, and debt is repaid.

Another equilibrium is one with zero private investment. Since $\Psi(0) < r$

the country cannot attract only a small but strictly positive amount of private capital. The government will have an incentive to tax any such amount at such a high rate that the after-tax return is noncompetitive. In this case tax revenues do not cover debt-service obligations. The country is insolvent. A certain threshold level of private investment is needed to generate a competitive after-tax return. Other equilibria with private capital in the range $(0, K^*)$ are also possible, with an after-tax return on capital equal to the world rate.

The potential for multiple equilibria can be modelled most starkly by eliminating taxation of the fixed factor, labor, and assuming that $t^*_L = T^L(P^*, K, L) = 0$, so that private capital income is the only tax base. The function

$$\Psi(K) = g^K_K - rP^*/K \tag{5.14}$$

is the actual after-tax return on capital. At the optimum,

$$\Psi(K) = r$$

while

$$\lim_{K\to\infty} \Psi(K) = g^K_K(P^*, K, L) < r$$

and

$$\lim_{K\to 0} \Psi(K) = -\infty$$

Continuity of g^K ensures that there are at least two equilibria in which $\Psi(K) = r$.

If we posit the Marshallian adjustment mechanism

$$\dot{K} = \lambda\,[\Psi(K) - r], \qquad \lambda > 0$$

then both the equilibrium with the maximum amount invested and that with $K = 0$ are stable. Figure 6.1 provides a simple illustration of this result. Stable equilibria are at $K = K^*$ and $K = 0$; $K = \tilde{K}$ is an unstable equilibrium.

In conclusion, the interaction of public and private borrowing gives rise to situations of multiple equilibria, some of which Pareto-dominate others. If the government must incur public debt before capital is allocated then the tax burden implied by that debt leads to ranges in which the after-tax return to private capital *increases* with the total amount invested. One equilibrium is the Pareto-optimal one, with a substantial amount of private investment

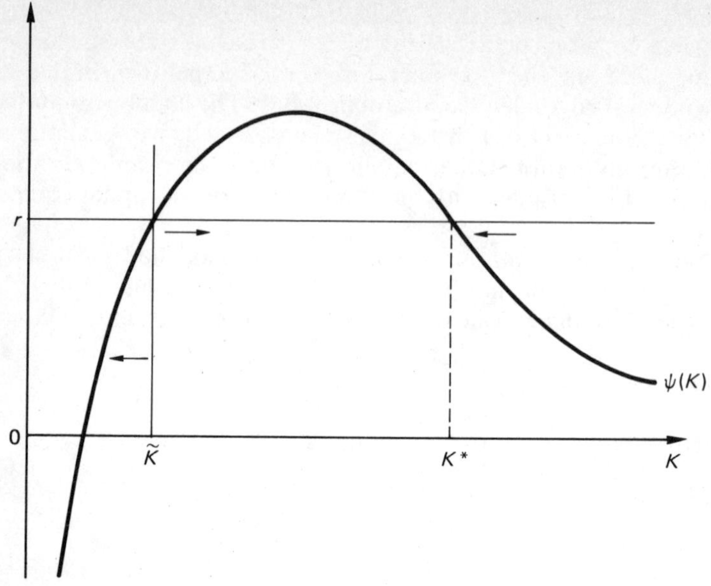

Figure 6.1 The anticipated after tax return on private investment and multiple equilibria

earning a competitive return and public loans repaid. No private investment (or a low level if capital controls keep some capital from escaping) and insolvency characterize another equilibrium.[15]

The model sketched here illustrates the potential for multiple equilibria in a very simple context. The result survives several modifications. Introducing the potential for willful default, rather than insolvency, in particular, would not change the character of the results as long as the temptation to default grows as the domestic tax base falls.

6. Conclusions

A frequent subject of Carlos Díaz-Alejandro's writings is the complex and often stormy interactions of foreign capitalists, domestic governments, and local entrepreneurs. An analysis of foreign investment that ignores the imperfect nature of property rights and contract enforcement in international markets cannot explain these relationships, Furthermore, the way that recipients and suppliers of capital organize capital transfer has important implications for the functioning of markets and for optimal policy in capital-importing countries. Recognizing these features of the world economy makes evident the fragility of the institutions that sustain movements of capital between countries, and the potential for instability and conflict that they generate.

In this paper we have considered the implications of alternative institutional arrangements for transferring capital between nations in the presence of country risk. The effort has been an exploratory one and the source of risk itself has not been discussed. Introducing uncertainty about the production process as well as the penalty would change the nature of the insurance that the option to default or expropriate implicitly provides. It would also, of course, introduce additional reasons why direct and portfolio investment would allocate risks differently.

Another issue is the interaction of foreign capital with domestic factor markets. What, in particular, happens, when default is an option domestically as well? Third, we have treated the stock of national capital as given. What implication do our results have for accumulation patterns in a dynamic context?

NOTES

1 This result supports pessimism about the potential for refinancing the bank loans of major debtors with direct private investment, a component of the Baker initiative.
2 Gersovitz (1988) discusses aspects of taxation of foreign investment in developing countries.
3 This is a very abstract representation of the penalty that may be imposed on recipients of foreign capital who do not honor contracts. In fact, the penalties are likely to be quite indirect, such as exclusion from: (a) future borrowing (Eaton and Gersovitz 1981a,b); (b) specialized inputs or technological know-how (Eaton and Gersovitz 1984); and (c) foreign trade (Gersovitz 1983; Kahn 1984; Alexander 1985). Eaton and Gersovitz (1983) contrast the penalties available to financial lenders and direct investors, whereas in this paper we investigate the implications of different ways of organizing the transfer of capital when the penalty is of the same type and magnitude. As argued in Gersovitz (1985) and Eaton et. al. (1986) the form of the penalty may have important consequences for comparative statics and for policy prescriptions. In this paper, we adopt the simple formulation of the penalty as a first step.
4 We arbitrarily resolve ties in favor of repayment.
5 Either lenders' risk neutrality or the perfect diversifiability of this country's risk of defaulting justifies this assumption.
6 This result is sensitive to the way in which the risk of default is introduced into the model. Since it is the penalty that is unknown at the time of the borrowing decision, default occurs in the well-endowed, low-penalty state. An alternative specification (used in Eaton and Gersovitz 1981a) is one in which the penalty is constant in *utility* terms and income is stochastic. Risk aversion consequently implies default in *poorly endowed* states. This insurance aspect of borrowing and default could imply that risk aversion makes *more* borrowing optimal.
7 An incentive, of course, might arise for borrowers to merge their projects into single firms. We do not pursue this issue here.

8 For some borrowers this cost could be negative. If, for example, a consequence of default is a loss of opportunities for international trade then τ^i might be negative for projects producing import substitutes.

9 All but the first play a role in Kahn's analysis. He assumes risk neutrality.

10 Again, alternative specifications of the source of uncertainty imply different results.

11 The contrast between the reactions of foreign investors to expropriation and to default was notable in the case of Peru in the 1970s; see Eaton and Gersovitz (1983).

12 If expropriation led to default on their borrowing by direct investors, then direct investors would transfer all risk to foreign lenders. The analysis would be the same as that of the previous section, only with foreign investors replacing domestic owners of firms as borrowers.

13 Again, the conditions that $1 + \varepsilon > 0$ and that ε not rise as K^f rises ensure that the second-order condition for a maximum is satisfied.

14 Again, alternative specifications of the nature of uncertainty can imply different results.

15 Diamond and Dybvig (1983) explain the potential for bank runs in a framework that is similar formally to this one. In their model a nonconvexity in dynamic technology, along with the existence of deposit contracts, leads to the possibility of runs. See also Eaton (1987).

REFERENCES

Alexander, Lewis S. (1985), Trade and sovereign lending. (Unpublished, Washington, DC: Federal Reserve Board of Governors.)

Bacha, Edmar Lisboa and Díaz-Alejandro, Carlos F. (1982), *International Financial Intermediation: A Long and Tropical View*, Essays in International Finance No. 147, Princeton, NJ.

Cuddington, John T. (1985), *Capital Flight: Issues, Estimates and Explanations.* Princeton Studies in International Finance, no. 58, Princeton, NJ.

Diamond, Douglas and Dybvig, Philip E. (1983), Bank runs, deposit insurance and liquidity, *Journal of Political Economy*, 91, 401–9.

Díaz-Alejandro, Carlos F. (1984), Latin American debt: I don't think we are in Kansas anymore, *Brookings Papers on Economic Activity*, 2, 335–89.

Díaz-Alejandro, Carlos F. (1985), Good-bye financial repression, hello financial crash, *Journal of Development Economics*, 19, 1–24.

Dooley, Michael P., Helkie, William, Tryon, Ralph, and Underwood, John (1986), An analysis of the external debt positions of eight developing countries through 1990, *Journal of Development Economics*, 22: 283–318.

Eaton, Jonathan (1987), Public debt guarantees and private capital flight, *World Bank Economic Review*, 1: 377–96.

Eaton, Jonathan and Gersovitz, Mark (1981a), Debt with potential repudiation: theoretical and empirical analysis, *Review of Economic Studies*, 48, 289–309.

Eaton, Jonathan and Gersovitz, Mark (1981b), *Poor Country Borrowing and the Repudiation Issue*, Princeton Studies in International Finance No. 4, Princeton, NJ.

Eaton, Jonathan and Gersovitz, Mark (1983), Country risk: economic aspects, in

Richard J. Herring (ed.), *Managing International Risk*. New York: Cambridge University Press.

Eaton, Jonathan and Gersovitz, Mark (1984), A theory of expropriation and deviations from perfect capital mobility, *Economic Journal*, 94, 16–40.

Eaton, Jonathan, Gersovitz, Mark and Stiglitz, Joseph E. (1986), The pure theory of country risk, *European Economic Review*, 30, 481–513.

Gersovitz, Mark (1983), Trade, capital mobility and sovereign immunity, Research Program in Development Studies Discussion Paper No. 108, Princeton University, Princeton, NJ.

Gersovitz, Mark (1985), Banks' international lending decisions: What we know and implications for future research. In Gordon W. Smith and John T. Cuddington (eds), *International Debt and the Developing Countries*. Washington, DC: The World Bank.

Gersovitz, Mark (1988), The effects of domestic taxes on foreign private investment. In David Newbery and Nicholas Stern (eds) *The Theory of Taxation for Developing Countries*. New York: Oxford University Press.

Harberger, Arnold (1976), On country risk and the social cost of foreign borrowing by developing countries. (Unpublished, University of Chicago.)

Harberger, Arnold (1985), Lessons for debtor-country managers and policy makers. In Gorden W. Smith and John T. Cuddington (eds), *International Debt and the Developing Countries*. Washington, DC: The World Bank.

Kahn, Robert B. (1984), External borrowing and the commons nature of foreign exchange. (Unpublished, Washington, DC: Federal Reserve Board of Governors.)

Khan, Mohsin S. and Ul Haque, Nadeem (1985), Foreign borrowing and capital flight: a formal analysis, *International Monetary Fund Staff Papers*, 32, 606–28.

COMMENT

Pedro S. Malan

At the time of the original invitation, the distinguished Organizing Committee of this Conference asked me to participate with comments on a proposed paper by Professors Eaton and Gersovitz, the provisional title of which was 'The Theory of Sovereign Borrowing'. A very good survey of the state of the arts in this area entitled 'The Pure Theory of Country Risk' has since been published by Eaton, Gersovitz and Stiglitz in the *European Economic Review*.[1]

I happen to believe that there is no such thing as a 'pure theory' of country risk or of sovereign borrowing. As indicated in the more analytical contributions to the book on debt, edited by Smith and Cuddington for the World Bank,[2] the theoretical basis for this discussion – to the extent that there is one – is available from conventional economic analysis of intertemporal optimization under constraints with elements of game theory, since the constraints entail perceptions of the other side's likely actions, responses and bargaining power.

This represents both a source of strength and of weakness when it comes to the relevance of this literature for actual policy discussions between debtors and creditors. The relative merit of the theoretically oriented writings on these topics lies in their attempt to organize, in an analytically meaningful way, the fundamentals of the problems involved in sovereign borrowing in decentralized markets under conditions of risk, uncertainties and externalities of all sorts for both borrowers and lenders.

The weakness of the purely theoretical approach lies in the fact that, as noted by Nordhaus, this literature is largely self-referential.[3] Its recent growth, however, has not been due to any major theoretical breakthrough or insight which opened an entirely new field, but to the recognition that we are facing now, in the late 1980s, an extremely important real world problem, the outcome of which is very uncertain.

Carlos Díaz-Alejandro was, and I am sure would have continued to be, very much involved in this debate, bringing to it his rare combination of historical perspective, rigorous empirical work, analytical soundness and an admirably open mind. I am also convinced that he would have read this paper with great interest; unfortunately the comments which follow are poorer for lack of opportunity to discuss the matter with Carlos, as we often did in the past. I am also sure that he would have approved the change of the focus of the paper from 'The theory of Sovereign borrowing' to the current 'Country risk and the organization of international capital transfer.'

The general theme of this paper is the way capital transfer is organized under conditions of sovereign borrowing, with risks of default for foreign portfolio investment and of expropriation for foreign direct investment. Enhancement of contracts in international markets looms large in this discussion. I should like to start with a brief comment on the meaning and usage of the terms default and expropriation in this paper.

We all know that cases of outright repudiation by the borrower or formal declaration of default by the lender are extremely rare in the history of sovereign debt of non-socialist countries. The truly interesting cases are the intermediate ones, marked by accumulation of arrears, restructurings, reschedulings, discussions about capacity and willingness to pay, reputation risks and so forth. In most real-world cases, cooperation often goes together with ever-postponed real confrontation and threats of limits being reached by the borrowers' ability, not willingness, to pay.

In this context, default or expropriation, even when loosely defined, are elusive words in the sense that they apply only to limit situations. In this paper, the 'penalty' for incurring either of them (equivalent to a loss of income) is not known in advance, i.e. at the time the loan or investment is made, but, according to the authors, is known 'exactly' (p. 14) at the time of repayment. I find it hard to accept the proposition that a sovereign country, acting as a single rational actor, would decide either to default/expropriate *or* to continue servicing its debt based on a single comparison between known payments and known penalty costs. Nonetheless, this is the story told by inequalities 2.3 on p. 111 and 4.4 on p. 117. In my mind, they express a black or white view when the picture has several shades of grey and innumerable possibilities of compromise or conflict amongst borrower and lenders short of default or expropriation. In addition, one has to recognize the importance of the domestic political debate within each sovereign borrowing country where the spectrum of views and changing perceptions often play a crucial role in determining the course of relationships with lenders. Theory is of little help in this area where politics and economics are closely intertwined.

The second cluster of issues that I should like to comment on relates to whether there is sufficient flexibility in the contracts under which capital is transferred given the contingencies that may arise. Eaton and Gersovitz suggest that this topic subsumes some important differences between lenders and direct investors and raise the issue of taxation policies in the host country.

I fully agree with Hellwig's analysis of the first question.[4] Although there were many factors linked to domestic policies of both debtor and creditor countries behind the international debt crisis, the problem was turned into a crisis largely as a consequence of (a) an asymmetrical allocation of risk in international borrowing and lending and (b) an exceptionally unfavorable realization of these very high risks in the early 1980s. Contingency mechanisms of some sort, absent from earlier contracts, are likely to emerge in future borrowings and they should be welcomed as imparting a less inequitable distribution of risks between lenders and borrowers.

Eaton and Gersovitz are probably right in noting the evident shortcomings of the institutional mechanisms that maintain movements of capital between countries and the potential for instability and conflict that they generate. Indeed, as far as currency loans are concerned, I fail to see why the increase in the prime rate from approximately 7 per cent in 1975–7 to nearly 19 per cent in 1980 and the doubling of LIBOR in the same period from 7 per cent to 14 per cent should have been seen by some as an absolutely normal feature of contracts with floating rates of interest. It is true that in many countries the tax treatment of remittances in the form of interest was much more favorable than the tax treatment of profits and dividends resulting in a sort of revealed preference for currency loans relative to direct investment. But as Eaton and Gersovitz note, quoting Harberger on p. 110, there is, in principle, justification for a tax on foreign borrowing as long as the marginal cost *to the country* of borrowing exceeds the average cost. But this seems now a remembrance of things past as the usually circumspect OECD noted in its 1985 Survey of External Debt of Developing Countries:

> The so-called 'privatization' of financial flows seen to have occurred in the late 1970s was essentially a kind of 'financial bubble' associated with temporary financial policy situations. . . . The cost of this episode to the countries concerned, and to the world economy, has nevertheless been high. . . . The 1970s appear in retrospect to have been a rather special phase rather than, as often seemed at times, a move in a new direction.[5]

The third cluster of issues raised in this paper relates to a problem which is likely to emerge under conditions of decentralized borrowing, namely the interactions between the public and the private sectors and particularly the vexing issue of stocks of public indebtedness to foreigners growing together with stocks of private assets held abroad.

It is important to note that since the eruption of the debt crisis in 1982, there has been a remarkable shift from private to public responsibility for debt, not because of new net lending but as a result of the redistribution of stocks of debt, with the public sector – under pressure from creditors – taking responsibility for previously nonguaranteed, purely commercial debt.[6]

This reliance on the government of the borrowing country to enforce private contracts with private foreign creditors created a serious internal transfer problem, which does not concern us here, but Eaton and Gersovitz are probably right in suggesting that 'prospective external debt service obligations may contribute to the private sector's fear . . . of taxation as a means for the government to raise funds to service debt. If capital located abroad escapes taxation and is free of expropriation risk, then capital flight can emerge as a *consequence* of heavy foreign borrowing' (p. 24).[7]

This sounds familiar, from the never-ending discussions among economists on the burden of national debt and the effects on expenditure and savings of anticipated future increases in taxation. But in highly indebted developing countries, debt-service obligations do not pose problems for future generations alone. They depress national income today and with the exception of a few cases, it defies both evidence and imagination to assume that this fall is always offset by larger private assets held abroad. These capital movements do exist but a good deal of international capital flows nowadays involve tax sheltering or tax evasion rather than normal portfolio diversification or socially productive resource transfers.

In conclusion, Eaton and Gersovitz have written a paper in which they have raised too wide a range of issues. They are surely right in noting in their concluding section that their effort has been exploratory and that an analysis of many interesting issues remains undone. But for both what they have included and for what they have not, I think Carlos Díaz-Alejandro would have liked reading this paper full of insights and suggestions for future work on a subject likely to remain with us for many years to come, and not just as an intellectual curiosity for academic economists.

NOTES

The author is Executive Director, The World Bank. At the time of the Conference, he was Director, General Analysis and Policies Division, Department of International Economics and Social Affairs, United Nations, New York.

1 *European Economic Review*, 30, 3 (1986), pp. 481–513.

2 Smith, Gordon and Cuddington, John (eds) *International Debt and the Developing Countries*. The World Bank, 1985.

3 See W. Nordhaus 'Comment' in *European Economic Review*, 30, 3 (1986), pp. 561–9.

4 See M. Hellwig, 'Comments' in *European Economic Review*, 30, 3 (1986), pp. 521–7.

5 *Financing and External Debt of Developing Countries*. 1985 Survey, OECD, 1986, p. 10.

6 The authors describe the Chilean widespread socialization of private debt on p. 114 but the phenomenon was generalized throughout the developing world. See *Country Exposure Lending Surveys*, US Federal Examination Council, several issues.

7 Curiously enough, in the sentence above, the authors write 'expropriation, or other forms of taxation' as if all forms of taxation were forms of expropriation.

7

How Integrated are World Capital Markets? Some New Tests

Maurice Obstfeld

Introduction

The vicissitudes of the international capital market are a recurring theme in the work of Carlos Díaz-Alejandro. Simple microeconomic theory shows how internationally integrated financial markets can improve global resource allocation by channeling the world flow of saving toward its most productive uses. A major message of Díaz-Alejandro's work, however, is that a realistic analysis of the international capital market must contend with the influence of factors that sometimes are difficult to model formally: moral hazards, political pressures, and even shifts in the prevailing paradigms of economic science. Over more than a century and a half, all of these factors have helped produce a series of booms and busts in international financial intermediation.

The booming world capital market of the five decades ended by the First World War provides a benchmark against which economists often have measured the adequacy of contemporary international capital flows. In that golden age, the market effected a continuing and substantial resource transfer from developed to developing countries in spite of occasional reverses.[1] The post-1945 world capital market appears to have been less vigorous on the whole. Only after the early 1970s did international lending expand to levels even comparable with those of the pre-1914 period. And since the early 1980s, the net resource transfer to developing countries has stopped and a widespread default on foreign debts has been averted (so far) only through the constant involvement of official financial agencies.

One important indicator of the difference between the pre-1914 and post-1945 capital markets has been the average magnitude of national current-account imbalances in the latter period. The current-account surplus, as the difference between a country's overall saving and its domestic investment, shows the amount of domestic savings being invested abroad, or, in the case of a deficit, the amount of foreign savings being borrowed to finance domestic investment. In 1965, countries classified by the World Bank as middle-income oil importers financed a mere 5 per cent of their domestic investment by drawing on foreign savings. The figure rose to 7.6 per cent in 1973 and to 15.4 per cent by 1980, but dropped sharply after 1982.[2] Compare these figures with the one-third to one-half of Argentine investment that Díaz-Alejandro (1970, p. 31) reckoned was financed by foreign capital in the years 1880–1914! For developed countries in the postwar era, current accounts have tended to be even smaller (as a percentage of GNP) than for industrializing countries. The recent United States current-account deficit, which in 1985 amounted to nearly 18 per cent of US domestic investment, is an extreme outlier in this respect.

The fact that current accounts have on the whole been so small since 1945 is a major puzzle for economists hoping to apply open-economy theory to open-economy policy problems. Our predictions about specific policy measures, however, depend crucially on whether the limited net capital flows we observe reflect an efficient global resource allocation, given countries' preferences and intertemporal transformation opportunities, or arise instead from such barriers to capital-market integration as official controls and sovereign risk. A growing empirical literature has taken several routes in trying to assess the freedom with which capital flows across national boundaries.

In an earlier paper (1986), I surveyed two important approaches taken in the empirical literature on world capital-market integration. The first of these approaches attempts to compare the returns available on assets located in different countries. Because asset returns are inherently uncertain, the conclusions drawn from an international comparison of asset returns inevitably rest on an assumed model of the pricing of risk. To avoid taking a stand on the appropriate asset-pricing model, my earlier paper restricted its discussion to assets whose returns would be the same in nearly all states of nature in a world of perfectly integrated capital markets. Evidence on the interest paid by onshore and offshore deposits denominated in the same currency seemed to me consistent with a high degree of international capital mobility.[3]

The second empirical approach I reviewed is based on a direct comparison of divergences between countries' saving and investment rates. This second approach, due to Feldstein and Horioka (1980) and Feldstein (1983), argues that the small size of average current accounts over long periods is indeed evidence that sizable barriers impede the free international movement of capital. I suggested that this interpretation of the data suffers from potentially serious identification problems, and presented quarterly time-series evidence with implications apparently different from those Feldstein and Horioka drew from their cross-sectional findings.

This paper develops additional evidence on the integration of world capital markets. The first set of tests I carry out is based on an international comparison of marginal rates of substitution between consumption on different dates. If residents of two countries have access to a nominally risk-free bond denominated in dollars, say, their common expected marginal rate of substitution of future for present dollars should equal the gross nominal return on dollar bonds. Tests of the international equality of expected intertemporal marginal substitution rates yield evidence consistent with a substantial degree of international capital-market integration after, but not before, 1973. These tests are naturally based on a particular model of intertemporal consumption choice, but direct estimation of the inter-country relationships implied by that model lends support to its assumptions. These last findings are relevant to the current debate in macroeconomics about the role of intertemporal substitution.

The second set of tests conducted here extends the work reported in my 1986 paper. For a sample of countries somewhat larger than the one I examined earlier, correlations between annual changes in saving and investment rates over the period 1948–84 look quite similar to those found in quarterly data. Surprisingly, however, the correlation coefficients are often lower before the mid-1960s than afterward. I argue that this finding throws further doubt on the interpretation of saving–investment correlation coefficients as structural parameters reflecting the response of domestic investment to shifts in national saving.

The paper is organized as follows. Section 1 examines the relationship between expected intertemporal marginal substitution rates in the United States, Germany, and Japan. Section 2 discusses some shortcomings of the data and methods used. As a partial check on the relevance of the conclusions drawn in section 1, section 3 estimates the model underlying that section's tests. Section 4 contains the new time-series estimates of saving–investment correlations for the postwar period.

1. A Test of World Capital-Market Integration

Recent work in finance and macroeconomics has drawn on consumption-based models of asset pricing developed by Breeden (1979), Lucas (1978), and others. These models extend to a stochastic setting Irving Fisher's (1930) celebrated account of intertemporal consumption choice under certainty. In the equilibria of the stochastic models, the joint distributions of asset returns and individual consumption levels satisfy a condition that generalizes Fisher's equality between marginal rates of intertemporal substitution in consumption and a relative intertemporal price.

Suppose that a typical consumer maximizes

$$E_t \, [\sum_{\tau=t}^{\infty} \beta^{\tau-t} U(c_\tau)] \tag{1}$$

subject to budget constraints, where $E_t\,[\cdot]$ is a conditional expectation based on time-t information, $\beta < 1$ is a subjective discount factor, c_τ is consumption on date τ, and the period utility function $U(\cdot)$ is strictly concave and differentiable. Then if R_{t+1} denotes the (possibly random) real time-(t+1) payoff on any asset relative to its real purchase price on date t, individual maximization forces the consumer's contingency plan for future consumption to obey the *expected* marginal equality

$$E_t[R_{t+1} \times \beta U'(c_{t+1})/U'(c_t)] = 1 \qquad (2)$$

This equation reduces to Fisher's marginal equality in the deterministic case.

In a world of integrated capital markets, equation (2) has strong implications about the *ex ante* relationship between consumption growth in different countries.[4] Consider two countries, a 'home' country and a 'foreign' country (which we make notationally distinct from the home country by using asterisks). Let P_t be the price level in the home country and i_t be the nominal interest rate on a risk-free one-period bond (such as a US Treasury bill). Then for this particular asset, equilibrium condition (2) takes the form

$$E_t[(1 + i_t)(P_t/P_{t+1}) \times \beta U'(c_{t+1})/U'(c_t)] = 1 \qquad (3)$$

for a representative home consumer. A similar relationship naturally links the corresponding foreign variables. Foreigners consume a basket of commodities which may differ from the one consumed at home. Let the currency exchange rate X_t denote the home-currency price of foreign currency. Then the home-currency price of the characteristic foreign consumption bundle is $X_tP_t^*$, and for a foreign consumer, the *ex post* real return on the home-currency bond is

$$(1 + i_t)(X_tP_t^*/X_{t+1}P_{t+1}^*)$$

According to (2), therefore, foreign residents plan their consumption so that the following condition holds:

$$E_t[(1 + i_t)(X_tP_t^*/X_{t+1}P_{t+1}^*) \times \beta^* U^{*\prime}(c_{t+1}^*)/U^{*\prime}(c_t^*)] = 1 \qquad (4)$$

Because the nominal interest rate i_t is part of the time-t information set, equations (3) and (4) together imply that

$$\begin{aligned} 1/(1 + i_t) &= E_t[(P_t/P_{t+1}) \times \beta U'(c_{t+1})/U'(c_t)] \qquad (5) \\ &= E_t[(X_tP_t^*/X_{t+1}P_{t+1}^*) \times \beta^* U^{*\prime}(c_{t+1}^*)/U^{*\prime}(c_t^*)] \end{aligned}$$

Equation (5) states that if residents of the home and foreign countries can invest in the same nominally risk-free asset, then their expected marginal rates of substitution between current and future units of the home currency must be equal. Of course, if residents of both countries also have access to a nominally risk-free foreign-currency bond paying the interest rate i_t^*, then the home and foreign expected marginal rates of substitution between current and future units of the *foreign* currency must also be equal:

$$1/(1 + i_t^*) = E_t\{[(P_t/X_t)/(P_{t+1}/X_{t+1})] \times \beta U'(c_{t+1})/U'(c_t)\} \tag{6}$$

$$= E_t[(P_t^*/P_{t+1}^*) \times \beta^* U^{*\prime}(c_{t+1}^*)/U^{*\prime}(c_t^*)]$$

Under the rational expectations assumption, equations (5) and (6) provide the testable predictions about consumption, price-level, and exchange-rate movements that underlie the statistical tests carried out in this section and the next one.[5]

Before going on to assume the additional restrictions needed to infer testable implications from (5) and (6), I want to make two points about these relationships. First, if the interest rates in equations (5) and (6) are offered by assets issued in the same location (for example, if they are London Eurocurrency deposit rates), the model yields expressions for the forward foreign-exchange premium, which is related to the nominal interest-rate differential through covered interest parity. The intertemporal consumption allocation conditions have been used in this way by Hansen and Hodrick (1983), Mark (1985), Campbell and Clarida (1986), and Cumby (1986) in attempts to model forward premia. In my 1986 paper, I observed that these tests, which do not involve assets located in different political or regulatory jurisdictions, are uninformative about capital mobility between countries. Nonetheless, the same basic theoretical framework can throw light on questions about international capital mobility if it is used to compare consumption paths in different countries. The marginal equalities in (5) and (6) do not require any particular location for the assets being considered, but they do require that residents of different countries be able to trade the same asset.

A second point about equations (5) and (6) is that they are not based on any assumption of purchasing power parity or perfect goods–market integration. The derivation of these equations requires only that measured exchange rates and price indexes reflect the true prices at which residents of the two countries can transform home or foreign money into the goods they usually consume.

To implement (5) and (6) empirically, however, two strong assumptions must now be made. First, it is assumed that consumers within a country are alike with respect to endowments and preferences, so that (5) and (6) may be tested using aggregate per capita consumption levels in the two countries. Second, it is assumed that preferences are identical across the two countries, such that the marginal utility of a consumption level c is given in both by

$$U'(c) = c^{-\alpha}, \ \alpha > 0$$

Thus, α, the reciprocal of the intertemporal elasticity of substitution, is the same between both countries, and $\beta = \beta^*$. There is no justification for the first assumption other than the absence of practical alternatives. The next section provides partial evidence that the data are consistent with the second assumption.[6]

The assumptions just made, together with (5) and (6), lead to the equations

$$E_t\left[\left(\frac{C_t}{C_{t+1}}\right)^{\alpha}\left(\frac{P_t}{P_{t+1}}\right)-\left(\frac{C^*_t}{C^*_{t+1}}\right)^{\alpha}\left(\frac{X_tP^*_t}{X_{t+1}P^*_{t+1}}\right)\right]=0 \qquad (7)$$

$$E_t\left[\left(\frac{C_t}{C_{t+1}}\right)^{\alpha}\left(\frac{P_t/X_t}{P_{t+1}/X_{t+1}}\right)-\left(\frac{C^*_t}{C^*_{t+1}}\right)^{\alpha}\left(\frac{P^*_t}{P^*_{t+1}}\right)\right]=0 \qquad (8)$$

According to (7) and (8), international discrepancies between *ex post* marginal rates of substitution are unpredictable on the basis of time-t information if everyone can trade the same nominally risk-free home-and foreign-currency bonds. Define the random variables η_{t+1} and η^*_{t+1} by

$$\eta^*_{t+1}=\left(\frac{C_t}{C_{t+1}}\right)^{\alpha}\left(\frac{P_t}{P_{t+1}}\right)-\left(\frac{C^*_t}{C^*_{t+1}}\right)^{\alpha}\left(\frac{X_tP^*_t}{X_{t+1}P^*_{t+1}}\right)$$

$$\eta^*_{t+1}=\left(\frac{C_t}{C_{t+1}}\right)^{\alpha}\left(\frac{P_t/X_t}{P_{t+1}/X_{t+1}}\right)-\left(\frac{C^*_t}{C^*_{t+1}}\right)^{\alpha}\left(\frac{P^*_t}{P^*_{t+1}}\right)$$

Then (7) and (8) can be expressed compactly as

$$E_t(\eta_{t+1})=0 \qquad (9)$$
$$E_t(\eta^*_{t+1})=0 \qquad (10)$$

Both η_{t+1} and η^*_{t+1} would be observable *ex post* if the preference parameter α were known. In the tests conducted in this section, I examine conditions (7) and (8) over a wide grid of possible values for α.

In principle, conditions (9) and (10) can be falsified empirically if any information known at time $t-1$ or earlier is useful in forecasting values of η and η^* dated t or later. In practice, however, attention must be restricted to some subset of the information which agents presumably use in forming their expectations. Because the factors that give rise to bond-market segmentation are likely to change only gradually over time, I follow the 'efficient-markets' tradition of testing whether past discrepancies in marginal substitution rates help forecast future discrepancies. For different assumed values of α, I thus estimate regression equations of the form

$$\eta_t=\gamma_0+\sum_{i=1}^{N}\gamma_i\eta_{t-i}+V_t$$

$$\eta^*_0=\gamma^*_t+\sum_{i=1}^{N}\gamma^*_i\eta^*_{t-i}+V^*_t$$

where V_t and V_t^* are errors orthogonal to information dated t–1 or earlier. For each assumed value of α, a test of the hypothesis

$$H_0: \gamma_0 = \gamma_1 = \ldots = \gamma_N = 0$$

tests whether people in different countries equate *ex ante* marginal rates of substitution of present for future units of home currency through intertemporal trading at the same home-currency interest rate. Similarly, given α, a test of the hypothesis

$$H_0^*: \gamma_0^* = \gamma_1^* = \ldots = \gamma_N^* = 0$$

tests whether people in different countries equate *ex ante* marginal rates of substitution of present for future units of foreign currency through intertemporal trading at the same foreign-currency interest rate.

The data used were quarterly series drawn from the International Monetary Fund's *International Financial Statistics* data tape. The per capita consumption series were defined as nominal consumption divided by population and deflated by the consumer price index (CPI). Price levels are CPIs and exchange rates are quarterly averages. Over a grid of ten α values ranging from $\alpha = 0.5$ to $\alpha = 25.0$, these data were used to construct η and η^* series between the United States and West Germany, and between the United States and Japan. Table 7.1 (United States–Germany) and table 7.2 (United States–Japan) report significance levels for F-statistics under the null hypotheses H_0 and H_0^* over the entire sample period 1962:II to 1985:II. The lag length for the test was set at $N = 8$ quarters.[7]

The results in table 7.1 are on the whole unfavorable to both null hypotheses. For all but the three highest values of α, both H_0 and H_0^* can be rejected at the 10 per cent significance level or below. Since α values of 7 or greater are implausibly high, the tests seem to indicate that over the entire period since 1962:II, expected intertemporal marginal substitution rates for dollars and Deutsche Marks have not been the same in the United States and Germany.

The results for the US and Japan show an even stronger rejection of the null hypotheses over the sample period as a whole. Except for the implausible cases $\alpha = 12$ and 25, both H_0 and H_0^* are always rejected at the 5 per cent level or below.

It is unlikely that the entire sample period studied in tables 7.1 and 7.2 is structurally homogeneous. In particular, the international capital market has expanded dramatically since the early 1970s, when a marked liberalization of industrial-country capital markets began.[8] One possible explanation of the rejections is that they reflect the influence of the earlier observations, which come from a period when international financial markets seem to have been less interdependent than they are today.

To check this possibility, I split the sample at 1973:I and conducted separate tests for the resulting subsamples. The results are reported in tables

Table 7.1 Tests of H_0 and H_0^* between the United States and Germany (sample: 1962:II–1985:II)

α	H_0 *Significance*	H_0^* *Significance*
0.5	0.093	0.091
0.75	0.074	0.075
1.0	0.060	0.062
1.5	0.042	0.046
2.0	0.035	0.039
3.0	0.040	0.045
5.0	0.084	0.089
7.0	0.117	0.121
12.0	0.152	0.155
25.0	0.284	0.291

The distribution of the test statistic is $F(9, 84)$ under either null hypothesis. The significance level is the probability under the null hypothesis of drawing a realization of the test statistic at least as high as the calculated value.

Table 7.2 Tests of H_0 and H_0^* between the United States and Japan (sample: 1962:II–1985:II)

α	H_0 *Significance*	H_0^* *Significance*
0.5	0.028	0.018
0.75	0.038	0.025
1.0	0.045	0.031
1.5	0.040	0.030
2.0	0.024	0.019
3.0	0.008	0.007
5.0	0.005	0.004
7.0	0.012	0.009
12.0	0.110	0.087
25.0	0.890	0.861

The distribution of the test statistic is $F(9, 84)$ under either null hypothesis.

7.3 (United States–Germany) and 7.4 (United States–Japan). The striking feature of the results in table 7.3 is that for all values of the inverse intertemporal substitution elasticity, the null hypotheses are always rejected at lower significance levels in the first subsample than in the second. This finding is consistent with the hypothesis that capital-market integration has increased since the early 1970s. In most cases, however, rejection of the null hypotheses in the first subsample is possible only at significance levels higher than 10 per cent. This result suggests that the test may be weak, so conclusions about the second subsample cannot be drawn with confidence in the US–Germany case.

Table 7.3 Subsample tests of H_0 and H_0^* between the United States and Germany

	1962:II–1972:IV		1973:I–1985:II	
	H_0	H_0^*	H_0	H_0^*
α	*Significance*		*Significance*	
0.5	0.074	0.069	0.562	0.566
0.75	0.110	0.108	0.520	0.526
1.0	0.135	0.138	0.479	0.490
1.5	0.213	0.226	0.414	0.429
2.0	0.235	0.256	0.369	0.388
3.0	0.190	0.210	0.347	0.367
5.0	0.149	0.160	0.497	0.507
7.0	0.146	0.153	0.674	0.680
12.0	0.161	0.166	0.842	0.853
25.0	0.228	0.235	0.899	0.920

Under either null hypothesis, the distribution of the test statistic is $F(9, 34)$ for the first subsample and $F(9, 41)$ for the second.

The subsample tests comparing the United States and Japan tell a somewhat stronger story. Table 7.4 reports that for the period ending in 1972:IV, both null hypotheses are rejected at extremely low significance levels (which in most cases are essentially zero). Nonetheless, the significance levels of the test statistics are all quite high for the period beginning in 1973:I. The results suggest that in the recent period, US and Japanese consumptions have behaved as if residents of the two countries had access to the same risk-free borrowing and lending opportunities in both dollars and yen. This was decidedly not the case before the early 1970s.

Another interpretation of the results comes from the fact that the *ex post* international differences between marginal rates of substitution become substantially more variable after the move to floating exchange rates in 1973. On this interpretation, the higher test significance levels found in the second subsample reflect a drop in the test's power caused by additional noise in the data, not an increase in world capital-market integration. In principle, this ambiguity can be resolved in the future when more data are available.

2. Discussion

Some important caveats apply to the interpretation of the previous section's results:

1 The consumption series I have used include expenditure on durable goods. Most recent studies of consumption use either expenditure on nondurables or expenditure on nondurables plus services. Both of these

Table 7.4 Subsample tests of H_0 and H_0^* between the United States and Japan

	1962:II–1972:IV		1973:I–1985:II	
	H_0	H_0^*	H_0	H_0^*
α	*Significance*		*Significance*	
0.5	0.000	0.000	0.654	0.605
0.75	0.000	0.000	0.773	0.723
1.0	0.000	0.000	0.866	0.824
1.5	0.000	0.000	0.950	0.928
2.0	0.000	0.000	0.955	0.940
3.0	0.000	0.000	0.869	0.843
5.0	0.000	0.000	0.747	0.705
7.0	0.000	0.000	0.776	0.748
12.0	0.001	0.001	0.874	0.869
25.0	0.002	0.002	0.985	0.983

Under either null hypothesis, the distribution of the test statistic is $F(9, 34)$ for the first subsample and $F(9, 41)$ for the second.

measures are only partial measures of consumption: implicit (or explicit) in the use of these measures is the arbitrary assumption that the excluded portion of consumption enters the utility function in a separable manner. As Mankiw et al. (1985) argue, however, the separability assumption is implausible. Since some degree of misspecification seems likely no matter what consumption measure is chosen, results based on the consumption measure utilized above are of interest. Future research should examine the sensitivity of the results to alternative consumption proxies.

2 Available published consumption data are seasonally adjusted. The first-order Euler condition (2) from which the tests are derived, however, applies to seasonally *unadjusted* data. Miron (1985) has employed seasonally unadjusted data for US consumption and shown that the estimation of equations like (2) may be quite sensitive to the use of seasonal prefilters.[9] The tests in this paper, however, are based on data in the form of inter-country differences. This may reduce the bias due to deseasonalization, particularly if deseasonalization practices are similar across countries.

3 The theory underlying equation (2) assumes that consumption is uniform over the time period beginning on date t, with the consumption decision made at the beginning of t and all variables dated t in the consumer's time-t information set. In reality, the data used are quarterly averages, so measured consumption over the quarter starting on date t incorporates information that accrues between dates t and $t+1$. Hall (1985) has raised this point in connection with empirical studies of the intertemporal elasticity of substitution in the US; since the issue is also important in the next section, I discuss it at greater length there.

4 If the conditional distributions of economic variables change over

time, estimation in a finite sample may yield misleading inferences even if unconditional distributions are constant. This problem is related to the 'peso problem' discussed in the literature on exchange market efficiency. At the very least, shifting conditional distributions will induce conditional heteroscedasticity into estimation problems, and econometric technique should take this feature of the data into account. Although Cumby and Obstfeld (1984) present evidence of conditional heteroscedasticity in data on exchange rates, interest rates, and prices, the estimates in the present paper assume the problem is unimportant. Clearly, future work will have to check on the validity of that assumption.

A more fundamental question is whether the model underlying the tests in this section has any claim to empirical validity. Because the tests are joint tests of certain propositions about capital mobility *and* a particular model of consumer behavior, test results have no implications about capital mobility if the model is wrong. It is therefore important to examine independent evidence on the adequacy of equations (1) and (2) as descriptions of economic behavior in the real world.

Much of the evidence on this question is discouraging. Studies of US consumption by Hansen and Singleton (1982) and by Mankiw et al. (1985) reject the model in many cases, often obtaining *negative* point estimates of the intertemporal elasticity coefficient α. Mark (1985) obtains estimates of α which, while positive, are in most cases imprecisely measured and implausibly high.

Some countervailing considerations suggest, however, that complete abandonment of the model given by (1) and (2) may be premature. In the study mentioned above, Miron (1985) finds that the model cannot be rejected for US data if seasonally unadjusted data are used. As I suggested earlier, estimates such as those in the present paper, which are based on inter-country differences, may be less sensitive to problems of seasonality. In addition, tests of Euler conditions that use data from only a single country must find appropriate data series on rates of return. Some researchers, such as Summers (1984), suggest that this is a major difficulty.

Several studies point to liquidity constraints as a possible cause of deviations from (2) in the aggregate. Zeldes (1985), for example, analyzes data from the Michigan Panel Study on Income Dynamics and finds that the Euler condition is rejected for families with low ratios of liquid wealth to income, but not for the others. From that finding, and from direct estimates of the Lagrange multipliers associated with binding borrowing limits, he concludes that liquidity constraints may lie behind the rejections of (2) by US aggregate data. International synchronization of monetary conditions could give rise to a high positive correlation between the fractions of households that are liquidity constrained in different countries. In this case, aggregate tests comparing consumption growth in different countries might be less sensitive than single-country tests to the presence of some liquidity constrained households.

Another possible cause of the disappointing results reported by Hansen and Singleton (1982) and others is the existence of preference shocks or other random factors that are unobserved by the econometrician but prevent (2) from holding exactly. To the extent that disturbances are correlated across countries, tests based on cross-country comparisons of consumption behavior may again yield less biased results.

It seems fair to describe the evidence on the underlying Euler condition as mixed at best. In the next section, I therefore report my own attempt to estimate the model using inter-country differences of US, German, and Japanese data. The model imposes several strong restrictions on the data. Rejection of these restrictions would call into question the interpretation given to the results of section 1. Conversely, results that are reasonably in accord with the model's predictions would suggest that the results of section 1 are relevant for evaluating world financial-market integration.

3. Cross-Country Tests of the Consumption Model

A test of the consumption model used in section 1 can be based on equations (7) and (8). To derive readily estimable equations, I follow Hansen and Hodrick (1983), Hansen and Singleton (1983), and Hall (1985) in assuming that growth factors for per capita consumption levels, price levels, and the exchange rate are lognormally distributed in equilibrium, that is, that the natural logarithms of these variables are normally distributed. No attempt will be made to write down a general-equilibrium model that explicitly derives a lognormal distribution for these endogenous variables from the distributions of the exogenous variables.

Denoting by lower case letters natural logarithms of the corresponding upper case variables, I assume that the vector

$$y_t' = \Delta(c_t, c_t^*, p_t, p_t^*, x_t)$$

is generated by the autoregressive process

$$[I - A(L)]y_t = A_0 + \mu_t$$

where I is the 5×5 identity matrix, A_0 is a 5×5 matrix of constants, and $A(L)$ is a polynomial in positive powers of the lag operator L. A lognormal model results from assuming that the vector μ_t of disturbances is covariance stationary and normally distributed. Thus, the conditional mean of y_t may vary over time, but because μ_t is distributed independently of the information set $\theta_{t-1} = (y_{t-1}, y_{t-2}, \ldots)$, the covariance matrix of y_t conditional on θ_{t-1} is a time-independent constant matrix.

The restricted information set θ_t is a subset of the broader information available to agents in the economy. Let $E_t'(\cdot)$ denote a conditional expectation with respect to the restricted information set, that is, $E_t'(\cdot) = E\{. \mid \theta_t\}$. Then equations (7) and (8) continue to hold if $E_t(\cdot)$ is replaced everywhere by $E_t'(\cdot)$

For the empirical exercise of this section, I drop the assumption that $\alpha = \alpha^*$ so that it can be tested against the data.[10] If the restricted expectations operator is applied to (7), the equation that results is therefore

$$E_t'[\exp(-\alpha\Delta c_{t+1} - \Delta p_{t+1})] = E_t'[\exp(-\alpha^* \Delta c_{t+1}^* - \Delta x_{t+1} - \Delta p_{t+1}^*)] \tag{11}$$

Lognormality now implies that (11) can be written as

$$\exp[E_t'(-\alpha\Delta c_{t+1} - \Delta p_{t+1}) + V_t'(-\alpha\Delta c_{t+1} - \Delta p_{t+1})/2]$$

$$= \exp[E_t'(-\alpha^*\Delta c_{t+1}^*) - \Delta x_{t+1} - \Delta p_{t+1}^*) + V_t'(-\alpha^*\Delta c_{t+1}^* - \Delta x_{t+1} - \Delta p_{t+1}^*)/2] \tag{12}$$

where $V_t'(\cdot)$ is a variance conditioned on θ_t. As noted earlier, these conditional variances are time-independent constants. Define the percentage change in the real exchange rate of the home currency as

$$\Delta q = \Delta x + \Delta p^* - \Delta p$$

Then (12) implies

$$E_t'(\Delta q_{t+1}) = \sigma + \alpha E_t'(\Delta c_{t+1}) - \alpha^* E_t'(\Delta c_{t+1}^*) \tag{13}$$

where σ is a constant that depends on the time-independent conditional covariances in (12).[11]

The economic intuition behind (13) is standard. In a deterministic, continuous-time analogue of the present model, the marginal utility of consumption in each country grows at a proportional rate equal to the difference between the rate of domestic time preference and the domestic real interest rate. By interest parity, the international difference between home and foreign real interest rates is the percentage change in the real exchange rate. Thus, the difference between the derivatives $\alpha(\mathrm{d}c/\mathrm{d}t)$ and $\alpha^*(\mathrm{d}c^*/\mathrm{d}t)$ is $\mathrm{d}q/\mathrm{d}t$ plus a constant reflecting any international time-preference difference. Equation (13) is the same condition in expectation, adjusted by a constant risk premium.

Equation (13) must be expressed in terms of observables before it can be estimated. Define the expectational errors

$$v_{t+1}^q = \Delta q_{t+1} - E_t'(\Delta q_{t+1})$$

$$v_{t+1}^c = \Delta c_{t+1} - E_t'(\Delta c_{t+1})$$

$$v_{t+1}^{c*} = \Delta c_{t+1}^* - E_t'(\Delta c_{t+1}^*)$$

Substitution of these expressions into (13) leads to

$$\Delta q_{t+1} = \sigma + \alpha \Delta c_{t+1} - \alpha^* \Delta c^*_{t+1} + v_{t+1} \tag{14}$$

where $v_t = v^q_t - v^c_t + v^{c^*}_t$. By construction, v_t is serially uncorrelated and uncorrelated with any variables in the information set θ_{t-1}. These properties of v_t imply that the parameters of (14) may be estimated by instrumental variables, with variables in θ_t serving as instruments.[12]

In a multi-country framework, there are also cross-equation restrictions that can be tested as an additional check on the model. Take the 'starred' country in (14) to be the United States. Then for Germany and Japan, (14) implies the relationships

$$\Delta q^{\mathrm{DM/\$}}_t = \sigma_1 + \alpha_{\mathrm{G}} \Delta c^{\mathrm{G}}_t - \alpha_{\mathrm{US}} \Delta c^{\mathrm{US}}_t + v^{\mathrm{GUS}}_t \tag{15}$$

$$\Delta q^{\mathrm{¥/\$}}_t = \sigma_2 + \alpha_{\mathrm{J}} \Delta c^{\mathrm{J}}_t - \alpha_{\mathrm{US}} \Delta c^{\mathrm{US}}_t + v^{\mathrm{JUS}}_t \tag{16}$$

Equations (15) and (16) can be estimated jointly under the restriction that α_{US} be the same in both equations, and that restriction can be tested.

Notice that the disturbances v^{GUS}_t and v^{JUS}_t in (15) and (16) are likely to be highly correlated contemporaneously, if only because both include as an additive component the innovation in US consumption. The two-equation system can therefore be estimated most efficiently by three-stage least squares, which takes the contemporaneous error covariance into account. The instrumental variables used in three-stage least squares estimation were a constant and the first through third lags of $\Delta q^{\mathrm{DM/\$}}$, $\Delta q^{\mathrm{¥/\$}}$, Δc^{US}, Δc^{G}, and Δc^{J}.

With three lags of the variables used as instruments, the remaining sample period is 1961:I–1985:II. Over that period, the estimated preference parameters are

$$\alpha_{\mathrm{US}} = \underset{(0.778)}{2.669}\,, \qquad \alpha_{\mathrm{G}} = \underset{(0.761)}{-0.432}\,, \qquad \alpha_{\mathrm{J}} = \underset{(0.428)}{0.808}$$

where standard errors are given in parentheses. The model restriction that the coefficient of Δc^{US} be the same in both (15) and (16) is not rejected by the data: the significance level of the χ^2 (1) test statistic is 0.355.

The results are somewhat favorable for the model, but not completely so. For the United States and Japan, the parameter estimates are of reasonable magnitude and quite significant. They are roughly consistent with the magnitudes found by Hansen and Singleton (1983), who also used a logarithmic specification but estimated Euler equations like (2) jointly with consumers' linear forecasting equations. In addition, the key cross-equation restriction implied by the model appears consistent with the data. The estimated intertemporal substitution parameter for Germany is negative, however, implying a convex utility function. Even though the German estimate is insignificant, its incorrect sign is troubling.

In light of the tests carried out in section 1, it is of interest to test the restriction $\alpha_{US} = \alpha_G = \alpha_J$ that was assumed there. The restriction can be rejected at the 2.5 per cent significance level.

A problem with the foregoing results arose already in section 1: we have good reasons for believing that the structure of world capital markets changed dramatically after the early 1970s. This structural change may be behind the model's uneven empirical performance, so it is informative once again to split the sample and perform separate subsample tests.

Estimation over the subsample 1961:I–1972:IV yields the estimates

$$\alpha_{US} = \underset{(0.501)}{0.897}, \qquad \alpha_G = \underset{(0.301)}{0.175}, \qquad \alpha_J = \underset{(0.242)}{0.067}$$

when the cross-equation restriction is imposed. The significance level of the test statistic for that restriction is 0.721. The parameters are all correctly signed, but smaller and less significant than those found over the complete sample. These characteristics of the estimates are unsurprising in view of the low variability of real exchange rates over the first subsample period compared to the second. The restriction that all the α's are equal cannot be rejected for this sample; the point estimate for the common value of α is 0.244, and its standard error is 0.164.

When the model is estimated over 1973:I–1985:II the results are

$$\alpha_{US} = \underset{(1.015)}{2.254}, \qquad \alpha_G = \underset{(1.306)}{0.804}, \qquad \alpha_J = \underset{(0.611)}{1.086}$$

and the cross-equation restriction cannot be rejected. (The significance level for the test statistic is 0.759.) These results are closer to the full-sample results, except that the German preference parameter is correctly signed. The parameter estimate is, however, insignificantly different from zero. The $\chi^2(3)$ test statistic for the hypothesis that all the α's are equal has a significance level of 0.693, so that hypothesis appears to fit the data. The estimate of α under this restriction is 1.240, with a standard error of 0.523. On the whole, the results from subsample two support the model, as well as the international equality of intertemporal substitution elasticities that was assumed in section 1.

As noted in the last section, Hall (1985) has argued that the time aggregation problem inherent in existing consumption data may bias results such as those reported above. He suggests lagging instruments an additional period, and shows that the results of Hansen and Singleton (1983) are quite sensitive to the timing of the instrument set. To check whether the time-aggregation issue raised by Hall has an important impact on the results, I now discuss estimates in which the first lag of each instrument used is omitted. Thus, the estimates below are based on an instrument set contain-

Table 7.5 Estimates of preference parameters for the United States, Germany, and Japan

	Sample: 1961:I–1985:II	
α_{US} = 2.009 ,	α_G = –0.937 ,	α_J = 0.964
(0.944)	(1.111)	(0.575)
Test of cross-equation restriction: $\chi^2(1)$ = 1.179, significance = 0.278		
Test of $\alpha_{US} = \alpha_G = \alpha_J$: $\chi^2(3)$ = 5.363, significance = 0.147		
	α = 0.632	
	(0.526)	
	Sample: 1961:I–1972:IV	
α_{US} = –0.091 ,	α_G = –0.101 ,	α_J = –0.037
(0.757)	(0.492)	(0.313)
Test of cross-equation restriction: $\chi^2(1)$ = 0.916, significance = 0.338		
Test of $\alpha_{US} = \alpha_G = \alpha_J$: $\chi^2(3)$ = 0.932, significance = 0.818		
	α = –0.062	
	(0.238)	
	Sample: 1973:I–1985:II	
α_{US} = 2.594 ,	α_G = –0.166 ,	α_J = 1.949
(1.363)	(1.507)	(0.896)
Test of cross-equation restriction: $\chi^2(1)$ = 0.021, significance = 0.884		
Test of $\alpha_{US} = \alpha_G = \alpha_J$: $\chi^2(3)$ = 1.885, significance = 0.597		
	α = 1.524	
	(0.767)	

Standard errors appears in parentheses. The α estimate reported after the test $\alpha_{US} = \alpha_G = \alpha_J = 0$ is the estimated common value of α under this hypothesis.

ing only a constant and the second and third lags of $\Delta q^{DM/\$}$, $\Delta q^{¥/\$}$, Δc^{US}, Δc^{G}, and Δc^{J}. The results are summarized in table 7.5.

The full-sample results are quite similar to those found using the original set of instrumental variables. Because of probable structural shifts, however, the subsample findings are of greater interest. For the 1961:I–1972:IV sample, the model appears to break down completely when the instruments are changed. All coefficients are incorrectly signed, quite insignificant, and small in absolute value. Once again, however, these results are to be expected in light of the relatively low capital-market integration and real exchange rate variability of the period.

The results for the second subsample, 1973:I–1985:II, are similar to those found with the original instrument set. The main differences are that the point estimate for Germany is once again negative while the point estimate for Japan is substantially higher. The cross-equation restriction easily fits the data, as does the restriction that the three α's are the same. The estimated common value of α is plausible, and the estimate is significant at the 5 per cent level.

Taken as a whole, the results point to the persistently insignificant and frequently incorrectly signed German preference parameter as the model's major empirical shortcoming. Another source of concern is evidence of some serial correlation in the equation residuals. Even though the procedure suggested by Hall (1985) does not make a dramatic difference for the parameter estimates, the timing problem Hall discusses may induce serial dependence in equation disturbances.[13] A more detailed specification analysis is therefore needed before firm conclusions can be drawn. Tentatively, however, it seems reasonable to view the results of this section as generally supporting the model used to construct the tests in section 1.

A potential criticism of this view comes from the empirical literature on the determinants of forward foreign-exchange premia. As Hansen and Hodrick (1983) showed, the lognormal model implies a constant expected return to forward speculation. Their empirical tests rejected the resulting model of the forward premium. The evidence on conditional heteroscedasticity reported by Cumby and Obstfeld (1984) also contradicts lognormality, as do Cumby's (1986) explicit estimates of forward-exchange risk premia, which vary significantly over time.[14] It is possible that the tests of this section are less sensitive to deviations from lognormality than tests using forward-market data. A closely related conjecture is that this paper's tests are less sensitive to peso problems, since the tests involve only a single asset. In future work, it will be important to check these conjectures by applying distribution-free estimation procedures of the type employed by Hansen and Singleton (1982) and Mankiw et al. (1985). Stronger tests can also be constructed by expanding the sample of countries.

4. More on the Correlation between Saving Rates and Investment Rates

In my 1986 paper I reported time-series estimates, for several countries, of the correlation between quarter-to-quarter changes in saving and investment rates. The sample period ran from around 1960 to the early 1980s. Those results were compared with the cross-sectional findings reported by Feldstein and Horioka (1980) and Feldstein (1983). I argued strongly in the paper that serious identification problems make it difficult to interpret saving–investment correlations as unambiguous evidence about capital mobility, either in a time-series or cross-sectional context. Nonetheless, the pattern of time-series correlations I found in the quarterly data seemed to me inconsistent with the Feldstein–Horioka conclusion that capital is essentially immobile in some long-term sense.

In this section I extend my earlier work by presenting time-series estimates of correlations between *annual* changes in saving and investment rates. There are four reasons why tests based on annual data are of interest. First, use of annual data allows me to expand the sample of countries and the sample period of the test. Second, annual data may be more reliable than quarterly data, which are often based on interpolation and other approximate procedures. Third, annual data are not subject to seasonality. Fourth, short-term capital movements that are essentially self-reversing (such as trade credits) should be less important in annual than in quarterly data. Thus, calculations based on annual data may come closer to addressing the issues of 'long-term' capital mobility that Feldstein and Horioka seem to have in mind.

The data I use are nominal yearly national account data from the *International Financial Statistics* data tape. Saving, S, is defined as gross national product (GNP) minus private plus government consumption. Investment, I, is gross fixed capital formation plus the change in stocks.[15] The correlations computed are those between $\Delta(S/\text{GNP})$ and $\Delta(I/\text{GNP})$, where Δ is now an annual first difference.

Table 7.6 reports the estimated correlation coefficients between year-to-year changes in the saving rate and the investment rate for ten countries. The sample period runs from around 1950 to 1984 in most cases, and because structural homogeneity is unlikely over such a long time span, I have split the sample period at 1967. The standard errors of these coefficients were calculated using the spectral estimator described in Obstfeld (1986).

Two major empirical regularities seemed to emerge from my earlier quarterly estimates. First, the estimated correlation coefficient r_{SI} between $\Delta(S/\text{GNP})$ and $\Delta(I/\text{GNP})$ seemed positively related to country size, and was statistically insignificant for some small countries and sample periods. Second, r_{SI} fell for all but one country between the 1960–72 period and the period beginning in 1973. I noted that the first regularity was consistent with a high degree of world capital-market integration because of the greater ability of larger countries to influence world interest rates. The second regularity seemed consistent with an increasing degree of capital mobility after 1973, a view that is also supported by the earlier results of the present paper.

Both of these stylized facts are to some extent overturned by the data in table 7.6. For most countries, r_{SI} actually *rises* between the first and second periods in spite of the presumed increase in the international mobility of capital. Further, the association between country size and r_{SI} is much less striking. Austria, for example, which had a very low r_{SI} value using quarterly data, has a rather high one in table 7.6. In contrast, the correlation coefficients for France (which was not in my earlier sample) are rather low.

The new estimates underline the pitfalls of drawing inferences about capital mobility from correlations such as those reported in the table. The change in current account patterns between the two subsamples probably has more to do with changing investment opportunities than with the extent of capital-market integration. It is plausible that emerging investment opportunities in Europe in the 1950s and early 1960s caused a pattern of investment increases financed by foreign (mostly American) savings. A relative scarcity of such opportunities from 1967 on would have tended to increase saving–investment correlation coefficients, in spite of increasing world financial integration. The reverse story certainly seems plausible for

Table 7.6 Saving–investment correlations based on annual data

Country	Period	Coefficient (s.e.)	Period	Coefficient (s.e.)
Australia	1953–66	−0.419 (0.272)	1967–84	0.420 (0.246)
Austria	1949–66	0.645 (0.288)	1967–84	0.723 (0.279)
Canada	1949–66	0.403 (0.233)	1967–84	0.792 (0.299)
France	1951–66	0.251 (0.248)	1967–82	0.520 (0.257)
Germany	1951–66	0.609 (0.288)	1967–84	0.789 (0.294)
Italy	1953–66	0.401 (0.335)	1967–84	0.746 (0.286)
Japan	1953–66	0.912 (0.368)	1967–84	0.773 (0.332)
Mexico	1953–66	0.819 (0.323)	1967–83	0.429 (0.269)
United Kingdom	1949–66	0.513 (0.258)	1967–84	0.512 (0.256)
United States	1951–66	0.946 (0.327)	1967–84	0.925 (0.316)

Standard errors are in parentheses. The estimated coefficients are correlation coefficients between the change in the saving rate, $\Delta(S/\mathrm{GNP})$, and the change in the investment rate, $\Delta(I/\mathrm{GNP})$, over the sample periods indicated. Details about the estimation method are given in Obstfeld (1986).

Mexico. The development of that country's oil resources is the probable cause of the sharp drop in its saving–investment correlation between the two subsample periods.

While it is difficult to place great weight on such explanations in the absence of complete structural models of saving and investment, the numbers do pose a challenge for those who argue that capital is essentially immobile. The capital immobility hypothesis is impossible to reconcile with many of the reported correlations, some of which do not differ significantly from zero at the 5 per cent level and most of which are comfortably distant from the value of unity that would characterize a closed economy. The correlation coefficients furnish statistical facts about saving and investment which future structural models will have to explain.

NOTES

Michael W. Klein provided excellent research assistance; Robert E. Cumby, Alberto Giovannini, and Marc Nerlove participated in helpful discussions; Jacob A. Frenkel and Mohsin S. Khan, my conference discussants, made useful comments; and members of the Penn macro lunch group offered valuable suggestions. All opinions and any errors, are, however, my own. Research support was provided by grants from the National Science Foundation and the Alfred P. Sloan Foundation.

1 Evidence on the absence of arbitrage opportunities between major financial centers also supports the view of a smoothly functioning world capital market in the decades before 1914. See, for example, Officer (1985).
2 See World Bank (1985), table A.7.
3 Researchers who have attempted to model risk explicitly have reached differing conclusions. Two recent examples are the papers of Wheatley (1985) and Jorion and Schwartz (1986).
4 Stulz (1981) presents a continuous-time analysis of open-economy asset pricing similar in spirit to the analysis carried out below.
5 I am assuming that domestic and foreign agents have identical information sets. (Clearly, nominal interest rates at which both sets of residents can transact are common information.) The tests carried out below do not require this assumption provided they are based on common lagged information. Interest taxes are ignored. This omission should have little effect on the tests if tax rates are similar across countries.
6 More precisely, the tests performed in the next section [which assume that (5) or (6) holds] do not reject the hypothesis that intertemporal substitution elasticities are the same in the US, Germany, and Japan.
7 The raw data run from 1960:I to 1985:II, but after first-differencing and then allowing for eight lags, only observations from 1962:II onward can be used in the regressions.
8 The expansion in international financial intermediation is documented and analyzed by Bryant (1985).
9 Singleton (1986) gives a useful theoretical discussion of the effect of prefiltering in estimating Euler-equation models.
10 The assumption $\beta = \beta^*$ is also inessential at this point. Relaxing that assumption

affects only the interpretation of the constant terms in the equations estimated below.

11 Of course, if (8) also holds, it can be used to derive an equation that differs from (13) only because of a different constant term, σ^*. The condition $\sigma = \sigma^*$ is, however, an equilibrium condition of the model if (7) and (8) both hold. This equality provides an additional restriction on the model which should be tested in future work.

12 Instrumental-variable methods are necessary because both Δc_t and Δc_t^* are correlated with v_t in general.

13 Hall's criticism also applies to the tests carried out in section 1. When those tests were re-run using regressions on lags two through nine of the dependent variable (rather than regressions on lags one through eight), the results were qualitatively the same. Not surprisingly, though, significance levels tended to be higher.

14 Fama (1984) and Hodrick and Srivastava (1986) report additional test results showing the variability of risk premia. Some indirect evidence comes from Hansen and Singleton (1983, pp. 262–4), who are able to reject a lognormal model in the closed-economy US context.

15 Government consumption includes government investment in the US data, while in the other countries government investment is included in I. When the alternative accounting convention was applied to the US, however, the estimation results were virtually the same.

REFERENCES

Breeden, Douglas T. 1979: An intertemporal asset pricing model with stochastic consumption and investment opportunities, *Journal of Financial Economics*, 7, 265–96.

Bryant, Ralph C. 1985: International Financial Intermediation: Underlying Trends and Implications for Government Policies. Paper prepared for the Second International Conference, Institute for Monetary and Economic Studies, Bank of Japan, Tokyo, May 1985.

Campbell, John Y. and Clarida, Richard H. 1986: The Term Structure of Euromarket Interest Rates: An Empirical Investigation. National Bureau of Economic Research Working Paper no. 1946.

Cumby, Robert E. 1986: Is it Risk? Explaining Deviations from Uncovered Interest Parity. Manuscript, New York University.

Cumby, Robert E. and Obstfeld, Maurice 1984: International interest rate and price level linkages under flexible exchange rates: a review of recent evidence. In John F.O. Bilson and Richard C. Marston (eds) *Exchange Rate Theory and Practice*, Chicago: University of Chicago Press (for the National Bureau of Economic Research).

Diaz-Alejandro, Carlos F. 1970: *Essays on the Economic History of the Argentine Republic*. New Haven: Yale University Press.

Fama, Eugene F. 1984: Forward and spot exchange rates. *Journal of Monetary Economics*, 14, 319–38.

Feldstein, Martin S. 1983: Domestic saving and international capital movements in the long run and the short run. *European Economic Review*, 21, 129–51.

Feldstein, Martin S. and Horioka, Charles 1980: Domestic saving and international capital flows. *Economic Journal*, 90, 314–29.

Fisher, Irving 1930: *The Theory of Interest*. New York: Macmillan.

Hall, Robert E. 1985: Real Interest and Consumption. National Bureau of Economic Research Working Paper no. 1694.

Hansen, Lars Peter and Hodrick, Robert J. 1983: Risk averse speculation in the forward foreign exchange market: an econometric analysis of linear models. In Jacob A. Frenkel (ed.) *Exchange Rates and International Macroeconomics*. Chicago: University of Chicago Press (for the National Bureau of Economic Research).

Hansen, Lars Peter and Singleton, Kenneth J. 1982: Generalized instrumental variables estimation of nonlinear rational expectations models. *Econometrica*, 50, 1269–86. [Errata in *Econometrica*, 52 (January 1984), 267–8.]

Hansen, Lars Peter and Singleton, Kenneth J. 1983: Stochastic consumption, risk aversion, and the temporal behavior of asset returns. *Journal of Political Economy*, 91, 249–65.

Hodrick, Robert J. and Srivastava, Sanjay 1986: The covariation of risk premiums and expected future spot exchange rates. *Journal of International Money and Finance*, 5 [Supplement], S5–S22.

Jorion, Philippe and Schwartz, Eduardo 1986: Integration vs. segmentation in the Canadian stock market. *Journal of Finance*, 41, 603–14.

Lucas, Robert E. Jr 1978: Asset prices in an exchange economy. *Econometrica*, 46, 1429–45.

Mankiw, N. Gregory, Rotemberg, Julio J. and Summers, Lawrence H. 1985: Intertemporal substitution in macroeconomics. *Quarterly Journal of Economics*, 100, 225–51.

Mark, Nelson C. 1985: On time varying risk premia in the foreign exchange market: an econometric analysis. *Journal of Monetary Economics*, 16, 3–18.

Miron, Jeffrey A, 1985: Seasonal Fluctuations and the Life-Cycle Permanent Income Model of Consumption. Manuscript, University of Michigan.

Obstfeld, Maurice 1986: Capital mobility in the world economy: theory and measurement. In Karl Brunner and Allan H. Meltzer (eds) *The National Bureau Method, International Capital Mobility, and Other Essays*. Carnegie-Rochester Conference Series on Public Policy no. 24 (supplement to the *Journal of Monetary Economics*). Amsterdam: North-Holland Publishing Company.

Officer, Lawrence H. 1985: Integration in the American foreign-exchange market, 1791–1900. *Journal of Economic History*, 45, 557–85.

Singleton, Kenneth J. 1986: Econometric Issues in the Analysis of Equilibrium Business Cycle Models. Manuscript, Carnegie-Mellon University.

Stulz, René M. 1981: A model of international asset pricing. *Journal of Financial Economics*, 9, 383–406.

Summers, Lawrence H. 1984: The after-tax rate of return affects private savings. *American Economic Review*, 74, 249–53.

Wheatley, Simon. 1985: Some Tests of International Equity Market Integration. Manuscript, University of Washington.

World Bank 1985: *World Development Report 1985*. New York: Oxford University Press.

Zeldes, Stephen 1985: Consumption and Liquidity Constraints: An Empirical Investigation. Working Paper no. 24–85, Rodney L. White Center for Financial Research, Wharton School, University of Pennsylvania.

COMMENT

Mohsin S. Khan

The paper by Obstfeld is a carefully done piece, and certainly very topical. Carlos Díaz-Alejandro was deeply concerned with the effects of capital flows on developing countries, and the problems they created for policymakers in these countries, so that this paper has a direct bearing on his interests. Even though Obstfeld focuses primarily on industrialized countries, and in particular on the US, Japan, and Germany, his analysis and results are of relevance to developing countries as well.

My comment on the paper is divided into two parts, dealing first with the evidence on capital mobility, and second with the theories and tests of international capital-market integration.

1. Evidence on Capital Flows

Obstfeld comes to the subject of international capital mobility with certain priors. He believes that there are capital flows between countries and that the empirical tests showing otherwise should be considered suspect. I feel that a number of economists would generally go along with Obstfeld's priors and would be equally troubled by existing tests, particularly those of Feldstein (1983) and Feldstein and Horioka (1980).

As has been mentioned, Carlos Díaz-Alejandro believed that capital movements in the context of developing countries were large and variable, and likely to create both short-run and long-run problems. What is the evidence on capital flows for developing countries? Table 7c.1 presents data on foreign borrowing and capital outflows for six high-debt Latin American countries over the period 1974–82.

The evidence of two-way flows is quite striking from the figures in table 7c.1. While in the case of Chile, and to some extent Brazil, there were limited outflows, for Argentina, Mexico, and Venezuela the ratio of capital outflows to external borrowing averaged around 70 per cent for the period 1974–82. Superficially at least one could argue that this is evidence of international equalization of risk-adjusted (with risk defined broadly to include risks of expropriation and bankruptcy in developing countries) returns. Further evidence on capital mobility in developing countries is

Table 7C.1 Gross external debt and capital outflows, 1974–82 (in billions of US dollars)

Country	*External debt*	*Gross capital outflows*	*Gross capital outflows as percentage of external debt*
Argentina	43.6	31.0	71.1
Brazil	90.5	11.6	12.8
Chile	17.3	0.2	1.2
Mexico	85.6	42.7	49.9
Peru	11.6	3.0	25.9
Venezuela	31.8	28.0	88.1

Source: Khan and Ul Haque (1987)

provided by Edwards and Khan (1985) using a variant of the interest arbitrage condition for financial assets.

Of course, evidence of two-way trade in financial assets does not imply that *net* trade in such assets has played a measurable role in equalizing rates of return on physical assets among countries. This is why one needs to perform the type of tests undertaken by Obstfeld here.

2. Theories and Empirical Tests

Obstfeld uses two types of tests to determine the degree of capital mobility among developing countries. The first compare intertemporal marginal rates of substitution, and the second look at correlations between savings and investment rates.

2.1 Comparison of Intertemporal Marginal Rates of Substitution

This is an interesting approach that involves an international comparison of the equality of expected marginal rates of substitution between future and present dollar bonds. The results confirm the author's expectations regarding capital-market integration, at least after 1973. One can quibble about assumptions underlying the theoretical model, such as equality of endowments and preferences of consumers in different countries, but by and large the results are pretty impressive.

There are four specific questions that arise when looking at the empirical tests contained in sections 1–3 of the paper.

1 What were the values of the parameters relating the intertemporal rates of substitution (γ_i), and were these stable over time? Only one check is made for stability (for 1973), but there may well be other points in time where the γ_i's shift.
2 What is the explanation for the negative value for the intertemporal

elasticity of substitution α for Germany over the period 1961–85? It is also puzzling that when estimates of α are obtained for subperiods, 1961–72 and 1973–85, the values turn out to be positive, and yet for the full period α is negative.

3 Was any check made for serial correlation in the estimation of equations (15) and (16)? If such correlation exists the tests for equality of the α's would be suspect.

4 If all the parameters are not significantly different from zero at the 5 per cent level, as for example is the case in the estimates for 1961–72, does it make much sense to go through a further test and conclude that the parameters are equal?

2.2 Correlation between Savings and Investment Rates

Obstfeld's second test extends his earlier critique of the Feldstein-Horioka analysis relating savings and investment rates using annual data. This bivariate link between savings and investment rates is, as Obstfeld recognizes, the *ultimate* structural relationship that is devoid of any policy implication.

While I share Obstfeld's misgivings about such tests, the results are still somewhat of a puzzle. While his tests show evidence of capital-market integration, such integration appears in some cases to have decreased since 1973! Penati and Dooley (1984) report quite different results from Obstfeld for 19 industrial countries. Those authors show that changes in net foreign assets are not sensitive to cross-country differences in rates of return (so that location of investment would be related to the location of savings) and furthermore they reject the hypothesis that changes in net foreign assets have become *more* sensitive to yield differentials. Given that we can observe capital mobility, it is easier to accept Obstfeld's overall results and difficult to take the Feldstein–Horioka and Penati–Dooley studies too seriously. Current account imbalances seem to reflect a variety of unanticipated shocks, and what we need to do is to investigate these in the context of a properly specified structural model.

In conclusion, the evidence provided by Obstfeld is an important contribution to the literature on capital mobility and capital-market integration. The results are, however, not as strong as one would have hoped, but undoubtedly future work building on Obstfeld's study will yield more robust evidence.

NOTE

The views expressed are the sole responsibility of the author.

REFERENCES

Edwards, Sebastian and Khan, Mohsin S. 1985: Interest rate determination in developing countries: a conceptual framework, *IMF Staff Papers*, September, pp. 377–403.

Feldstein, Martin 1983: Domestic saving and international capital movements in the long run and the short run. *European Economic Review*, March/April, pp. 129–51.

Feldstein, Martin and Horioka, C. 1980: Domestic savings and international capital flows. *Economic Journal*, June, pp. 314–29.

Khan, Mohsin S. and Ul Haque, Nadeem 1987: Capital flight from developing countries. *Finance and Development*, March, pp. 2–5.

Penati, Alessandro and Dooley, Michael 1984: Current account imbalances and capital formation in industrial countries, 1979–81. *IMF Staff Papers*, March, pp. 1–24.

Part III

LIBERALIZATION OF TRADE AND EXCHANGE CONTROLS

8

Economic Liberalization and the Equilibrium Real Exchange Rate in Developing Countries

Sebastian Edwards

1. Introduction

Carlos Díaz-Alejandro's interests were remarkably broad: they ranged from the economic history of Latin America, to the functioning of international financial markets, to the technology of cement plants.[1] There were, however, two interrelated topics to which Díaz-Alejandro kept coming back time after time: the role of international trade in the development process, and the importance of exchange rate policies. He first addressed the exchange rate problem in his 1961 MIT dissertation, later published as *Exchange Rate Devaluation in a Semi-Industrialized Country: The Experience of Argentina, 1955–1961* (MIT Press, 1966). In this work, which has become a classic on the subject, Díaz-Alejandro developed a number of important insights including the by-now popular idea that under certain circumstances devaluations can be contractionary.[2] In his later work, Díaz-Alejandro came back to the exchange rate issue with renewed interest; he was particularly concerned with understanding the behavior of real exchange rates in the developing countries.[3]

Possibly Díaz-Alejandro's most prominent work on the role of trade policy in the development process is contained in his monumental volume on the economic history of Argentina. In it he forcefully argued that during the post-Second World War period, Argentina had neglected the potential role of international trade as an engine of growth. The importance of international trade in the development process is also a dominant aspect of Díaz-Alejandro's work on the Colombian economy. Throughout his work on the relation between trade and growth, Díaz-Alejandro emphasized that maintaining an 'appropriate' exchange rate policy was essential for the success of trade liberalization reforms aimed at moving a country towards an export-oriented development strategy. The maintenance of the real exchange rate at its 'appropriate' (or realistic) level should be interpreted as meaning that the actual value of the real exchange rate should not depart significantly from its equilibrium value. In other words, in this Díaz-Alejandro context, an 'appropriate' real exchange rate is one that does not become misaligned and especially overvalued (Díaz-Alejandro, 1984a).

The purpose of the present paper is to investigate the way in which the adoption of an export-oriented policy, through the liberalization of the external sector, affects the *equilibrium* value of the real exchange rate. Surprisingly perhaps, in spite of the increasing importance of issues related to trade liberalization, much of the policy discussion on the relation between commercial policies, liberalization, and real exchange rate has been quite confusing.[4] This paper seeks to clarify and integrate some of the issues involved by formally developing two simple general equilibrium models to investigate the relation between changes in commercial policies and the real exchange rate.

2. The Traditional Literature

In the economic development policy literature on tariffs, liberalization and development strategies, it has long been recognized that there is a relation between tariffs level and the equilibrium value of the real exchange rate. Most of this discussion, however, has been quite vague and has been carried out in a partial equilibrium context. The vagueness in this policy literature has stemmed, in part, from the confusion that for some time now has surrounded the concept of 'the' real exchange rate. In fact, as discussed in more detail below, there are a number of competing definitions for 'the' real exchange rate, and often one is not sure which concept a particular author has in mind.

The traditionally accepted view among policymakers has been that a reduction in tariffs in a small country will always 'require' a real (equilibrium) depreciation to maintain external balance. The argument usually given is based on a partial equilibrium interpretation of the elasticities approach to exchange rate determination, and runs along the following lines: a lower tariff will reduce the domestic price of importables, and consequently increase the demand for imports. This, in turn, will generate an external imbalance (i.e., a trade account deficit), which, assuming that the Marshall–Lerner condition holds, will require a (real) devaluation to restore equilibrium. This view is clearly captured by the following quote from Balassa (1982, p. 16): '[E]liminating protective measures would necessitate a devaluation in order to offset the resulting deficit in the balance of payments.' On the other hand, according to Harry Johnson (1966, p. 159):

> One of the assumptions commonly made in the context of liberalization of trade by underdeveloped countries is that such liberalization would necessarily involve a balance of payments deficit and the consequent necessity of devaluation. . . .

The proposition that a reduction (or elimination) of tariffs will necessarily result in an equilibrium real depreciation has also been made in the shadow pricing literature. Some authors have proposed that the shadow exchange rate should be computed as the equilibrium real exchange rate under conditions of free trade (Bacha and Taylor, 1971). It has then been postulated that an elimination of existing trade impediments will result in a higher equilibrium real exchange rate (i.e., in a real depreciation). For example, for the case of a small country which faces initial trade equilibrium, Bacha and Taylor (1971, p. 216) proposed the following expression for the free trade real exchange rate:

$$e^F = e(1+t)^\gamma$$

where e^F is the free trade equilibrium (real) exchange rate, e is the existing equilibrium (real) exchange rate prior to the elimination of tariffs, t is the level of the tariffs and $\gamma = \eta_M/(\varepsilon_x+\eta_M)$, for η_M elasticity of demand or level of demand for imports and ε_x elasticity of supply for exports.

More recently, using a slightly different model, Taylor (1979, p. 207) has insisted on this point (where the same notation applies):[5]

> [S]uppose that a pre-existing tariff is reduced or removed altogether . . . [t]hen [the real exchange rate] e will rise. . . . [T]he result can be called the *free-trade* exchange rate [e^F].
> [N]aturally, e/e^F is less than 1. . . .

A common feature of most early models is that they ignored, among other things, the presence of intermediate inputs. This problem was acknowledged by Harry Johnson (1966) in an article that uses effective rates of protection to analyze the effect of tariff changes on the equilibrium exchange rate (see also Corden, 1971, chapter 5). Johnson pointed out that once intermediate goods were allowed into the picture the reduction or removal of tariffs could result either in a devaluation *or* in an *appreciation*. In Johnson's words (1969, p. 159): '[T]ariffs structures may bring about a situation in which appreciation rather than depreciation would be necessary to preserve equilibrium under liberalization. . . .' The reason for this is intuitively clear. With intermediate goods it is possible that some activities will have a negative effective rate of protection; that is the tariff *structure* will impose a tax on value added in those activities. Consequently, the removal of tariffs will reduce the magnitude of this tax and, according to Johnson's model, will result in higher production of these goods. The effects of eliminating the negative rates of effective protection could be such that a balance of payments surplus could result, with the consequent required *appreciation* of the equilibrium real exchange rate (see also Corden, 1971).[6]

Most traditional treatments of the relationship between commercial policy and the real exchange rate have tended also to (implicitly or explicitly) ignore the presence of nontradable goods.[7] However, once nontradables are allowed into the picture the effect of tariff changes on the real exchange rate can be different from those effects obtained from simpler partial equilibrium models (Edwards, 1987b). In sections 3 and 4 of this paper two alternative models with nontradables are used to analyze formally the relation between tariff liberalization and the equilibrium real exchange rate. It is shown that although in principle, within the context of a general equilibrium framework, a commodity trade liberalization can result in either equilibrium real depreciation or appreciation, the real depreciation case is somewhat more plausible.

3. Tariffs and the Real Exchange Rate in a Factor-Specific Model

In this section the relation between tariff liberalization policies and the equilibrium real exchange rate in a model with sectoral factor specificity is presented. An important property of this model is that changes in the demand for nontradables play a predominant role in determining the new equilibrium real exchange rate. This contrasts with the more standard model of section 4 where the behavior of the real exchange rate is independent of the demand for nontradables. As is pointed out below the model in this section can be interpreted as capturing the short- or medium-run effects of the tariff reform.

Since much of the confusion found in the policy literature on the subject stems from the existence of numerous, and often contradictory, definitions of real exchange rate, I begin this section with a brief discussion on what we mean by *real exchange rate*. In the actual formal analysis, I use alternative definitions as a way to contribute toward the clarification of this issue.

3.1 Real Exchange Rate: Alternative Definitions

Currently there are at least four or five competing definitions of 'the' real exchange rate. While this is not per se serious, it does generate some communication problems.[8] Although most writers define 'the' real exchange rate as a relative price, there are disagreements on which relative price should be called 'the' real exchange rate. According to an early definition 'the' real exchange rate is equal to the nominal exchange rate (E) corrected (i.e., multiplied) by the ratio of 'the' foreign price level (P^*) to 'the' domestic price level (P). This definition has often been called the purchasing power parity (PPP) real exchange rate, $e_{\text{PPP}} = EP^*/P$. Depending on whether P and P^* are CPIs or WPIs, or GDP deflators, e_{PPP} will be the relative price of consumption or production baskets.[9]

More recently, however, most authors have defined the real exchange rate in the context of dependent economy-type models as the relative price of tradable to nontradable goods (see, for example, Dornbusch, 1974, 1980; Krueger, 1978, 1983; Mussa, 1983, Frenkel and Mussa, 1984). Assuming that the law of one price holds for tradables and that there are no taxes on trade, the real exchange rate is defined by these authors as: $e = EP_T^*/P_N$, where P_T^* is the world price of tradables, and P_N is the domestic price of nontradables.

It is interesting to compare the tradables–nontradables relative price definition with the PPP definition of the real exchange rate. Assuming that P and P^* in the PPP definition are geometrically weighted averages of tradable and nontradable prices, with weights, α, $(1-\alpha)$, β and $(1-\beta)$, it is possible to write $P = P_N^{\alpha} P_T^{1-\alpha}$ and $P^* = P_N^{*\beta} P_T^{*(1-\beta}$. Further assuming that the country in question is small, that the law of one price holds for tradable goods (i.e., $P_T = P_T^* E$) and that E is fixed and equal to 1, it is possible to find the relation between percentage changes in the real exchange rate (e) and in the PPP real exchange rate (where, as usual, the 'hat' operator ($\hat{}$) represents percentage change:

$$\hat{e} = (1/\alpha)\hat{e}_{ppp} + (\beta/\alpha)\,(\hat{P}_T^* - \hat{P}_N^*)$$

It may be seen that, in general, changes in the two definitions of the real exchange rate will differ (i.e., $\hat{e} \neq \hat{e}_{ppp}$). Moreover, e and e_{ppp} can even move in opposite directions, depending on the behavior of foreign relative prices (P_T^*/P_N^*).[10]

The above discussion has ignored taxes on international trade. However, if there are these type of taxes, a decision should be made on whether to define a real exchange rate inclusive or exclusive of them. If it is assumed that tradables are subject to a uniform protective tax of rate t, an index that takes into account the effect of protection on competitiveness can be defined as $e_T = e(1+t)$. Obviously, if the tax on tradables does not change, e_T and e will move at the same rate: $\hat{e} = \hat{e}_T$.

In fact, most theoretical analyses rooted in the dependent economy model have chosen to use e_T as 'the' real exchange rate. However, a limitation of this definition is that it assumes that all tradable goods are subject to the same tax. In a many-goods economy, the different tradable goods are subject to taxes at different rates. For example, most importables are subject to differentiated tariffs or import quotas, while some exportables are often subject to taxes. For this reason, in applied work, it has been proposed to define sector-specific (or goods specific) indexes of the real exchange rate corrected by the effects of taxes (or subsidies).[11] For example, if sector j is subject to a tax of t_j this index will be $e_{Tj} = EP_j^*(1+t_j)/P_N$. Again, of course, if taxes on j and world relative prices do not change, e and e_{Tj} will move at same rate. If, on the other hand, the tax on sector j is altered, with relative world prices constant, changes in e_{Tj} and changes in e will be linked by the following simple relationship: $\hat{e}_{Tj}/(1+t_j) = 1 + \hat{e}/(1+t_j)$. For this reason, and due to the difficulty in obtaining reliable time series of taxes on trade, most empirical studies have concentrated on real exchange rate definitions given by e or e_{ppp} rather than e_T.[12]

The above discussion has clearly illustrated the semantic confusion that surrounds the policy literature on real exchange rates. If authors are not careful to clearly state what concept they are referring to, significant misunderstandings can ensue. An additional difficulty arises with defining the *equilibrium* real exchange rate.[13]

3.2 Tariff Liberalization and Equilibrium Relative Prices

In this section I use a fairly simple general equilibrium model to analyze how a tariff liberalization affects the equilibrium value of five alternative definitions of the real exchange rate. It is hoped that by looking at this set of definitions, instead of at only one of them, the ongoing confusion in policy discussions will be (somewhat) clarified. In particular I focus on: (a) the PPP definition $e_{\text{ppp}} = E(P^*/P)$; (b) the dependent economy definition of relative prices of tradables to nontradables, excluding taxes on trade, $e = EP_T^*/P_N$; (c) the domestic relative price of tradables to nontradables, $e = P_T/P_N$; (d) the domestic relative price of importables to nontradables, $e_{TM} = P_M/P_N$; and (e) the domestic relative price of exportables, $e_{TX} = P_X/P_N$.

Assume a real model of a small country which produces competitively importables (M), exportables (X) and nontradables (N), using capital and labor. The nominal exchange rate is fixed and imports are initially subject to an import tariff of r. The capital account is assumed to be closed, and there is no international borrowing (see below, however). Also, in order to focus on the behavior of the equilibrium real exchange rate we set all monetary considerations aside. Capital is sector-specific, whereas labor can move freely across sectors. In this Ricardo–Viner specification, domestic factor prices are not linked to foreign factor prices and the Stolper–Samuelson theorem does not hold. Production technology and resource allocation can be summarized by a revenue function, R, which gives the maximum revenue obtainable given factor supplies, F, and relative prices. It is also assumed that the revenue function is twice differentiable in all arguments.[14] Consumer preferences and consumption decisions, on the other hand, are summarized by a twice-differentiable expenditure function, E, which gives the minimum expenditure required to achieve a level of utility W. A useful property of revenue functions is that their partial derivatives with respect to prices yield the corresponding supply functions. In a similar way the partial derivatives of E with respect to prices yield the Hicksian demand functions. Assuming that the nominal exchange rate is equal to 1, and using the price of exportables as the numeraire, the model can be written as

$$R(1,p_M,p_N;F) + \tau\left(E_{P_M} - R_{P_M}\right) = E(1,p_M,p_N;W) \tag{2}$$

$$R_{P_N} = E_{P_N} \tag{3}$$

$$p_M = p_M^* + \tau;\ p_X = p_X^* = 1 \tag{4}$$

$$P = \alpha P_M + \beta P_N + \varepsilon P_X;\ \alpha + \beta + \varepsilon = 1 \tag{5}$$

$$P_T = \delta P_M + (1-\delta)P_X \tag{6}$$

Equation (2) is the economy's budget constraint, where $(E_{P_M} - R_{P_M})$ are imports and $\tau\ (E_{P_M} - R_{P_M})$ are import revenues which are assumed to be handed back to the public in a nondistortionary fashion. Equation (3) establishes that the nontradable goods market is always in equilibrium. Naturally, the combination of equations (2) and (3) implies that this economy is also in external balance. Equation (4) specifies that in this economy importables are subject to a (specific) tariff τ. P in equation (5) is an index of the general price level, whereas P_T in equation (6) is an index of the price of tradables.

The equilibrium real exchange rate is defined (for any of the five real exchange rate concepts discussed above) as that value of the real exchange rate (RER) for which internal and external equilibrium hold simultaneously, given (long-term sustainable) values of other exogenous variables such as tariffs, international terms of trade, technology and preferences.[15] According to equations (2) and (3), then, this economy is initially in internal and external equilibrium, and the initial real exchange rate is at its equilibrium level. Then, in this context, a change in the RER induced by an exogenous shock should be interpreted as changes in the equilibrium real exchange rate.[16]

The modeling strategy is first to analyze how changes in the tariff will affect the equilibrium relative price of nontradables, N and then to look at how the five different definitions of equilibrium real exchange rate are affected. Totally differentiating equations (2) and (3) and using equation (4) we find that

$$\frac{dp_N}{d\tau} = \frac{E_W}{\Delta}\left\{ \tau\,(E_{p_M p_M} - R_{p_M p_M})\, C_N - (1-\tau C_M)\,(R_{p_M p_N} - E_{p_M p_N}) \right\} \tag{7}$$

where $C_N = E_{p_N}W/E_W$, $C_M = E_{p_M}W/E_W$ are pure income effects on demands for nontradables and tradables, $\Delta = E_W\{\tau\,(R_{p_N p_M} - E_{p_N p_M})\,C_N - (1-\tau C_M)$ $(E_{p_N p_N} - R_{p_N p_N})\} > 0$ under stability (see appendix A).

The sign of $d_{p_N}/d\tau$ in equation (7) is undetermined, indicating that in this general setting a tariff reduction can result in either a reduction or an increase of the price of nontradables relative to exportables. There are two sources for this ambiguity. There are income and substitution effects that work in opposite directions, and there is a possibility of complementarity in consumption between nontradables and importables. That is, $E_{p_N p_M} \gtrless 0$.[17] However, at this level of aggregation it is highly unlikely to have this type of cross-effect that results in complementarity in consumption; for this reason, in what follows it is assumed that $E_{p_N p_M} > 0$ and $R_{p_N p_M} < 0$ so that $(1-\tau C_M)$ $(R_{p_M p_N} - E_{p_M p_N}) < 0$. However, even in this case the ambiguity with respect to the sign of $dp_N/d\tau$ remains.

The term $\tau(E_{p_M p_M} - R_{p_M p_M})\, C_N$ is the income effect, and is only relevant if initially there was a large tariff in place (i.e., $\tau \neq 0$). The reduction in the tariff increases welfare and thus the demand for nontradables, exercising upward pressure on their prices. Under the assumption of gross substitutability in consumption, the substitution effect works in the opposite direction: the tariff liberalization reduces the domestic price of importables generating an incipient excess supply of N, which requires a reduction in its price. Whether the income or substitution effects dominate will depend crucially on the values of C_N and on the initial level of the tariff. Assuming a very small initial tariff, i.e., $\tau \approx 0$, equation (7) reduces to:

$$\frac{\mathrm{d}p_N}{\mathrm{d}\tau} \approx \frac{(R_{p_M p_N} - R_{p_N p_M})}{(E_{p_N p_N} - R_{p_N p_N})} > 0 \tag{8}$$

In this case we can say unambiguously that a tariff liberalization will result in a reduction of the price of nontradables relative to exports. Of course if $C_N = 0$, $\mathrm{d}p_M/d\tau > 0$ even if $\tau > 0$.

In general, under most circumstances it can be expected that unless the initial distortion is *very* high (i.e., the initial τ is very large), the substitution effect will dominate. Consequently, although we have seen that rigorously $\mathrm{d}p_N/\mathrm{d}\tau$ cannot be signed, under most plausible assumptions, i.e., when all goods are gross substitutes and the substitution effect dominates, we have $\mathrm{d}p_N/\mathrm{d}\tau > 0$.

Having found $\mathrm{d}p_N/\mathrm{d}\tau$ in equation (7), all we require are straightforward arithmetic manipulations to find how the alternative definitions of equilibrium real exchange rates react to a tariff liberalization policy. Table 8.1 summarizes the results obtained in the more general case, where the expression for $\mathrm{d}p_N/\mathrm{d}\tau$ is given by equation (7). From this table it is clear that in general, for many of these definitions, it is not possible to know a priori how the equilibrium real exchange rate will change following a trade liberalization. Moreover, even under our simplifying assumptions of dominating substitution effect, the changes in some of the different RER definitions result in opposite signs! For example, assuming that the substitution effect dominates in equation (7), $\mathrm{d}p_N/\mathrm{d}\tau > 0$ and $\hat{e}/\hat{\tau} < 0$, as postulated by traditional partial equilibrium policy analyses. Moreover, even in this case $\hat{e}_{\text{ppp}}/\hat{\tau} \gtrless 0$ and $\hat{e}_T/\hat{\tau} \gtrless 0$.

The results in equation (7) of table 8.1 were derived assuming that tariffs on all importables were reduced by the same amount. In reality, however, liberalization reforms seldom work that way. In most instances only some tariffs are reduced. If only tariffs on a subset, k, of importables are reduced while for the other m importables tariffs are maintained, we have that $\mathrm{d}p_N/\mathrm{d}\tau_k = (E_w/\Delta\ \{(E_{p_k p_k} - R_{p_k p_k})C_N - (1-\tau C_M)\ (R_{p_N p_k}) + \tau(E_{p_k p_M} - R_{p_k p_M})C_N)$. Of course, since $E_{p_k p_M}, R_{p_k p_M} \gtrless 0$ additional sources of sign ambiguity emerge for $\mathrm{d}_{p_N}/\mathrm{d}\tau_k$.

3.3 Extensions

Wage Rigidity The previous discussion has been carried out under the assumption of fully flexible factor and commodity prices. This, however,

Table 8.1 Tariffs and 'the' equilibrium real exchange rate: the special factor case

Real exchange rate definition
(a) $e_{PPP} = EP^*/P$; $\hat{e}_{PPP}/\hat{\tau} = -\{\gamma_M(\tau/P_M) + \gamma_N(\tau/P_N)(dp_N/d\tau)\}$
(b) $e = EP^*_T/P_N$; $\hat{e}/\hat{\tau} = -\ (\tau/P_N)(dp_N/d\tau)$
(c) $e_T = P_T/P_N$; $\hat{e}_T/\hat{\tau} = \{\phi_M(\tau/P_M) - (\tau/P_N)(dp_N/d\tau)\}$
(d) $e_{TM} = P_M/P_N$; $\hat{e}_{TM}/\hat{\tau} = \{(\tau/P_M) - (\tau/P_N)\ (dp_N/d\tau)\}$
(e) $e_{TX} = P_X/P_N$; $\hat{e}_{TX}/\hat{\tau} = \hat{e}/\hat{\tau}$

γ_M, γ_N and ϕ_M are positive weights.

may not be the more relevant case for a number of LDCs. The analysis can be easily expanded to the case where some factors have a fixed price. Assume, for example, that, as is the case in numerous developing countries, the wage rate w is fixed at a level $\bar{w} \geq R_L$, where R is the unconstrained revenue function, and L is the labor force. In this case, then, we have to define a constrained revenue function ($\widetilde{R}$):[18]

$$\widetilde{R}(\bar{w},p_M,p_M,K) = \max_{q,L} \left\{ \left(q^X + p_M q^M + p_N q^N \right) - \bar{w}L \right\} \tag{9}$$

where q^i, $i = X,M,N$, refers to output of exportables, importables and nontradables. Also, the nontradables market equilibrium condition is replaced by:

$$\widetilde{R}_{p_N} = E_{p_N} \tag{10}$$

where $\widetilde{R}_{p_N}$ is the partial derivative of the constrained revenue function (9) with respect to the price of nontradables. Neary (1985) has shown that under fixed factor prices the following relation exists between restricted and unrestricted revenue functions:

$$\widetilde{R} = R\{p_M,p_N,\widetilde{L}(\bar{w},p_M,p_N,K)\} - \bar{w}\widetilde{L}(\bar{w},p_M,p_N,K) \tag{11}$$

where $\widetilde{L}$ is the amount labor employed in the constrained case.

It is easy to find how the relative price of nontradables reacts to a tariff reduction in an economy with factor specificity and fixed real wages.[19] In order to facilitate the comparison with the case of flexible factor prices, $d\widetilde{p}_N/d\tau$ is expressed in terms of the derivatives of the *unconstrained* revenue function:

$$\frac{d\widetilde{p}_N}{d\tau} = \frac{E_W}{\widetilde{\Delta}}\left[\left\{\tau C_N\left(E_{p_Mp_M} - R_{p_Mp_M}\right) - (1-\tau C_M)\left(R_{p_Mp_N} - E_{p_Mp_N}\right)\right\}\right.$$
$$\left. + \left\{\left(R_{Lp_M}/R_{LL}\right)\tau C_N + (1-\tau C_M)\left(R_{Lp_N}/R_{LL}\right)\right\}\right] \tag{12}$$

where

$$\widetilde{\Delta} = \Delta - \left\{ \tau \left(R_{Lp_M} / R_{LL} \right) C_N + (1 - \tau C_M) \left(R_{Lp_N} / R_{LL} \right) \right\} \tag{13}$$

Since $R_{Lp_N} > 0$ and $R_{LL} < 0$, it follows that $\widetilde{\Delta} > \Delta$. Also the inspection of (12), (13) and (7) reveals that,

$$\frac{\mathrm{d}\widetilde{p}_N}{\mathrm{d}\tau} < \frac{\mathrm{d}p_N}{\mathrm{d}\tau} \tag{14}$$

That is, under wage rigidity the equilibrium relative price of nontradables will be less responsive to changes in tariffs. This means that under these circumstances it is not sufficient that the substitution effect dominate in order for a tariff liberalization to result in a decline of the relative price of nontradables. Moreover, it is now possible to have a number of pseudo-paradoxes where changes in tariff levels can result in a real depreciation with wage flexibility, but in a real appreciation under wage rigidity.

Import Quotas The case of import quotas can be analyzed in a quite straightforward fashion by defining 'virtual prices' as in Neary and Roberts (1980). The use of virtual prices, of course, assumes that the quota is allocated competitively via an auction mechanism. In this case the relaxation of a binding import quota will result in a lower virtual price for importables, which can be analyzed in a way perfectly analogous to our previous discussion. Obviously, the reason why our tariff discussion can be applied directly to the case of quotas is that under the assumptions made here there is an equivalence between tariffs and quotas.

Intermediate Goods Intermediate goods can also be incorporated quite easily through the definition of net outputs (Dixit and Norman, 1980, p. 160). In this case an additional source of ambiguity with respect to the sign of $\mathrm{d}p_N/\mathrm{d}\tau$ emerges. The reason, of course, is related to Johnson's (1966) effective protection case discussed above. The tariff liberalization, by reducing the tax on the importation of inputs, not only eliminates negative effective protection in some importable sectors, but also reduces costs of nontradables generating forces towards a downward shift in the supply of nontradables.

Changes in International Terms of Trade This model can be used directly to analyze how exogenous changes in the international terms of trade will affect the equilibrium real exchange rate. This was another topic of great interest to Carlos Díaz-Alejandro. For example, in 1982 he published an empirical study on the relation between exchange rates and the Argentinian real exchange rate between 1913 and 1976, where he found strong evidence that in that country improvements in the international terms of trade had led to real exchange rate appreciation (see Díaz-Alejandro, 1982). The empirical relation between the international terms of trade and the real exchange rate was again picked up in his 'In Toto I don't think we are in Kansas any more.'

In terms of the model presented above, the main difference between an exogenous change in the international price of importables and a policy-induced change in the import tariff of the same magnitude resides in the different magnitudes of the income effects. In particular $\mathrm{d}W/\mathrm{d}p_M^* = \mathrm{d}W/\mathrm{d}\tau + (E_{p_N p_N} - R_{p_N p_N})\,(E_{p_M} - R_{p_M})/\Delta$, where the second term on the right-hand side is negative. The effect of a reduction of the international price of M on p_N is given by:

$$\frac{\mathrm{d}p_N}{\mathrm{d}p_M^*} = \frac{\mathrm{d}p_N}{\mathrm{d}r} - \frac{E_W}{\Delta}\left(E_{p_M} - R_{p_M}\right)C_N \tag{15}$$

where the second term on the right-hand side is positive. It is interesting to compare the effects on p_N of changes in τ and in p_M^*. For example, a number of authors have argued that whereas a tariff reduction will lead to a real depreciation (i.e., $\mathrm{d}p_N/\mathrm{d}\tau > 0$ for the *e* definition of RER), an improvement in the terms of trade will result in a real appreciation (i.e., $\mathrm{d}p_N/\mathrm{d}p_M^* < 0$). It is clear from equation (15) that for these results to hold simultaneously, $E_W(E_{p_M} - R_{p_M})C_N/\Delta$ has to be 'sufficiently large'; that is, the income effect associated with the terms of trade deterioration has to be sufficiently large. (For a detailed discussion on this subject see Edwards and van Wijnbergen, 1987.)

Transfers This model can also be used to analyze the effects of international transfers. Denoting the transfer as H it follows that:[20]

$$\frac{\mathrm{d}p_N}{\mathrm{d}H} = \frac{E_W}{\Delta} C_N > 0 \tag{16}$$

It is interesting to interpret a transfer from abroad as capital inflows resulting from a relaxation of capital controls in a small country. This means that if, as was the case in the recent Southern Cone liberalizations, following the opening of the capital account, foreign funds flow into the country ($\mathrm{d}H > 0$), the relative price of nontradables will increase, generating a real appreciation for every definition of the RER used here. In fact Díaz-Alejandro (1981a) was one of the first observers who perceptively noticed the importance of this real appreciation in the frustrating Southern Cone experiments.

The (highly likely) possibility of $\mathrm{d}p_N/\mathrm{d}H$ and $\mathrm{d}p_N/\mathrm{d}\tau$ having the same sign is at the core of recent policy discussions on the appropriate order of economic liberalization in the developing countries (Edwards, 1984). Equation (16) also highlights the fact that once capital inflows are reduced, p_N will have to decline. If, however, due to wage rate rigidities this is not possible, unemployment will result as was the case in Chile (see Edwards and Cox Edwards, 1987).[21]

International Borrowing and Lending Although the transfer problem framework provides a useful benchmark for analyzing the effects of opening the capital account, the results obtained may be somewhat misleading.

Alternatively the model of section 3.2 can be transformed into a two-period model with endogenous investment and restricted foreign borrowing as in Edwards and van Wijnbergen (1986). The results, in terms of the reaction of p_N, will under most circumstances be the same as those discussed here.[22] An interesting application of the two-period model is to investigate how expected changes in the tariff in the future will affect the path of p_N. Since in that setting, foreign borrowing is possible, consumers will try to smooth consumption and will increase their demand for nontradables in both periods 1 and 2. As a result, in the first period there will be positive pressure on p_N, even though the tariff in that period will still be on. On the other hand, the expected reduction of τ will affect the consumption rate of interest, and present consumption on all goods will tend to be reduced. The final outcome can be either a higher or lower p_N in period 1. In order to provide some idea of how the case with foreign borrowing works, the general model is presented in appendix B.

4. Trade Reform and the Equilibrium Real Exchange Rate in the Mobile Factor Case

The discussion of the preceding section assumed that capital was fixed and that it could not move across sectors following a relative commodity price shock. The importance of that assumption lies in the fact that factor prices become independent of world commodity prices. As a result, demand conditions for nontradables play a crucial role in determining the real exchange rate reaction to changes in τ or p^*_M. In the present section, the more traditional case with full intersectoral factor mobility is analyzed. To the extent that the fixed factors Ricardo–Viner model of section 3 is considered a short-run model, the one in the present section can be viewed as a medium- or intermediate-run model.[23] The comparison of both cases will give us some (rough) idea of the dynamics of the real exchange rate following a trade liberalization reform.

Consider the case of a small economy that, as before, produces exportables (X), importables (M) and nontradables (N), using two intersectorally mobile factors of production, capital (K) and labor (L). As before, it is assumed also that the worldwide common technology is characterized by constant returns to scale, that there is perfect competition, that there is a fixed unitary nominal exchange rate and that there is an initial tariff on the importation of M. Under these circumstances, and ruling out specialization, the world prices of exportables (p^*_x) and importables (p^*_M) plus the tariff (τ) determine unequivocally the rewards of both factors, w and r.[24] These factor rewards, under the assumption of competition, determine the nominal price of nontradables (p_N). Demand conditions for nontradables, in turn, determine total production of nontradables and total factors used in their production. This leaves a certain amount of factors, K and L, that are used in the production of exportables and importables in a traditional Heckscher–Ohlin fashion. (For a discussion of the effects of changes in tradable goods' prices on production in the context of similar models, see Corden and Neary (1982), Edwards (1986a) and Edwards and van Wijnbergen (1987)).

The model can be presented in traditional Jones (1965) notation by equations (17) and (18), where once again the price of X is taken as the numéraire. Note that, as long as there is no specialization, there is no need to specify the demand side to find the effects of tariff changes on prices, factor rewards and the real exchange rate. However, to find their effect on output, demand considerations are required.

$$a_{LW}W + a_{KM}r = p_M;\ a_{LX}w + a_{KX}r = 1;\ a_{LN}W + a_{KN}r = p_N \tag{17}$$

$$p_M = p^*_{\mathrm{M}} + \tau;\ p_X = p^*_{\mathrm{X}} = 1 \tag{18}$$

where the a_{ij}'s are input–output coefficients. As in section 3, I will analyze how changes in τ will affect the five different definitions of real exchange rate e_{PPP}, e, e_T, e_{T_M} and e_{T_X}.

Consider first the more plausible case for LDCs where exports are the most labor-intensive commodity, with imports being the more capital intensive. The capital–labor ratio for nontradables lies in between $(K/L)_M$ and $(K/L)_X$.[25] As before the strategy is to first find how p_N reacts to changes in τ. From equation (18) it is clear that this requires knowledge of how wages and the rate of return will change.

The effect of a reduction of price of M on factor rewards and the relative price of nontradables p_N can be analyzed using figure 8.1, which is the dual to the well-known Lerner–Pearce diagram. The initial equilibrium is given by the intersection of the three isocost curves MM, XX and NN. These curves present the combinations of wages and rental rates of capital that result in a constant cost of producing these goods with the existing technology. The slopes of these curves are equal to the capital–labor ratio. The reduction of the price of M will result in a leftward shift of the MM curve toward $M'M'$. This is because now, in order to maintain equilibrium between domestic costs and the world price of importables, plus the tariff, lower combinations of wages and rental rates will be required. New long-run equilibrium will be obtained at B where the new $M'M'$ curve intersects the XX curve. As the Stolper–Samuelson theorem indicates, the reduction of the price of M in an economy where exportables are labor intensive will result in higher wages and lower rental rates (i.e., $W_1 > W_0$, and $r_1 < r_0$). The new equilibrium point B is below the NN isocost curve, indicating that as a consequence of the tariff reduction, the price of nontradables in terms of exportables has to decline. As a result the isocost curve for N will move down until it intersects the other two curves at B.

Straightforward manipulation of equations (17) and (18) gives us the formal expression for the change in p_N following a change in τ:

$$\frac{\hat{p}_N}{\hat{\tau}} = \left[\frac{\theta_{KX} - \theta_{KN}}{\theta_{KX} - \theta_{KM}}\right](\tau/p_M) \tag{19}$$

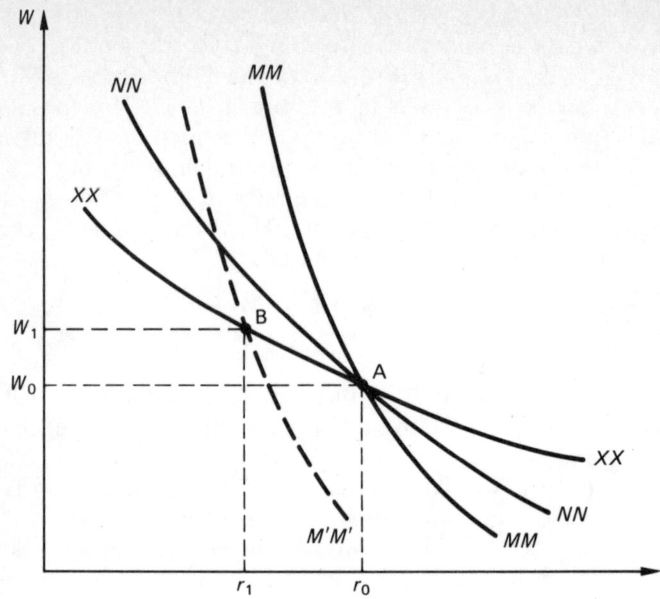

Figure 8.1 Wage–rental frontiers

where $\theta_{KX} = a_{KX}r/p_X$; $\theta_{LX} = 1 - \theta_{KX}$; $\theta_{KM} = a_{KM}r/p_M$; and $\theta_{LM} = 1 - \theta_{KM}$. Since our capital-intensity assumptions mean that $\theta_{KX} < \theta_{KN} < \theta_{KM}$, equation (19) implies that $\hat{p}_N/\hat{\tau} > 0$.

It is interesting to notice that in the present case of full factor mobility the degree of ambiguity regarding $\hat{p}_N/\hat{\tau}$ is much reduced in relation to the model in section 3. For example, if the relative capital intensities are reversed to $\theta_{KX} > \theta_{KN} > \theta_{KM}$, we still get that $\hat{p}_N/\hat{\tau} > 0$. Only if it is assumed that nontradables are at an extreme of the capital-intensity ranking (i.e., $\theta_{KM} < \theta_{KX} < \theta_{KN}$ or $\theta_{KN} < \theta_{KX} < \theta_{KM}$) can we get $\hat{p}_N/\hat{\tau} < 0$. This, however, is a rather implausible case for a developing country. Moreover, when nontradables are at one of the extremes of the relative capital labor ranking, it is more likely that we will have specialization in production; in that case, of course, the present framework has to be modified by explicitly bringing in the demand for nontradables.

Table 8.2 contains a summary of the reactions of the different definitions of e to changes in τ. Ruling out the case where nontradables are at an extreme of the capital-intensities ranking, we get unambiguous signs for a number of definitions of e:

$$\hat{e}_{\text{PPP}}/\hat{\tau} < 0; \hat{e}/\hat{\tau} < 0; \hat{e}_{TX}/\hat{\tau} < 0$$

This, of course, is the traditional result which indicates that a tariff liberalization will result in an equilibrium real depreciation. Also, notice that since under $\theta_{KX} < \theta_{KN} < \theta_{KM}$, $(\theta_{KX} - \theta_{KN})/(\theta_{KX} - \theta_{KM}) < 1$, $(\hat{e}_{TM}/\hat{\tau}) < 0$.

Table 8.2 Tariffs and real exchange rates: the mobile factor case

Real exchange rate definition
(a) $e_{PPP} = EP^*/P$; $\hat{e}_{PPP}/\hat{\tau} = -(\tau/P_M)\left\{\gamma_M + \gamma_N \frac{(\theta_{KX}-\theta_{KN})}{(\theta_{KX}-\theta_{KM})}\right\}$
(b) $e = eP_T^*/P_N$; $\hat{e}/\hat{\tau} = -\,(\tau/P_M)(\theta_{KX}-\theta_{KN})/(\theta_{KX}-\theta_{KM})$
(c) $e_T = P_T/P_N$; $\hat{e}_T/\hat{\tau} = (\tau/P_M)\{(\phi_M - (\theta_{KX}-\theta_{KN})/\theta_{KX}-\theta_{KM})\}$
(d) $e_{TM} = P_M/P_N$; $\hat{e}_{TM}/\hat{\tau} = (\tau/P_M)\{1 - (\theta_{KX}-\theta_{KN})/(\theta_{KX}-\theta_{KM})\}$
(e) $e_{TX} = P_X/P_N$; $\hat{e}_{TX}/\hat{\tau} = \hat{e}/\hat{\tau}$

γ_N, γ_M and ϕ_M are positive weights.

By assuming nonspecialization in the above discussion, it has been possible to ignore the role of the demand for nontradables. However, it is possible that as a result of the relative price shock, this country will specialize in the production of X and N, while consuming M, X and N. Using the notation from section 3 in this case we have:

$$(\hat{p}_N/\hat{\tau}) = (\tau/P_M)E_W\,\{\tau E_{p_M p_M} C_N + (1-\tau C_M)E_{p_M p_N}\}/\Delta', \tag{20}$$

where as before $\Delta' > 0$.

As in section 3, the analysis presented here can be extended easily in several directions. With full intersectoral factor mobility, the existence of factor price rigidities is likely to lead to specialization in the nontradables and one of the tradables, as Brecher (1974) has shown.[26] The case of quotas can also be analyzed using the 'virtual prices' trick. The consequences of opening the capital account will, to a large extent, depend on whether, as a consequence, specialization in N and X will result. It is interesting to note that in this case if, as it is the most plausible case, $\hat{p}_N/\hat{\tau}) > 0$, then $\hat{p}_N/\hat{p}_M^*$ can never be positive.

5. Concluding Remarks

In this paper the effects of tariff changes on the *equilibrium* real exchange rate have been analyzed in some detail. It was indicated that according to the traditional policy literature, in small countries, a tariff reduction will necessarily lead to an equilibrium real depreciation, and that a terms of trade improvement will provoke an equilibrium real appreciation. It was then shown that these propositions theoretically are not strictly correct. More specifically, it was shown that within the context of two simple general equilibrium models of a small open economy with no capital movements, the effects of terms of trade and tariff changes on 'the' equilibrium real exchange rate are ambiguous, and will depend on factors such as relative capital intensities among importables, exportables and nontradables; signs and magnitudes of cross-elasticities of demand and supply; and relative importance of income effects. (This was the case for all five definitions of RER considered.)

The discussion presented above has ignored the welfare effects of trade liberalization and has taken for granted that it is desirable for the LDCs to actually open their economies to the rest of the world. Although a complete analysis of this issue is well beyond the scope of this paper, it is important to discuss briefly a few issues. First, in all but one of the models presented here (the factor-specific model with wage rigidities), it is desirable to liberalize fully the economy, opening it up to commodity trade. Moreover, if the country in question is small, under these models the best option is to reduce tariffs to zero instantaneously. Of course, from an actual policy perspective this sounds both inapplicable and incorrect. The reason, of course, is that in most of the models discussed above there are no distortions or rigidities besides the initial tariffs. The exception is the factor-specific model with real wage rigidity in section 3.2. In fact that case the reduction of an import tariff will lead to unemployment, and *may* result in a welfare reduction of the complete operation. However, in order to add additional real-world features, more general intertemporal models with different types of rigidities should be built (Edwards and van Wijnberger, 1987).

This paper has shown that the analytics of the relation between commercial policies and the equilibrium real exchange rate are fairly simple. At the empirical level, however, we still don't know too much about the magnitudes of the coefficients involved. The lack of completely adequate data should by no means detract analysts from seriously attempting to understand the reaction of the RER to exogenous shocks. As Díaz-Alejandro (1986, p. 418) argued: '. . . policy makers groping for a real effective exchange rate compatible with a more open and stable economy would gain much from knowing how that variable relates at least to the expected terms of trade and to "normal" capital movement.'

APPENDIX A: STABILITY CONDITION IN THE NONTRADABLE MARKET

Dynamic adjustment in the nontradable market is given by:

$$\dot{p}_N = \sigma(E_{p_N} - R_{p_N}) \text{ for } \sigma > 0 \tag{A.1}$$

Stability requires that

$$\frac{\mathrm{d}\dot{p}_N}{\mathrm{d}p_N} < 0$$

Totally differentiating (A.1) we obtain:

$$\frac{\mathrm{d}\dot{p}_N}{\mathrm{d}p_N} = (E_{p_N p_N} - R_{p_N p_N}) + C_N E_W \frac{\mathrm{d}W}{\mathrm{d}p_N} \tag{A.2}$$

Using equation (3) in the text to eliminate dW we obtain:

$$E_W\{ (R_{p_N p_M} - E_{p_N p_M}) C_N \tau - (1 - \tau C_M)(E_{p_N p_N} - R_{p_N p_N}) \} > 0$$

This means that the determinant Δ in equation (7) is positive.

APPENDIX B: THE INTERTEMPORAL CASE

In this appendix a two-period version of the model developed in the paper is presented. As before, superscripts refer to periods (i.e., R^2 is the revenue function in period 2); subscripts refer to partial derivatives with respect to that variable (i.e., $R^1_{q^1}$ is the partial derivative of period 1's revenue function relative to q^1 (the price of nontradables in period 1); $R^2_{q^2p^2}$ is the second derivative of R^2 with respect to q^2 and p^2):

$$R^1(1,p^1,q^1;V) + \delta^* R^2(1,p^2,q^2;V) + \tau^1(E_{p^1} - R^1_{p^1}) + \delta^* \tau^2(E_{p^2} - R^2_{p^2}) =$$

$$E\{\pi^1(1,p^1,q^1), \delta^* \pi^2(1,p^2,q^2), W\} \qquad \text{(B.1)}$$

$$R^1_{q^1} = E_{q^2} \qquad \text{(B.2)}$$

$$R^2_{q^2} = E_{q^2} \qquad \text{(B.3)}$$

$$p^1 = p^{1*} + \tau^1 \qquad \text{(B.4)}$$

$$p^2 = p^{2*} + \tau^2 \qquad \text{(B.5)}$$

where the following notation is used (see Edwards and van Wijnbergen, 1986):

τ^i; $i = 1,2$	Specific tariffs in period i.
δ^*	World discount factor, equal to $(1+r^*)^{-1}$, where r^* is world real interest rates (in terms of tradables).
$E(\ .\ )$	Intertemporal expenditure function.
$\pi^i(1,p^i,q^i)$	Exact price indexes, which under assumptions of homotheticity and separability, correspond to unit expenditure functions.
W	Total aggregate welfare.

Equation (B.1) is the intertemporal budget constraint, and states that present value of income – generated through revenues from production R^1 $\delta^* R^2$, plus tariffs collection – has to equal present value of expenditure. Given the assumption of perfect access to the world capital market, the discount factor used in (B.1) is the world discount factor δ^*. Equations (B.2) and (B.3) are the equilibrium conditions for the nontradables market in periods 1 and 2; in each of these periods, the quantity supplied of N ($R^1_{q^1}$ and $R^2_{q^2}$) has to equal the quantity demanded. Given the assumptions about preferences (separability and homotheticity) the demand for N in period i can be written as:

$$E_{q^i} = E_{\pi^i} \pi^i_{q^i} \qquad \text{(B.6)}$$

Equations (B.4) and (B.5) specify the relation between domestic prices of imports, world prices of imports and tariffs.

The current account in period 1 is equal to the difference between income and total expenditure in that period:

$$CA^1 = R^1(\ ) + \tau^1(R_{p^1} - E_{q^1}) - E_{\pi^1}\pi^1 \tag{B.7}$$

From the inspection of equations (B.1)–(B.5) it is apparent that exogenous shocks in, say, the international terms of trade, will affect the vector of equilibrium RERs through two interrelated channels. The first one, which has been subject to some discussion in the literature, is related to *intratemporal* effects of terms of trade shocks on resource allocation and consumption decisions. For example, as a result of a temporary worsening of the terms of trade, there will be a tendency to produce more and consume less of M in that period. This, plus the income effect resulting from the worsening of the terms of trade will generate an incipient disequilibrium in the nontradables market which will have to be resolved by a change in the equilibrium q. In fact, if we assume that there is an absence of foreign borrowing, these intratemporal effects will be the only relevant ones. However, with capital mobility, as in the current model, there is a second intertemporal channel through which changes in exogenous variables will affect the vector of equilibrium RERs. For example, in the case of a temporary worsening of the terms of trade, the consumption discount factor $\pi^2\delta^*/\pi^1$ will be affected, altering the intertemporal allocation of consumption. In the rest of the paper we will emphasize the role of this intertemporal effect.

NOTES

A previous version of this paper was presented at the Carlos Díaz-Alejandro Memorial Conference, Helsinki, 23–25 August 1986. I have benefitted from comments by Gus Ranis and Louka Katseli. The research was partially financed by the National Science Foundation (Grant SES 84 19932).

1 See for example Díaz-Alejandro (1970).
2 On contractionary devaluations see, for example, Katseli (1983) and Edwards (1986a).
3 See, for example, Díaz-Alejandro (1986).
4 Of course, there have been some exceptions. See for example, Krueger (1978) and Harberger (1986).
5 It should be noted that Bacha and Taylor (1971) and Taylor (1979) are using slightly different models. See the original references for details.
6 On modern criticisms of the concept of effective rate protection see, for example, Bhagwati and Srinivasan (1983), Jones and Neary (1984), and Corden (1984).
7 A notable exception is Corden (1971, ch. 5). See also Dornbusch (1974).
8 See Edwards (1988) for a discussion on real exchange rate measurement problems.
9 For simplicity we are ignoring issues related to multilateral exchange rates. See, however, Edwards (1988).
10 A common confusion that sometimes appears in the literature is to use the concepts of the real exchange rate and the terms of trade interchangeably. Of course, since the terms of trade are defined as the relative price of exportables to importables, and the real exchange rate is usually defined as the relative price of tradables to nontradables, there is no reason for them to be equivalent. In fact, there are circumstances where these two variables will tend to move in the opposite direction. Williamson (1983) has recently stressed the importance of distinguishing between the terms of trade and the real exchange rate. Also Katseli (1984) has recently shown, using a cross-country data set, that these two variables have tended to behave quite differently in recent years.
11 See, for example Krueger (1978).
12 Recently, Harberger (1986) has proposed yet another definition for the real exchange rate: $e_H = E/P_G$, where as before E is the nominal exchange rate, and P_G is a 'general' domestic price level. In this case e_H is the relative price of the domestic basket in terms of a unit of foreign currency. In terms of the discussion in this paper, e_H is equivalent to e. For this reason we will not deal specifically with e_H.
13 For the purpose of the present paper a general definition that can be applied to any of the competing concepts of real exchange rate is provided. The equilibrium real exchange rate is defined as that relative price which simultaneously equilibrates the external and internal sectors for given long-term equilibrium values of other key variables such as international terms of trade, capital inflows and commercial policies. These other variables are usually called the 'fundamental' determinants of the equilibrium real exchange rate. 'Internal equilibrium' implies that there is full employment. For discussions see, for example, Williamson (1983), Katseli (1984) and Edwards (1988).
14 The existence of more factors than goods assures that R is twice differentiable.
15 Since in this model there is no foreign borrowing, the equilibrium RER is defined

in temporal terms. In models with foreign borrowing and lending the equilibrium RER is defined in intertemporal terms. For this type of intertemporal model see, for example, Edwards (1987b) and the section on extensions below.

16 In this model it is assumed that the actual RER is always at its equilibrium level. In that sense, there is no RER misalignment. On equilibrium and disequilibrium RERs see, however, Edwards (1987a).

17 Of course the possibility of complementarity between any two goods arises because we have a three-goods model.

18 See Neary (1985). See also ch. 8 of Dixit and Norman (1980). Notice that in the analysis that follows it is assumed throughout that all three goods are produced. This is possible, thanks to the assumption that the Stolper–Samuelson theorem does not hold. See section 4 for further discussions on the subject.

19 An important point is whether real wages are actually fixed, or if they are only inflexible downwards.

20 Edwards (1984) used transfers to analyze the behavior of the real exchange rate following a liberalization of the capital account.

21 On the Southern Cone also see Díaz-Alejandro (1981), Edwards (1985), Corbo (1985), Hanson and de Melo (1985) and Calvo (1986).

22 The main difference will be that under that framework the funds obtained from abroad will also be used to increase the capital stock.

23 The long run will be given by the case with capital accumulation and population growth.

24 An important question that crucially impinges on the nature of the results that follow is whether it is reasonable to assume nonspecialization. Jones (1974) discusses the case of many commodities (one of them nontradable) and two factors and shows that the production possibilities frontier will be flat. Changes in world price of importables and exportables or in tariffs, however, will shift the position of the production possibilities frontier. The case I focus on here corresponds to that depicted in fig. 9 of Jones' (1974) paper, where over a reasonable range the two tradables and the nontradable are produced. This, of course, requires that the aggregate capital–labor ratio *net* of capital and labor employed in the *NT* sector falls between the capital–labor ratios in each traded sector that guarantees zero profits at positive activity levels for given world traded goods prices. Since these latter two ratios will in general be different, the set of equilibria characterized by incomplete specialization has positive measure. In section 4.2 I discuss the case of specialization in nontradables and one of the tradables.

25 It is assumed that there are no capital-intensity reversals and that the capital intensities in value terms correspond to those in physical terms.

26 Notice, however, that starting from nonspecialization, rigid real wages will generate no additional problems. The reason, of course, is that under our assumptions of relative capital intensities the tariff removal will result in an *increase* in the real wage.

REFERENCES

Bacha, E. and Taylor, L. 1971: Foreign exchange shadow prices: a critical review of the current theories. *Quarterly Journal of Economics*, 85, 197–224.

Balassa, B. 1982: Reforming the system of incentives in developing economies. In B.

Balassa (ed.), *Development Strategies in Semi-Industrial Economies*, Oxford: Oxford University Press.

Bhagwati, S. and Srinivasan, T.N. 1983: *Lectures in International Trade*. Cambridge, MA: MIT Press.

Brecher, R. 1974: Minimum wages and the pure theory of international trade. *Quarterly Journal of Economics*, 88, 98–116.

Calvo, G. 1986: Fractured liberalism. *Economic Development and Cultural Change*.

Corbo, V. 1985: Chilean economic policy and international economic relations since 1970. In G.M. Walton (ed.), *The National Economic Policies of Chile*, Greenwich CT: JAI Press.

Corden, W.M. 1971: *The Theory of Protection*, Oxford: Oxford University Press.

Corden, W.M. 1984: The normative theory of international trade. In P. Kenen and R. Jones (eds.), *Handbook of International Economics*, vol. I, Amsterdam: North-Holland.

Corden, W.M. and Neary, J.P. 1982: Booming sector and de-industrialization in a small open economy. *Economic Journal*, 825–48.

Díaz-Alejandro, C.F. 1970: *Essays on the Economic History of the Argentine Republic*. New Haven, Connecticut: Yale University Press.

Díaz-Alejandro, C.F. 1981a Southern Cone stabilization plans. In W.R. Cline and S. Weintraub (eds.), *Economic Stabilization in Developing Countries*, Washington DC: Brookings.

Díaz-Alejandro, C.F. 1981b: Latin America in depression, 1929–39. In M. Gersovitz et. al. (eds.), *The Theory and Experience of Economic Development*, New York: Allen & Unwin.

Díaz-Alejandro, C.F. 1984a: Exchange rates and terms of trade in the Argentine Republic: 1913–76. In M. Sryquin and S. Teitel (eds.), *Trade, Stability, Technology and Equity in Latin America*, New York: Academic Press.

Díaz-Alejandro, C.F. 1984b: No less than 100 years of Argentine economic history. In G. Ranis et al. (eds), *Comparative Development Perspectives: Essays in Honor of Llyod G. Reynolds*, Boulder, Colorado: Westview.

Díaz-Alejandro, C.F. 1984c: Latin American debt: I Don't Think We are in Kansas Any More. *Brookings Papers on Economic Activity*, 2, 335–89.

Díaz-Alejandro, C.F. 1986: Comment on Harberger, In S. Edwards and L. Ahamed (eds), *Economic Adjustment and Exchange Rate in Developing Countries*, Chicago: University of Chicago Press.

Dixit, A. and Norman, V. 1980: *Theory of International Trade*, Cambridge: Cambridge University Press.

Dornbusch, R. 1974: Tariffs and nontraded goods. *Journal of International Economics*, May 4,: 117–85.

Dornbusch, R. 1980: *Open Economy Macroeconomics*, New York: Basic Books.

Edwards, S. 1984: The order of liberalization of the external sector. *Princeton Essays on International Finance*, N156.

Edwards, S. 1985: Stabilization and liberalization: an evaluation of the years of Chile's experiment with free-market policies, 1973–1983. *Economic Development and Cultural Change*, January, 33, 223–54.

Edwards, S. 1986a: The order of liberalization of the current and capital accounts of the balance of payments. In A. Choksi and D. Papageorgiou (eds.), *Economic Liberalization in Developing Countries*, Oxford: Blackwell.

Edwards, S. 1986b: The liberalization of the current and capital accounts and the real exchange rate. Paper presented at American Economic Association Meetings.

Edwards, S. 1987a: Exchange rate misalignment in developing countries. CPD Working Paper, The World Bank, Washington.

Edwards, S. 1987b: Tariffs, terms of trade and real exchange rate in an intertemporal model of the current account. NBER Working Paper.

Edwards, S. 1988: Exchange Rates in Developing Countries. Cambridge, MA: MIT Press.

Edwards, S. and Cox Edwards, A. 1987: *Monetarism and Liberalization: The Chilean Experiment*, Cambridge, MA: Ballinger.

Edwards, S. and van Wijnbergen, S. 1986: The welfare effects of trade and capital market liberalization. *International Economic Review*, Feb. 27, no. 1, 141–8.

Edwards, S. and van Wijnbergen, S. 1987: Tariffs, real exchange rates and the terms of trade: on two popular propositions in international economics. *Oxford Economic Papers*, (forthcoming).

Frenkel, J.A. and Mussa, M. 1984: Asset markets, exchange rates and the balance of payments: a reformulation of doctrine. In R.J. Jones and P. Kenan (eds.), *Handbook of International Economics*, Amsterdam: North-Holland.

Hanson, J. and de Melo, J. 1985: External shocks, financial reform and liberalization attempts in Uruguay. *World Development*.

Harberger, A. 1986: Economic adjustment and the real exchange rate. In S. Edwards and L. Ahamed (eds.), *Economic Adjustment and Exchange Rates in Developing Countries*, Chicago: University of Chicago Press.

Johnson, H.G. 1966: A model of protection and the exchange rate. *Review of Economic Studies*, 33, 159–63.

Jones, R.W. 1965: The structure of simple general equilibrium models, *Journal of Political economy*, 73, 557–72.

Jones, R.W. 1974: Trade with many commodities. *Australian Economic Papers*. 13, 225–36.

Jones, R.W. and Neary, J.P. 1984: The positive theory of international trade. In R. Jones and P. Kenen (eds.), *Handbook of International Economics*, Amsterdam: North-Holland.

Katseli, L. 1983: Devaluation: a critical appraisal of the IMF's policy prescriptions. *American Economic Review*, May. 73, no. 2, 359–63.

Katseli, L. 1984: Real exchange rates in the 1970s. In J. Bilson and R. Marston (eds.), *Exchange Rates in Theory and Practice*, Chicago: University of Chicago Press.

Krueger, A.O. 1978: *Foreign Trade Regimes and Economic Development: Liberalization Attempts and Consequences*. Cambridge, MA: Ballinger.

Krueger, A.O. 1983: *Trade and Employment in Developing Countries*, Chicago: University of Chicago Press.

Mussa, M.L. 1974: Tariffs and the distribution of income: the importance of factor specificity. *Journal of Political Economy*, 82, 1191–204.

Neary, P. 1985: International factor mobility, minimum-wage rates, and factor price equalization: a synthesis. *Quarterly Journal of Economics*, 100, no. 3, 551–70.

Neary, J.P. and Roberts, K. 1980: The theory of household behavior under rationing. *European Economic Review*. 13, 25–42.

Taylor, L. 1979: *Macro Models for Developing Countries*, New York: McGraw-Hill.

van Wijnbergen, S. 1984: The Dutch disease: a disease after all? *Economic Journal*, 94, 41–55.

Williamsom, J. 1983: *The Exchange Rate System*. Washington DC: Institute for International Economics.

COMMENT 1

Louka T. Katseli

This session deals with the interaction between trade policy and the real exchange rate. Carlos Díaz-Alejandro in fact pointed out that it is possible to learn a great deal about a country's economic history from inspecting the behavior of its real exchange rate. The real exchange rate is perhaps the most important relative price in a small, open economy.

As a number of studies have shown, the behavior of the real exchange rate is dependent on a number of interdependent factors:

1 structural characteristics, i.e. the flexibility of the economy to external shocks captured by the elasticity of supply and demand;
2 policy, especially exchange rate and incomes policy not to speak of macro policy;
3 the degree of interaction between the real and the financial side of the economy, for example the interaction between the trade and capital account in the balance of payments;
4 expectations regarding future developments which affect behavior in financial markets but also pricing decisions; and finally
5 institutional factors regarding price formation, the workings of the financial system etc.

Thus it is not surprising that there is still a gap between our simple theoretical models and empirical work. Given the state of the art, it is hard in the context of partial or general equilibrium models to produce very meaningful testable propositions that are founded in theory but then can be used to understand economic developments. As a result, in our empirical work we often introduce a number of extraneous parameters or appeal selectively to one of the factors above, institutional or structural, to help us 'explain' developments.

The wiser among us resort then to history and through the study of specific societies and the study of structural change proceed inductively rather than deductively first to ask specific questions, then to search for and use the appropriate methodology, to analyze data and thus proceed to further our understanding of economic behavior. But this approach is not only extremely time-consuming; it requires above all knowledge that transcends the boundaries of economics, the ability to go from the specific to the general both selectively and effectively and the intellectual modesty to accept the limitations of one's theorizing and to admire the richness and variety of human manifestations. These, in my view, were distinguishing characteristics of Carlos Díaz-Alejandro. And it is not coincidental that during all his professional life he struggled successfully to reach a balance between the specific and the general, the concrete and the abstract, the historical and the mathematical, always questioning the fundamentals and exploring their repercussions. He merged, as few others did, the study of history with economics; as a history professor of mine used to say, 'big things happen when two sciences meet.'

Sebastian Edwards in his paper gives us a hint of the complexity of the issues involved with regard to real exchange rate behavior. He provides a useful and concise presentation of the effects of a one-shot tariff reduction on the equilibrium real exchange rate in models with fixed and/or mobile factors of production. It is particularly useful in that it distinguishes ambiguities regarding the effect on the real exchange rate that have to do with the definition of the real exchange rate as opposed to ambiguities that concern the relative magnitude of the income vs substitution effects in the Ricardo–Viner model or the capital-intensity ranking of nontradables in the fully mobile factor model. It is also useful in that it presents a typical model of a small open economy that can easily be extended to cover different exogenous disturbances beyond a tariff reduction. The author himself uses it to analyze the effects of a reduction in quotas, changes in the price of intermediate inputs or importable final goods as well as of a positive transfer, identical here with capital-account liberalization. Wage rigidity has also been introduced.

It could also be used, and this has actually been done elsewhere, to analyze the effects of a nominal devaluation on the real exchange rate or the effects of emigrant remittances in developing countries, again a positive transfer into the economy. Exactly because of the simplicity and the flexibility in specification that this type of modelling allows, it has been used by many authors in the past especially in the development literature and more recently in the international finance literature. Harberger, for example, in his 1964 article on inflation uses a similar specification to look at the effects of exchange rate devaluation on the price of home goods. Of course, in the absence of a real wealth effect or a tariff, in his work there is no income effect as such but only substitution effects.

As the literature expanded, most of the ambiguities in the sign of derivatives have been noted and discussed in one context or the other. For example, the ambiguity regarding the relative size of income vs substitution effects in this paper is equivalent to that regarding the relative size of the real wealth effect in models with money, such as Connolly and Taylor's 1976 article on 'Adjustment to Devaluation with Money and Non-traded Goods.' Similarly, the role of relative capital intensities in the determination of the real exchange rate has been dealt with in the context of the Scandinavian model and more recently in Corden and Jones' 1976 article on 'Devaluation, Non-flexible Prices and the Trade Balance for a Small Country.'

Given that we have virtually exhausted the potential results derived from this type of modelling, it might be interesting to step aside and ask some broader questions regarding the effects of trade liberalization on the real exchange rate.

The author already presents some interesting insights from earlier work of his where he analyzes the effects on relative prices of expected changes in tariffs in a two-period model with and without access to foreign borrowing. This in my view is a more promising route. Liberalization after all, is a process that could involve either a gradual adjustment over time that is fully expected (such as entrance to the European Community by Southern European countries), or, as in a few cases, an unexpected change in relative prices. Expectations will influence the behavior of agents both with regard to their behavior in financial markets (official or unofficial) but also with regard to pricing decisions in both commodity and factor markets.

Initial conditions also would seem to play an important role. If tariff reduction takes place in the context of an IMF-type program, it is highly likely that the balance of payments is in deficit, that foreign borrowing is restricted and that there are entrenched expectations of a future devaluation even if the devaluation has not already taken place. Liberalization in that case might result in hoarding of importables, an increase in the price of nontradables and the outflow of financial capital, not to speak of unemployment in the import-competing sector. The key once again is expectations. If on top of this the fiscal system is not adequately developed, the repercussions of tariff reductions on the budget deficit have to be taken into account. Finally, the ability of the financial system to ease the burden of adjustment of import-competing firms is an important factor which is usually underestimated.

The possibility of perverse effects is lessened if trade liberalization is seen as part of a medium-term development program that aims at the restructuring of the productive base of the economy and in that context aims at gradually redressing relative price distortions.

In that light, it will be extremely informative to look at actual country experiences and develop potentially a typology of behavior based on a consistent analytical framework that would however take into account differences in structural characteristics, initial conditions and policy outcomes.

Here, however, we come back to the point raised earlier about the need to look analytically at economic history, something which Carlos knew how to do. It is now for some of us to continue his efforts.

COMMENT 2

Gustav Ranis

This is an interesting, well-crafted and meaty paper, both in its theoretical and empirical sections. It is justifiably critical and endeavors to correct some of the imprecision in the existing literature focused on linking import liberalization and the exchange rate. Nevertheless, given the restricted capacity of the general equilibrium model it deploys, it cannot keep its promise of shedding additional light on some recent real-world LDC experience. In other words, Edwards quite appropriately appeals to the two main themes of Carlos Díaz-Alejandro's life and work, i.e. the relationship between trade and growth, and the specific role of the exchange rate in that context. But through no fault of his, the paper represents an unfinished symphony; it has very little to say about the relationship between trade and growth, and it can only give a very restrictive explication of the role of the exchange rate in relation to trade.

Let me be more specific. After pointing to the confusion surrounding the literature which cavalierly uses different definitions of the real exchange rate Edwards turns to modeling the effects of liberalization on the equilibrium exchange rate, using five alternative definitions of the real exchange rate. It is important to note that his most 'long-term' model extends only to permitting capital to move between the three sectors, exportables, importables and nontradables, with the possibility of opening to the world capital market only referred to briefly. My problem, therefore, is not with the model as such, but with the fact that, while painting on a very restricted canvas, Edwards claims too much. He seems to forget that he is dealing with the impact of tariff liberalization on the equilibrium exchange rate, in implicit disregard of the fact that there are many other things going on which affect the equilibrium exchange rate, e.g., monetary policy, wage policy, fiscal policy, reserve policy, exchange controls, just to cite a few. Thus, if one really wants to deal with the notion of an equilibrium exchange rate in the context of growth, the existence of so much else needs to be made explicit, even if it can't all be dealt with at once. As Edwards himself points out, depending on the initial conditions, the equilibrium exchange rate and the real exchange rate don't necessarily move together.

Secondly, and perhaps more serious, even if we accept the equivalence of the initial equilibrium exchange rate with the effective rate, it is clearly treated as a spot concept in this paper, tied very much to the short-term balance of trade equilibrium, not really very useful in a dynamic or growth-related context. More on this later. The overall problem is not with what Edwards does, but with what he claims to be doing, i.e., relating import liberalization to growth and potentially illuminating actual growth experience in the Southern Cone with the help of the model.

It is indeed very useful to be reminded that there are these different real exchange rate definitions in the literature and that some may go up and others down as a consequence of import liberalization, and that indeed we have to be more careful. But the basic point, I think, is that the exchange rate is not an end in itself and that different definitions are probably used for different political and policy-relevant purposes. Carlos Díaz-Alejandro himself often referred to the 'appropriate' exchange rate. He clearly had an economic performance 'bottom line' in mind. Possibly a better way of thinking about the problem is to view the real exchange rate as a 'target' relative to some set of intertemporal objectives and constraints, i.e., in terms of the policy variables which can be adjusted over time, partly in response to such excessive shocks as the terms of trade, and in terms of such policy adjustments as import liberalization, both dealt with specifically in this paper. A good demonstration of this paper's weakness is that even when Edwards allows for capital inflows in the brief extension to his basic model, he views this as an appreciation of the equilibrium exchange rate. But this clearly should not hold in the case of a developing country where some level of long-term capital inflows must surely be viewed as normal – quite aside from the role of the short-term speculative movements which he undoubtedly had in mind.

A weakness with his general equilibrium concept for policy purposes shows up in Edwards' discussion of terms of trade shocks. For example, why shouldn't an increase in the current account surplus due to favorable terms of trade lead – at least in part – to an increase in reserves instead of to an appreciation of the real exchange rate? If we had completely instantaneous market clearance and full price–wage flexibility – as Max Corden has pointed out – government policy could have a real effect only if there is asymmetric information available to different parties.

It is clear that all systems experience some policy oscillation, but some, for example the East Asian cases, have oscillation superimposed on a long-term (if gradual) liberalization trend, while those in Latin America experience oscillation in the absence of a clear trend. To understand this real-world phenomenon, which is basically Edwards' objective, one needs at least three ingredients missing in this paper: a more dynamic perspective reaching beyond the static general equilibrium tools deployed here; a broader view than the binary relationship between import liberalization and the exchange rate; and finally, if at all possible, an effort to endogenize the policy changes themselves within a political economy context. Even two out of three is a tall order, and more than one has a right to expect from the simple model which is presented here in a highly workman like fashion. Perhaps the only thing the author should really be held accountable for is not explicitly recognizing the limitations of his model.

9

Smuggler's Blues at the Central Bank: Lessons from Sudan

William H. Branson and Jorge Braga de Macedo

1. Introduction: Real Devaluation and the Trade Balance

The usual analysis of the effects of real devaluation on trade flows assumes a high degree of substitutability among final goods in consumption and among uses of inputs in production. Thus the typical analysis assumes that all goods are final goods with domestic production of import-competing goods and domestic consumption of exportables. A real devaluation, by reducing the relative price of domestic output, encourages substitution from imports to home goods in consumption, and from production for the home market to production for export. This high degree of substitutability is usually reflected in an assumption that import demand and export supply both have high elasticities with respect to the real exchange rate. The result is a presumption that real devaluation will improve the trade balance.

The structure of trade in some developing countries, especially in sub-Saharan Africa, suggests a different analysis and result, however. This was previously argued by Branson (1986) in the case of Kenya, and is also applicable in Sudan. These countries have as a high proportion of their imports, intermediate inputs (such as oil) and capital equipment. These are inputs into a production structure that is to some degree rigidified by the existing capital stock, reducing the short-run price elasticity of demand for imports. These countries' exports are dominated by agricultural output whose supply is inelastic in the short run.

With inelastic import demand and export supply, a real devaluation will tend to expand export revenues and import receipts in proportion to their initial values in home currency, while leaving them unchanged in foreign exchange. If the trade balance is initially in deficit, the real devaluation may increase the deficit in home currency, deflating domestic demand, with little gain in foreign exchange. This makes real devaluation potentially counter-productive as part of a stabilization program.

This ineffectiveness of real devaluation as stabilization policy does not imply that the nominal exchange rate should be held constant in the face of a domestic inflation, however. In this circumstance, import duties and export subsidies would have to be escalated to counter the potential erosion of the trade balance. This escalation of trade barriers generates a rising black market premium and offers increasing incentives to smuggling, already a pervasive problem in the African countries. As a consequence, the central bank would find it more and more difficult to hold the nominal exchange rate constant. This leads us to consider a *passive* exchange rate policy of stabilizing the *real* exchange rate by moving the nominal rate in line with domestic inflation.

If such passive policy is not accompanied by the elimination of trade barriers, however, the black market premium will not disappear. Unless exchange rate policy and trade policy are consistent with each other, the smuggler's blues will reach the central bank. Indeed, this is the major lesson to be learnt from the recent experience of Sudan, as shown in section 6 below.

Section 2 presents a basic model of the trade balance, to show the consequences of rigidity in import demand and export supply. We note as a by-product that wage indexation can introduce a rigidity that replicates the results with inelastic export supply and import demand.

Sections 3 and 4 of the paper analyze the interaction of trade barriers, smuggling and the black market premium. We first introduce domestic inflation and trade barriers to show the necessary escalation of the latter to maintain the trade balance with a fixed nominal exchange rate. We then show the effect of smuggling on legal as well as total trade, and relate the rate of increase in the black market premium to the rate of escalation of trade barriers. With a passive exchange rate policy and a constant level of trade barriers, the black market premium will be constant. We finally introduce capital account considerations, showing how they exacerbate the rise in the premium if the unreported trade balance is in surplus, and conversely. Section 5 shows how the goal of real exchange rate stability may be attained.

2. Devaluation in the 'Rigid' Economy

In this section we lay out a simple model of export and import supply and demand that illustrates the problems of the 'rigid' economy. The model is essentially the same as the one sketched in Branson (1972) and developed in Branson and Katseli (1982). The duality with wage indexation can also be demonstrated easily in this framework.

Export supply and demand can be described by the following two log-linear equations, normalized on the home currency price of exports p_x for supply and the foreign exchange price q_x for demand.

$$\text{Supply:} \quad \ln p_x = \ln p_n + s_x^{-1} \ln X^s \tag{1}$$

$$\text{Demand:} \quad \ln q_x = \ln q - d_x^{-1} \ln X^d \tag{2}$$

Here X is the quantity of exports, p_n is the cost of production of home goods and q is the cost of foreign substitutes for our exports. We can interpret p_n as the opportunity cost of exports in the home economy; later we will identify the rate of growth of p_n as the domestic inflation rate. Foreign inflation would be interpreted as growth in q. Stating export supply in terms of the home currency price reflects the assumption that costs of producing exports are given in home currency. Stating demand in terms of the foreign exchange price reflects the assumption that exports compete with foreign goods in demand.

Supply and demand in the export market are brought together by the exchange rate as 'translator' between p_x and q_x:

$$\text{Translator:} \quad \ln p_x = \ln e + \ln q_x \tag{3}$$

The exchange rate is stated in terms of units of home currency per unit of foreign exchange: an increase in e is a devaluation of the home currency.

The export supply and demand model of equations (1) – (3) can be used to track movements of export price and quantity as functions of the domestic inflation rate $\hat{p}_n$, the foreign inflation rate $\hat{q}$ and changes in nominal exchange rate $\hat{e}$. Total differentiation of equations (1) – (3) gives the solutions for $\hat{p}_x$ and $\hat{X}$:

$$\hat{p}_x = k(\hat{e} + \hat{q}) + (1-k)\hat{p}_n \tag{4}$$

$$\hat{X} = ks_x(\hat{e} + \hat{q} - \hat{p}_n) \tag{5}$$

Here the parameter $k \equiv d_x/(d_x + s_x) > 0$. The movement in the home currency price of exports is a weighted average of foreign influences $(\hat{e} + \hat{q})$ and home influences $\hat{p}_n$. The relative price of exports in terms of home goods p_x/p_n is proportional to the real exchange rate $E = eq/p_n$, and the same is true of the quantity of exports. If the economy is 'small' in the export market, $d_x \to \infty$ and $k \to 1$ also, so that there are no home influences on relative prices and $\hat{X} = s_x\hat{E}$.

If we impose the 'rigid' economy assumption that $s_x = 0$, export revenue is fixed in foreign exchange. In home currency, export revenue moves proportionately to the change in e, with p_n and q constant:

$$\hat{p}_x + \hat{X} = \hat{e} \tag{6}$$

The duality result with domestic wage indexation can be obtained by assuming that $\hat{p}_n = \hat{e} + \hat{q}$ with devaluation. This would be the result if nontraded goods prices were a mark-up over wages, and wages are indexed to the CPI. See Branson (1985) for the derivation. With $\hat{p}_n = \hat{e} + \hat{q}$ from equations (4) and (5) we obtain again the result in equation (6). This is the duality between wage indexation as commonly practiced in Western Europe and the rigidity of $s_x = 0$, which may be more relevant in Africa.

We can re-interpret the duality result in a scenario of an ongoing domestic inflation with $\hat{p}_n =$ the rate of growth of domestic money. If the economy is rigid, there is no fall in export quantity. However, the profit squeeze that follows from the fall in p_x/p_n indicates that in the long run resources will exit the export-producing sector.

The 'passive' exchange rate policy sets $\hat{e} = \hat{p}_n$ = the money growth rate, with $\hat{q}$ assumed to be zero. This holds the quantity X constant with $\hat{e} = \hat{p}_n$ in equation (5). The home currency price of exports p_x rises at the same rate as p_n; from equation (4) with $k = 1$, $\hat{p}_x = \hat{e} = \hat{p}_n$. This holds p_x/p_n constant, preventing the profit squeeze in the export sector. The result is that the passive exchange rate policy with $\hat{e} = \hat{p}_n$ 'insulates' the exportable sector from the domestic inflation.

The analysis for imports follows by analogy, except that the relevant rigidity is on the demand side. Import demand and supply are given by:

$$\text{Demand:} \quad \ln p_m = \ln p_n - d_m^{-1} \ln M^d \tag{7}$$

$$\text{Supply:} \quad \ln q_m = \ln q + s_m^{-1} \ln M^s \tag{8}$$

Here p_n represents competition from import-competing home goods, and q represents foreign costs of production of imports. The small-country assumption sets $s_m = \propto$, whereas, in the 'rigid' economy, $d_m = 0$. The translator between p_m and q_m gives us the third equation,

$$\text{Translator:} \quad \ln p_m = \ln e + \ln q_m \tag{9}$$

The solutions for changes in import price and quantity $\hat{p}_m$ and $\hat{M}$ are obtained from total differentiation of equations (7) – (9). They are:

$$\hat{p}_m = k'(\hat{e} + \hat{q}) + (1 - k')\hat{p}_n \tag{10}$$

$$\hat{M} = -k'd_m(\hat{e} + \hat{q} - \hat{p}_n) \tag{11}$$

Here $k' \equiv s_m/(s_m + d_m)$. The formal analogy to the export solutions is obvious. In the small country, $k' \rightarrow 1$ as $s_m \rightarrow \propto$. In the 'rigid' economy, $d_m = 0$ and $k' = 1$ also. Thus the rise in import payments is equal to the devaluation.

The duality result can be obtained by again imposing $\hat{p}_n = \hat{e}$ and $\hat{q} = 0$ in equations (10) and (11). As in the export case, this result can be reinterpreted to study the effects of a passive exchange rate policy in the face of domestic inflation. With an infinitely elastic supply of imports, the rise in domestic costs relative to import prices, p_n/p_m, squeezes profits in the import-competing sectors. If the economy is 'rigid,' there is no increase in the quantity of imports in the short run. But the profit squeeze in the import-competing sector, to the extent it exists, would augur a longer run rise in imports.

A passive policy that sets $\hat{e} = \hat{p}_n$ releases this pressure. The home currency import price p_m rises at the same rate as p_n; from equation (10) with $k' = 1$, $\hat{p}_m = \hat{e} = \hat{p}_n$. This holds p_m/p_n constant, eliminating the profit squeeze in the import-competing industries, actual or potential.

Combining the equations for import payments and for export receipts, both in terms of home currency, we see that in the 'rigid' economy they increase in proportion to the change in the exchange rate. This means that the increase in import payments exceeds that in export receipts if the trade balance showed a deficit at the time of devaluation. So in the 'rigid' economy, real devaluation may be counterproductive. However, the passive policy would hold a balanced trade position in the face of a domestic inflation, with the quantities of exports and imports constant:

$$\hat{p}_x + \hat{X} = \hat{p}_m + \hat{M} = \hat{e} = \hat{p}_n \tag{12}$$

devaluation in the 'rigid' economy. Here, there is no movement in the foreign exchange trade balance, regardless of the initial condition: the passive policy insulates the trade balance from the domestic inflation. This may be about the best we can expect exchange rate policy to do in a 'rigid' economy.

3. Fixed Exchange Rates and Trade Barriers

An alternative to the passive policy of moving the exchange rate with domestic inflation is to hold the nominal exchange rate constant and use escalating trade barriers to offset the effect on trade quantities. The basic idea is that rising import duties and export subsidies could offset the effects on resource allocation from the increasing divergence between nontraded goods prices and export and import prices.

The model of export supply and demand is modified by introduction of a subsidy on top of the export price received by the seller. We illustrate the case with ad valorem subsidy at rate s that multiplies the export price p_x by a subsidy factor $\sigma = 1 + s$. Thus the price actually received by exporters is σp_x, and export supply becomes:

$$\ln p_x + \ln \sigma = \ln p_n + s_x^{-1} \ln X^s \tag{13}$$

Equilibrium in the export market is shown in figure 9.1. The demand curve is equation (2) of section 2 in non-log, or exponential, form. The underlying supply curve, the one without a σ term, is equation (1). The subsidy factor σ shifts this supply curve down to give the equilibrium intersection at E_0. This shows a higher export volume and a combination of a lower price paid by the buyer abroad and a higher price inclusive of the subsidy received by the home producer than at the unsubsidized equilibrium E_0'. The figure shows that if p_n, the domestic price, is rising due to domestic inflation and if the nominal exchange rate e is constant, the export subsidy factor σ must rise at the same rate to hold the quantity X_0 constant.

This result implies an increasing rate of growth of the actual subsidy rate, since $\hat{\sigma} = \dot{s}/(1 + s)$, where $\dot{s}$ is the increase in the subsidy rate. The need for an increasing subsidy rate to provide a constant rate of growth of the subsidy factor can be seen from a simple example. If initially $s = 0$, imposition of a 10 per cent subsidy will yield an increase of 10 per cent in σ. But if the subsidy rate is 50 per cent, so $\sigma = 1.5$, to increase σ by 10 per cent, s will have to increase from 0.50 to 0.65, or 30 per cent.

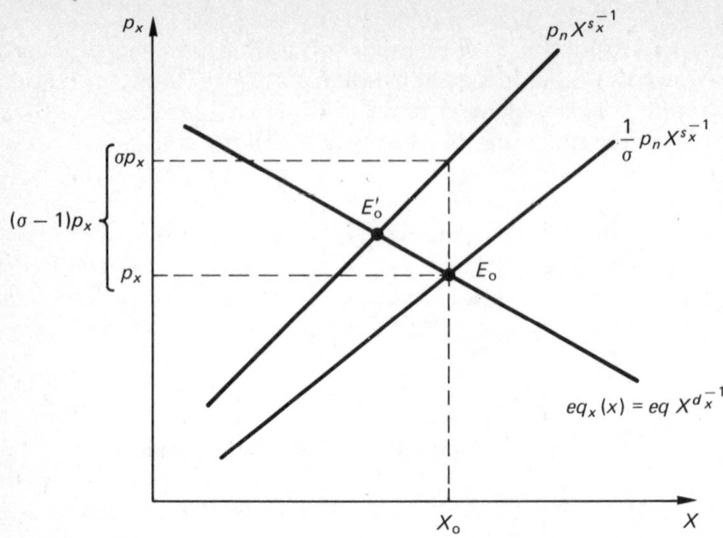

Figure 9.1 Export subsidy

The equilibrium between export demand and subsidized supply in equations (13), (2) and (3), and in figure 9.1, is expressed in equations (14) and (15) for changes in export quantity and market price net of subsidy:

$$\hat{p}_x = k(\hat{e} + \hat{q}) + (1 - k)\,(\hat{p}_n - \hat{\sigma}) \tag{14}$$

$$\hat{X} = ks_x\,\{(\hat{e} + \hat{q}) - (\hat{p}_n - \hat{\sigma})\} \tag{15}$$

The subsidy factor σ enters both solutions in tandem with the domestic price index p_n. If an inflation driven by domestic money growth or other domestic factors is increasing the domestic price index p_n, and policy keeps the nominal exchange rate e constant, then a growth rate of the export subsidy factor σ that equals the rate of inflation $\hat{p}_n$ would be needed to hold the quantity of exports X constant.

Thus in an environment of domestic inflation with rapid monetary growth, a policy of fixing the *nominal* exchange rate would destabilize the *real* exchange rate E; in particular, if p_n grows rapidly, an attempt to fix the nominal rate would yield a real appreciation of the exchange rate and shrinking exports. As we see below, this has been the policy response in Sudan – stabilizing the nominal rate against movements in the real rate.

A regime that attempts to eliminate the effects of stabilizing the nominal rate in the face of a major appreciation of the real rate requires, from equations (14) and (15), a rate of increase of the export subsidy factor equal to the domestic inflation. The subsidy factor σ would have to rise at the domestic inflation rate $\hat{p}_n$ to hold $X = X_0$ in figure 9.1. The subsidy rate itself would have to grow at an increasing rate to provide $\hat{\sigma} = \hat{p}_n$. This would, of course, create an ever-increasing incentive to false-invoice sales as exports to obtain the subsidy. This is part of the problem we see in developing countries attempting to hold nominal exchange rates in the face of domestic inflation. The policy increases incentives to move transactions to the illegal sector.

The movement in an import tariff needed to hold the quantity of imports constant in the face of a domestic inflation with a fixed nominal exchange rate can be shown by analogy to the export subsidy model. With an import tariff, import demand becomes:

$$\ln p_m + \ln \tau = \ln p_n - d_m^{-1} \ln M^d \qquad (16)$$

The demand curve gives the total price in home currency that importers pay, inclusive of the tariff factor $\tau = 1 + t$. In equation (16), p_m is the home currency price the sellers of imports receive, t is the ad valorem tariff rate added by the government and τp_m is the price paid by the domestic purchaser.

The equilibrium in the import market with the import tariff factor τ is shown in figure 9.2. The supply curve is equation (8) in section 2 in exponential, or non-log, form. The non-tariff demand curve without a τ term is the demand curve of equation (7). These would yield the non-tariff equilibrium E_0'. The tariff factor τ shifts the demand curve inclusive of the tariff down, giving the tariff-inclusive equilibrium at E_0. This shows a lower import quantity M_0 than without the tariff, with a lower price received by the seller p_m and a higher price paid by the domestic buyer τp_m.

It is clear from figure 9.2 that for a given foreign price index q, tariff factor

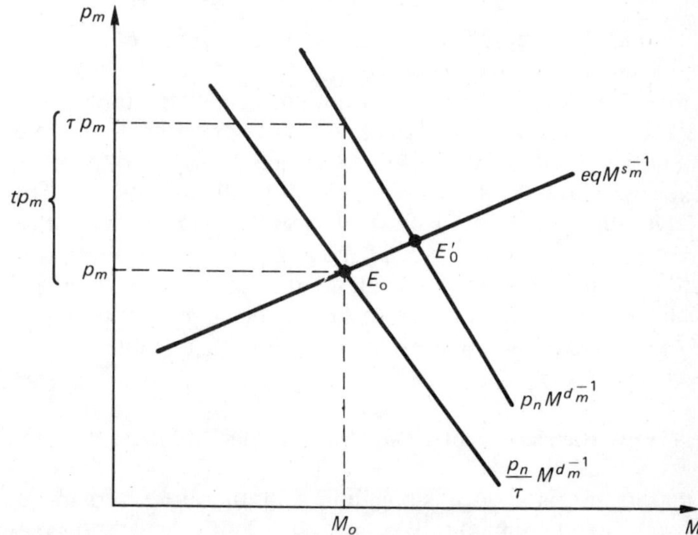

Figure 9.2 Import tariff

τ and exchange rate e, an increase in domestic prices represented by p_n would shift the demand curves up, increasing import prices and quantities. To prevent the increase in import quantity in the face of a domestic inflation given by $\hat{p}_n$, the tariff factor τ would have to increase at the same rate. This would hold M at M_0 as p_n increases. So, analogously to the export case, the import tariff factor τ would have to grow at the same rate as domestic inflation to hold the quantity of imports constant.

As in the export case, a constant growth rate of the tariff factor τ requires an increasing rate of increase in the actual tariff rate, since $\hat{\tau} = \dot{t}/(1 + t)$. To achieve a 10 per cent increase in the tariff factor τ (to offset a 10 per cent domestic inflation), if initially $t = 0$ (no tariff), a 10 per cent tariff will do. If initially $t = 0.50$, a 30 per cent increase is needed.

The equilibrium between import supply and demand inclusive of the tariff in equations (16), (8) and (9), and in figure 9.2, is expressed in equations (17) and (18) for changes in import quantity and market price net of the import tariff:

$$\hat{p}_m = k' (\hat{e} + \hat{q}) + (1 - k') (\hat{p}_n - \hat{\tau}) \tag{17}$$

$$\hat{M} = -k' d_m \{(\hat{e} + \hat{q}) - (\hat{p}_n - \hat{\tau})\} \tag{18}$$

The tariff factor $\hat{\tau}$ enters both equations in tandem with domestic inflation $\hat{p}_n$. With a domestic inflation driven by money growth and with a fixed exchange rate, a growth of the tariff factor τ equal to the inflation rate would be needed to hold the quantity of imports M constant.

Consider now the quota alternative to the tariff of figure 9.2. If the domestic price level is rising, the non-tariff demand curve shifts up continuously. If a quota of M_0 is imposed, the gap between the demand price given by $p_m M^{d_m^{-1}}$ and the supply price given by $eqM^{s_m^{-1}}$ grows continuously. This gap is the same as the tariff wedge tp_m.

Thus in an environment of a domestic inflation characterized by $\hat{p}_n$ both the tariff and the subsidy factors would have to grow at the same rate to hold trade quantities constant with a fixed nominal exchange rate. If tariffs and subsidies grow more slowly, import quantity will rise and export quantity fall. But, with the tariff and subsidy factors growing at the domestic inflation rate ($\hat{\sigma} = \hat{\tau} = \hat{p}_n$), the regime with a fixed nominal exchange rate would offer ever-increasing incentives to smuggling, through false invoicing or other means. This, in turn, would generate a rising black market premium, which would make the fixed nominal exchange rate unsustainable.

4. Trade Barriers, Smuggling and the Black Market Premium

Rising import tariffs induce smuggling and therefore provide an extra obstacle to the fixed nominal rate policy. An importer will tend to smuggle if the tariff is so high that it pays to purchase foreign exchange in the black market at a premium $\pi = e^b/e$ greater than one, given that the good imported may be confiscated by the government. Denoting the probability of success in smuggling by z, if $z\tau > \pi$, the importer will tend to smuggle more. We assume that the probability of success depends on the ratio of smuggled to legal imports, denoted by $m = S_m/L_m$ so that, given trade barriers and the premium, an importer will choose m such that expected profits are maximized. Associated with the optimal m, there will be a probability of success $z(m)$ and a domestic price which can be expressed as a weighted average of the tariff factor and the premium, with $\tau > \pi$ a necessary condition for import smuggling to occur.

Rising subsidies, on the other hand, reduce the incentive to smuggle exports but if the subsidy is smaller than the black market premium weighted by the probability of success, or $\sigma < z\pi$, it will pay to smuggle more. Profits will be maximized for a smuggling ratio $x = S_x/L_x$, associated with a probability of success $z(x)$ and a domestic price of exports which can also be expressed as a weighted average of the subsidy factor and the premium, with $\sigma < \pi$ a necessary condition for export smuggling to occur. As a consequence, smuggling requires that $\tau > \sigma$ initially, a condition which is necessarily met when we have an export tax since then $\sigma < 1$. The nature of the smuggling equilibrium is discussed in Macedo (1987), and can be adapted to our purposes.

Since tariff (or subsidy)-inclusive domestic prices are a weighted average of the premium and the tariff, domestic prices, net of tariff or subsidy, differ from the domestic currency value of foreign prices at the official exchange rate by the difference between the premium and trade barriers:

$$\hat{p}_x = \hat{e} + \hat{q}_x + \beta_x(\hat{\pi} - \hat{\sigma}) \tag{19}$$

where $\beta_x = \pi x z(x)/\{\sigma + \pi x z(x)\}$;

$$\hat{p}_m = \hat{e} + \hat{q}_m + \beta_m(\hat{\pi} - \hat{\tau}) \tag{20}$$

where $\beta_m = \pi m/\tau + \pi m)$.

We interpret planned smuggled imports as the flow demand for black market foreign exchange and successfully smuggled exports as the flow supply of black market foreign exchange. This determines the long-run black market premium consistent with balanced legal and illegal trade.

As before, we set foreign prices q at unity. Then if legal exports equal legal imports ($L_x = L_m$) and successfully smuggled exports pay for planned smuggling imports $\{z(x)S_x = S_m\}$, the smuggling ratios which satisfy the trade balance equilibrium are such that:

$$z(x)x = m \tag{21}$$

Using equation (21) to solve for the black market premium and the smuggling ratios in terms of trade barriers, it can be shown that these only depend on the ratio $\varrho = \tau/\sigma$, with a coefficient capturing the inverse of the sum of the elasticities of the demand for and supply of black market foreign exchange with respect to trade barriers. An increase in τ increases smuggling whereas an increase in σ decreases smuggling. In long-run equilibrium, the black market premium is a weighted average of τ and σ. It can be expressed as:

$$\hat{\pi} = \hat{\tau} - \{\alpha_m/(\alpha_m + \alpha_x)\}\hat{\varrho} \tag{22}$$

where $\alpha_m(\alpha_x)$ is the elasticity of demand for (supply of) black market foreign exchange.

Using equation (22) in equations (19) and (20) we obtain changes in net domestic prices as a function of changes in trade barriers:

$$\hat{p}_x = \hat{e} + \hat{q}_x + (1 - k_B)\,\beta_x\,\hat{\varrho} \tag{19'}$$

where $k_B = \alpha_m/(\alpha_m + \alpha_x)$;

$$\hat{p}_m = \hat{e} + \hat{q}_m - k_B\beta_m\hat{\varrho} \tag{20'}$$

An increase in ϱ, or in the tariff (relative to the subsidy) raises (lowers) the domestic net price of exports and lowers (raises) the domestic net price of imports because of the induced increase (decrease) in smuggling. Since higher import tariffs increase smuggling which lowers import prices and raises export prices, whereas higher export subsidies reduce smuggling which raises import prices and lowers export prices, we see that smuggling improves the net terms of trade. This improvement in relative prices is offset by the induced increase in the probability of detection, which leads to greater confiscation by the government and thus less consumption.

Note also that in the benchmark case where $\tau = \sigma = \pi = 1$, the β coefficients become the share of import smuggling (or of successful export smuggling) in total trade, denoted by β_o. We can then write the condition for the smuggling equilibrium to exist as $\beta_x > \beta_o > \beta_m$.

The smuggling model summarized above can now be adapted to the model of section 3. Under the simplifying assumption that the government does not resell confiscated smuggled goods, exports supplied by home producers (X^s) are greater than exports demanded by foreign consumers (X^d) and greater than legal exports (L_x) whereas imports demanded by home consumers (M^d) are smaller than imports supplied by foreign producers (M^s) but still greater than legal imports (L_m). The wedges between X^d and L_x and between M^s and L_m involve the smuggling ratios for exports and imports respectively. However, the wedges between X^s and L_x and between M^d and L_m involve those same smuggling ratios multiplied by the probability of success in smuggling for X^s and M^d; they can be expressed as a function of the ratio of trade barriers:

$$\hat{X}^s = \hat{L}_x + \{\beta_x/(\alpha_x + \alpha_m)\}\hat{\varrho} \tag{23}$$

$$\hat{X}^d = \hat{L}_x + \{\beta_o/(\alpha_x + \alpha_m)\}\hat{\varrho} \tag{24}$$

$$\hat{M}^s = \hat{L}_m + \{\beta_o/(\alpha_x + \alpha_m)\}\hat{\varrho} \tag{25}$$

$$\hat{M}^d = \hat{L}_m + \{\beta_m/(\alpha_x + \alpha_m)\}\hat{\varrho} \tag{26}$$

The equality of the wedge between exports demanded and legal exports on the one hand and between imports supplied and legal imports on the other is a consequence of the long-run equilibrium condition expressed in equation (21). This wedge affects the foreign exchange price and disappears for the small open economy.

Before substituting for quantities in the log differential of the demand and supply equations from sections 2 and 3 and solving the model for prices and legal quantities, we note that the solution will be the same as in section 3 if $\hat{\varrho} = 0$, so that the rule $\hat{p}_n = \hat{\tau} = \hat{\sigma}$ still keeps total import and export quantities constant. The difference, of course, is that the black market premium is growing at the same rate $\hat{\pi} = \hat{p}_n$, independently of the changes in the official exchange rate.

It is convenient to write the solution relative to the no-smuggling model of section 3, denoted by an L superscript. We then have:

$$\hat{p}_x = \hat{p}_x^L + A_x^{-1} \{ \beta_x(1 + \alpha_x d_x) - \beta_o \} \hat{\varrho} \tag{27}$$

$$\hat{L}_x = \hat{X}^L + A_x^{-1} \{ \beta_x d_x(\alpha_x s_x^{-1}) - \beta_0 s_x \} \hat{\varrho} \tag{28}$$

where $A_x = (\alpha_x + \alpha_m)(d_x + s_x)$.

$$\hat{p}_m = \hat{p}_m^L - A_m^{-1} \{ \beta_m(1 + \alpha_m s_m) - \beta_0 \} \hat{\varrho} \tag{29}$$

$$\hat{L}_m = \hat{M}^L + A_m^{-1} \{ \beta_m s_m(d_m \alpha_m^{-1}) - \beta_0 d_m \} \hat{\varrho} \tag{30}$$

where $A_m = (\alpha_x + \alpha_m)(d_m + s_m)$.

We see that the net price of exports (imports) is always higher (lower) than without smuggling, and that, in the case of a small economy, these price effects are larger.

Quantities legally traded are ambiguous. In the 'rigid' economy, legal trade falls but a rise in the value of imports and exports requires that the foreign exchange elasticities be greater than one:

$$\hat{p}_x + \hat{L}_x - \hat{p}_x^L - \hat{X}^L = \{ \beta_x/(\alpha_x + \alpha_m) \} (\alpha_x - 1) \hat{\varrho} \tag{31}$$

$$\hat{p}_m + \hat{L}_m - \hat{p}_m^L - \hat{M}^L = \{ \beta_m/(\alpha_x + \alpha_m) \} (\alpha_m - 1) \hat{\varrho} \tag{32}$$

Total trade may rise or fall, except for the small, rigid economy. Adding equation (23) to equation (28) and equation (26) to equation (30), we obtain:

$$\hat{X}^s = \hat{X}^L + (\alpha_x + \alpha_m)^{-1} \{ (\beta_x - \beta_o)(1-k) + \beta_x k s_x \alpha_x \} \hat{\varrho} \tag{33}$$

$$\hat{M}^d = \hat{M}^L + (\alpha_x + \alpha_m)^{-1} \{ (\beta_m - \beta_o)(1-k') + \beta_m k' d_m \alpha_m \} \hat{\varrho} \tag{34}$$

It is seen that total exports rise with ϱ whereas total imports may fall. For the small country ($k = k' = 1$), total trade rises. A country with monopoly power on the import side, say $k' = 0$, would see a fall in total imports but, since $\beta_x > \beta_o$, a country with monopoly power on the export side would still increase its total exports relative to the no-smuggling situation.

The smuggling model shows therefore that, even in the 'rigid' economy, legal trade will fall only if tariffs are rising faster than subsidies. However, the black market premium will be growing at the same rate as trade barriers.

To analyze this phenomenon we need to model the short-run black market premium, which importers and exporters take as given because it makes the stock of black market foreign exchange willingly held, as in Macedo (1982). In this connection, the importance of a given short-term premium is that in order for smuggling to exist, it must be such that $\tau > \pi > \sigma$. Alternatively put, the observed premium provides a lower bound for import tariffs and an upper bound for export subsidies.

The analysis is in Macedo (1987). For our purposes, it is sufficient to stress that if the reported trade balance is zero, the unreported trade balance in foreign currency is given by:

$$B \sim q_m S_m[\hat{\pi} - \hat{\tau} + \{\alpha_m/(\alpha_m + \alpha_x)\}\hat{\varrho}] \tag{35}$$

When the premium is higher than the weighted average of trade barriers, the unreported balance is in surplus and vice versa. The effect of capital flight is therefore to exacerbate the rise in the premium as given by equation (22) above.

5. Exchange Rate Stability

Exchange rate stability is desirable in a developing country because it eliminates a major source of uncertainty as the traded-goods sectors develop. As we saw above, an attempt to stabilize the *nominal* exchange rate in the face of domestic inflation will require increasing trade restrictions and the rising incentives they provide for illegal activity. An alternative objective is stabilization of the *real* exchange rate so as to insulate the traded-goods sectors and the trade balance from domestic inflation. To stabilize the *real* exchange rate, the nominal rate e should be moved to offset the home inflation differential. For a constant E, the nominal rate e would follow the rule

$$\hat{e} = \hat{p}_n - \hat{q} \tag{36}$$

Once we have accepted, on principle, that the objective for exchange rate stabilization is the real exchange rate, we face the question: to which nominal rate do we apply the rule given in equation (36)? The dollar rate? The sterling rate? An average? Do we use import or export weights in forming the average? The general answer to these questions is that the real effective exchange rate can be stabilized by applying the rule of equation (36) to a nominal effective rate, where the same set of weights is used in calculating the effective nominal rate e and the effective traded-goods price q. In the absence of market power in either export or import markets for a small country like Sudan, the appropriate choice is likely to be total trade weights. Thus the nominal effective rate and traded-goods price can be formed by making a weighted average across the sum of exports and imports by trading partner. The nominal exchange rate of a selected numéraire currency such as the US dollar can then be moved so that the effective nominal rate follows equation (36).

6. Lessons from Sudan

To put the lessons from Sudan in perspective, recall that, after the first oil crisis, the Sudanese authorities embarked on a development program designed to make their country the 'bread basket' of the Gulf states. The eagerness of these states to provide development aid to the Sudan as well as the significant migration of Sudanese workers toward the Gulf would seem to have relaxed the foreign exchange constraint. Nevertheless, when Sudan negotiated with the IMF in 1978, it was already in a difficult financial situation. Nashashibi (1980) illustrates the decline in the competitiveness of major crops in the mid-1970s. Hussain and Thirwall (1984) find the same tendency after the 1978 devaluation. It is as yet unclear whether the deterioration of Sudan's solvency in 7 years of agreements with the IMF is mostly attributable to errors in policy or policy advice. An alternative hypothesis, put forth by Brown (1984, 1985), argues that both the United States and the Arab countries managed to use the IMF's 'seal of approval' to continue lending to a friendly government. The ability of Sudan to continue dealing with the IMF despite arrears on its debt to the Fund is consistent with this hypothesis at least before negotiations with the IMF broke down in late 1984.

During the period since 1973, there were many changes in exchange rate arrangements in Sudan, involving both multiple official exchange rates (official, commercial, special, etc.) and the free – or black market – rate. This is also, to some extent, the pattern in Egypt, as shown in Macedo (1982). Some figures comparing the basic official dollar rate with the free dollar rate are shown in table 9.1, while figure 9.3 reports a real effective exchange rate index using the basic official rate against fifteen major trading partners. The underlying data are reported in Branson and Macedo (1987). Here we note that, prior to the nominal depreciation of 1978, the measure of p_n/q had increased by 7 per cent and 14 per cent respectively in 1977 and 1978.

The combination of steadily accelerating inflation and irregular movement of the nominal exchange rate resulted in the unstable movement in the real effective rate. After the late 1960s, the real effective rate fell in an unstable manner to 1980. This real appreciation was bad for output of traded goods and the trade balance. The instability of year-to-year movement in the real rate raises risk and may reduce investment in the traded-goods sector.

The situation worsened after 1980. A sharp real appreciation came in 1981 as the nominal rate was held nearly constant against a rising domestic inflation. The sharp devaluation in 1982 gave a large depreciation in the real

Table 9.1 Exchange rates in the Sudan (1973–84 yearly averages)

	Piastres/Dollar		*Free market premium*	*1976 = 100*		
	Official	*Free*		*CPI relative to US*	*Real official*	*Real free*
1973	35	64	1.83	80	125	121
1974	35	67	1.91	91	110	112
1975	35	74	2.11	104	96	108
1976	35	66	1.89	100	100	100
1977	35	66	1.89	108	93	93
1978	38	72	1.89	120	91	91
1979	42	77	1.83	142	85	82
1980	50	88	1.76	156	92	85
1981	53	103	1.94	178	85	88
1982	94	143	1.52	209	129	104
1983	130	193	1.48	264	141	111
1984	130	244	1.88	303	122	122

Sources: Official, consumer prices *IFS*.
Free 1973–8 *Picks's Currency Yearbook*, average of monthly data.
1979–84 Bank of Sudan, average of daily data.

effective rate, and the nominal appreciation (!) in 1984 resulted in an appreciation of the real rate back to its level in 1980.

The 1979 partial unification of the official rates, rather than being part of any agreement with the IMF, seems to have been an initiative of the Sudanese authorities. The accompanying financial liberalization, whilst very gradual, turned out to have very severe consequences because, while broadening the market where a free exchange rate was determined, it did not induce a more credible official exchange rate policy.

Thus the reforms continued to be implemented in 1980 and 1981, with further measures toward 'the simplification and unification of the exchange rate' as mentioned in the *Annual Report* of the Bank of Sudan. In September 1980, according to Awad (1985), the official rate became 60 piastres per dollar, the special rate 80 piastres while the free market rate was at 125 piastres, a premium of 2.08, much higher than the average of 1.76 reported in table 9.1.

The Bank of Sudan set the date of the unification of the exchange system in November 1981, at 90 piastres per dollar, but it only lasted a few months. In March 1982, the commercial rate rose to 135 piastres, only slightly below the free market rate of 145. In November, the official rate was set at 130 piastres and the commercial rate at 175, again very close to the free market rate. While the official rate remained at that level until 10 February 1985 (when it became 250 piastres) the commercial rate was raised to 180 piastres in March 1983, and to 210 piastres in October 1984. Before that, however, the official rate was only applicable to the imports of petroleum and some

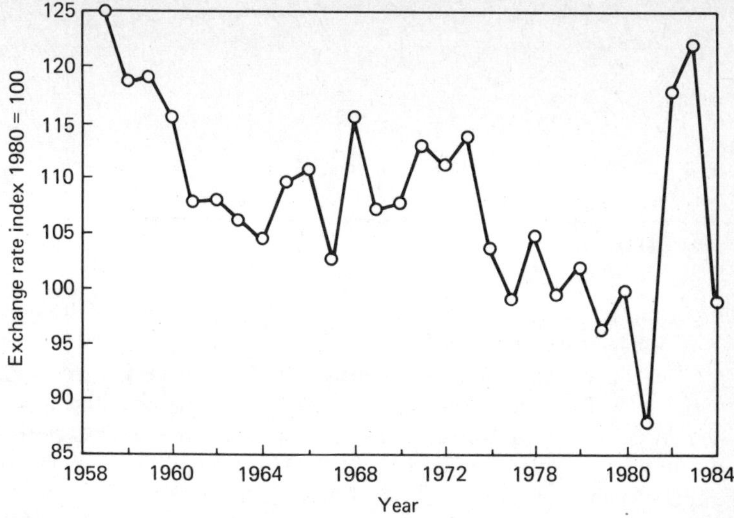

Figure 9.3 Real exchange rate of Sudan (15 country weights: total trade)

pharmaceuticals because agricultural exports were valued at a combined rate of 142 piastres (obtained by weighing the official rate with ¾ and the commercial rate with ¼). Indeed, by then the commercial rate itself was only applicable to specific 'priority' imports. This is why the official exchange rate policy was not credible, and the free market premium became a signal of the inability of the authorities to manage the economy and was accordingly viewed with suspicion by the central bank. This may well have exacerbated the potential of informal financial markets for bubbles and crashes, as indeed became reality in early 1985: from 26 January to 6 February 1985, the black market rose from 360 to 500 piastres to the dollar, when the official rate was raised from 130 to 250 piastres.

While during the IMF period there continued to be continuous changes in exchange rate policy, the major difference compared with the previous period is the decline in the premium and the real devaluation against the dollar. This started in 1979 for the free market exchange rate and continued until 1984. For the official rate, it is limited to the period 1981–3. But, as before, the shift of transactions to the commercial rate makes the true pattern look less volatile than the numbers reported in table 9.1 indicate. Similarly, the 'strong dollar' causes mostly differences in magnitude: to a real depreciation of 66 per cent against the dollar in 1982–3, corresponds a 40 per cent depreciation against major trading partners.

Using data reported by private dealers to the central bank, Macedo (1986) characterizes the Khartoum black market for foreign exchange. The data are subject to caveats, since the authorizations to private dealers were revoked from 10 February 1983 through to the end of January 1984, at which

Table 9.2 Share of unreported transactions 1981/2

	Debit	*Credit*	*Net*
Trade	27	33	25
Invisibles	33	44	–
Remittances	100	55	50
Current account	31	46	–

Source: Macedo (1986).

time the commercial banks virtually ceased to deal in foreign exchange since they would not use the free market rate.

From table 9.2 we get smuggling ratios of 0.37 ($^{27}/_{100-27}$) for commodity imports and 0.49 for commodity exports. These reflect the importance of smuggling in government transactions (cotton and oil exports, petroleum and sugar imports) as well as for livestock. The smuggling ratio for remittances reported in table 9.2 is about 1 but, in a 1983 study of Sudanese workers abroad, discussed by Harris (1986), this ratio is as high as 7.27, so that as a share of output they would represent 37 per cent rather than 5 per cent. Even if such a figure is grossly exaggerated, it seems clear that the stock of foreign exchange held by Sudanese determines the premium in the short run, as postulated in our analysis.

To the extent that these remittances are spent on imports, only a small part of the stock of foreign assets held by Sudanese residents is directed to supply foreign exchange to the Khartoum black market. This may account for the low level of net inflows or outflows reported in Macedo (1986).

The structure of the free market by currency composition shows a share of about ¾ for the US dollar in 1982–4. Similarly, the number of authorized dealers increased from five to nineteen during 1984, but many of them had a very small share of the market so that the average number-equivalent Herfindahl index for the year is 6. Still, this shows a substantial degree of competition. For example, Dixit (1985) finds an index of 8 for US auto firms, counting divisions as separate entities. Despite the caveats about the quality of the data, this evidence illustrates how in Sudan the black market has offset the effects of official exchange rate policy leading to movements in the premium that were determined by stock demand for foreign assets as well as smuggling activity.

In sum, the failure to match movement in the nominal exchange rate to relative inflation sharply destabilized the real effective rate after 1980. The attempts at stabilizing the nominal exchange rate destabilized the real rate, discouraging investment in the traded-goods sectors and providing incentives for illegal activity, so the smuggler's blues made their way to the central bank!

NOTE

An earlier version was presented at a WIDER Conference in memory of Carlos Díaz-Alejandro, Helsinki (Finland), 23–25 August 1986. We are grateful for the comments received then. The title of the paper was partially suggested by Waterbury (1984).

REFERENCES

Awad, M.H. 1985: Some Thoughts on the Devaluation of the Sudanese Pound, draft Khartoum.

Branson, W.H. 1972: The trade effects of the 1971 currency realignments, *Brookings Papers on Economic Activity*, 1, 15–58.

Branson, W.H. 1985: The dynamic interaction of exchange rates and trade flows. In T. Peeters et al. (eds), *International Trade and Exchange Rates in the Late Eighties*, Amsterdam: North-Holland, pp. 133–60.

Branson, W.H. 1986: Stabilization, stagflation, and investment incentives: the case of Kenya. In S. Edwards and L. Ahamed (eds.), *Economic Adjustment and Exchange Rates in Developing Countries*, Chicago: University of Chicago Press, pp. 267–88.

Branson, W.H. and Katseli, L.T. 1982: Currency baskets and real effective exchange rates. In M. Gersovitz et al. (eds), *The Theory and Experience of Development*, London: George Allen & Unwin, pp. 194–214.

Branson, W.H. and Macedo, J. 1987: Smugglers' Blues at the Central Bank: Lessons from Sudan, NBER Working Paper no. 2220, April.

Brown, R. 1984: On Assessing the Effects and Rationale of IMF Stabilization Programme in Sudan since 1978. Institute of Social Studies, the Hague, Netherlands, Working Paper no. 12.

Brown, R. 1985: A Background Note on the Final Round of Austerity Measures Imposed by the Nimery Regime: June 1984 to March 1985, draft. Development Studies Research Center, University of Khartoum.

Dixit, A. 1985: Optimal Trade and Industrial Policies for the US Automobile Industry, draft. Princeton University, August.

Harris, J. 1986: Macroeconomic Adjustment in Sudan. Paper presented at a WIDER Conference, Helsinki, August.

Hussain, N. and Thirwall, A.P. 1984: The IMF supply-side approach to devaluation: an assessment with reference to Sudan. *Oxford Bulletin of Economics and Statistics*, May.

Macedo, J. 1982: Currency inconvertibility and export competitiveness: a model of the 'Dutch disease' in Egypt. *Journal of Development Economics*, December.

Macedo, J. 1986: The Foreign Exchange Market in the Sudan, draft. Princeton University.

Macedo, J. 1987: Currency Inconvertibility, Trade Taxes and Smuggling. NBER Working Paper no. 2177, March.

Nashashibi, K. 1980: A supply framework for exchange reform in developing countries: the experience of Sudan. *IMF Staff Papers*, March.

Waterbury, J. 1984: The Sudan Blues, draft lyrics from Khartoum.

COMMENT 1

Edward P. Buffie

This paper wrestles with a central policy problem confronting many LDCs, namely, what policy package should be adopted to eliminate a payments deficit? Branson and Macedo argue that, though devaluation is of limited effectiveness in economies plagued by technological and institutional rigidities, it is still preferable to use the exchange rate instead of trade taxes to redress problems of external imbalance. The problem with using trade taxes is that in an inflationary world *real* import tariff and export subsidy rates must be increased continuously to stabilize the price of tradables relative to nontradables. For example, to prevent the relative price of importables from declining, the ad valorem tariff rate t must be increased each period by

$$\hat{t} - \hat{P}_N = \hat{P}_N / t > 0$$

where P_N stands for the price of nontradables and a circumflex denotes the percentage change in a variable. Thus, equiproportionate increases in import tariffs and export subsidies differ from a steady crawl of the currency in that they create ever-increasing incentives to divert trade activities into illegal channels.

While I think this point about the limitations of trade taxes is basically valid, I have some difficulty with the paper's analysis of devaluation and the conclusion that a passive exchange rate policy is appropriate for the Sudan. It is argued that in the face of either zero trade elasticities or a rigid real wage, devaluation will fail to improve the trade balance and will contract aggregate output. The rigid economy case of zero trade elasticities does not strike me as particularly relevant. There is now a fairly substantial empirical literature which supports the view that both export and import elasticities are sizeable in LDCs. In fact, over 10 years ago Díaz-Alejandro wrote in a survey paper that the results of empirical studies allow one to speak of the 'rout of export pessimism.'

With respect to the second argument put forward by Branson and Macedo, I have doubts about whether analysis based on the assumption of an economy-wide rigid real wage is of much relevance for a highly agrarian economy like the Sudan's. In any case, however, the duality result that in the presence of a rigid real wage a devaluation is just as ineffective as in a rigid economy is conditional on the special assumption that the percentage increase in the price of nontradables equals the percentage increase in the wage rate. With this pricing rule, devaluation is ineffective because it cannot alter relative prices. Letting w denote the nominal wage and α_i the consumption share of good i, we have

$$\hat{P}_N = \hat{w} = \alpha_T \hat{P}_T + \alpha_N \hat{P}_N$$

or

$$\hat{P}_N = \hat{P}_T$$

since $\alpha_T + \alpha_N = 1$.

To the best of my knowledge, there are no models of imperfect competition that generate the pricing rule $\hat{P}_N = \hat{w}$. And with competitive market clearing prices, if the nominal money supply does not increase by the same percentage amount as the exchange rate, the relative price of nontradables will decline, producing a fall in the product wage in the tradables sector and a rise in the product wage in the nontradables sector. The wealth effect, the rise in the relative price of tradables and the fall in the tradables sector product wage then all work to improve the trade balance.

Turning to the effect on aggregate output, Branson and Macedo assert that a contractionary outcome is likely because, if a deficit exists initially, a devaluation can cause a worsening in the trade balance measured in domestic currency and hence a decrease (over time) in the money supply. But if this is the only contractionary effect at work, it is easily neutralized by an offsetting increase in domestic credit that maintains the domestic money supply. Moreover, in the small open economy a decrease in the money supply is necessarily contractionary only if firms in the nontradables sector are initially constrained by a lack of effective demand. With a rigid real wage and flexible prices, a decrease in the money supply lowers the relative price of nontradables. The product wage falls in the tradables sector and rises in the nontradables sector, so the impact on aggregate employment is generally ambiguous.

I think Branson and Macedo are correct to emphasize the possibility of a contractionary outcome but, in my view, the analysis should focus on how devaluation alters the relative prices of imported intermediate inputs and capital goods. A real devaluation raises the relative prices of these critical inputs to the nontradables and quota-protected sectors. The impact on aggregate employment turns on the nature of factoral substitution patterns, differences in sectoral factor intensities and the precise degree of real wage rigidity. The higher price for imported capital goods lowers investment in the quasi-nontradables sectors and may lower aggregate investment as well if the tradables sectors do not expand strongly or if capital is a less important factor of production in these sectors.

It is important to determine the effects of a real devaluation because few LDCs are in a position to follow the passive exchange rate policy recommended by Branson and Macedo. In an inflationary economy with a zero current account deficit the nominal exchange rate ought, of course, to keep apace of other prices in order to prevent a deterioration in the real exchange rate and the payments balance. But typically countries face the more difficult task of altering relative prices so as to eliminate a payments deficit.

This raises the issue of whether a real devaluation delivers the best package of relative price changes. At present, we lack the empirical information on substitution patterns involving imported inputs, the characteristics of sectoral technology, the responsiveness of investment to the supply price of capital goods etc. that is needed to ascertain whether devaluation is likely to prove employment and growth contractionary. In light of this uncertainty about the repercussions of a real devaluation, it is worth investigating whether other policies such as export subsidies or lower wage taxes for tradables sectors might not offer more favorable macroeconomic trade-offs.

REFERENCES

Díaz-Alejandro, C.F. 1975: Trade policies and economic development. In P.B. Kenen (ed.), *International Trade and Finance: Frontiers for Research*, New York: Cambridge University Press.

COMMENT 2

Francisco Thoumi

This is an interesting paper, although its title is somewhat misleading since it deals with smuggling in the Sudan only as an illustration of the applications of a model developed extensively in the essay.

The theoretical part of the paper develops an export supply and import demand model for a rigid economy typical of many LDCs. The model shows that given inelastic short-term import demand and export supply functions, a devaluation is unlikely to be effective in eliminating a current account deficit. However, in the presence of domestic inflation, a passive exchange rate policy of devaluations to follow *pari passu* the difference between domestic and international inflation rates is a very effective way to prevent a balance of payments crisis as an alternative to a fixed nominal exchange rate which would require continuously growing import tariffs and export subsidies which in turn would make smuggling increasingly attractive and will induce a growing level of illegal trade and overinvoicing of exports.

The final pages of the paper argue that beginning in 1977, inflation in the Sudan accelerated, and that the nominal exchange rate was kept constant until a year later when it was devalued. From then on, further changes in the nominal exchange rate were made in discrete jumps which created a very unstable real exchange rate and varying differences between the official, commercial and black market rates. The evidence presented is hard to evaluate since the free (black) market foreign exchange premium in the post-1977 period is not higher than in the pre-1977, low inflation, stable period. Thus while it can be argued that increased inflation brought in higher real exchange rate instability, it did not appear to have increased the average black market premium. Thus, it is not clear that the increase in the inflation rate affected the incentives to smuggle as predicted by the model.

The final pages of the paper discuss some estimates of the share of black market transactions as a percentage of the 'private' and 'official' current account for 1982, 1983, and 1984, the 1981/2 share of unreported transactions of total trade and exports of three main products and imports of two products. Weighted averages are also provided. For scholars interested in the study of the impact of smuggling, these data could be extremely interesting. However, while the reader is referred to several publications, there is no discussion of the methodology used in producing these estimates and of their limitations. The paper concludes stating that contraband and the black foreign exchange market cannot be ignored in the design of exchange rate policy.

While this paper presents an interesting theoretical model, the relationship between the model and the data presented in its support is at best awkward and most readers will find it somewhat confusing. One reason for confusion is the fact that the model built is a current account one, which is used to explain the determination of the exchange rate. Of course, the observable exchange rates, particularly those of the black market, are strongly affected by factors other than the profitability of smuggling such as the expectations of devaluation, the difference between domestic and international exchange rates, the political stability of the country, the legality of capital movements etc. Thus, the black market premium alone says very little about smuggling.

If one were to focus the model more on smuggling, one would modify it to make it somewhat more reflective of the dimensions of smuggling in which other estimations could be made. First, a difference in the probability of interdiction of contraband between illegally imported and exported goods should be made. Normally, the probability of catching smuggled imports is higher than that of catching smuggled exports as the latter could only be done at the border crossing while the former could be done any time after the illegal crossing and before consumption. This difference is especially relevant in the Sudan since most exports are quite homogeneous commodities whose origin is easily disguisable after they leave the country. Second, it would be useful to break up exportable and importable goods into easy and difficult to smuggle categories. Goods with high value to volume and weight ratios are easier to smuggle than those with low ratios. (Cocaine is easier to smuggle than marihuana.) This would open up the possibility of studying the impact of smuggling using disaggregated production data. For example in the household appliance sector, refrigerators have to compete very little with smuggled goods while the opposite happens with toasters, blenders etc. Thus, when tariffs and contraband increase, one could expect a change in the output composition of local industry which could be tested.

The changes suggested are likely to produce a model which is easier to quantify at a micro level, and which could produce more useful results for the policymakers such as guidelines for contraband control expenditures, selective protection etc.

The general conclusion that contraband should be taken into account in policy design, while valid, contributes little to policymakers as they already do that, even though they do not always openly acknowledge it. For example, monetary and fiscal policies in Colombia have been influenced by the large inflow of illegal drug exports. In this country, the glut of foreign exchange also caused large overinvoicing of exports and phantom, non-existing exports were used to launder drug dollars, a phenomenon which was taken into account to lower export subsidies. Gasoline prices in Ecuador are subsidized, but the subsidy is lower near border towns to lower the incentives for foreigners to fill up that country. Thus policy-makers in many countries already recognize the existence of contraband, and react to it.

Part IV

STABILIZATION AND ECONOMIC REFORM

10

Incredible Reforms

Guillermo A. Calvo

1. Introduction

The objective of this paper is to examine the role of credibility in connection with trade and financial reforms. The current discussion of these reforms is undoubtedly keenly aware of the importance of credible policies in insuring their full success (see, e.g., Edwards, 1985b), but it is perhaps also fair to say that reference to the credibility problem is usually tangential, and has not been explicitly incorporated into the standard analytical structures.

In order to help focus our attention on the central issues, section 2 of the paper will develop two very simple but highly suggestive examples. The first example examines the implications of a trade liberalization policy when the public does not fully believe that the policy will be continued in the future. In sharp contrast, the second example is developed in the context of a closed economy; we study a model with heterogeneous individuals, where in equilibrium there is a set of individuals who are net borrowers, and, consequently, a set of individuals who are net lenders. The central question that we ask in this context is about the effects of a stabilization policy that is not expected to last beyond the 'present' period. In both examples, policies that would be optimal under full credibility turn out to be inoptimal under incomplete credibility. We show that the outward symptoms that credibility is interfering with otherwise optimal policies may be (a) excess borrowing, in the first example, and (b) unintended income redistribution in the second example.

The themes of these examples are expanded into more realistic (if not intellectually more satisfying) variations in section 3, where we explore the role of durable goods, of the real exchange rate and of the banking system.

Section 4 is devoted to discussing the possible sources of incomplete credibility, and the paper is closed with some conclusions in section 5.

2. The Examples

This section will present two bare-bone examples that help illustrate some important consequences of imperfect credibility (to be defined more precisely below).

2.1 *Open Economy, Identical Individuals*

Consider an economy consisting of one representative individual whose utility function is of the following form:

$$u(c_1,x_1)+\beta u(c_2,x_2) \tag{1}$$

where c and x are internationally tradable goods, and the subscript indicates time (time 1 is the present and time 2 the future); constant β (> 0) is the discount factor.[1] We assume that the international relative price of c and x is constant and equal to unity. We begin our discussion by assuming, in addition, that the only barrier to trade is an import tariff on good c (which we denote by τ). Therefore, the budget constraint for the representative individual (using x as the unit of account, and x_2 as the numéraire)[2] becomes:

$$(1+r)\left\{(1+\tau_1)c_1+x_1\right\}+(1+\tau_2)c_2+x_2 = (1+r)(y_1+g_1)+y_2+g_2 \tag{2}$$

where r is the international interest rate (i.e., the international own-rate-of-interest on c and x), and y and g denote the mana-type endowment of good x and government lump-sum transfers, respectively. Notice that under these assumptions, c is the importable, while x is the exportable good.

We further assume that the government rebates all the proceeds of the tariff back to the public in the form of lump-sum taxes; thus, since we are abstracting from any other distortion, we have, in equilibrium,

$$g_t = \tau_t c_t \tag{3}$$

Clearly, under the present assumptions, 'free trade forever' is the optimal (i.e., utility-maximizing) solution; obviously, this would be achieved by setting

$$\tau_1 = \tau_2 = 0 \tag{4}$$

Under more realistic circumstances, however, the present authorities can at best hope that the future authorities will also set $\tau_2 = 0$. Imagine, for example, that the representative consumer expects $\tau_2 > 0$, what happens then? If the present authorities can only control τ_1, it is quite clear that only by accident will the optimal present tariff be equal to zero, for $\tau_1=0$ would eliminate the distortion between x_1 and c_1, but not the one involving c_1 and c_2, for example; thus, no credibility in free trade forever implies that free trade today is a second-best solution. The optimal today policy is thus conditioned by today's expectations about tomorrow's policy.

Let us now consider the case where the present authorities actually know that $\tau_2=0$, but the public believes the latter to be positive. As argued above, $\tau_1=0$ is not going to be optimal in general;[3] but consider the possibly normal case in which, when $\tau_1=0$ but τ_2 is expected to be positive, the current account deteriorates in period 1 with respect to the case where τ_2 is expected to be zero; clearly, this would be a situation where there would be 'excessive borrowing from abroad.' The first-best could, however, be attained easily by setting $\tau_1=0$ and imposing controls on capital mobility so that the public will not borrow more than is warranted by the first-best optimum. This shows that under imperfect credibility, the optimal policy may consist of opening up the trade account, keeping some quantitative control on the capital account.[4]

An alternative optimal policy is to impose a tax on capital inflows[5] (and, hence, a subsidy on capital outflows). In our example, if all government revenues are returned to the public in the form of lump-sum taxes, it is easy to see that an optimal policy consists of setting $\tau_1=0$, and the capital-inflows tax at a level such that the resulting domestic interest rate induces a level of savings equal to the one associated with full credibility. It is interesting to note, however, that this kind of solution requires knowing expected τ_2 in addition to the first-best level of savings (the latter being the only piece of information required by the capital-controls solution outlined above).

The above discussion illustrates a point which is in fact quite general. The existence of expectations which are not consistent with first-best policy is equivalent to the existence of an intertemporal distortion. Therefore, unless the distortion can be completely removed – in other words, unless the first-best policy is fully credible – attaining the first-best solution will require the introduction of additional distortions, possibly ones of an intertemporal nature. Moreover, our examples suggest that quantitative controls on capital mobility could be easier to implement than a tax on international capital flows, given that the latter would, in addition, require information about expectations of future tariffs.[6]

2.2 Closed Economy, Heterogeneous Individuals

In the next example we will assume that there are two individuals in the economy (who, however, behave in a price-taking way). They have identical tastes, but different (homogeneous) output endowments. Furthermore, if the latter are denoted by y_t^j where t denotes time ($t=1,2$), and j the individual ($j=1,2$) we assume

$$y_1^1 = y_2^2 = 0 \tag{5a}$$

$$y_2^1 = y_1^2 = 1 \tag{5b}$$

Clearly, in any reasonable equilibrium, individual 1 will turn out to be the borrower, while individual 2 will be the lender.

The preference ordering of individual j is represented by the following Selden-type risk-neutral utility function (Selden, 1978):

$$u(c_1^j) + \beta u\,(\hat{c}_2^j) \qquad \beta > 0 \tag{6}$$

where c_1 is consumption in period 1, and $\hat{c}_2$ is expected consumption in period 2, i.e.,

$$\hat{c}_2^j = E\{y_2^j + (y_1^j - c_1^j)\,(1+i)\,/\,(1+\pi)\,\} \tag{7}$$

where E is the expectations operator conditional on information available[7,8] at time 1, and i and π are, respectively, the nominal interest rate and inflation rate between periods 1 and 2 (more details on these concepts will follow).

Selden labeled the above type of utility functions OCE (ordinary certainty equivalent); the present rendition assumes risk neutrality, because second-period utility depends on just the expected value of second-period consumption.

In this example the only stochastic variable in equation (7) is π, the rate of inflation, since endowments are nonstochastic, and the nominal interest rate, i, is specified at time 1. Thus equation (7) can more simply expressed as

$$\hat{c}_2^j = (y_1^j - c_1^j)(1 + R) \tag{8}$$

where

$$1 + R = (1 + i)E\{(1 + \pi)^{-1}\} \tag{9}$$

Therefore, R can be interpreted as the expected 'real' rate of interest (i.e., the expected own-rate-of-interest on output).

The first-order condition for individual j's maximization problem [i.e., maximize equation (6) subject to equation (8)] is, thus, pleasantly standard

$$u'(c_1^j)/u'(\hat{c}_2^j) = 1 + R \tag{10}$$

Therefore, quite conventionally, equations (5), (8) and (10) determine c_1^j given R, and the latter is determined by the following market-clearing condition:

$$c_1^1 + c_1^2 = 1 \tag{11}$$

(equilibrium in the time 2 output market is ensured by Walras' Law). We will denote the general equilibrium level of R by R^*. For simplicity, we also assume R^* to be unique.

By equation (9), it follows that the equilibrium nominal interest rate, i^*, satisfies

$$1 + i^* = (1 + R^*)/E\{(1 + \pi)^{-1}\} \tag{12}$$

This implies, of course, that the nominal interest rate is affected by the expected rate of inflation. The absence of 'money' or risk aversion in the model implies, in addition, that the 'real rate of interest,' R^*, is impervious to changes in inflationary expectations.[9] On the other hand, the actual or ex post real rate of interest, R^a, is determined by the actual or ex post rate of inflation, π^a, by the familiar formula

$$1 + R^a = (1 + i^*)/(1 + \pi^a) \tag{13}$$

Thus far, we have modeled the economy in an essentially nonmonetary fashion; hence, the next order of business is to motivate the existence of concepts like the nominal interest rate and the rate of inflation. We will do this in this section by relying on a somewhat arbitrary scenario, which will, however, help us get to the core of the main issues in a very direct manner (extensions are discussed in section 3.2).

Imagine that there is a law which requires all contracts to be expressed in a unit of account called 'National Pride,' NP, and let the price of output in terms of NP be called the price level, P. In this context, the rate of inflation, π, is just the proportional rate of growth of P between periods 1 and 2; on the other hand, the nominal interest rate, i, would be the own-rate of interest on NP from period 1 to period 2. The problem with this construction is, of course, that P is undetermined. We will, however, assume that P_t, t=1,2, is determined by some 'monetary authority.' This closes the model.

The first observation that we wish to make is that there is nothing contradictory if the monetary authority announces that the value of P_2 will be chosen by some random procedure. Given our assumption of risk neutrality, individuals will be indifferent between writing loan contracts in terms of output with R^* as the rate of interest, or in terms of NPs with i^* as the interest rate. This implies, in particular, that utility at time 1 – as measured by equation (6) – is, in equilibrium, completely indepedent of the probability distribution of π.

Ex post (i.e., when period 2 arrives), however, the level of utility will depend on the realization of π, π^a. By equations (7), (8) and (13), we have that, in equilibrium,

$$c_2^j - \hat{c}_2^j = (y_1^j - c_1^j)(R^a - R^*) \tag{14}$$

This is perfectly intuitive. It says that if individual j is a net lender (borrower), his actual second-period consumption will be larger (smaller) than expected if the ex post real interest rate exceeds the equilibrium real rate of interest.

Suppose the government announces that the price level will be fully stabilized, i.e., $\pi = 0$. If the public believes the announcement and the government is true to its promises, then $R^a = R^*$. Alternatively, if individuals hold point expectations, and inflation is expected to be π^e, then the only way to generate the same allocation of consumption across individuals, as under full credibility, is for the government to depart from the announcement and set $\pi^a = \pi^e$. If instead, the government insists on sticking to its announcement, then, by equation (14), there will be a re-allocation of consumption. Consider, for the sake of realism, a situation where the stabilization policy is not credible and $\pi^e > 0$; then equation (14) implies that there will be an ex post transfer from borrowers to lenders if the stabilization program is implemented, i.e., type 1 individuals [recall equation (5)] are going to be worse off than expected.

In order to gain further understanding of the kind of dilemma faced by the policy maker, imagine that the latter tries to maximize the utility of the least well-off individual in society (i.e., he is a 'maximiner'). For the sake of definiteness, let us consider the case in which $\beta = 1$. Under the above assumptions, it is easy to see that with no government intervention, we have $R^* = 1$, and

$$c_1^j = \hat{c}_2^j = 1/2 \qquad j = 1,2 \tag{15}$$

Hence, if $\pi^a = \pi^e$, there is no further need for government intervention, because both individuals enjoy equal utility from the perspective of both time 1 and time 2. But, going back to our previous discussion, consider the situation where $\pi^e > \pi^a = 0$. Time 1 utility is still the same for both individuals; however, now the policy maker knows that second-period utility will be lower for the type 1 individual (the borrower) than for the type 2 individual (the lender). In other words, the lack of credibility generates, per se, an undesirable income distribution. Thus, if for reasons outside the present formulation of the model,[10] the policy maker values price stability, but the zero-inflation policy is not credible, he faces a nontrivial maximization problem; the example suggests that only by fluke will $\pi^a = 0$ be the optimal policy if $\pi^e > 0$.

Quite aside from the credibility issue, the example also gives a microfoundation to the classical view that price stability – interpreted as being equivalent to a low price-level variance – should be one of the primary goals of monetary policy (see, for example, Laidler, 1984). The example is particularly interesting because it shows that a positive price-level variance can cause ex post damage even when contingent markets *à la* Arrow–Debreu are available and the costs associated with money-demand 'triangles' *à la* Bailey–Harberger are totally absent.

3. Durable Goods, The Real Exchange Rate and Banks

The objective of this section is to extend the above examples to account for some phenomena that are both realistic and important. The discussion will be organized around the key words of the section's title.

3.1 Durable Goods

The possibility of storage is of obvious significance in situations in which trade liberalization is not fully credible.[11] To understand its implications, we will assume, in the context of the open-economy model of section 2.1, that both goods are storable without cost between period 1 and 2. Thus, denoting the stocks of c and x accumulated at time 1 by S_c, and S_x respectively, the left-hand side of the budget constraint (2) becomes

$$(1 + r)\{(1 + \tau_1)(c_1 + S_c) + x_1 + S_x\} + (1 + \tau_2)c_2 + x_2 \tag{16}$$

Clearly, S_c and S_x are constrained to be nonnegative, and the right-hand side of equation (2) remains the same.[12] On the other hand, since the second-period consumption of c and x will be $c_2 + S_c$ and $x_2 + S_x$, respectively, the utility function (1) becomes

$$u(c_1,x_1) + \beta u(c_2 + S_c,x_2 + S_x) \tag{17}$$

A brief examination of equations (16) and (17) reveals that

$$(1 + r)(1 + \tau_1) < (1 + \tau_2) \Rightarrow S_c > 0 \text{ and } c_2 = 0 \tag{18}$$

Moreover, one can show that $S_c = 0$ if the above inequality is reversed. Futhermore, if $r > 0$ – a maintained assumption – then $S_x = 0$. The intuition of the above results is quite straightforward. Thus, for instance, equation (18) simply says that if the future value of period 1 c – i.e., $(1 + r)(1 + \tau_1)$ – is smaller than the future value of period 2 c – i.e., $(1 + \tau_2)$ – then it will be optimal for the consumer to buy the whole of second-period consumption at time 1, and keep it in storage until period 2.

In sum, only stocks of good c are ever going to be accumulated; furthermore, with the exception of the borderline case where the first inequality in equation (18) becomes an equality sign, inventories of good c are positive only if the first inequality in equation (18) holds true, in which case all purchases of good c occur in period 1.

The logic leading to equation (18) shows immediately that, unlike the no-storage case of section 2.2 the capital-controls policy *cum* trade liberalization is not going to lead the economy to the first-best solution in general. To see this, notice, firstly, that with a positive interest rate, the first-best optimum is characterized by no inventory accumulation (i.e., $S_c = S_x = 0$); and, secondly, that, for any given level of first-period expenditure, one can find a sufficiently high expected τ_2, such that individual-optimal $S_c > 0$, which proves the earlier assertion.[13] More intuitively, capital controls may fail in attaining the first-best because they can only determine the level of total expenditure, not its composition in terms of c, x and S_c.

A lesson from the above analysis is that liberalization programs which are not fully credible may require not only controls on international capital mobility, but also controls on the accumulation of durable goods.[14] This is perhaps worth emphasizing because there seems to be the conviction in some policy circles that in order to ensure a successful trade liberalization program only controls on the capital account of the balance of payments may be necessary. Our example shows that lack of credibility may lead to an 'overaccumulation of capital' (inventories in the example). In more general models, however, the possibility of *under*accumulation also exists.[15] This ambiguity is interesting, because it indicates that unless the nature of the credibility problem is well understood, there is no a priori strong case for a subsidy or a tax on capital accumulation.

3.2 The Real Exchange Rate

The real exchange rate (i.e., the relative price of 'tradable' with respect to 'nontradable' goods) has played a prominent role in the recent South American stabilization fiascos (see Corbo, 1985; Edwards 1985a; Harberger, 1982; Díaz-Alejandro, 1981; Calvo, 1983, 1986a), and has also surfaced as a salient characteristic of the recent US stabilization policy (see Mussa,

1985). Fortunately, this is a variable which is easy to incorporate in our models. For example, in the model of section 2.1, one could include 'leisure' l, in the utility function; hence, instead of (1) we get

$$u(c_1,x_1,l_1) + \beta u(c_2,x_2,l_2) \tag{19}$$

In addition, we could assume that output is produced by means of labor and some fixed factor; thus, letting total labor endowment be $\bar{l}$, we assume, recalling the notation of section 2.1, that

$$y_t = F(\bar{l} - l_t) \qquad F'(\,.\,)>0 \tag{20}$$

for some concave production function $F(.)$ Therefore, in a competitive equilibrium we have

$$w_t = F'(\bar{l} - l_t) \tag{21}$$

where w is the wage rate in terms of exportables, and also in terms of importables (recalling that, by assumption, the international relative price of c with respect to x is unity). Therefore, since leisure is, indisputably, a pure 'home good', w qualifies for an index of (the inverse of) the real exchange rate.

With this extension, we can perform the exercises of section 2.1; the welfare results are going to be similar. Among the symptoms of lack of credibility, however, the extended version will show 'abnormal' variations in the real exchange rate. Thus, for instance, if the liberalization is not expected to last into period 2, and a current account deficit develops, leisure may turn out to be unduly high,[16] resulting in an appreciation in the real exchange rate with respect to its full credibility level (i.e., a rise in w over the level attained if credibility was perfect).

3.3 Banks

The simple lesson of the example of section 2.2 is that financial intermediation may be harmful in the presence of price uncertainty. Our motivation for choosing that particular example was the observation in countries like Chile and Argentina that the risk of an unscheduled devaluation seems to have led to high ex post real interest rates (see Edwards, 1985a; Calvo, 1986a). In fact, the example suggests that the banking liberalization policies that were implemented in these countries may have contributed to the politically untenable wealth redistribution that took place. This implication will perhaps become more evident if we conduct our analysis in terms of slightly more realistic examples. We turn to that in what follows.

Consider a small open economy in which, initially, there is no domestic intermediation; thus, borrowers get funds from the international market at the going real interest rate, and lenders place their funds at the same rate of interest in the same international market. Assuming that the international price level is perfectly certain, we can think of this transaction as being specified in terms of output. If, in addition, we assume that the international own-rate of interest on output is equal to zero and the discount factor is equal to 1, as specified at the end of section 2.2, it follows that in equilibrium the current account will be balanced. In fact, the equilibrium outcome would be similar to that in the closed economy of section 2.2 if all intertemporal transactions were specified in terms of output.

The above modifications of the example show that the latter can be readily applied to an open economy. In this context, the price level, P, could be thought of as the exchange rate if the international price level is assumed constant and equal to unity. Consequently, π would stand for both the rate of inflation and the rate of devaluation. The model can, therefore, be applied immediately to examine situations in which the government announces the rate of devaluation,[17] but the public thinks that there is some probability that actual π, π^a, may depart from the announcement.

Quite clearly, if the public continues dealing with the rest of the world for its capital transactions – or internal transactions are exclusively done in terms of output – then uncertainty or lack of credibility about the rate of devaluation would have no ex ante or ex post welfare effects.

Imagine, however, that banks or, more generally, financial intermediaries are created, but they are required by law to denominate their transactions in terms of domestic currency, and price indexation of interest payments is prohibited. If there is no cost of intermediation, it follows that the equilibrium nominal interest rate would be i^* as given by equation (12). Thus, to the extent that some transactions are done through the banking system,[18] incomplete credibility about the exchange rate policy will lead to the income redistribution problems discussed in section 2.2.

Obviously, if domestic currency does not serve any purpose, as in the above-mentioned model, then the solution to all of this economy's problems is to simply express all transactions in terms of foreign currency ('dollarization' or 'goldarization'). In practice, however, the fisc's dependence on the inflation tax is the key inducement for countries to run into high inflation. But to model this we have to introduce a motive for holding money.

In order to generate a demand for money one can follow the usual practice of putting real monetary balances in either utility or production functions; thus, for example, one can assume that the utility function (6) takes the following form:

$$u(c_1^j) + v(m^j) + \beta u(\hat{c}_2^j) \tag{22}$$

where m^j is the real stock of 'money' (demand deposits in the ensuing interpretation) held by individual j; the other variables are defined as in section 2.2.

We introduce banks in the following manner. These are institutions that take demand deposits and make loans denominated in the domestic currency.[19] We define i as the nominal one-period interest on bank loans; i_m as the nominal one-period interest on demand deposits; and σ as the minimum cash/deposits ratio. Consequently, abstracting from intermediation costs, competitive banks will set

$$i_m = (1-\sigma)i \tag{23}$$

Real income of individuals is still assumed to be given by equation (5); in addition, however, we assume that in period 1 each individual is endowed with H units of the domestic currency. Recalling that there are only two individuals, 'high-powered' money supply at the beginning of period 1 is equal to $2H$.[20]

We will define b^j as the output-denominated bonds held by individual j; x^j as the bank loans received by individual j in terms of output of period 1; and R^* as the international own-rate of interest on output.

In order to emphasize the potential damage caused by a competitive banking system, it will be convenient to assume, as in section 2.2, that $\beta = 1 = 1 + R^*$. Therefore, the budget constraint of individual j is given by the following set of equalities:

$$H/P_1 + y_1^j = c_1^j + b^j + m^j - x^j \tag{24a}$$

$$y_2^j + b^j + m^j(1 + i_m)/(1 + \pi) - x^j(1 + i)/(1 + \pi) = c_2^j \tag{24b}$$

Since the individuals are risk-neutral (*á la* Selden) equation (12) holds in equilibrium; thus, in equilibrium,

$$1 + i = 1/E\{(1 + \pi)^{-1}\} \tag{25}$$

Hence, by equations (23), (24) and (25), recalling that $\hat{c}_2^j$ is the expected value of c_2^j, we get

$$\hat{c}_2^j = y_1^j + y_2^j + H/P_1 - c_1^j - \sigma[1 - E\{(1 + \pi)^{-1}\}]m^j \tag{26}$$

Consider now the case where the government has a claim on output with present value equal to $2H/P_1$. Furthermore, we assume that there is perfect currency convertibility at the exchange rates P_t, $t = 1,2$, and that any accumulation of reserves at the central bank is invested in the international bond. Thus, since no one will plan to hold domestic money in period 2, it follows, recalling that $R^* = 0$, that the government would exactly deplete its wealth in period 2 if it set $P_2 = P_1$, i.e., if it maintained a fixed exchange rate. On the other hand, if $P_2 > P_1$, the government will be left with positive wealth. Therefore, if for reasons outside the model, the government derived some utility from period 2 wealth, there would be a temptation to generate a positive rate of devaluation (i.e., set $P_2 > P_1$).

Let the optimal quantity of money, m^F, be defined, as usual, as the value of m^F at which $v(m)$ is maximized. Then it is quite apparent that any benevolent planner (maximiner, utilitarian or equalitarian) will try to achieve the equilibrium where

$$m^j = m^F \tag{27a}$$

$$c_t^j = (1 + H/P_1)/2 \tag{27b}$$

for $j = 1,2$ and $t = 1,2$. There is, in fact, one way to decentralize this solution and, not too surprisingly, it coincides with Friedman's (1969) rule of setting the rate of inflation equal to (minus) the real rate of return. Let us check the validity of this assertion.

Given that the equilibrium real rate of return is zero (by assumption), Friedman's rule calls for setting $\pi = 0$ with probability 1. Hence, by equations (22) and (26), under this rule consumers will plan a constant consumption path; in addition, m^F will be attained because the opportunity cost of holding money is zero [i.e., the term multiplying m^j in equation (26) is zero]. Finally, it follows from equations (5) and (26) and the previous observations that equation (27b) will be satisfied QED.

It goes without saying that the above proof relies on the implicit assumption that $\pi = 0$ with probability 1 is a credible policy target. If, as indicated above, the government was tempted to depart from the announcement, then it is quite conceivable that the public will attach some positive probability to π being greater than zero, which would make the first-best optimum unattainable, unless $\sigma = 0$. We will discuss the last possibility in what follows.

By definition, $\sigma = 0$ corresponds to the situation where banks are totally free and hold no currency reserves. Since the public is assumed to hold only bank deposits, no one in this economy demands currency in equilibrium. By equations (23) and (26), it is quite clear that the optimum quantity of money will obtain. Furthermore, condition (27b) holds *if* c_2^j is substituted for $\hat{c}_2^j$; in the present case, however, the actual value of c_2^j could very well differ from its expected value. To see this, notice that the real value of deposits in the banking system will at least be

$$2m^F \tag{28}$$

The latter is fully intermediated by the system, and hence lent to somebody in nominal terms at the rate i given by equation (25) [notice, incidentally, that when $\sigma = 0$ we have, by equation (23), that $i = i_m$], thus possibly leading to the redistribution problems discussed in section 2.2.[21] We will now take a closer look at the equilibrium financial flows intermediated by the banking system.

Intuition would seem to indicate that individual 1 – recall equation (5) – will be the one who borrows from the bank. But this is not necessarily so when $\sigma = 0$, because an individual could deposit the amount m^F by simultaneously borrowing the same amount from the bank. This is, however, only one of several possible configurations. Imagine, for example, that in order to open a deposit account at a bank, individuals have to have nonbank resources (i.e, they cannot open a bank account with funds borrowed from the banking system). Furthermore, for the sake of simplicity, let us consider the case where $H = 0$; clearly here, individual 1 will borrow from individual 2 directly (say, in output terms) to open his bank account for a total of m^F, while individual 2 could, in principle,[22] deposit m^F by transferring to the bank part of his first-period income. Hence, liquidity preference alone determines that the banking system ends up with $2m^F$ real units of loanable funds. Let us consider the special case where $m^F = 1/4$. By equations (5), (22) and (26), and recalling that $\beta = 1 + R^* = 1$, we have,

$$c_t^j = 1/2 \qquad j = 1,2 \quad \text{and} \quad t = 1,2 \tag{29}$$

Therefore individual 2 will simply consume 1/2, lend 1/4 directly to individual 1 and deposit m^F (= 1/4) in period 1; on the other hand, individual 1 will borrow 1/4 from individual 2 to invest in m^F, and 1/2 (= $2m^F$ = loanable funds of banking system) from banks for consumption in period 1.

Since the bank is a pure intermediary, the above configuration implies that individual 2 lends to individual 1 real output of 1/2; the bank-loan contract, however, is specified in nominal terms with the nominal interest rate given by equation (25). Obviously then, lack of credibility in the $\pi = 0$ policy will lead to the same type of period 2 redistribution problems that were discussed above (in this section), and in section 2.2.

In sum, free banking helps the economy in decentralizing the optimum quantity of money, but it may result in an undesirable ex post (or period 2 in our examples) income distribution. Consequently, optimal planning, whatever the objective function, is likely to call for some control in bank intermediation (e.g., a nonzero σ) when credibility is imperfect.[23]

4. Sources of Incomplete Credibility

Thus far, our discussion has assumed that nonconformity of expectations with announcements – which we chose to call 'lack of credibility' – is exogenous to the model. This is, of course, unrealistic. Consequently, in this section we will discuss some of the possible sources of lack of credibility. It should be made clear from the outset, however, that we are going to make no serious attempt at fully articulating the present discussion with that of the previous sections.

Perhaps a useful way to start the discussion is to ask ourselves: Why should policy announcements be credible in the first place? Economists do not seem to agree on the relevant model and politicians do not seem to be bothered greatly by the concept of 'scientific truth'; so, why should the average citizen pay much attention to mere promises of future action?. He is, after all, accustomed to hearing that the original policy had to be revised for 'technical reasons,' or, because 'the last government was more preoccupied with speculation than with production,' and so on.

Some announcements are not credible simply because they *are* incredible. The revisions alluded to above are sometimes just a consequence of the fact that the announced policy was 'too' simple. Simple announcements are a great political temptation, because the simpler the policy announcement, the larger the number of people who can understand what is being said. The drawback is that except for the less gifted or the religious converts, the announcement is doomed not to be fully credible. This is a serious problem, because the alternative of making highly detailed – and, very likely, also very technical – announcements is not necessarily a better solution; tons of announcements in 'small print' may just go unread, their potential credibility ignored.

The point that emerges from these remarks is that there may be a fundamental communications problem involved in the credibility issue: if the announcement is simple it may be noncredible, and if it is going to be credible it may not be at all simple, invalidating the message.

Simplicity may become a major issue in situations that require a fundamental overhaul of the monetary and fiscal system. For example, if the problem is to stop a hyperinflation, a simple solution might be to announce a freeze on money supply and to balance the government budget by raising taxes. In practice, however, the process of achieving those targets may be, at the very least, time consuming, implying that the relatively straightforward economics of a once-and-for-all policy adjustment may not be a very useful guide for the private sector to figure out, say, the future rate of inflation. The economics of this type of situation are quite complex; therefore, as far as the public is aware of the implementation problems, expectations might behave very much as if they were generated quite independently of the (simple) policy announcement, and, even more worrisome, expectations might be quite unrelated to the policy that the policy maker has *truly* in mind. Thus, the policy maker will have to live with a reality which may not be too different from the one in which policy announcements are not fully credible, as in the examples of previous sections, unless he/she has the incredible ability to read people's minds under those circumstances.[24] The exogeneity of expectations from the point of view of the policy maker, however, does not imply that expectations are going to be independent of his actions. The problem is that the policy maker would not know the nature of that interdependence. From his perspective, expectations would be very much like a 'moving target' with unknown laws of motion. This gives some support to our earlier conjecture that quantity controls could dominate taxes, given that the effective use of the latter would require a fairly good knowledge about the state of expectations.

Thus, returning to the original question ('Why should policy announcements be at all credible?'), we seem to be converging on the following partial answer: 'There does not seem to be a good reason for "simple" policy announcements (the typical ones in practice) to be credible, unless we are dealing with a very simple situation.' In the process of reaching that conclusion we also cast some doubts on the advisability of making oversimplified announcements.

Another independent reason for lack of credibility is what is usually called 'time inconsistency of optimal policy.' This is an issue that has received a great deal of attention from macroeconomists (e.g., Kydland and Prescott, 1977; Calvo, 1978; Barro and Gordon, 1983; Fischer, 1980; Lucas and Stokey, 1983). The situation is characterized by the fact that the policy maker has a temptation to depart from the preannounced policy, even when he/she was the designer of the policy that he/she feels like changing.

The basic ingredients for time inconsistency are that (a) announcements are processed by rational individuals in a way that is understandable (processable?) by the policy maker, and that (b) the set of policies available to the policy maker at a given point in time is not sufficient for achieving the first-best.[25] The proof is intuitive: since policy announcements do not lead the economy to the first-best, the policy maker may prefer not to continue with the announced policy once the contribution of the announcement to getting closer to the first-best dissipates (i.e., when 'tomorrow' arrives, and 'today's' expectations become inoperational).

Time inconsistency is a real possibility as is amply testified to by many interesting examples in the literature. To the extent that point (b) is highly relevant in practice, time inconsistency may also be an important policy issue. It should be kept in mind, however, that point (a) must also apply; otherwise, if the policy maker was not able to predict the impact of his promises on people's expectations, the incentives for time inconsistency would tend to vanish. In practice, this probably means that time inconsistency is a relevant problem when departure from announcements amounts to much more than mere 'fine tuning.' Time inconsistency may, therefore, not be extremely relevant in explaining inflation in the US economy, but it may nonetheless be an important consideration for substantial reforms like those designed to stop hyperinflation.

As was pointed out above, the possibility of time inconsistency on the part of the policy maker involves the existence of some relevant information on the relationship between expectations and policy announcements. Therefore this source of imperfect credibility is, in principle, inconsistent with our examples' assumption that expectations are exogenous. Fortunately, however, the examples are not misleading with respect to the first-best policies, because being able to achieve the first-best eliminates all incentives for time inconsistency.

In sum, our discussion has indicated that credibility problems are more likely to be encountered when policy is aimed at resolving complex and substantial politico-economic disturbances. Somewhat paradoxically, for different reasons, credibility problems tend to be exacerbated at the extremes of very good and of very bad communications between the public and the policy makers, due to time inconsistency and oversimplifications, respectively.

5. Conclusions

Our central examples have shown that lack of full credibility is an important factor in determining the nature of optimal policy. Simple policies that disregard this factor may result in situations that are far from optimal. Unfortunately, the correct appreciation of the 'state of beliefs' in a given country usually requires a highly sensitized 'nose' which cannot be obtained unless one has a rather deep understanding of the relevant history and institutions. Thus, in a way, this paper casts serious doubts on economic advice that comes from 'instant' country experts who oftentimes know the country only through the pages of the IFS.

A worrisome conclusion of the analysis is that optimal policy could require controls that may be difficult to implement, and which may interact with credibility in ways which we, as economists, are still far from understanding fully. Hence, although this paper has uncovered reasons to criticize policy that disregards the credibility issue, the solutions discussed in the text can at best be considered tentative.

In view of the above, what can be said about the role of the economic advisor? A somewhat clear implication is that the economic advisor should, at the very least, make the politician extremely conscious of the importance of credibility; in order to do that, however, the advisor will probably have to 'bone up' on the politics of the situation since, otherwise, the politician will be left with a warning whose meaning will be hard for him to understand. This is an important point. The economic advisor has to be able to express his ideas in a way which is understandable to noneconomists, which in the present context will probably mean that we will have to take into consideration the politico-historical moment at which the advice is given. Clearly, this requires a solid grasp of the above-mentioned 'noneconomic' factors, a subject on which the professional economist seldom receives any training.

In this paper we have emphasized how easy it is for a policy – particularly for one that entails radical reforms – not to be fully credible. On the other hand, we had very little to contribute by way of remedies for the credibility syndrome. This does not mean, of course, that the problem can be ignored. As recent Latin American history seems to indicate, credibility is not helped by pretending that the problem does not exist, and much less by relying on advisors who ignore its key role.[26]

NOTES

The research reported in the paper was funded by a grant from the National Science Foundation.

1 In addition, we assume $u(.,.)$ is strictly concave, and exhibits positive partial derivatives.

2 More specifically, spot prices at time t (t=1,2) are given in terms of good x at time t (this is the meaning of good x being the unit of account), while each term in the sum defining the budget constraint is given in terms of x_2, i.e., good x in the future (x_2 is, thus, the numéraire).

3 An obvious solution to the problem would be for the government to find a way to precommit itself to setting τ_2=0. In practice, however, this may be hard to implement because future administrations (some of them not even known to the general public at present) would have to be involved in the decision.

4 This solution is similar to some of the proposals discussed in Edwards (1985b) concerning the optimal staging of liberalization policies. However, imperfect credibility, although frequently mentioned in this literature, is not normally mentioned in support of the capital-control proposition outlined in the text.

5 We define a capital inflow (outflow) as an accumulation (decumulation) of debt on the part of the domestic economy.

6 See Calvo (1986c) where some of the above issues are discussed in a dynamically richer model.

7 Notice that E is not indexed by j, meaning that all individuals share the same information. This assumption, however, is not essential for our results.

8 $u(\cdot)$ is assumed to be strictly concave and increasing.

9 Notice that if individuals had 'point expectations,' or, more precisely, if the distribution of π was concentrated at a single point, say, π^e, then equation (12) implies the following, undoubtedly more familiar, expression:

$$1+i^* = (1+R^*)(1+\pi^e)$$

10 More realistic extensions of the model are discussed in the next section.

11 See, for example, Edwards (1985a) for a discussion and references in regard to the recent liberalization program in Chile. Calvo (1986c) shows that the existence of durable goods when liberalization plans are not credible could bring about a substantial welfare loss.

12 Obviously, for $t=1$, equation (3) will be modified to read

$$g_1=\tau_1(c_1+S_c)$$

13 Similar difficulties are present if a tax on capital flows is used to try to achieve the first-best solution.

14 This observation raises serious questions about the efficacy of quantitative controls in a world of heterogeneous capital goods. In fact, we conjecture that the greater the degree of capital diversity, the more attractive an interest rate policy would be, despite the drawbacks pointed out before.

15 For example, there will tend to be underinvestment in industries that would be profitable only if the liberalization policy is expected to last.

16 This would be the case if, for instance, the expectation that the liberalization program will be terminated after one period leads to a higher consumption of c and x, and l is complementary with the last two.

17 The pre-announcement of the exchange rate was at the center of the recent stabilization programs of Argentina, Chile and Uruguay. See Corbo (1985), Edwards (1985a), Harberger (1982), Díaz-Alejandro (1981), Rodriguez (1982) and Calvo (1983, 1986a).

18 Recall that individuals would be indifferent about the unit of account in which loans are specified. Thus, banks would be able to survive even though individuals are in the position to specify their capital-market transactions (with the rest of the world) in terms of output.

19 This captures the impact of the common regulation that prohibits banks from exchange-risk exposure. We could have allowed banks to operate in foreign exchange, but none of the ensuing results would be essentially changed if *some* deposits are denominated in terms of the domestic currency.

20 This may differ from the stock of high-powered money at the end of the period because perfect currency convertibility will be assumed.

21 Since in this case no one holds domestic currency, there would be no obvious reason for the government to make a surprise devaluation. The temptation will return, however, as soon as δ becomes positive; thus, the present discussion approximates a situation in which δ is positive but 'small.'

22 Conditions for insuring this will be specified below.

23 This result stands in sharp contrast with the situation of perfect credibility, where under otherwise very similar assumptions, a strong case for free or, at least, freer banking can be made. See Calvo (1986b).

24 Notice that our arguments are consistent with the hypothesis of rationality, i.e., that individuals utilize all of their available information; the cases that we are describing correspond to situations where the individual information sets do not coincide with that of the policy makers, and the latter do not fully know what variables are contained in the information sets of the private sector.

25 Notice that condition (a) was not necessary for the 'simplicity' arguments presented above.

26 Carlos Díaz-Alejandro has, on several occasions, expressed his misgivings about simple-minded advice in connection with Latin American countries (see Díaz-Alejandro, 1981, 1983, 1985).

REFERENCES

Barro, Robert J. and Gordon, David B. 1983: A positive theory of monetary policy in a natural-rate model. *Journal of Political Economy*, 91, 589–610.

Calvo, Guillermo A. 1978: On the time consistency of optimal monetary policy. *Econometrica*, 46, 1411–28.

Calvo, Guillermo A. 1983: Trying to stabilize: some theoretical reflections based on the case of Argentina. In Pedro Aspe A., Rudiger Dornbusch and Maurice Obstfeld (eds.), *Financial Policies and the World Capital Market: The Problem of Latin American Countries*, Chicago: University of Chicago Press.

Calvo, Guillermo A. 1986a: Fractured liberalism: Argentina under Martinez de Hoz. *Journal of Economic Development and Cultural Change*, 511–34.

Calvo, Guillermo A. 1986b: Welfare, banks and capital mobility in steady state: the case of predetermined exchange rates. In L. Ahamed and Sebastian Edwards (eds.), *Structural Adjustment and the Real Exchange Rate in Developing Countries*, Chicago: University of Chicago Press for the National Bureau of Economic Research.

Calvo, Guillermo A. 1986c: On the costs of temporary liberalization/stabilization experiments. Paper presented at the VIth Latin American Meetings of the Econometric Society, Cordoba, Argentina, July.

Corbo, Vittorio 1985: Reforms and macroeconomic adjustments in Chile during 1974–84. *World Development*, 13, 893–916.

Díaz-Alejandro, Carlos F. 1981: Southern cone stabilization plans. In William R. Cline (ed.), *Economic Stabilization in Developing Countries*, Washington, DC: The Brookings Institution.

Díaz-Alejandro, Carlos F. 1983: Stories of the 1930s for the 1980s. In Pedro Aspe A., Rudiger Dornbusch and Maurice Obstfeld (eds.), *Financial Policies and the World Capital Market: The Problem of Latin American Countries*, Chicago: University of Chicago Press.

Díaz-Alejandro, Carlos F. 1985: Good-bye financial repression, hello financial crash. *Journal of Economic Development*, 19, 1–24.

Edwards, Sebastian 1985a: Stabilization with liberalization: an evaluation of ten years of Chile's experiment with free-market policies, 1973–1983. *Journal of Economic Development and Cultural Change*, 223–54.

Edwards, Sebastian 1985b: The order of liberalization of the external sector in developing countries. *Essays in International Finance*, International Finance Section, Princeton University, no. 161.

Fischer, Stanley 1980: Dynamic inconsistency, cooperation and the benevolent dissembling government. *Journal of Economic Dynamics and Control*, 2, 93–108.

Friedman, Milton 1969: The optimum quantity of money. *The Optimum Quantity of Money and other Essays*. Chicago: Aldine.

Harberger, Arnold C. 1982: The Chilean economy in the 1970s: crisis, stabilization, reform. *Carnegie–Rochester Conference Series on Public Policy*, 17, 115–52.

Kydland, Finn E. and Prescott, Edward C. 1977: Rules rather than discretion: the inconsistency of optimal plans. *Journal of Political Economy*, 85, 473–91.

Laidler, David 1984: Misconceptions about the real-bill doctrine: a comment on Sargent and Wallace. *Journal of Political Economy*, 92, 149–55.

Lucas, J., Robert, E. and Stokey, Nancy L. 1983: Optimal fiscal and monetary policy in an economy without capital. *Journal of Monetary Economics*, 12, 55–94.

Mussa, Michael 1985: Nominal exchange rate regimes and the behavior of real exchange rates: evidence and implications. Presented at the *Carnegie–Rochester Conference Series on Public Policy*, November 22–3.

Rodriguez, Carlos A. 1982: The Argentinian stabilization plan of December 20th. *World Development*, 10, 226–38.

Selden, Larry 1978: A new representation of preferences over 'certain uncertain' consumption pairs: the 'ordinal certainty equivalence' hypothesis. *Econometrica*, 46, 1045–60.

11

External Shocks and Policy Reforms in the Southern Cone: A Reassessment

Vittorio Corbo and Jaime de Melo

1. Introduction

Few reform packages have led to as much controversy as the Southern Cone reforms in Chile, Argentina and Uruguay. Carlos Díaz-Alejandro, a close observer, was well aware of this when he stated cautiously that '. . . it is often difficult to establish where scientific economics ends and political preference begins' (Díaz-Alejandro, 1981, p, 120). While not eschewing his centrist position, Díaz-Alejandro knew where to draw the line between scientific economics and political preferences and showed much foresight in his interpretations of Southern Cone reforms. In his early appraisal of Southern Cone stabilization plans, he foresaw, among other difficulties, the risks of using the exchange rate to bring down inflation. He wrote:

> Reliance on a preannounced and declining rate of exchange rate devaluation as the key instrument to lower inflation also appears as excessively risky. Stubborn inflation in the prices of nontraded goods can lead to overvaluation. . . . Preannounced exchange rates reduce the uncertainty of financial speculators while increasing that of exporters, a peculiar trade-off. . . . Yet if the preannounced and slower devaluation pace fails to reduce inflation fairly quickly, expectations will grow that sharper devaluations lie ahead. The government will be faced with the 1950s dilemma of giving in to such expectations, rekindling after all the inflationary spiral and losing any remaining credibility, or adopting very contractionary policies to validate the overvalued exchange rate. (Díaz-Alejandro, 1981, p. 135)

Later on, in 1982, before the impending financial crisis, he forewarned about the moral hazard problem created by outright financial sector deregulation unaccompanied by appropriate banking sector supervision. He wrote:

> The combination of preannounced or fixed nominal exchange rate, relatively free capital movements, and domestic and external financial systems characterized by the moral hazard and other imperfections discussed

above set the stage not only for significant microeconomic misallocation of credit, but also for macroeconomic instability, including the explosive growth of external debt. . . . That macroeconomic instability would occur even assuming tranquil circumstances, but it is of course exacerbated by external shocks hitting economies made particularly brittle and vulnerable by that combination of policies and institutions. (Díaz-Alejandro, 1985, pp. 15–16)

Díaz-Alejandro's insights aside, currently received wisdom about the outcomes of Southern Cone reform sometimes gives the impression of a state of disarray analogous to the economic disorder in the three countries themselves, as their dismal record unraveled in the early 1980s. Some observers, notably in the press, have concluded that the reform effort as a whole was a failure. Others, including the present authors (Corbo and de Melo, 1985, 1987), have suggested that the microeconomic reforms were successful and that most of the problems that emerged resulted from inadequate macroeconomic policies. Still others have blamed a large part of the failure on unfavorable external shocks (Sjaastad, 1983).

This paper uses the benefit of hindsight to examine these controversial reforms once more – their pervasiveness, their implementation and the contribution of external factors to their overall failure. Section 2 summarizes the reforms, setting the scene for sections 3 and 4 in which we assess the role of external shocks using both straightforward decomposition analysis and counterfactual simulations derived from an econometric model. The model is used again in section 5 to attempt to quantify the relative importance of the imprudent macroeconomic policies referred to by Díaz-Alejandro. Having established that external shocks were not a predominant factor, in section 6 we summarize briefly how inconsistent policies combined to produce economic disarray in the Southern Cone in the early 1980s.

2. Synopsis of the Reforms

2.1 Stabilization

In all three countries, the reform process began against a background of severe macroeconomic imbalances, reflected in unsustainable balance of payments positions and high inflation.[1] Not surprisingly, the authorities' first priority was stabilization – a strategy that would still be recommended today, because an up-front stabilization effort lends credibility to liberalization and helps to reduce real exchange rate fluctuations. Up-front stabilization is also necessary when inflation is high, because of some of the latter's main adverse side-effects: (a) volatility in relative prices, which reduces the information content of prices; (b) sharp real exchange rate variations stemming from the periodic use of the exchange rate to reduce inflation; and (c) increasing concentration of financial transactions in instruments with short-term maturities because of uncertainty about future inflation levels.

Until early 1978, the three countries followed orthodox stabilization strategies, emphasizing control of the money supply and reductions in fiscal deficits. For Chile and Uruguay in particular, external shocks caused by falling commodity terms of trade exacerbated balance of payments difficulties and intensified the contractionary effects of the orthodox stabilization packages. Moreover, by the middle of 1978, much had been done to deregulate the financial system in each country. Not only had the interest rate ceilings that had applied to financial transactions for the past 20 years been eliminated; in Argentina and Uruguay, financial transactions with the outside world as well had been deregulated.

It was roughly at this point, i.e., after substantial deregulation of their respective financial systems, that policymakers in all three countries became convinced that increasing worldwide capital mobility meant that they could do little to control the money supply. Switching to an exchange-rate-based approach to stabilization through preannounced future exchange rate values (the tablita) – which Díaz-Alejandro foresaw as storing up future troubles – seemed an attractive option, especially given the belief that this approach would avoid the contractionary effects of orthodox stabilization packages because people would rapidly lower their inflationary expectations.[2] The exchange-rate-based stabilization was abandoned in March 1981 in Argentina, in June 1982 in Chile and in November 1982 in Uruguay.

2.2 Liberalization

After three decades of import substitution and extensive price controls and interest rate controls, the economies of the three Southern Cone countries had by the early 1970s become some of the most distorted among middle-income developing countries. Trade policies in all three countries were similarly and strongly biased in favor of import-substituting industrialization (ISI) and against exports. All three countries had tried mild trade liberalization experiments – Chile in the late 1960, Argentina in the second half of the same decade and Uruguay in 1959. In each case, there was a return to a very restrictive trade regime with widespread tariff and nontariff barriers. The fragmentary available evidence indicates high average effective rates of protection to domestic sales in each country: 84 per cent in Argentina (1969); 151 per cent in Chile (1974); 384 per cent in Uruguay (1969). The variability of protection across sectors, an indicator of distortion in incentives, was also very high in the three countries, and for no good economic reason; rather, it was the piecemeal result of pressures imposed by different domestic interest groups. Financial markets were also highly regulated, while nonprice allocation of credit and strongly negative real interest rates were widespread and longstanding.

With the exception of domestic financial market deregulation, which proceeded rapidly in all cases, the sequencing of liberalization in the late 1970s and early 1980s differed in each country. Uruguay removed all controls on capital flows and many commodity price controls early on, but progressed more slowly on the liberalization of foreign trade. Uruguay also rationalized its fiscal system the most, eliminating the income tax and moving to a value added tax (VAT). Chile, on the other hand, also introduced a VAT and implemented a deep rationalization of public expenditures, transforming a large public sector deficit (close to 25 per cent of GDP in 1973) to a surplus by 1978. Chile also went the farthest in eliminating domestic price controls and reducing trade barriers, but maintained controls on short-term capital flows for a long period. Chile also maintained important labor market regulations. Argentina eliminated price controls, eliminated most restrictions on medium-term (more than 1 year) capital flows and removed quantitative import restrictions (with some important exceptions) before implementing some ad hoc tariff reductions. Uruguay virtually eliminated price controls by the end of 1979, but adopted only minimal commercial policy reforms to lower protection.

The evidence of persistently high effective protection to domestic sales in Argentina and Uruguay makes it clear that liberalization by no means affected all markets. In fact, contrary to popular belief, only Chile experienced extensive trade liberalization, moving in 5 years toward a uniform 10 per cent tariff which was achieved in June 1979; in Argentina and Uruguay, where liberalization was much less widespread, pressure from foreign competition was only felt at the height of real exchange rate overvaluation. For example, redundant protection in Uruguay was only eliminated in 1981; at that time the bias against export sales was still 35 per cent.

As stated above, rapid and pervasive deregulation of domestic financial markets was a common feature of the reforms in all three countries. Prior to deregulation, nonprice allocation of credit and strongly negative real interest rates had been widespread and longstanding. The reforms began by progressively eliminating ceilings on interest rates, and then reduced restrictions on financial intermediaries. Argentina went from 100 per cent reserve requirements and directed credit programs to a decentralized fractional reserve system. The Chilean government began loosening its control of the financial system by allowing nonbank intermediaries to operate without interest rate controls. Then, over several years, it removed interest rate ceilings for commercial banks and returned state-owned commercial banks to the private sector. In Uruguay, dollar deposits were legalized and directed credit programs were progressively dismantled starting in 1974. Later, in 1977, controls on entry to the banking system were also lifted.

With respect to international capital flows, the sequencing and speed of reforms differed from country to country. Uruguay legalized unrestricted movements of private capital as early as 1974, and reached full convertibility by early 1977. Argentina eliminated most controls on capital movements in 1979. Chile progressively deregulated medium-term capital flows, eliminating global limits on borrowing in 1979 and restrictions on monthly inflows in April 1980. Restrictions on short-term capital inflows were not dismantled until late 1981, however.

Finally, in all three countries, there was relatively little liberalization of labor markets. These markets continued to be controlled through penalties or prohibitions on labor dismissals, together with legislated wages and/or wage indexation. Thus, while the weakening of trade union power in the early stages of the reforms amounted to a degree of de facto deregulation, the Southern Cone countries did little to promote greater labor mobility, which is a necessary condition for efficient resource reallocation under any revised system of incentives.

To sum up, along with the lifting of domestic price controls, with the exception of trade liberalization in Chile, the most extensively implemented liberalization program in all three countries was the deregulation of financial markets. This is not surprising: one might reasonably expect much less resistance from threatened interest groups to the reduction of restrictions in this area than, say, to reduction of trade barriers or removal of protective labor market regulations (where, as just noted, very little was indeed done). Eventually, all three countries also decontrolled short-term external capital flows – a liberalization measure rarely carried out in developing countries – but only Uruguay adopted a fully liberalized regime in this area.

The controversy this paper deals with concerns the latter part of the reform period. Starting in middle to late 1978, all three countries switched from an orthodox approach to stabilization policy based on control of the money supply to an exchange-rate-based approach. The idea of the new approach was that by preannouncing future exchange rates (reflecting declining rates of devaluation) inflationary expectations could be curbed while avoiding the standard contractionary effects of orthodox stabilization packages. As Díaz-Alejandro perceived early on, such an approach was risky. Proponents of the approach, however, have argued that it is the concurrent external shocks (the oil price hike of 1979 followed by the rise in interest rates in 1981) which were the proximate cause of failure of the reform package in each country.

Before turning to an examination of their relative importance, consider the facts to be explained: these are summarized in figure 11.1 which traces the quarterly real exchange rate, real GDP and ex post interest rate trajectories during 1977–82 in each country. A similar pattern of real exchange rate appreciation, acceleration of GDP growth and a U-shaped trajectory of real interest rates developed in all three countries. Were these trajectories mostly determined by external events, internal events or, more plausibly, a combination of the two?

3. Assessing External Shocks via Decomposition Analysis

We start our assessment of the role of external events by a decomposition analysis of changes in terms of trade and interest rates. This is a common approach to analyzing the welfare effects of interest rates and terms of trade changes (Balassa, 1984; Mitra, 1987; Sachs, 1985). Its theoretical justification is given by Dornbusch (1985) in terms of a two-period model. Dorn-

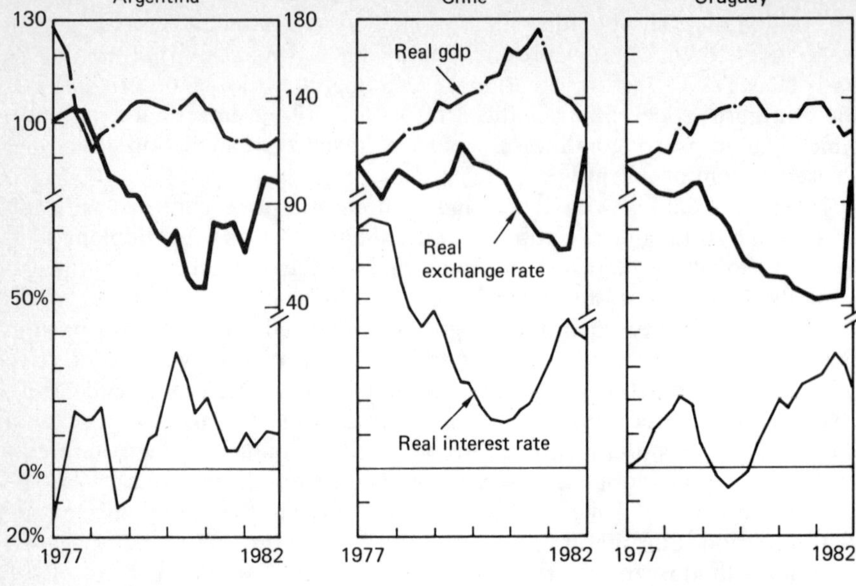

Figure 11.1 Real exchange rates and real interest rates during the active crawling peg (real exchange rate index on right-hand scale, real interest rate and GDP index on left-hand scale)

busch shows that maximization under perfect competition by households and firms subject to an intertemporal budget constraint yields marginal welfare effects of external disturbances arising from real interest rate, terms of trade and external debt changes.

A decomposition of the unfavorable impact of external events is provided in table 11.1. The methodology is the same as the one used by Sachs (1985). The table offers quantified estimates of how important terms of trade and interest rate shocks were for the Southern Cone countries. The interest rate shock, which began to be felt after the rise in US interest rates starting at the end of 1979, not only affected the cost of new borrowing but also interest charges on existing debt. Not surprisingly, this latter effect was particularly strong in the three countries during 1982–3 because much of their debt was contracted at variable interest rates through syndicated commercial bank loans. As table 11.1 shows, for the 1982–3 period, the combination of declining terms of trade and increasing interest costs amounted to 12.2 per cent of GNP in Chile, 6.7 per cent of GNP in Argentina but only 1.0 per cent of GNP in Uruguay.

Comparing the relative contribution of external shocks during each sub-

Table 11.1 External shocks: 1974–83 (% of GDP)

	Terms of trade (1)			*Interest rate* (2)			*Total* (3) = (2) + (1)		
	1974–8	*1979–81*	*1982–3*	*1974–8*	*1979–81*	*1982–3*	*1974–8*	*1979–81*	*1982–3*
Argentina[a]	−2.9	−0.3	−0.3	n.c.	2.8	−6.4	−2.9	2.5	−6.7
Chile	−5.7	−1.9	−4.8	n.c.	0.2	−7.4	−5.7	−1.7	−12.2
Uruguay	−7.6	−0.4	1.9	n.c.	0.9	−2.9	−7.6	0.5	−1.0

n.c. – not calculated.

Methodology. The real income effect of terms of trade changes is computed from import and export unit value indices in *ECLA* weighted by the import share of GDP. The interest rate effect is calculated as

$$\frac{i - \hat{P}_T}{1 + \hat{P}_T}; \ \hat{P}_T = (\hat{P}_X + \hat{P}_M)\, 0.5$$

where $\hat{P}_X$ and $\hat{P}_M$ are percentage changes in the export and import price indices and the interest rate effect is computed from the world debt tables (1986) as the ratio of interest payments to disbursed debt and expressed in terms of GDP by multiplying by the debt to GNP ratio. $\hat{P}_M$ is measured by the export unit value of industrial countries from the IFS. The same methodology is used in Sachs (1985). Changes are computed with respect to the previous period.

[a] For Argentina the periods are 1976–8, 1979–80 and 1981–2.

period, it is notable that terms of trade shocks were significant during 1974–8 when stabilization was based on the orthodox approach and that during 1979–81 when signs of unsustainability of the exchange-rate-based stabilization program were appearing, the external environment was favorable for two of the three countries (Argentina and Uruguay). This is to be expected since the cost of foreign borrowing was low in that period of excess world liquidity. And in spite of the oil price hike of 1979, the adverse terms of trade shock was small for the three countries. Thus, we conclude from this first-round examination that external shocks were not important during the inception of the exchange-rate-based approach to stabilization.

The estimates of external shocks during 1982–3, however, show large magnitudes for Chile and Argentina. The large terms of trade effect for Chile during 1982–3 reflects the spike in copper prices in 1980–1. However, as we argue below, in the three countries a part of the interest rate shock – which reflects the increase in the interest rate and the increased volume of debt – was endogenous as it occurred when public debt was accumulating to finance private capital flight when doubts about the sustainability of exchange-rate-based stabilization set in. In Argentina and Uruguay, increased debt resulted mostly from capital flight[3] and in Chile from expenditure-led trade deficits.

The decomposition analysis is useful but the methodology rests upon assumptions that exclude the possibility that government policies may affect private sector behavior which in turn would lead to a change in the external position of the country. Thus, we are not able to take into account in this decomposition that the increased external borrowing which took place in the early 1980s was at least partly induced by the exchange-rate-based stabilization policy. Therefore we move on to an analysis which incorporates many of the issues Díaz-Alejandro was concerned with when he first assessed Southern Cone stabilization plans.

4. An Econometric Model to Analyze External Shocks

In this section we formulate a small macro model to assess in a quasi-general equilibrium framework the contribution of external and domestic factors to output growth and debt accumulation.[4] The model is then estimated for Chile and Uruguay[5] with annual data for the period 1962–83. The model adapts an earlier quarterly model presented in Caballero and Corbo (1985) for the analysis of the effects of real exchange rate changes. In that paper, specifications and estimation issues are fully described. The model's treatment of the external sector is quite similar to the Computable General Equilibrium (CGE) simulation model used by Condon et al. (1985) to examine the role of external shocks in Chile during 1977–81. However, in that exercise no parameter estimation was undertaken and adjustment frictions were not included in the analysis as they are here.

4.1 The Model

To isolate the importance of external shocks, we disaggregate the model into five goods: two exportables (manufacturing and nonmanufacturing); two importables (oil and nonoil);[6] and one nontradable. Besides oil, two goods are consumed domestically, nonoil importables and nontradables. Two-stage budget allocation determines demand for these two goods. On the production side, supply functions come from optimization with ad hoc lags to capture adjustment dynamics. Identities implied by the general equilibrium feature of the model allow us to determine nontradable prices and hence the real exchange rate. Finally, a Phillips curve reflects wage stickiness. This implies that a sudden contraction after a boom may have strong real effects because of increases in unemployment caused by rising real labor costs.

The general structure of the model is presented below with the specific changes (e.g., ad hoc lags and dummy variables) required for the application of the model to Chile and Uruguay discussed later along with estimation issues.

Expenditure

$$C = \alpha_o C_{-1} + \mu(DY - \alpha_o DY_{-1}) + e_t \tag{1}$$

Imports $(P_M \cdot M \equiv \text{OILM} \cdot P_{\text{OIL}} + \text{NOM} \cdot P_{\text{NO}})$

$$\log(\text{NOM}) = \beta_o + \{1/(1-\beta_1)\}\ \{\log(P_c) - \log(P_{\text{NO}})\} + \log(N \cdot C) \tag{2}$$

Exports $(P_X \cdot X \equiv P_{\text{XNM}} \cdot X_{\text{NM}} + P_{\text{XM}} \cdot \hat{\text{XM}})$

$$\log(\text{X}_{\text{NM}}) = \gamma_{01} - \gamma_{11}\ \{\log(W) - \log(P_{\text{XNM}})\} - \gamma_{21}\ \{\log(P^i_{\text{XNM}}) - \log(P_{\text{XNM}})\} + k_{\text{XNM}} \tag{3}$$

$$\log(\text{X}_{\text{M}}) = \gamma_{02} - \gamma_{12}\ \{\log(W) - \log(P_{\text{XM}})\} - \gamma_{22}\ \{\log(P^i_{\text{XM}}) - \log(P_{\text{XM}})\} + k_{\text{XM}} \tag{4}$$

Nontradable Price and Phillips Curve

$$\log(P_{\text{N}}) = \theta_{11}\log(W) + \theta_{12}\log P_{\text{OIL}} + (1-\theta_{11} - \theta_{12})\log P_{\text{NO}} + \theta_{14}\{\log(E) - k_{\text{N}}\} \tag{5}$$

$$\Delta\log(W) = \theta_{21} + \Delta\log(P_c) + \theta_{22}\ \{\log Y) - \log(N)\} \tag{6}$$

$$\log(P) = \phi_o \log(P_N) + \phi_1 \log(P_X) + (1 - \phi_0 - \phi_1) \log(P_{OIL}) \tag{7}$$

Identities

$$B \equiv P_x \cdot X - P_M \cdot M \tag{8}$$

$$Y \equiv (N \cdot C\, P_c + B)/P \tag{9}$$

$$DY \equiv [P \cdot Y - \mathrm{INT}]/(P_c \cdot N) \tag{10}$$

Price Definitions

$$\log(P_c) \equiv \psi_{11} \log(P_{NO}) + (1-\psi_{11}) \log(P_N) \tag{11}$$

$$\log(p^i_{XNM}) \equiv \psi_{12} \log(P_{OIL}) + \psi_{22} \log(P_{NO}) + (1-\psi_{12}-\psi_{22}) \log(P_N) \tag{12}$$

$$\log(p^i_{XM}) \equiv \psi_{13} \log(P_{OIL}) + \psi_{23} \log(P_{NO}) + (1-\psi_{13}-\psi_{23}) \log(P_N) \tag{13}$$

$$\log(P_M) \equiv \psi_{14} \log(P_{OIL}) + (1-\psi_{14}) \log(P_{NO}) \tag{14}$$

$$\log(P_X) \equiv \psi_{15} \log(P_{XM}) + (1-\psi_{15}) \log(P_{XNM}) \tag{15}$$

where Δ is the log difference operator, the subscript index -1 indicates a one-period lag and the symbols are as follows:

C : private consumption plus investment (per capita)
DY : disposable income (per capita)
e_t : Expectational error (orthogonal to information available at $t-1$)
P_M : imports price
M : imports volume
OILM : oil imports
P_{OIL} : oil price
NOM : nonoil imports
P_{NO} : nonoil import price
P_c : private consumption (plus investment) deflator
E : total expenditure
P_X : exports price
X : exports volume
X_{NM} : nonmanufacture exports
P_{XNM} : nonmanufacture exports price
X_M : manufacture exports
P_{XM} : manufacture exports price
W : nominal wage
P^i_{XNM} : input price in nonmanufacture exports
P^i_{XM} : input price in manufacture exports

k_{XNM} : log of capital in nonmanufacture exports
k_{XM} : log of capital in manufacture exports
k_N : log of capital in nontradables
P_N : nontradable price
N : population
P : GDP deflator
B : Balance of trade
Y : GDP
INT : net foreign interest payments (abroad) in local currency

The most important novelty, with respect to the model in Caballero and Corbo (1985), is equation (1), the aggregate expenditure function. Here we interpret the residual of this equation to indicate an expectational error. This interpretation, necessitated by our analysis, has implications for estimation. Caballero (1986) justifies the estimation procedure adopted here. The hypothesis is that there are two groups of individuals, one that is not subject to a liquidity constraint and behaves according to the permanent income hypothesis, and one which is subject to a liquidity constraint. For the former group, Hall (1978) showed that assuming that this group has a separable utility function, consumption follows a martingale. For the non-liquidity constrained group, we describe consumption by the process:

$$C'_t = \alpha_0 C'_{t-1} + e_t \tag{16}$$

where C'_t is per capita consumption of the group that is not liquidity constrained and e_t is an expectational error with

$$E(e_t / I_{t-1}) = 0 \tag{17}$$

We assume that the rest of the population is absolutely liquidity constrained and thus spends all its income. Thus for this second group we assume:

$$C''_t = DY''_t \tag{18}$$

Aggregating equations (16) and (18), we obtain the per capita consumption equation (1) above, i.e.,

$$C_t = \alpha_O C_{t-1} + \mu(DY_t - \alpha_O DY_{t-1}) + e_t$$

where α_O is a constant and μ is the fraction of the population that is liquidity constrained.

Equation (2) and a similar one for nontradables [used to derive equation (5)] are obtained from a two-stage budgeting process, with the first stage determining the level of expenditure for each period and the second stage assigning the expenditures to nontradable and nonoil importables. Equations

(3) and (4) are derived from profit maximization subject to a homogeneous Cobb–Douglas technology. Two–stage budgeting and technology are thus standard and similar to the specification in Condon et al. (1985). Equation (5) is derived from market clearing for nontradables using a demand equation similar to equation (2) and a supply equation like equations (3) and (4).

The second important feature of the model is equation (6), the Phillips curve. The realism of this specification allows us to capture stickiness in price adjustment, an important feature when an economy must adjust to an external shock.[7] Next is equation (7), the GDP deflator, where the weights are constant and estimated through a regression.

Following are identities (not estimated) and price definitions. Identity (8) is the balance of trade and nonfactor services, identity (9) is the GDP expenditure identity and (10) is the definition of GDP after net foreign interest payment. Equations (11) to (15) are price definitions. The weights entering the cost functions for exports are obtained from the 1977 input–output table of Chile and from Uruguay's manufacturing census of 1978.

4.2 *Estimation Issues*

Estimation problems arise because e_t is only orthogonal to the information set I_{t-1} which does not contain DY_t. As e_t is a revision of the expectations on permanent income, the 'news' component of DY_t will most likely be correlated with e_t. We approach the estimation problem by estimating equation (1) by instrumental variables, using instruments that belong to the information set I_{t-1}. The use of full information maximum likelihood (FIML) does not restrict the instruments to the information set I_{t-1}, hence it is inconsistent.

Earlier, we argued (Corbo et al. 1986) that a 'bubble' developed in the Southern Cone countries in the early 1980s. Our residual in equation (1) corresponds to a revision on expectation formation so it is not able to capture the beginning and the bursting of the 'bubble' or any unexpected change in its size. The residual can, however, take account of the expected 'bubble' once it exists.

The procedure we suggest is to first estimate equation (1) by instrumental variables (IV), and then to investigate its residuals. A large positive residual followed by a systematic high level of consumption is taken as evidence of a revision in expectations. If present, we interpret this break as signaling the start of a bubble, and we introduce a dummy variable to capture this effect in the simulation. Moreover, if the break is not a bubble but rather an unexpected increase in wealth, the dummy variable procedure is still justified since our model cannot capture this type of unexpected change unless it originates in the liquidity constrained population.

For Chile we went further. For the 1980–2 period, we added the residual from the instrumental variable estimation of equation (1). We call this a nonpredictable bubble evolution.

For Uruguay, where data availability was not as good as in Chile, we had to do some aggregation before estimating. Furthermore, when we estimated equation (1) by IV we could not estimate the rest of the model by FIML because the model did not converge. Therefore, we had to estimate the complete model by FIML. In this case, we used the residuals obtained from the FIML estimation of equation (1) for the period 1979–83. We also had to aggregate the two export equations in the Uruguay model. Moreover, in the simultaneous estimations we had to impose the nominal export price effect obtained from the ordinary least squares estimation. In the estimation no restrictions were imposed on the coefficient of domestic costs.

The models finally estimated appear in table 11.2. They differ from the basic model in that the former included three additional elements: (a) dummy variables, (b) dynamic components and (c) prior information. For the Chile model, note that equations (12) and (13) have already been substituted away in equations (3c) and (4c) which also contain the input cost shares (ψ_{12}, ψ_{22}, ψ_{13}, ψ_{23}) obtained from the 1977 input–output table. For Uruguay note that two equations (4u) and (15u) do not appear because no distinction is made between manufactured and nonmanufactured exports.

The values of the estimated coefficients and their standard errors appear in table 11.3. Coefficients in the Uruguay estimation for which there is no standard error (i.e., in table 11.3) correspond to parameters taken as fixed in the *last* step of estimation.[8] Because the estimated models are different, there is no one-to-one relation between the meaning of the coefficients in Chile and Uruguay. The overall fit of the estimated model is quite good for both countries. In the case of Uruguay, however, the crisis of the early 1980s, had many elements that the model could not completely account for. Because prediction errors are accumulated in the dynamic simulations, we decided to use a dummy variable (solely for the simulation) to bring the 'control' close to the true value of the endogenous variables. We only connected the debt accumulation through the import and export equations. These modifications result in good fits for the 1980–3 period as a whole, though not for the actual timing of the crisis. We are thus able to make the counterfactual simulations reported below more meaningful.

5. The Relative Importance of the External Shocks: Some Counterfactual Simulations

We now use the parameter estimates of table 11.3 to quantify the contribution of external and domestic factors to the dynamic pattern of output growth and debt accumulation. Table 11.4 presents the historical evolution of the terms of trade, GDP and external debt for the two countries. These data serve as inputs for the simulation runs for the 1981–3 period on the hypothesis of no external shocks. We simulate the absence of external shocks by maintaining the national accounts terms of trade index at its value for 1980 (a good year) in table 11.4, and by assuming that interest rates remain at their average level of 1974–9. As the results below will show, the

Table 11.2 Models for econometric estimation[a]

Chile	Uruguay
(1c) $C = \alpha_0 C_1 + \mu (DY - \alpha_0 DY_{-1}) + \text{BUBCH}^{b}$	(1u) $C = \alpha_0 C_{-1} + \mu (DY - \alpha_0 DY_{-1}) + \text{BUBUR}^{e}$
(2c) $\log(\text{NOM}) = \beta_0 + \beta_{11} \{\log(P_c) - \log(P_{\text{NO}})\} + \log(N \cdot C) + \beta_{12}\, \text{DU75}^{c}$	(2u) $\log(\text{NOM}) = \beta_0 + \beta_{11} \{\log(P_c) - \log(P_{\text{NO}})\} + \log(N \cdot C) + \beta_{12} \cdot \text{DU75}$
(3c) $\log(\hat{X}_{\text{NM}}) = \gamma_{01} - \gamma_{11} \{\log(W) - \log(P_{\text{XNM}})\} - 1.5121\, \gamma_{11} \{\log(P_{\text{N}}) - \log(P_{\text{XNM}})\} - 0.7968\, \gamma_{11} \{\log(P_M) - \log(P_{\text{XNM}})\} + k_{\text{XNM}} + \gamma_{21} \log(\text{XNM}_{-1}) + \gamma_{31}\, \text{D734}^{d}$	(3u) $\log(X) = \gamma_{01} + \gamma_{11} \log(P_c) + \gamma_{12} \log(P_x) + \gamma_{13} \log(X_{-1}) + \gamma_{14} \log(\text{time})$
(4c) $\log(\hat{X}_{\text{M}}) = \gamma_{02} - (1 + \gamma_{13}{}^{*}\, \text{DU75}) [\gamma_{12} \{\log(W) - \log(P_{\text{XM}})\} + 4.0358 \cdot \gamma_{12} \{\log(P_{\text{N}}) - \log(P_{\text{XM}})\} + 0.293 \cdot \gamma_{12} \{\log(P_{\text{OIL}}) - \log(P_{\text{XM}})\} + 1.8338 \cdot \gamma_{12} \{\log(P_{\text{NO}}) - \log(P_{\text{XM}})\} + k_{\text{XM}} + \gamma_{14}\, \text{DU75}$	

(5c) $\log(P_N) = \theta_{11}\log(W) + \theta_{12}\log(P_{OIL}) + (1-\theta_{11}-\theta_{12})\log(P_{NO}) + \theta_{14}\{\log(E) - k_N\}$	(5u) $\Delta\log(P_N) = \theta_1\,\Delta\log W + (1-\theta_1)\,\Delta\log(P_M) + \theta_{14}\,\Delta(\log E - k_N)$
(6c) $\log W - \log(P_c) = \phi_{11}\{\log(W_{-1}) - \log(P_{c-1})\} + \phi_{12}\{\log(W_{-2}) - \log(P_{c-2})\} + \phi_{13}\{\log(\mathrm{GDP}) - \log(N)\}$	(6u) $\Delta\log(W) = \phi_{11}\,\Delta\log(P_c) + \phi_{12}\,\Delta\log(P_{c-1}) + \phi_{13}\cdot\{\log(\mathrm{GDP}_{-1}) - \log(N_{-1})\}$
(7c) $\Delta\log(P) = \psi_{21}\cdot\Delta\log(P_N) + (1-\psi_{21})\cdot\Delta\log(P_X)$	(7u) $\Delta\log(P) = \psi_{21}\cdot\Delta\log(P_N) + (1-\psi_{21})\cdot\Delta\log(P_X)$
(8c) $\log(P_c) = \psi_{11}\log(P_{NO}) + (1-\psi_{11})\log(P_N)$	(8u) $\Delta\log(P_c) = \psi_{21}\,\Delta\log(P_{NO}) + (1-\psi_{11})\,\Delta\log(P_{NO})$
(9c) $\log(P_M) = \psi_{14}\log(P_{OIL}) + (1-\psi_{14})\log(P_{NO})$	(9u) $\log(P_M) = \psi_{14}\log(P_{OIL}) + (1-\psi_{14})\log(P_{NO})$
(10c) $\log(P_X) = \psi_{15}\log(P_{XM}) + (1-\psi_{15})\log(P_{XNM})$	

[a] Models estimated with annual data for 1962–83. Estimation procedures described in the text.
[b] BUBCH is the variable that captures the bubble component and takes values 3.77, 9.54 and −2.50 for 1980, 1981 and 1982 respectively. As a reference, $C_{1980} = 79.08$.
[c] DU75 is a dummy variable that takes value 1 from 1975 on and zero otherwise.
[d] D734 is a dummy variable that takes value 1 for 1973–4 and zero otherwise.
[e] BUBUR is the variable that captures the bubble component. It takes values 600, 1400, −110, −2000 and −1000 for the period.

Table 11.3 Model estimates

Coefficients (standard error)	*Chile*	*Uruguay*
α_0	0.39	1.01
	(0.07)	(0.02)
μ	0.89	0.42
	(0.01)	(0.17)
β_0	−1.99	−4.92
	(0.03)	(1.27)
β_{11}	1.17	0.82
	(0.08)	(0.21)
β_{12}	0.44	0.32
	(0.03)	(0.14)
γ_{01}	−2.28	5.52
	(0.17)	(2.80)
γ_{11}	0.06	−0.15
	(0.01)	(0.03)
γ_{21}	0.38	–
	(0.03)	
γ_{31}	−0.28	–
	(0.04)	
γ_{02}	−0.98	–
	(0.07)	
γ_{12}	−0.03	0.30
	(0.02)	
γ_{13}	−8.15	0.56
	(5.14)	(0.21)
γ_{14}	1.15	−0.44
	(0.09)	(0.35)
$\gamma_{12} \cdot \gamma_{13}$	0.28	–
	(0.09)	
θ_{11}	0.21	1.04
	(0.03)	
θ_{12}	0.18	n.a.
	(0.04)	
θ_{14}	1.14	−0.009
	(0.11)	(–)
ϕ_{11}	1.41	1.015
	(0.07)	(–)
ϕ_{12}	−0.45	−0.004
	(0.07)	(–)
ϕ_{13}	0.02	−0.0004
	(0.02)	(–)
ψ_{11}	0.06	−0.0199
	(0.003)	(–)
ψ_{21}	0.98	0.922
	(0.02)	(–)
ψ_{14}	0.18	0.335
	(0.05)	(–)
ψ_{15}	0.05	n.a.
	(0.002)	

n.a.: Not applicable. – : See text.

Table 11.4 Terms of trade, GDP and debt: 1980–3 (historical data)

	Chile			*Uruguay*		
	Terms of trade[a]	*GDP*[b]	*External debt*[c]	*Terms of trade*[a]	*GDP*[b]	*External debt*[c]
1980	100.0	1.00	11.0	100.0	1.00	1.1
1981	90.1	1.06	14.7	104.0	1.02	1.4
1982	80.4	0.91	17.4	104.0	0.92	1.7
1983	79.9	0.90	18.2	116.0	0.87	2.5

[a] National account terms of trade: 1980 = 100.0.
[b] GDP, real index: 1980 = 1.0.
[c] External debt in billions of US dollars.

Table 11.5 Simulating external shocks: Chile

Accumulated 1980–3	*Actual*	*Experiment E1* *TOT=100* *R*=7.54%	*Experiment E2* *'Bubbleless'* *(1981–3)* TOT=100, *R*=7.54%	*Experiment E3* *'Bubbleless'* *(1981–3)* Actual TOT and *R*
GDP[a] (%)	−9.98	6.53	8.31	−2.78
GDP[b] (%)	−3.4	2.1	2.7	−0.9
Δ Debt[c]	7214	5.009	1338	1992
Debt[d]	18 201	15 900	12 217	12 871

TOT = terms of trade index; *R* = international interest rate.

[a] Accumulated rate of growth (1980–3).
[b] Average annual rate of growth (1980–3).
[c] Debt 1983 − Debt 1980 in millions of current dollars.
[d] Debt at the end of 1983, in millions of current dollars.

Actual values for international interest rate were: 1980 = 10.980; 1981 = 13.320; 1982 = 13.020; and 1983 = 9.820.

general conclusion is that only a small part of the countries' poor performance during the early 1980s was due to unfavorable external conditions.

5.1 Chile

The results of our simulation experiments for Chile appear in table 11.5. We perform three experiments. In the first experiment, E1, we assume that the terms of trade index for the period 1981–3 remains at its 1980 level (TOT = 100) while the average international interest rate, *R*, paid on foreign debt remains for 1981–3 at the average for the 1974–9 period (*R* = 7.54 per cent). In the second experiment, E2, we assume for both the terms of trade and the average interest rate the same trajectory as in experiment E1, but we assume that no 'bubble' occurred, that is, we remove the dummy from the consumption function in equation (lc) and we leave lagged consumption endogenous.[9] The third experiment, E3, is similar to the second except that we use the actual trajectory for the terms of trade and for the international interest rate.

Starting with experiment E1, we find that even if the 1980 terms of trade and 1974–9 international interest rate had been in place in the 1981–3 period, GDP growth would have been only 2.1 per cent per year; by the end of 1982, the debt would have reached 15.9 billion dollars (the historical value given in table 11.3 was 18.2 billion). Thus, according to our model, even without external shocks, the performance of the Chilean economy during 1981–3 would have been much worse than in the 1976–80 period. Critical causal factors include the drop in the real exchange rate, the increase in real wages and slow capital accumulation during 1976–80, all of which slowed GDP growth.

Consider now the likely outcome if there had been no external shocks and if expenditure had not been allowed to grow so rapidly. This is experiment E2. The outcome of this simulation shows an average GDP growth rate of 2.7 per cent during 1981–3 and an external debt of only 12.2 billion dollars. This more favorable outcome is achieved by the following mechanisms. With a normal expenditure path, growth would have been less in 1981 but borrowing and real wage increases would also have been less. Lower real wages have raised employment and output, especially in the nontradables sector. Production of nontradables would also have gained from the higher disposable income available with lower interest payments.

Robustness is added to these results by performing the same experiment but instead assuming the actual trajectory of the terms of trade and interest rates. This is the experiment E3. Now the average drop in GDP would have been only −0.9 per cent per year and the level of debt only 12.9 billion dollars. These results compare very favorably with the actual GDP and debt trajectories. Indeed, 1980–3 average GDP growth was only −3.4 per cent and the debt at the end of 1983 was 18.2 billion dollars (table 11.3). Thus, we conclude that the bubble in expenditures that developed in the late 1970s played a large role in both the accumulation of external debt and in the slowdown in the rate of growth.

5.2 Uruguay

Our simulations for Uruguay appear in table 11.6. The conclusions are in line with those for Chile. Actual and control values are reasonably close to one another to go ahead with counterfactual simulations. As for Chile, experiment E1 corresponds to a favorable external environment: the average interest rate for 1981–3 is set at $R = 10$ per cent instead of the actual average of 12 per cent. Experiment E2 maintains the same external environment as E1 but we remove the dummy from the consumption function in equation (1u). Experiment E3 is the same as E2 except that actual terms of trade and interest rate trajectories are used. Experiment E1 shows that even

Table 11.6 Simulating external shocks: Uruguay

Accumulated 1979–83	Actual	Control	*Experiment E1* R=10% (1981–3)	*Experiment E2* 'Bubbleless' (1981–3)	*Experiment E3* 'Bubbleless' actual external condition (1981–3)
GDP (%)[a]	−7.9	−9.0	−3.2	5.5	−0.1
GDP (%)[b]	−2.0	−2.3	−0.8	1.4	0.0
Δ Debt[c]	1590	1592	737	460	811
Debt[d]	2523	2525	1670	943	1708
Consumption per capita (%)[e]	−15.1	−13.1	−9.8	1.6	−1.8
Average consumption per capita (%)[f]	−4.0	−3.5	−2.6	0.4	−0.4

[a] Accumulated rate of growth (1979–83).
[b] Average annual rate of growth (1979–83).
[c] Debt 1983 − Debt 1979 in millions of current dollars.
[d] Debt at the end of 1983, in millions of current dollars.
[e] Accumulated rate of per capita private consumption growth (1979–83).
[f] Average rate of per capita private consumption growth (1979–83).

under favorable external conditions the average rate of output growth would still have been −0.8 per cent, a gain of only 1.5 per cent over our control data and again a poor performance. Debt accumulation would have been cut by a third, again similar to Chile. Given that the national accounts terms of trade were improving during the counterfactual simulation period in Uruguay, external shocks were *much* less important in Uruguay than in Chile. Again, external shocks fail to explain the crisis.

The next experiment, E2, shows, as in Chile, that a more 'reasonable' consumption path maintaining favorable external conditions would have achieved much better results in terms of GDP at the end of 1983, and a substantial reduction in debt.

As in the Chilean case, in experiment E3 we also simulate the path of a 'bubbleless' economy with the actual external conditions. Again, the performance is much better than in our control. The economy would have stagnated but the smoother path would have lowered the external debt level of 1983 by one-third. In concluding, it should be recalled that many of the erratic movements in Uruguay's private consumption were beyond Uruguayan control as they reflected the unstable Argentine economy rather than a speculative path generated by inconsistent macroeconomic policies.

6. Policy Inconsistencies Once Again

We have established that 'excessive' expenditure goes a long way toward explaining the collapse of the Chilean and Uruguayan economies in the early 1980s. We have attributed 'excessive' expenditure to inconsistent macroeconomic policies without being specific about the nature of these inconsistencies. We conclude by detailing the various forms that the inconsistencies took in each of the Southern Cone countries.

To begin with, in all three Southern Cone economies, the deregulation of the domestic financial systems was not accompanied by an information system that could allow for early warning concerning the quality of loans. Furthermore, as pointed out by Díaz-Alejandro (1985) and documented for Chile by Galvez and Tybout (1986), cross-ownership between financial and nonfinancial firms facilitated many internal transactions where loans were given without proper risk evaluation.[10] Not surprisingly, when the macroeconomic crisis unraveled in the early 1980s the financial system entered into a major crisis.[11]

Next, signs of inconsistency in the three countries' macroeconomic policies became apparent in the early 1980s. In Argentina (with an externally financed public sector deficit of over 10 per cent of GDP and no prospect of fiscal reform), doubts about further external financing of the deficit and the sustainability of the exchange rate regime set in as early as the first half of 1980. This was made worse by the April 1980 collapse of the BIR (Banco de Intercambio Regional) which produced a 25 per cent increase in the money supply in a single month. The absence of a commitment about future exchange rate policy by President-elect Viola accelerated private capital outflows. The 10 per cent devaluation introduced in February 1981 was a case of 'too little and too late' and only exacerbated the crisis.

In Chile, a fiscal surplus equal to 2.1 per cent of GDP was achieved in 1979–81, but it was accompanied by large expansion in private expenditure leading to a current account deficit of 14.6 per cent of GDP in 1981. The expansion in private expenditure was facilitated by easy access to external credit on very favorable terms. The introduction of a preannounced and declining rate of exchange rate devaluation together with backwards wage indexation based on at least 100 per cent of previous CPI inflation was bound to result in a lengthy period of real appreciation (Corbo, 1985b). On the other hand, the deregulation of domestic financial markets tended to increase real returns on domestic financial assets. With the continuous lifting of controls on capital inflows and the lessening of uncertainty about devaluation produced by the policy of preannounced exchange rates, large portfolio adjustments occurred, yielding large capital inflows that provided easy access to 'cheap' foreign credit to fuel the expansion in private expenditure. Real exchange rate appreciation followed (Corbo, 1985a; Corbo, 1987; Harberger, 1982; Edwards, 1985). Then concerns about the sustainability of the exchange set in. This reduced private capital inflows from 1.6 billion dollars in the second half of 1981 to 0.9 billion dollars in the first half of 1982.

In the case of Uruguay, the fiscal position, which had improved continuously up to 1980, started to deteriorate in 1981 with an underfunded social security reform. Meanwhile, the real exchange rate appreciated by 27.4 per cent between 1978 and 1981. Furthermore, with the collapse of the stabilization attempt in Argentina, Uruguay's real appreciation vis-à-vis Argentina was even larger (Hanson and de Melo, 1985). Emerging doubts about the sustainability of the *tablita* were reflected in increased private capital outflows starting in 1981 (de Melo, 1987). To some extent, capital outflows were due to the collapse in Argentina, but these outflows could have been mitigated, had Uruguay adjusted its parity after Argentina abandoned the *tablita*.

Capital flight was evident in Argentina and Uruguay (and to a lesser extent in Chile) *before* their economies were hit by the adverse external developments of the early 1980s, when changes in the mix of fiscal and monetary policies in the industrial countries (especially in the US) produced an unanticipated world recession, an appreciation of the US dollar, a drop in the terms of trade and a sharp increase in international interest rates. Nevertheless, the debt crisis that followed and the consequential interruption of voluntary capital flows had severe adverse consequences for all three countries and for other countries that had become used to, or had encouraged the existence of, a large gap between expenditures and output. Specifically in the Southern Cone countries, real exchange rate appreciation (together with increasing budget deficits in Argentina and Uruguay) made their economies far too dependent on foreign financing as early as 1981. In Chile, the borrowing was by the private sector, in Argentina and Uruguay by the public sector.

In this paper, we have argued that when the international debt crisis that followed the Mexican crisis broke in August 1982, the Southern Cone countries were already in serious trouble. The debt crisis closed the option of using public borrowing to finance private capital outflows, but *private* sector adjustment had started earlier. All the August 1982 crisis implied was a faster cut in absorption and a faster real depreciation. The econometric model we have estimated supports our argument that in Chile the recession was deepened by the downward inflexibility of nontradable prices and wages in a regime with backward wage indexation and that the crisis would have been dampened or avoided with consistent macroeconomic policies. In Uruguay too, 'excessive' expenditure was also apparent and the recession was deepened by the large real appreciation vis-à-vis Argentina as expenditures were rapidly shifted to Buenos Aires. An exchange rate policy that would have taken into account more closely developments in Argentina would have dampened the recession.

NOTES

We are grateful to Juan Carlos de Pablo and Carlos Massad for comments on a previous version of this paper. We thank Ricardo Caballero and Gabriel Castillo for research assistance, Myriàm Bailey and Maria Ameal for word processing and Peter Bocock for editorial help.

1 There is now a large literature on these reforms, though most writing is country-specific (Corbo, 1985a; Edwards, 1986; Fernandez, 1985; Hanson and de Melo, 1985; Harberger, 1982; Nogues, 1986; Rodriguez, 1983). For further elaboration of the reforms in a comparative framework, see McKinnon (1982), Edwards (1985), Corbo et al. (1986), Corbo and de Melo (1987) and references therein.

2 How the program was supposed to work during the transition is explained in Rodriguez (1982). Dornbusch (1982) contrasts the orthodox and new approaches to stabilization.

3 Corbo et al. (1986, table 3) estimated capital flight of $29.8 billion for Argentina during 1979–83 and $2.2 billion for Uruguay during 1979–83.

4 The use of the term 'quasi' denotes that not all budget constraints are explicitly incorporated in the model as they are, for instance, in CGE simulation models.

5 We tried to estimate a similar model for Argentina but we were unsuccessful. This is not surprising because there were numerous changes in the structure of the economy during the sample period.

6 Oil imports are taken as exogenous.

7 This link is absent not only in the decomposition analysis above, but in most CGE exercises assessing the impact of external shocks.

8 Some parameters correspond to the values obtained with limited information procedures. Others were approximated by iterating over the procedures with the parameters of primary concern taken as given. This process continued until no significant change in the likelihood function was obtained. Lack of convergence of the complete model but convergence of each of the sections independently suggests some identification problem, a very difficult problem to solve in non-linear models.

9 That is, we do not add the error of the equation to the simulation of consumption.

10 In the case of Uruguay, Melo et al. (1985) show that, starting in 1981, when sustainability of the *tablita* had already set in, firms borrowed in order to pay out dividends, an indication that a bailout was expected.

11 Aspects of the financial crisis are further discussed in Barandiaran (1984), Díaz-Alejandro (1985), Zahler (1985) and Tybout (1987).

REFERENCES

Balassa, B. 1984: Adjustment policies in developing countries: a reassessment. *World Development*, 12, 955–72.

Barandiaran, E. 1984: Nuestra Crisis Financiera. *Estudios Publicos*, Fall, 89–122.

Caballero, R. 1986: Testing Liquidity Constraints: International Evidence. Mimeo, MIT, January.

Caballero, R. and Corbo, V. 1985: Explaining the Trade Balances: A General Equilibrium Approach. World Bank Discussion Paper no. DRD141, November.

Condon, T., Corbo, V. and Melo, J. de 1985: Productivity growth, external shocks, and capital inflows in Chile: a general equilibrium analysis. *Journal of Policy Modelling*, 7 (3), 379–406.

Corbo, V. 1985a: Reforms and macroeconomic adjustments in Chile during 1974–84. *World Development*, 13 (8), 893–916.

Corbo, V. 1985b: International prices, wages and inflation in an open economy: a Chilean model. *The Review of Economics and Statistics*, 67 (4), 564–73.

Corbo, V. 1987: The use of the exchange rate for stabilization purposes: the case of Chile. In M. Connolly and C. Vega (eds.), *Economic Reform and Stabilization in Latin America*, New York: Praeger, pp. 111–38.

Corbo, V. and Melo, J. de 1985: Liberalization with stabilization in the Southern Cone of Latin America: overview and summary, *World Development*, 13 (8), 863–6.

Corbo, V, and Melo, J. de 1987: Lessons from the Southern Cone policy reforms. *World Bank Research Observer* 2(2), 111–42.

Corbo, V., Melo, J. de and Tybout, J. 1986: What went wrong with the recent reforms in the Southern Cone. *Economic Development and Cultural Change*, 34 (3), 607–40.

Díaz-Alejandro, C. 1981: Southern Cone stabilization plans. In W. Cline and S. Weintraub (eds.), *Economic Stabilization in Developing Countries*, The Brookings Institution, pp. 119–47.

Díaz-Alejandro, C. 1985: Good-bye financial repression, hello financial crash. *Journal of Development Economics*, 19 (1/2), 1–24.

Dornbusch, R. 1982: Stabilization policies in developing countries: what have we learned?. *World Development*, 10 (9), 701–30.

Dornbusch, R. 1985: Policy and performance links between LDC debtors and industrial nations. *Brookings Papers on Economic Activity*, 2, 303–68.

Edwards, S. 1985: The Order of Liberalization of the External Sector: An Analysis Based on the Southern Cone Experience. Mimeo, December.

Edwards, S. 1986: Monetarism in Chile 1973–1983: analytical issues and economic puzzles. *Economic Development and Cultural Change*, 34 (3), 535–60.

Fernandez, R. 1985: The expectations management approach to stabilization in Argentina during 1976–82. *World Development*, 13 (8), 871–92.

Galvez, J. and Tybout, J. 1986: Microeconomic adjustments in Chile during 1977–81: the importance of being a grupo. *World Development*, 13 (8), 969–94.

Hall, R. E. 1978: Stochastic implications of the life cycle–permanent income hypothesis: theory and evidence. *Journal of Political Economy*, 86 (6), 971–87.

Hanson, J. and Melo, J. de 1985: External shocks, financial reforms, and stabilization attempts in Uruguay during 1974–83. *World Development*, 13 (8), 917–40.

Harberger, A. 1982: The Chilean economy in the 1970s: crisis, stabilization, liberalization, reform. In K. Brunner and A. H. Meltzer (eds.), *Economic Policy in a World of Change*, Amsterdam: North-Holland, pp. 115–57.

McKinnon, R. 1982: The order of economic liberalization: lessons from Chile and Argentina. In K. Brunner and A. Meltzer (eds.), *Economic Policy in a World of Change*, Amsterdam: North-Holland, pp. 159–201.

Melo, J. de 1987: Financial reforms, stabilization and growth under high capital mobility: Uruguay 1973–83. In M. Connolly and C. Gouzalez-Vega (eds), *Economic Reform and Stabilization in Latin America*, Praeger, pp. 229–49.

Melo, J. de, R. Pascale and J. Tybout 1985: Microeconomic adjustments in Uruguay during 1973–81: the interplay of real and financial shocks, *World Development*, 13(8), pp. 995–1015.

Mitra, P. 1987: Adjustment to external shocks in selected semi-industrial countries: 1974–81. In P. Ferri and G. Ragazzi (eds.), *Adjustment to Shocks: A North–South Perspective*. Amsterdam: North-Holland.

Nogues, J. 1986: The nature of Argentina's policy reforms during 1976–81. *World Bank Staff Working Papers*, no. 765.

Rodriguez, C. A. 1982: The Argentine stabilization plan of December 20th. *World Development*, 10 (9), 226–38.

Rodriguez, C. A. 1983: Politicas de Estabilizacion en la Economia Argentina. *Cuadernos de Economia*, April.

Sachs, J. 1985: External debt and macroeconomic performance in Latin America and East Asia. *Brookings Papers on Economic Activity*, 2, 523–74.

Sjaastad, Larry 1983: Failure of economic liberalism in the Cone of Latin America. *The World Economy*, March, 5–26.

Tybout, J. 1987: A firm-level chronicle of financial crises in the Southern Cone. *Journal of Development Economics* (forthcoming).

Zahler, R. 1985: Las Tasas de Interes en Chile: 1975–82. Mimeo, ECLA, Santiago, Chile.

COMMENT 1

Carlos Massad

From the very interesting paper by Corbo and de Melo, we learn three main lessons:

1 The microeconomic reforms implemented in the Southern Cone countries (financial deregulation and trade and financial liberalization) were successful and most problems that emerged resulted from inadequate macroeconomic policies.
2 One outstanding mistake was to use the exchange rate for stabilization purposes.
3 External shocks were unimportant in provoking the crisis of 1982–3.

I do agree with the authors on the need to undertake reforms in the early 1970s and on their criticism of the pre-reform situation. I disagree however with their conclusion of success of the particular reforms undertaken. Let's first take up financial deregulation.

Financial deregulation in Chile was more or less simultaneous with a drastic reduction of the public sector deficit, a phased reduction of trade tariffs and controls to a uniform rate of 10 per cent and a relaxation of controls to capital inflows, although not to capital outflows. In Argentina, financial deregulation came together with a rapid elimination of controls to capital movements and virtually no change in the trade area. In Uruguay, the sequence and speed was somewhere in between.

However, in the three countries the governments had to come in and bail out the financial system, one way or another, to avoid a catastrophe. Such intervention began long before the exchange rate came clearly out of line. Some of my friends in the central banks and commercial banks at the time are still fighting legal battles to protect or to recover their freedom.

Why did this happen? I believe it did because financial reform and financial deregulation are not the same thing. In relatively small economies, links between financial and nonfinancial enterprises are common and difficult to prevent. Banks and nonfinancial firms share expectations about the future including the permanent or transitory character of a given government policy. This is particularly important for the financial sector, as policy 'reforms' of any kind can have a pervasive effect on the asset portfolio of financial institutions without similar effects on their liabilities. If the 'permanency' of such reforms is doubted, banks will not stay away from lending to distressed borrowers, endangering the quality of their portfolio and driving interest rates to unbelievable levels. Deregulation also brings with it different forms of moral hazards, Ponzi schemes and the like.

Corbo and de Melo's paper neglects bank supervision, a fundamental element in any financial reform. Financial deregulation, without bank supervision, instead of improving credit and investment allocation, as Corbo and de Melo assert, has in practice endangered the whole financial system, allocated credit inefficiently and stimulated capital outflow (a point I shall refer to later on) while provoking a substantial redistribution of wealth.

The second microeconomic reform characterized as successful is trade and capital account liberalization. Here, my reading of the evidence is that the record is somewhat mixed. Both Argentina and Uruguay liberalized the capital account first, and then the trade account. Chile followed the opposite sequence. Perhaps as a consequence, interest rates in Argentina and Uruguay never reached, for extended periods of time, the unbelievable levels reached in Chile between 1975 and 1980 (and also in 1981 if rates are measured in dollars) but their rates of inflation never approached rates abroad as those in Chile did for a brief period of time in 1981–2. Argentina and Uruguay maintained a substantial deficit in their public sector and consequently expanded domestic credit, while Chile rapidly reached public sector equilibrium. However, in the three cases we find substantial increases in expenditure, mainly consumption expenditures, probably as a consequence of the wealth effects produced by capital inflow.

In Argentina, more than in Uruguay, the public sector imbalance fed the disequilibrium. In this sense, macroeconomic policies got in the way of the microeconomic reforms. But not in Chile: there, it was the excess expenditure of the private sector, financed with foreign borrowing, which led the way to impending catastrophe. I argued 5 years ago that the real exchange rate revaluation in Chile between 1980 and 1981 was the consequence of the *micro* policies adopted: a reduction of tariffs which increased the price of capital goods relative to consumption goods (as the latter were very heavily taxed before the reform); a deregulation of the financial system which in fact reduced real interest rates for consumption (as consumption could previously find financing only in informal markets at extremely high rates) while increasing real rates for other credit users; a strong incentive to borrow abroad as domestic rates exceeded foreign rates appropriately measured; and domestic banks relying on foreign borrowing, the lowest cost funding source, for their own survival in the market.

It was the micro policies in Chile which led to revaluation, not the rigid pegging of the peso to the dollar. Without financial deregulation and capital account liberalization, given the fact that the public sector was in surplus, the private sector would have found no financing for excess spending which led to a deficit in the current account of the balance of payments equivalent to 14 per cent of GDP.

In all three countries, but particularly in Argentina, financial deregulation and capital account liberalization enhanced international portfolio diversification.

Argentinians were buying banks in the US. Part of foreign borrowing was based on back-to-back guarantees with foreign exchange deposits abroad, as a form of covering for the risk of new policy shocks. In a way, deregulation and capital account liberalization contributed, perhaps decisively, to so-called capital flight. Portfolio diversification should be considered a normal phenomenon in a world of open capital markets, deriving from profit maximization and risk avoidance considerations.

The third lesson we learn from Corbo and de Melo is that external shocks played little role in the 1982–3, or for that matter, the 1982–6, debacle.

Unfortunately, the version of their paper I had at my disposal beforehand did not include a description of the model on which they base their conclusions. So here my own comments are only of a very preliminary character.

First, a few facts: terms of trade for Latin America were, on the average for 1982–5, not too different from those of 1930–5. For the non-oil-exporting countries, terms of trade at the end of 1985 were below the worst figures ever registered. Efforts to expand exports after 1981 have resulted in an increase in volume, but a reduction in value. Latin American exports at the end of 1985 were below those of 1981, measured in dollars.

The financial markets have dried out, to a point where the region as a whole is transferring real resources abroad (trade surplus) at a rate of about 4 per cent of GDP per year, as compared to an inflow of the order of 1 per cent per year on average for the period 1960–80.

After the First World War, Germany had to pay war reparations to the victors. Reparations plus interest payments never exceeded 25 per cent of exports. When capital outflows began in 1931, and reparation plus interest payments and capital outflows reached 36 per cent of exports, a special commission of the BIS determined that Germany would be justified in not abiding by her commitment to continue making war reparation payments. These figures are substantially below those registered in Latin America in 1985.

Why is it that the crash came for all countries more or less at the same time? Is it because, by mere chance, they all made the same mistakes at the same time, despite the fact that they are supposed to be more or less independent decision-making units? Or is it because the constraints they face are similar? What would have happened in Corbo and de Melo's model if they had assumed continued foreign borrowing beside better interest rates and terms of trade? Without the external shock, the timing and magnitude of the generalized economic crisis in Latin America are very difficult to explain.

The international environment has changed substantially since 1981. At present, international trade is not growing as it did in the 1960s and 1970s, new external financing is not available and macroeconomic imbalances prevail in the world economy.

Should these external conditions induce some change in the prescription, either in the nature, speed and/or sequence of the reforms suggested? Does the change in external conditions affect the credibility of certain policy packages? The answer to these questions may be quite relevant to policy making today.

This is not to justify wrong macroeconomic policies or to take the blame off square shoulders. It is just to emphasize, as Corbo and de Melo do, the need to take due account of initial conditions, both external and domestic, in any program.

This emphasis on recognizing a changing environment is evident in Carlos Díaz-Alejandro's work. He was particularly sensitive to such changes and to their implications for policy, a virtue needed today perhaps more than ever.

COMMENT 2

Juan Carlos de Pablo

In deriving lessons from the liberalization and stabilization programs applied in the 'Southern Cone' in the late 1970s and early 1980s, Corbo and de Melo provide a useful basis for improving future decision making. (The dream of everyone systematically connected with economic policy is to observe at least new 'sins' in policy making, and not merely the replication of old ones.)

Among the many facts and lessons pointed out by the authors I want to emphasize the following: (a) when the rate of inflation is greater than 50 per cent per year, stabilization is a prerequisite to liberalization, because at the mentioned rate of inflation the 'noise' existing in the economic system (particularly the intensity and unexpectedness of changes in relative prices) is so great that it neutralizes the 'signals' of the liberalization process; (b) during the orthodox stabilization plans (implemented before the '*tablita*-like' stabilization plans) the three Southern Cone economies did well by historical standards (despite the fact that the initial conditions were far from ideal).

My basic comment to Corbo and de Melo's paper is indeed a proposal: to suggest they should complement their research with more research that visualizes the same issue from another perspective.

To illustrate my proposal I want to quote from the original version of the paper, where the authors say: 'It is now clear that borrowing abroad to finance the fiscal deficit and monetization of nonperforming commercial bank loans were inconsistent with the *tablita* and that the liberalization episode was doomed from the start because of inconsistent macro policies.'

What did the authors mean by 'it is now clear?.' As far as I know, no economist in the world is today a candidate for the Nobel prize in economics for having discovered, during or after the late 1970s, that economies cannot operate in the middle and the long run unless fiscal, monetary and exchange rate policies are consistent. The mentioned consistency requirement, I am sure, can be found in most economic textbooks written not just in this century, but since the very beginning of our profession (in this connection, I am deliberately ignoring the technical literature that was fashionable in the late 1970s in Latin America).

Corbo and de Melo's analysis is basically ex post, but if the lessons derived in the paper were 'well-known' in the economic literature before the design and implementation of the economic policies under consideration, then the mentioned analysis should be complimented by another that, starting from the replication of the ex ante considerations that were relevant in the decision making under analysis, can help improve future decision making.

My feeling about the outcome of the research I am suggesting is that the problem under consideration resulted from a combination of 'governmental despair' and lack of checks and balances in the economic profession in general (both in the countries involved and in the rest of the world), in academia as well as in international organizations (i.e., in the IMF).

The case of Argentina is quite clear. By the end of 1978, that is, after almost 3 years in office, the military and Martínez de Hoz had accomplished many reforms, but the rate of inflation since 1976 continued to fluctuate around 8 per cent per month, a level considered intolerable in Argentina at that time. In addition to this the economy had experienced an important recession since mid-1977, with a revival towards the end of 1978. So, obviously, the minister of economics was asked 'to reduce inflation without interrupting the recovery of the economy.' That is what I call 'governmental despair.'

Under these conditions, the demand for 'ideas' looks for the 'supply' of ideas in a rather particular way. If some very respectable economists say that it is possible to accomplish both goals simultaneously by adopting a '*tablita*-like' stabilization program, if the rest of the profession does not say anything – loudly enough to be heard by the decision makers! – and if the Fund does not say anything either, then we have what I call lack of checks and balances.

This example, I am afraid, can be found in other countries at that time, as well as at other times (in my opinion the problem I am mentioning occurred again in some Latin American countries in mid-1985, with plans like Austral in Argentina and Cruzado in Brazil), and probably also can be extended to the case of supply-side economics in the United States. In other words, the issue merits close attention since it is more systematic than expected.

Some colleagues, although agreeing with the importance of my suggestion, could argue that we as economists are not professionally prepared to deal with this issue, transferring the research proposal to sociologists or political scientists. I do not agree with this at all. My impression, as well as my personal experience of following the Argentine economic policy, on a daily basis, for more than 20 years, is that we economists do have a lot to say about this, and that although research from other disciplines is welcome, we have a comparative advantage in ex ante, and accordingly, recreated ex ante, analysis. I hope that current research efforts at the National Bureau of Economic Research, the World Bank and WIDER, on the analytical economic history of the last two decades of some developing countries, take into account this suggestion.

Part V

MACROECONOMIC THEORY AND POLICY IN DEVELOPING COUNTRIES

12

The Relevance for Developing Countries of Recent Developments in Macroeconomic Theory

W. Max Corden

An earlier version of this paper was prepared, at the suggestion of Carlos, as background for a proposed World Bank project on macroeconomic policy in developing countries in which he, Ian Little and I were involved.

It was not easy to understand the sometimes obscure rational expectations literature (and perhaps I have still not got it right). In any case, dear Carlos gave me a lot of work to do, and I shall always remember him for putting me on to a somewhat painful but, I hope, fruitful reading course. Carlos was often skeptical about 'the latest' developments in theory, at least when extreme conclusions were drawn from them, but he did believe in 'keeping up', and that there was always something to be learnt from the great minds pouring out technically sophisticated papers from the major US universities. This paper is written in the same spirit.

The paper is rather long and those who are familiar with the field and just want to read about developing countries could omit sections 1 and 3.

In making revisions I am indebted to comments from John Cuddington and Mohsin Khan.

This paper reviews the recent literature of macroeconomic theory in developed countries (called DCs here). To a great extent this is an American literature, though I shall also refer to some approaches more popular in Europe. The paper considers the relevance of various discussions and models for developing countries (LDCs). Much of the paper is concerned with the 'rational expectations revolution' and its possible relevance for studying macroeconomic policies in LDCs.

It is impossible to specify some standard DC model, or perhaps some textbook written for DCs, and then relate it to a standard LDC model, or to a particular LDC, hence clearly bringing out differences between the models or bringing out the way in which the DC model (or the textbook) needs adjusting to suit the particular LDC. The reasons are (a) that DC macroeconomic theory since the destruction of the Keynesian consensus is not sufficiently consolidated, and (b) the great diversity of the characteristics and experiences of the LDCs. Every idea that can be found in the recent DC literature can be shown to have some relevance for some LDC somewhere, and the DC literature is so extensive that one could never successfully claim that an issue important for any LDC has been completely neglected in the DC literature. For this reason every generalization made below must be thoroughly qualified.

1. Keynesian Economics and Rational Expectations

The central message of Keynesian economics is that demand management through monetary and fiscal policies can successfully stabilize output and employment, and possibly raise the average level of employment over a longer period. The recent DC theoretical literature seeks to explain to what extent Keynesian nominal demand policies can work when some allowance is made for rational behaviour. This literature can really be regarded as having three parts. In the first part it is assumed that market-clearing wages and prices are continuously established, and the question is then asked whether Keynesian effects can still be generated through policy surprises. The second part seeks to explain existence of nominal rigidities, especially wage rigidities. The third part, which is the most interesting and relevant for the present discussion, is concerned with the role of policy surprises and the scope for policy activism, given some rigidities.

1.1 Market-Clearing Approach

Suppose that there was instantaneous market clearing, any increase in nominal demand in a particular market thus leading to a rise in the relevant price. Surprise shocks in nominal demand, e.g. an increase in the money supply, would still have *real* effects if their implications were initially misunderstood. This is an 'incomplete information' problem.[1] For example, if a nominal demand expansion leads to a rise in prices and nominal wages, without necessarily any change in real wages, but it is misunderstood either as a rise in real wages (so leading to greater labour supply) or as representing a rise in real profitability (so leading to an expansion by firms and so greater labor demand), then nominal demand policies would have real effects.

This type of story (the Lucas supply function) has been given much prominence in the DC theoretical literature. The argument of the rational expectations theorists is that it is not possible to surprise private agents consistently. If the government is following some kind of policy rule, that rule will be discovered in due course. On average, nominal demand changes will thus come to be expected, and then they will not be misunderstood when they happen.

There is an objection to this approach. It seems implausible that firms or workers misunderstand a general expansion or contraction of demand when these actually happen. They may not understand why they happen, and may have failed to anticipate them, but with complete and instantaneous price and wage flexibility it is not really necessary to anticipate events. If one believes that prices and wages are very flexible in response to market conditions one should, therefore, not expect nominal demand policies to generate real output and employment changes, even when the policies are unexpected.

The whole discussion only becomes interesting once some rigidities in prices and wages, or at least significant lags in their adjustment to changing conditions, are introduced.

1.2 Explaining Nominal Rigidities

An extensive literature seeks to explain nominal rigidities, especially wage rigidity, as part of an efficient maximizing process. It is notable that nominal wages are (more or less) rigid downwards, and also somewhat sluggish upwards, even in a country like the United States where trade unions are relatively weak. There are explanations both in terms of explicit and implicit contracts. Explicit contracts with unions tend to be longer term in the US than in other DCs, so that there has been a particular emphasis on such contracts. One explanation is in terms of negotiation costs, including the costs and delays involved in the process of organizing collective agreed positions (the 'logic of collective action').

One explanation rests on the willingness of employers to accept the risks for their profits of demand fluctuations, employees being risk-averse and unable to insure adequately against income fluctuations. There is an implicit contract literature, which cannot be summarized here (see Azariadis and Stiglitz, 1983). Most explanations for wage rigidities seem to be explanations of real rather than nominal rigidities, and only the difficulties of indexation (which, surely, are not so great) can explain why rigidities that are intended to be real turn out to be nominal. If there is learning, then the experience of inflation would lead to increased use of indexed contracts – as is indeed the case in several LDCs.

1.3 Policy Surprises and Rational Expectations

We come now to the most important development, namely the interaction between nominal rigidities, especially wage rigidity, and whether 'policy surprises', i.e. nominal demand policies, are expected or not. By introducing some nominal rigidities into a rational expectations framework, results that are essentially Keynesian can be obtained (see Fischer, 1977, 1980).

The literature with which we are now concerned assumes that nominal wages are fixed at intervals on some rational basis, taking into account expectations about market conditions, the general price level and so on but, after being fixed, are not changed for some time. There may be overlapping contracts, so that the general wage level gradually and continuously responds to changing expectations, even though particular wage rates stay fixed for limited periods.

Given, then, the assumption of short-term nominal rigidities, demand policies would have no real effects if (a) they are determined at the same times as prices and wages are fixed, (b) the principles of the demand policy are known to the private agents, (c) these policies are based on information that is available to the private agents as much as to the government and (d) the private agents interpret information available to them correctly. Absence of assumptions (b) and (c) means that there is 'asymmetric information'.

Assumption (d) is usually implicit in the rational expectations literature, though it is hardly discussed. Assumptions (b) and (c) are the key rational expectations assumptions, at least when interpreted as representing tendencies. The argument of rational expectations theory has been that, for demand policies to be effective, at least one of these two assumptions must not apply. There must be some element of surprise.

These rather extreme conclusions are changed radically when assumption (a) is removed, i.e. that policy is no more flexible than wage rates.

It is quite possible that wages are rigid for a longer period than demand policy. The government may have more flexibility than, say, the labour market. There is (my term) 'asymmetric flexibility'. In that case, Keynesian demand policies may be effective even though there is no information asymmetry.

The government can then adjust its policies in the light of new information, but, even though the information is also available to, and absorbed by, private agents (so that expectations are rational), wages are not adjusted, or are adjusted less. The policy regime, which includes the pattern of policy reactions to new information obtained by the government, is known by the private agents from the start and is adhered to by the authorities. The 'surprise' is embodied in the new information, rather than in the policy.

The general conclusion is that the more government demand policies can surprise private agents (essentially by being unsystematic) *or* the longer the periods of wage rigidity relative to policy rigidity, the more likely is it that Keynesian demand policies would have some real effects. But if real wage outcomes turn out to be consistently different from those intended by the private agents then presumably private agents will learn, and adapt their behaviour accordingly. If it is usual for important new information about labour market conditions and demand policies to emerge after wage contracts have been made, then, presumably, the contract periods will be shortened.

2. Are There Keynesian Effects in LDCs?

The central question is how relevant all this is for LDCs. Many macromodels that have been constructed specifically with developing countries in mind have Keynesian elements, i.e. there is some degree of wage and price rigidity, or at least sluggishness of adjustment. Hence it is certainly a widespread view that Keynesian effects *are* relevant for LDCs. Important examples are the paper by Krugman and Taylor (1978), which deals with the possible contractionary effects of devaluation, and the paper by Khan and Knight (1981), which is concerned with stabilization policy when the exchange rate is fixed.

One might hold the view that prices and nominal wages in some LDCs, or even in most of them, are very flexible, more so than in most DCs, principally because trade unions are more important in the latter. This does *not* mean that there are not considerations making for structural unemployment or for supply rigidities of various kinds. If at the same time one dismisses the argument that significant Keynesian effects can be obtained from unexpected nominal demand policies purely because their effects would be misunderstood by private agents, then it follows that one would not get Keynesian effects in such LDCs. Nominal demand policies would not have real effects irrespective of whether they were expected or not. Only when there are significant short-term *nominal* rigidities are Keynesian policies and analysis relevant.

A major issue for LDCs is usually the effectiveness of nominal devaluation. Some degree of rigidity of nominal wages or of prices of non-tradables is required for a nominal devaluation to lead to real devaluation. It is well-known that the wage reaction to a devaluation is crucial. If nominal wages were flexible downwards there would be no need for exchange rate adjustment, while if real wages are rigid, nominal exchange rate adjustment will have no real effects (aside from any real balance effect).

This is the way in which the Keynesian issue primarily presents itself in small open economies with large tradables sectors. Keynesian policy consists then essentially of using the exchange rate as an instrument of policy. If an LDC finds that it has unemployment in its tradables sector, and if it is believed that the Keynesian assumptions (the conditions required for policy effectiveness) do apply, then a government could engage in depreciation combined with monetary expansion. If the exchange rate floated, it could engage in monetary expansion with endogenous depreciation. Employment would then increase even while the current account is kept at its original level.

In addition, Keynesian assumptions may apply in non-tradables sectors, or some of them, notably the construction industry. It would then be possible to increase employment by nominal demand expansion, leading possibly to lower real wages achieved in part through the depreciation that demand expansion brings about. Monetary and fiscal policies could then stabilize domestic demand when there are fluctuations emanating from private investment. A question then is to what extent such fluctuations originating domestically are important.

The crucial issues are empirical, and a good deal of work on this has already been done. There is evidence in some LDCs of some degree of nominal rigidity, sufficient to cause devaluations or monetary expansion above previous (presumably expected) levels to have short-term effects. But usually the effects are eroded after a few years.[2] Is there then a short-term non-vertical Phillips curve, perhaps with adaptive expectations, so that it gradually shifts in an unfavourable direction as nominal demand expands? Must a devaluation be unexpected at the time that nominal wages and prices are initially fixed, if it is to be effective?

If there is some degree of nominal rigidity lasting for a significant time, as there is in the United States, then all the issues discussed in the DC literature become potentially relevant. One must then go on to ask why anything should ever be rigid in nominal, rather than real terms? Certainly long-term labour contracts of the US kind are not common in LDCs. The strength of labour unions, of course, varies very greatly among LDCs. They are strong in the urban sectors of a few LDCs.

3. The Rational Expectations Revolution

In the *General Theory* expectations were exogenous (animal spirits) and played a part in determining the inducement to invest. They played no role in determining nominal wages. The crucial role of expectations,[3] and, above all, of expectations that turned out to be consistently wrong, was seen by Friedman and Phelps when they sought the logic of the non-vertical Phillips curve. Backward-looking expectations with learning – formalized by the concept of adaptive expectations – formed the basis for the expectations-augmented Phillips curve, which led to the policy conclusion that demand management could maintain unemployment below the natural rate, but that this would require accelerating inflation.

'Rational expectations' was the next logical step. Expectations would surely be forward-looking. Mistakes would not consistently be made. Private agents would make use of all information available, not just observing the past rate of inflation, and would feed this information into their model or models of the economy. If agents find their models of the economy to be consistently in error they will gradually discard them, until they develop or accept the right model.

This approach raises many questions. How does one really know what is the right model? It has been remarked many times that even quite respectable economists have many models, and the faith that 'truth will prevail' may seem a little naive. Does history really teach that mistakes of a similar kind are not made again and again? For many persons (and politicians in power, also) the opportunity to learn from their own mistakes is limited because decisions on particular matters are infrequent or even 'one-off'. In any case, the central theme is that 'individuals should not make systematic mistakes in forecasting the future'. This sets limits to the ability of governments to manipulate the economy by tricking private agents. Eventually governments will be found out and private agents will adapt.

The 'rational expectations revolution' usefully focuses on the role of expectations. Every policy, indeed every policy discussion, every policy announcement and every event that has a possible implication for future policy, generates expectations by private agents, and these will have effects on economic behaviour that must be taken into account. Private agents will not ignore readily available information. While they will take into account the costs of obtaining information – and hence it may be optimal for them not to be fully informed, on average – one cannot assume that they can be readily misled.

Clearly, the simplest versions of rational expectations thinking require considerable qualifications. In particular the extent of the capacity of private agents to assimilate given information is crucial. Presumably there is some kind of production function where information is the input and understanding the output. It is also crucial, as has been noted frequently, what the mental model of the economy is into which the information is fed. In all these respects, in any given economy, different agents can differ. The information may only be available to some and not to others, perhaps because the costs of obtaining the information are greater for some than for others. There may be economies of scale in obtaining information. All agents (like economists themselves) will not have the same model of the economy. If agents have different abilities to obtain or process information, some being more 'rational' than others, the outcome may or may not be dominated by the more rational agents (Haltiwanger and Waldman, 1985).

In considering the relevance of all this for LDCs there is another consideration, to which I now turn.

4. Systematic and Benign Government Policies

4.1 Are Government Policies Systematic?

The literature puts a great emphasis on the effects of 'systematic' (and hence, in principle, predictable) government policies. The two policies that people usually have in mind are the old-fashioned Keynesian fine-tuning policy of adjusting nominal demand with the aim of offsetting private sector instabilities, and the Friedman policy of a constant rate of money supply growth. Because of the difficulties of measuring money and the unpredictability of velocity, the Friedman recommendation should be transmuted into advocacy of a constant rate of nominal GNP growth.

When one seeks to apply this idea of 'systematic policies' to LDCs, one wonders to what extent their policies, or significant aspects of their policies, can be described as systematic. Some LDCs have stable governments and stable economic philosophies. (Indeed the economic policy stability in certain LDCs, for example India, is greater than in some developed countries.) In other cases it would be hard to describe policies as systematic in any sense. Particular governments or ruling groups, or particular finance ministers, may have systematic policies in mind, but there is no 'system' about the changes in governments. In other cases there may not be any conscious system, and governments may continuously fail to achieve what they want to achieve, and lurch about from crisis to crisis.

On the other hand, a detached observer may be able to observe some systematic responses. For example, external shocks may always lead to crises and apparently to confused policy responses. But a detached observer taking a long view may indeed see regularities. If one stretches the term a bit, the apparently chaotic policies or non-policies might be described as 'systematic'. The situation greatly differs between countries, and the degree of predictability of the policies and the explicit or implicit 'system' in policy responses to shocks is definitely worth studying carefully. The probability that particular governments or finance ministers survive in power in the relevant policy period is clearly crucial. But, taking all this into account, the great emphasis in the DC macroeconomic literature on private agents' reactions to systematic policies by governments seems out of proportion when seen from the point of view of LDCs and possibly many DCs also.

4.2 Benign, Optimizing Government and the Political Economy Issue

Underlying Keynesian thinking was the idea of government as a benign, well-informed optimizer of the national interest, manipulating, in effect, the various rigidities – principally, nominal rigidities – in the private sector, and stabilizing the economy by offsetting the destabilizing activities of the private sector. In an open economy the latter aspect can be readily extended to allow for destabilizing effects coming from abroad, which may have originated from the policies of foreign governments rather than the private sector.

In a very broad sense rational expectations theory (at least when applied to macroeconomics) can be regarded as operating within the same framework as Keynesian theory even though its principal contribution has been to highlight the doubtful assumptions that crude Keynesianism requires for its validity. The implicit assumption is still an optimizing government which can be organized effectively to pursue whatever policies are desirable, whether fine-tuning policies or policies that operate subject to well-defined rules, which the government will adhere to.

A key characteristic is that there is a concept of 'the' government or 'the' central bank. The government acts on the private sector, and the private sector *reacts through the market place*, i.e. through product price and wage reactions. The whole elaborate edifice of rational expectations theory is concerned with this two-way relationship, and, above all, with whether the government can 'trick' the private sector into behaviour that the latter would not engage in if it had full information and made full use of that information.

The problem is that the focus is not at all on the motives of governments, nor on the way in which the private sector acts *directly* on governments through the political process, rather than responding through the market.

4.3 The Crucial Macroeconomic Issues for LDCs

The important macroeconomic issues for LDCs, and possibly for some DCs also, seem to be right outside the scope of rational expectations theory. What are the macroeconomic objectives of different governments at different times? How do pressure groups act on them? How do finance ministers and central banks balance one pressure against another?

There is a 'political' market in which pressure groups operate. Government policies certainly affect private sector behaviour, but the private sector, in turn, affects the government. This is, of course, only one aspect of the political economy issue. Policy is likely to be influenced by the interests of politicians as a class, and of various categories of government employees. Public choice theory might shed light on some of these issues, though its formal development appears to be relevant only for countries with democratic institutions.

An interesting aspect of the existing political economy literature concerns the argument that politicians take a short-term election-orientated view (Nordhaus, 1975). Given that a demand expansion may (in a Keynesian model) raise employment before it raises inflation, the politicians' high discount of the future may lead to excessive inflation from a national welfare point of view. In the recent LDC context, if Keynesian effects are *not* significant, the short-term benefit to the politicians may be higher public spending financed by foreign borrowing, while the longer term cost may be not just inflation but also the problems caused by the need for repayment of foreign loans. One question is whether government's discount rates appeared to be consistently lower in cases where governments were more stable, i.e. felt themselves more securely in power. To what extent did the more insecure governments buy support through current account deficits?

5. The Rational Expectations of Government

There appears to be a surprising gap in the literature. Rational expectations theorists have assiduously explored many questions with regard to the private sector, but have not asked these with regard to the policies of governments.

Is all available information made use of by government decision makers? What are the costs of acquiring information, and in what circumstances will it pay not to acquire all possible information? What is the model into which the public decision makers feed their information?

If there are 'wrong' models and 'right' models, do the right models eventually prevail because politicians or decision makers with the right models survive, or win over those with wrong models? (In other words, does truth prevail?) Could outcomes be improved if there were more provision of information to public decision makers and more education in the 'right' models? Perhaps this is where the policy advice of the International Monetary Fund and the World Bank fits in?

This discussion suggests an empirical programme, a kind of extension to the public sector of the empirical programme yielded by the rational expectations revolution. What have been the expectations of government decision makers at various times, and were these expectations justified by the information available at the time? Did different government decision makers (including different political parties) have different expectations, and, if so, was this because the information was different, or the models were different?

One should also focus on the ability to assimilate given information even when the model is given. This is a matter of how efficient the bureaucracy and the political system are. Do policy shifts reflect changing information, changing ability to assimilate information, changing models or changing objectives? If the objectives have changed, is it because given power groups or individuals have changed their objectives, or because the weighting given to different pressure groups or individuals in power has changed, with each having a different but constant objective? It seems obvious to me that these questions need to be considered when any assessment of LDC macroeconomic policies is made.

6. The Neo-Ricardian Theorem and LDCs

An important feature of DC fiscal theory is the rediscovery of, and emphasis on, the so-called 'Neo-Ricardian equivalence theorem'.[4] We consider here the effects of a bond-financed government deficit.

It used to be argued that the extra bonds represent net wealth in the hands of the public. The public does not take into account the extra tax obligations in the future that the government incurs when it borrows from the public (whether the local public or abroad). The new idea is that rational taxpayers *will* take this into account. The Ricardian theorem in its extreme form is that private savings will increase to provide for the future tax obligations: a bond-financed deficit does *not* increase net wealth, because the increased holding of bonds in private hands is offset by the wealth-reducing effect of the higher expected taxes. Thus a budget deficit will not increase national expenditure; it will only shift the pattern of expenditure. If the deficit resulted from a rise in government spending, the pattern of spending will shift from private to public. Extra public dissaving will be matched by extra private savings. This represents an application of rational expectations theory to fiscal policy.

Has this idea any relevance for LDCs? To begin with, in LDCs deficits tend to be money-financed. As long as the increase in the money supply is not expected to increase inflation or the current account deficit, but is just expected to lead to extra output along Keynesian lines, there should not be any Neo-Ricardian effect. On the other hand, if inflation is expected, the expectation of an erosion of the real value of money holdings (the inflation tax) would lead to higher savings. But the most relevant case for some LDCs may be one where the situation is essentially non-Keynesian and a fixed exchange rate prevents or moderates inflation. Much or all of the budget deficit will then be reflected in a current account deficit.

In that case the government does not pay any interest to the central bank or to any local citizens, but the central bank must either reduce its foreign exchange reserves (and so forgo interest earnings), or the government must borrow abroad. In one way or another, interest obligations are incurred, as well as obligations eventually to repay foreign loans, or a future need to rebuild the reserves is foreseen. The perceived net wealth of taxpayers who foresee these consequences will decline and (if they are rational) they would then increase their savings, and hence produce an offsetting reduction in the current account deficit. If the private sector reactions were instantaneous and completely offsetting (both very unlikely) a current account deficit would not result at all. Extra deposits by the private sector with the banking system, or reduced borrowing abroad, would exactly offset the increased borrowing by the government.

The practical question is whether there might be any tendency to such offsetting savings behaviour in LDCs. What motivates private saving and dissaving behaviour in LDCs? Is there any degree of Ricardian rationality? Private households and firms may foresee that government borrowing abroad could create difficulties for the future. They may come to expect foreign pressures to raise taxes or reduce government expenditures, leading to policies which might cause social disruption, and they might then wish to take precautions. But such precautions would not necessarily consist of building up domestic-currency-denominated financial assets. They might wish to build up stocks of goods, of gold or – most likely – of foreign-currency-denominated assets.[5]

Properly adjusted and broadened, the Ricardian theorem could then have some relevance for LDCs. There is plenty of experience available for testing it, some of which suggests that (in the light of hindsight) appropriate foresight was not always shown by the private sector, possibly because the very same analyses which led governments to think that certain policies would have favorable consequences led the private sector to the same conclusion.

One might conclude with a very general point: the fiscal policies of LDC governments may create various expectations about future consequences (a) in the minds of the country's own citizens, including taxpayers, and (b) in the minds of operators in the world capital market. These expectations can have early effects on private savings, on private investment and on the desired portfolio balance between domestic-currency- and foreign-currency-denominated financial assets, and hence on the exchange rate in a floating rate system or the overall balance of payments in a fixed exchange rate system. These forward-looking expectational effects must be taken into account in any analysis of current fiscal policy.

7. Non-market-clearing Models

A sophisticated literature has elaborated non-market-clearing models. These assume price and wage rigidities (usually with no capital markets) and spell out the general equilibrium implications of various policies.[6] The prices and wages are not endogenous, not even to the extent that they are in old-fashioned (non-expectations-augmented) Phillips curve models. Nothing is said about the explanations for the rigidities. The rigidities are nominal, which may also imply real wage rigidity. But real wage rigidity and neo-classical effects are not the focus.

One might regard these models as being more thorough expositions and explorations of the popular Keynesian pre-Phillips curve model. Their special contribution is to spell out the general equilibrium effects of excess demands and supplies in various markets. But no allowance is made for the effects on factor and goods prices of the various possible policies that are explored.

If there is evidence of Keynesian effects in an LDC in the short run then these models have some relevance. But they neglect the feedback effects of policies on wages and prices, so they are clearly limited. Particularly in countries with high and variable rates of inflation, the central assumptions are implausible. On the other hand, in many LDCs one would hardly expect instantaneous market clearing in all the main markets, so these models may be at least as useful as the cruder rational expectations models. But I doubt whether they tell us much more than the simple Keynes-with-Phillips curve models.

8. Real Wage Rigidity

The tendency to real wage rigidity downwards, possibly post-tax, and at least in the short run, has been noticed in Europe and other developed countries outside the United States since 1973, and has played an important part in post-oil shock analyses. There is now a large DC literature built around the real wage rigidity assumption.

8.1 Explaining Real Wage Rigidity

It is not difficult to explain some involuntary unemployment and real wage rigidity downwards in terms of the 'efficiency wage' hypothesis (Yellen, 1984). In a static model it can also be explained by trade unions exercising their monopoly power at the expense of the unemployed. It is a little more difficult to explain why the real wage demanded by unions does not fall sufficiently in response to shocks, such as the oil price shock. Thus static or equilibrium real wage rigidity (i.e. maintenance of real wages above full employment levels) is easier to explain than dynamic real wage rigidity. There may be information problems, there may be problems of understanding (using the 'wrong model' or being unable to feed information efficiently into the right model) and the logic of collective (in)action may dictate slow adjustment. There may be a probability at least that the negative shock is temporary, which might justify maintenance of real wage levels when there are costs of negotiating and of explaining required real wage cuts to trade union members.

Potentially, rational expectations theory is fully applicable to this issue, even though it is no longer focused on explaining the determination of *nominal* wages and prices, and hence no longer concerned with analysing the Keynesian question of the efficacy of nominal demand management. One has to explain the real wage expectations on which wage demands are based. What is the information base of these expectations, what are the implicit models of the economy used and so on?

8.2 Raising Employment with Real Wage Rigidity

Various policies have been proposed for getting around the rigidity with the objective of increasing employment. They are all clearly applicable to LDCs.

One possible approach hinges on the assumption that the rigidity is post-tax, not pre-tax, and that it is not only downwards but also upwards. The idea is to reduce tax rates on labor incomes or on goods consumed by wage earners, a policy which would then lead to a decline in pre-tax real wages (to maintain constant post-tax wages) and hence to higher employment (Corden, 1981). The hope is that the higher tax base resulting from the higher employment will prevent a fall in government revenue.

Another possible solution involves short-term borrowing abroad, the borrowed funds allowing taxes to be kept low and so post-tax wages high; the funds are repaid later when productivity is higher and the rigid post-tax real wage can be sustained without borrowing. Such borrowing may also allow public sector real wages to stay higher than otherwise.

A third approach is to tax sectors of the economy where real incomes are not rigid, using the revenue to subsidize the real-wage rigid sectors. An indirect and rather inefficient way of doing this would be through particular forms of trade protection, this being the implicit model of the Cambridge (England) protectionists.

8.3 Real Wage Rigidity and LDCs

The real wage rigidity assumption was implicit (and occasionally explicit) in the Latin American structuralist models. Ideas coming from structuralism may have been rediscovered in the more recent Europe-orientated literature. Furthermore, real wage rigidity in one sector of a two-sector economy is central to the Harris–Todaro model, which seeks to explain a form of structural unemployment in LDCs. But this model has not been used for analysing macroeconomic policy.

For LDCs the idea may have to be extended from just having downwardly rigid urban real wages to allowing for at least two real wage categories – government employee real wages and private sector urban real wages. Furthermore, rigidities of particular categories of government expenditure, and also rigidities of some rural incomes, might be added. One may have to categorize the various real incomes in the country (presumably post-tax, and allowing for real incomes derived from particular forms of government expenditure) in terms of the degree of their rigidity downwards. Presumably there would be two government policy instruments: first, fiscal policy, which would include not only the level of the budget deficit (leading to a current account deficit and hence foreign borrowing) but also the mix of taxes and of government expenditure; and secondly, incomes policy.

9. Supply-Side Models and Sectoral Income Effects

Models which do not actually assume that the real wage is rigid downwards, but where all wage adjustments are explicitly in real terms, have been developed. Such models allow for rational behaviour and seem very relevant for many countries. They allow negative supply shocks to produce both an increase in unemployment *and* some fall in real wages as part of a trade union optimizing response. In such cases the real wage is unresponsive to nominal demand shocks, but has some degree of flexibility – though not sufficient to maintain constant employment – in response to real shocks. Models of this kind, focusing on the effects of supply-side shocks on real factor prices and allowing for sluggishness in real wage adjustment and optimizing behaviour, are expounded in Bruno and Sachs (1985), where further references are also given.[7]

Some shocks, whether nominal or real in origin, may cause real wages to rise, but the shocks may be temporary in nature, and yet real wages may not fall when the original shock is reversed, the rigidity being downwards, but not upwards. This is surely the common situation in DCs as well as LDCs. Yet it is hard to derive such reactions from a model of rational behaviour. If the favourable shock was known to be temporary to start with, so that its reversal is expected, rational behaviour would not lead to a rise in real wages in the first place (or, at least, not one so great that it needed later to be reversed), unless the future were heavily discounted. On the other hand, if it was expected to be permanent initially, so that its reversal was unexpected, rational behaviour should lead the trade unions to lower their real wage targets or demands when new information about the reversal of the shock comes in.

One can imagine a body of *real* macroeconomic theory which is very different from the sort of macroeconomics discussed in the DC textbooks and which focuses on real rigidities and sectoral income effects. A literature in this direction is growing up, though it is hardly yet consolidated. Tendencies in this direction can be found in Corden (1985), Prachowny (1984) and Bruno and Sachs (1985), and various papers by Scandinavian authors.[8]

The 'booming sector and Dutch disease' literature comes into this general category. It has been developed with respect to both DCs and LDCs and is concerned primarily with a special issue: the sectoral real income effects, as well as overall macroeconomic consequences, of a sectoral real income boom (Corden, 1984). In effect the Dutch disease models package various aspects of macroeconomics to examine a particular problem, but the special aspect is the emphasis on real income and output effects on different sectors.

10. Large Group Interaction and Game Theory

Macroeconomic policy and events can be conceptualized as the outcome of a game played between two or more large actors in an economy. Recent theorizing, mostly in Europe, or by economists primarily influenced by non-US institutional environments, might be relevant for some LDCs.

In the simplest model (originating in Scandinavia) the actors are the government and the trade union movement (Calmfors, 1982). The first has fiscal policy as its instrument of choice and the second has the real pre-tax wage level. The outcome yields the current account of the balance of payments and the level of employment. If money is explicitly introduced, the price level and, perhaps, the exchange rate would also be included in the story. There are several variants of such models, including those where one party is pre-committed to a policy, or to a reaction function, while the other one then optimizes. Such models could be extended to more than two actors. The corporate sector could be added and the government could have both monetary and fiscal policy as instruments. Various game theory issues, including the crucial one of credibility of threats, arise.

Models of this kind have a great ring of reality about them for many DC economies outside the US, more than many of the contributions of rational expectations theorists. The models can either assume that each party has full information, or that there is an 'asymmetric information' situation, the withholding of information and the surprising of the other parties being part of the game.

The principal weakness of the game theory approach is that governments are not really independent of the private actors. This point was made earlier. Groups or classes within a country further their interests not just through their wage (or other income) demands in the market place but also by *directly* influencing government policies. While in some LDCs the government controls the unions, in some other countries, including many DCs, the unions significantly influence the government.

In considering the applicability to LDCs of this new body of theory, two observations can be made: (a) organized groups vary in different countries, and the trade unions are often weak. There may be a variety of interest groups to take into account, but if they are not well organized, the model is inappropriate; (b) in most cases one would guess that the interest groups exercise their power much more directly on governments, i.e. through the political process, than, as in the models mentioned, through adjusting their nominal wages or product prices in response to varying government policies. As noted earlier, interactions through both the political process *and* the market place (especially the labour market) have to be taken into account.

11. Conclusion

There is a standard body of theory for small open economies which takes into account the distinction between tradables and non-tradables, between absorption and switching, between real and nominal devaluation and so on, and which can incorporate capital mobility and allow for sectoral distribution effects. This body of theory is clearly relevant for developing countries, but is so well-known that it has not been expounded here. The aim has *not* been to expound macroeconomic theory for developing countries but rather to look reflectively at the significance of various recent developments in theory, and also possible further developments that are not yet fully incorporated in this standard theory, and see whether these can be of use for the study of the macroeconomic experiences of developing countries. At the risk of over simplification, the main conclusions can be summarized as follows:

1 A crucial question concerns the extent to which there are *nominal* rigidities in LDCs, and especially the length of time nominal devaluations have real effects. Of course, the latter is not a new question, there being an extensive empirical literature dealing with it.
2 The rational expectations approach raises some interesting issues about the reaction of private agents to government behavior. It needs to be considered to what extent private sector behaviour in LDCs suggests evidence of 'rationality' in the sense in which the literature uses the term, both in its reactions to aggregate demand (primarily money supply and exchange rate) policies, and budget deficit policies.
3 One might ask to what extent policies in various LDCs are 'systematic', or can ever be so, either in the usual narrow sense, or in a broad sense.
4 The political economy of governments' macroeconomic policies needs to be investigated. Essentially this involves seeking to explain the policies of governments at various times and especially examining the effects of pressure groups on them. The point has been made that, while in orthodox theory the effects of the government on the private sector are studied, it is also necessary to examine the effects through the 'political market' of

the private sector (as well as of government employees and politicians) on government policy.

5 The expectations of governments need to be analysed. Are they 'rational', i.e. what information and what models do policy makers use, and what is their ability to process information? An empirical programme which is an extension to the public sector of the empirical programme yielded by the rational expectations revolution, is suggested.

6 The Neo-Ricardian theorem may have some relevance for LDCs, particularly because government or central bank borrowing abroad could lead to some offsetting private savings behaviour. More broadly, fiscal policies, notably the expectations of the difficulties that deficits might generate, are likely to lead to reactions by the private sector. Forward-looking expectations must be taken into account in analysing current fiscal policies.

7 Models involving post-tax real wage rigidity, or at least some sluggishness in real wages, are relevant for many LDCs, as are various solutions that have been explored for maintaining or increasing employment when there is such rigidity. These models may need to be extended to allow for several sectors, and there is scope for a body of theory that focuses on real rigidities and sectoral income effects.

8 Models with large group interaction, using game theory, may be useful for analysing macroeconomic behaviour in some developing countries, but if interest groups are not well organized, such models are not really relevant. Furthermore, interaction through the political process rather than through the market place may be more important.

NOTES

The paper was written in 1985 at Nuffield College, Oxford and the Australian National University, and revised in April 1986 when I was Visiting Professor at Harvard University. I wish to thank all the institutions, as well as the World Bank.

1 This market-clearing approach is set out systematically in Barro (1984, ch. 18), and originated with Lucas, Barro and Sargent and Wallace (see n. 3 below).

2 The literature on the effectiveness of devaluation is generally concerned with 'competitiveness', rather than real wages. A well-known paper is Connolly and Taylor (1976). See also Warr (1984) and Khan and Knight (1985) which both contain further references. Recent Southern Cone experience certainly suggests that nominal exchange rate policy has real effects, i.e. that there are nominal wage and price rigidities. Some empirical work on the real effects of monetary policy, mostly in Latin America, is available. There is an excellent summary and review in Khan and Knight (1985). See especially Hanson (1980) and the references given there, as well as Edwards (1983) and Leiderman (1984). It appears, at least from Hanson (1980), that there is a significant relation between output and unexpected inflation, though there must always be some doubt as to what is really the 'expected' inflation.

3 Classic articles on the applicability of the rational expectations idea to macroeconomics are Sargent and Wallace (1976) and various papers by Lucas, reprinted in

Lucas (1981). For a clear statement of implications, see Lucas and Sargent (1979). Important contributions have also come from Barro, and his current views can be found in Barro (1984). The textbook by Sheffrin (1983) is particularly useful. It contains an extensive bibliography. An excellent reference is Fischer (1980), which contains both sympathetic and critical analyses of the rational expectations approach.

4 See Barro (1974), Barro (1984, p. 381) and references given in the latter.

5 As far as I know, empirical work on the applicability of the neo-Ricardian hypothesis for LDCs has not been published so far. Mohsin Khan has pointed out to me that the data suggest that the savings–GDP ratio is pretty stable even for countries with large shifts in public dissavings, and this could be a Ricardian equivalence effect. An interesting example is Chile 1979–80, where a private financial deficit replaced the budget deficit, which had been practically eliminated.

6 See Barro and Grossman (1976), Malinvaud (1977), Muellbauer and Portes (1978) and Cuddington et al. (1984). The latter book discusses some of the broader issues, including the causes of rigidities.

7 See also Calmfors and Horn (1985) and Calmfors (1985) and references cited in these two papers as well as various papers presented at a Stockholm conference on Trade Unions, Wage Formation and Macroeconomic Stability, published in the *Scandinavian Journal of Economics*, 87(2), 1985.

8 The connection with elements of Latin American structuralism and the neo-structuralist model building of Taylor is obvious. I have not attempted to survey or analyse this literature. The best-known reference is Taylor (1983).

REFERENCES

Azariadis, Costas and Stiglitz, Joseph E. 1983: Implicit contracts and fixed-price equilibria. *Quarterly Journal of Economics*, 48, Supplement, 1–22.

Barro, Robert J. 1974: Are government bonds net wealth?. *Journal of Political Economy*, 82, 1095–117.

Barro, Robert J. 1984 : *Macroeconomics*. New York: Wiley.

Barro, Robert J. and Grossman, Herschel 1976: *Money, Employment and Inflation*. Cambridge: Cambridge University Press.

Bruno, Michael and Sachs, Jeffrey D. 1985: *Economics of Worldwide Stagflation*. Cambridge, MA: Harvard University Press.

Calmfors, Lars 1982: Employment policies, wage formation and trade union behaviour in a small open economy. *The Scandinavian Journal of Economics*, 2.

Calmfors, Lars 1985: Trade unions, wage formation and macroeconomic stability – an introduction. *The Scandinavian Journal of Economics*, 87 (2).

Calmfors, Lars and Horn, Hendrik 1985: Classical unemployment, accommodation policies and the adjustment of real wages. *The Scandinavian Journal of Economics*, 87.

Connolly, Michael and Taylor, D. 1976: Testing the monetary approach to devaluation in developing countries. *Journal of Political Economy*, August, 849–59.

Corden, W. Max 1981: Taxation, real wage rigidity and employment. *Economic Journal*, 91, 309–30.

Corden, W. Max 1984: Booming sector and Dutch disease economics: a survey. *Oxford Economic Papers*, 36, 359–80.

Corden, W. Max 1985: *Inflation, Exchange Rates and the World Economy*. Oxford: Oxford University Press.

Cuddington, John T. and Löfgren, Karl-Gustaf 1984: *Disequilibrium Macroeconomics in Open Economies*, Oxford: Blackwell.

Edwards, Sebastian 1983: The short-run relation between growth and inflation in Latin America: comments. *American Economic Review*, 73, 477–82.

Fischer, Stanley 1977: Long-term contracts, rational expectations and the optimal money supply rule. *Journal of Political Economy*, 85, 191–206.

Fischer, Stanley (ed.)1980: *Rational Expectations and Economic Policy*. Chicago: National Bureau of Economic Research.

Haltiwanger, John and Waldman, Michael 1985: Rational expectations and the limits of rationality: an analysis of heterogeneity. *American Economic Review*, 75, 326–40.

Hanson, J. A. 1980: The short-run relation between growth and inflation in Latin America. *American Economic Review*, 70, 972–89.

Khan, M. S. and Knight, M. D. 1981: Stabilization programs in developing countries: a formal framework. *IMF Staff Papers*, 28, 1–53.

Khan, M. S. and Knight, M. D. 1985: *Fund-Supported Adjustment Programs and Economic Growth*, IMF Occasional Papers no. 41.

Krugman, Paul and Taylor, Lance 1978: Contractionary effects of devaluation. *Journal of International Economics*, 8.

Leiderman, L. 1984: On the monetary-macro dynamics of Colombia and Mexico. *Journal of Development Economics*, 14, 184–201.

Lucas, Robert E. 1981: *Studies in Business-Cycle Theory*. Cambridge, MA: The MIT Press.

Lucas, Robert E. and Sargent, Thomas J. 1979: After Keynesian macroeconomics. *Quarterly Review*, Federal Reserve Bank of Minneapolis, pp. 1–16.

Malinvaud, Edmond 1977: *The Theory of Unemployment Reconsidered*. Oxford: Blackwell.

Muellbauer, John and Portes, Richard 1978: Macroeconomic models with quantity rationing. *The Economic Journal*, 88, 788–821.

Nordhaus, William 1975: The political business cycle. *Review of Economic Studies*, 42, 169–90.

Prachowny, Martin F. J. 1984: *Macroeconomic Analysis for Small Open Economies*. Oxford: Clarendon Press.

Sargent, Thomas and Wallace, Neil 1976: Rational expectations and the theory of economic policy. *Journal of Monetary Economics*, 4, 1976, 1–44.

Sheffrin, Steven M. 1983: *Rational Expectations*. Cambridge: Cambridge University Press.

Taylor, Lance 1983: *Structuralist Macroeconomics*, New York: Basic Books.

Warr, Peter G. 1984: Exchange rate protection in Indonesia. *Bulletin of Indonesian Economic Studies*, 20, 53–89.

Yellen, Janet L. 1984: Efficiency wage models of unemployment. *American Economic Review*, Papers and Proceedings, 74, 200–5.

13

Indian Macroeconomic Policies

Vijay Joshi and I.M.D. Little

1. Introduction

Development economics can and does no longer ignore short- and medium-run macroeconomic policies and their effects on long-run growth, however difficult to analyse these may be. The old dichotomy between the World Bank's concern with development and the IMF's concern with stabilization and balance of payments viability is dead.

Something needs to be said about the meaning of 'macroeconomic policy', and this is especially true of a highly controlled economy such as that of India. The range of policies here considered as 'macro' includes the conventional items of fiscal and monetary policy, the exchange rate regime adopted and the management of the balance of payments. Governmental revenues and expenditures apart, these areas of policy all involve controls. In particular, imports, the use of foreign exchange, borrowing abroad, foreign investment in India, interest rates and domestic credit are all subject to control.[1] These controls both designedly and inadvertently affect the allocation of resources to particular activities: this aspect of the control system has been much studied but is here ignored. We are interested only in the effect of controls on aggregates, the overall level of imports, capital movements, domestic credit and the level of investment and savings – allocational or efficiency aspects are regarded as falling within the domain of microeconomics. One particular control measure which may on the face of it appear to be microeconomic in its effects is in fact a major instrument of macroeconomic policy, that is the handling of imports and stocks of foodgrains. This is because, in India, the variability of the monsoon can be a more dominant influence than any change in the external environment.

India exhibits none of the extremes of external shock and policy change, or of outcomes such as accelerated growth or lasting major recessions accompanied by large increases in unemployment, or inflation and debt-servicing problems, features that attract swarms of economists to the study of the 'Southern Cone', Brazil, Mexico and Korea. But the fact that the dog did not bark, or only yelped a little, itself requires explanation, for there have been considerable disturbances. For instance, although external shocks were relatively small, not exceeding 3 per cent of GNP in any year, India periodically suffers an internal exogenous shock from drought, which has caused a decline of agricultural production of as much as 15 per cent in a year, and a 5 per cent decline of GDP.

India's macroeconomic policies have been essentially conservative and cautious. Budgetary deficits at least until the 1980s have been kept to a very small proportion of GNP. When inflation has begun to climb, monetary growth has fairly soon been reduced with the desired effect. Macroeconomic policy has thus been more Friedmanite than Keynesian. Foreign borrowing has been cautious, and capital movements strictly controlled. Apart from one devaluation in 1966, exchange rate policy has also been conservative: after the breakdown of Bretton Woods the rupee was pegged to the pound, and later to a small basket of major currencies[2] (sterling remaining the currency of intervention). When reserves proved inadequate, the balance of payments has been managed largely by variations in the stringency of import controls, but also by variations in borrowing.

This relative conservatism needs to be explained. India is a country with manifold internal divisions and rivalries. Her political system is democratic, but concentrates much power in the bureaucracy, as well as in the hands of a small political elite. These characteristics might lead one to wrongly expect the populist excesses so common elsewhere in the Third World. Similarly, Indian governments unlike many in the Third World are very sensitive to inflation and react fairly quickly to suppress it.

The conservatism also needs to be questioned. India has in real terms avoided the most turbulent outcomes (except where loss of agricultural output is unavoidably due to the drought). But India has also grown slowly. This slow growth has not been uniform, but the trend has not deviated since 1950 from the 'Hindu rate of growth',[3] despite a strongly rising level of savings and an increasing share of government in both output and investment, despite the 'green revolution' and despite the rise and fall of the influence of the Planning Commission. Would India have done better in the long run if she had adopted Keynesian policies, used the exchange rate and interest rates more actively as policy instruments or borrowed more freely? Or, would bolder macropolicies and free use of such 'macroprices' as the exchange rate and interest rates have made little difference to so highly controlled an economy? Alternatively, if India had been much less controlled (and had therefore, most probably, grown faster) would she have been able to avoid the turbulence suffered by some more open economies?

Interesting questions are also posed by the apparent success of essentially monetarist policies. India was twice able in our period to reduce inflation very quickly, and *prima facie* without very serious loss of industrial output or unemployment. This suggests considerable price and wage flexibility, and contrasts with the experience of many industrialized and Latin American countries.[4] This is a matter that demands much more research than it seems to have attracted. What were the costs of the monetary squeezes, and who bore them?

Lastly, although we have categorized India as a low-inflation economy and have described her policies as conservative, it is important to notice that this is not so true now as earlier. Although inflation has proceeded in a stop–go manner (almost inevitable in a monsoon economy) the trend has been exponential even if mildly so, and the same is true of the rate of growth of the monetary aggregates. Government borrowing from the Reserve Bank averaged about 1 per cent of GNP before the second oil shock, but has increased to about 2 per cent since. India has also resorted to commercial borrowing from 1981–2 onwards with new commitments running at more than $1 billion a year.[5] It is too early to say whether these straws in the wind portend a shift to a more Latin American style, or whether they will have any effect on the trend rate of growth.

A good deal has been written about the intricacies of Indian controls, and the consequential price distortions which result in apparently irrational production and trading incentives, and the delays and corruption they cause. But almost nothing seems to have been written to explain India's relatively untypical macroeconomic policies, or to question whether they have been conducive to long-run development. We do not answer the questions raised above in this article, which does little more than clear the ground and point the way to future work.

2. Political Economy

Among the features of Indian economic management that most demand explanations are (a) budgetary conservatism and the related fear of inflation, and (b) deep distrust of the price mechanism, with its corollary, the very extensive use of controls. The first of these is especially surprising in view of the serious conflicts and rivalries within the subcontinent. There are the inevitable state rivalries of a federal system, and even independence movements. There is urban–rural conflict, and there are deep communal and linguistic problems. Class conflict (whether one defines classes in terms of production roles, or relative incomes) has been less a feature than in many economies, largely because of the caste system and the other rivalries mentioned; but it spottily and increasingly manifests itself.

How is it that the central government has not felt the need to throw money at these problems? To a limited extent it has done so, but it has been within the confines of small deficits (at least until very recently).[6] In India charismatic leaders have occasionally appealed directly to the masses for support, but their appeals have not involved the large deficits or inflationary wage increases of such populist policies in Latin America, or even France.

There are various lines of explanation of fiscal conservatism. These are often also explanations of the distrust of the price mechanism, and the belief in administered development.

2.1 A Deep Historical and Cultural Conception of the State as a Guardian and Protector, Reinforced both by British Rule and by the Independence Movement

The British created a small, high-minded, highly elitist bureaucracy with a Gladstonian fiscal outlook.[7] Congress, when it became an independence movement, was imbued with Gandhian austerity. Nehru dominated the Indian political and economic scene from independence to his death. His economic views were highly heterodox by British standards, but not in the fiscal sphere.[8] Nehru was a Kashmiri Brahmin, and was also a Fabian socialist who had suffered an upper-class English education. All of these go with a distrust of business, and some of them at least with ignorance of the allocational role of the price mechanism, admiration for Russian planning and genuine concern for the poor. Permitting inflation would harm the poor, and could be seen as a loss of control and an abrogation of the proper role of the state.

Nehru's ideas did not conflict with those of the Indian Civil Service. Before independence, the civil service administered law and order, with little need to understand economics or business. Faced, after independence, with the extraordinary new demands of development, it naturally thought in terms of *administering* it, in conformity not only with Nehru's philosophy but probably with the views of almost all members of the Congress party.[9]

The role of the Indian bureaucracy needs further consideration. To what extent is it an overt political force? Of course, all bureaucracies make minor political decisions and even major ones when faced with a weak government, or a weak minister. But some political theorists assign a more leading role to the bureaucrats. The Latin American theory of the 'bureaucratic authoritarian' state suggests that the 'army and civil service, ostensibly created to serve the "peoples will", instead arrogate to themselves the task of defining the goals of the state which they make to coincide with their own'.[10] As they see it, these goals require considerable intervention in the working of the economy, which inevitably creates new disequilibria and further intervention. This multiplication of tasks is in the interests of an expanding bureaucracy.

This view of the bureaucracy is certainly consistent with the fact that administration and defence have grown twice as fast as GDP, but since there has been no conflict in these matters between the ruling Congress and the bureaucracy nothing is proved. There is furthermore the fact that the salaries of high civil servants have been much reduced in real terms since independence. Indeed, it has been suggested that governmental sensitivity to inflation stems from the fact that these salaries are not indexed (nor are those of the politicians). But if the bureaucracy is powerful enough to induce political action to restrain inflation in its own interests, then it is surely powerful enough to see to it that its own salaries are indexed. It may be that the austerity of the first two post-war decades has left a tradition that is not easy to break in any overt manner. Although corruption has reached serious proportions one cannot say that the Guardian state has been succeeded by a 'bureaucratic–authoritarian' or quasi-predatory state. India does not fit easily into any classification.

There have been several moves towards some limited liberalization, with limited objectives in mind. Most intellectuals seem to oppose such moves, retaining their inherited distrust of the price mechanism as the fulcrum of the colonial economic system, while radical protest against any decontrol verges on the hysterical. There has never been a political constituency for making a 'bonfire of controls'. The Swatantra party has this aim, but it seems that its support is too narrowly based for it to make much headway.

The moment of truth will come if India ever acquires a government that is determined to unshackle the economy from its controlling fetters. Would it find it impossible to implement a planned programme of liberalization? It is very doubtful whether this moment of truth has arrived: whatever Mr Gandhi's own views, many other influential members of the Congress party would seem to remain convinced that no more than very tentative liberalization is appropriate.

2.2 India is a Democracy. Two Cheers?

It may be suggested that democracies are less prone to inflation than authoritarian governments for the simple reason that inflation is unpopular and elections have to be won. Our hunch is that a comparative study would not support this hypothesis. But Indian democracy differs from others. By and large Indian parties do not compete directly for individual votes with programmes based on class interests. Votes are still largely determined by caste and community membership, or 'delivered' in so-called 'vote banks' by shifting alliances of dominant castes or factions, especially in rural areas. It remains, however, rather obscure as to why this might increase the sensitivity of a ruling party to inflation, though it is possible that the party might fear that inflation would lead to a development of class interests.

2.3 One Cheer for Controls?

Control of credit made it easier for the government to finance itself at negative real rates during the 1970s. The commercial banks have been required to buy government paper at controlled rates of interest. A rapidly mounting burden of interest, the 'dept trap' was thus avoided. This is further discussed in section 4.

In one other respect, controls and distrust of the price mechanism may have helped to restrain inflation. Except for one major devaluation, which was widely regarded as a political disaster, the exchange rate has been pegged, and this may have helped to maintain some internal price discipline.

2.4 Past Inflation

It is often suggested that past experience of very high or hyperinflation makes governments, once the inflation has been mastered or burnt itself out, particularly wary of policies that may lead in that direction. There are certainly some examples: Germany, China, Taiwan, for instance. Some systematic comparative work would however, seem to be required. India experienced a fairly severe inflation (and a major famine in Bengal) during the Second World War. The inflation was around 40 per cent per annum from 1940 to 1943, not in the class of hyperinflation.[11] However, it was over 100 per cent in 1943, the year of the Bengal famine, and it is possible that this contributed to a lasting anti-inflationary ethos, and shaped subsequent attitudes and policies towards food prices, food supply management and buffer stocks.

3. India 1966–85 – A Chronological Sketch

This sketch is intended as background to the more focused, albeit brief, review of trends of monetary, fiscal and exchange rate policies that follows in section 4.

3.1 From 1966 to 1970

The wars with China (1962) and Pakistan (1965) resulted in large increases in defence expenditure. It rose from around 2 per cent of net national product (NNP) before 1962 to around 4 per cent between 1962 and 1972. Aid was suspended during the Pakistan war, and was resumed at a lower real level only after the devaluation of the rupee in 1966, which came shortly after but was otherwise unconnected with the choice of Mrs Gandhi as prime minister. The devaluation achieved little in the economic sphere, partly because of the disastrous droughts in 1966 to 1967. Politically, devaluation was a disaster, being attacked from all sides as a surrender to reactionary capitalist advice stemming from the International Bank for Reconstruction and Development (IBRD) and Agency for International Development (AID).[12] Mrs Gandhi would never have permitted another *overt* devaluation (but the rupee was effectively devalued in the 1970s). The suspension and resumption of aid, combined with its apparent leverage over Indian policies, also increased the popularity of measures to achieve greater economic independence.

The disastrous droughts and the very large grain imports in 1966 and 1967 (food imports rose to about one-third of the import bill) did result in a shift of attention towards agriculture, increased agricultural investment and rapid official acceptance and encouragement of the green revolution. From 1967 to 1971 net cereal production rose by about 50 per cent (the wisdom of hindsight shows, however, that there was no change in the long-run trend!).

Agricultural recovery in India is often hailed as a new dawn, while its decline leads to despair and to ignorant foreign comment to the effect that India is a 'basket case', not worth aiding. NNP also staged a recovery growing at 5.5 per cent p.a. in this period, though industry recovered only slowly from the recession caused by the drought years. This slow recovery may be partly attributed to the fact that in response to the inflation caused by the droughts of 1965/6 and 1966/7, the government imposed restrictive fiscal policies. The overall public deficit was reduced from Rs 4 billion in 1965–6 to Rs 0.6 billion in 1969/70. This, and the fall in aid, was associated with a fall in public investment that was concentrated on the transport and communication sectors, and also a fall in the trend of investment in electricity, gas and water supply.[13] These 'economies' gave rise to shortages in these key non-traded sectors which have persisted ever since. It is noteworthy that the government preferred to cut investment rather than risk inflation by running budget deficits. It would surely have been better, had it been feasible, to maintain investment by augmenting public revenue.

Drought and the devaluation made nonsense of the projections of the Third Five Year Plan and its initiation was delayed until 1969. The Planning Commission came under severe criticism, and lost power and prestige. Always only advisory, its plans had nevertheless been strongly indicative to central ministries, state governments and even to the cabinet itself. It seems that these indications have never since been taken as seriously as in the days of Nehru, and central influence over state governments has been reduced.

In 1967 the Congress party lost heavily at the polls. In 1969 Mrs Gandhi in populist mood resolved a longstanding debate by nationalizing the commercial banks, a move which led directly to a split in the Congress party and her emergence as the dominant leader of the ruling wing.

3.2 From 1970 to the First Oil Price Shock

The 1970s opened well, with a record harvest in 1970/1, low inflation (5.1 per cent) and above-average growth of GDP (5.6 per cent). Mrs Gandhi won a famous victory in the 1971 elections, campaigning on the slogan 'abolish poverty'. Her popularity rose further as a result of the Indian victory in the Pakistan/Bangladesh war of independence of that year, a war that again resulted in a suspension of aid. It also left a costly legacy of 10 million refugees from East Bengal.

Overall government current expenditure rose by no less than 22 per cent between 1970/1 and 1971/2, a period during which wholesale prices only rose by 5.6 per cent, so that the rise in real expenditures was very large. Of the increase of nearly 13 billion rupees, less than 3 billion was for the defence budget, but provision for the refugees cost another Rs 3.25 billion (about Rs 1.25 billion was recouped however from earmarked aid). It was not long before the economic situation deteriorated. Agricultural production fell in 1971/2, but was still above trend. The 1972/3 harvest was very bad, with an 8 per cent fall in agricultural production (and a slight fall in GDP). The world price of wheat (and many other commodities) began to rise sensationally in the summer of 1972. Unfortunately India delayed purchases, finally buying less than the government had authorized, with the result that there was a fall in the availability of food grains in 1973.[14] Money supply was allowed to grow rapidly M_3 rising by 16 per cent in 1971/1 and 18 per cent in 1972/3. Food prices rose 25 per cent between July 1972 and July 1973. There was widespread rioting in Gujerat, and famine in Maharashtra. The government nationalized the wholesale trade in wheat in the spring of 1973: this probably made matters worse, and the trade was again 'privatized' in 1974. The spurt of inflation caused the authorities to initiate a policy of restraint in 1973, which became quite savage in 1974, when expenditure was cut and taxes and interest rates were raised.

With the new alignment of exchange rates between major currencies in 1971, India had to make a choice. Either luckily or cleverly (see section 4), a sterling peg was chosen: there was, however, very little movement in the real exchange rate from 1970 through 1974.[15]

3.3 From the First Oil Price Shock to 1979

Preceding paragraphs make it clear that the oil shock was superimposed on an economy already suffering the economic and political trauma resulting from the very bad harvest of 1972/3, combined with, it appears, some mismanagement.

Expressed as a proportion of GNP, the deterioration in India's terms of trade was small compared to most other oil-importing LDCs.[16] But India is a low-trading country and the balance of payments effects were large. The current account changed from a small surplus of Rs 280 million in 1972/3 to a deficit of Rs 9.6 billion in 1974/5, the latter representing only 1.4 per cent of GDP but 25 per cent of the value of exports – this change could be accounted for almost entirely by the rise in the price of oil.[17] There was no loss of reserves as a result of an increase in aid and drawings on the IMF low-conditionality tranches. After 1974/5 the current account turned round and was in surplus to the tune of over Rs 10 billion in 1976/7 and remained in surplus until 1980/1.

This remarkable turnaround from a deficit of almost Rs 10 billion to a surplus of Rs 10 billion in 2 years was mainly due to a change in the resource balance (Rs 15 billion), supported by an increase in transfers (remittances) of nearly Rs 5 billion. Exports rose by 60 per cent (39 per cent in volume), and imports by 18 per cent (nil in volume).[18] Some additional export incentives were given, but the large changes in the real effective exchange rate, a fall of 17 per cent,[19] was much more important.[20] While there may have been some favourable non-price factors, it is hard to believe that the real effective exchange rate did not play an important role.

In a study of macroeconomic management it is essential to ask to what extent the turnaround was due to policy decisions, or to natural equilibrating forces or to luck. And where policy was involved, we also have to ask whether the policy measures with favourable outcomes were actually intended to produce those outcomes.

We saw that in 1973 the government, alarmed by the price rises that were caused largely by the bad harvest but also by rising world prices, began to restrain the growth of the money supply. Prices continued to rise rapidly in 1974, and restrictive policies, both monetary and fiscal, were strengthened during the first half of the year. Public investment fell in real terms, and some non-fiscal restrictions on income growth were also introduced. These measures were supported by a good 1973/4 rabi (winter) harvest, and by increased imports of grain in 1974 (5 million tons). The inflation came to a halt, and prices actually fell in the autumn, and continued their fall into 1975 (despite rather poor harvests in calendar 1975). The disinflationary policies were not, apparently, very painful. Industrial production which had scarcely risen from 1972/3 to 1973/4 rose by 3.2 per cent, 7.2 per cent and 9.6 per cent in the following 3 years. The reasons why a 20 per cent inflation could be eliminated in so short a time, in contrast to the painful experience of many other countries, cries out for further analysis (in the future!).

The disinflationary policies had three obvious effects. First imports were restrained, and here the fall in public investment was probably of particular importance. Secondly the 'pull of the home market' was reduced, encouraging exports. Thirdly, and almost certainly most important, the real exchange rate was devalued as India became less inflationary than the world (the tying to sterling also helped, but was less important, see note 19). The disinflationary policies were set in motion to combat inflation, not to cure an unviable balance of payments. They began before the oil price shock, and when they were intensified in 1974, there was no very threatening payments problem. The current balance deficit of 1973/4 had been easily financed by an increase in aid, and low-tranche drawings on the IMF, with only a small use of reserves, and the same was true for the larger deficit of 1974/5. Other structural policies may have played some small role. The government did intensify the search for oil, but there was as yet little increase in output. There was also some increase in export subsidies, but the incentive effect was small compared to the real devaluation. Finally however, the luck of the monsoon did play a role. The 1975/6 harvest was exceptional and huge stocks of cereals were accumulated (reaching 17 million tons by the end of the year). In 1975 imports of cereals had been higher (at 7.5 million tons) than at any time since 1967, but in 1976/7 they were virtually eliminated.

The period of the turnaround coincides with Mrs Gandhi's Emergency (June 1975 to March 1977). But the Emergency was not caused by macroeconomic events. Nor does it appear to have had more than marginal macroeconomic effects. Tax collection was improved, and remittances may have been increased, but though useful this was small beer. It is also suggested that fear of disciplinary action led to a release of hoarded food stocks.

In March 1977 Mrs Gandhi lost the election she had proclaimed in January. The Janata government succeeded, with Morarji Desai as premier, and the Emergency was over. Nothing much of note occurs in the next 2 years (the Janata government fell in December 1979), except in the negative sense that India was very slow and half-hearted in making use of the large reserves of both foreign exchange and cereals that had accumulated, and continued to accumulate until the second oil price shock and the disastrous harvest of 1979/80. Imports were liberalized to some extent in 1976/7 and 1977/8, but the continued policy of almost total protection of Indian manufacturing prevented any upsurge. This may be a good example of how micro-policies can affect or inhibit macroeconomic flexibility. However, money supply grew rapidly, fuelled by the rise in reserves. M_3 rose at over 20 per cent p.a. between 1975/6 and 1978/9. It is a puzzle, needing further thought, that inflation remained low. India was criticized at the time for not using its large reserves, but it has to be noted that they came in very handy in the aftermath of 1979.

Imports did rise faster than exports, but the rising level of remittances kept the current account balance positive, albeit declining after 1976/7. It remained positive until 1980/1. Aid fell sharply after 1976/7;[21] it was, after all, only going to swell the reserves which reached a level equal to more than 9 months imports by the end of 1978/9. (IMF drawings were also 'repaid'.) The good harvest of 1977/8 resulted in some further accumulation of cereal stocks, which reached a level of 21 million tons in July 1979. Apart from liberalizing imports, an increase in public investment would have been the obvious way of stimulating the economy: but central government capital expenditure stayed level from 1975/6 to 1977/8, and there was a consolidated government surplus taken over these 3 years.

3.4 The Second Oil Price Shock, and Beyond

As in 1973/4 the oil price shock was a small proportion of GNP,[22] and India was among the least affected of the oil-importing LDCs. Between 1978/9 and 1980/1 the resource balance deteriorated by Rs 4.3 billion. The current account deteriorated by less (Rs 2.3 billion) to about the Rs 2 billion, mainly because of a further growth in remittances. The deficit was reduced only very slowly in the following 3 years, in sharp contrast to what happened after the first oil shock. As a proportion of exports these deficits were around 20 per cent, as compared with the 25 per cent of 1974/5. There was no such great turnaround as after the first oil price shock.

The second shock, like the first, was imposed upon perhaps the worst harvest since Independence, agricultural production falling by 15 per cent in 1979/80 and GDP by over 5 per cent. This caused food prices to rise by 8.4 per cent in 1979/80 and 11.3 per cent in 1980/1. These price rises were less than in 1973/4 and 1974/5, because some 14 million tons of cereals were released from stocks. There were no net imports, so the bad harvest did not significantly affect the current balance of payments. The wholesale price index, influenced also by world prices, rose by more than food prices, by 17 per cent and 18 per cent in the same 2 years. The government's reaction to this inflation was much less fierce than to the earlier inflation. Only in 1981/2 did the growth of the money supply become less than accommodating, and inflation of the wholesale price index fell to an average of about 7 per cent in the following 3 years – as against 2 per cent in the 3 years after 1974. The overall public sector deficit which reached 3.0 per cent of GDP in 1980/1 was reduced to 1.9 per cent in 1981/2 and 1.6 per cent in 1982/3. Further to this, public sector investment rose by 4 per cent in real terms in 1980/1 contrasting with a fall of 14.5 per cent in 1974/5; moreover it rose by about 10 per cent p.a. in each of the following 3 years.

Thus on this occasion the (incomplete) adjustment of the balance of payments deficit was not primarily due to deflationary measures. Exports were relatively sluggish, rising by only 3.6 per cent p.a. in real terms from 1978/9 to 1983/4. Though in large part due to a slowdown of world trade, it should also be noticed that exports received no boost from a depreciating real exchange rate, since on this occasion India's inflation exceeded that of its main trading counterparts and rivals. The real exchange rate appreciated by 14 per cent between 1979 and 1981.[23] This appreciation was slightly offset by various export incentives, but the contrast with the second half of the 1970s remains.

The behaviour of imports was also different. After the first oil shock the volume of imports fell to a lower real level for 3 years, much the largest proportional fall being in capital good imports. In contrast there was a large rise in the volume of imports, especially capital goods, after the second shock. Comparing the 3 years before and after 31 March 1980, the volume of imports rose by 50 per cent and capital good imports by 100 per cent. The overall total was held down (relatively) by the successful import substituting 'adjustment' programme in oil. The volume of petroleum imports peaked in 1980/1. Between then and 1983/4, there was a 40 per cent fall. India now imports about one-third of its oil, against two-thirds in the 1970s.[24] The large rise in imports can be attributed to liberalization, to the overall rise in investment and to a greater public share of investment associated with very import- and capital-intensive 'adjustment' programmes of import substitution in energy (oil and coal) and fertilizers.[25].

It would be nice to be able to record that the more expansionary policies of the 1980s, including the large rise in public import-substituting investment, had resulted in some acceleration of industrial output. The reverse has been the case. Industrial output rose at only 3.4 per cent p.a. from 1980/1 to 1983/4. As a result, incremental capital–output ratios (ICORs) which fell after 1974 with expanding manufactured exports and production, have risen again to their highest levels.

How was the deficit financed? In 1980/1 India drew Rs 8.15 billion from the IMF Trust Fund and the Compensating Financial Facility, and in November 1981, it agreed a very large Extended Fund Facility arrangement for SDR 5 billion over 3 years (about Rs 50 billion), only 3.9 billion of which had been used when India terminated the arrangement in May 1984.[26] Apart from the IMF finance, concessional flows rose above the level of the 1970s, and IBRD loans increased. Reserves were run down from their very high level, equal to 9 months imports in 1978/9, to a 'normal' level of 3 months imports in 1981/2. Thereafter India resorted to commercial borrowing for the first time in any significant amounts and new commitments have recently risen to more than $1 billion a year.[27] As of the end of 1984/5, the debt to GDP ratio was 17 per cent, still a low figure compared to most developing countries. The terms of borrowing have hardened as the proportion of non-concessionary loans has risen, but the debt service ratio was still at the modest level of 15.5 per cent.[28]

4. Fiscal, Monetary and Exchange Rate Policy

It is clear from the previous section that there has been a creeping evolution in the past 20 years towards increasing public sector deficits, and inflation. India in recent years is also relying more on foreign borrowing. The inflation has come in fits and starts, associated both with bad harvests and import price rises. Monetary and fiscal policies have been successful in reducing inflation, but the reaction appears to come when inflation is already well underway, and after a period when the money supply was allowed to increase rapidly. Public investment has been rather erratic. Export growth has also been erratic, and is closely associated with the real exchange rate, which in turn is closely associated with the rate of inflation (given India's reluctance to use the nominal exchange rate very actively). The dynamics of all this awaits further analysis. Meanwhile in the rest of this section we discuss some of the problems connected with the conduct of fiscal, monetary and exchange rate policies, and the medium- to long-term issues that arise.

In an economy in which borrowing from the central bank is a major source of government receipts, the distinction between fiscal and monetary policy gets rather blurred. Some overlap is therefore unavoidable in the discussion under these two headings though it should be noted that since the Reserve Bank does have some instruments to offset the impact of its lending to the government on high-powered money (or 'reserve money' in Indian usage) the distinction does not vanish entirely.

Some traditional questions about fiscal and monetary stabilization policies cannot be answered without further study. For example, has fiscal policy exacerbated the real cycle? Fiscal contraction has generally been undertaken in response to inflationary pressures arising from weather-induced reductions in food output. An important instrument of fiscal contraction has been reductions in public investment which have intensified the deflationary effects of agricultural decline on industrial output. Would it have been feasible, by following alternative policies (more vigorous food imports and distribution; external borrowing) to have maintained a more even path of public investment? Would a more stable path of public investment have reduced industrial fluctuations and perhaps have even improved the trend rate of industrial growth?

Some obvious questions about monetary policy also suggest themselves. Would the acceleration of inflation in the 1970s have been prevented by monetary targeting, and at what cost if any in terms of the growth of output? Of course, monetary targeting requires controlability of reserve money, an issue which we comment on below. But it also requires a stable demand for money function and a stable money multiplier. The evidence in favour of such stability is mixed and needs further investigation. On exchange rate policy, the evidence is clearer; we argue below that there is a strong presumption that more active use of the exchange rate after the second oil price shock would have increased industrial output, and reduced the need for commercial borrowing.

In discussing fiscal and monetary policy in this section, we largely ignore the above traditional questions regarding stabilization and concentrate on 'the micro–macro link'. A fashionable view about Indian economic policy is that it was unsound microeconomically but sound macroeconomically and further that these phenomena were positively linked; in other words, that the controls which led to microeconomic inefficiency actually made macroeconomic balance easier to attain. There is indeed something to be said for this view. There is an obvious sense in which India's insulation from world trade and capital markets and her financial controls, both reduced the direct impact of the external shocks of the 1970s and facilitated swift adjustment to the shocks that did penetrate the economy.

Nevertheless there is much to be said on the other side. The following subsections show that in a subtle, creeping way, the microeconomic inefficiencies, acting in combination with political changes, have reduced macroeconomic flexibility over time.

This is to be seen in fiscal policy (the rise in tax evasion, the inflation inelasticity of tax revenues and public enterprise profits, the growth of subsidies), in monetary policy (the lack of a bond market, the very limited ability to use interest rates as a macroeconomic instrument) and in exchange rate policy (the creation of industrial interests vested in the control system, a reduction in the elasticity of supply).

4.1 Fiscal Policy

A noteworthy feature of recent Indian economic performance is the deterioration in public finances after the second oil price shock, a deterioration serious enough to make the financing of public sector outlay in the Seventh Five Year Plan (1985/6 to 1990/1) look highly uncertain. The budgetary deficit, the consolidated government and public sector borrowing requirements and net Reserve Bank of India (RBI) credit to the government have all increased in recent years as a proportion of GNP.[29]

The consolidated government's tax take as a proportion of GNP rose substantially during the 1970s but has stagnated in recent years. One important reason is that agriculture (which contributes more than a third of national income) is free from direct taxation. Agriculture is a state subject under India's federal constitution and politics at the state level are dominated by rural interests. The central government has not made any serious attempt to persuade the state governments to grasp this particular nettle.

Tax evasion has become an important problem. This is one reason for the falling share of direct taxes in national income . But there is also evasion of indirect taxes. It is well-known that the unorganized and small-scale sectors are 'tax havens'. Presumably the growth of evasion is partly the result of the system of controls. Changing public morality and the dilution over time of the austere ethos of the Indian national movement have also contributed.

Indirect tax revenue is inelastic with respect to inflation not merely because of the large number of specific taxes but also because many taxed products have administered prices that are adjusted discontinuously. Finance ministers faced with the need for increasing revenues have for the most part obtained them by increasing indirect tax rates and tariffs. The indirect tax structure has become exceedingly complicated with much cascading of taxes on intermediate goods. The recognized inefficiency of this structure has increased the pressure for tax reduction.

Conflict between the centre and the states has sharpened in the past decade, and this has had a bad effect. The Finance Commissions that govern the division of revenues have had a 'gap-filling approach', so the states have been able to secure larger shares of taxes collected by the centre by showing bigger deficits. This has reduced the tax effort of the states and is one reason for the worsening financial position of the centre which now regularly has a deficit balance on current revenues and expenditures.

Though non-tax revenues have risen, they are making an inadequate contribution. The outstanding problem here is the low profitability of public sector enterprises. The overall gross rate of return on capital employed in public sector enterprises is around 12 per cent. Excluding the highly profitable oil sector, however, the return is only 5 per cent (and would be considerably lower on an inflation-accounting basis). There are many prominent loss-makers in mining, heavy engineering, metals, chemicals and pharmaceuticals, indeed in the entire range of manufacturing industry. State electricity boards are notorious for their inefficiency. In addition the government has, for employment-protection reasons, taken over many 'sick' units, particularly in the textile industry, which survive only with subsidies from the budget.

There are many reasons for the low profitability of public sector units. One reason is their inappropriate pricing policies. There is a tendency to keep down administered prices of key producer goods. But the problem is recognized to be deeper than that. It relates to the lack of penalties for inefficiency in an economy in which there is very little external competition, and not much internal competition either. No substitute for competition has been devised to enforce efficiency. Public sector managers are not accountable for financial performance. There is known to be a great deal of political interference in the running of public sector enterprises. An important assumption in the financing projections for the Seventh Five Year Plan is the doubling of the contribution of public sector enterprises as a proportion of GNP. It is not at all clear how this is going to be achieved.

Subsidies (of which 70 per cent relate to food, fertilizers and exports) have grown rapidly. Central government subsidies have grown from 0.7 per cent of GDP in 1973/4 to around 2 per cent of GDP in 1984/5. Growing export subsidies represent an attempt at partial redressal of export profitability given the reluctance to devalue the nominal exchange rate. In the case of food, it seems to be a political constraint that procurement prices cannot be reduced even if there is a bumper crop. There are similar political difficulties in raising the issue prices of fertilizers (which particularly benefit the larger, richer farmers) to keep up with the rising cost of inputs. There are many other subsidies representing, in the opinion of some observers, an attempt to buy off various pressure groups (see the reference to P. Bardhan in section 2).

Government interest payments, which can be both cause and effect of the deterioration in public finances, have grown rapidly as a proportion of GDP from about 1.7 per cent in 1975/6 to about 3 per cent at present and are expected to rise further in the Seventh Plan. Public debt ratios have shown a deteriorating trend in the last 10 years. Internal public debt (net of borrowing from the Reserve Bank) was 32 per cent of GNP in 1972/3; it fell to 19 per cent in 1974/5 largely because it was eroded by inflation; since then it has doubled to 40 per cent in 1984/5. (If borrowing from the Reserve Bank is not excluded, the corresponding figures are 45 per cent in 1972/3, 38 per cent in 1974/5 and 57 per cent in 1984/5.) It is worth noting that internal public debt ratios did not fall during the inflation of 1979/80–1980/1 unlike during that of 1973/4–1974/5. This reflects the larger government borrowing in the later period. In the 1980s there has been some upward adjustment in government borrowing rates which has contributed to the rise in public debt ratios but that is not the only or the main reason.

The rise in the internal public debt ratio might be regarded as the inevitable by-product of a rising public investment ratio, and not per se alarming. It is alarming only if it shows an explosive tendency. There are some disturbing trends in this respect. On the one hand, the real rate of return on public sector investment is very low. In the past this has been offset by the low (and often negative) real rate of interest on government borrowing. However there is pressure for the latter to rise for various good reasons (discussed further in the section on monetary policy). Controlled interest rates on lending to the government and to various priority sectors have sharply reduced bank profitability. For this and various other reasons connected with reaping some of the benefits of financial liberalization, there is a move to require the government to pay market-related positive real rates of interest on its borrowing. The short-term effect of this would be to raise government interest payment further; and the move may not work unless higher interest rates induce greater efficiency and profitability in public sector enterprises. (It is doubtful if this could be achieved without other measures to increase efficiency).

India's external borrowing was cautious during the 1970s and that seems sensible given the fact that foreign exchange reserves were comfortably high. In the more aggressive strategy adopted in response to the second oil price shock, commercial borrowing has increased sharply and, as already noted in section 1, was running at more than $1 billion for each of the last 3 years. There is nothing wrong with such borrowing if it finances investments with a high return, and if export growth can be kept up. The latter proviso has not, unfortunately, been realized; as discussed below, exchange rate management is partly to blame.

4.2 Monetary Policy

By law, and in practice, the Reserve Bank is subservient to the Finance Ministry, and monetary arrangements in India severely constrain the scope for a monetary policy that is independent of the government budget.[30] The government's borrowing requirement is met in substantial measure by the banking system in general and by the Reserve Bank in particular. The Reserve Bank holds 90 per cent of outstanding treasury bills and 30 per cent of outstanding government securities. Borrowing from the Reserve Bank adds directly to reserve money; from 1970 to 1985, net Reserve Bank credit to government constituted a staggering 97 per cent of additions to reserve money. (This figure does, however, mask some changes; for example, from 1975 to 1977, rising foreign exchange reserves were the dominant influence on reserve money and the Reserve Bank was not entirely successful in sterilizing this inflow.)

Since the Reserve Bank cannot control government deficits and has to lend to cover them, monetary policy is in effect largely concerned with making room for the government in reserve money expansion. The cash reserve ratio (CRR) which regulates the cash reserves of commercial banks has been used frequently. By law, the CRR has an upper limit of 15 per cent (though of course Parliament could change the law). Starting from 5 per cent in 1973, the trend has been firmly upward. Currently the CRR stands at 12 per cent. The banks must also obey the statutory liquidity ratio (SLR) which specifies the proportion of their deposit liabilities they must invest in government securities. By law, the upper limit on the SLR is 40 per cent; starting from 25 per cent in 1970 it has been increased in steps to its current level of 37 per cent. Raising the SLR does not directly reduce reserve money but captures bank credit for government use; however, for any given level of government expenditure, it indirectly reduces the government's need to borrow from the Reserve Bank and therefore reduces reserve money expansion. Other financial institutions such as the nationalized life insurance companies are also required to hold a substantial proportion of their assets in government securities. Interest rates are administered; the whole rate structure is constrained by government borrowing rates. Government borrows cheaply and also stipulates that banks lend cheaply to various 'priority' sectors such as small-scale industry and agriculture. Banks have to direct 40 per cent of their credit to these sectors in addition to obeying SLR requirements. As a result, deposit rates are kept low and lending rates to organized private manufacturing industry are kept high. Even so, bank profitability is very low.

In the above structure, there is no scope for open market operations (the captive government bond market is not going to absorb more low-yielding securities than it has to) and little scope for interest rate policy. Another instrument of monetary policy is discretionary lending (or 'refinance' in Indian usage) to commercial banks by the Reserve Bank. The Reserve Bank can vary reserve money by changing the credit thresholds that qualify banks for refinance. This potentially could be important but is not so in practice. Reserve Bank refinance is primarily aimed at 'priority' activities such as food procurement and export credit, and therefore can be varied only within narrow limits.

The above account implies that the CRR is effectively the only instrument of monetary control. But the CRR is a blunt instrument which cannot discriminate between banks. In using it, the Reserve Bank runs the risk of disclocating financial markets (as indeed happened in the last quarter of 1981/2). This may partly account for its reluctance to use the CRR more savagely after 1975 to sterilize balance of payments surpluses.

There is one other instrument which deserves some comment, namely quantitative credit controls. The official line of the Reserve Bank used to be (and to some extent still is) that it exercises direct control not merely over the allocation of bank credit but also over its total volume. In earlier years, there seems to have been some confusion within the Reserve Bank on this subject. The links between reserve money and total money supply were imperfectly understood and it would appear that the Reserve Bank fell prey to the rhetoric of planning and believed that the volume of bank credit could be controlled directly and independently of reserve money creation. This belief weakened monetary control for it had the result that the growth of reserve money (through government borrowing and external influences) was not regularly monitored. The Reserve Bank consequently tended to react rather late to pressures increasing the money supply. However, many years of overshooting of credit targets (banks finding ways round reserve ratios and defaulting on them, as one would expect if reserve money growth and demand for credit are strong) has dispelled much of the confusion; continuous monitoring of monetary and credit aggregates during the Extended Fund Facility programme also helped in this process.

The above monetary framework has led to two effects: (a) there has been upward pressure on the growth of money supply; government borrowing from the Reserve Bank has increased reserve money, and the Reserve Bank has been understandably reluctant to squeeze private sector liquidity beyond a point for fear of hurting production, and (b) monetary management has been inflexible and jerky because of the lack of sensitive policy instruments.

There are currently suggestions in India that the above complex of problems should be attacked by breaking the link between government deficits and the money supply.[31] Under this scheme, the government would meet all its requirements by borrowing from the market. Since the SLR cannot be raised indefinitely (without disastrous effects on bank profitability), this would require raising treasury bill and government bond coupon rates substantially. If successful, such a change would make open market operations and interest rate variations genuine instruments of policy. However, there are two serious transitional difficulties in the scheme (which the government has not yet agreed to). First, as already mentioned, the increasing share of government has not destabilized public finances despite the low real rate of return on public investment because the government has borrowed at negative real rates. If interest rates on government borrowing rise without an increase in the efficiency of public investment, the public finance problem will get worse. Secondly, during the transition, the private sector would suffer a powerful 'crowding out' in the credit market with consequent effects on output. Thus, it is not easy to get out of the box of government financial controls.[32] The Chakravarty Committee (see note 30) has also come out in favour of monetary targeting (the target taking the form of a *range*) in order to control inflation. Though the Committee did not emphasize this, controlling money growth is an especially important issue given India's great reluctance to alter the nominal exchange rate. Any such suggestion of course requires that reserve money should be controllable which raises the problems discussed above.

4.3 Exchange Rate Policy

One may distinguish between (a) the designation currency, i.e. that in terms of which the rupee's exchange rate is announced, (b) the intervention currency, i.e. that which the Reserve Bank normally buys and sells and (c) the peg currency, or basket of currencies, i.e. that in terms of which the value of the rupee is kept fixed or within a certain range.

It was said in section 3 that after the experience of the 1966 devaluation Mrs Gandhi would never have permitted another *overt* devaluation. After the dollar cut loose from gold in August 1971, the dollar briefly became the designation and the peg currency. But in December 1971 after the Smithsonian realignment of major currency rates, sterling was chosen as the designation, intervention and peg currency, and remained so until September 1975. The effect of this was that the *effective* nominal exchange rate (against a trade-weighted basket of ten currencies) was devalued by 20 per cent over the same period: but the rupee was not overtly devalued.

It should be possible to ascertain, and certainly interesting to know, the exact reasons for the choice of sterling. It could have been a clever anticipation of the weakness of sterling on the part of those (or someone) who believed that the rupee should be effectively devalued. Or it may have been a political reaction against the dollar peg resulting from the very bad US/Indian relations due to the war in Bangladesh. After 1975 the peg was

Table 13.1 Changes in exchange rates and exports

	Real exchange rate, RER (percentage change)	*Nominal exchange rate, NER (percentage change)*	*Share of world exports (vol) (percentage change)*	*Export volume (percentage per annum)*
1974–9	−23	−12	+26	+11[a]
1979–83	+15	+1	+2	+0.6
1983–5	−3[b]	−11[b]	probably negative	probably negative

[a] Economic Survey 1985/6, table 6.5 implies +8.4% p.a.
[b] Author's estimate.

Sources: Joshi (1984, table 2), for exchange rates; Ahluwalia (1985, table 5), for export volumes.

altered to a basket of currencies with undisclosed weights, though sterling remained the designation and intervention currency (for old times sake?). The perfectly sensible reason given was that this would reduce undesirable variations in the nominal effective rate (though it seems possible that a further effective devaluation was feared and thought undesirable, if sterling remained the peg). The margin permitted around the peg was 2.5 per cent, raised to 5 per cent in January 1979. Officially, the peg has not been changed since 1975, but this did not prevent a fall in the nominal effective rate of 7 per cent by 1983, and about 17 per cent by 1985.

But it is necessary to concentrate on the behaviour of the real effective exchange rate as a measure of competitiveness (we use the same broad ten-country measure as for the nominal effective rate). We saw in section 3 that there was a large fall (devaluation) in the rate after 1974, mainly as a result of the fact that India's prices were rising more slowly than those of its competitors, but partly because the rupee was pegged to sterling until September 1975 (this was responsible for most of the fall in the nominal exchange rate, NER). India's exports rose as never before or since. From 1979 to 1983 the reverse happened. Exports stagnated. Table 13.1 speaks for itself.

The authorities seem to have been able to engineer a fall in the NER in the most recent period (probably because of the fall in the dollar), but nowhere near enough to wipe out the large appreciation of the rupee between 1979 and 1983.

Some of the reasons why India has not adopted a more active exchange rate policy were discussed in section 3 – the hangover from the 1966 devaluation and a general inherited distrust of the price mechanism. But there are other more rational, though in our opinion misguided, reasons. India is still the intellectual home of elasticity pessimism, despite a mass of contrary evidence both from India and from all over the world. This is not the place for an elaborate refutation. A relatively sophisticated version of the argument is that the supply response would be weak unless many other reforms were made, and these are politically impossible. No doubt there is something in this argument. But the rapid growth of exports in the second half of the 1970s suggests that exports can respond well even when little is done to increase the elasticity of supply. Other common arguments are deployed, that it would be bad for public finance and bad for income distribution. We have not examined the validity of these arguments, but doubt their significance. Almost certainly it is more important that the export lobby is weak, and that the import-substitution lobby appears to believe that a devaluation (associated with liberalization) would not improve their profits and might even reduce them.

4.4 Concluding Observations and Questions

1 Indian macroeconomic management has been cautious and conservative. But is this changing? More inflation seems to be tolerated, and though it arises in fits and starts, with the monsoon, there is undoubtedly a rising trend. Budget deficits seem to be becoming more of a habit. Commercial borrowing at quite high real interest rates is now resorted to, although this was not the case in the 1970s when real interest rates were often negative.

Is it possible that a decline in personal morality is related to an increase in public irresponsibility?[33] If so, this would make it hard to continue to entertain the image of the civil service as a band of dedicated guardians, which was our explanation of the conservatism of the policies they used to uphold.

2 A pattern in economic management was descernible in the 1960s and 1970s. A bad monsoon caused inflation, which scared the raj. There was some procrastination in the hope of a quick natural reversal. If it did not come, and inflation rose further to around 15 per cent or more, there was a monetary and fiscal crackdown that was successful. So far as industry is concerned, this was procyclical. The correct response would have been rather to increase supply, by running down stocks of cereals, and using reserves or borrowing to increase imports. Nevertheless the control of inflation in an inflationary world paid handsome dividends.

3 A more expansionary policy on the above lines has been attempted in the 1980s. But the reduction in world inflation and a rise in Indian inflation has resulted in sluggish export growth. As a result, the performance of the economy has been worse than in the second half of the 1970s. The key role of the real effective exchange rate seems to be inescapable.

4 We have suggested various ways in which the micro-control system reduces the flexibility of macroeconomic policy. The manner in which the economy reacts to macroeconomic policy also requires much further investigation.

5 Many of our observations need further substantiation, and many loose ends have been left. More research should be rewarding.

NOTES

1 Industrial licensing is another very important control, but it is peripheral to our present range of interest.

2 The composition is not officially disclosed.

3 So dubbed by Raj Krishna (3.6 per cent p.a., or about 1.5 per cent per capita p.a.). Our repeated assertions of unchanging trends are substantiated as follows. Tests for changes in the trend rate of growth were made for GNP, agricultural production and cereal production for the period 1950 to 1984. The trends were 3.60 per cent p.a., 2.60 per cent p.a., and 2.57 per cent p.a. respectively. The samples were then split at 1968 and 1979. In no case did the Chow test for parameter stability reveal any evidence whatever of a change in trend. For instance, when the sample was split at 1968 the Chow test figures were 1.24 for GNP, 0.60 for agricultural production and 0.59 for cereal production. The figure of 1.24 shows that the hypothesis that the better fit is obtainable by splitting the example, and *not* due to chance, can be easily rejected at the 10 per cent likelihood level. Figures below 1 imply that the trend of the first period fits the second period better than it did the first! When the sample was split at 1979, the test figures were 1.15 for GDP, 0.93 for agricultural production and 0.76 for cereal production. Our thanks are due to Dr T. Jenkinson, Merton College, Oxford for making these tests.

4 India, however, is not unique in this respect. Taiwan in 1974 brought an inflation of around 40 per cent (over the previous 12 months) down to near zero in a few weeks. Indonesia may be another example.

5 Ahluwalia (1985, p. 10).

6 It has been argued that a large increase in subsidies and other current expenditure since the mid-1960s results from conflict between three dominant classes, the rich farmers, the industrial bourgeoisie and the professionals. See Bardhan (1984), chs. 6, 7, and 8).

7 The second volume of Philip Woodruff's account (1953) of the men who ruled India is appropriately subtitled *The Guardians*. Of course, Britain ruled elsewhere, and ex-British colonies have not always been financially conservative. But nowhere else was there such a longstanding hierarchical bureaucracy created with the traditions of the ICS. In Africa, indirect rule was more the theory and practice of government.

8 The size of the Third Plan became an important political issue in 1959. Nehru strongly supported a large plan. But neither he nor anyone else argued that it should be supported by inflationary financing.

9 '. . . the Congress inherited an administrative structure, which it had to use for a new purpose. Its ideas became, not to disrupt the status quo, but to build up its "socialistic pattern" of economy on the foundation of the existing order without any violent disturbance. In the prosaic task of reformation, the Congress Party, in the opinion of its critics, has tried to convert every problem of rational reconstruction into an administrative problem. . . . There is an effort to continually add to new responsibilities, instead of a desire to stimulate the growth of non-official endeavours to any appreciable extent.' N.K. Bose, 'Social and cultural life of Calcutta, pp. 27–8, quoted by George Rosen (1966, p. 71).

10 Findlay (1986).
11 Thingalaya (1969).
12 The devaluation and its economic and political consequences have been fully analysed in Bhagwati and Srinivasan (1975).
13 Srinivasan and Satyanarayana (1977).
14 Veit (1976, p. 236).
15 Relative to an export weighted basked of ten currencies.
16 The effects of both the terms of trade and a slow down in exports resulting from a reduced rate of growth of world trade for the period of 1974–6 have been calculated by Balassa (1984). The average effect on India was 2.1 per cent of GNP. Of twenty-five countries with unfavourable shocks, only Argentina and Mexico suffered less than India.
17 See Ahluwalia (1985, table 2).
18 Figures from Ahluwalia (1985): the Economic Survey 1985/6 gives a somewhat lower figure of 31 per cent for the increase in export volume.
19 Joshi (1984, table 2). The *nominal* effective exchange rate also fell by 5 per cent: thus the chosen peg (sterling) helped, but changes in relative prices were more than twice as important.
20 It has been estimated that the net incentive rate rose from 2.6 per cent in 1974/5 to 5.9 per cent in 1976/7. See Martin Wolf (1982, table 4.7).
21 In a sense, the rise in remittances was an endogenous result of the rise in oil prices. But it was not, and could hardly have been, anticipated.
22 Balassa and McCarthy (1984) estimate 3.0 per cent average over the period of 1978–9. This figure includes the estimated effects on exports.
23 Joshi (1984, table 2).
24 However, production is thought to have reached a plateau, so that India's energy dependence will again increase.
25 Ahluwalia (1985, p. 19).
26 The conditions of this IMF loan, and the inevitable criticism that was aroused in India, are extensively discussed by Catherin Gwin, 'Financing India's structural adjustment: the role of the Fund', in John Williamson (1983). The IMF demanded little if anything that was not in line with the government's own intentions: The critics on the left were opposed to the increases in administered prices and indirect taxes that were designed to keep the public sector deficit within bounds. They blamed the external deficit on the liberalization of imports, and demanded a return to yet more inward-looking policies.
27 Ahluwalia (1985, p. 10).
28 IBRD 1985 Report p. 144.
29 In Indian budgets, the 'budgetary deficit' is defined narrowly: it includes treasury bills issued but excludes RBIs purchases of long-dated government securities (which are actually treated as 'market borrowing'!). As a result, the budgetary deficit understates the increase in net Reserve Bank credit to the government.
30 For an authoritative discussion of monetary policy in India, see *Report of the Committee to Review the Working of the Monetary System*, Reserve Bank of India, 1985. The Committee was chaired by Professor Sukhamoy Chakravarty.
31 This suggestion has been made by the Chakravarty Committee.
32 Carlos Díaz-Alejandro would have liked these points; he was impressed by the difficulties of financial liberalization in other contexts.
33 See, e.g. Acharya (1985) for a discussion of both public and private corruption.

REFERENCES

Acharya, S. 1985: *Aspects of the Black Economy in India*. GOI, Ministry of Finance.

Ahluwalia, M.S. 1985: Balance of Payments Adjustment in India. 1970–1 Report to the Group of Twenty-Four, UNDP/UNCTAD.

Balassa, B. 1984: Adjustment policies in developing countries, a reassessment. *World Development*, 12(9).

Balassa, Bela and Desmond McCarthy, F. 1984: Adjustment Policies in Developing Countries, 1979–83, An Update, World Bank Staff Working Papers, no. 675.

Bardhan, Pranab 1984: *The Political Economy of Development in India*. Oxford: Blackwell.

Bhagwati, Jagdish N. and Srinivasan, T.N. 1975: *Foreign Trade Regimes and Economic Development: India*. National Bureau of Economic Research.

Bose, N.K. 1958: Social and cultural life of Calcutta. *Geographical Review of India*, December.

Economic Survey 1985/6, GOI, Ministry of Finance.

Findlay R. 1986: Trade Development and the State. Mimeo.

Joshi, Vijay 1984: The nominal and real effective exchange rate of the Indian rupee 1977–83. *Reserve Bank of India Occasional Papers*, 5 (1).

Report of the Committee to Review the Working of :he Monetary System. Reserve Bank of India, 1985.

Rosen, George 1966: *Democracy and Economic Change in India*. California: University of California Press.

Srinivasan, T.N. and Satyanarayana, N.S. 1977: Economic performance for the third plan and its implications for policy. *Economic and Political Weekly*.

Thingalaya 1969: A century of prices in India. *Economic and Political Weekly*, 25 January.

Veit, Lawrence, A. 1976: *India's Second Revolution*. New York: McGraw-Hill.

Williamson, John 1983: *IMF Conditionality*. Washington DC: Institute for International Economics.

Wolf, Martin 1982: *India's Exports*. Oxford: Oxford University Press.

Woodruff, Philip 1953: *The Men Who Ruled India*, vol II: *The Guardians*. London: J. Cape.

COMMENT

John Williamson

Max Corden's paper represents an attempt to give effect to an idea of Carlos Díaz-Alejandro, to survey the intellectual capital accumulated in recent years by Northern macroeconomists with a view to transferring it to the South. Judging by the rather meagre haul presented in Corden's paper, I think one has to say that this was not one of Carlos's more inspired suggestions.

Given the focus of Northern macroeconomics over the past decade, it was presumably inevitable that a large part of Max's paper would be devoted to the two principal theorems of the new classical macroeconomics, the policy ineffectiveness theorem and the neo-Ricardian theorem. At the end of the day Max concurs with my own judgement, which is that an awful lot of intellectual energy has been wasted chasing these hares in the North. I would, however, have liked to see him warn the South against a similar dissipation of intellectual resources in distinctly more emphatic terms, and avoid giving comfort to the neoclassical school by endorsing the view that policy needs to be able to 'trick' the public if it is to be effective. On any broader view, policy may be effective *inter alia* by improving the public's information base.

The reasons for believing that we can with a clear conscience apply the standard body of theory and brush aside the new classical assault include the following:

1 the dependence of the policy ineffectiveness theorem on the counterfactual assumption of ubiquitous market clearing;
2 the dependence of the theorem on everyone having the same model of the world;
3 the empirical evidence, of which the most decisive yet is in my judgement John Helliwell's (1986) recent presidential address to the Canadian Economic Association, in which he explains short-run output variations by a supply-side factor utilization model that gets some limited additional explanatory power from Keynesian variables but none from distinctively new classical ones;
4 Blanchard's (1985) insight that lives are finite, which – like liquidity

constraints – results in aggregate demand being influenced by the size of the budget deficit;

5 the empirical estimate of Masson and Knight (1986) that an increased budget deficit is about 57 per cent offset by increased private saving, rather than 100 per cent offset as claimed by the neo-Ricardian theorem;

6 the Brazilian empirical literature of the 1970s, which found that money was non-neutral in the short run in an economy where money illusion was surely long dead but which still had a contract structure that gives strong inertia to the inflationary process.

On the other hand, there are a couple of points that have emerged in this brand of the Northern literature that are not mentioned by Max but seem to me to deserve recognition. I think in particular of the Lucas Critique and time inconsistency. One should also recognize that rational expectations form a key ingredient in much macromodelling. (It is only when one links rational expectations with their illegitimate twin, ubiquitous market clearing, that one generates the theorem about policy ineffectiveness.) For example, if one thinks of the problem of credibility, a policy cannot be expected to command credibility unless it is consistent with rational expectations. On the other hand it is a mistake to *rely* on expectations always being rational, as the recent history of the overvalued dollar has shown.

Towards the end of his paper Max comes to areas where recent Northern macroeconomics has more to offer: non-market-clearing models, real wage rigidity, supply-side shocks, etc. But, with due respect to Bruno and Sachs (1985), my own judgement is that in this field the work in the South has got further than that in the North. I think in particular of that staple of the Brazilian macroeconomic literature, the two-sector (fixprice/flexprice) model. One might instance also the rich literature on the experience of the Southern Cone, largely inspired by Carlos Díaz-Alejandro, and represented at this conference by Vittorio Corbo, Sebastian Edwards, Ricardo Ffrench-Davis and credibility Calvo. If one is going to look for a transfer of macroeconomic technology between North and South, maybe one ought to be looking for a reverse transfer. Perhaps that would have made a more interesting and substantive paper than Max managed to get out of his subject.

Let me now say a few words about the Joshi/Little paper on India. Unfortunately I am not an expert on India, and I am therefore in no position to tie up the loose ends, of which there are a lot, as the authors recognize with admirable honesty.

The stylized facts of the Indian case are, first, that growth of almost everything has been amazingly constant. When I protested to Ian that surely constant output growth meant that at least there was an acceleration in per capita growth, because population growth had fallen, he told me that I was mistaken. Second, financial policies have been distinctly conservative as compared with Latin America and, in recent years, with Africa. The third major fact is that the exchange rate has been kept at an overvalued level, at least tolerated and perhaps welcomed as a support for a rather dirigiste system of trade controls.

The main question that the paper asks is 'Why did India pursue that set of policies?' I suppose I am one of those people whom Charlie Kindleberger would never have admitted to MIT, since I think that a more interesting question is: 'Was it a good thing that policies were what they were?' There are hints in the paper that in the authors' view a better strategy was available. This would have involved a more competitive exchange rate, with the resulting trade balance improvement used partly to permit a more liberal import regime. But should the benefit not also have been taken partly in higher reserve accumulation in good years, which would then have permitted less need for deflation in bad years? From the way Ian talked at the conference one might get the impression there would have been no payoff from that, because he described how the economy bounced back to its trend growth path as soon as the deflation was over. But the paper asserts that the forced economies in public investment in the early 1970s gave rise to shortages in key non-traded sectors which have persisted ever since, and claims that it would have been better, had it been feasible, to maintain investment by augmenting public revenue. My intuition says that the judgement in the paper is more plausible than the judgement offered verbally at the conference. Hence I think the presumption is that there would have been advantages in a more active policy of attempting to even out shocks. (Actually a 'more active' policy might have meant less activism in the sense of pushing taxes up and down, had one had those extra reserves with which to maintain demand in bad years.) Indian policy does not, however, seem to be moving in that direction: from what one reads in the paper, the main recent change is a downgrading of the objective of price stability.

Doubtless this shift away from financial conservatism will be construed as a move towards 'Keynesianism'. To those of us with the quaint view that 'Keynesian' ought to be used to describe policies of which Keynes would have approved, and who recall his aversion to inflation and his caution in endorsing increased deficit financing in Britain in 1937 (Moggridge, vol. XXI, pp. 404–9), this will seem quite anomalous. In this view a more Keynesian policy would be that of which Joshi and Little seem to approve, involving a more competitive exchange rate with a part of the trade balance benefits being hoarded in good years to permit less deflation in years when the monsoon fails. Whatever the label to be applied to such a policy shift, I hope that in their future work Joshi and Little will question the notion that more inflation is a promising way of raising the 'Hindu rate of growth' and confront squarely the normative question regarding an appropriate macroeconomic strategy for India.

REFERENCES

Blanchard, Olivier 1985: 'Debt, deficits, and finite horizons'. *Journal of Political Economy*, April.

Bruno, Michael and Sachs, Jeffrey 1985: *Economics of Worldwide Stagflation*. Cambridge, MA: Harvard University Press.

Helliwell, John F. 1986: 'Supply-Side Macroeconomics'. Presidential Address to the annual meeting of the Canadian Economic Association, Winnipeg, May.

Masson, Paul R. and Knight, Malcolm 1986: 'The International Transmission of Fiscal Policies in Major Industrial Countries'. IMF Staff Papers, vol. 33, no. 3, September.

Moggridge, D. (ed.), 1982: *The Collected Writings of John Maynard Keynes*, vol. XXI, *Activities 1931–39: World Crises and Policies in Britain and America*. London: Macmillan.

Part VI

NEW DEVELOPMENTS IN OPEN ECONOMY MACROECONOMICS

14

New Channels in the Transmission of Foreign Shocks

Edmund S. Phelps

The Mundell–Fleming model has been called the workhorse of open-economy macroeconomics. To have exerted so strong an influence over so long a timespan is a tall achievement, of course. Yet it is surprising that this workhorse should have so many satisfied drivers. It takes as constant some things that are variable, such as the price mark-up, and it takes as freely variable some things that are at least momentarily constant, such as a country's stock of customers. It seems unlikely that a workhorse so simply built will pull well and true in every task. One of the virtues of Carlos Diaz-Alejandro, whom we are honoring on this occasion, was his sense that models are all ponies, none of them fit for carrying the heavy burden of the analysis, but there are lots of them waiting to serve.

A serious disability of the prevailing open-economy macro-model is its narrow view of the channels by which foreign disturbances are transmitted to the home country. As is now rather widely expounded in international economics textbooks, the orthodox view holds that a rise of the real interest rate abroad, whether that is due to a fiscal stimulus or a monetary tightening in the rest of the world, tends to drive up the real interest rate in the home country – and the nominal interest rate too, absent any change in economic activity or the exchange rate that would lower the expected rate of inflation. This tendency, of course, is the potent fruit of the perfect capital mobility postulate, which was the fundamental paradigmic shift that the Mundell–Fleming model introduced and exploited.

A way of memorizing these results is to remember that the model likens the world economy to a balloon. If the foreign fiscal authorities inflate more the overseas part of the balloon the home part will inflate further in sympathy. If the foreign monetary authorities squeeze the overseas part of the balloon – a sort of supply shock – the air thus expelled will again inflate the domestic part. It is perfectly true that the increase in the world real interest rate originating abroad may reduce home investment expenditures and some of these may have fallen on nontradable capital goods produced domestically. However, the rise of aggregate home output and employment is unambiguous, which implies that exports net of imports must more than fill, or offset, any slack arising in the capital-goods sector. A real depreciation of the home currency is the means to this end.

It would be nice to be able to demonstrate neatly and easily the truth of the above propositions. But where is the official revised version of the orthodox model descending from Mundell–Fleming? That framework, with its 'our consumer good' and 'their consumer good,' has always made it awkward to discuss real-interest effects anyway. It might be more natural to build another model, one in the spirit of Mundell–Fleming, that focusses on capital spending. (In fact, a great deal of trade, especially trade between Europe and North America, is the exchange of capital goods.) Here is such a model.

There is output Z^C of a consumer good, which is tradable, and output Z^I of a nontradable capital good needed for producing Z^C. The price of the former in wage units is denoted $\widetilde{p}$ and the real price of the latter is denoted q. The LM equation says that the actual-and-expected inflation rate must make up the excess of the nominal domestic interest rate (h) over the worldwide home-and-abroad real rate, r^*. The surrogate IS equation has the proportionate rate of change of q making up the excess of r^* over the 'marginal productivity of capital' (in terms of the consumer good). The increase of the capital stock, K, is determined by Z^I. Both Z^I and Z^C are increasing functions of their own-price to wage ratios.

$$\frac{\dot{\widetilde{p}}}{\widetilde{p}} = h\left\{qZ^I(q\widetilde{p}) + Z^C(\widetilde{p}, K), \frac{\widetilde{m}}{\widetilde{p}}\right\} - r^* + \frac{\dot{W}}{W}$$

$$\frac{\dot{q}}{q} = -\,q^{-1}F^K(\widetilde{p}) + r^*$$

$$\dot{K} = Z^I(q\widetilde{p}) - G^K - \delta K$$

An increase of r^* tends to drive up p and thus $Z^C + qZ^I$.

Other Channels

When Jean-Paul Fitoussi and I began to ponder the causes of the 1980s slump in Europe we were skeptical of the view taken by some that all, or the great part, of this tremendous decline could be explained by tightened money and heightened fiscal austerity in Europe. Looking back, I think we perhaps underestimated the degree to which money tightened in the late 1970s and continued to tighten in the early 1980s. On the other hand, the indexation of wages that pervades Europe certainly shortens the effectiveness of monetary policy tightening, and the impressions of fiscal austerity that budget data as late as 1983 may have given were soon erased as the dwindling of inflation eliminated the inflation tax in calculations of the inflation-adjusted high-employment budget surplus.

Fitoussi and I suspected that the phenomenal rise of real interest rates throughout the world in the 1980s and the tremendous fall of European currencies against the dollar – the two most striking shocks of that period – played a part in Europe's deepening slump. If Europe's own policies were not so draconian as to have produced the slump single-handedly, the unexplained part of the slump might be attributable to external shocks and these were the largest, at any rate the most visible, external disturbances. But the orthodox open-economy macro-model gave no comfort to this hypothesis. On the contrary, that model implies that the increased world real interest rate must have been stimulative for Europe and the currency depreciation in Europe must have been the means by which the enlarged European output, spurred by the increased velocity of money, could be sold.

To argue that the shocks elevating the world real interest rate and kicking up the dollar – presumably the move toward tighter money in the United States in the early 1980s, the three-stage reduction of tax rates on income known as the Reagan tax cut, and the remarkable investment subsidies that were introduced in 1981 and largely removed in 1985 and 1986 – were contractionary for Europe therefore made it necessary to construct new models of the international transmission of economic shocks. Fitoussi and I developed three new two-country models in a recent monograph.[1] Here I shall briefly sketch the arguments that these three models make, then proceed to a dynamic one-country model closely related to (though far from identical to) one of the three two-country models in Fitoussi and Phelps.

The first model differs from the orthodox model in having customer markets rather than perfect markets obeying the law of one price. A simple situation is examined in which, to begin with, European suppliers have all the European customers and American suppliers have all the American customers; yet every supplier calculates the loss or gain of customers resulting in the future from a loss or gain of competitiveness relative to the 'average' supplier. In this two-country model, American monetary tightening or American fiscal stimulus (or both) drives up the real interest rate there while in the initial situation described it has no impact directly upon the real interest rate in Europe, given the real exchange rate. For interest rate parity the dollar must jump to a higher level. Since European suppliers' customers are not induced to buy more on this account – the customers are all Europeans initially – the real depreciation of the European currency has no expansionary effect in Europe. Its only role is to raise the price level until real balances have grown scarcer to the point where the interest rate in Europe has risen to match the American level. But this fall of real cash balances implies a fall of output and employment in Europe. Expressed another way: the rise of the real interest rate implied by the American shock (or shocks) dictates a fall of European output and thus also of the European demand for real balances; so the amount of real balances supplied must be made to fall likewise.

In diagrammatic terms, the American IS shifts up and the American LM shifts in. For the European LM to intersect the unshifting European IS at the same elevated real interest rate reached in America, there must be a real depreciation in Europe. That will shift LM in by causing producers to raise their mark-ups, since European suppliers have less to fear from their American competitors when the rise of the dollar puts the latter at a competitive disadvantage. To the extent that the increased world real interest rate itself induces European suppliers to raise their mark-up, less depreciation is needed. It should be added that any upward push on the mark-up resulting from an increase of the real exchange rate or of the real interest rate will feed back, to the extent there is indexation, to money wages, and this induced wage push will produce another upward push on the price level, thus setting the stage for another wage push, and so forth. The model will function under full indexation in the same manner as when indexation is partial or nil.

The second new two-country model introduced in the monograph is reminiscent of the two-sector growth models and capital theories of yesteryear. There is, for convenience, just one consumer good in the world and one capital good. Here I concentrate on full indexation in Europe, thus a predetermined real wage over the near term, and nontradability of each country's capital-good output. The frictions of customer markets are banished, so producers in Europe throw out an inelastic supply of the consumer good onto the world consumer-good market, the amount of which is determined by Europe's pre-given real wage. In this model a tightening of American monetary policy, assuming that it drives up the real interest rate in America, drives down the real price of the capital good in Europe that investing firms there are willing to bid, with the consequence that output and employment in the capital-goods sector fall (and the price level rises to eliminate the excess supply of real balances); no surprise, you might say, but remember that it is opposite to the prediction of Mundell–Fleming. Even more striking are the implications for fiscal stimulus abroad. A foreign fiscal stimulus such as increased tax benefits to investment in America, in driving up the worldwide real interest rate, likewise drives down the real price of investment-goods output in Europe with the same doleful consequences for output and employment there.

In diagrammatic terms, the upward shift of the American IS or the inward shift of the American LM spells a rise of the real interest rate common to both countries. An upward movement along Europe's negatively sloped IS is thus entailed, implying a contraction of output and employment there. To clear the money market there must be a nominal depreciation of the European currency, which will serve to drive up the nominal price (and wage) level and so reduce the supply of real balances.

It was not until our book was completely written that we became aware of the strength of these results from the first two models. The sole function of currency depreciation, nominal or (as in the first model) real as well, is to shift up Europe's LM in order to rendezvous at the lower output and higher interest point on the IS curve that is dictated by the foreign shocks. The depreciation does not shift Europe's IS curve at all. Hence the slope of

Europe's LM curve does not matter at all. The imported rise of the real interest rate might have an electrifying impact upon the velocity of money in Europe; but the induced fall in the amount of real cash balances demanded merely augments the rise of the price level and fall of real balances needed to restore portfolio balance. In short, we hit upon models in which currency depreciation serves as the adjustment mechanism to move the LM curve as required, while the Mundell–Fleming model happens to have portrayed the real exchange rate as the mechanism serving to adjust the IS curve to an unshifting LM curve. In the one-country dynamic model that I shall analyze in the next section the Fitoussi–Phelps mechanism and the Mundell–Fleming mechanism are allowed to coexist and to compete for the upper hand. But before undertaking that act of reconciliation let me touch upon the last model in Fitoussi and Phelps.

The last of the three two-country models studied in the monograph focusses upon the demand for labor. The motif running through this analysis is that the amount of labor demanded is not simply determined by the real wage, given the marginal productivity relations derived from production functions. The real interest rate figures as well. In a way this point was already implied by our second model: the fall of the real price of the investment goods being produced shifts downwards the schedule of the marginal *real-value* productivity of labor. But here we have in mind the notion of the firm's workforce as a kind of investment in view of training and other recruitment costs; also, its value to the firm is in part to provide against future manpower emergencies in view of the frictions impeding instantaneous hiring and training. When the real interest rate is driven up by one or more foreign shocks the present level of this investment by the firm becomes too expensive, and the firm is led to suspend for a while its accustomed replacement hiring and training and even possibly to lay off some existing employees or consign them to early retirement.

Another way by which the increased real interest rate affects the demand for labor is more prosaic, yet, as an empirical matter, quite important. Capital formation in Europe is curtailed as a result of the increased cost of capital. The rate at which Europe adds Japanese electronic gear and American aircraft and French communication equipment to its capital stock is reduced. Hence the demand for labor schedule either falls, or rises less rapidly. Juxtaposed against some tendency for nominal or real wages to continue to rise at the normal rate, pending a palpable worsening of labor-market conditions, the result is a slowing of employment and a rise of the unemployment rate – until such restorative processes as may exist begin to take the upper hand. We enter here into the world of international power politics. Who – which countries – shall have the lion's share of the capital stock that the world capital market has to allocate? To some extent many countries are competing for a larger share of the world's capital stock and of the world's production. On this one point, at least, one can reasonably condemn recent American policy.

> [T]he most serious indictment cf the American fiscal stance is that it has artificially diverted capital investment to America . . . from Europe and the rest of the world. By what rights did the United States do that? . . . There is a 'beggar-thy-neighbor' aspect to the American fiscal maneuver.[2]

'Interest Shock' in a Small Open Customer Market Economy

In the Fitoussi–Phelps monograph the models are dynamic, at least in some key respects, but the otherwise formal analysis was informal about the consequences for the present employment level (and other present variables) of the impact of the foreign shocks upon certain expected-rate-of-change variables: the expected rate of currency depreciation and the expected rate of inflation. It was persuasively argued that releasing these expected rate-of-change variables from the pound of *ceteris paribus* and equating them to the actual rate of change would certainly moderate the impact of the foreign shocks on present variables but never reverse that impact. At this writing Slobodan Djajic and I are at work on a formal dynamic analysis of a two-country customer market model with the purpose of confirming the Fitoussi–Phelps propositions.

Here I present a formal dynamic analysis of a less complex model. It is a (one-country) model of a small open economy competing in a worldwide customer market that was prepared for a Paris conference on deficit spending in 1985 and recently published in the new journal from INSEE.[3] Besides the greater formality, the present analysis differs in focussing upon the effects of a world real-interest rate shock rather that the effects of a domestic deficit. The method of analysis follows that being used in the work with Djajic.

The model is a six-equation system with the following variables, all of which are in logs with the exception of interest and inflation rates: output, z; the price of output, p; the nominal wage w; the nominal interest rate, i; the nominal exchange rate, e; and the current stock of customers, x. A fiscal parameter, g, measures the log of the fraction of output purchased by the government, and the money supply is another constant, the log of which is denoted m. The time rate of change of a variable (here always a logarithm) is indicated with the Newtonian dot. Starred variables denote exogenous levels of foreign variables. In this notation the system is:

$$\text{(GG)} \quad z = -n(p - e - p^* - z^*) + x + g \qquad (1)$$
$$\text{(PP)} \quad p = b_w w + (1 - b_w)(e + p^*) + b_{z^*} z^* + b_r r^* \qquad (2)$$
$$\text{(Dw)} \quad \dot{w} = \Phi(z - \widetilde{z}) \qquad (3)$$
$$\text{(LM)} \quad m - p = 1_z z - 1_i i \qquad (4)$$
$$\text{(De)} \quad \dot{e} = i - (r^* + \dot{p}^*) \qquad (5)$$
$$\text{(Dx)} \quad \dot{x} = \delta(e + p^* - p), \quad \delta > 0 \qquad (6)$$

We have in mind here the constant-cost case, briefly studied in the original

Phelps–Winter model, in which the stock of customers already garnered from the world market by the representative firm does not directly influence its optimal price. For simplicity we have followed the Paris model in taking as negligible the domestic component of a representative firm's stock of customers; so only the typical foreign customer's money income and the firm's price matter for the amount demanded by the typical customer. The PP equation has been simplified in form by omitting the shadow price of customers, but the crucial real-interest rate variable is explicitly present.

Upon substituting into the three differential equations the other relationships, we have the following linear system:

$$\begin{bmatrix} \dot{w} \\ \dot{x} \\ \dot{e} \end{bmatrix} = \begin{bmatrix} -\Phi n b_w & \Phi & \Phi n b_w \\ -\delta b_w & 0 & \delta b_w \\ \dfrac{(1-1_z n)\, b_w}{1_i} & \dfrac{1_z}{1_i} & \dfrac{\{1_z n b_w + (1-b_w)\}}{1_i} \end{bmatrix} \begin{bmatrix} w - \overline{w} \\ x - \overline{x} \\ e - \overline{e} \end{bmatrix}$$

where the steady-state levels, indicated by an overbar, satisfy

$$\begin{aligned} \overline{z} &= \tilde{z} \\ \overline{z} &= z^* + \overline{x} + g \\ \overline{e} &= \overline{p} - p^* \\ \overline{p} &= \overline{w} + (b_z/b_w)\, z^* + (b_r/b_w) r^* \\ \overline{m} - \overline{p} &= 1_z \overline{z} - 1_i \overline{i} \\ \overline{i} &= r^* + \dot{p}^* \end{aligned}$$

The continuing (Keynesian) problem of this economy is to adjust its nominal wage to make real balances compatible with the full-employment demand for them evaluated at a nominal interest rate equal to the foreign level, $r^* + \dot{p}^*$.

Regarding stability properties we first calculate that

$$\Delta = \delta b_w \Phi / 1_i > 0$$

$$Tr = -\Phi n b_w + \frac{\{1_z n b_w + (1 - b_w)\}}{1_i} \gtreqless 0$$

We are free to suppose that the parameters are such as to make two of the roots of the system negative and the other root positive, as desired to ensure convergence to the steady state along a uniquely determined path. Since $\Delta > 0$, this property must result if $Tr < 0$ although that condition is not necessary for the result.

Under this uniquely determined convergence to the steady state the trajectory makes the exchange rate, the jumpy costate variable, a time-invariant function of the wage and stock of customers, which are our two state variables:

$$e - \bar{e} = u_1 (w - \bar{w}) + u_2 (x - \bar{x})$$

where it may be calculated, letting $\bar{\varrho}$ denote the positive root,

$$u_1 = 1 - \frac{1}{1_i\bar{\varrho}} < 1$$

$$u_2 = u_1 \frac{\Phi}{\varrho} - \frac{1_z}{1_i\varrho}$$

Collecting our results about the determination of the steady-state values of the above three variables and the above results we have the following comparative-statics propositions of particular interest here:

$$d\bar{e} / dr^* = \bar{\varrho} + u_1 \, (b_r/b_w) \gtreqless 0$$

$$dz/dr^* = nb_w \{ \bar{\varrho} - \frac{1}{\bar{\varrho}1_i} \cdot \frac{b_r}{b_w} \} \gtreqless 0$$

The last finding states that the orthodox mechanism, according to which the increased real interest rate abroad expands domestic output by increasing the domestic nominal interest rate and thus spurring the velocity of money, must contest against our unorthodox mechanism, according to which the increased real rate of interest contracts output by swelling the price mark-up and thus curtailing the supply of real cash balances. (It should be borne in mind that in supressing wage indexation for the sake of simplicity we have robbed the unorthodox effect of one of its weapons.) Our unorthodox effect *must* triumph if 1_i is close enough to zero.

A brief technical aside is in order on the difference between the above finding and the analysis in the Fitoussi–Phelps monograph. In the latter, the currency depreciation triggered by the rise of the world real interest rate is the mechanism by which the LM curve is shifted up the negatively sloped IS curve, so the slope of the LM curve plays no apparent role, stability properties aside. In the present model, the currency depreciation, assuming that to occur, shifts the negatively sloped IS curve up against the possibly negatively sloped LM Curve as it simultaneously shifts inwards the LM curve. That fact provides an intuitive explanation of why in the present model the parameter b_r is of crucial importance.

Perhaps that aside will raise more questions than it will answer, however! Why is it that in Fitoussi–Phelps the currency depreciation is incapable of producing a happy ending out of the foreign interest shock, as it apparently only shifts inwards the LM curve, while in the present model it would assuredly work in the orthodox direction if b_r is small enough? The answer lies in the point that in the monograph all customers of the home firms were home residents, at least initially, as we looked in: hence the currency depreciation was powerless to do any good in the near term – it could only do harm by raising the mark-up. But in the present model virtually all the customers of domestic firms are foreigners: here, by implication, currency depreciation does more good than harm – but must contend against the direct effect on the mark-up of the increase in the world real rate of interest.

Concluding Comments

It is interesting to see how two really quite simple models, the one analyzed here and the customer market model studied in the monograph, open up a vista of international transmission connections that are surprisingly complex. It appears less and less likely that we shall be able to extract tight qualitative predictions from qualitative models about international transmission phenomena, and that we shall have to turn more to econometric and statistical research – but not, I hope, econometric models that squish everything into the mold of some traditional theoretical model without regard to the rich theoretical possibilities that exist and yet have hardly begun to be explored.

NOTES

The author is McVickar Professor of Political Economy. Columbia University. The themes of this paper are the result of an earlier collaboration with Jean-Paul Fitoussi. The further analysis here has drawn extensively on a joint paper with Slobodan Djajic. Any errors or quirks in the present paper are my responsibility though.

1 Fitoussi, Jean-Paul and Phelps, Edmund S. *The Slump in Europe* (Oxford: Blackwell, 1988).
2 Phelps, Edmund S. 'Appraising the American fiscal stance.' In M. J. Boskin, J. S. Flemming and S. Gorini (eds.) *Private Saving and Public Debt* (Oxford: Blackwell, 1987), pp. 100–1.
3 Phelps, Edmund S. 'The significance of customer markets for the effects of budgetary policy in open economies.' *Annales d'Economie et de Statistique*, 1 (3) (September 1986), pp. 101–17.

15

Trade, Capital Flows and Dynamics of the Real Exchange Rate

Pentti J. K. Kouri

Introduction

The motivation for this paper is an old and important issue in balance of payments theory: what is the role of the real exchange rate in effecting international capital transfers? The issue goes back to the famous debate between Keynes and Ohlin regarding the transfer problem: Keynes argued that a transfer payment imposes a secondary burden on the paying country in the form of a terms of trade deterioration while Ohlin argued that a transfer could be effected without any changes in relative prices by expenditure adjustments in the paying and receiving countries. As we know, the issue hinges on whether the spending patterns are different in the two countries. If each country has a higher propensity to spend on domestic than on foreign products, a transfer requires a terms of trade deterioration or real depreciation in the paying country to be effected. The existence of non-traded goods is another reason why, even with identical spending patterns with respect to traded goods, real depreciation (increase in the relative price of traded goods) is required to effect a capital transfer.

The Keynes–Ohlin debate lies behind the elasticities–absorption debate in devaluation theory, and has more recently surfaced in a controversy concerning the role of the exchange rate in current account adjustment, particularly with reference to the US deficit problem. One school of thought, notably Mundell and McKinnon, argues that there is no obvious relationship between the real exchange rate and the current account: elimination of the US current account deficit requires the elimination of the US budget deficit and changes in the investment-saving balances in the US and in the surplus countries. In line with Ohlin, Mundell and McKinnon argue that a change in the saving-investment balances would change the current account deficit *without* any changes in the dollar exchange rate. Another school of thought represented by Bergsten, Dornbusch, Feldstein, Krugman and Marris, amongst others, takes the Keynesian position and argues that a real depreciation of the dollar is required to eliminate the trade deficit without a decline in total output and employment.

In the Ohlin world, an increase in saving causes an outflow of capital and a simultaneous decline in imports and/or an increase in exports. Equilibrium in the balance of payments is not perturbed and no exchange depreciation is required. In the world envisaged by Keynes, the automatic improvement in the trade account brought about by expenditure adjustments falls short of the ex ante outflow of capital caused by the increase in saving, and therefore a depreciation of the domestic currency is required to effect the outflow of capital. Ex post the magnitude of the capital outflow is less than the initial ex ante increase in saving. Thus although capital is perfectly mobile at an exogenous world interest rate, the effective inflow or outflow of capital is not infinitely elastic at the world interest rate. The friction is not in the flow of capital but in the adjustment of the balance of trade. This point has an obvious bearing on the finding of Feldstein and Horioka, that national saving and investment rates are highly correlated (Feldstein and Horioka, 1980). As Frankel argues in a recent paper (Frankel, 1986), the high correlation need not be evidence of imperfect capital mobility but rather of imperfect integration of goods markets.

The starting point of this paper is the Keynesian, or in the current debate, the mainstream perspective on the transfer problem. I assume a world of perfect capital mobility in which financial capital moves freely and instantaneously across national boundaries. However, the Ohlin transfer condition is not met: to effect net capital movements through trade account surpluses or deficits, real exchange rate changes are necessary. The vision is one of a world in which financial markets put the real economy under continuous stress as disturbances and policies give rise to capital movements which the world trading system can adjust to only with difficulty.

To analyze the dynamics of capital transfer, we develop a dynamic model of an open economy that integrates the determination of the balance of trade with the determination of capital flows and the saving–investment balance. Both the elasticities and the absorption approach are integrated into the analysis: they are two sides of the same pair of scissors and both are needed to determine the real exchange rate, the real interest rate, the terms of trade and the balance of trade.

Purchasing power parity does not hold in the model: shifts in trade and the saving–investment balance change the equilibrium terms of trade. Changes in the real exchange rate are required to effect capital transfers. Fiscal policies and commercial policies have effects on the real exchange rate both in the short run and in the long run. The 'real interest rate parity' (Frankel, 1986) does not hold either, although capital is perfectly mobile. The domestic real interest rate is affected by policies and disturbances together with the real exchange rate. An implication of the failures of the purchasing power parity and the real interest rate parity is that shifts in the investment–saving balance are not fully offset by equal changes in the current account.

Money is in the background of the analysis. Prices are assumed to be flexible and the central bank is assumed to follow Wicksell's rule and stabilize the domestic price level P rather than forcing P to adjust to M, as Friedman's rule requires. With P stabilized, there is a one to one relationship between the nominal exchange rate and the real exchange rate. This feature of the model eliminates the usual channel through which expectations influence the exchange rate, namely the effect of expected depreciation or appreciation on money demand (as in Dornbusch and Fischer, 1981). In our model the real exchange rate itself is inherently a speculative price – its value cannot be determined except with reference to future expectations. We assume rational expectations and derive conditions for a rational expectations equilibrium to exist. Nonexistence of equilibrium or the existence of a continuum of equilibria is shown to be possible if a modified Marshall–Lerner condition fails to hold.

The issues analyzed in this paper have been discussed in a number of recent papers. Of particular importance are the papers of Frenkel and Razin (1986a, 1986b), which develop the open economy version of Blanchard's (1985) ingenious overlapping generations model and analyze the effects of fiscal policies. Also relevant are the papers of Dornbusch and Fischer (1981), and Mussa (1985). Our paper takes a modelling approach that is different from that of Frenkel and Razin and is also concerned with a different set of issues. It can be thought of as a synthesis of Dornbusch and Fischer (1981) and Mussa (1985) on the one hand and Blanchard (1985) on the other.

The model is developed next, followed by an analysis of its dynamic properties. The most important part of the paper consists of two sections that apply the model to the analysis of the effects of various unanticipated and anticipated shocks and policies. The model reduces to a simple diagram, the usefulness of which these exercises hopefully demonstrate. The paper concludes with a summary.

The Model

We consider a textbook open economy that produces one composite good that can be either exported or consumed at home. Export demand is not infinitely elastic at an exogenously given price but instead is a decreasing function of the relative export price. Domestic prices are flexible and full employment prevails. Monetary policy stabilizes the internal purchasing power of money, measured by the consumer price index. Capital is perfectly mobile and the domestic interest rate must always equal the world interest rate adjusted for the expected rate of change of the exchange rate. Consumption and savings decisions are derived from intertemporal optimization by finitely lived agents (Blanchard 1985). Expectations are rational. From these ingredients we obtain a dynamic model that explains the behavior of the terms of trade, the current account and the net stock of foreign assets and their response to various anticipated and unanticipated shocks and policies. The terms of trade is shown to behave like a speculative asset price.

If a modified Marshall–Lerner condition fails, either no rational expectations equilibrium exists or there is a continuum of such equilibria.

Building Blocks

The demand side of the model is derived from the optimal choices of finitely lived economic agents with uncertain income and lifespan. We assume that the representative agent chooses his consumption–savings plan and money demand so as to maximize the expected utility of consumption over an uncertain lifetime. As in Blanchard (1985), the probability of death is assumed to be constant.

$$\text{Max } E_t \int_t^\infty \{ u(c_\tau^h, c_\tau^m) + \ell(M_\tau/P_\tau)\}\, c^{-\delta\tau} d\tau \tag{1}$$

$$= \text{Max } \int_t^\infty \{ u(c_\tau^h, c_\tau^m) + \ell(\mathrm{m}_\tau)\}\, e^{-(\delta+\varrho)\tau} d\tau$$

We assume that the utility function $u(\ )$ is separable in the following way:

$$u = u\{v(c_\tau^h, c_\tau^m)\} \equiv u(c) \tag{2}$$

where $u(x)$ = a logarithmic function in x, $v(c_\tau^h, c_\tau^m)$ = a homothetic utility function of c^h and c^m.

We shall define $c \equiv v(c_\tau^h, c_\tau^m)$ as real consumption. With the assumption of homotheticity, the agent's choice problem can be divided into two parts. First he chooses the optimal lifetime consumption and money demand plan $\{c_\tau, m_\tau\}$:

$$\text{Max } \int_t^\infty \{u(c_\tau) + \ell(m_\tau)\}\, e^{-(\delta+\varrho)\tau} dT \tag{3}$$

Second, he chooses the composition of consumption $\{c^h, c^m\}$ so as to minimize the cost of achieving a level of real consumption or utility equal to c:

$$\Phi(P^h, eP^m, c) = \min c_\tau^h p_\tau^h + c_\tau^m e_\tau p_\tau^m \tag{4}$$

subject to $v(c_\tau^h, c_\tau^m = c_\tau$ *where* $\Phi(\ \ )$ is the expenditure function associated with the utility function $v(\ \ )$. The homotheticity of $v(\ \ )$ implies that $\Phi(\ \ )$ is separable in prices and utility.

$$\Phi(P^h, cP^m, c) = p(P^h, ep^m)c = P \cdot c \tag{5}$$

where

$$P = p(P^h, eP^m) = \min c^h P^h + c^m eP^m \;\; s.t. \;\; v(c^h, c^m) = 1 \tag{6}$$

is the optimal consumption deflator associated with the utility function $v(\ \ )$

(the price of 'one unit of utility'). From equation (5) we have the following relationship between the nominal exchange rate e and the 'real exchange rate' λ:

$$e = (p/Pm)p(\lambda,1) = (p/Pm)e(\lambda) \tag{7}$$

Proportionate price changes satisfy:

$$\hat{p} = \theta^h\hat{p}^h + \theta^m(\hat{e} - \hat{p}^{\mathrm{m}}) \tag{8}$$

where θ^h and θ^m are the expenditure shares of domestic and imported goods, respectively. The solution of (3) yields the Hicksian compensated demand functions for c^h and c^m:

$$c^h = c^h(\lambda)c;\ c^m = c^m(\lambda)c \tag{9}$$

or in terms of proportionate changes

$$\hat{c}^h = -\theta^m\eta\hat{\lambda} + \hat{c}; \quad \hat{c}^{\mathrm{m}} = \theta^h\eta\hat{\lambda} + \hat{c} \tag{10}$$

where η is the elasticity of substitution between c^h and c^m.

Next we have to determine the level of consumption $\{c_\tau\}$ and money demand $\{m_\tau\}$. The latter is obtained simply by setting the marginal utility of money $1'(m_\tau)$ equal to the marginal opportunity cost of holding money, or the nominal rate of interest, R_τ. This gives us:

$$m_\tau^d = M_\tau^d/P_\tau = L(R_\tau)c_\tau \tag{11}$$

The level of consumption is now obtained by maximizing the expected present discounted utility of consumption subject to the agent's intertemporal budget constraint:

$$\max E_t\textstyle\int_t^\infty u(c^h)c^{-\delta\tau}\mathrm{d}\tau = \int_t^\infty u(c^h)e^{-(\delta+\varrho)\mathrm{T}}\mathrm{d}\tau \tag{12}$$

subject to:

$$E_t\textstyle\int_t^\infty c^h \exp\{-\int_t^\infty r(s)\,\mathrm{d}s\}\,\mathrm{d}\tau = \int_t^\infty c^h \exp\{-\int_t^\infty [r(s) + \varrho]\,\mathrm{d}s\}\,\mathrm{d}\tau \tag{13}$$

$$= E_t\textstyle\int_t^\infty (y_\tau - T_\tau - R_\tau m_\tau^d) \exp\{-\int_t^\infty r(s)\,\mathrm{d}s\}\,\mathrm{d}\tau + a_t$$

$$- \textstyle\int_t^\infty (y_\tau - T_\tau - R_\tau m_\tau^d) \exp\{-\int_t^\infty [r(s) + \varrho + \mu]\,\mathrm{d}s\}\,\mathrm{d}\tau + a_t$$

where ϱ, is the probability of death and μ, the probability of 'retirement' (after which the agent receives no labor income).

The left-hand side is equal to the expected present discounted value of consumption. We assume the existence of a perfect insurance market and therefore the uncertainty of the lifespan and of income simply increases the rate of discount by the probability of death (see Blanchard, 1985) and by the probability of retirement. The first term on the right-hand side is the expected present discounted value of labor income, net of taxes and the cost of money balances. The second term is the market value of financial assets. All financial assets are perfect substitutes (except for money) and yield the same expected rate of return $\{r(\tau)\}$.

The dynamic optimization problem defined by equations (11) and (12) is familiar (see Blanchard, 1985) and its solution implies that consumption must satisfy the following differential equation:

$$\dot{c}_\tau = \{r(\tau) + \mu - \delta\}c_\tau - \varrho(\delta + \varrho)a_\tau \tag{14}$$

From equation (13) the stock of wealth evolves according to

$$\dot{a}_\tau = \{r(\tau) + \varrho\}a_\tau + y_\tau - T_\tau - R_\tau m_\tau^\delta - c_\tau \tag{15}$$

Differential equations (14) and (15) determine the optimal consumption and asset accumulation plans together with (12) and the initial condition on a_τ. We do not have to solve for the consumption function, however, since we can use equations (14) and (15) directly.

We now have a complete specification of the behavior of the representative agent. The behavior of the aggregate economy is the same because of the assumption that population is constant (we normalize population to be equal to one). The domestic demand side for the private sector is thus completely described by equations (9), (11), (14) and (15).

The government consumes only domestic products, collects taxes, receives the seignorage from money creation and incurs debt in domestic currency. The budget constraint is given by:

$$\dot{b}_\tau = r(\tau)b_\tau + T_\tau + R_\tau m_\tau - g_\tau \tag{16}$$

where $b_\tau = B_\tau/P_\tau$ = net public debt held outside the banking system.

To complete the demand side, we need to specify foreign demand for domestic products. In this regard we treat foreign consumption as exogenous. Foreign demand for domestic products is then given by:

$$x^h = x^h(\lambda)c^* \tag{17}$$

In terms of proportionate changes, we have:

$$\hat{x}^h = -{}^*\theta^m\eta^*\hat{\lambda} + \hat{c}^* \tag{18}$$

Regarding the supply side, we assume that output is fixed at full employment. We also assume that labor is the only input.

Equilibrium Conditions

We are now ready to write down the equilibrium conditions of the model. First we have the condition of equilibrium in the domestic output market:

$$c^h + g^h + x^h = c^h(\lambda)c + g + x^h(\lambda)c^* = y \tag{19}$$

Solving this for λ gives us the terms of trade equation:

$$\lambda = \lambda(c;g,c^*) \tag{20}$$

Totally differentiating this we obtain, after a little manipulation:

$$\hat{\lambda} = \frac{1}{c^h\theta^m\eta + x^{h^*}\theta^m\eta^*}(c^h\hat{c} + g\hat{g} + x^hc^*) \tag{21}$$
$$= \frac{\lambda}{c^m\eta_m + x^h\lambda\eta_x}(c^h\hat{c} + g\hat{g} + x^h\hat{c}^*)$$

where η_m and η_x are the (compensated) price elasticities of import and export demand, respectively.

All the coefficients are unambiguously positive: an increase in real demand improves the terms of trade.

The second equation defines the dynamics of consumption [see equation (14) above]:

$$\dot{c}_\tau = \{r(\tau) + \mu - \delta\}c_\tau - \varrho(\delta + \varrho)\,(Fe/p + B/P) \tag{22}$$

We shall assume that the central bank stabilizes the internal purchasing power of money. P is therefore constant and $\pi = 0$. For convenience we also assume that P^m is constant. From equation (6) $\hat{e}$ is then equal to $-\theta^h\lambda$. Assuming rational exchange rate expectations, we then have $\pi_e = \hat{e} = -\theta^h\lambda$, and substituting from equation (21):

$$r(\tau) = \mathrm{r}^* + \hat{e} = r^* - \theta^h\lambda = r^* - \alpha\theta^h\hat{c} \tag{23}$$

where $\alpha = c^h\lambda/\,(c^m\eta_m + x^h\lambda\eta_x)$ is the elasticity of the terms of trade with respect to domestic consumption. Substituting this in differential equation (22), we get one of the two basic equations of our model:

$$\dot{c} = (1+\sigma\theta^h)^{-1}\,(r^* + \mu - \delta)c - \varrho(\delta + \varrho)\,(1+\alpha\theta^h)^{-1}\{Fe(c;g,c^*) + B/P\} \tag{24}$$

$$= c(c,F;r^*,c^*,g,B/P)$$

For future reference we note that:

$$\partial\dot{c}/\partial c = (1+\alpha\theta^h)^{-1}(r^* + \mu - \delta) + \varrho(\delta + \varrho)\,(1+\alpha\theta^h)^{-1}\,(F/ec)$$

which can be positive or negative; $\partial\dot{c}/\partial F$ is equal to $-\varrho(\delta + \varrho)\cdot e(1+\alpha\theta^h)^{-1}$ and is therefore always negative.

The second basic differential equation of the model governs the accumulation of foreign assets or, as the case may be, liabilities:

$$\dot{F} = \lambda x(\lambda)c^* - c^m(\lambda)c + r^*F = TB(\lambda,c;c^*) + r^*F \tag{25}$$

To complete the model, we have the equilibrium of money demand and supply:

$$m^d \equiv M^d/P = L(R_\tau)c = M^s/P \tag{26}$$

This equation determines the supply of money: we assume that the central bank adjusts M^s so as to stabilize P.

The model is now complete and it reduces to differential equations (24) and (25) and the terms of trade equation (20). Its dynamic properties are analyzed next.

Dynamics

The linearized form of the two differential equations is given:

$$\dot{c} = a_{11}(c-c^*) + a_{12}(F-F^*) \tag{27}$$

$$\dot{F} = a_{21}(c-c^*) + a_{22}(F-F^*) \tag{28}$$

where (c^*,F^*) is the solution of $c(c,F) = 0$ and $f(c,F) = 0$, and the coefficients (a_{ij}) are given by:

$$a_{11} = (r^* + \mu - \delta)/(1+\alpha\theta^h) + \varrho(\delta + \varrho)\alpha\theta^h\,(F/ec)/(1+\alpha\theta)$$

$$a_{12} = -\varrho(\delta+\varrho)e/(1+\alpha\theta^h)$$

$$a_{21} = -\{c^m\eta_m + \lambda x^h(\eta_x - \theta^h)\}/(c^m\eta_m + \lambda x^h\eta_x)$$

$$a_{22} = r^*$$

The balance of trade, *TB*, may be a decreasing or an increasing function of the terms of trade, depending on whether the Marshall–Lerner condition holds:

$$\partial TB/\partial\lambda = -\lambda x^h(\eta_x - 1) - c^m\eta_m \tag{29}$$

Substituting from (15) into (25) we get the reduced form capital flow or current account equation:

$$\dot{F} = f(c,F;f^*,c^*,r^*) \tag{30}$$

After some manipulation, the partial derivative of the current account with respect to domestic consumption is equal to

$$-\{c^m\eta_m + \lambda x^h(\eta_x - \theta^h)\}/(c^m\eta_m + \lambda x^h\eta_x)$$

while the partial derivative with respect to foreign demand is equal to

$$\lambda x^h\theta^h/(c^m\eta_m + \lambda x^h\eta_x)$$

which is always positive. $\partial\dot{F}/\partial c$ can, however, be of either sign.

Proposition I

An increase in domestic consumption worsens, leaves unchanged or improves the balance of trade depending on whether $c^m\eta_m + \lambda x^h(\eta_x - \theta^h)$ is positive, zero or negative.

Proof

Obvious. Note that this condition is less strict than the Marshall–Lerner condition, since θ^h is less than one.

A necessary and sufficient condition for (c^*,F^*) to be a saddle point is that the determinant of the matrix (a_{ij}) is negative. It is convenient to write this condition in the following way:

$$|a_{21}| > a_{11}a_{22}/a_{12} \tag{31}$$

where $|a_{21}|$ is the Marshall–Lerner expression. For $r^* = 0$, the Marshall–Lerner condition is both a sufficient and necessary condition for saddle point stability. If the rate of interest is small, a_{11} is likely to be negative and condition (31) is less strict than the Marshall–Lerner condition; if the rate of interest is high, the reverse is the case. We shall assume below that condition (31) holds and thus (c^*,F^*) is a saddle point and a unique perfect foresight equilibrium exists locally.

If condition (31) does not hold, there are two possibilities. Either the trace of the matrix (a_{ij}) is positive or it is negative (or zero). If it is positive [and (29) fails], both characteristic roots have positive real parts. In that case, (c^*,F^*) is unstable and no perfect foresight equilibrium exists. If it is negative, both real parts are negative and in that case there is a continuum of equilibria: whatever the initial level of consumption and the initial terms of trade, the economy converges to (c^*,F^*). This peculiar possibility, noted in Kouri (1982), arises if the country is a net debtor with F negative, and

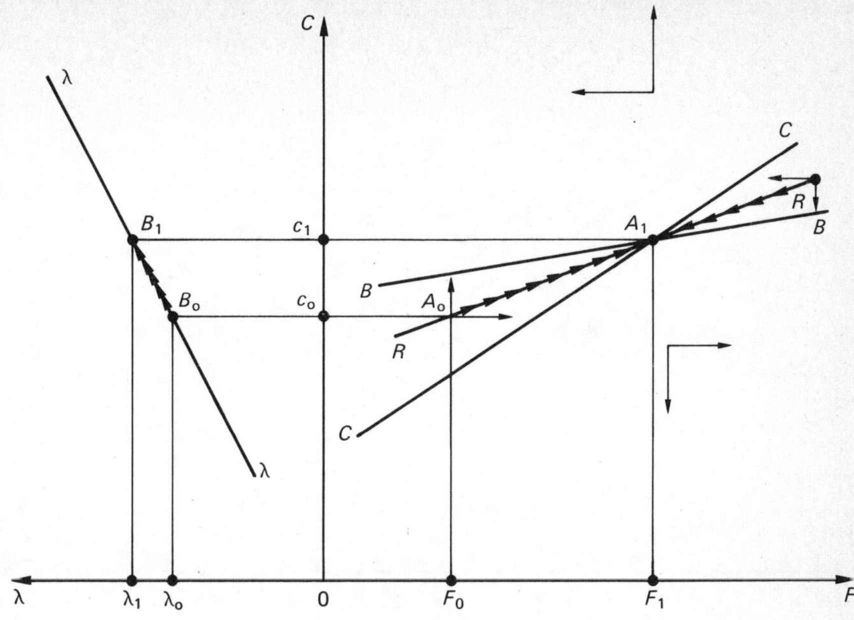

Figure 15.1 A creditor country

$r^*+\mu$ less than δ. An equally peculiar case is one in which the trace is zero [this would be the case if ($r^* = 0$, $B/P = 0$ and $\mu = \delta$)]. In that case, the solution of the system of two differential equations is a continuum of limit cycles: the economy rotates around (c^*,F^*) forever on whatever circle it gets on initially.

We shall focus our attention on the case when the long-run equilibrium is a saddle point and a perfect foresight equilibrium exists. The dynamics of the model with this assumption is illustrated in figure 15.1

It is assumed there that $\partial\dot{c}/\partial c$ is positive and that the net stock of foreign assets is positive in long-run equilibrium.

The CC schedule is defined by setting $\dot{c}$ equal to zero in equation (23). It is upward sloping when $\partial\dot{c}/\partial c$ is positive. Consumption is constant along the CC schedule, increases above it and decreases below it. The BB schedule is defined by setting $\dot{F}$ equal to zero in equation (24). It is upward sloping if the modified Marshall–Lerner condition holds. Assuming that condition (31) holds, it is less steep than the CC schedule. The stock of foreign assets is constant along the BB schedule, decreases above it and increases below it.

Long-run equilibrium obtains at the intersection of the CC and the BB schedules. It is clear from the phase diagram that the equilibrium is a saddle point: there is only one path that leads to it with expectations continuously fulfilled. This is the perfect foresight or rational expectations equilibrium of the model (the RR schedule in figure 15.1). In the diagram, the economy

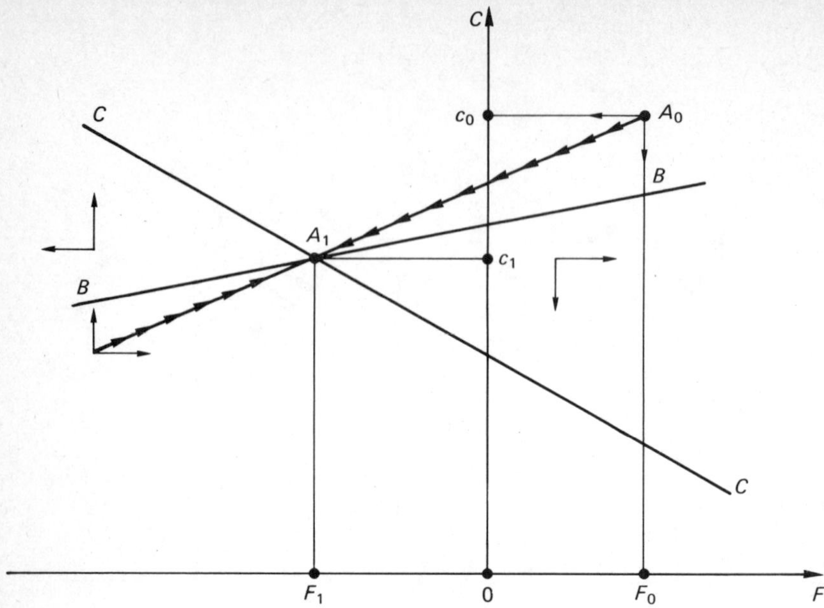

Figure 15.2 A debtor country

starts with a stock of foreign assets equal to F_0. The initial equilibrium level of consumption is equal to c_0, implying a surplus on the current account. Over time the stock of foreign assets and consumption increases, while the currency appreciates in real terms.

Throughout this adjustment process the domestic interest rate is below the foreign rate of interest. Long-run equilibrium is eventually reached with $r = r^*$, $c = c^*$, $F = F^*$ and $\lambda = \lambda^*$. Figure 15.2 illustrates the dynamics of the model when $\partial \dot{c}/\partial c$ is negative and the country is a net debtor. As long as condition (31) holds, long-run equilibrium is still a saddle point and there is a unique rational expectations equilibrium illustrated by the RR schedule.

Adjustment to Anticipated and Unanticipated Disturbances

In this section we put our model to use and analyze the adjustment of the economy to various disturbances originating whether on the trade account or on the capital account.

In figure 15.3 we study adjustment to an unanticipated increase in export demand. The economy is initially in equilibrium with consumption equal to c_0 and the terms of trade equal to λ_0. An increase in foreign demand shifts the BB schedule to B′B′ and the $\lambda\lambda$ schedule to $\lambda'\lambda'$. Because of the increase in foreign demand, the relative price of domestic products increases from λ_0

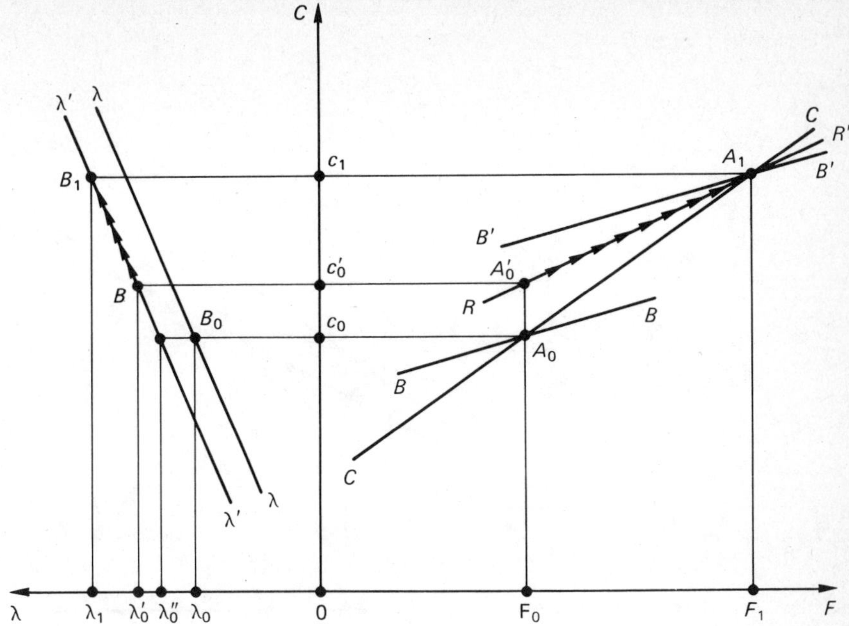

Figure 15.3 An Increase in export demand

to λ_0''. This terms of trade improvement causes an increase in domestic consumption as well, which in turn leads to a further improvement in the terms of trade. New equilibrium is achieved on the new R′R′ schedule with an unchanged stock of foreign assets, a higher level of consumption (c_0') and improved terms of trade (λ_0'). The short-run marginal propensity to consume is less than one, and as a result there is an increase in saving, causing a surplus on the current account. As the stock of foreign assets increases, consumption increases further, the terms of trade continue to improve while the current account surplus declines. Eventually a new long-run equilibrium is reached at (λ_1,c_1,F_1). Throughout the adjustment process the domestic interest rate is below the world interest rate both in nominal and in real terms. Sustained real interest rate differentials are thus possible despite the fact that we have perfect capital mobility.

This example shows clearly how an exogenous increase in export demand causes real appreciation and an increase in saving, capital outflow and surplus in the current account. This result is consistent with Laursen and Metzler but at variance with the implications of some other models and theories of current account determination. The familiar Mundell–Fleming model, for example, assumes away the Laursen–Metzler effect and implies that an increase in export demand has no effect on the saving–investment balance. An optimizing model that assumes infinitely lived agents with

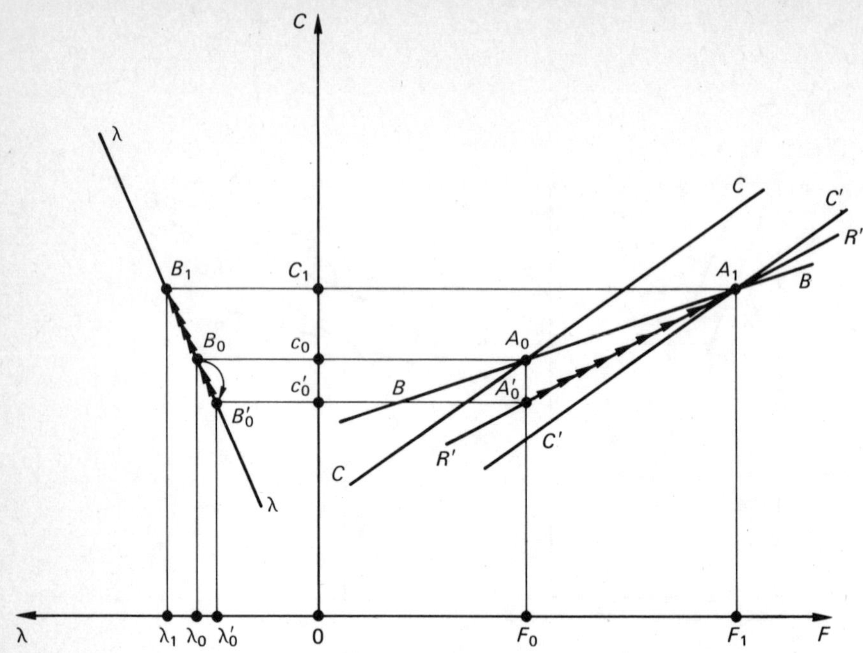

Figure 15.4 An Increase in saving

constant time preferences *à la* Ramsey also implies that a permanent increase in export demand has no effect on the current account (Svensson and Razin, 1983). An alternative optimizing model with infinitely lived agents and varying time preference *à la* Uzawa (Obstfeld, 1982) implies that an increase in export demand causes a deficit on the current account.

Next we consider adjustment to an increase in saving. This is shown as a shift in the CC schedule in figure 15.4. There is an immediate decline in consumption from c_0 to c_0'. The terms of trade deteriorate from λ_0 to λ_0' and the current account moves to surplus to effect the transfer of capital. The capital transfer is achieved both by means of lower absorption and by real depreciation of the domestic currency. Again there is no conflict between the elasticities and the absorption perspectives on current account determination: they are the two sides of the same pair of scissors.

With the current account in surplus the stock of foreign assets increases. Consumption also increases and the terms of trade improve as the economy adjusts to a new long-run equilibrium with a permanently higher level of consumption (c_1) and an improved terms of trade (λ_1) relative to the initial position.

Throughout the adjustment process the domestic interest rate is below the world interest rate both in nominal and in real terms. Despite perfect capital mobility, an increase in domestic saving thus still reduces the domestic interest rate.

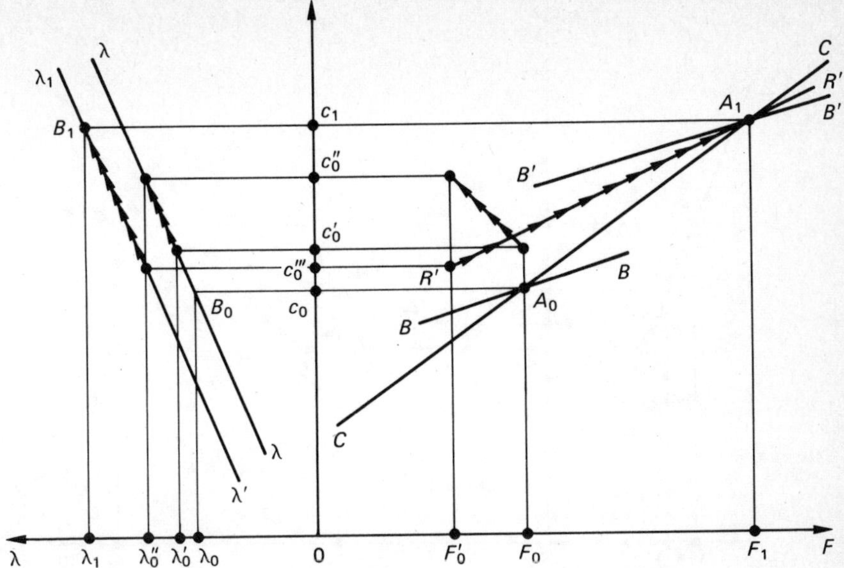

Figure 15.5 Anticipated increase in export demand

Next we consider the adjustment of the economy to an anticipated future increase in export demand (adjustment to an expected increase in oil revenue would look the same).

In figure 15.5, the increase in export demand shifts the BB schedule to B′B′ when it happens and the $\lambda\lambda$ schedule to $\lambda'\lambda'$. Before the increase occurs, the dynamics of the system is defined by the CC and the BB schedules. The expectation of a future increase in export demand causes an immediate increase in consumption from c_0 to c_0', a deterioration in the current account and a real appreciation of the domestic currency from λ_0 to λ_0'. Following the initial impact, consumption continues to increase and the terms of trade improve at an accelerating rate. The domestic real rate of interest declines on impact and continues to decline as the date of the export shock comes closer. When the increase in export demand actually occurs, consumption is at c_0' and the terms of trade are equal to λ_0''. Immediately at that point consumption declines to c_0''' while the terms of trade remain unchanged at λ_0''. The terms of trade cannot jump except at the initial point when the news about the future increase in export demand hits the market – otherwise there would be an arbitrage opportunity with infinite profit. The reason why consumption paradoxically declines when export demand increases is that the real rate of interest increases at that point as the rate of appreciation slows down. From another perspective, consumption must decline to make room for the increase in export since output is fixed at full employment. After the increase in export demand has occurred, the current

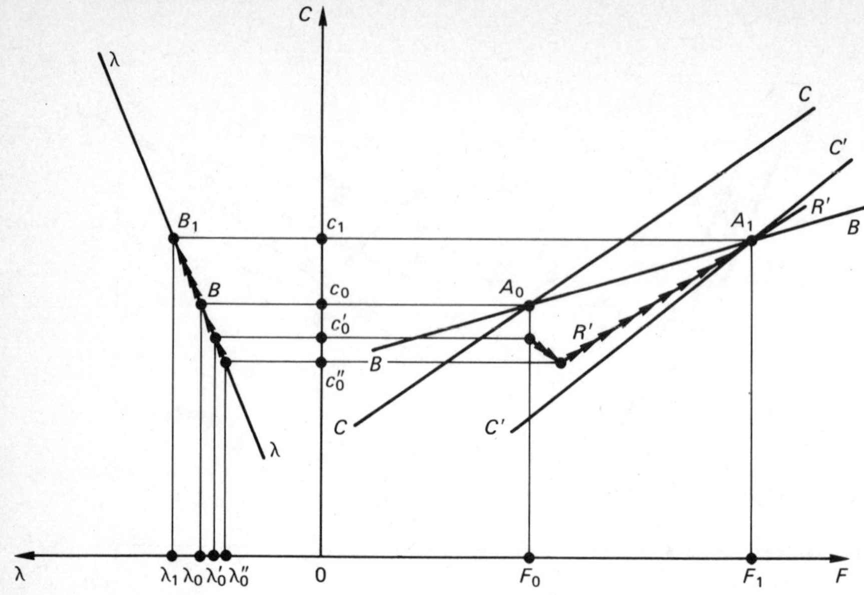

Figure 15.6 Anticipated increase in saving

account moves from a deficit to a surplus and the economy moves along the new RR schedule to a new long-run equilibrium with consumption at c_1 and the terms of trade at λ_1.

The ultimate effects of an unanticipated shock and an anticipated shock are the same, but as is evident from the above analysis, the adjustment paths are very different. In one case we observe appreciation of the currency and a surplus on the current account and in the other case the currency appreciates while the current account is initially in deficit and then moves on to a surplus. This point is made by Dornbusch and Fischer (1981) with reference to a descriptive open economy model.

Adjustment to an anticipated future increase in savings is illustrated in figure 15.6. The increase in saving causes the CC schedule to shift to C′C′ at some future date. The economy is initially in equilibrium with consumption at c_0 and the terms of trade at λ_0. As the news hits the market, the currency depreciates from λ_0 to λ_0', the rate of interest increases in anticipation of continued depreciation, consumption declines and the current account moves to a surplus. The currency continues to depreciate at an accelerating pace and the interest rate increases before the disturbance occurs. At the time of the disturbance, consumption is at c_0'' and the terms of trade at λ_0''. Immediately thereafter, the currency begins to appreciate, the rate of interest declines and consumption begins to to increase as the economy moves to a new long-run equilibrium.

This example shows yet another pattern between the current account and

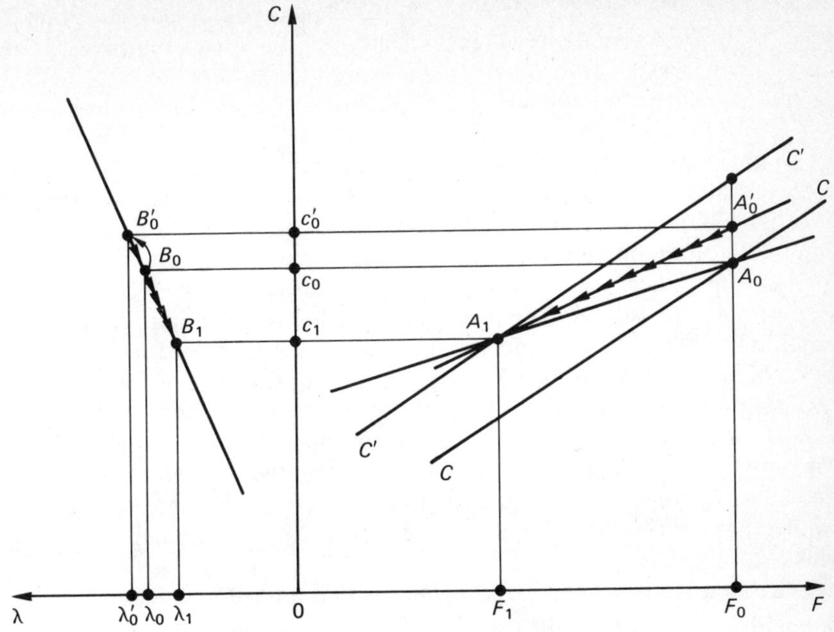

Figure 15.7 An increase in public debt

the exchange rate. A surplus in the current account initially is associated with currency depreciation and then with appreciation.

Adjustment to Policy Changes

We conclude with a discussion of the dynamic effects of changes in government policies. The effect of budget deficits on the exchange rate and the balance of trade has been a subject of active debate and research. Blanchard (1985) shows clearly how a budget deficit causes a deficit in the balance of trade, but in his model real appreciation is not required to effect the transfer of capital. Nor does the budget deficit have any effect on the real rate of interest in the world capital market. Frenkel and Razin (1986a, 1986b) develop an analysis of the effects of budget deficits on the terms of trade and real interest rates in a two-country setting similar to ours. Our model is also well suited to the analysis of the dynamic effects of fiscal policies. We assume in figure 15.7 that the government makes a once-and-for-all lump sum payment to the private sector and finances it by issuing debt. This causes the CC schedule to shift left to C′C′. There is an immediate increase in consumption to c_0' and an appreciation of the currency to λ_0'. As a result, the current account moves to a deficit. Over time, the stock of foreign assets declines, while the currency depreciates throughout the adjustment process.

Eventually a new long-run equilibrium is reached with a reduced level of consumption at c_1, a depreciated currency at λ_1 and an improved trade balance matching a permanent decline in foreign interest income.

Thus the short-run beneficial effects of the budget deficit are more than offset by the long-run adverse effects.

As a final case, we consider the effects of an import tariff on the balance of payments and the exchange rate. In models that treat capital flows as exogenous, an import tariff has no effect on the balance of trade: its effect is completely offset by an appreciation of the currency. In our model, however, an import tariff changes consumption and saving as well and thus has an effect on the capital account, too.The effects of an import tariff are illustrated by figures 15.8a and 15.8b. The left-hand side of these diagrams shows the domestic terms of trade as a function of the level of consumption. Assuming that the central bank continues to stabilize the domestic price level, the nominal exchange rate is a decreasing function of the domestic terms of trade and thus can be read directly from the diagram. The relative price faced by foreigners is equal to $(1+t)\lambda$, where t is the rate of tariff. We assume that tariff revenue is distributed as a transfer payment to households.

The reason why we need two diagrams is that a tariff may either improve the balance of trade or worsen it. The effect on the domestic terms of trade is also ambiguous. Whether a tariff improves the trade balance or worsens it depends on whether the rate of tariff is less than or greater than $1/(\eta_x-1)$ – the optimal rate of tariff. This is the rate of tariff that maximizes the balance of trade subject to the condition that the level of real consumption remains unchanged.

Figure 15.8a assumes that the rate of tariff is less than optimal. In such a case, an increase in the rate of tariff improves the balance of trade and shifts the BB schedule up to B′B′.

There is an immediate increase in consumption to c_0', but real income increases more and the current account moves to a surplus. With the current account in surplus, the stock of foreign assets and consumption increase over time until a new long-run equilibrium is reached with consumption at c_1 and stock of foreign assets at F_1.

The effect of the tariff on the domestic terms of trade and on the exchange rate is ambiguous. The decline in export demand shifts the $\lambda\lambda$ schedule to the right. For the domestic terms of trade to improve, domestic consumption must increase enough to offset the decline in foreign demand. This is assumed in the diagram where the terms of trade initially improve and subsequently continue to improve, reaching long-run equilibrium at λ_1.

Figure 15.8b illustrates the case when the rate of tariff is increased above its optimal level. In this case consumption is reduced, the current account moves into a deficit and the terms of trade deteriorate.

The effect of an import tariff on the real rate of interest can also be read from figures 15.8a and b. In the first case the rate of interest is reduced during adjustment as a result of the increase is real income; in the second case the rate of interest in increased.

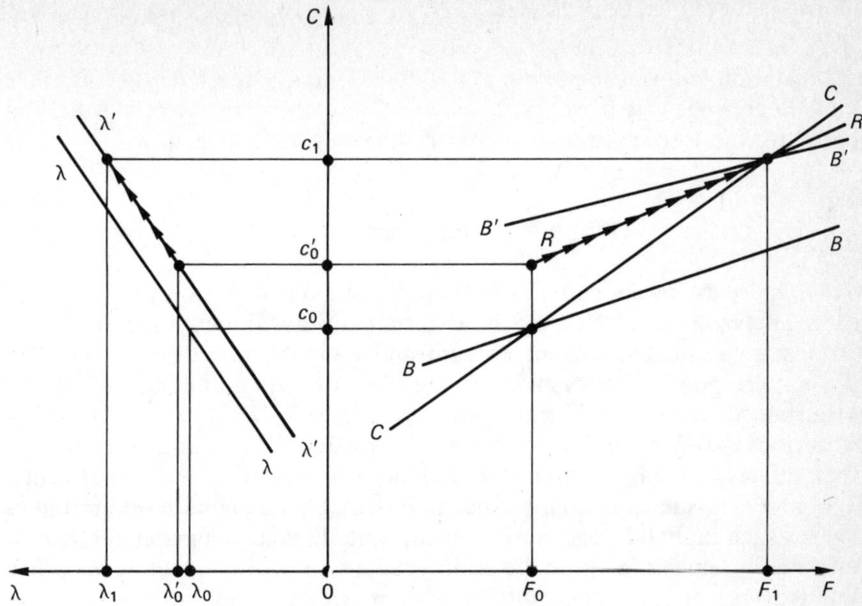

Figure 15.8a An import tariff: an improvement in the balance of trade

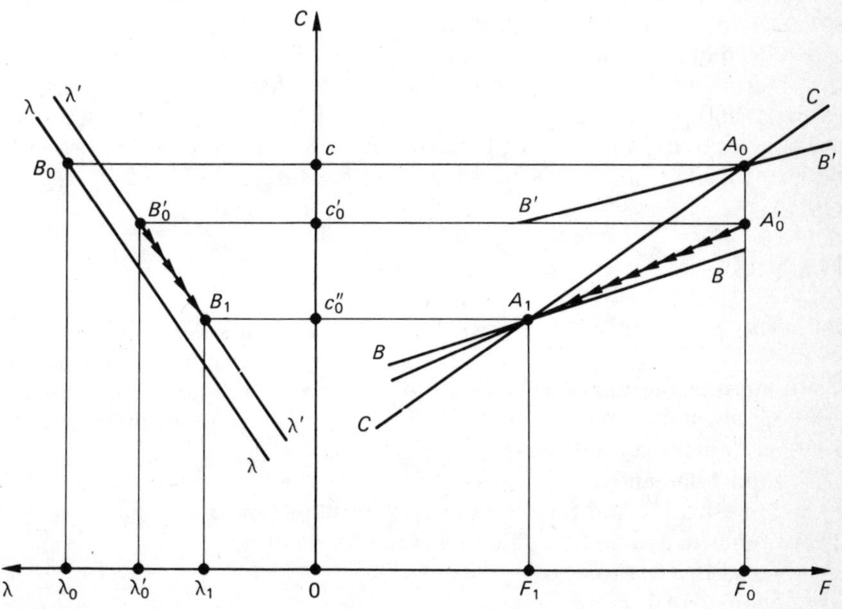

Figure 15.8b An import tariff: a deterioration in the balance of trade

In summary, our model explains why a country might be tempted to use trade restrictions to achieve a virtuous cycle of trade surpluses, currency appreciation, a lower interest rate and higher and increasing real consumption. Such policy, if it works, does so only at the expense of the trading partners who lose more than the tariff-imposing country gains.

Conclusion

This paper has developed a dynamic model of an open economy that enables us to analyze in a simple way the determination of the exchange rate, the interest rate and the current account and their evolution over time. The dynamic response of markets to various anticipated and unanticipated real disturbances can be easily traced using the *cc*, BB, $\lambda\lambda$ diagram. The effects of various government policies can also be analyzed easily and derived from their effects on the opportunities and choices of optimizing economic agents. The model assumes rational expectations and its dynamic equilibrium is always such that all information is incorporated in current prices. Only new information causes jumps in the exchange rate, or in other asset prices. With this feature, our model is fully consistent with the modern asset market perspective on exchange rate determination.

We assume that capital transfers require changes in the real exchange rate to be effected and therefore the real exchange rate becomes a crucial variable in the balance of payments adjustment process. Indeed, it can be viewed as the price that equilibrates the balance of payments. From this perspective, our model integrates the balance of payments view of exchange rate determination with the asset market view. In doing so, the paper brings the determinants of trade and capital flows to the forefront of exchange rate analysis, and provides a framework within which we can go beyond monetary policies to explain the past behavior of exchange rates, and to prescribe policies for their more orderly behavior in the future.

APPENDIX I

Notation

c = domestic consumption
y = real income
g = government consumption
x^h = export demand
c^h = domestic demand for the domestic consumer good
c^m = domestic demand for the imported consumer good
r^* = world interest rate
r = domestic real interest rate
R = domestic nominal interest rate

F = net stock of foreign assets (in foreign currency)
b = net real stock of public debt
a = financial wealth of the private sector
M = nominal supply of money
P = domestic price level
π = expected rate of change of P
P^h = domestic currency price of the domestic good
P^m = foreign currency price of the imported good
e = nominal exchange rate
$\lambda = P^h/eP^m$ = the terms of trade
δ = subjective rate of time preference
ϱ = probability of death
μ = probability of retirement

REFERENCES

Blanchard, Olivier 1985: Debt, deficits and finite horizons. *Journal of Political Economy*, 95, (2), 223–47.

Dornbusch, Rudiger and Fischer, Stanley 1981: Exchange rates and the current account. *American Economic Review*, 70 (5), 960–71.

Feldstein, Martin and Horioka, Charles 1980: Domestic saving and international capital flows. *Economic Journal*, 90, 314–29.

Frankel, Jeffrey A. 1986: International capital mobility and crowding-out in the US economy: imperfect integration of financial markets or of goods markets? In R.W. Hafer (ed.), *How Open is the US Economy*, Lexington, MA:, Lexington Books.

Frenkel, Jacob and Assaf, Razin 1986a: Fiscal policies in the world economy. *Journal of Political Economy*, 94 (3).

Frenkel, Jacob and Assaf, Razin 1986b: Real exchange rates, interest rates and fiscal policies. *Economic Studies Quarterly*, August.

Kouri, Pentti 1982: Balance of payments and the foreign exchange market: a dynamic partial equilibrium model. In J. Bhandari and B.H. Putnam (eds.), *Flexible Exchange Rates*, Cambridge: Cambridge University Press.

Kouri, Pentti 1983: Intertemporal balance of payments equilibrium and exchange rate determination. *Banca d'Italia Discussion Paper*, no. 5.

Mussa, Michael 1985: The real exchange rate as a tool of commercial policy. *NBER Working Paper*, no. 1577.

Obstfeld, M. 1982: Aggregate spending and the terms of trade: is there a Laursen–Metzler effect? *Quarterly Journal of Economics*, May.

Obstfeld, M. 1986: Capital flows, the current account, and the real exchange rate: consequences of liberalization and stabilization. In L. Ahmed and S. Edwards (eds.), *Exchange Rate Policies in Developing Countries*, Chicago: University of Chicago Press.

Svensson, Lars and Razin, Assaf 1983: The terms of trade and the current account: the Harberger–Laursen–Metzler effect. *Journal of Political Economy*, 91, 97–125.

Part VII

INTERNATIONAL TRADE, FACTOR MOBILITY AND DEVELOPMENT

16

New Trade Theory and the Less Developed Countries

Paul Krugman

Since this paper is dedicated to the memory of Carlos Díaz-Alejandro, it may not be inappropriate to begin on a personal note. My own work on the relationship between industrial organization and international trade began in 1977, when I was just beginning my teaching career at Yale University. At the time, this line of work seemed to some of my colleagues to be of doubtful value and interest; and sometimes I wondered myself if it was the right thing to work on. Fortunately I had Carlos as a colleague and friend. He served as a sounding board for ideas that were often badly expressed at first, and a source of encouragement when my work initially met with little outside acceptance. Without the support of a few close colleagues, Carlos prominent among them, I am sure that I would have abandoned an effort that in the end has rewarded me better than I deserve. We all know the work that Carlos published under his own name; we should also give him an important share of the credit for the work that he encouraged from younger economists.

In one respect I am afraid that the 'new' theories of international trade and investment have so far disappointed Carlos's expectations. From the beginning he urged that new theory be applied to the trade problems of less developed countries. Yet somehow the results of research have often seemed to suggest that the theory applies only to the problems of advanced countries. The first generation of industrial organization/trade models in the intra-industry trade literature led to the apparent conclusion that unconventional trade based on scale economies rather than comparative advantage will be prominent only between similar economies. This appears to imply that the new theory applies to North–North trade, but that North–South trade can continue to be analyzed with conventional tools. [As Stewart (1984) has emphasized, the new tools are relevant to South–South trade as well, a point I will return to. However, the sheer logic of relative purchasing power insures that South–South interactions are smaller than either of the other kinds of trade.]

More recently, the work on strategic trade policy following from the contributions of Brander and Spencer clearly has been inspired by the problems of competition among advanced countries. The models are admittedly abstract, and complete in their internal logic, but the scenarios they depict are inspired by the rivalry of Airbus and Boeing, Texas Instruments versus NEC. Very recently several attempts at empirical quantification of strategic trade policy arguments have been made (Dixit, 1985; Baldwin and Krugman, 1986; Venables and Smith, 1986). These attempts so far rely entirely on cases drawn from the advanced countries (and indeed mostly on the US–Japan rivalry).

The question is whether the lack of LDC applications of new theory reflects a genuine lack of applicability, or a bias in the research agenda. What I will argue in this paper is that the latter is the case. Understanding trade and trade policy in the less developed world requires taking account of increasing returns and imperfect competition as much as, if not more than, trade analysis in the developed world. If the research has not yet appeared to make this clear, it is because advanced-country-issues have temporarily pre-empted the limited supply of economists working on these issues. My intention in this paper is to indicate as best I can how the field can be widened to include poor nations as well.

The paper is in three parts. The first part is a brief review of the central ideas of the new theory of international trade and investment that has emerged over the last decade, with special emphasis on those aspects of the theory that may be relevant to less developed countries. The second part asks what features of LDCs mandate a difference in approach or emphasis in our analysis of their trade problems. Finally, the third part illustrates some of the discussion with a simple model of North–South trade in the presence of economies of scale in the provision of export infrastructure.

The 'New' Trade and Investment Theory: Central Ideas

The 'new' theory of international trade and investment arose from a marriage of an old idea with a new approach to modelling. The old idea is that much trade is due not to underlying differences between countries but to arbitrary specialization to realize economies of scale. This idea is by itself hardly revolutionary: Ohlin emphasized the role of economies of scale repeatedly, and we might argue that Adam Smith had the idea first. As long as the role of scale economies remained poorly formalized, however, it tended to be neglected and even forgotten in many discussions of trade. What turned it into a new theory was the addition of the 'new' industrial organization approach of the 1970s. The essence of this approach was to try, wherever possible, to model issues of industrial organization as the outcome of noncooperative games among firms and possibly other players.

Now of course such modelling often does violence to reality. If nothing else, oligopolies are rarely truly noncooperative. It was precisely the recognition of the lack of any really good models of oligopoly that led economists such as Johnson (1967) to dismiss the idea of modelling imperfect competition in trade. The breakthrough in the 1970s was that economists dared to be silly, on the valid grounds that even an imperfect model can add insight. The next breakthrough will be to bring the process full circle, by making the new theories empirically relevant.

What does the new theory tell us? On the positive side, the theory gives us an expanded account of the sources of international trade and specialization. More controversially, the new theory suggests that trade policy may have quite different effects from those predicted in conventional models. One way to think about these effects is in terms of the effect of policy on market power (something that of course could not be an issue in traditional competitive trade theory). First, trade policy can affect the monopoly power of domestic firms in their home market; this issue was noted a generation ago, but has resurfaced as both a practical and theoretical concern. Second, trade policy can in some models be used to reduce the market power of foreign firms in the domestic market (whether these firms supply that market by exporting or through direct foreign investment). This raises the possibility of an active trade policy aimed at extracting monopoly profits from foreign firms. Finally, and most controversially, trade policy may, as Brander and Spencer argue, be used to reinforce the market power of domestic firms in their competition in foreign markets.

As a prologue to our discussion of the relevance of new theory to less developed countries, let us consider each of these insights briefly.

The Sources and Nature of International Trade

The new theory of trade does not reject comparative advantage as a determinant of international trade. Instead, it supplements it. The basic view is that the pattern of trade is determined only up to a point by countries' tastes, technologies and resources. These underlying factors determine certain features of the trade pattern, but do not determine its complete detail. The reason is that the complete pattern of trade also reflects specialization due to economies of scale, and this additional specialization typically includes an arbitrary or historical element. Thus in many of the models described in Helpman and Krugman (1985) we find that net trade in factor services embodied in goods is determined by national resources, but that trade in individual products is determined by the requirement that production of increasing returns goods be geographically concentrated. *Where* the production of any one good is concentrated is indeterminate, so that there is a level of arbitrariness or randomness to the pattern of trade.

In the most popular models of this kind, the idea that trade represents an overlay of arbitrary scale-economy specialization on a comparative advantage base takes a more specific form. The numerous models of 'intra industry trade' (Dixit and Norman, 1980; Krugman, 1979, 1980, 1981; Lancaster, 1980; Ethier, 1982; Helpman, 1981) postulate that scale economies apply to individual product varieties within an 'industry' characterized by a common technology. The result is that comparative advantage applies at the level of industries, determining the pattern and volume of *inter*industry trade. What is left is specialization on individual products within each industry, so that the effect of scale economies shows up in *intra*industry trade. In simple models it is then easy to show that the relative importance of intra-trade as opposed to inter-trade will be greater, the more similar are countries; i.e., noncomparative advantage trade is identified with intraindustry trade among similar countries.

While this is an attractively tidy way to present the concept of increasing returns-based trade, for less developed countries it is important to point out that the identification of scale-economy trade with intraindustry trade is not a necessary one. In the first place, it will often be the case, even for large countries, that scale economies apply to product lines so large that their exploitation requires *inter*industry trade. The most spectacular example is of course the aircraft industry: Boeing assembles its wide-bodied commercial jets, which account for more than half the world market, in *one* plant in Seattle. For smaller countries such examples are legion. A single scale efficient auto assembly plant, oil refinery, pulp mill, etc., will exceed the domestic market size of many developing countries. So trade to realize economies of scale for such countries will necessarily be interindustry rather than intraindustry.

Beyond this point is a more subtle one. It is easy to imagine scenarios where scale economies that in a technological sense apply only at an intraindustry level nonetheless give rise to 'linkage' effects at an interindustry level. In Helpman and Krugman (1985) we note that when there are nontraded intermediate goods produced subject to increasing returns, the result is to encourage the formation of 'industrial complexes' composed of the intermediate goods and their consumers. These industrial complexes tend to concentrate in a single country, and this concentration will be reflected in interindustry specialization and trade. Indeed, it is possible for the level of specialization to become even more aggregative, because backward and forward linkages can tie several traded goods sectors into the same industrial complex.

What all of this means is that the equivalence 'scale-economy trade = intraindustry trade', while a useful first approximation for North–North trade, can be seriously misleading when we think about the trade of less developed countries. As I will argue below, scale economies may have a larger role in the trade of these countries than is generally appreciated.

Trade Policy and Domestic Market Power

The relationship between trade and market power is at one level an obvious one. No matter how concentrated a domestic industry, it will have little market power if the industry is a small part of a world market, and the domestic market is open to imports. Clearly, also, trade restrictions can create domestic market power where there would be little or none under free trade.

It is in the details of the relationship between trade policy and domestic market performance that some more careful modelling effort is needed. Modelling efforts here predate the rest of the 'new' theory, and have gone in two main directions; both are relevant to the needs of less developed countries. The first is the proposition, advanced by Eastman and Stykolt (1962), that protection leads to excessive entry and an inefficient scale of production. The second is the proposition, advanced by Bhagwati (1965), that the effects of protection depend on its form, with quotas worse than tariffs.

The Eastman–Stykolt proposition is that protected firms will take advantage of a tariff or quota to raise prices. This increase in prices will at first raise profits. However, if entry into the industry is possible, additional firms will enter until excess profits have been more or less completely absorbed by reduced efficiency due to lower scale. Harris and Cox (1984) have given the Eastman–Stykolt analysis a strong revival, using it as a key element for their analysis of the costs of Canadian protection. The relevance to LDCs is also apparent: anecdotes about the proliferation of inefficient-scale firms in LDCs, for example in the auto industry, are legion. The assumption that inefficient entry raises average costs, but without any explicit model of this process, underlies some estimates of the costs of LDC protection.

The influence of the form of protection on domestic market power is also easy to describe. A tariff does not completely insulate domestic firms from foreign competition: if they raise their prices too high, imports can still come in. A quota, by contrast, establishes a fixed limit. If domestic firms raise prices, the quota premium will also rise. The result for a single domestic monopolist facing competitive foreign suppliers was noted by Bhagwati (1965): a quota will always lead to a higher domestic price and lower domestic output than a tariff that produces the same level of imports.

While Bhagwati's analysis has become the standard exposition, however, it falls short of providing an adequate description of the real problem. The reason is that it assumes somewhat arbitrarily that there is only a single monopolistic domestic firm, with all other agents acting competitively. The first natural extension would be to imagine that a single domestic firm confronts a single foreign competitor. This case has been analyzed by Krishna (1984), who shows that some unexpected technical difficulties arise in modelling equilibrium. In the end, however, Bhagwati's insight is confirmed, with an additional insight as well: a quota can in effect serve as a coordinating device that raises the profits of both the domestic and the foreign firm.

Trade Policy and the Market Power of Foreign Firms

The analysis of the effect of trade policy on domestic market power seems to suggest extra costs to protectionist policies. When we turn to trade policy and the market power of foreign firms, however, we find instead that we now have a possible argument in favor of trade activism. The reason is that under certain circumstances a tariff or other policy might be used to extract part of the difference between foreign firms' selling prices and their marginal costs.

The end result can look something like the standard optimal tariff argument, where a part of the tariff is reflected in improved terms of trade rather than higher internal prices. It is important, therefore, to stress the differences in the imperfect competition case. In the traditional optimal tariff literature the ability of a country to improve its terms of trade depends on its being large enough to affect the relative prices of its import and export goods on world markets. For tariffs to extract rent from foreign firms, this is not necessary. All that is needed is that the foreign firms sell at prices above marginal costs, and be able to discriminate in price between domestic and other markets.

The simplest scenario for rent extraction, described by Brander and Spencer (1981), is that where a single foreign monopolist sells to domestic consumers without domestic competition. To eliminate the standard optimal tariff considerations, let us assume that the firm has constant marginal cost, i.e., the foreign supply curve is not upward sloping in the usual sense. Suppose that in this situation the home government imposes a tariff. What can be shown easily is that, provided the demand curve is not too convex, the tariff will not be fully passed on in domestic prices. That is, part of the tariff will be absorbed out of foreign monopoly rent. For example, if the demand curve is linear, only half of a specific tariff will be passed on to consumers, the other half being absorbed by the foreign firm.

An even stronger possibility for rent extraction via tariffs arises if foreign firms are trying to deter entry by domestic competitors. Brander and Spencer point out that if a foreign firm is engaging in limit pricing, the limit price will not change with a tariff. In this case a tariff that does not lead to an abandonment of the limit-pricing strategy will be absorbed entirely by the foreign firm.

If simple tariffs can extract rent, other policies, such as two-part tariffs, could do so even more effectively. Return to the case of a foreign monopoly without domestic competition. Here a fee charged for the right to sell to the domestic market would allow rent extraction without any rise in domestic prices. In fact, it is apparent on reflection that the optimal policy is to combine a fixed fee for right of access with an import *subsidy*, inducing the foreign firm to charge precisely its own marginal cost.

The Brander–Spencer analysis was intended to apply to tariffs against foreign suppliers who produce outside the country. However, it also applies in principle to multinational firms that produce inside the country. Suppose that a foreign-based firm has special expertise that allows it to produce some good more cheaply than domestic firms. Then there will be an opportunity for mutual gain if that firm is allowed to establish a subsidiary. However, there will usually be a gap between the profit the firm could earn under *laissez-faire* and the minimum necessary to induce it to come. Again, charging a fee for the right to operate could, in principle, insure that the country, not the firm, appropriates the rent implicit in this gap.

The idea of using trade policy to extract rent from imperfectly competitive foreign firms may sound like too subtle a policy to be believable. There would certainly be problems of implementation, but we may offer an analogy that makes the idea seem much more reasonable. In ordinary domestic transactions, we are all accustomed to dealing with oligopolies that charge prices well above their marginal cost. It is a commonplace that large agents can often bargain with these oligopolies, getting prices below the market level. This is the main reason why firms seek to centralize at least some of their outside purchases under the control of a central supply department. But if corporations can bargain with their suppliers for below-market prices, so, in principle, can countries. If we follow the logic of this argument to its conclusion, what it seems to indicate is that the new theory provides a justification for marketing boards, not for exports, but for imports. Imagine a small country with a highly competent and honest administration. Would it be unreasonable for such a country to centralize its purchases of a few commodities when we know that large buyers are able to negotiate substantial price discounts?

Strategic Trade Policy

We now come to the most controversial area of new trade theory. In a series of papers that have quickly become extremely well-known, Brander and Spencer (1983, 1984, 1985) suggested that government policy can play the same role in international competition that 'strategic' moves, such as investment in excess capacity, play in domestic competition. A government, by subsidizing exports, could allow national firms credibly to threaten aggressive moves, and thus deter competition by foreign firms. By shifting monopoly rents from foreign to domestic firms, such a strategic trade policy can raise national income at other countries' expense.

The strategic trade policy argument has obvious relevance to industrial country competition where only a few firms compete for a world market – Boeing versus Airbus, Caterpillar versus Komatsu. Given the explosive politics of this competition in the 1980s, the result has been an intense scrutiny of the concept, with critical papers by Eaton and Grossman (1986), Dixit and Grossman (1984), Dixit (1986a), Grossman (1986), Krugman (1984b) and others. The upshot of this literature has been the conclusion that policy recommendations in this area are very sensitive to the subtle aspects of competition. For example, Brander and Spencer showed that with Cournot competition, an export subsidy will raise national income. Eaton and Grossman showed, however, that if firms compete on prices rather than quantities, then an export *tax* turns out to be the right policy. Issues of entry are also crucial – will rents simply be competed away?

Most recently, several authors have attempted to calculate the prospects for strategic trade policy using more or less real data. In the most complete exercise of this kind, Dixit (1985) analyzes the US auto market. His calculations suggest that fairly sizable tariffs could be justified as a second-best policy, but that the gains from such a policy are small. In a first-best policy purely domestic instruments eliminate most of the role for trade policy. Other recent exercises, by Baldwin and Krugman (1986) and Venables and Smith (1986), are less complete but point in a similar direction: Baldwin and Krugman show that protection can have large nonconventional effects on trade flows, but does not in the case they study turn out to benefit the protectionist country. Venables and Smith find that fairly sizable tariffs are optimal in the industries they study, but the welfare gains from these tariffs are quite small.

Special Characteristics of Less Developed Countries

We now turn to the question of the relevance of all this new theory to less developed countries. To do this, we need to ask what makes these countries different. What characteristics of LDCs require a different emphasis in our modelling than that which is appropriate for advanced countries?

Now LDCs are clearly fundamentally different from advanced countries. Their poverty and low productivity are themselves *prima facie* evidence that markets do not work as well as they should. The mix of still-powerful traditional forces and the pressures generated by the perception of relative backwardness generate a political economy that is very different from anything in the advanced world. For our purposes here, however, we need to focus more specifically on differences that bear on the appropriate choice of trade models. Without necessarily ruling out the possibility of other important differences, I would suggest four key characteristics that may define how we should adapt our theory to the Third World. These are the following:

Small Size Although a few less developed countries have huge populations, many are quite small. And their GNP is of course smaller still, relative to advanced countries. Even a huge, relatively affluent LDC like Brazil has a GNP only about 5 per cent as large as that of the US or the EC.

Primary Product Exports Advanced countries mostly, though not exclusively, export manufactured products. Less developed countries still mostly export primary products, though this is much less true than it used to be.

Difference in Resources Because advanced countries are both richer and somewhat more open than LDCs, North– North trade is larger than North–South trade, which in turn is larger than South–South trade. This means that trade for an advanced country typically means trade with another country that has similar resources, technology, etc., while for an LDC it typically means trade with very different economies. Germany trades mostly with Western Europe; so does Turkey.

Import-Substituting Industrialization Virtually all developing countries have attempted to promote economic growth through import substitution. Inward-looking policies are now out of intellectual fashion, but they have not been reversed in many countries, and the legacy of these policies for economic structure is still evident throughout the Third World.

Let us consider in more detail how each of these factors might affect the relevance of different pieces of the new trade theory.

Size

The markets for manufactured goods in most LDCs are extremely small by advanced country standards, even in those with large populations, because the population is poor and still on the early portions of the Engel curve. The small size of markets, while it may not require a fundamental change in our theory by itself, certainly requires a change in emphasis. In particular, it affects the relative importance of the three linkages we suggested earlier between trade policy and market power.

Consider first the link between protection and the market power of domestic firms. This only matters when the minimum efficient scale of production is large enough relative to the domestic market that protection creates a serious oligopoly or monopoly problem. In LDCs the domestic market will often be so small that the range of goods for which this is the case is much more extensive than industrial economists accustomed to the United States might imagine. And the scale problems will be very acute in sectors where scale economies are normally regarded as significant. To use the overworked example of autos once again, there is probably *no* less developed country with a domestic market large enough to support even a *single* fully integrated auto company at efficient scale (say around 500 000 autos a year). Yet the Eastman–Stykolt dynamics insure that the tiny domestic markets are often served by three or five manufacturers.

Turning next to the possibility of extracting monopoly rent from foreign firms, it is unclear whether small size is an advantage or a disadvantage for countries. On one side, one might imagine that small countries will have less bargaining ability than large. On the other hand, one can think of two advantages. First, the ability to create tailor-made trade policies in a centralized fashion may be greater for a small, relatively simple economy than for a huge advanced one. Second, foreign firms may be willing to grant more concessions to small negotiators than to the large ones precisely because concessions to a small country do not cost as much, or threaten to create precedents, as dangerous as those to large nations. [For an interesting discussion of the advantages of being weak for such strategies as the 'puppy dog ploy' and 'judo economics', see Dixit (1986b).] The important point here in any case is that the conventional view that optimal tariff arguments are irrelevant to small countries does not apply to tariffs and other policies that aim at extracting rent. Finally, small size does reduce the role for strategic trade policy *à la* Brander and Spencer. Small countries will rarely be the home base for companies that have a substantial share of the world market (although small advanced countries can sometimes play this role, e.g., the Netherlands for Phillips). Even where a country does have a major share of some product, the ability to play strategic games will presumably be less when the country is small, because the government will have difficulty being a credible first-mover. For example, suppose that a government from a very small country promises a domestic firm an export subsidy. The firm's competitors abroad may well reason that an aggressive response on their part will place so large a burden on the country's finances that the policy will not be maintained.

So the small size of LDCs, at least in economic terms, seems to suggest that we emphasize domestic monopoly power and rent extraction, rather than strategic moves against foreign competitors, as the potential roles for government policy.

Export of Primary Products

Once upon a time it was customary to view the categories of less developed countries and primary product exporters as virtually identical. This is clearly much less true now, but it is still true that a higher proportion of LDC exports consist of primary products. The main point about primary products relevant to this discussion is that their technology is rarely characterized by economies of scale large relative to the relevant markets. Obviously this is true of agricultural production. Even in mineral production, it seems impressionistically that it is rare that a single mine accounts for a large share of world output, and when it does happen it is usually due to a quirk of geology rather than technology. This may seem to suggest that increasing returns therefore play a limited role in the trade pattern of LDCs. Yet we should qualify this view: I would venture a guess that scale economies and the associated phenomenon of arbitrary specialization play a larger role in primary product trade than most people think.

The reason is that there is really no such thing as an unprocessed export. Even tropical agricultural exports require an infrastructure of transportation lines, port facilities, warehouses, etc., to get them to the world market. Often they also require at least some preliminary processing in the field or soon after. There may also be inputs into the agricultural process that require some kind of infrastructure subject to economies of scale. So even if the crop is raised by atomistic family farmers, there may still be important scale economies that give the overall pattern of primary-product trade a definite noncomparative advantage element.

Perhaps the point can best be illustrated with a crude hypothetical example. (We will develop a model that formalizes this example in the next section.) Suppose that along a coast there are a number of countries that could all produce an export crop, say bananas. We imagine that these countries are all initially identical in their resources. However, to export bananas requires construction of a piece of infrastructure – say a banana dock – that cannot be built below some minimum scale. Let us finally suppose that the world market is sufficiently small that only a few banana docks can profitably be built – say one or two.

What would happen in this example? One or two countries would be chosen as sites for docks, and they would become the exporters of bananas. *Which* countries took on this role would be indeterminate. Obviously the countries that became banana republics would be drawn from the set of those with banana-friendly environments, so that comparative advantage would in an aggregate sense continue to hold. But the detailed pattern of trade would reflect an additional, arbitrary element. This is an example of the point we noted in our review of the new theory of trade, that linkages can lead to scale-economy-based specialization even in industries that themselves are devoid of increasing returns.

We can pursue the example further if we notice that it would be likely that the shift into banana export would generate some rents for the countries chosen. The arbitrary location of banana production would then have real consequences for the distribution of national welfare. Countries might then attempt to compete for the privilege of having a dock, which would be strategic trade policy re-appearing in a different guise.

How realistic is this example? The real world is much more complex than the example. Yet one wonders whether, for example, the climate and location of Chile explain why it supplies 80 per cent of the winter grapes in the US, or that of Ivory Coast explain why it has been so much more successful than its neighbors in exporting beans suitable for instant coffee. Economic policies are surely important, but some random specialization is probably present as well.

Difference in Resources

Because the advanced countries loom so much larger in world trade than less developed countries, they are both each others' main trading partners and the main trading partners of each individual LDC. If we view this with the standard theory of intraindustry trade in mind, we seem to be led back to the conclusion that the new theory is much less important for LDCs than for DCs. Germany, trading mostly with other advanced countries, also engages in a great deal of intraindustry, noncomparative advantage trade. Brazil, trading mostly with countries richer than itself, engages in the interindustry trade that reflects the country's comparative advantage.

The counterargument to this conclusion is similar to that we have just made about primary products. Intraindustry trade and the role of scale economies, while related, are not synonymous. We can imagine scenarios like our banana story in which the pattern of trade of particular LDCs does reflect increasing returns as well as comparative advantage, even though from a global point of view North–South trade may be almost purely determined by comparative advantage. This may be even more true of LDC exports of manufactured goods than it is of their exports of primary products. In manufacturing it is easy to imagine that scale economies in the provision of intermediate inputs and services will cause groups of manufactured exports to be 'industrial complexes' in the sense we described in the last section. The result will be that only some countries out of the set of potential exporters will actually realize this potential.

Also, we should note that whether or not a country's exports reflect non-standard motives for trade, many of the new arguments about trade policy hinge not on the reason for a country's trade pattern but on the market structure of either its import suppliers or its import-competing industries. If the import-competing industries are imperfectly competitive, the issue of the effect of protection on market power will arise even if a country's trade is wholly determined by comparative advantage. If foreign suppliers are oligopolists who sell at prices above their marginal cost, a country can try to extract rent even if its own economy is perfectly competitive. So even if the hypothesis that North–South trade reflects more than comparative advantage turns out to have little force, this does not mean that the new theory is without application.

Import Substitution

The long and unhappy history of import substitution policies in less developed countries raises two important links with new theories of trade policy. One link is liable to misinterpretation: the revival of the infant industry argument in some recent literature. The other is vitally relevant: the protection/market power/entry linkage.

Several authors have published papers that in effect offer a refurbished version of the infant industry argument. The traditional version of this argument relied either on imperfect capital markets or external economies to explain why temporary protection was needed to establish an industry. In the new version, advanced in Krugman (1984a), Venables (1985), and visible to some extent in Dixit and Kyle (1985), the emphasis is instead on increasing returns internal to a firm. A protected home market allows firms to move down their marginal cost curves (or down their learning curves in a dynamic model), lowering costs and raising market shares in all markets. A striking conclusion of this literature is that a protected domestic market may actually serve as a springboard for increased exports. Recent simulation analyses by Baldwin and Krugman (1986) and Venables and Smith (1986) seem to confirm the importance of this effect for several actual industries.

The problem with applying the new infant industry argument – better described as the argument for 'import protection as export promotion' – to LDCs is that it depends on the domestic market being fairly large. The privileged access of domestic firms to the home market can only be a significant strategic asset if the home market is large enough to matter. Yet this can hardly ever be the case for LDCs, none of which account for more than 2 or 3 per cent of the world demand for any manufactured good.

On the other hand, the concern over the role of protection in creating excessive market power for and/or entry by domestic firms is especially valid for LDCs. Not only are their markets small, but the history of import substitution has led to a characteristic pattern of quantitative restrictions rather than tariffs, with rates of effective protection much higher than anything seen in the advanced countries.

These observations together suggest an important point: even though some of the developers of new trade theories have been described as 'new protectionists,' there is nothing in the theory so far that would restore intellectual respectability to the strategy of import substitution. Import substituting industrialization looks even worse in the new theory than in standard theory.

Increasing Returns and North–South Trade: A Simple Model

In this part of the paper I lay out a simple model designed to illustrate three points. The first is that even when North–South trade as a whole is determined by underlying comparative advantage, increasing returns in the provision of infrastructure can play a crucial role in the detailed structure of that trade. The second is that the indeterminacy characteristic of trade driven by increasing returns can matter, with lucky countries doing better than the unlucky ones. Finally, we will see that even small, primary-product-exporting countries can still face both the opportunities and the dilemmas that are now familiar from the analysis of strategic trade policy among advanced countries.

The model is a formalization of the 'banana competition' story outlined above. We envisage a large number of countries able to produce an export commodity, with the problem, however, that exporting requires an indivisible investment in infrastructure. In equilibrium, only some of the potential exporters will actually get the infrastructure they need. It is this linkage effect that drives the results.

Assumptions of the Model

We assume that there are m identical countries, each capable of producing two goods: bananas and corn. The countries are assumed to have no domestic demand for bananas. Thus they sell their output of bananas, if any, on the world market. We will assume that their collective consumption of corn is small enough relative to the world as a whole that it is acceptable to treat the banana market using partial equilibrium analysis; thus the world price of bananas in terms of corn will be represented as an inverse demand curve:

$$P = D(Q) \tag{1}$$

where Q is total exports of all banana producers.

Within each country, it will be assumed that labor is the only factor of production. For reasons that will be soon become clear, however, it will be desirable to allow for the possibility of an upward-sloping supply curve of bananas. We can do this by imagining that workers differ in their relative aptitude in the banana and corn sectors. Without loss of generality, let us assume that each potential banana republic has a labor force of 1, and that the workers in that labor force are indexed by z. Let $b(z)$ be the productivity of worker z in the banana sector, and $c(z)$ be her productivity in the corn sector. Then we will reorder the workers so that $A(z) = b(z)/c(z)$ is decreasing in z.

Now consider the response of workers to changes in the price. Let p be the internal price of bananas. As we will see, this price will generally be lower than the world price P. A worker will be able to earn an income $pb(z)$ in the banana sector, or $c(z)$ in the corn sector. Clearly, all workers for whom $A(z) > 1/p$ will prefer to grow bananas. It follows that there will be an upward-sloping curve of bananas for each country,

$$p = S(q) \tag{2}$$

where q is an individual country's production.

We assume, however, that a country cannot export bananas without infrastructure. Specifically, let us suppose that there is a minimum size banana dock that must be built at a cost F (in terms of corn) to allow banana export. We assume initially that there is free entry into the provision of docks. We also assume throughout that the equilibrium number of docks is smaller than the number of potential banana exporters.

Market Equilibrium

The first step in characterizing market equilibrium is to note that as long as there are more countries than docks, there will be at most one dock per country. The reason is that an entrepreneur never has any reason to compete for local bananas with another dock when she has the option of opening a dock in virgin territory, with a pure monopsony over the local supply.

The next step is to characterize the position of the dock owners in the banana market. Here there is an important question of the choice of strategy variables. On one side, we might imagine that dock owners simply charge a toll for the right to export. A noncooperative game between the dock owners would then involve a Bertrand-like competition in toll rates per banana. Such a game is of considerable interest, but it also raises some problematic technical issues, and will not be considered here.

Instead, we will view dock owners as active middlemen, United Fruit style. Each dock owner is, of course, a local monopsonist. We will treat her as an active oligopolist on the world market. In particular, I will assume that dock owners play Cournot, with each treating the deliveries of all the others as given.

This leads to the following description of behavior: a dock owner will perceive the marginal cost of bananas to be the domestic price plus the effect of a marginal purchase in raising the price of inframarginal units:

$$MC = p + q(\partial p/\partial q) \tag{3}$$

Similarly, a dock owner will perceive the marginal revenue from banana sales to be the world price, less the effect of increased sales on inframarginal units:

$$MR = P + q(\partial P/\partial Q) \tag{4}$$

In equilibrium, of course, we have

$$MR = MC \tag{5}$$

implying

$$P - p = q(\partial p/\partial q - \partial P/\partial Q)$$

i.e., the wedge between world and domestic prices reflects the combined monopoly and monopsony power of dock owners.

Since all banana-exporting countries are assumed to be identical, they will export identical quantities:

$$Q = nq \tag{6}$$

where n is the number of active exporters, assumed less than m.

Finally, we turn to the question of entry. Ignoring integer constraints, docks will be built until no profits are earned net of fixed cost. Thus our final equilibrium condition is

$$q(P - p) = F \tag{7}$$

Interpreting the Equilibrium

The first point to notice about the market equilibrium implied by equations (1)–(7) is that it has the characteristic new theory combination of determinate aggregates with indeterminate detail. The number of banana exporters n is fixed by underlying factors, as is the per country export q and hence the volume and price of world banana trade. However, *which* countries export bananas is indeterminate. The surprising point is that this indeterminacy occurs even though banana production itself is assumed to be an increasing-cost activity. The reason is, of course, the linkage effect of increasing returns associated with the activity of exporting.

In many of the models considered in recent literature on increasing returns and trade, the indeterminacy does not matter for welfare – the possibly numerous equilibria produce different trade flows but the same distribution of income. In this model, however, the difference between equilibria *does* matter. Those countries that are chosen as the sites of docks gain relative to those that are not.

Figure 16.1 illustrates the situation of a representative banana republic.

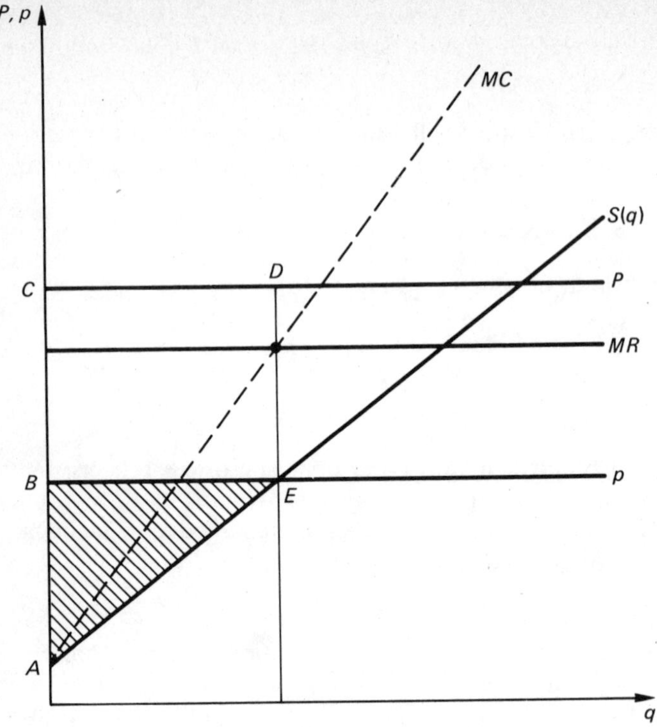

Figure 16.1 Optimal price and quantity for banana exporters

The world price P and the perceived marginal revenue MR are shown as horizontal schedules; in general they will of course be affected by the individual dock owner's actions, but that is not essential to the story. We also show the domestic supply curve $p = S(q)$, and the corresponding marginal cost curve. In equilibrium, the area $BCDE$ would be just equal to the fixed cost F. Thus a dock owner would earn no profit, and would be indifferent between building a dock or not.

The country, however, is not indifferent to the choice. The shaded area ABE represents a producer surplus that the country gains if the dock is constructed. Recalling our production model, this producer surplus takes the form of higher earnings for a part of the population: inframarginal workers end up earning more if the country does export bananas than if it does not. So the accident of who ends up with the docks may be a consequential matter for national welfare.

Strategic Trade Policy

This simple model clearly shows that even small, primary-product exporters can find that they have both an incentive to engage in strategic trade policy and a problem of policing their competition.

The incentive is simply the shaded triangle in figure 16.1. A country can gain if it can insure that it gets a dock. If no other country follows an activist policy, this can be accomplished by offering a small subsidy to the construction of a dock; since firms are otherwise indifferent about which country gets the privilege, even an infinitesimally small subsidy will be sufficient.

From the point of view of other potential banana exporters, however, this is a beggar-thy-neighbor policy. Suppose that they respond in kind. Then a noncooperative subsidy war will clearly lead to the complete dissipation of the gains from exporting. With free entry by dock operators, the benefits of the subsidy war will not be captured as profits. Instead they will be absorbed partly by a proliferation of docks, partly by a fall in the world price. From the point of view of potential banana exporters, it is clear that the game has the structure of a prisoner's dilemma: each country is better off subsidizing, whatever its rivals do, yet the outcome of a subsidy war is to leave everyone no better off and possibly worse off than *laissez-faire*.

This model is clearly even more of a caricature than most of the simple illustrative models that are the staple of new trade theory. I hope, however, that it makes its point. This is that the characteristic issues of new trade theory need not arise only in the context of industrial country trade.

Final Remarks

I have tried to suggest in this paper how the new theory of international trade might be adapted to the special concerns of less developed countries. It is certainly not correct to suppose that the rethinking of international trade that has taken place in recent years applies only to the most advanced countries. The emphasis will necessarily be indifferent, but economies of scale and imperfect competition are probably, if anything, more important for LDCs than for industrial countries.

The main question is not whether the new theory should be applied to LDCs, but what our priorities in research should be. Here I would urge that history not repeat itself. In the initial development of the new trade theory, it was inevitable that purely abstract models led the way. It was necessary to demonstrate the possibility of new ways of explaining trade, and of new ways of thinking about trade policy; and at least at first the liberating effect of that demonstration excused the lack of operational models and real-world applications. As we turn our attention to less developed countries, however, it should not be necessary to demonstrate the *possibility* of unconventional models once again (though I have been somewhat guilty of that here). What we need is operational models that can be applied to real problems. Exactly how this may be done is still unclear: perhaps a mixture of econometrics, computable general equilibrium models, 'calibrated' partial equilibrium models and case-study methods. The point is that it seems unlikely that much can be contributed simply by rewriting the already excessive stock of theoretical new trade papers with a slight Southern hemisphere twist.

And finally, the political economy caution that has been uppermost in the minds of new trade theorists is even more important as the theory moves south. New trade theory offers some subtle arguments for sophisticated government policy, but it could all too easily be used as a cloak for crude protectionism. This is a problem even in the US, where free trade is a powerful ideology. In LDCs the propensity to protect is stronger, there is a long history of wildly uneconomic trade policy and the vested interest in intellectually indefensible trade policy is surely very powerful. Let us try not to allow new trade theory to be used to provide undeserved respectability to bad old trade policies.

REFERENCES

Baldwin, R. and Krugman, P. (1986): 'Market Access and International Competition: A Simulation Study of 16K Random Access Memories', NBER Working Paper no. 1936.

Bhagwati, J. (1965): 'On the Equivalence of Tariffs and Quotas' in R. Baldwin, ed., *Trade, Growth, and the Balance of Payments*, Chicago:Rand-McNally.

Brander, J. and Spencer, B. (1981): 'Tariffs and the Extraction of Foreign Monopoly Rents under Potential Entry', *Canadian Journal of Economics* 14, 371–89.

Brander, J. and Spencer, B. (1983): 'International R&D Rivalry and Industrial Strategy', *Review of Economic Studies* 50, 707–22.

Brander, J. and Spencer, B. (1984): 'Tariff Protection and Imperfect Competition' in H. Kierzkowski, ed., *Monopolistic Competition and International Trade*, Oxford: Oxford University Press.

Brander, J. and Spencer, B. (1985): 'Export Subsidies and International Market Share Rivalry', *Journal of International Economics* 18, 83–100.

Dixit, A. (1985): 'Optimal Trade and Industrial Policy for the US Automobile Industry', mimeo, Princeton University.

Dixit, A. (1986a): 'Trade Policy: An Agenda for Research' in P. Krugman, ed., *Strategic Trade Policy and the New International Economics*, Cambridge: MIT Press.

Dixit, A. (1986b): 'Issues of Strategic Trade Policy for Small Countries', mimeo, Princeton University.

Dixit, A. and Grossman, G. (1984): 'Targeted Export Promotion with Several Oligopolistic Industries', mimeo, Princeton University.

Dixit, A. and Kyle, P. (1985): 'The Use of Protection and Subsidies for Entry Promotion and Deterrence', *American Economic Review* 75, 139–52.

Dixit, A. and Norman, V. (1980): *Theory of International Trade*, Cambridge: Cambridge University Press.

Eastman, H. and Stykolt, S. (1962): 'A Model for the Study of Protected Oligopolies', *Economic Journal* 70, 336–47.

Eaton, J. and Grossman, G. (1986): 'Optimal Trade and Industrial Policy under Oligopoly', *Quarterly Journal of Economics*, May.

Ethier, W. (1982): 'National and International Returns to Scale in the Modern Theory of International Trade', *American Economic Review* 72, 389–405.

Grossman, G. (1986): 'Strategic Export Promotion: A Critique' in P. Krugman, ed., *Strategic Trade Policy and the New International Economics*, Cambridge: MIT Press.

Harris, R. and Cox, D. (1984): *Trade, Industrial Policy, and Canadian Manufacturing*, Toronto: University of Toronto Press.

Helpman, E. (1981): 'International Trade in the Presence of Product Differentiation, Economies of Scale, and Monopolistic Competition: A Chamberlinian–Heckscher–Ohlin Approach', *Journal of International Economics* 11, 305–40.

Helpman, E. and Krugman, P. (1985): *Market Structure and Foreign Trade: Increasing Returns, Imperfect Competition, and the International Economy*, Cambridge: MIT Press.

Johnson, H. (1967): 'International Trade and Monopolistic Competition Theory' in R.E. Kuenne, ed., *Monopolistic Competition Theory*, New York: Wiley.

Krishna, K. (1984): 'Trade Restrictions as Facilitating Practices', mimeo, Harvard University.

Krugman, P. (1979): 'Increasing Returns, Monopolistic Competition, and International Trade', *Journal of International Economics* 9, 469–79.

Krugman, P. (1980): 'Scale Economies, Product Differentiation, and the Pattern of Trade', *American Economic Review* 70, 950–9.

Krugman, P. (1981): 'Intra-industry Specialization and the Gains from Trade', *Journal of Political Economy* 89, 959–73.

Krugman, P. (1984a): 'Import Protection as Export Promotion: International Competition in the Presence of Oligopoly and Economies of Scale' in H. Kierzkowski, ed., *Monopolistic Competition and International Trade*, Oxford: Oxford University Press.

Krugman, P. (1984b): 'The US Response to Foreign Industrial Targeting', *Brookings Papers on Economic Activity* 1:1984, 77–131.

Lancaster, K. (1980): 'Intra-industry Trade under Perfect Monopolistic Competition', *Journal of International Economics* 10, 151–75.

Stewart, F. (1984): 'Recent Theories of International Trade: Some Implications for the South' in H. Kierzkowski, ed., *Monopolistic Competition and International Trade*, Oxford: Oxford University Press.

Venables, A. (1985): 'Trade and Trade Policy with Imperfect Competition: The Case of Identical Products and Free Entry', *Journal of International Economics* 19, 1–19.

Venables, A. and Smith, M.A.M. (1986): 'Trade and Industrial Policy under Imperfect Competition', *Economic Policy* 3.

COMMENT 1

G.K. Helleiner

Carlos Díaz-Alejandro devoted much of his life and work to the translation of what seemed to be sensible and accepted historical and policy propositions in the South into intellectually respectable arguments in the North. He spoke frequently of the frustration and mutual misunderstanding created when experienced and thoughtful Southern policy makers are confronted with young, intellectually vigorous 'modern' (and usually Northern) economists. 'More in sorrow than in anger', as he would sardonically put it, hotshot Northern analysts frequently seem to explain the errors of their ways to unimpressed Southern decision makers: 'Hocus-pocus. Mumbo-jumbo. Therefore you are wrong.' Carlos worked, with a subtle combination of inductive and deductive approaches, historical and institutional knowledge, and policy sense, to build Southern perceptions into forms that Northern academe would understand and perhaps eventually accept. He often saw himself, he said, as 'a lawyer for the South' and he wished there were more of them. Of course, he also worked this process the other way round. He sought to introduce what he saw as the relevant basics of mainstream economics, as developed in the North, into the context of the quite different political and social cultures of the South. As others have said, he was that increasingly rare phenomenon – a civilized and humane economist – and therefore was intensely interested in the relativity of science and the sociology of knowledge. Carlos was a bridge builder. I am not a trained analyst of group behaviour but I can already see, and so can many of you, the effect of his absence upon the social and intellectual dynamics at this very meeting.

I am sure that it was because of his interest in intellectual bridge-building that he welcomed and had such high hopes for 'the new trade theories'. I think he would have liked Paul Krugman's paper very much – not so much because it contains new interpretations of history or new policy conclusions (for, actually, it contains neither) but because of the respectability of the argument in the current Northern intellectual context. The 'new trade theory' has placed scale economies and market imperfections (market power) at *centre* stage when they were previously, particularly in large economies like the US, more like intellectual curiosities. In the developing countries – and, indeed, in small economies more generally (certainly in Canada and, I suspect, in Finland) – scale economies and market power have a much longer history of mainstream trade economists' concern. What has been going on in the 'new' trade theory is a major shift in what large countries' trade theoreticians think is important. *I* like the paper.

Let me divide what I have to say into three parts:

1 comments on scale economies;
2 comments on market imperfections;
3 comments on import substitution policies.

I agree with Paul that both scale economies and market imperfections are probably more important in developing countries than they are in the countries where the 'new theory' is being developed, and that we need more research on these matters in the developing country context.

1. Scale Economies

1 Scale economies in infrastructure are deployed in this paper to explain the substantial, apparently random, degree of specific primary export development as among country locations. Comparative advantage *is* relevant; but Third World economic historians have always known and said that it still leaves a lot to be explained. It will be helpful to them to have analytical backing from the 'new' trade theory.

2 Krugman's emphasis on the importance of scale economies in the exports of small countries, quite apart from the intraindustry trade phenomenon with which the argument has often been linked, is also welcome. Whether the specialized exports developed by smaller countries are recorded as *intra*industry or *inter*industry trade is often purely a matter of statistical definition. It is helpful to cut scale economy arguments loose from these less important statistical matters, as it has been in smaller countries all along. This analysis will no doubt also help large countries better understand why small countries still see the GATT's total *prohibition* of export subsidies (as against mere binding and codification of import barriers) as biassed against them.

3 One is also reminded by this emphasis on scale, though the point is not made in the paper, that economic integration efforts in the developing world were *always* motivated less by competitive efficiency considerations than by the swapping of protection for import-substituting industries enjoying scale economies. Whether they performed as expected is another matter. Scale economies *have* long figured in LDC trade policy in a major way.

4 The current policy makers most likely to identify with the dilemmas (prisoner's type) of strategic trade policy makers in his two-good, one-factor, indivisible infrastructure and monopsony model are probably those seeking to enter world markets for unskilled labour-intensive products. Noncooperative subsidy wars leading to the dissipation of the gains from

exports today loom less large in the banana republics than in the pajama ones. In this case, *domestic* scale economies (docks) have less to do with outcomes, I suspect, than do the scale economies (and other barriers to entry) in *international* transport, storage, information systems and marketing that generate buyer market power. There may be subsidy wars *without* docks. In more detailed modelling it turns out that the degree of internalization of export trade (i.e. foreign ownership) also affects the equilibrium outcome in any individual industry and country.

2. Market Imperfections

Carlos was among those who believe that market structure matters in international exchange. He didn't say that *only* market structure matters or that it *always* matters, but his skepticism of competitive assumptions in the analysis of many financial, commodity and other markets was clear – particularly so in his little (1978) AER article.

Krugman introduces market power to trade policy considerations in three spheres – with respect to (1) circumstances in purely local developing country markets; (2) market power possessed by suppliers of imports to developing countries; (3) market power enjoyed by buyers of developing country exports. Let me consider each in turn.

1 As far as domestic competitive effects of trade policy are concerned it is nowadays insufficient to elaborate the tale only in terms of Bhagwati-style, or, as Krugman aptly suggests, more complex, analyses of import trade. Export quotas and voluntary export restraints also generate quite different consequences according to the assumptions made concerning market structure in the exporting country. It may be tedious, but nonetheless also fruitful, to work out the differential implications of different degrees of competition in trading as opposed to production activities; bilateral as opposed to global import or export quotas; internalized as against arms-length trade; and other such elements of a highly complex reality. Once one leaves the relatively easy competitive assumptions, the potential for – admittedly, rather boring – PhD theses in the 'new' theories is vast.

2 Market power on the part of suppliers of goods and services, and the possibility of extracting monopoly profit for the purchasing country by adroit use of government policy, even in small or developing countries, have a long history. That is, after all, what much of the clamour over relations with foreign investors is all about. Industrial organization approaches to the analysis of transnational corporate activity – whether involving direct investment (which can be thought of as a package of services) or not – have been *de rigeur* for some time now. The services of firm-specific assets owned by foreign firms, on which they earn monopoly profit, are sought by developing country purchasers at minimum prices. Beating the price down is part of a

game that has been analysed in an existing theoretical and empirical literature. It is, at first sight, a little startling to see these business school issues apparently being 'taken over' by the 'new' trade theory. On reflection, though, I think – with Krugman – that they should have been in mainstream trade theory all along.

What Paul has emphasized – moving away from the traditional argument that optimal tariffs are irrelevant for small countries – is the segmentation of national markets, and the possible capacity of sellers both to exercise market power in individual national markets and to price discriminate among them. How important these are is an empirical question. So is the question of whether developing countries do better or worse than others; or whether client states fare better than rebels. It forces us, altogether healthily I think, to consider the structure of *global* markets for individual products – how concentrated they are, what entry barriers there may be, how segmented they are and what the key influences on noncompetitive market price determination really are.

Krugman argues that in the case of foreign monopoly or oligopoly without domestic competition a fixed fee for the right of market access or right of establishment would extract monopoly rent without domestic price increases such as tariffs, which may also do the trick, might engender. Perhaps some state trading and countertrading really *is* rather like this. The fee (rent) is not necessarily collected by the state! Such gains may, however, be largely socialized where negotiations take many weeks in an expensive local hotel. Paul's rationale for consolidated import purchasing begins to blur with that for consolidated 'one-stop' foreign investment screening offices. Such proposals have been around for decades – sometimes extended into proposals for *internationally* coordinated import purchasing and/or screening systems for direct investment and technology imports. There has also been some experience with them. The 'catch' is in a little sentence that he sneaks in just before his policy suggestion: 'Imagine a small country with a highly competent and honest administration.' How many of these are there?

In this context, Carlos would probably want also to remind us of the major role of political influence and power in these matters. In his paper in the Kindleberger volume on direct foreign investment in Latin America, as I recall, he spoke of the important role of gunboats and marines (today there are new instruments of subversion and threat) in bringing recalcitrant governments towards a healthier respect for the need for adequate returns for US firms.

3 Krugman suggests that Brander–Spencer style strategic export subsidies (or, on some assumptions, taxes) may seem a little far-fetched for many small developing countries. The credibility of their threats *is* small. On the other hand, if a world market that can be efficiently supplied from a number of developing country sources is itself limited, e.g. by Northern global quotas or inelastic demand, strategic export policies may well govern intercountry distribution among these countries themselves. Threats to one

another may be credible enough. And we are back to the danger of export subsidy wars.

Market power issues *are* certainly found on the buying side of developing countries' exports. There must be important barriers to entry, some of which, as Krugman notes, relate to scale economies in downstream activity, in many primary commodity markets – else why, for instance, do the banana and bauxite markets look like they do? (Carlos used to ask where they were!) For all their faults, export marketing boards *did* have a rationale.

3. Import Substitution

Paul Krugman still thinks rather little of import substitution. He has previously shown, in the spirit of the 'new' approaches, that protection against imports may serve as a subsidy ('a springboard') for exports, and there are empirical examples of this phenomenon. He now rather overstates, I think, the unimportance of such policy in developing countries. He states (p.358), 'The privileged access of domestic firms to the home market can only be a significant strategic asset if the home market is large enough to matter.' Right. He then resumes – 'Yet this can hardly ever be the case for LDCs, none of which account for more than 2 or 3 per cent of the world demand for any manufactured good.' This is surely both theoretically and empirically wrong – theoretically, because of the high potential for product differentiation (the conventional argument for small country specialization) and the potentially large relative role of domestic sales for individual risk-averse firms, and empirically, because Korea has evidently successfully been doing it. I cannot resist adding that many analysts of import substitution and virtually all economic historians would still deliver a Scotch verdict (i.e. unproven) on the inevitability of national losses from import substitution. That doesn't make them advocates, certainly not advocates of doing it badly. It just makes them more humble.

I spoke earlier of Third World and small country intellectual currents that had differed from those in the so-called 'mainstream'. The reason that I especially like this paper is that it helps to bridge the very sort of intellectual gap that Carlos tried to bridge. It helps to widen the 'mainstream'. I hope that our host institution, WIDER, will take up Paul's implicit challenge and help to develop some of the more empirical and operationally oriented research that he recommends.

COMMENT 2

Ronald W. Jones

New Trade Theory and the Less Developed Countries

Paul Krugman has put forward the argument that some of the recent advances in trade theory, especially those dealing with imperfect markets and economies of scale, are of relevance to less developed countries even though most existing work seems tied to problems of larger, wealthier developed economies. I find little with which to disagree in his clear survey of the issues. Indeed, I find his claims to be rather modest. I think I would be tempted to argue more strongly that the assumptions which characterize what he calls the 'new trade theory' are if anything more applicable to LDCs then to advanced economies.

To the extent that the new theory attempts to provide a rationale for the large volume of intraindustry trade it may appear to be addressed primarily to trade among Western European countries, North America and Japan. But, as Krugman stresses, the phenomenon of increasing returns may apply to less developed countries even if primarily in the background role of providing infrastructure or intermediate inputs to traditional primary productive activity. It is with respect to the importance of imperfect competition that I think Krugman has undersold his product.

An almost uniform characteristic of LDCs is their small size – especially in terms of produced income. Any nation has a set of regulations and controls that helps to isolate that region and its economic participants from the competitive pressures in the rest of the world. The complexity and restrictiveness of such regulations generally do not increase in proportion to the size of a country so that, in parlance borrowed from more traditional trade theory, one might characterize LDCs as regulation-abundant compared with private economic activity relative to advanced countries. The necessity of analyzing economic behaviour among small numbers of participants, with the imperfections in markets characteristic in such a setting, seems especially clear for less developed regions. As well, new analysis concerning the interaction of private groups and government needs to be developed. Krugman stresses the role of government in providing a credible basis for expansion of domestic oligopolists in world markets. This may be merely the thin edge of the wedge. There are a number of other ways in which firms and government interact in arriving at regulations and controls which spill over to affect a region's trade pattern. I suspect that new trade theory, which has borrowed extensively from the field of industrial organization, could also make use of recent developments in social choice theory and political science in modelling endogenous policy formation. Some work along these lines by Krueger, Bhagwati, Mayer and Brock and Magee has already appeared. My point is that small numbers of private agents and relatively heavy intrusion of government regulations make the traditional assumption of large, competitive markets *prima facie* less relevant for LDCs than for advanced economies.

One of the points clearly put forth by Krugman with which I concur is the distinction between the use of commercial policy to improve a country's terms of trade and the use of such policy to extract rents from foreign firms. According to traditional theory, small countries cannot influence their terms of trade by using tariffs and quotas, thus removing the main rationale for an activist trade policy. To the extent that foreign suppliers are imperfectly competitive, however, and earn rents selling in the local market, the small country may be able to capture some of these rents by use of a tariff. In one case the small country cannot improve its terms of trade, in the other it can.

The latter possibility, that rents earned by an imperfectly competitive supplier can at least in part be taxed away, seems to depend upon the ability to discriminate among markets. Krugman puts forth the analogy of oligopolistic sellers in domestic markets who are willing to bargain with various buyers in order occasionally to sell below market price. The danger for such sellers is that these buyers might turn around to sell to others at below market price if markets cannot be kept separate. This is less likely to occur in the case in which countries levy a duty on goods obtained from a foreign monopolistic supplier.The instruments of commercial policy serve to *create* a separation of markets in which price discrimination can take place. A tariff which lowers the net price paid by a country typically raises the domestic price paid by any local resident; domestic purchasers are not in a position to spoil the market by reselling. An exception, of course, must be made if duties paid can be reimbursed if a good is re-exported.

Krugman seems sensitive to the charge that recent developments in trade theory based on increasing returns and imperfect competition provide a basis for a new protectionism. In his paper Krugman states, 'Import substituting industrialization looks even worse in the new theory than in standard theory.' If small countries can levy tariffs and improve their terms of trade by expropriating rents from foreign imperfect competitors, they are at the same time encouraging domestic import substitution. Contrary to Krugman's assertion, the assumptions of the new theory appear to provide an invitation for active commercial policy on the part of small LDCs.

One of the standard arguments for protecting an industry in a small LDC is the infant-industry argument. A modern variation on this theme is Krugman's 'import protection as export promotion.' As he observes, this requires not only economies of scale (internal to the firm in his case), but a sufficiently large domestic market. The latter is typically not available in LDCs so that, he argues, this line of support for commercial policies for LDCs is less relevant than it is to larger economies. However, tax agreements whereby host countries often get first crack at incomes generated by productive activities suggest an alternative type of commercial policy which by-passes the need for a large domestic market. Subsidies can be used to attract foreign producers to a country's shores, not to supply the domestic market but to produce for the world market. The resulting world allocation of resources would reflect a blend of strategic trade policies as featured in the 'new trade theory' and the differential pull of national productivity. The latter, as analyzed in other recent work in trade theory, would involve both the standard ingredients of comparative advantage for factors trapped within national frontiers and the relative attractiveness (as measured by differences in absolute advantage) of countries as competitors for internationally mobile factors.

Elements of the new theory blend in other ways with more traditional concerns. Some of the bold conclusions of the new theory, e.g. the use of industrial targeting to promote an oligopolistic sector in foreign markets, have been criticized by Dixit and Grossman. They demonstrate how adding just a few extra firms may substantially alter the results: a subsidy to one firm may be wiped out by increased costs to other firms, e.g. if they use in common some resource fixed in supply (skilled technical personnel in their case). One traditional characteristic of standard trade theory has been its concern with simple general equilibrium models in which the effects of disturbances in one sector can be traced throughout the economy. The pattern typically revealed when one sector benefits by technical progress, resource discoveries or externally based price rises is that some other sectors are made worse off. This is the Dutch disease, a more modern manifestation of the doctrine of comparative advantage. Even in settings heavily infected by imperfect competition, artificial moves aimed at helping one sector may be balanced by induced deterioration in others. The division between 'new' and 'traditional' trade theory may not be that pronounced.

Finally, let me add a few remarks about Krugman's mini-model of banana republics faced with the problem of requiring docks before their produce can be exported to world markets. In each potential exporting country two commodities, corn and bananas, can be produced, under conditions of increasing costs. Bananas are not consumed locally, and therefore are of no use unless they can be exported. This requires the construction of a dock of minimum (and fixed) size, which can be provided by dock owners at given cost in corn units, F. It is assumed that there are more countries (each identical in size and conditions of production) than the equilibrium number of docks. Dock owners have potential monopsony power in buying up bananas in any country, while facing together a downward-sloping world market demand curve for bananas. In providing bananas for the world market dock owners are assumed to be Cournot-type oligopolists, aware of the downward pressure on market price which increased sales from a single dock entails, but expecting other dock owners to keep their sales unchanged. There is assumed to be free entry into the provision of docks, so that profits to dock owners from their exercise of joint monopsony and oligopoly powers are driven down to zero.

As Krugman notes, such an equilibrium leaves some countries without docks, and these countries are worse off than those which have obtained docks and export bananas. The type of diagram commonly used in standard trade theory to illustrate production possibilities and prices can be utilized to illustrate the position of a country which has obtained a dock. The transformation schedule captures the assumption that bananas are produced subject to increasing costs. Production takes place at point C. The slope of tangent line BC reflects the relative price of bananas before they are exported, p. The steeper line, DC, represents the price of bananas to world consumers, P. If entry of potential dock owners drives the amount paid for the use of dock facilities down to the level of fixed costs, F, distance BD represents this value. Consumers in the country are only interested in the quantity of corn available. Distance AB denotes the gain to such consumers from being located in a country possessing one of the few docks required in the banana trade. This is what Krugman refers to as producer surplus.

If the government of this country pays a fixed amount, BD, for the use of the dock, it might be tempted to expand production and exports of bananas if it ignored the effect on world prices. For example, production at E would in such an event increase the country's surplus. However, such action, especially if followed by action in other countries, would depress the world price of bananas. Banana producers would nevertheless be tempted to expand production beyond the point which maximizes returns to dock owners since the latter are exercising monopsony power. A solution whereby competition among dock owners keeps their returns equal to fixed cost, F, and those countries with docks act as Cournot oligopolists and set perceived marginal revenue equal to the cost of producing bananas, p, entails larger output for each country with a dock but fewer such countries. When dock owners possessed monopsony powers, they acted so as to spread output over a larger number of countries and curtail output in any single country.

Although competition among dock owners might keep their returns down to cost, it is difficult to conceive of an equilibrium in which some countries gain while others, with identical cost conditions, do without. As Krugman suggests, subsidies paid to attract dock facilities could wipe out gains for all. An alternative route would involve collusion among all potential banana republics, an OBEC if you will (Bananas instead of Petroleum). Such a solution replaces the Cournot-type of myopia concerning other producers' reaction to own output increases with a single profit-maximizing strategy. Some redistribution scheme would be required to keep nonproducers from attempting to obtain docks. In this sense OBEC would consist largely, if not primarily, of countries not producing bananas. World output of bananas would fall short of Krugman's oligopolistic solution and I think it is an open question whether an average OBEC member's profits would exceed the producer's surplus *BA* for a country which happens to possess dock facilities in Krugman's solution. In any case, the OBEC route offers banana republics a return that in order scenarios is competed away.

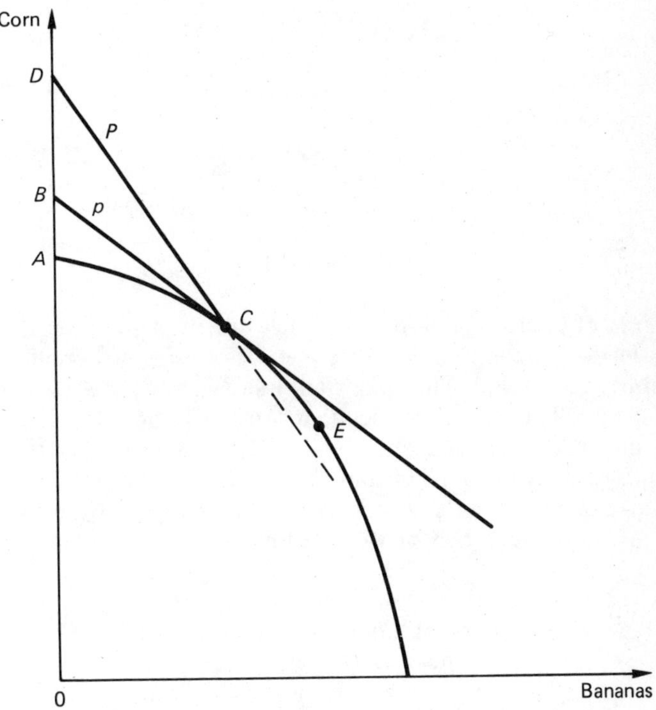

Figure 16C.1 General equilibrium solution of Krugman model

17

Policy-Induced Inflows of Foreign Capital in the Presence of Rigid-Wage Unemployment

Richard A. Brecher

1. Introduction

In the theory of international trade and investment, a great deal of attention has been devoted to the welfare consequences of using tariff policy to attract inflows of foreign capital. This important issue was analysed in a pioneering paper by Mundell (1957),[1] in subsequent work of Bhagwati (1973), Hamada (1974), Minabe (1974)[2] and Brecher and Díaz-Alejandro (1977), and in more recent studies by Brecher and Findlay (1983), Srinivasan (1983) and Jones (1984), among others. A central theme emerging from much of this literature is the serious risk of welfare loss from tariff-induced inflows of capital from abroad.[3]

Most (if not all) of the theoretical work on this topic has dealt with flexible-wage full-employment models.[4] In national debates about economic policy, however, a key benefit of foreign investment is supposed to be its impact on domestic unemployment. In this regard, the existing theory is not closely tailored to the concerns of policy makers.

To address these concerns, the present paper follows Brecher (1974a, 1974b) in allowing for unemployment caused by a real wage floor that is institutionally imposed throughout the entire labour market of the home economy, within a two-country, two-good, two-factor model of a world engaged in free international exchange of goods.[5] This model is then extended to permit unrestricted capital movements across national borders. Once the minimum-wage model of international trade and investment has been outlined in section 2, the employment and welfare consequences of using trade policy to generate capital inflows (or outflows) are analysed in section 3. Then, in section 4, we explore the use instead of subsidies on foreign investment itself, as an alternative (more direct) policy for generating capital flows between countries. Next, allowing simultaneous taxes (subsidies) on international movements of both goods and capital, section 5 determines the optimal policy package for the home country. Some concluding remarks are offered in section 6.

2. The Basic Model

Let us begin with the standard Heckscher–Ohlin–Samuelson model of a trading world with two 'large' countries that produce two consumer goods using two primary factors. Both the home and foreign economies have fixed endowments of capital and labour, which are perfectly mobile domestically but completely immobile internationally. The capital/labour endowment ratio is smaller at home than abroad. The two countries, however, have the same technology for goods X and Y that are produced under constant returns to scale, with the former good being capital intensive relative to the latter at any wage/rental ratio in common. Producers maximize profits while consumers maximize utility in a world characterized by perfect competition and no externalities.

To the entire labour market of the home economy, now add a real wage floor of $\bar{w}$ units in terms of (say) good Y. Assuming that this minimum wage rate is institutionally set above the full-employment level, we generate some home-country unemployment, which prevents the wage from rising above the floor. In view of Samuelson's (1949) well-known one-to-one correspondence between product and factor prices, the relative price of good X (in terms of Y) within the home country remains fixed at (say) $\bar{p}$ and the real rental rate of capital at home stays correspondingly constant at $\bar{r}$ (in terms of good Y), given that home production is assumed to be incompletely specialized at all times. As we know from Brecher (1974a, 1974b), moreover, the product-transformation and trade-offer curves of the minimum-wage economy are both linear in the region of incomplete specialization, with total labour employment being positively (negatively) related to home output and excess supply of the labour-intensive (capital-intensive) good. Thus, assuming free international trade, we see that any excess world supply in the market for good Y (X) is cleared by a fall (rise) in home employment at constant prices.

Free trade, furthermore, ensures equality between the home product-price ratio (fixed at $\bar{p}$) and its foreign counterpart, denoted p^*. Thus, from the factor–price equalization theorem, we also have equality between the home wage and rental rates ($\bar{w}$ and $\bar{r}$) on the one hand and their foreign counterparts w^* and r^* on the other, assuming that foreign production is also diversified at the outset. In other words, the wage floor in the home economy uniquely fixes relative product prices and real factor rewards for the world as a whole.

Now let capital become perfectly mobile internationally. Since the home and foreign rental rates are equal simply because of free trade in goods, capital is indifferent between flowing from and remaining in its country of origin.[6] This factor's world distribution needed to clear international product markets, moreover, is indeterminate: at fixed prices (and constant employment of labour), shifting a unit of capital from one economy to the other would not lead to any imbalance in world markets, as we know from Mundell's (1957) reasoning. Since such a shift leads to no commodity-market disequilibrium, there would be no change in the level of home employment. Thus, all equilibrium distributions of the world's capital stock imply the same degree of (home) unemployment and a unique level of welfare for each country.

Without loss of generality, assume that the *laissez-faire* equilibrium is characterized by no actual movement of capital, and that we obtain the Heckscher–Ohlin pattern of trade with the relatively labour-abundant home economy exporting the labour-intensive good. International capital movements, however, will be induced by the various taxes and subsidies analysed below.

3. Trade Policy

Suppose now that the home government imposes a tariff on imports of good X, thereby creating a wedge between the home and foreign prices of this good. Since the home price ratio is fixed at $\bar{p}$ by the minimum wage, p^* must therefore fall by the amount of the tariff. Thus, in view of the Stolper–Samuelson theorem, there is a corresponding decline in the foreign rental rate on capital. With r^* less than $\bar{r}$ for this reason, we begin to have a rise in K, which denotes the net flow of capital services from the foreign to the home country.

To determine the resulting tariff-induced equilibrium, it is convenient to return temporarily to free trade with no actual movement of capital, and then proceed via the following comparative-static decomposition into two conceptual stages. First, before the tariff is imposed, let the (indeterminate) level of foreign investment in the home country be exogenously increased to the point at which home imports of good X have fallen (in view of the Rybczynski theorem) to zero. As we saw above, adopting such a level of investment under free trade has no impact on prices, employment or welfare. Second, levy the tariff, which clearly has no effects since it is imposed on a zero level of imports. This conclusion for the minimum-wage economy is a straightforward extension of a full-employment result obtained by Mundell (1957).

A further inflow of capital with some significant consequences, however, can be generated by adding also a home subsidy on *exports* of good X. Given $\bar{p}$, p^* falls by the amount of this subsidy, thereby pushing r^* below $\bar{r}$ as before. The resultant inflow of capital cannot cease as long as both countries are incompletely specialized, since the rental rate in each country would remain constant as would the positive difference $\bar{r} - r^*$. Since we are assuming that home production stays diversified, the foreign economy must eventually become completely specialized. Because capital is leaving for the home country, moreover, it is the capital-intensive good X that is no longer produced by the foreign country, in view of the Rybczynski theorem.

To determine the resulting equilibrium level of foreign investment, it is convenient to return temporarily to free trade but let the (indeterminate) level of K be arbitrarily set at $\bar{K}$, which denotes the minimum capital flow needed to extinguish foreign production of good X. Given $\bar{K}$, the rental rate of capital is still equalized internationally, but any further inflow of this factor would raise r^* above $\bar{r}$ by the Law of Diminishing Marginal Productivity. Thus, $\bar{K}$ is the only level of capital inflow consistent with equilibrium.

To determine the export subsidy's impact on employment and welfare, we therefore start with free trade and assume (without loss of generality) a capital inflow of $\bar{K}$, which will not be affected by the policy action. Our basic model can thus be stated as follows, given the conventional assumption that the subsidy is financed in lump-sum fashion:

$$e(\bar{p}, u) = g(\bar{p}, \bar{K}, L) - \bar{r}\bar{K} + sx(\bar{p}, u, \bar{K}, L) \tag{1}$$

$$e^*(\bar{p} - s, u^*) = g^*(\bar{p} - s, \bar{K}) + \bar{r}\bar{K} \tag{2}$$

$$x(\bar{p}, u, \bar{K}, L) + x^*(\bar{p} - s, u^*, \bar{K}) = 0 \tag{3}$$

where s is the specific subsidy (in terms of good Y) imposed on home exports of good X, and hence $p^* = \bar{p} - s$; u is the level of home welfare; L is the level of home employment; e, g and x respectively are the home country's expenditure function, revenue function and compensated excess-demand function for good X;[7] and asterisks indicate the corresponding symbols of the foreign country.[8]

Taking total differentials in equations (1) through (3), we find that

$$\begin{bmatrix} -\bar{w} - sx_L & 1 - sx_u & 0 \\ 0 & 0 & 1 \\ x_L & x_u & x_u^* \end{bmatrix} \begin{bmatrix} \mathrm{d}L \\ \mathrm{d}u \\ \mathrm{d}u^* \end{bmatrix} = \begin{bmatrix} x \\ x^* \\ x_p^* \end{bmatrix} \mathrm{d}s \tag{4}$$

where subscripts of a function indicate partial derivatives (e.g. $x_u \equiv \partial x / \partial u$ and $x_u^* \equiv \partial x^* / \partial u^*$); $e_u = e_u^* = 1$ at the initial position, because marginal utilities there are set at unity, without loss of generality; and we have used the well-known properties that $e_p^* - g_p^* = x^*$ and $g_L = \bar{w}$.

Using Cramer's Rule, we can solve equation (4) to find that

$$\begin{bmatrix} \mathrm{d}L \\ \mathrm{d}u \\ \mathrm{d}u^* \end{bmatrix} (x_L + \bar{w}x_u) = \begin{bmatrix} (1 - sx_u)\tilde{x}_p^* - xx_u \\ (\bar{w} + sx_L)\tilde{x}_p^* + xx_L \\ (x_L + \bar{w}x_u)x^* \end{bmatrix} \mathrm{d}s \tag{5}$$

where the uncompensated import-demand function for good X in the foreign country is $\tilde{x}^*(\bar{p} - s, \bar{K}) \equiv x^*\{\bar{p} - s, v^*(\bar{p} - s, \bar{K}), \bar{K}\}$, with $v^*(\bar{p} - s, \bar{K})$ being a type of indirect utility function obtained by solving for u^* in equation (2); and $\tilde{x}_p^* = x_p^* - x^*x_u^*$ from the Slutsky decomposition.

To investigate the effects of a 'small' subsidy,[9] we may set $s = 0$ in equation (5), thereby obtaining

$$\frac{dL}{ds} = \frac{(\tilde{x}_p^* - xx_u)}{(x_L + \bar{w}x_u)} \tag{6}$$

$$\frac{du}{ds} = \frac{(\bar{w}\tilde{x}_p^* + xx_L)}{(x_L + \bar{w}x_u)} \tag{7}$$

$$\frac{du^*}{ds} = x^* \tag{8}$$

When considering these equations, note that: $x = -x^* < 0$, since the home economy is exporting good X; $x_u > 0$, because we assume that neither good is inferior in home consumption; $\tilde{x}_p^* < 0$, given a well-behaved offer curve for the foreign country; and $0 < x_L$, which is simply minus the Rybczynski effect that a labour employment increase has on home production of good X.

As we can see from equation (6), $dL/ds \gtreqless 0$ as $m - \eta^* \gtreqless 0$, where $\eta^* \equiv -p^*\tilde{x}_p^*/x^*$, which is the uncompensated price elasticity of foreign import demand for good X; $m \equiv \bar{p}x_u/e_u$, which is the home country's marginal propensity to consume this good; and, at the initial equilibrium, $p^* = \bar{p}$ (since $s = 0$ there) and $e_u = 1$ (as assumed above). In other words, the subsidy raises employment if and only if we satisfy the well-known condition for the Metzler Paradox in the traditional flexible-wage model without international capital mobility.[10] This condition in the traditional model would ensure that a subsidy on exports of good X paradoxically lowers the home relative price of this product, by creating an excess world demand for good Y at constant home prices. In the present minimum-wage model, however, this excess demand for the labour-intensive good would raise employment instead.[11] If the Metzler Condition is considered to characterize the 'perverse' case, then the subsidy-induced inflow of foreign capital would 'normally' be expected to accompany a reduction in home employment.

Although the subsidy's impact on employment cannot be unambiguously signed, we immediately see from equation (7) that $du/ds < 0$. Thus, even if the subsidy leads to an expansion in employment, this possible benefit is never large enough to offset the subsidy-induced deterioration in the terms of trade. In other words, the overall result of this policy is a decline in national welfare of the home country.

From equation (8), however, we know that $du^*/ds > 0$. This necessary improvement in the foreign country's welfare is not surprising, since the subsidy simply improves this country's terms of trade.

Because a subsidy to induce a capital inflow causes an unambiguous deterioration in home welfare and normally leads to a decline in employment, a natural question to ask is whether the minimum-wage economy can gain from trade policy designed to generate an *outflow* of capital. The simplest way to explore this question, without having to replace the foregoing set of equations (1) through (8), is to let X (instead of Y) be the labour-intensive good that the home country is initially exporting in the *laissez-faire* equilibrium. A subsidy on exports of good X reduces the relative foreign price of this product below $\bar{p}$ to $\bar{p} - s$ as before; but this reduction now pushes r^* above $\bar{r}$ (given the assumed change in relative factor intensities of the two goods), thereby attracting home capital into the foreign country. Thus, K is now negative at its equilibrium level $\bar{K}$. At the same time, the Rybczynski effect $- x_L$ becomes positive (under the new factor-intensity ranking), and the expression $x_L + \bar{w}x_u$ is correspondingly negative.[12]

Under these circumstances, equation (6) can be manipulated (in essentially the same way as before) to show that $\mathrm{d}L/\mathrm{d}s \gtreqless 0$ as $\eta^* - m \gtreqless 0$. Thus, in contrast to our previous case, a rise in employment is the normal result of subjecting exports to a subsidy that generates an outflow of home capital.

As might therefore be surmised, this subsidy may now raise home welfare. Since the numerator of equation (7) is equivalent to $-(\bar{w}\eta^* + \bar{p}x_L)x^*/\bar{p}$, we would have $\mathrm{d}u/\mathrm{d}s > 0$ if (for example) the foreign offer curve is sufficiently elastic (i.e. η^* is sufficiently large).

At the same time, in view of equation (8), $\mathrm{d}u^*/\mathrm{d}s > 0$ as before. In other words, an export subsidy imposed by the home government always raises foreign welfare, regardless of the relative factor intensity of home exports and irrespective of the direction of subsidy-induced movements of capital.

As the above results suggest, using trade policy to attract foreign capital is always welfare-inferior and normally employment-inferior to a *laissez-faire* strategy. Ironically, moreover, we saw that there are normally employment gains and possibly welfare improvements to be had from a trade subsidy that induces an outflow of capital from the minimum-wage economy. Under either the inflow-attracting or outflow-generating policy, however, the foreign country benefits unambiguously.

4. Subsidizing Foreign Investment

Suppose instead that the home government implements a subsidy on inflows of foreign capital, while pursuing free international trade in goods. When this subsidy is added to $\bar{r}$, the total return to foreign capital inflows exceeds r^* (still equal to $\bar{r}$ since $p^* = \bar{p}$). As before, the resultant inflows must eventually lead one country to specialize completely in production. Once again, we assume that the foreign country ceases to produce the capital-intensive good X, while home production remains diversified.

In equilibrium, we must have $\bar{r} + \sigma = r^*$, where σ is the specific subsidy (in terms of good Y) on inflows of foreign capital. This equality implies that K is a monotonic increasing function $k(\sigma)$ of σ, since the Law of Diminishing Marginal Productivity ensures that r^* is a monotonic decreasing function of the quantity of capital utilized within the foreign economy. Thus, our basic model can be respecified as follows:

$$e(\bar{p}, u) = g\{\bar{p}, k(\sigma), L\} - (\bar{r} + \sigma)k(\sigma) \tag{9}$$

$$e^*(\bar{p}, u^*) = g^*\{\bar{p}, k(\sigma)\} + (\bar{r} + \sigma)k(\sigma) \tag{10}$$

$$x\{\bar{p}, u, k(\sigma), L\} + x^*\{\bar{p}, u^*, k(\sigma)\} = 0 \tag{11}$$

Taking total differentials in these three equations, while recalling that foreign output of good X remains constant at zero (in which case $x_K^* = 0$), we find that

$$\begin{bmatrix} -\bar{w} & 1 & 0 \\ 0 & 0 & 1 \\ x_L & x_u & x_u^* \end{bmatrix} \begin{bmatrix} dL \\ du \\ du^* \end{bmatrix} = \begin{bmatrix} -k - \sigma k' \\ k \\ -x_K k' \end{bmatrix} d\sigma \tag{12}$$

where $k' \equiv dk/d\sigma$. Equation (12) can be solved by Cramer's Rule to obtain

$$\begin{bmatrix} dL \\ du \\ du^* \end{bmatrix} (x_L + \bar{w}x_u) = \begin{bmatrix} (k + \sigma k')x_u - kx_u^* - x_K k' \\ -(k + \sigma k')x_L - \bar{w}(kx_u^* + x_K k') \\ (x_L + \bar{w}x_u)k \end{bmatrix} d\sigma \tag{13}$$

To investigate the effects of a small subsidy,[13] set $\sigma = 0$ in equation (13), which thus gives

$$\frac{dL}{d\sigma} = \frac{\{(x_u - x_u^*)k - x_K k'\}}{(x_L + \bar{w}x_u)} \tag{14}$$

$$\frac{du}{d\sigma} = \frac{-\{(x_L + \bar{w}x_u^*)k + \bar{w}x_K k'\}}{(x_L + \bar{w}x_u)} \tag{15}$$

$$\frac{du^*}{d\sigma} = k \tag{16}$$

Note that $k' > 0$, since K is a monotonic increasing function of σ; and $x_K < 0$ by the Rybczynski theorem.

If $x_u > x_u^*$ in equation (14), then $dL/d\sigma > 0$. In this case, the subsidy payments transferred from the home to the foreign country tend to create an excess world supply equal to $(x_u - x_u^*)k$ in the market for good X, because the marginal propensity to consume this good is lower in the (transfer-receiving) foreign economy than in the (transfer-giving) home country. This excess supply is increased by the amount $-x_K k'$, due to the subsidy-induced inflow of capital. To clear the world market for good X, we thus need a rise in employment. Alternatively, if $x_u < x_u^*$, there might be an excess world demand for this good, requiring a fall in employment. The present possibility of a rise in employment does not appear to be associated with any obviously paradoxical condition, in contrast to what we saw in the case of an export subsidy that induced an inflow of foreign capital within the previous section.

According to equation (15), the sign of $du/d\sigma$ cannot be unambiguously determined. Intuitively, although the subsidy payments to foreign capital detract from home income, employment may rise for reasons discussed above. Thus, unlike the subsidy on exports of the capital-intensive good in the previous section, the present subsidy on foreign investment may indeed raise home welfare.

In view of equation (16), $\mathrm{d}u^*/\mathrm{d}\sigma > 0$. From the foreign perspective, the home country's subsidy is simply a transfer payment, whose size depends on the amount of foreign capital invested at home. Thus, as in the previous section, the foreign country can only gain from the home subsidy.

If a subsidy is put instead on outflows of home capital, we end up having k negative with foreign specialization complete in the capital-intensive good. To analyse this scenario without replacing equations (9) through (16), simply let σ now be negative (so that a fall in it represents a rise in the subsidy), and respecify Y again as the relatively capital-intensive good (so that r^* is still capital's marginal product in the industry operating abroad). Given the respecified factor-intensity ranking, $x_L + \bar{w}x_u$ becomes negative as before, x_K reverses its sign to become positive in view of the Rybczynski theorem and $x_L + \bar{w}x_u^*$ is now negative.[14] Note, however, that k' remains positive.

Thus, if $x_u > x_u^*$ in equation (14), then $\mathrm{d}L/\mathrm{d}(-\sigma) < 0$, meaning that the subsidy now lowers employment in contrast to what happens under the opposite factor-intensity ranking. On the other hand, when $x_u < x_u^*$, the subsidy-induced change in employment is ambiguous in sign as before.

From equation (15), we see that $\mathrm{d}u/\mathrm{d}(-\sigma) < 0$, meaning that the subsidy must diminish home welfare. Intuitively, this policy lowers r^* below $\bar{r}$ and hence reduces the repatriation of earnings by the initial stock of capital invested abroad. Evidently, this negative impact on welfare must outweigh any possible gain in employment. The present unambiguous conclusion regarding the subsidy-induced change in home welfare contrasts with the (ambiguous) result obtained under the previous factor-intensity ranking.

From the viewpoint of the foreign country, however, the subsidy is beneficial as before. As we can see from equation (16), $\mathrm{d}u^*/\mathrm{d}(-\sigma) > 0$.

Thus, in comparing subsidies on foreign investment with those on international trade, we observe some differences and some similarities. As far as employment is concerned, the effects of a trade subsidy normally depend only on whether capital flows in or out, whereas the same thing cannot be said for an investment subsidy (if $x_u < x_u^*$). Regarding home welfare, the effect is negative or ambiguous when an inflow of foreign capital results from a subsidy on international trade or investment, respectively; but these conclusions must be interchanged when the subsidies induce outflows of home capital. In the case of foreign welfare, however, either type of subsidy has a positive impact, regardless of the direction in which capital is induced to move.

5. Optimal Policy

Let us now examine how taxes (subsidies) on international trade and investment can be simultaneously chosen to provide the minimum-wage country with its highest attainable level of welfare. (As we shall see, a third instrument will also be part of the optimal policy package.) Once again, home production will be assumed to remain diversified, whereas the foreign economy at the policy-induced equilibrium will produce only good Y and hence import X. For the sake of concreteness, moreover, our analysis will focus on the case in which X is the relatively capital-intensive good and the optimal flow of capital is from the foreign to the home country, although the discussion could be readily adapted for other circumstances.

The policy problem for the home government is to maximize $U(C_x, C_y)$ by choosing Q_x, p^* and K subject to the following constraints:

$$C_x = Q_x - \tilde{x}^*(p^*, K) \tag{17}$$

$$C_y = [\alpha(1 + K) - \beta Q_x] + p^*\tilde{x}^*(p^*, K) - R(K)K \tag{18}$$

where U is the home country's social welfare function, assumed to be strictly quasi-concave with positive marginal utilities; C_x and C_y are the home consumption levels of goods X and Y, respectively; Q_x is home output of good X; r^* may be expressed as a monotonic increasing function $R(K)$ of K, for reasons given above; the home endowment of capital is set equal to 1 by choice of units; α represents the average product of capital in producing good Y at home; and β is the ratio of α to the average product of capital in good X within the home economy. As we know from Brecher (1974b), the expression in square brackets on the right-hand side of equation (18) gives the output of good Y along the minimum-wage product-transformation curve, which is a Rybczynski line (for changes in labour employment) whose intercept (α) and slope (β) are fixed by $\bar{w}$.

The first-order conditions for this maximization may be expressed as follows:

$$q = \beta \tag{19}$$

$$q - p^* = \frac{x^*}{\tilde{x}_p^*} \tag{20}$$

$$\alpha - r^* = [1 - (q - p^*)x_u^*]KR' \tag{21}$$

where $q \equiv U_x/U_y$, which gives the consumer price ratio at home; R' ($\equiv \mathrm{d}R/\mathrm{d}K$) > 0, since R is a monotonic increasing function of K; and, in view of Kemp's (1966) calculations, $\tilde{x}_K^* = x_u^*KR'$ since we now set $e_u^* = 1$ at the optimal (rather than initial) equilibrium. Recall, moreover, that $\tilde{x}_p^* < 0$, $x^* > 0$ and $K > 0$ under present assumptions. An examination of equations (19) through (21) will now enable us to characterize the optimal policy package.

The Rybczynski line for labour is known to be steeper than the domestic price line for producers, when goods X (capital-intensive) and Y (labour-intensive) are measured on the horizontal and vertical axes, respectively. In other words, $\beta > \overline{p}$. This inequality and equation (19) imply that $q > \overline{p}$. Thus, the optimal equilibrium requires a tax (equal to $q - \overline{p} > 0$) on production of good X.

From equation (20), $q < p^*$. Thus, we need also an optimal tax (of $p^* - q > 0$) on exports of good X. This call for a tax (rather than subsidy) on trade holds as well for the full-employment case analysed previously by Kemp (1966) and Jones (1967) and more recently by Brecher (1983) and Brecher and Feenstra (1983).

Given equation (21), $\overline{r} - r^*$ is equivalent to $\overline{r} - \alpha + [1 - (q - p^*)x_u^*]KR'$. In this expression $\overline{r} - \alpha < 0$, because the average exceeds the marginal product of capital, whereas $[1 - (q - p^*)x_u^*]KR' > 0$, since q falls short of p^* as we derived above. Thus, $\overline{r} - r^*$ is ambiguous in sign, implying that the optimal policy towards foreign investment may be either a tax (equalling $\overline{r} - r^* > 0$) or a subsidy (of $r^* - \overline{r} > 0$) on inflows of capital from abroad. This ambiguity does not apply to the full-employment case, in which foreign investment should be taxed under our assumption about specialization abroad.[15]

It is worth remarking also that the optimal policy package for a full-employment economy involves the simultaneous application of only two instruments, as opposed to the three required in the minimum-wage case. The extra policy in the presence of the wage floor is needed to eliminate the *laissez-faire* distortion between the consumer's domestic rate of substitution, q $(= \overline{p})$, and the producer's domestic rate of transformation β $(> \overline{p})$.[16] Of course, if the minimum-wage economy were able to subsidize the hiring of labour directly, unemployment could be entirely eliminated, and the rest of the optimal policy package would be the same as for the full-employment case.

6. Conclusion

The present paper has re-evaluated the costs and benefits of policy-induced inflows of capital from abroad, after adapting the standard trade-theoretic model to include minimum-wage unemployment within the policy-imposing country. The analysis has reconfirmed earlier reservations about the welfare effects of using trade policy to attract foreign capital, and has added to these reservations by showing that the capital inflows would normally correspond to a drop in employment. Ironically, moreover, employment gains would normally result if trade policy is adjusted to cause an outflow of home capital, in which case welfare might also improve, Alternatively, when international capital movements are induced instead by a direct subsidy on inflows or outflows of this factor, the employment effects are generally ambiguous in sign, whereas the welfare consequences are negative in the case of capital outflows but ambiguous for inflows. Although policy applied solely to either international trade or foreign investment may be incapable of improving home welfare, both types of instruments can be simultaneously applied to obtain an optimal policy package, which includes also a production tax.

NOTES

Gratefully acknowledged are helpful comments and suggestions from Ngo Van Long, J. Peter Neary, Lawrence L. Schembri, Kar-yiu Wong, participants at the Conference in Memory of Carlos Díaz-Alejandro at the World Institute for Development Economics Research and participants of the Sixth Annual Conference on International Trade Theory at the University of Western Ontario. Of course, the author alone is responsible for any remaining errors or shortcomings.

1 Although Mundell's paper is remembered mainly for its proposition about substitutability between international commodity and factor movements, see also his section entitled 'An Argument for Protection?'.

2 Hamada's article and the article by Minabe draw attention to a related contribution of Uzawa (1969).

3 For the quite different consequences of foreign investment in the presence of an import quota (instead of a tariff), however, see Buffie (1985) and Dei (1985).

4 Although MacDougall (1960) did provide a few concluding comments on the employment gains from inflows of foreign capital, these comments were not related to the question of tariff policy.

5 Earlier analyses of departure from the standard flexible-wage full-employment assumption have been provided by Haberler (1950), Johnson (1965), Bhagwati (1968a), Findlay (1973, chapter 5) and Lefeber (1971). More recent treatments include, for example, Krueger (1977), Schweinberger (1978) and Neary (1985).

6 If we dropped our assumption that technology is identical for the two countries, generally at most one of them would be diversified in production at the free-trade mobile-capital equilibrium, since only by chance would $r^* = \bar{r}$ when $p^* = \bar{p}$ under global diversification in this case. Nevertheless, relaxing the identical-technology assumption would not essentially affect our main results below, because they too involve completely specialized production for one country in the policy-induced equilibrium.

7 The properties of these functions are well-known from duality theory; see, for example, the recent textbook by Woodland (1982). The value of x is negative when the home country exports good X (as in the present subsidy-induced equilibrium), but positive if the country imports this good (as in our *laissez-faire* situation described in section 2).

8 Because the foreign use of labour remains constant at the full-employment level, it has been suppressed (without consequence) from the set of arguments of the g^* *and* x^* functions.

9 A 'large' subsidy would have qualitatively the same effects, provided that we assume $1 - sx_u > 0$, where this inequality is simply the well-known Vanek (1965)–Bhagwati (1968b)–Kemp (1968) condition needed to ensure a *unique* value of x for each world price ratio along the subsidy-inclusive offer curve of the home country.

10 Kemp (1969, p. 96) provides a general statement of the Metzler condition that, in present notation, may be expressed (for a specific subsidy instead of an *ad valorem* tax on trade) as $mp^*/(p^* + s) - (1 - sx_u)\eta^* > 0$ and simplified (for our small subsidy) to $m - \eta^* > 0$.

11 Thus, trade policy's impact on employment in the presence of international capital mobility is qualitatively the same as what Brecher (1974a) found for the case in which capital does not move between countries.

12 This expression is the change in x for a small increase in L (given $\bar{p}$ and $\bar{K}$) under free trade, as may be readily verified by noting that $\mathrm{d}u/\mathrm{d}L = \bar{w}$ when $s = 0$ in equation (1). Now that X is the labour-intensive good, an increase in employment lowers excess demand for this (normal) commodity.

13 Qualitatively the same effects would hold for a large subsidy.

14 To verify this last point, begin with the well-known facts that $\bar{p}x_L + y_L = -\bar{w}$ and $\bar{p}x_u^* + y_u^* = 1$, where $y[\bar{p}, u, k(\sigma), L]$ and $y^*[\bar{p}, u^*, k(\sigma)]$ are the compensated excess-demand functions for good Y at home and abroad, respectively. Given these facts, $x_L + \bar{w}x_u^* = -(y_L + \bar{w}y_u^*)/\bar{p}$, which is negative because $y_L > 0$ (by the Rybczynski theorem) and $y_u^* > 0$ (given normality in consumption).

15 If both countries were diversified at the optimum, the function $R(K)$ in equation (18) would be respecified as $R(p^*)$ with $R' \equiv \mathrm{d}R/\mathrm{d}p^* > 0$, and the right-hand sides of equations (20) and (21) would be replaced respectively by $(x^* - KR')/\widetilde{x}_p^*$ and $(q - p^*)\widetilde{x}_K^*$. In this case, it might be optimal to subsidize both international trade and foreign investment *simultaneously*, in contrast to what Jones (1967) has shown for the full-employment model.

16 The point made in this and the next sentence have been established by Brecher (1974b) in the absence of international capital mobility.

REFERENCES

Bhagwati, Jagdish N. 1968a: The theory and practice of commercial policy: departures from unified exchange rates. *Special Papers in International Economics* (Princeton, NJ: International Finance Section, Department of Economics, Princeton University), no. 8, January.

Bhagwati, Jagdish N. 1968b: Gains from trade once again. *Oxford Economic Papers*, 20, 137–48.

Bhagwati, Jagdish N. 1973: The theory of immiserizing growth: further applications. In Michael B. Connolly and Alexander K. Swoboda (eds.), *International Trade and Money* (Toronto, Ontario: University of Toronto Press).

Brecher, Richard A. 1974a: Minimum wage rates and the pure theory of international trade. *Quarterly Journal of Economics*, 88, 98–116.

Brecher, Richard A. 1974b: Optimal commercial policy for a minimum-wage economy. *Journal of International Economics*, 4, 139–49.

Brecher, Richard A. 1983: Second-best policy for international trade and investment. *Journal of International Economics*, 14, 313–20.

Brecher, Richard A. and Díaz-Alejandro, Carlos F. 1977: Tariffs, foreign capital and immiserizing growth. *Journal of International Economics*, 7, 317–22.

Brecher, Richard A. and Feenstra, Robert C. 1983: International trade and capital mobility between diversified economies. *Journal of International Economics*, 14, 321–39.

Brecher, Richard A. and Findlay, Ronald 1983: Tariffs, foreign capital and national welfare with sector-specific factors. *Journal of International Economics*, 14, 277–88.

Buffie, Edward 1985: Quantitative restrictions and the welfare effects of capital inflows. *Journal of International Economics*, 19, 291–303.

Dei, Fumio 1985: Welfare gains from capital inflows under import quotas. *Economics Letters*, 18, 237–40.

Findlay, Ronald 1973: *International Trade and Development Theory* (New York, NY: Columbia University Press).

Haberler, Gottfried 1950: Some problems in the pure theory of international trade. *Economic Journal*, 60, 223–40.

Hamada, Koichi 1974: An economic analysis of the duty-free zone. *Journal of International Economics*, 4, 225–41.

Johnson, Harry G. 1965: Optimal trade intervention in the presence of domestic distortions. In Robert E. Baldwin et al. (eds.), *Trade, Growth and the Balance of Payments: Essays in Honor of Gottfried Haberler* (Chicago, Illinois: Rand-McNally).

Jones, Ronald W. 1967: International capital movements and the theory of tariffs and trade. *Quarterly Journal of Economics*, 81, 1–38.

Jones, Ronald W. 1984: Protection and the harmful effects of endogenous capital flows. *Economics Letters*, 15, 325–30.

Kemp, Murray C. 1966: The gain from international trade and investment: a neo-Heckscher–Ohlin approach. *American Economic Review*, 56, 788–809.

Kemp, Murray C. 1968: Some issues in the analysis of trade gains. *Oxford Economic Papers*, 20, 149–61.

Kemp, Murray C. 1969: *The Pure Theory of International Trade and Investment* (Englewood Cliffs, NJ: Prentice-Hall).

Krueger, Anne O. 1977: Growth, distortions, and patterns of trade among many countries. *Princeton Studies in International Finance* (Princeton, NJ: International Finance Section, Department of Economics, Princeton University), no. 40, February.

Lefeber, Louis 1971: Trade and minimum wage rates. In Jagdish N. Bhagwati et al. (eds.), *Trade, Balance of Payments, and Growth: Papers in International Economics in Honor of Charles P. Kindleberger* (Amsterdam: North-Holland).

MacDougall, G.D.A. 1960: The benefits and costs of private investment from abroad. *Economic Record*, 36, 13–35.

Minabe, Nobuo 1974: Capital and technology movements and economic welfare. *American Economic Review*, 64, 1088–100.

Mundell, Robert A. 1957: International trade and factor mobility. *American Economic Review*, 47, 321–35.

Neary, J. Peter 1985: International factor mobility, minimum wage rates, and factor-price equalization: a synthesis. *Quarterly Journal of Economics*, 100, 551–70.

Samuelson, Paul A. 1949: International factor-price equalisation once again. *Economic Journal*, 59, 181–97.

Schweinberger, Albert G. 1978: Employment subsidies and the theory of minimum wage rates in general equilibrium. *Quarterly Journal of Economics*, 92, 361–74.

Srinivasan, T.N. 1983: International factor movements, commodity trade and commercial policy in a specific factor model. *Journal of International Economics*, 14, 289–312.

Uzawa, H. 1969: Shihon Jiyuka to Kokumin Keizai (liberalization of foreign investments and the national economy). *Economisuto*, 23, 106–22 (in Japanese).

Vanek, Jaroslav 1965: *General Equilibrium of International Discrimination: The Case of Customs Unions* (Cambridge, MA.: Harvard University Press).

Woodland, A.D. 1982: *International Trade and Resource Allocation* (Amsterdam: North-Holland).

COMMENT 1

Albert Berry

Richard Brecher's model, involving the effects of capital flows in an economy with a minimum wage distortion, adds an interesting aspect to the analysis of the welfare effects of policy-induced capital flows. Apart from the relevance of the specific case, where the imperfection is a minimum wage, the variety of results, the sometime ambiguity of results and the occasional surprising result all serve to warn us that few conclusions are very robust across the various imperfections and institutional twists to which an economy may be subject. Since I see no errors and only one slight problem of presentation in the paper, I will focus on questions of relevance and on some extensions of possible interest in the LDC context.

The minor criticism involves the relationship between the home country's utility and its level of employment. The basic welfare analysis focuses on a standard utility function into which the level of employment does not enter, and the terminology seems also to imply that the employment level does not directly affect social welfare. 'Evidently this negative impact on welfare must outweigh any possible gain in employment'). If it is indeed the case that no change in employment could outweigh even a small change in utility as defined in the formal model, then it is unclear why we should be interested in the employment level. If employment is to be seen as in principle entering the social welfare function then one should either put it there, or at least modify the terminology to reflect the fact that when utility as measured moves in one direction and employment in the other, the more broadly defined welfare result is ambiguous.

This is, of course, a parsimonious model, so one must feel around a little for its real-world implications. The present model appears less relevant to LDCs than to developed countries both because so few LDCs could be considered large *vis-à-vis* their trading partners and because the specification of an economy-wide minimum wage would not be appropriate to the typical LDC. Perhaps also the greater mobility of capital between developed countries makes the model of more interest in their context. One might hypothesize that the European economy could be analysed with benefit using the leads provided here.

Certainly, though, the question of capital flows is more than a little relevant for many LDCs at this time, and insights could be gleaned from a model which, among other things, shrank the home country into a small one and modified the specification of distortions. Though minimum wages (or unions or other institutional factors) certainly do push some wages in LDCs above their market clearing levels, their application is not economy wide; more often the coverage is small. As a result, open employment is not their only nor necessarily their major effect; the major effect more likely is a wage gap between the 'protected' or 'formal' or 'high-wage' sector and the rest of the economy. While the high-wage sector suffers from this distortion, it typically benefits from a capital market distortion and sometimes also has a technological advantage. The dual economy with capital intensity favoured in one sector (both distortions working in the same direction as far as factor proportions are concerned) and labour intensity in the other is often alleged to be a hallmark of LDCs. A capital inflow would be eminently desirable in this case, since it could not only raise national income in the standard neoclassical way (i.e. by lowering the relative return to capital held by foreigners) but it could erase the efficiency loss due to the distortions. If the capital market distortion takes the form of a maximum price of capital, it would disappear when enough foreign capital flowed in so that access to capital at market prices was generalized. The increase in the marginal product of labour resulting from the higher L/K ratio would eradicate the minimum wage distortion also. Depending on which was eradicated first, the relative growth of the high-wage and the high-capital-cost sectors would vary.

How productive such a capital inflow might be, and hence whether a subsidy to induce it would be desirable, depends on the institutional underpinning of the labour and capital market distortions. One limiting possibility, that just considered, is where the maxima and minima are independent of the market-determined rates for the variables in question. At the other extreme, the factor price gaps could be fixed in absolute terms or as a proportion of the market-determined value, in which case the analysis of the effects of capital inflows becomes more complicated and interesting. While the benefits are obviously less than in the previous case, one might surmise that there would be benefits roughly comparable to those characterizing the no distortion case unless there is reason to believe that the distortion loss would rise with the increase in capital in the system. Additional capital would seem likely, though not certain, to put more pressure on the capital market distortion than on the labour market distortion. If before, with capital scarcer, its cost to favoured clients was fixed say at industrial country levels (with that to non-favoured clients much higher), maintenance of a constant gap between the two prices would necessitate a clearly 'low' rate to favoured clients, e.g. below industrial country levels or perhaps even negative.

In the presence of inflation such low charges are common, less so when prices are fairly stable. Meanwhile, there is probably no such obvious reason to expect a labour market distortion based on union power, for example, to narrow as capital flows in. In any case, if the capital market distortion does narrow but the labour market one does not, firms in the 'high-wage' sector will be disadvantaged relative to those in the 'high-capital-cost sector' and the distribution of production will shift in favour of the latter. Since there is no general presumption as to which sector has higher total factor productivity (the very meaning of the concept becoming subtle in such a context), especially since either may have 'better' technology but be prevented from winning the competitive contest by the existence of the factor market distortions, one cannot generalize as to the effects of differential distortion reduction. There is even less presumption as to the relative social efficiency of the 'marginal' firms in each sector, the ones which would expand (or be created) or contract (or disappear) during the cited shift. For those who believe that 'small is beautiful', the shift would be expected to raise the output of the economy; for those who favour size and modernity, the opposite expectation would be held.

My own guess would be that capital inflow could be expected to reduce both factor market distortions because I suspect these tend to be a function both of per capita income and of its rate of change (which could be accelerated by the inflow). Subsidized inflow would therefore seem an interesting option. But the main message of the above is that careful study of the factor market distortions and their likely response to capital inflow is a matter of some importance.

In the real world there are of course capital flows and capital flows. Portfolio or bank capital, much of which flowed to the LDCs in the 1970s, could appropriately be analysed in the rather simple model considered here. Direct foreign investment is a different kettle of fish, and the current discussion of whether LDCs should now be encouraging it in light of their debt problems raises more complicated questions – about the industrial organization context of the investing foreign firms, about what sorts of technological transfer tend to be involved, and so on.

Although policy-induced capital flows are certainly an important issue in LDCs, and I believe Brecher's model helps to begin the conceptualization of policy analysis involving direct subsidies/taxes on those flows, the same does not strike me as true with respect to trade subsidies/taxes which could affect capital flows. The additional link in the causal chain would probably do in any attempt at policy-relevant analysis using such a simplified model. Certainly the capital flows associated with exports subsidies can be important, but market structure and technology transfer considerations would probably have to be introduced before much of interest could be said. This is not, of course, to say that this part of Brecher's discussion might not find applications in other contexts.

A final note on some contemporary considerations of the 1980s. One of the striking revelations of the economic difficulties so many LDCs have had in recent years is the downward flexibility of real wages in the modern sector. Cuts of 20 to 40 per cent have been, if not common, at least not uncommon. It remains to be analysed to what degree these can be achieved without rapid inflation. Evidence also remains too patchy to generalize on whether the modern–traditional sector earnings gap has typically widened, narrowed or remained unchanged. In any case the observed wage flexibility (or lack of total inflexibility) renders the benchmark Brecher model of less direct relevance to LDC questions. But the variant discussed above retains its usefulness, and the urgency of a better understanding of the determinants of downward wage flexibility and of the magnitude of factor market distortions is heightened.

COMMENT 2

Anne O. Krueger

Richard Brecher's paper provides a neat analysis of the ways in which mobility of foreign capital affects the impact of wage rigidities on patterns and welfare effects of trade. It is an appropriate and fitting tribute to Carlos Díaz-Alejandro. Although Carlos's interests ranged widely over the development field, many of his major contributions centered on issues involving trade and capital flows. Indeed, he and Brecher earlier co-authored a seminal paper in which they demonstrated that, in the Heckscher–Ohlin model, a capital inflow would be welfare-reducing for a labor-abundant country in the presence of tariffs. This followed because a capital inflow would result in an absolute increase in the production of the import-competing good and a decrease in the production of the exportable (via the Rybczynski effect) with a consequent inward shift in the country's true consumption possibility set.

In this paper, Brecher extends that analysis, and his own earlier work on the effects of trade for a labor-abundant country which then imposes an economy-wide binding minimum wage above that which would prevail at full employment. In the standard two-by-two-by-two model, he assumes that a labor-abundant country, in a world in which factor price equalization prevails, imposes a binding minimum wage above that consistent with full employment.

As usual, Brecher chooses his assumption carefully and well to obtain meaningful results with a minimum of inessential detail. Nonetheless, the model is intuitively hard to follow for the following reasons: (a) he assumes that the legislated minimum wage becomes the new world-wide factor-price-equalized wage with unemployment in the home country; (b) likewise, when the labor-abundant minimum-wage-ridden country imposes a tariff, he assumes that the foreign price ratio falls by the full amount of the tariff (since the given wage and rental determine home prices); (c) in most of the discussion, the labor-abundant country is exporting the capital-intensive commodity; and (d) in order to induce a capital inflow (starting with factor price equalization) into the labor-abundant country producing and exporting the capital-intensive good, he must introduce yet another policy instrument (e.g., an export subsidy) and thus have the initially capital-abundant country producing and exporting the labor-intensive good! After analyzing these cases, Brecher concludes by considering the optimal combination of tariffs on trade and taxes/subsidies on capital flows in the presence of a wage floor.

The assumption that factor price equalization prevails must surely limit the analysis to some extent. One wonders, for example, how a labor-abundant country (where the real wage is increased through trade in the Hecksher–Ohlin world) might 'legislate' an increase in the world-wide real wage. If one assumes that Brecher's model is applicable to a large country (the United States? – but it is probably not labor-abundant despite Leontief) and a small rest of the world, there could clearly be some monopoly power over the wage derived from the country's large proportion of the total world labor supply. If, however, one were to apply the analysis to any single labor-abundant country in the world economy, one would have to conjecture that the elasticity of demand for labor in that country was extremely high, and that the real solution, within the Heckscher–Ohlin model, to any significant increase in the real wage would be zero production (as producers in the rest of the world were confronted with the same rental on capital due to capital mobility and a lower real wage.).

Clearly, the results would be different in a world of complete specialization, although it is difficult to formulate such a model and then to examine the impact of capital flows. If a labor-abundant country (where the wage would, by hypothesis, initially be lower than in the rest of the world) imposed a minimum wage, it would produce less of its exportable with open unemployment. A higher real wage for those employed would lower the return on capital (as all capital was employed with less labor in the single industry) and, if there were capital mobility (perhaps less than perfect), probably induce a capital outflow. While the terms of trade of the country might improve (because the entire fall in income with unemployment would represent reduced production of the exportable), it would require a Metzler–Paradox situation for that effect to outweigh the welfare loss associated with reduced real income.

There is little to comment on with regard to each of Brecher's solutions, except to note that the question of whether general equilibrium conditions are satisfied occasionally arises. For example, in his first tariff-induced equilibrium, he assumes that at the free trade position, home imports of good X would have been equal to zero. This in turn implies either that demand conditions were very different in the two countries or that factor endowments were much the same. With no initial trade, he assumes an export subsidy and a capital inflow sufficient to extinguish foreign production of X. If there is a new equilibrium, it must be one in which the initially labor-abundant country (which could not have been very labor-abundant since there were no imports) was initially not engaged in trade, and then adopted a policy of subsidizing exports of the capital-intensive good, which in turn would induce a capital inflow, since the rate of return on capital in the home country at the higher domestic price of the exportable would exceed the real marginal product of capital which was then paid as rental on capital from abroad. Only in the case where unemployment is sufficiently reduced (which once again raises the question of the degree of monopoly power of the country) is there any conceivable welfare gain for the home country.

In general, welfare of the rest of the world always increases when the minimum-wage-ridden country adopts trade policy or capital-tax or subsidy measures. This follows automatically from the fact that the terms of trade improve. Moreover, employment in the home country would normally fall further if there were capital inflows. Welfare of the minimum-wage-imposing country is always reduced when trade policy induces a capital inflow, and home country welfare is more likely to increase with a capital outflow than with a capital inflow. At this point, we would have the labor-abundant country improving its welfare by exporting capital! A first-best policy for the home country is, naturally, the removal of the minimum wage (or a wage subsidy). Alternatively, three policy instruments – tax on production of X, tax on exports of X and a tax or subsidy on capital flows – are needed to achieve a first-best optimum.

Brecher's analysis is an important contribution pointing to the probable economic costs of labor market interventions in open economies. The links between labor market policies and trade policies, and the negative impact of labor market intervention for most developing countries, have heretofore been largely neglected in the literature. As such it is a welcome contribution to knowledge and deals with an important subject. Understanding the effects of alternative policies and providing an analysis of first-best, second-best, *n*th best and policies that will not work at all have been an important development in trade theory over the past several decades. Often, that understanding has undermined the arguments of politicians defending trade policies as an instrument: even if they move in the right direction, there are other, superior, policies that will achieve the same or better results with less costs. Brecher's analysis extends that important tradition to key issues.

One cannot, however, resist pointing out that Brecher's analysis, like all of the analysis in this tradition, once again underscores our naïvete as economists when we address policy issues: on the one hand it is assumed that an 'exogenous' minimum wage regulation exists and cannot be altered; on the other hand, wise, rational and disinterested policy makers are thereupon assumed to be able to measure a complex set of parameters, and then to implement three policies, all of which are probably highly sensitive to the empirical estimates. It is interesting to inquire what underlying model of policy making implies that this may be the case. Certainly, a first question would be whether, if the minimum wage were government-imposed, it could not be removed. Alternatively, even if the wage were otherwise 'exogenously' determined, one would have to have some model of policy formulation in which complex trade and tax instruments could be manipulated to achieve social goals whereas regulations that impacted on wage determination and workers' welfare could not be. This is especially so in the Brecher model, where the income of capital owners is largely unaffected by the minimum wage, because of capital mobility.

In either case, the answer to this question would imply a certain model of political decision making. This model might be special groups, irrationality and ignorance of the politicians or something else. But to assume that any one of these (or other explanations) holds with respect to reasons why the wage rigidity cannot be tackled but that disinterested policy makers will costlessly and effortlessly measure and implement trade and tax instruments seems a bit inconsistent.

This is no criticism of Brecher, whose contribution is important, but rather of the profession. Carlos Díaz-Alejandro was becoming increasingly interested in these sorts of 'political economy' questions before his death, as his perceptive analysis of developing countries' economies and policies led him to conclude that policy making was neither exogenous nor entirely rational. Had he lived, our understanding of political–economic interactions in policy formulation and implementation would no doubt be more advanced than it is. One can only hope that others will address them, and delve into these issues.

18

North–South Models and the Evolution of Global Interdependence

Ronald Findlay

International trade as a fundamental influence on the economic life of every nation in the world is a relatively recent phenomenon in history. Transport costs long confined specialization and exchange to relatively contiguous regions and localities. The exception was trade in commodities of very high value relative to weight and bulk – hence the predominance of the precious metals and stones, silks and spices in the romantic early history of international commercial relations. Trade between Europe, on the one hand, and Asia and Africa on the other, was no exception. In exchange for Eastern silks and spices Europe had little alternative but to offer bullion, for millenia. An Arab commercial geography of the ninth century, *The Book of the Routes and the Kingdoms*, lists 'eunuchs, slave girls and boys' as the first three items in its account of commodities exported from Europe, than which there can be 'no more salient symptom of economic backwardness' as David Landes remarks.[1]

Although the European voyages of discovery in the latter half of the fifteenth century are rightly regarded as opening a new era in the history of the world, Landes points out that 'the relative autonomy of the European commercial system remained intact' and 'the rest of the world, then, remained as before primarily a source of luxuries and non-necessaries, of spices and medicaments, rare woods, costly fabrics, fine porcelains, elegant furnishings.' Sugar, coffee, tea and tobacco were the key commodities of global trade and colonial rivalry between the maritime European powers in the 1500–1800 era, along with the infamous slave trade that the cultivation of sugar spawned. This global trade, however, was in the opposite direction to the traffic noted by the Arab geographer, not to Europe itself but to the New World opened up by the Europeans. How did Europe pay for these imports? Guns, clocks and trinkets accounted for some of the payment but bullion, transferred from the New World to Asia, must have been the main item, so that the 'Great Drain,' as the European deficit with Asia was called since Roman times, continued, though by a circuitous route.

All this was transformed by the Industrial Revolution which created the so-called 'nineteenth-century pattern' of world trade, with manufactures exported from Europe in return for primary products of all kinds from Asia, Africa, the Americas and Australia. This era was also marked by the export of capital from Europe which was used to create the physical infrastructure necessary for the flow of primary exports on such a vast scale. This pattern had its heyday in the 1870–1914 era, picked up again in the 1920s and survived through the Great Depression up to the Second World War. It was towards the close of this era, illustrating the Hegelian dictum that the owl of Minerva spreads its wings only when shades of night are falling, that D.H. Robertson (1937), in his famous essay, said that 'the specializations of the nineteenth century were not simply a device for using to the greatest effect the labors of a given number of human beings; they were above all an "*engine of growth*".'

Robertson in 1937, and many others long after him, were pessimistic about the subject of his essay, 'The Future of International Trade.' In the newly independent countries of Asia and Africa, and in Latin America as well, economists and policy makers generally tended to feel that world trade would not continue to grow as it had in the previous era. As we all know, however, world trade for the next two and a half decades grew at a rate that put the nineteenth century to shame.

The structure and pattern of this rapidly growing trade also altered drastically. As Robertson presciently remarked, 'proficiency in the arts of mechanized industry could not remain forever the monopoly of the nation, or even of a group of nations, that had just learnt to use them.' These arts were diffused in the nineteenth century itself to the United States and later to Japan, so that the concept of the industrial 'core' or 'center' of the world economy has had to be enlarged to permit the entry of former primary exporters. In the last two decades they have spread also to the 'newly industrializing countries,' particularly the East Asian quartet of Korea, Taiwan, Hong Kong and Singapore and to Brazil. Import substitution for manufactures, both in response to the rise in capital–labor ratios and growth of market size as well as in response to deliberate protective measures, has caused manufacturing to become an increasingly important sector even in economies that continue to export mainly primary products. Another major influence on the pattern of world trade has been mechanization and the scientific revolution in agriculture, particularly with respect to the prairies of North America and other temperate zones. Combined with massive population growth in the tropical areas this has led to increasing net import of cereals from the temperate industrial 'center' by the tropical 'periphery.'

How does the theory of international trade relate to the broad outlines of the evolution of global interdependence described here? The answer seems to be not much, beyond the very basic and general point that differences in natural resources, capital and technology generate mutually beneficial trade. Our beloved textbook 'two-by-two-by-two' model pays little attention to characterizing each of the partners in this threefold dichotomy, so that we can speak blandly of countries *A* and *B*, factors *L* and *K* and commodities *X* and *Y* without differentiating them in any meaningful respect.

While this bloodless abstraction may reflect the mechanistic and ahistorical thrust of so much in neoclassical economics it need not necessarily be so. There is no reason why one cannot adapt the structure of neoclassical models to reflect some of these historical interests and concerns. In the rest of this paper I shall explore three different models, each designed to correspond, in 'stylized' fashion, to a particular phase in the evolution of the world economy, initially conceived as divided between a 'center' and a 'periphery' or 'North' and 'South.'[2]

1. Asymmetrical Interdependence and the 'Nineteenth-Century Pattern'

The germ of the analysis in this section of the paper is Robertson's fundamental insight quoted in the introduction about trade as the 'engine of growth' in the nineteenth century. Findlay (1980) provides perhaps the simplest way in which this insight can be captured in a dynamic model of trade and growth. In this model the North is viewed as an industrial center or 'workshop of the world,' *à la* Manchester and Birmingham, while the South is a plantation economy adjoined to a hinterland of subsistence agriculture. The North is modelled as a one-sector neoclassical economy as in Solow (1956), while the South is a one-sector dual economy as in Lewis (1954). The manufactures produced by the North serve both as consumer and capital goods, while the primary products produced by the South are purely consumer goods. Both economies demand both goods, so that trade is essential, with the terms of trade determined by reciprocal supply and demand in the usual fashion.

Each of the two goods is produced by a constant returns to scale neoclassical production function, with capital and labor as inputs. History endows each economy with an initial stock of capital (accumulated manufactures) and the North with its labor force. Competitive factor markets generate full employment of the Northern labor force, with the real wage and the return to capital in that economy determined by the marginal productivity principle. Given the proportion of income saved, the investment demand for manufactures by the North is determined. Consumption demand for manufactures and primary products is specified by a homothetic utility function identical for all consumers with the demand for each good varying inversely with the relative price.

In the South the real wage is given, in terms of the primary product. In conjunction with the initially given stock of capital, this determines the demand for labor, and hence employment in the South and the output of primary products, by the marginal productivity principle applied to profit-maximizing plantation owners. The distribution of income between profits and wages in the South is also thereby determined. It is assumed that capitalists spend a fixed fraction of profits on investments. Thus the South's demand curve for manufactures for investment purposes is a rectangular hyperbola, with the quantity demanded increasing in the same proportion as the relative price falls. Consumption out of profits, and all of wages, are spent on primary products and manufactures according to a homothetic utility function, with consumption demand for each good varying inversely with the relative price. With supplies of both goods determined, and demand for both goods in each region specified as a function of relative prices or the terms of trade, the short-run or momentary equilibrium of the system is determined by the equality of supply and demand in either one of the markets, which will also equate the value of exports and imports for each region.

Turning to the dynamics of the system, the growth rate of the labor force of the North is an exogenously given parameter, n, which can be considered as the sum of the growth rate of population and the rate of labor-augmenting technical progress. It is thus the growth rate of labor in terms of 'efficiency units.' The growth of the capital stock in the North is given by the fixed propensity to save out of income, denoted s, which together with n, completely determines the dynamics of factor supply for the North.

The growth rate of capital in the South is governed by what Joan Robinson called the 'Anglo-Italian' equation, with the rate of accumulation equal to the prospensity to save out of profits, σ multiplied by the rate of profit, denoted ϱ. With the real wage given, the production function for the primary products determines the capital–labor ratio in the South by the equality of the marginal product of labor to the given real wage. Hence, employment and capital both grow at the same rate $\sigma\varrho$ in the South, and therefore so also does the output of primary products.

The rate of profit ϱ is equal to the marginal product of capital in primary products, evaluated in units of manufactures at the prevailing terms of trade. The profit rate and hence the growth rate in the South therefore vary directly with the terms of trade. Because of the South's dependence on the North for capital goods, the terms of trade vitally influence the growth rate of the South.

The growth rates of the two regions are linked by the terms of trade. Very favorable values of this variable that result in the growth rate of the South being higher than in the North, will imply that demand for manufactures is growing faster than demand for primary products since income elasticities of demand are unitary by the assumptions made. Thus, as in the early work of Johnson (1954), the terms of trade must deteriorate for the South, resulting in a slackening of growth in that region. The mechanism operates in reverse when growth is lower in the South than in the North.

This verbal description of the model can now be summarized concisely by a few equations. Outputs in each region can be written in per capita form as

$$q = q(k_N) \tag{1}$$

$$\pi = \pi(k_S) \tag{2}$$

where q and π denote per capita output of manufactures and primary products and k_N and k_S the capital–labor ratios in North and South. The given real wage $\bar{w}$ in the South and profit maximization by the plantations results in

$$\pi(k_S{}^*) - \pi'(k_S{}^*)k_S{}^* = \bar{w} \tag{3}$$

where k_S^* is the unique value of k_S that satisfies (3).

The terms of trade, denoted θ will be determined at each instant by the balance of trade condition

$$a(\theta)q(k_N) = \lambda\beta(1/\theta)\pi(k_S)\,\theta \tag{4}$$

where $a(\theta)$ is the proportion of per capita income q in the North spent on primary products, β is the proportion of per capita income π in the South spent on manufactures (both for consumption and for investment) and λ is the ratio of employment, L_S, in the South to employment, L_N, in the North. Employment in the South is determined by the total capital stock at each instant divided by k_S^*. Thus k_N and λ are state variables of a dynamic system, with given values at any moment of time, so that equation (4) can always be solved for the short-run equilibrium value of the terms of trade θ.

The equations of motion for the system are

$$\dot{k}_N = sq(k_N) - nk_N \tag{5}$$

$$\dot{\lambda} = \sigma\varrho\,(k_N,\lambda) - n \tag{6}$$

with

$$\frac{\partial \dot{k}_N}{\partial k_N} = sq'\,(k_N) - n < 0$$

$$\frac{\partial \dot{\lambda}}{\partial k_N} = \frac{\sigma\,\partial\varrho}{\partial k_N} > 0$$

$$\frac{\partial \dot{\lambda}}{\partial \lambda} = \frac{\sigma\,\partial\varrho}{\partial \lambda} < 0$$

The first of these inequalities is the usual stability condition for the Solow model. The second and the third follow from the familiar Marshall–Lerner condition of trade theory. An increase in k_N here raises Northern income and hence creates an excess demand for primary products, thus raising θ and hence ϱ. An increase in λ creates an excess supply of primary products, thus lowering θ and ϱ. Note that $\dot{k}_N$ is independent of λ, leading to the vertical schedule for $\dot{k}_N = 0$ in figure 18.1, while the $\dot{\lambda} = 0$ schedule is upward sloping. The 'steady-state' values of k_N and λ determined by the intersection of the loci are denoted k_N^* and λ^*.

From the steady-state equations we can derive

$$\theta^* = \frac{nk_S^*}{\sigma\pi'\,(k_S^*)k_S^*} \tag{7}$$

$$\lambda^* = \frac{a(\theta^*)q(k_N^*)}{\beta(1/\theta^*)\pi(k_S^*)\theta^*} \tag{8}$$

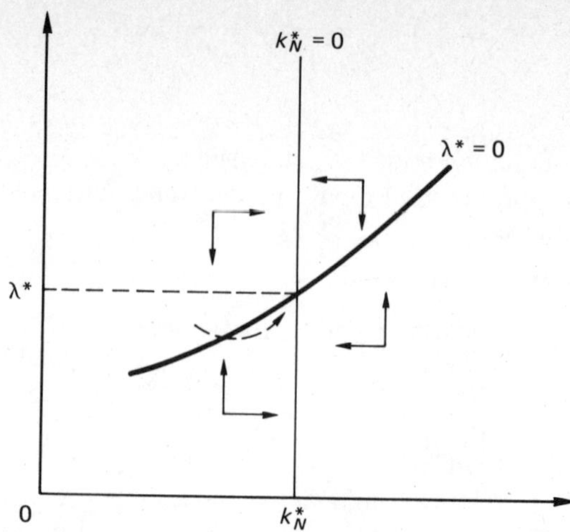

Figure 18.1 Phase diagram of Solow-Lewis model

From equation (7) we see that θ^* is the ratio of steady-state investment in the South in physical terms (units of manufactures used to equip newly employed workers) to the constant level of profits measured in units of primary products, determined by the fixed wage w and the profit-maximizing capital–labor ratio $k_s{}^*$.

From equation (8) we obtain the steady-state employment in the South per worker in the North as the ratio of steady-state Northern imports per capita to Southern imports per capita evaluated at θ^*.

Though we have solved for the 'steady-state' of the dynamic system constituted by equations (5) and (6) this term should not be interpreted too literally in the present context. As Lewis and other writers have themselves stressed, the 'surplus labor' regime is at best a transitional one in the morphology of a developing economy. Eventually sustained growth will drain the surplus pool and so restore tightness and an endogenous wage to the labor market. We thus have what we may term a 'quasi' steady-state towards which the system tends so long as it remains characterized by a fixed real wage and surplus labor.

This model can illustrate some key features of the 'nineteenth-century pattern' that Robertson, and following him Nurkse (1959), identified:

1 The exogenous growth of the North, arising from technological progress, is the 'engine' that drives the world economy as a whole, transmitting growth to the South via the expansion of trade.
2 The size of Northern markets for the primary exports of the South determines the scale of the plantation sector, in terms of capital, employment and output, relative to the North.
3 The terms of trade link the growth rates of the two regions of the world

economy together, deteriorating for the South when its growth exceeds that of the North, thus preventing an equalization of per capita incomes.

4 Increases in the rate of saving and 'once-for-all' technological improvements in the North leave the terms of trade unchanged in the long run, while they would deteriorate the terms of trade in the long run for the South. There is a basic 'asymmetry' in the pattern of dependence between North and South.

The last two implications should be associated with the views of Prebisch (1950) rather than those of Robertson and Nurkse. Note, however, that unlike Prebisch we define an equilibrium level of the terms of trade rather than predict a presumably unbounded permanent decline.

One aspect of the nineteenth-century pattern stressed by both Robertson and Nurkse, and which we have so far ignored, is the role of international capital mobility. As Robertson put it:

> Thus the volume of trade was kept at a high level by two closely connected facts – first, the fact that the new countries keenly desired a type of goods, which we may think of for short as steel rails and girders, which the older countries were particularly fitted to supply, and secondly, the fact that the old countries did not demand immediate payment for these goods, but were willing in effect to supply them on tick, so that the volume of trade was continuously larger than it would have been had it depended solely on the opportunities for simultaneous barter.

This vitally important feature has been incorporated thoroughly and elegantly into the model outlined above by Burgstaller and Saavedra-Rivano (1984). Investment by the North in the South equalizes the profit rates at every instant, leading to the establishment of a Northern enclave within the plantation economy of the South, 'crowding out' some of the native Southern capital. The introduction of capital mobility raises per capita incomes in the North while having possibly deleterious consequences for the South in terms of capital ownership and perhaps even employment. The pattern of asymmetrical interdependence of the world economy in the model is thus both enriched and enhanced by the work of these authors.

The fact that the supply of primary products is perfectly elastic at the relative price θ^* in the long run has an interesting implication for tariff policy, pointed out by Kiguel and Wooton (1985). Any tariff levied by the North must reduce its own welfare in the long run, since the terms of trade of the South must be invariant at θ^*. The South, however, does have monopoly power in the long run and so can improve its terms of trade by the imposition of tariffs. It is the domestic price ratio, and not the terms of trade, that has to satisfy equation (7) and so the long-run impact of any tariff levied by the South is entirely on the North. The South, however, will be damaged by the consequent decline in the import demand of the North resulting from the worsening of its terms of trade. The relevant trade-off for the South is therefore between improving its terms of trade and worsening its employment relative to the North. An 'optimum' tariff can be defined, once the weights on these two objectives and a rule for the distribution of the tariff revenue are specified, as Kiguel and Wooton demonstrate.

2. Import Substitution for Manufactures in the South

The analysis of the previous section has ignored the possibility of manufacturing production in the South. Particularly since the Second World War Robertson's prediction that the 'arts of mechanized industry' would be quickly diffused across the globe has been coming true with a vengeance. The structural relationships between North and South would obviously be altered in a major way once this aspect is taken into account.

The asymmetrical pattern of North–South relationships explored in the previous section does not in any way imply that the South will necessarily be better off by 'delinking' itself from the North. The general aspects of this issue have been dealt with by Díaz-Alejandro (1978) himself, in a typically wise and insightful essay. Our task here is the more narrowly analytical one of seeing how the Solow–Lewis model of the world economy is modified once the open dual economy of the South has a two-sector structure.[3]

Let us begin with a 'quasi steady-state' in which the South, let us say, is impatient with growth under complete specialization at the same rate n as in the North and decides to 'delink' and establish its own manufacturing sector. What will be the effect on growth, employment and other relevant variables of this decision?

In figure 18.2 we display a unit isoquant for the primary product and the capital–labor ratio and relative factor prices associated with the given real wage $\bar{w}$ in terms of the primary product. We assume that the capital–labor ratio in manufacturing exceeds that in the primary product, i.e., manufacturing is relatively capital-intensive. Depending upon the technological efficiency of this sector in the South there will be a certain number of units, say x, of manufactures that can be produced at the same factor cost as one unit of primary output. Thus, in figure 18.2, the isoquant for manufactures tangential to the factor price line is the one that corresponds to x units of output. The price of a unit of primary products in the South, under competitive domestic markets with a ban on trade with the North, must therefore be x units of manufactures. It must be the case that x is less than θ^*, since otherwise manufacturing would have been viable under free trade, so that we have

$$g_a = \sigma\varrho_a = \sigma x\pi'(k_s^*) < \sigma\theta^*\pi'(k_s^*) = n \tag{9}$$

where g_a and ϱ_a refer to the autarky growth and profit rates of the South.

Given the capital stock, employment under autarky can be determined by the condition that domestic demand (for both consumption and investment) for manufactures equals supply, with the same condition also holding true of course for primary products by Walras' Law. Since under free trade the

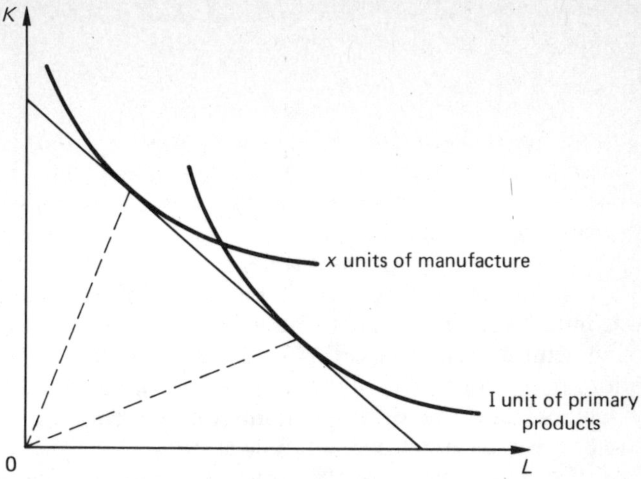

Figure 18.2 Relative prices and capital labor ratios under incomplete specialization

economy was completely specialized, and primary products are less capital-intensive than manufactures, it is clear that employment in the South must contract at the moment it opts out of the 'system,' with the overall capital–labor ratio rising to a value in between the capital–labor ratios of the two sectors that ensures balanced growth of the economy henceforth at the rate g_a.

Thus autonomy or self-sufficiency in this case is purchased at a heavy price, an initial decline in employment as well as a permanent decline in the rate of growth of capital, employment and national income below that obtainable under free trade. Whatever the frustrations and inequities of 'dependency' under complete specialization, it does not follow that 'inward-looking' development as advocated by Samir Amin and others is a better alternative. Note that we are not criticizing this policy on grounds of consumer welfare, as in the usual neoclassical critiques, but in terms of employment and growth, which is presumably what Marxist theoreticians are in favor of.

Suppose, however, that manufacturing production in the South is sufficiently competitive to become viable under free trade at some world price $\tilde{\theta} > \theta^*$. Thus the South would completely specialize only when $\theta > \tilde{\theta}$ and would experience growth rates higher than n in this case. The resulting decline in the South's terms of trade would be arrested when $\theta = \tilde{\theta}$, since it is now able to produce some manufactures for itself. Once θ hits $\tilde{\theta}$ on its way down the South would start to put some of its capital stock into the production of manufactures and a process of relative import substitution would begin.

The growth rate of capital and the rate of profit in the South in this situation would be given by

$$\tilde{g} = \sigma\tilde{\varrho} = \sigma\tilde{\theta}\pi'(k_s^*) > n \tag{10}$$

The South's export of primary products will grow at n, the same rate as Northern demand. Domestic demand for manufactures will be met increasingly by domestic production, though imports will of course grow in absolute terms at the same rate as exports. The growth rate of the capital stock $\tilde{g}$ will be higher than the growth rate of employment, and the capital–labor ratio of the economy will rise from the capital–labor ratio in the primary sector, to which it was initially equal, towards an upper limit set by the capital–labor ratio in manufacturing. The proportion of the labor force in manufacturing must therefore rise accordingly. In the terminology of the Heckscher–Ohlin model the capital–labor ratio of the economy will move up within the limits of the 'cone of diversification' defined by $\bar{w}$ and $\tilde{\theta}$.

A process of 'catching up' with the North will now be fully under way, with a rising capital–labor ratio and per capita income in the South accompanied by industrialization and structural change as manufacturing expands faster than primary output.

The assumption of a constant real wage, however, would now need to be altered. As the South industrializes with an increasing capital–labor ratio, the real wage would eventually rise in the 'modern' sector, now consisting of both factories and plantations. A rising real wage, and the associated falling rate of profit, would check the expansion of the South at a faster rate of growth than the North, and restore balanced growth between the two regions. The labor market of the South would now also be characterized by full employment of a given labor force and an endogenously determined real wage. It is assumed that the South's labor force grows at the same rate as the labor force of the North.

In order to introduce a variable real wage for the South in a model of balanced growth of the world economy, with incomplete specialization in the South, we plot the two functions between w and θ shown in figure 18.3. The *NN* curve shows the relationship between w and θ implicit in equation (7). As w increases k_S increases and therefore $\pi'(k_S)$ decreases, by the usual factor–price frontier relationship in the primary sector. From equation (7) we see that θ would increase in the same proportion that $\pi'(k_S)$ falls. The *SS* curve is the familiar Stolper–Samuelson relationship between w and θ. Since primary products are relatively labor-intensive θ must increase as w increases. The slope of *NN* must be steeper than *SS* at the intersection point of the two curves. This is because the proportionate increase in θ on *SS* must be less than on *NN*, since on *NN* it increases in proportion to the fall in the real rental $\pi'(k_S)$, whereas it is a weighted average of the proportional changes in the two factor prices on *SS*. We denote the values of w and θ that satisfy both these relationships as w^* and θ^*.

Define the capital-labor ratios corresponding to w^* in manufacturing and primary production as $k_1^*(w^*)$ and $k_2^*(w^*)$ respectively. Then, to any

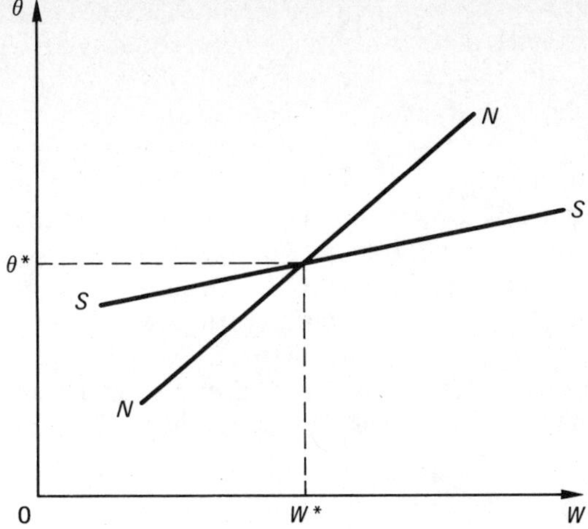

Figure 18.3 The real wage and the terms of trade

capital-labor ratio k_S in the South we can find the proportion α of the employed labor force that is engaged in manufacturing from the equation

$$k_S = \alpha k_1{}^* (w^*) + (1-\alpha)k_2{}^* (w^*) \tag{11}$$

Per capita income, wages and profits in the South can all be readily derived for any value of k_S and corresponding value of α. Income and profits per capita are clearly an increasing function of k_S also, given the relative price θ^*.

By the Rybczynski Theorem the output of manufactures per employed worker in the South is an increasing function of k_S, while the output of primary products is a decreasing function, since α must rise in equation (11) if k_s rises, given $k_1^* (w^*)$ and $k_2^* (w^*)$. Per capita income in the South is

$$y_S = w^* + \pi' (k_2^*)\, k_S \tag{12}$$

which is an increasing function of k_S since w^* and $\pi' (k_2^*)$ are constants. Per capita demand for primary products in the South is therefore an increasing function of k_S, since the income elasticity of demand is unitary. Thus the per capita supply of primary exports from the South, which we define as $e(k_S)$, is a decreasing function of k_S.

We can now determine k_S^*, the capital–labor ratio of the South consistent with balanced growth of the world economy. The steady-state per capita demand for import of primary products in the North is determined as before by θ^* and k_N^*. Denoting this per capita import demand of the North as m (θ^*, k_N^*) the condition of balanced trade yields the equation

$$\lambda e\,(k_S) = m(\theta^*, k_N^*) \tag{13}$$

where λ, the ratio of employment in the South to employment in the North is now a constant since there is no longer any surplus labor in the South. We thus obtain k_s^* as the unique value of k_s that solves equation (13).

The dualistic labor market of the South that we used in the 'nineteenth-century pattern' model of the previous section was thus a transitional phase in the evolution of the world economy. The 'quasi steady-state' for that model eventually leads toward the 'true' steady-state of the present model. The South must still be a net importer of manufactures, however, since the North does not produce any primary output of its own. The next section will attempt to fully restore symmetry to the world economy by leaving open the direction of the net import of manufactures.

It would be useful to undertake several exercises in comparative statics and dynamics on the model of this section but they will have to be postponed to a later paper.

3. The Restoration of Symmetry

> The fabric of the world has its center everywhere and its periphery nowhere.
>
> Nicholas of Cusa
> (Quoted in Heinz Pagels *Perfect Symmetry*)

The Industrial Revolution of the eighteenth century is slowly being diffused over the world, and the time is perhaps not too far off when we will have 'one world' from an economic point of view, in place of the present plurality. Thus the distinction between North and South, Center and Periphery, will cease to be an appropriate way of viewing international economic relations. This is not to say at all that trade would cease, but only that the asymmetry in the pattern of structural interdependence that we have stressed in the first two sections will be removed. What will undoubtedly remain to distinguish the nations of the world will be geographical location and the associated variety in the bounty of nature with which each one of them is endowed. The temperate and tropical zones in particular will be sharply differentiated in natural resources, with cereal and livestock products as the realm of the former's comparative advantage and the traditional sugar, coffee, tea, cocoa and so on as the realm of comparative advantage of the latter. The arts of manufacture, meanwhile, have lost their ties to Lancashire or the Ruhr and are as much at home in Singapore or Sao Paulo.

What sort of model would be appropriate to reflect this restoration of economic symmetry in the midst of geographical diversity? I propose an adaptation and transformation of a three-good model first put forward by Arthur Lewis in his 1954 article but developed more fully in his 1969 Wicksell Lectures. In his model the temperate zone produces food and steel, while the tropical zone produces food and coffee. While entirely appropriate to the 'nineteenth-century pattern' of our first section, Lewis himself in other writings has pointed to the temporary nature of the industrial monopoly of the North and has looked forward to the day when the South would 'internalize the engine of growth,' with its own production of capital goods and other manufactures.

Suppose then that the 'North' (more accurately the temperate zone) produces 'wheat' and manufactures, while the 'South' (the tropics) produces 'coffee' and manufactures. Each region consumes all three goods but produces only two, i.e., manufactures and a regionally specialized primary product. As before, manufactures can be both consumed and invested. Unlike Lewis, who used a Ricardian model with labor as the sole factor of production, we postulate constant returns to scale neoclassical production functions, with capital and labor as inputs, for both sectors in both regions. We assume that wheat is capital-intensive relative to manufactures in the North, whereas coffee is labor-intensive relative to manufactures in the South. The technology for manufactures may be the same in both regions, or superior in either one. Utility functions are homothetic in each region, so that income elasticities of demand are all unitary. Labor grows exponentially in each region at the rate n, in terms of efficiency units, i.e., the engine of growth beats uniformly in North and South, instead of being transmitted from the former to the latter by the demand for primary imports. For simplicity, we shall assume that saving only takes place out of profits in both regions, so that each region has its own 'Anglo-Italian' equation in the steady state

$$\sigma_i \varrho_i = n \qquad i = N,S \tag{14}$$

Since n and σ_i are constants, the rate of profit in each region in the steady-state can be determined from equation (14). The Stolper–Samuelson relationships between relative prices and the rate of profit in each region in turn specify the price ratio in each region

$$p_i = \phi_i(\varrho_i) \qquad i = N,S \tag{15}$$

where p_N is the ratio of the price of wheat to the price of manufactures and p_S is the ratio of the price of coffee to the price of manufactures. The relative price of wheat and coffee will of course be the ratio of p_N to p_S. Real wages in each region will also be determined by the factor–price frontiers in each region, given the rates of profit. The steady-state conditions of equation (14) thus tie down the structure of commodity and factor prices in each region and for the world economy as a whole. The factor prices determine the capital–labor ratios in both sectors of both regions.

We now have to turn to the determination of equilibrium quantities. This can be done as follows. Given k_N, per capita income and profits in the North are specified and thus also the demands for all three goods in the North at the steady-state price ratios $p_N{}^*$ and $p_S{}^*$. The per capita output of wheat and manufactures in the North is also determined, and hence the per capita excess supply of wheat as well. We can now determine the value of k_S that will generate the excess demand for wheat that will clear the world market for this commodity. Raising k_N will increase the excess supply of wheat in the North, since that is the capital-intensive good. Hence k_S will have to increase as well in order to clear the world market. We thus can define a positively sloped locus between k_N and k_S along which the world market for wheat is in equilibrium at the steady-state price ratios $p_N{}^*$ and $p_S{}^*$. A corresponding locus between k_S and k_N, along which the world market for coffee is in equilibrium, can also be constructed. Since production of coffee is labor-intensive an increase in k_S will reduce excess supply so k_N must be reduced to keep the world coffee market in balance. This locus is therefore negatively sloped. The intersection of the two loci determines the steady-state capital–labor ratios $k_N{}^*$ and $k_S{}^*$ for the two regions. In this three-good model the world market for manufactures must be in equilibrium if the markets for the other two goods are. Since trade must balance, manufactures will be exported by whichever region has a deficit on its trade in primary products, the exchange of wheat for coffee.

Having now determined the values of all variables, prices as well as quantities, in the steady-state the next task is the question of convergence of the world economy to the steady-state. At the initial moment of time history will endow North and South with a particular per capita capital stock, $k_N(0)$ and $k_S(0)$. At that moment markets will have to clear. At each price ratio p_N and p_S we can determine the supply and demand for all three goods in the world economy from the information on technology, preferences and the two initial capital stocks. We can vary these two price ratios until the wheat and coffee markets are cleared, and hence the market for manufactures as well. Corresponding to these short-run equilibrium price ratios the Stolper–Samuelson relations will yield real wages and profit rates for each region. The rates of change of k_S and k_N will be determined by the equations

$$\dot{k}_i = \sigma_i \varrho_i (p_i)\, k_i - n k_i \qquad i = N,S \tag{16}$$

As k_N and k_S shift over time in response to condition (16) they will generate new values of p_N and p_S and hence of ϱ_N and ϱ_S. We shall demonstrate that the dynamic system defined by equation (16) is stable, since the characteristic roots of the associated Jacobian matrix, evaluated at the steady-state, are both negative.

The partial derivatives are

$$\frac{\partial \dot{k}_N}{\partial k_N} = (\sigma_N \varrho_N - n) + k_N \sigma_N \frac{\partial \varrho_N}{\partial p_N}\ \frac{\partial p_N}{\partial k_N} \tag{17}$$

$$\frac{\partial \dot{k}_N}{\partial k_S} = \sigma_N k_N \frac{\partial \varrho_N}{\partial p_N}\ \frac{\partial p_N}{\partial k_S} \tag{18}$$

$$\frac{\partial \dot{k}_S}{\partial k_S} = (\sigma_S \varrho_S - n) + k_S \sigma_S \frac{\partial \varrho_S}{\partial p_S}\ \frac{\partial p_S}{\partial k_S} \tag{19}$$

$$\frac{\partial \dot{k}_S}{\partial k_N} = \sigma_S k_S \frac{\partial \varrho_S}{\partial p_S}\ \frac{\partial p_S}{\partial k_N} \tag{20}$$

Evaluated at the steady-state the first terms in equations (17) and (19) become zero. By the assumptions on technology and demand we have

$$\frac{\partial \varrho_N}{\partial p_N} > 0, \frac{\partial p_N}{\partial k_N} < 0, \frac{\partial \varrho_S}{\partial p_S} < 0, \frac{\partial p_S}{\partial k_S} > 0$$

from which we it follows that

$$\frac{\partial \dot{k}_N}{\partial k_N} < 0, \frac{\partial \dot{k}_S}{\partial k_S} < 0 \tag{21}$$

so that the so-called 'trace' condition for stability is satisfied. The assumptions on technology and demand also imply that

$$\frac{\partial p_N}{\partial k_S} > 0, \frac{\partial p_S}{\partial k_N} > 0$$

so that we have

$$\frac{\partial \dot{k}_N}{\partial k_S} > 0, \frac{\partial \dot{k}_S}{\partial k_N} < 0 \tag{22}$$

which together with equation (21) ensures that the 'determinant' condition is also satisfied. Hence the system is stable in the neighborhood of the steady-state solution.

The phase diagram of the dynamic system is plotted in figure 18.4. The $\dot{k}_N = 0$ locus is upward sloping and the $\dot{k}_S = 0$ locus is downward sloping, in view of equations (21) and (22). The arrows indicate the direction of movement in k_N and k_S towards the intersection point denoting the steady-

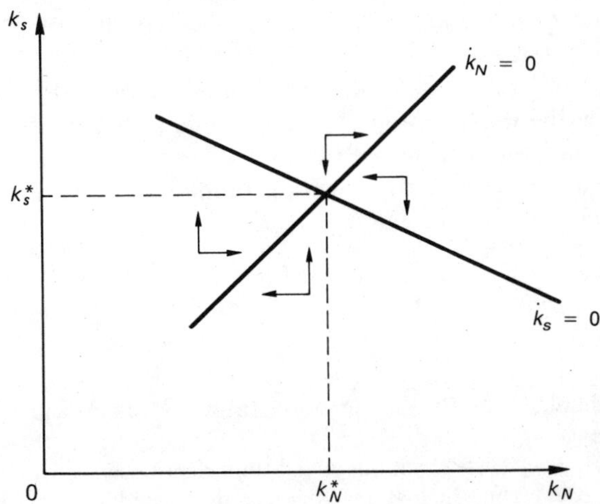

Figure 18.4 Phase diagram of symmetric North-South model

state values k_N^* and k_S^*. These values of the capital–labor ratios in the two regions correspond exactly to those obtained by our previous argument, clearing the markets for wheat and coffee at the steady-state price ratios p_N^* and p_S^*.

This final model of our sequence has two particular characteristics that should be emphasized – symmetry and the ability to be consistent with a 'role reversal' between North and South. Thus initially we may have $k_N(0) > k_S(0)$ by a wide margin, so that real wages are higher and rates of profit lower in the North, which is also the exporter of manufactures because the low $k_S(0)$ forces the South to concentrate its resources on coffee production. In the steady-state, however, the rates of profit and real wages will depend only on the propensities to save out of profits. If $\sigma_S > \sigma_N$ then $\varrho_S^* < \varrho_N^*$ and $w_S^* > w_N^*$. Per capita incomes could have initially been lower but may end up ultimately higher in the South. We could also have $k_S^* > k_N^*$ even though initially $k_N(0) > k_S(0)$, so that the South ends up with a higher capital–labor ratio and a heavy concentration in manufactures, which it exports to the North so that the direction of trade in this commodity becomes reversed.

These conclusions hold even if the regions have identical technology in manufacturing. The intuition that this cannot be, since wheat is more capital-intensive than manufactures, which is in turn more capital-intensive than coffee, would be true in a Heckscher–Ohlin model with three commodities and two factors but is false in relation to the present model. The reason is that the Heckscher–Ohlin model assumes that it is technically feasible for all countries to produce all commodities, with factor endowment the sole arbiter of whether a particular country produces a particular commodity or not. Here we have a 'climate' factor of a Ricardian sort, which makes it impossible for the South to produce wheat and the North to produce coffee. Thus it is possible for the South to have a higher capital–labor ratio, a lower profit rate and a higher real wage, in spite of the ordering of the factor intensities for the three goods.

Once again the model can be extended in many ways. Particularly interesting would be the introduction of international capital mobility but I have imposed too much already on the patience of my discussants. There is one set of comments – kind, generous, wise, probing – that alas none of us at this conference will ever receive again.

NOTES

I would like to thank Andre Burgstaller, José Antonio Ocampo and T.N. Srinivasan for their comments.

1 See Landes (1978). This article gives a brilliant brief survey of the history of commodity exports from the less developed to the more highly developed regions of the world. Mintz (1985) gives a fascinating account of the role that one of the

2 Other North–South models are Bacha (1978), Taylor (1983), Krugman (1982) and most important of these commodities, sugar, played in the development of the modern world economy.
Vines (1984). An extensive survey is given by Ocampo (1986).
3 Two-sector open dual economies are investigated in Findlay (1973, ch. 5) and Findlay (1982). Analytically this model is identical to the Heckscher–Ohlin–Samuelson model with a fixed real wage, as in Brecher (1974).

REFERENCES

Bacha, E.L. 1978: An introduction to unequal exchange from Prebisch–Singer to Emmanuel, *Journal of Development Economics*, 5, 319–30.

Brecher, R.A. 1974: Minimum wage rates and the pure theory of international trade. *Quarterly Journal of Economics*, February.

Burgstaller, A. and Saavedra-Rivano, N. 1984: Capital mobility and growth in the North–South model, *Journal of Development Economics*, 15, 213–37.

Díaz-Alejandro, C.F. 1978: Delinking North and South: unshackled or unhinged? In A. Fishlow et al. (eds.), *Rich and Poor Nations in the World Economy*, New York: McGraw-Hill.

Findlay, R. 1973: *International Trade and Development Theory*. New York: Columbia University Press.

Findlay, R. 1980: The terms of trade and equilibrium growth in the world economy. *American Economic Review*, June.

Findlay, R. 1982: Protection and growth in a dual economy. In M. Gersovitz et al. (eds.), *The Theory and Experience of Economic Development*, London and New York: Allen & Unwin.

Johnson, H.G. 1954: Increasing productivity, income-price trends and the trade balance. *Economic Journal*, September.

Kiguel, M. and Wooton, I. 1985: Tariff policy and equilibrium growth in the world economy. *Journal of Development Economics*, 19, 187–98.

Krugman, P.R. 1982: Trade, accumulation and uneven development. *Journal of Development Economics*, 8, 149–61.

Landes, D. 1978: The Great Drain and industrialization: commodity flows from periphery to center in historical perspective. *Economic Growth and Resources*, International Economics Association. London: St Martins Press.

Lewis, W.A. 1954: Economic development with unlimited supplies of labor. *Manchester School*, May.

Lewis, W.A. 1969: *Aspects of Tropical Trade 1883–1965*. Stockholm: Almquist and Wiksell.

Mintz, S.W. 1985: *Sweetness and Power*. New York: Viking Press.

Nurkse, R. 1959: *Patterns of Trade and Development*. Stockholm: Almquist and Wiksell.

Ocampo, J.A. 1986: New developments in trade theory and the LDCs. *Journal of Development Economics*, 22 129–70.

Prebisch, R. 1950: *The Economic Development of Latin America and its Principal Problems*. United Nations.

Robertson, D.H. 1937: The future of international trade. *Economic Journal*, September.

Solow, R.M. 1956: A contribution to the theory of economic growth. *Quarterly Journal of Economics*, February.
Taylor, L. 1983: *Structuralist Macroeconomics*. New York: Basic Books.
Vines, D. 1984: North–South growth model along Kaldorian lines. *Center for Economic Policy Research*, Discussion Paper Series, no. 26.

COMMENT 1

José Antonio Ocampo

1. A Personal Note on Carlos Díaz-Alejandro

I became a student of economics in the late 1960s, during what was certainly one of the most exciting periods in the history of Western universities. I have ever since been a firm believer in the virtues of the open intellectual environment of those days. I was thus extremely fortunate to have Carlos as my professor and dissertation advisor at Yale University, since a similar point of view was not widespread in the economics profession in the United States at the time and is even less common today.

As professor of international economics and development, Carlos was a firm believer in and practitioner of pluralism. I thus enjoyed the opportunity to read and take seriously the work of Little, Scitovsky and Scott, as well as that of Emmanuel and Hymmer, which had produced some of the most important pieces of research on both sides of the debate on LDCs at the time. He also took seriously and made very important contributions to the development of Latin American structuralist thinking. In that regard, he openly shared the view that North–South issues could only be understood from a global perspective. Finally, but obviously not less important, he was deeply imbedded in the study of economic history. Some of the most vivid recollections of my student days relate, in fact, to friendly chats on the work of the Cuban Marxist historian Manuel Moreno Fraginals, for whom he had great admiration, and to repeated discussions on the origins of industrialization in Latin America.

Ronald Findlay's paper is very much in this tradition of Carlos. Indeed, this and previous papers of the author (Findlay, 1980, 1981) are some of the most serious and uncommon efforts by a mainstream economist to understand and reformulate old structuralist ideas. His work, as well as contributions by Taylor, Vines and others, has in fact placed the old terms of trade debate in a new context (see Ocampo, 1986, for a review of the recent debate). The present paper is also an interesting attempt to understand with simple models the basic dynamics of whole historical periods. Finally, it is an analysis of North–South issues from a global perspective.

2. The Nineteenth-Century Pattern

In the first model of the paper, the North is a Solow economy completely specialized in the production of manufactures and the South is a Lewis economy completely specialized in the production of primary commodities. This model brings to the foreground at least four interesting features of North–South interactions. First of all, the North is the 'engine of growth' of the world economy. Secondly, initial disparities in income are reproduced, as equilibrating mechanisms operate to equalize the rates of growth in both regions if the elasticities of demand for both goods are unitary and there is no technical progress. As we will see shortly, however, this statement refers only to the modern sector in the South compared to income in the North and not to the Southern economy as a whole. Third, basic asymmetries in the pattern of dependence between North and South come out, particularly with regard to the role of technical progress. While in the North productivity improvements lead to higher per capita income, in the South they are 'exported' through lower terms of trade, a Prebisch-type result. Finally, contrary to neoclassical trade theory, free trade and capital inflows are suboptimal for the South.

Other interesting results could be obtained with a similar model, under slightly different assumptions. First, if the unit elasticity assumption is relaxed, the conclusion of a steady-state pattern with constant terms of trade and equal rates of growth between North and South cannot hold. In this case, if the South produces income-inelastic commodities, it would either face slower growth or a deterioration of the terms of trade in the long run; in both cases, income inequality in the world economy will increase. On the other hand, if continuous technical change is introduced at similar rates in North and South, there would be again a tendency to a deterioration of the terms of trade of the South and a widening income gap, as long as productivity improvements are not diffused in the traditional sector.

Finally, it should be pointed out that the paper does not say anything on those workers in the South who are not employed in the 'modern' export sector. Given the basic assumptions of the model, we will assume that they go into traditional agriculture. Thus, ruling out changes in productivity, GDP growth in the South is a weighted average of export and population (natural) growth. It may be increasing faster or slower than the former. If the 'engine of growth' beats fast enough, the latter would be true, and the nineteenth-century trade pattern would in fact lead to a narrowing down of income differentials between North and South, due to structural change in LDCs. But if Northern growth is not fast enough, structural change in LDCs would be too slow and income disparities would increase.

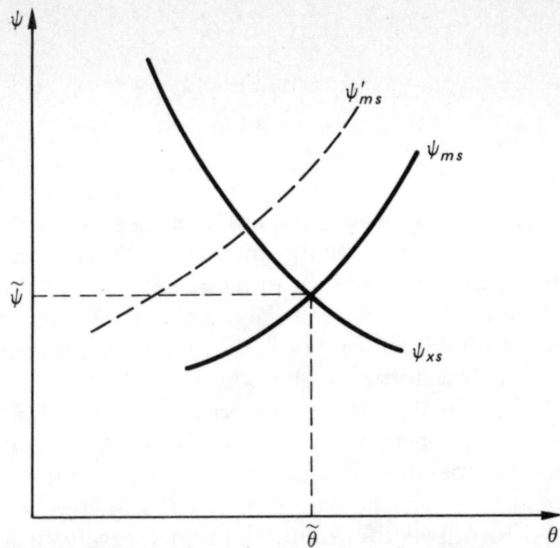

Figure 18C.1 Determination of the terms of trade (θ) and the rate of profit in the South (φ) when it produces primary goods and industrial commodities

3. The Origins of LDC Industrialization

The second part of the paper is a model of 'natural import substitution' in the South. As the Northern economy slows down, export growth and the terms of trade decrease in the South and industrialization becomes a natural strategy. This explanation of the origins of industrialization is very similar to Carlos's analysis of the 1930s (see Díaz-Alejandro, 1984) and one of the traditional interpretation of the origins of industrialization in Latin America. In fact, it is hard to understand such a large-scale process at a specific stage of development in a different way. However, as Carlos and Latin American structuralists have emphasized, active state intervention was required to get the process started. In a sense, state intervention operated as a catalyst rather than as the engine of industrialization in the South!

The essential idea can also be captured in a simple diagram (Fig. 18C.1). Let w be the real wage in the South in terms of exportables; k_{xs} and k_{ms} be the capital–labor ratios in export and manufacturing production ($k_{ms} > k_{xs}$) and π_{xs} and π_{ms} be per capita output of export and manufacturing goods in the same region. We will assume all these coefficients to be constant.[1] The relative world price of manufactures in terms of primary commodities is θ. The capital stock is made up of manufacturing goods. The rate of profit in export activities in the South (φ_{xs}) is:

$$\varphi_{xs} = (\pi_{xs} - w)/\theta k_{xs} \tag{1}$$

The rate of profit in the export sector thus depends inversely on θ, as shown in the diagram. The rate of profit in manufacturing production in the South (φ_{ms}) is:

$$\varphi_{ms} = (\theta\pi_{ms} - w)/\theta k_{ms} \tag{2}$$

As θ rises, the real wage in terms of manufacturing goods falls and the rate of profit in manufacturing production increases. There is thus a positive relation between φ_{ms} and θ as shown in figure 18C.1.

If the terms of trade of the South are high enough ($\theta < \widetilde{\theta}$), manufacturing production is not profitable in the South and the nineteenth-century model applies. However, as the terms of the South deteriorate (θ rises), due to falling natural growth in the North [see equation (7) in Findlay's paper], manufacturing eventually becomes profitable in the South under free trade. At this point ($\theta = \widetilde{\theta}$), the terms of trade of the South are determined by the intersection of φ_{xs} and φ_{ms} in the diagram. The intersection also determines the unique rate of profit in the South ($\widetilde{\varphi}$) and the rate of growth of the capital stock in the 'modern' sector ($\widetilde{g} = \sigma\widetilde{\varphi}$, where σ is the savings rate out of profits). Slower growth in the North will not result in a deterioration of the terms of trade or in slower growth for the South once this point has been reached. By industrializing, the South can thus effectively overcome dependence on the Northern 'engine of growth'!

This introduces, however, an interesting dimension to tariff policy in LDCs. If manufacturing consumer and capital goods can be differentiated (but they have identical production functions) and tariffs are levied only on the former, equation (1) above is unaffected, but equation (2) becomes:

$$\varphi'_{ms} = [\theta(1+t)\pi_{ms} - w]/\theta k_{ms} \tag{3}$$

where t is the tariff rate. Thus $\varphi'_{ms} > \varphi_{ms}$ for any θ as shown in the diagram. Thus, a new equilibrium is found at which the South enjoys better terms of trade and faster growth in the modern sector, which now includes manufacturing as well as export production. Note that this is true even if initially $\theta < \widetilde{\theta}$, if we impose high enough tariffs. The costs and benefits of tariff policy have some common elements but also some differences with respect to those considered by Kiguel and Wooton (1985). As in optimum tariff argument in the nineteenth-century model, the gain in the terms of trade for the South is reflected in lower demand for primary commodities in the North and thus in lower employment in the export sector in the South [a fall in $a(\theta^*)$ in equation (8) of Findlay's paper]. This effect is stronger if the increase in investment demand in the South outweighs the reduction in import demand for consumer goods [i.e., if $\beta(1/\theta^*)$ in equation (8) increases]. There is, however, an important difference. In the nineteenth-century model, the rate of growth of the modern sector in the South cannot be affected by tariff policy in the long run. This is no longer true once we bring industrialization into the analysis. Thus, a new optimum tariff argument can be developed, the magnitude of which will depend on the relative weight of gains from increasing growth and manufacturing employment in the long run and better terms of trade, versus the reduction in employment in export activities and consumer welfare losses in the process. Optimal tariffs will also depend on the difference in capital intensities in manufacturing and export production[2] and on how tariff revenues are redistributed.

The source of the gain from faster industrial growth depends, as in the previous model, on productivity gains from transferring workers from the traditional sector to either export or manufacturing production. There might be limits to this process, however, as the rate at which workers can be drawn out of the traditional sector is limited. Thus, if the rate of growth of employment in the modern sector is fast enough, w will certainly rise, shifting down both φ_{xs} and φ_{ms} and thus the rate of growth of the capital stock. This element should also be included in the analysis of optimum tariffs. An interesting corollary can be derived: if export (i.e., Northern 'natural') growth is fast, the attraction of active tariff policy for the South is reduced, but protectionism becomes more attractive when the Northern engine has lost dynamism. 'Forced' industrialization is thus complementary to 'natural' import substitution, in the sense in which I have been using the term.

The negative relation between export growth and industrialization captures only part of the story of manufacturing development in LDCs. In fact, as the traditional balanced–unbalanced development literature emphasized, there are significant scale economies in the process of industrialization. Thus, as export growth proceeds and the market for manufacturing goods increases, the Southern production function for at least some types of industrial commodities improves and thus φ_{ms} in the diagram shifts up. Thus, after some period of development on nineteenth-century lines, protectionism becomes increasingly attractive for the South. It is this complementarity between industrialization and the size of the market created by export development, together with the effect of the collapse of primary commodity markets and the increasing attraction of protectionism in these circumstances, which explain the strength of the industrialization process experienced by many LDCs, particularly in Latin America, in the 1930s.

4. The North–NICs Model

The last model of the paper is an interesting mélange of Heckscher–Ohlin, Lewis and Pasinetti. The interesting feature of the model is that symmetry is restored into the world economy. It may be relevant to understand the interaction between the North and the Newly Industrializing Countries at present. An interesting conclusion could be drawn, however, by including into the analysis a third region, a 'Deep South,' which is still completely specialized in the production of primary commodities and imports only manufacturing goods. The terms of trade of the Deep South would thus be determined by the NICs. If the growth rate of the core (North–NICs) economy falls, so would the rate of profit in this model and thus the relative price of labor-intensive commodities, i.e., primary goods. Thus, contrary to nineteenth-century patterns, the Deep South would actually enjoy a terms of trade improvement when the growth of the world economy is reduced! This is a peculiar result, which requires additional theoretical exploration in North–South modelling.

NOTES

1 In fact, w, k_{xs} and π_{xs} are constant, but k_{ms} and π_{ms} depend on w/θ and thus change with θ.

2 In this regard, it is interesting to note that capital intensity in manufacturing production will increase with the tariff level.

REFERENCES

Díaz-Alejandro, Carlos F. 1984: Latin America in the 1930s. In Rosemary Thorp (ed.), *Latin America in the 1930s: The Role of the Periphery in World Crisis* (Macmillan, London).

Findlay, Ronald 1980: The terms of trade and equilibrium growth in the world economy. *American Economic Review*, 70, 291–9.

Findlay, Ronald 1981: The fundamental determinants of the terms of trade. In Sven Grassman and Erik Lündberg (eds.), *The World Economic Order: Past and Prospects* (Macmillan, London).

Kiguel, Miguel A. and Wooton, Ian 1985: Tariff policy and equilibrium growth in the world economy. *Journal of Development Economics*, 19, 187–98.

Ocampo, José Antonio 1986: New developments in trade theory and LDCs. *Journal of Development Economics*, 22, 129–70.

COMMENT 2

T. N. Srinivasan

Like most of the participants of this conference, I came to know Carlos from his early days at Yale prior to my return to India. Strange as it may seem to some, I was (and to an extent still am) an ardent admirer of Fidel Castro, even after Carlos was disenchanted with Castro. I recall our long arguments, and his always pleasant, courteous and amused tolerance of the views on Cuba of someone who had never set foot in that country. Again, we differed on the Kissinger Commission Report. We also had our differences on the appropriate analytical framework for the economics of development, but we both believed that any analysis that ignored economic history was incomplete at best and irrelevant at worst. All of us will certainly miss his masterly and skilful use of economic history, economic theory and data in analysing contemporary issues.

Ron Findlay's paper, if I may paraphrase him, attempts to adapt the neoclassical models to reflect historical interests and concerns thereby correcting what he calls their mechanistic and ahistorical thrust. Through three parsimoniously constructed and elegantly exposited models, he derives conclusions that are consistent with three stylized patterns characterizing the evolution of global interdependence starting from what he calls asymmetrical interdependence of a South specialized in producing and exporting primary products to a North which specializes in manufactures which also serve as capital goods. Because of the South's dependence on the North for capital goods, the terms of trade vitally influence the growth rate of the South. Northern growth through technological improvement is the Robertsonian engine of world growth in this model. He then introduces the possibility of producing manufactures in the South. This substantially alters the dependence of the South on the North. As long as manufacturing is efficient under free trade in the South, prospects for the South in the global economy become much brighter. But if it is not, inward-looking development based on inefficient manufactures can only hurt the South. The third pattern is of the neoclassical nirvana of symmetric interdependence in which there is no presumption either that the South imports manufactures forever, or that the Southern per capita income is lower than that of the North forever.

Since Ron is unlikely to have made any errors of deductive logic, and I did not discover any, as a discussant I have few options but to quibble about some of his assumptions and approach. To begin with, except briefly in his local stability analysis at the end of the paper, most of Ron's discussion is on the steady-state properties of the model. I recall the late Joan Robinson once characterizing steady-state models as ahistoric and she was absolutely right in doing so. After all, initial conditions, i.e. history, do not matter at all in Ron's models and regardless of initial conditions each economy converges to the same steady-state. But comparative dynamics of steady-state equilibria corresponding to different combinations of basic parameters, whether based on neo-Ricardian or Neoclassical models, can be thoroughly misleading. Most of the relevant action of interest (i.e. gains and losses) in response to a change in policy parameters lies in the transition path from one steady-state to another. Indeed, if I may refer to the literature on optimizing planning models of the 1960s, the steady-state was used essentially as a less arbitrary way compared to other ways of imposing terminal conditions on a finite horizon model. The policy interest of the solution lay not in its convergence to the steady-state or in the steady-state itself, but in the choices it suggested for the initial periods.

In a two-country world, the insistence on the existence of a steady-state forces one to make some rather implausible assumptions. For instance, one has to assume that the growth of labour endowment in efficiency units is the same in both countries. This implies the implausible story that if the natural rate of growth of labour is different in the two countries, the rates of Hicks neutral technical progress differ in an offsetting way so as to maintain the same rate of growth of efficiency units of labour in the two countries!

In Findlay's model the savings behaviour differs between the two countries. The capitalists of the South save a proportion of their profits while the workers consume all theirs. The capitalists and workers of the North on the other hand save a constant proportion of their income all their lives! Neither savings behaviour is endogenously derived from intertemporal utility maximization. One could view the assumed fixity of the savings ratio relative to what would have been intertemporally optimal as a distortion. Given such a distortion, neither the non-steady-state consumption path nor its asymptotic steady-state in one country can be meaningfully compared from a welfare point of view with the corresponding path of the other country. On the other hand, even if one viewed the savings assumptions as purely descriptive, it is far from obvious that the description is valid for an indefinite future as the steady-state analysis would imply.

Finally, Findlay's model does not include a feature of international exchange, namely transfer of technical knowledge among trading partners and, even more important, its influence on the pace of innovation around the world. But then there are not many models even in a closed economy context that adequately capture the essential aspects of the process of innovation.

19

Sources of Technological Divergence Between Developed and Less Developed Economies

Raaj Kumar Sah and Joseph E. Stiglitz

Developed and less developed countries differ in numerous ways. Incomes per head are different, capital stocks are different, the levels of education of their citizens differ. Whether a cause or consequence of these differences, some of the most salient differences are related to technological change and innovation. Firms in many developed countries appear to be constantly looking around for new technologies, for better and more efficient ways of doing things; firms in the newly industrialized countries (NICs) and those LDCs aspiring to become NICs appear to be searching among available technologies for those which will most improve their productivity, while firms in the less successful LDCs are often slow to abandon the traditional ways of doing things. Though exceptions to this polar characterization can be found, the fact remains that the technological gap between many poorer LDCs and the developed countries has not significantly narrowed over the past 50 years.

Indeed, this constitutes one of the central puzzles facing development economics. Why is it that the growth rates and income levels of various countries have not converged faster than they have? There is some evidence (Baumol, 1986) that for a significant number of countries, there has in fact been divergence rather than convergence. Traditional neoclassical growth theory (Solow, 1956) predicts that in the long run, the growth rates in all countries should be related only to the rate of technological progress and the rate of population growth; growth rates in per capita income should be related only to the rate of labor-augmenting technological progress, and differences in levels of per capita consumption should be related to differences in savings rates.[1]

In this paper, we describe several different perspectives on the sources of non-convergence. Our emphasis is on one important aspect common to all of these perspectives, namely, that an economy can have multiple *equilibria*. That is, some societies may be characterized by high levels of innovation and others by low levels of innovation. One perspective is based on certain characteristics of technology. Some aspects of this approach have been pursued elsewhere by Stiglitz (1987), Lucas (1985) and others. The other is based on socioeconomic considerations, and this paper will explore these.

The objective of this paper is to provide an overview of these alternative perspectives and to sketch some simple models illustrating the points at issue, rather than to provide a detailed development of any of these approaches.

The paper is organized as follows: in section 1 we discuss the sources of multiplicity of equilibria in general terms. In section 2 we describe an approach which emphasizes individuals' learning about certain aspects of the economic environment. These models of social osmosis have been developed by Sah (1985, 1987a, 1988a) to analyze patterns of crime, corruption and other phenomena. Section 3 provides a general discussion of the sources of positive feedback which give rise to a multiplicity of innovative equilibria. Section 4 provides a brief discussion of several other perspectives which deal with the role of individuals' preferences (tastes) and with the birth and death of organizations. Section 5 presents certain aspects of the technological perspective.

This paper is dedicated to the memory of Carlos Díaz-Alejandro.[2] He inspired our attempt to broaden the perspectives with which we look at economics, particularly the problems of economic development. He had the rare ability to combine the techniques of modern economics with the insights and vision of an economic historian. He was not confined by the straightjacket imposed by the conventional paradigms: he knew those paradigms well, and he knew their strengths and weaknesses. He was a social scientist: his objective was to understand the development process in all of its ramifications, and to do this, he was willing to use whatever techniques and viewpoints that he thought helped obtain insights. We think he would have liked what we have attempted here. We would have vastly profited from his reactions to our analysis. We miss him.

1. Outline of the Theory

In this paper, we wish to put forward a theory of social equilibrium, in which it will turn out that in equilibrium some societies may be characterized by high levels of innovation, and others by low levels. (This view is sharply different from the kind of technological determinism popular in the late eighteenth and nineteenth centuries.) A central hypothesis underlying our analysis is that a major determinant of the survival value of any characteristic in the population – as well as a major determinant of the behavior of individuals in any society or organization – is the nature of the environment. But economic environments are endogenous. The nature of the environment should be explained by the theory. Of course, a central aspect of that environment is the mix of characteristics of those who make up the population. Thus, the mix of characteristics and behaviors of individuals in the environment is central in determining the kinds of characteristics which have survival value and in determining observed behaviors, the kinds of actions which individuals undertake. The mix of characteristics and behaviors at one date determines the set of characteristics and behaviors at later dates.

Specifically, we argue that society may be characterized by a high level of innovativeness, or by a low level of innovativeness. We explore a number of mechanisms through which the environment affects individuals' decisions to be innovative, and through which individuals' decisions to be innovative affect the socioeconomic environment. Several of these mechanisms can be expressed in conventional supply and demand terms: the demand for 'innovativeness' is an increasing function of the fraction of the population which is innovative; and the supply of innovativeness at any time is an increasing function of the fraction of individuals who are innovative in the previous period and of how well those innovative individuals have done. As a result there may exist multiple equilibria, in one (or several) of which there is a relatively small fraction of individuals who are innovative, while in others this fraction may be relatively large. Which of the multiple equilibria an economy exhibits at any particular time is partly a consequence of the historical path the economy has taken. Thus, the rate of technological progress in a society may depend explicitly on its history.

1.1 Feedbacks and Multiplicity of Equilibria

The principal source of multiplicity of equilibria here (as in other economic models) is positive feedback. To see this most clearly, consider the traditional economic model of a single market. Such models stress the role of negative feedbacks. An increase in the demand for some commodity results in an increase in price, and the increase in price brings forth an increase in supply, which dampens the initial price response. We draw the demand curve as downward sloping, the supply curve as upward sloping, and there is a unique equilibrium. Thus, if p is the price, $D(p)$ is the demand, $S(p)$ is the supply and $e(p)$ is the net demand, then the equilibrium condition

$$e(p) = D(p) - S(p) = 0 \tag{1}$$

yields a unique equilibrium if the derivatives D_p and S_p are respectively negative and positive.

We know, of course, that it is easy to generate analogous models with multiple equilibria. If the demand for a commodity increases the demand for a factor, and if the preferences of the owners of this factor are relatively intensive in that commodity, then there may be multiple equilibria. In one equilibrium, the factor has a high income because the demand for the commodity which uses that factor is high, and the demand for that commodity is high because the factor income is high. In another equilibrium the factor income is low because the demand for the commodity using that factor intensively is low, and the demand for that commodity is low because the factor income is low.[3] Still, by and large, economists believe that such effects are not too large, and that our conventional demand and supply stories, with their unique intersection, provide a good description of most markets.

This intuition, however, becomes much less reliable when we consider aspects of the economic environment in which prices do not play a central and direct role. The actions of one individual or group of individuals may have effects on others which are not mediated through the price system. These effects are like externalities. The nature of these interactions frequently gives rise to multiple equilibria; indeed, these provided the basis of the traditional Big-Push theories of development (Rosenstein-Rodan, 1943).[4]

1.2 The Screening Model: An Example

An illustration of non-price interactions giving rise to multiple equilibria is provided by the screening model of Stiglitz (1975, 1984). There are two types of individuals, the more able, with productivity γ_1, and the less able, with productivity γ_2. A fraction *m* of the population is more able. The more able can obtain certification of their ability, at a cost of *c*. If they do, they receive a wage corresponding to their ability. If a fraction θ of the more able get certified, then the average productivity (and the wage) of those who do not get certified is

$$W(\theta) = [(1-\theta)m\gamma_1 + (1-m)\gamma_2]/[(1-\theta)m + (1-m)] \tag{2}$$

Hence, the net gain from screening for someone with screening costs *c*, when the fraction of the able population obtaining the credential is θ, is

$$\gamma_1 - w(\theta) - c \tag{3}$$

The equilibrium is characterized by

$$\gamma_1 - W(\theta) = c \tag{4}$$

with corner solutions at

$$\theta = 0 \text{ if } \gamma_1 - w(0) < c$$

$$\theta = 1 \text{ if } \gamma_1 - w(1) > c$$

As more individuals obtain screening, the wage of the unscreened is reduced, so that the return to screening is increased. It is easy to see, as in figure 19.1, that there may exist multiple equilibria.

In the simplest of such models, with *only* positive feedbacks and identical individuals, equilibria naturally entail corner solutions in which either everyone or no one takes some action (in Stiglitz' model, obtaining a particular education level).[5] It is easy, however, to construct multiple interior equilibria by allowing both positive and negative feedbacks or differences among individuals.

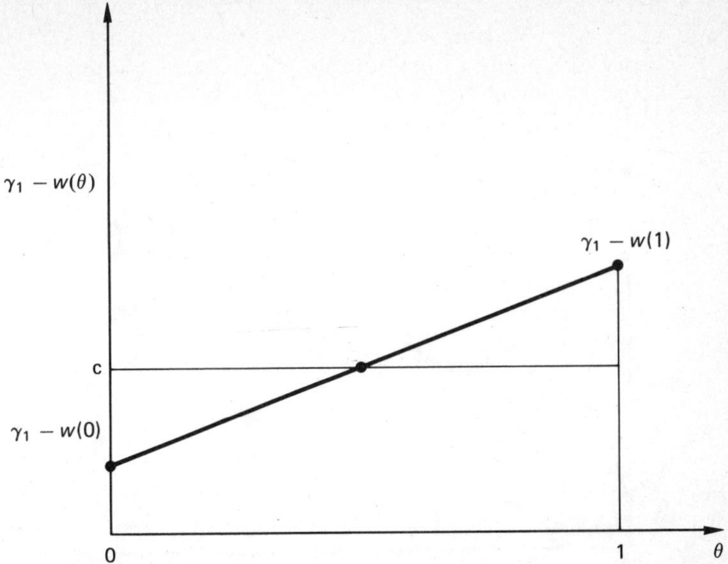

Figure 19.1 Multiple equilibria with corner solutions in screening model

1.2.1 Multiple Equilibria with Individual Differences Assume there is a distribution of costs of certification, $F(c)$. Then those with the lowest certification costs will get certified. As more individuals get certified, the benefits of certification increase but the costs of the marginal individual becoming certified also increase. Equilibrium is characterized by

$$F[\gamma_1 - W(\theta)] = \theta \tag{5}$$

Figure 19.2 shows the possibility of multiple interior equilibria.[6]

Related models are also useful in a variety of circumstances. Stiglitz (1974) has used such a model as a basis for multiple equilibria involving discrimination, where one group with some easily identifiable characteristic is caught in one equilibrium, say with a low level of education, and another group is in another equilibrium, say with a high level of education. Employers pay wages which reflect the productivity of the workers, given the information which is available to them, and workers in each group choose their optimal level of education, given the wages being paid by firms to members of their group. Starrett (1976) has analyzed alternative economic explanations of some of the radical views concerning income distribution.[7]

1.2.2 Multiple Equilibria with Positive and Negative Feedbacks Negative feedbacks arise naturally in many economic models and, in conjunction with positive feedbacks, give rise to multiple equilibria. In our example, if those who are identified as the more able work in different jobs than the less able

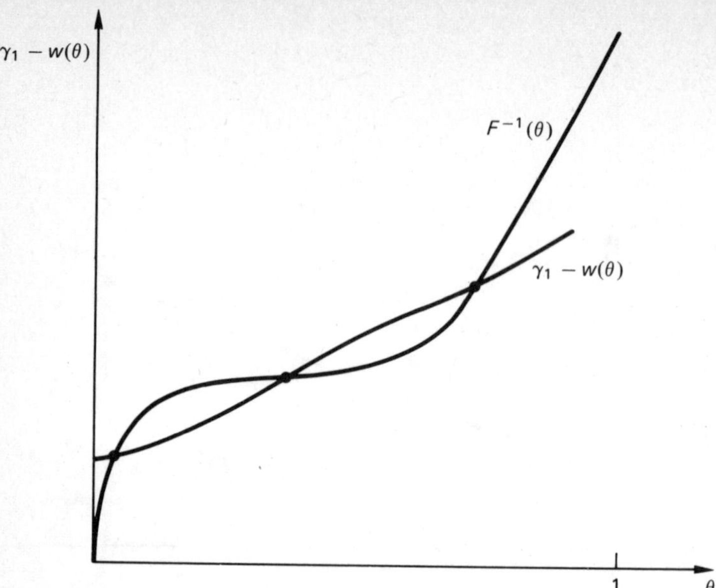

Figure 19.2 Multiple equilibria with individuals differing in costs of screening. $F^{-1}(\theta)$ gives the cost of screening at the θth percentile of the population

(the unskilled), then as more able individuals are identified, diminishing returns set in. Assume, for instance, that there is a production function of the form

$$Q = G(E_s, E_u)$$

where Q is output, E_s is effective skilled labor supply (number of individuals assigned to skilled jobs, multiplied by their average productivity) and E_u is the effective unskilled labor supply. Assume G exhibits constant returns to scale. We assume that the type 2 (unskilled) workers have zero productivity when assigned to the skilled job, but type 1 (skilled) workers are still more productive than type 2 workers when assigned to unskilled jobs. With appropriate normalizations, we denote the 'effective' units of labor of a skilled individual assigned to a skilled job as 1, of a type 1 worker assigned to an unskilled job as γ_1 and of a type 2 worker assigned to an unskilled job as γ_2. If the total population is L, and the fraction of type 1 workers screened is θ, then if all of the able who are identified as such are assigned to skilled jobs

$$E_u = [(1 - \theta)m\gamma_1 + (1 - m)\gamma_2]L$$

and

$$E_s = \theta mL$$

Let $e = E_u \backslash E_s$; let $W_s(\theta)$ and $W_u(\theta)$ be the skilled and unskilled wage, respectively, when a fraction θ of the able are screened; and let $g = G/E_s$ be output per effective unit of skilled labor, which, by the assumption of constant returns to scale, is just a function of e. Then

$$W_s = g(e) - eg'$$

$$W_u = g'(e)h$$

where h is a measure of the average productivity of the unscreened:

$$h = [(1 - \theta)m\gamma_1 + (1 - m)\gamma_2]/[(1 - \theta)m + (1 - m)]$$

In competitive equilibrium, all of the more able who are so identified will be assigned to skilled jobs, so long as

$$W_s > g'(e)\gamma_1 = W_u\gamma_1/h$$

and we focus attention on that situation here.[8] Equilibrium then entails

$$W_s - W_u = c$$

Differentiating with respect to θ, we obtain

$$\mathrm{d}(W_s - W_u)/\mathrm{d}\theta = -[g'' E_u/L^2\theta m(1-\theta m)]\,\mathrm{d}e/\mathrm{d}\theta - g'\mathrm{d}h/\mathrm{d}\theta$$

where $g' < 0$, $\mathrm{d}e/\mathrm{d}\theta < 0$ and $\mathrm{d}h/\mathrm{d}\theta < 0$. The second term is positive (the positive feedback effect that we identified earlier), while the first term is negative, as a result of diminishing returns. As figure 19.3 illustrates, it is easy to construct examples in which there are multiple interior equilibria, with varying proportions of the more able identifying themselves. In each, the *difference* between the wage of the skilled and the wage of the unskilled

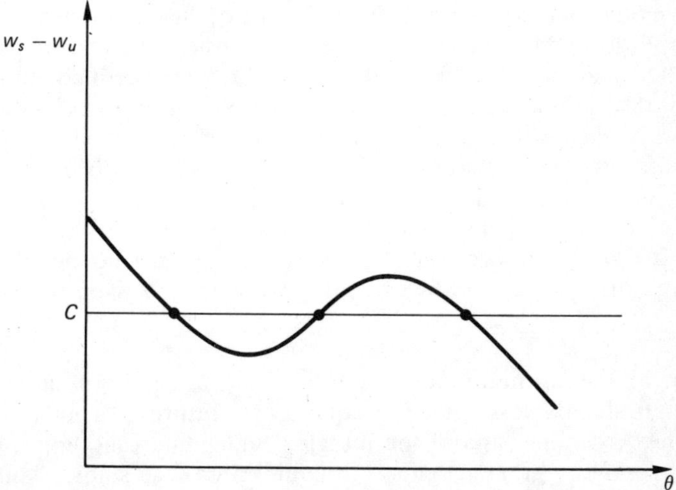

Figure 19.3 Multiple interior equilibria with fixed wage differential

is fixed, but as more individuals are screened, the skilled wage falls; hence, the equilibrium in which the fewest able are screened Pareto dominates the other equilibria.

1.3 Innovation and Multiple Equilibria

In the discussion below, we consider several alternative reasons why there may be important positive feedbacks associated with having more innovation (more innovative individuals) in an economy, resulting in a multiplicity of equilibria, with some equilibria characterized by low levels of innovation, others by a higher level. Several of these models involve multiple equilibria associated with differences in individuals arising from differences in information about the environment or about the returns to being innovative, from differences in their characteristics which affect the 'costs' of being innovative or from differences in tastes.

1.4 Dynamics

Most of this paper focuses on steady-state (long-run) equilibria. But, associated with each of the models there are dynamics which describe the evolution of the economy over time and which determine whether any particular equilibrium is stable or unstable. The dynamics are interesting in their own right. Because the dynamics associated with each of the different perspectives we explore in this paper differ, the analysis of the dynamics may also provide suggestions for discriminating among theories. Understanding dynamics may also be important for identifying policy interventions to move the economy successfully from one equilibrium to another.[9]

1.4.1 Dynamics in the Screening Model Some of the central dynamic issues are again illustrated by our screening model. Consider the version presented above where individuals differ in their costs of being certified. Individuals base their decisions about education (certification) on *expectations* concerning the wages they will receive if they are, or are not, certified. The simplest assumption is that expectations are based on wages *currently* being received by those who are certified and those who are not. This is the simplest extrapolative model. Firms are assumed to adjust wages quickly (relative to the time it takes to change education norms) to reflect true mean values of marginal productivities. In this view, the dynamics are given by

$$F[\gamma_1 - W(\theta_t)] = \theta_{t+1}$$

Let θ^* be an equilibrium that is a solution to (5). Equilibria in which, for values of θ slightly less than θ^*, equilibrium returns to being screened exceed the screening costs of the marginal individual (and conversely for values of θ slightly greater than θ^* in equilibrium) are stable, while other equilibria are unstable. Thus, in figure 19.2 the first and third equilibria are stable.

For this model to be a good description, individuals do not have to know the actual value of $\theta(t)$. What is important is that they know (or have beliefs about) the returns to being certified, which are a function of $\theta(t)$.

One could argue about the reasonableness of our expectations hypothesis on the grounds that it is too simplistic, particularly in the simple environment which we have postulated. Individuals should learn that $\theta(t)$ is not equal to $\theta(t-1)$. If they learn to correctly extrapolate, this would, of course, alter their behavior. If they come to believe that all others are also learning the process by which decisions are made, then the only possible equilibria are the Nash equilibria, the solutions to equation (5). More generally, it should be apparent that the nature of dynamics and the resulting equilibria depend on the expectation formation processes. We discuss some limited processes below.[10] The next section describes individuals' learning and its consequences in certain circumstances in which individuals have limited information and knowledge. In section 3 we discuss some effects of other information-generating mechanisms. In section 6.2 we argue why the introspection-based predictions emphasized in many strategic models may not be an appropriate description of many complex situations in which individuals find themselves.

2. Individuals' Learning about some Aspects of the Environment

In this section, we emphasize the role of individuals' learning about certain relatively intangible economic aspects of their environment which might be important in their decision to innovate. For concreteness, we begin by describing some elements of the analysis Sah (1985, 1987a, 1988a) has developed to explain certain patterns of phenomena such as crime, corruption and honesty. The assumptions underlying an individual's behavior are as follows:

1 As part of his decision making, an individual needs to predict some environmental variables about which public or market-based information is unavailable. For instance, in an individual's choice to undertake an illegal tax transaction, he needs to estimate the probabilities of encountering a corrupt versus non-corrupt tax bureaucrat. The difficulties of ascertaining this probability are obvious; not surprisingly, in most countries there are no statistics – let alone good statistics – on the proportion of corrupt tax bureaucrats.

2 The relevant information on which an individual bases his estimates and decisions is highly limited. It consists of his own past experiences, and it may also partly reflect observations gathered from others. The information is quite obviously limited, partly because there are increasing costs of acquiring more personal or indirect observations. Indirect observations further entail costs of miscommunication.

3 There is a significant stochastic element to any individual's observations,

and hence to his information and beliefs, and the observations are affected by actual past variables. Thus, if a larger fraction of tax bureaucrats were actually corrupt in a past period of an individual's life, then his observations concerning that period will partly, and stochastically, reflect this fact.

4 The emphasis here is on those types of individual decisions in which strategic considerations are not central. For instance, since an individual can encounter any of a large number of tax bureaucrats, it is reasonable to assume that the individual does not believe that his actions will significantly affect actions undertaken by others. (We discuss strategic considerations later in the paper.)

To see some of the consequences of this type of analysis in the context of technological change, consider a stylized model in which an individual chooses to be either an innovator or a non-innovator ('bureaucrat') in each period.[11] Define a variable $x^h(t, \lambda)$ such that $x^h(t, \lambda) = 1$ if a person with characteristics h, who has lived for λ periods, is an innovator in period t. $x^h(t, \lambda)$ is zero otherwise. Let $y(t)$ denote the number of innovators in period t. Thus

$$y(t) = \sum_{\lambda=0}^{L-1} \sum_{h} x^h(t, \lambda) \tag{6}$$

where L represents the life span of an individual.

For simplicity, we assume that in any period, the individual interacts with one other individual, and his pay-off depends both on what he does (i.e., whether he chooses to be an innovator) and on what the other individual has done. For an individual who chooses to be an innovator in a period, let U^{11} be the utility if he encounters an innovator, and let U^{12} be his utility if he encounters a bureaucrat. For an individual who chooses to be a bureaucrat in a period, let U^{21} and U^{22} denote the corresponding utilities. Assume for the moment that[12] $U^{11} > U^{21}$ and $U^{22} > U^{12}$. That is, being an innovator is better if one were to encounter an innovator, and being a bureaucrat is better otherwise. Then, the assumptions outlined earlier imply that the probability that an individual will choose to be an innovator will be influenced by the number of innovators in some of the past periods. That is, $Pr[x^h(t, \lambda) = 1] = g[y(t -), \ldots, y(t - \lambda)]$. From equation (6) therefore one obtains a relationship

$$y(t) = f[y(t-1), \ldots, y(t - L + 1)] \tag{7}$$

This relationship has the property that the current number of innovators in the population will be higher if the number of innovators has been higher in the past, and that the economy can have multiple steady-states.[13]

3. Sources of Positive Feedback in Innovation

Recall the stylized assumption made above that it is better for an individual to be an innovator if he were to encounter an innovator. Such a reward structure can arise from a variety of sources. The response a worker gets to a new idea proposed to his boss depends on whether his boss is 'innovative' (or acts innovatively) or not.

In other circumstances interactions involve several individuals. Most changes in methods of production require the acquiescence of many individuals. Changes in production are, at least to some extent, 'political' decisions. An owner who finds a better way of producing a widget must convince his banker to lend him money. Another dimension, which is perhaps far more important in LDCs than in developed countries, is that an owner or a manager also needs to obtain approval from a variety of government officials.

Positive feedbacks such as these also arise indirectly, through the negative effects of non-innovative individuals on innovators, and conversely, through the negative effects of innovators on non-innovators. A bureaucrat may have the power to suppress an innovation, or at least to make it more difficult for an innovation to occur. Innovative individuals on the other hand can create situations where the routines loved by bureaucrats are simply unproductive. In all of these cases, the return to being innovative depends (positively) on the fraction of those with whom one must interact that are innovative; and the individual's beliefs about this depend on past experience.

In still other cases, the return to being innovative depends more directly on the number of innovative individuals in the economy.[14] It may depend positively on the number of those in other industries who are engaged in innovation, for often ideas which prove useful in one context can be transferred to another. Moreover, the return to the inventors, to those who generate new ideas, depends in part on how likely it is that their ideas will be implemented, and with what speed. When there are many individuals systematically engaged in the search for new ideas the likelihood is increased that an invention will be readily adopted. Thus, there is positive feedback between the number of inventors and innovators, with the possibility of a high-level equilibrium and a low-level equilibrium.[15] Institutionally, this is partly reflected in the existence of organizations and firms, such as venture capital firms in more developed countries, who specialize in searching for and financing new ideas.

Thus, a greater 'supply' of innovation leads to the development of institutions which facilitate innovation. But there are other ways by which an increase in the amount of innovation increases an economy's innovative capacity. The ability to learn is itself learned; though some learning occurs in educational institutions, most learning occurs in social contexts, in which no charge is imposed for the learning externality.

There may, of course, also be a negative feedback: with a fixed stock of ideas, the greater the number of individuals engaged, say, in a patent race, the lower the expected return to each. Our hypothesis is that, at least in many situations, the positive feedbacks dominate this negative feedback.

Finally, the nature of any organization depends on the demands imposed on that organization for adaptation, which is itself a function of the society's state of innovativeness.[16] The supply of innovation gives rise, in a sense, to its own demand. In unchanging environments, there is little demand for individuals and institutions who know how to cope with changes, those who specialize in the collection, processing and dissemination of information. Further, the return to searching for new ideas may be lower, simply because there are fewer ideas floating around; there is a certain synergy in the production of new ideas.

Note that the model outlined in the previous section captures those types of interactions where market or public information is relatively scarce or has low accuracy.[17] On the other hand, many of the kinds of positive feedbacks we have discussed in this section would exist even if there were publicly available accurate information, say about the number and details of venture capital firms, and the variables representing the demands and remunerations associated with various kinds of jobs and qualifications. The information structure of the economy (what information is collected and how it is transmitted) obviously affects the stochastic distribution of information, and this, in turn, may affect not only the dynamics, but even the nature of the long-run steady-states to which the economy converges.

Still, in all of these models, the effect of the past is felt, though the nature and the magnitude of this effect will be determined by the nature of the available information-generating processes. The positive feedbacks which we discussed in the preceding paragraphs still give rise to multiple steady-states; there may be no long-run convergence either in levels of income or growth rates.

3.1 An Example

The following simple model provides an illustration of this non-convergence. As we noted in section 1 it is easier to construct multiple equilibria assuming differences among individuals; here we assume that for some individuals the cost of being innovative is greater than for others. As in the model of section 2 we shall focus on situations where the returns to pursuing a particular action depend on the actions taken by the individuals with whom one interacts; we shall also assume that there is a sufficiently large number of individuals so that no one believes that his actions will have any effect on the actions taken by others, that is, we ignore all strategic considerations. Unlike section 2, we shall (at least initially) assume individuals know the fraction of individuals undertaking different actions.

For simplicity we assume that there are two strategies, $\propto$ (innovative) and β (non-innovative or bureaucratic). Individuals interact pair-wise. When individual i pursues strategy $\propto$ and individual j, with whom he interacts, pursues strategy β, the pay-off to individual i is $\pi(\propto,\beta)$. When both pursue strategy $\propto$, the pay-off is $\pi(\propto,\propto)$; when both pursue β it is $\pi(\beta,\beta)$. We assume that while individuals have the same 'gross' pay-off function, individuals differ in the cost of undertaking strategy $\propto$ versus strategy β. Assume that pursuing $\propto$ costs c dollars more than pursuing β, and that the distribution of c in the population is given by $F(c)$. Assume that individuals believe that a fraction θ of the population is pursuing strategy $\propto$. Then the expected gross pay-off to pursuing strategy $\propto$ is

$$\theta\pi(\propto,\propto) + (1-\theta)\pi(\propto,\beta)$$

All of those for whom $c < c^*$ will pursue $\propto$, where c^* is defined by

$$c^* = [\theta\pi(\propto,\propto) + (1-\theta)\pi(\propto,\beta)] - [\theta\pi(\beta,\propto) + (1-\theta)\pi(\beta,\beta)] \qquad (8)$$

Then equilibrium is defined by

$$c^* = \{F(c^*)\pi(\propto,\propto) + [1-F(c^*)]\pi(\propto,\beta)\} - \{F(c^*)\pi(\beta,\propto) + [1-F(c^*)]\pi(\beta,\beta)\} \qquad (9)$$

or, alternatively,

$$\theta^* = F[c(\theta^*)] \qquad (10)$$

where $c(\theta)$ is the value of c associated with that individual who is indifferent between the two strategies when a proportion θ of the population pursue strategy $\propto$. At θ^*, the number of individuals pursuing strategy $\propto$ makes it worthwhile for precisely that fraction, θ^*, to pursue strategy $\propto$. A corner equilibrium is defined by

$$\pi(\propto,\beta) - \pi(\beta,\beta) < c_{\min}$$

When everyone is pursuing β, it pays the individual for whom the cost of pursuing $\propto$ is the least to pursue β. Another equilibrium is defined by

$$\pi(\propto,\propto) - \pi(\beta,\propto) > c_{\max}$$

When everyone is pursuing $\propto$, it pays the individual for whom the cost of pursuing $\propto$ is the highest to pursue $\propto$.

It is apparent that if

$$\pi(\propto,\propto) - \pi(\propto,\beta) - \pi(\beta,\propto) - \pi(\beta,\propto) + \pi(\beta,\beta) > 0$$

then as more individuals pursue $\propto$, the expected return to pursuing $\propto$ increases. There may exist multiple equilibria as illustrated in figures 19.4 and 19.5. A sufficient condition for the existence of multiple equilibria is that

$$\pi(\propto,\beta) - \pi(\beta,\beta) < c_{\min} \qquad (a)$$

$$\pi(\propto,\propto) - (\propto,\beta) > c_{\max} \qquad (b)$$

(a) and (b) ensure that there exist two corner equilibria.

The analysis so far has focussed on steady-states. If for generations the

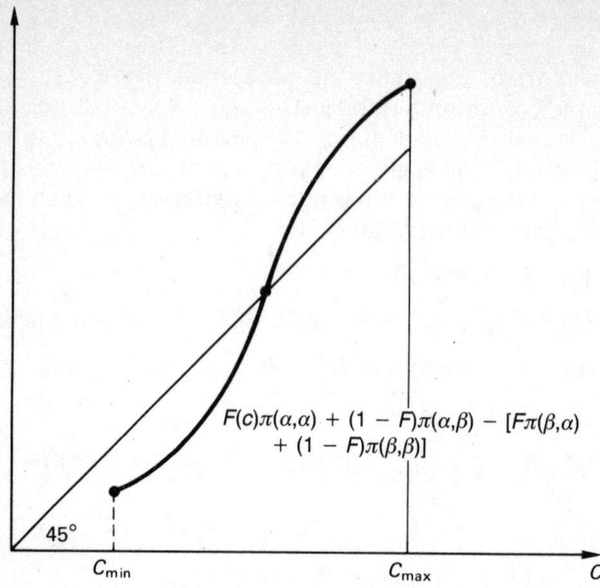

Figure 19.4 Multiple equilibria in willingness to innovate (corner solutions)

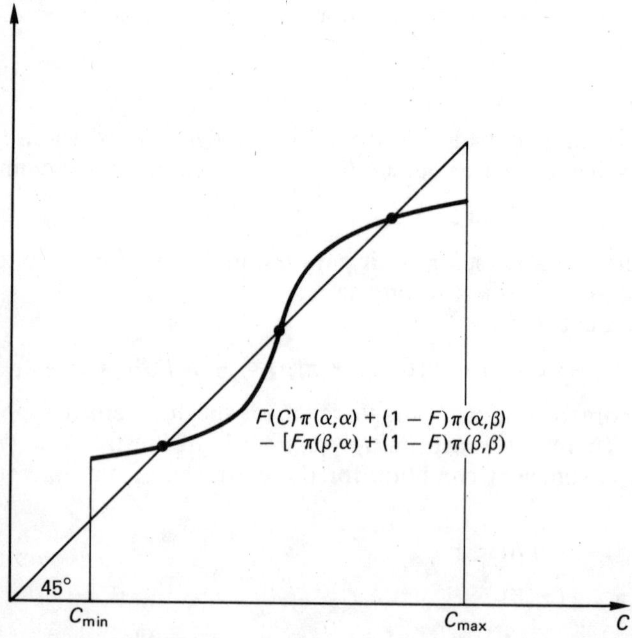

Figure 19.5 Multiple equilibria in willingness to innovate (interior solutions)

fraction of those who have acted innovatively is θ^*, it is plausible that individuals both know this and come to expect that the chances that the next individual they encounter will act innovatively is θ^*. But this does not explain how the equilibrium is attained. How do individuals come to know $\theta(t)$, and, even were it possible for them to know $\theta(t)$, how do they use that information to predict what $\theta(t+1)$ will be?

The great strength of the models discussed in section 2 is that they explicitly model a learning process. The particular learning process modeled has the property that, even in the steady-state, individuals never learn about the aggregate value of θ^* defined above. In some contexts, however, it is plausible to assume that the dispersion of beliefs about the aggregate value of θ decreases over time, and that a model similar to the one described in this section may provide a good description of the steady-states.

4. Other Perspectives

We have repeatedly shown externalities associated with technical change giving rise to positive feedbacks, which in turn give rise to multiple innovation/bureaucratic equilibria. Externalities similar to those discussed earlier can arise from several other sources. In this section, we analyze situations in which the distribution of characteristics in the population is affected not by decisions, but by either processes of taste acquisition or natural selection.

4.1 Tastes

It is not only capacities and beliefs which are learned, as was emphasized in the previous two sections, but also tastes. Tastes for innovation or for routinization can be acquired. Scitovsky (1976) has emphasized the basic psychological tension between 'novelty' and 'excitement' on the one hand, and 'comfort' or 'routineness' on the other. Those who like change become impatient in an environment in which they are asked to do repetitive, routine tasks. On the other hand, workers who are accustomed to routine tasks often complain when they are assigned to jobs requiring non-routine behavior. How the tension between novelty and routine gets resolved can be affected by the environment. A basically innovative personality placed in a bureaucratic environment may become a routine lover.

Though the details of the mechanisms of preference formation and change are not fully understood, many observers have noted that intrinsic preferences change,[18] particularly in intra-organizational contexts. Consider, for instance, an intra-organizational context where there are two types of managers, innovators and bureaucrats. While the latter enjoy routines and well-established patterns of behavior, the former enjoy change. If tastes are acquired then junior workers will tend to duplicate their superiors' preferences. Different kinds of preferences can, therefore, generate externalities.

4.2 Birth and Death Processes

Another aspect of organizations which we now examine is that new organizations appear to inherit some of the traits of the organizations which have spawned them. That is, an organization spawned by an innovative organization will be more innovative than an organization spawned by a bureaucratic organization. Note, however, that since the creation of a new organization is, in some sense, an innovative act, it seems reasonable that new organizations are more likely to be innovative than bureaucratic, and as organizations age they are more likely to become bureaucratic.

Let x denote the fraction of innovative organizations. Let $b^1(x)$ and $b^2(x)$ denote the birth rates innovative firms associated respectively with an innovative and a bureaucratic firm. Let $d(x)$ denote the death rate of innovative firms. Then equilibrium in the fraction of innovative firms is represented by

$$xb^1(x) + (1-x)b^2(x) = xd(x) \tag{11}$$

which can be restated as

$$x = b^2(x)/[d(x) - b^1(x) + b^2(x)] = c(x) \tag{12}$$

The derivatives of d, b^1 and b^2 (denoted respectively by d_x, b^1_x and b^2_x) have ambiguous signs in general. For instance, if innovative firms simply become bureaucratic with age, at some constant rate, then $d_x = 0$. If the number of innovative firms increases the effective degree of competition, then $d_x > 0$. If, on the other hand, bureaucrats make the life of innovators more difficult, $d_x < 0$. The sign of b^2_x is also ambiguous. While it is reasonable to postulate that an increase in the fraction of innovative firms decreases the profitability of bureaucratic behavior, it is not apparent whether low profits of bureaucratic firms spawn more births of innovative firms (because the relative gains to those with more innovative characteristics striking out on their own becomes more apparent), or whether low profits spawn fewer births of innovative firms (because the apparent lack of profitable opportunities attracts less entry).

In general, therefore, $c(x)$ can take on a variety of shapes. It can be, at least through a range, upward sloping (similar to the curve in figure 19.1), giving rise to multiple social equilibria. There may be a stable bureaucratic equilibrium, an equilibrium with a preponderance of bureaucratic firms and another stable innovative equilibrium with a preponderance of innovative firms. This is because, within the bureaucratic environment, it simply does not pay to be very innovative; and within innovative environments, bureaucrats cannot easily survive.

5. The Technological Perspective

The simple neoclassical model, which predicts a convergence of rates of growth, employs a number of stringent assumptions. We do not wish to overemphasize the contrast between the technological perspective and the perspectives discussed in previous sections. In particular, several of the arguments for positive feedbacks were based on technological considerations, on the externalities which arise between the amount of innovation in one sector and productivity in another. Our focus, here, is on certain properties of economic aggregates, rather than the behavior of individual units (individuals, organizations) which was the center of concern in preceding sections. Research in this area has attempted to identify what alternative technological assumptions give rise to multiple equilibria, e.g., one equilibrium in which there is a high rate of technological change and another in which there is a low rate.

Three aspects of technology which give rise to multiple equilibria have been identified.

1 Much of technological learning is a by-product of production (Arrow, 1962). Learning curves associated with different products and different technologies may differ markedly.
2 Much of technological learning is localized. That is, accretions in knowledge that are relevant to one technology may have little bearing on other technologies. Spill-overs are far from uniform (Atkinson and Stiglitz, 1969).
3 The process of learning is, itself, learned. Thus, just as Adam Smith emphasized the importance of specialization in production, the importance of specialization in learning has become increasingly apparent. Just as the worker who specializes in producing pins becomes more proficient in pin production unless he suffers from boredom, so too might the individual who specializes in research become more proficient in doing that.[19]

These observations concerning technological learning have important implications for economic theory and policy.[20] Among them are the following.

5.1 Multiplicity of Equilibria

It is possible to show that one consequence of the above technological hypotheses is that there may be multiple long-run equilibria. Assume, for instance, that more capital-intensive technologies have a greater capacity for learning.[21] That is, the rate of increase in productivity associated with any increment in production is greater in such technologies. Then some economy may be trapped in a low-level equilibrium, with a low capital–labor ratio and a low rate of technological progress, even though there exists another equilibrium with a high capital–labor ratio and a high rate of technological progress. Thus, this model provides an explanation of the non-convergence of rates of growth as well as levels of income.

There is one problem with this explanation. In the context of an international economy in which knowledge, and individuals who have the knowledge, can move across national borders, less capital-intensive economies have potential access to the information available in more developed countries. At the same time, however, the theory of localized technological change may provide a part of the explanation for why such knowledge, developed by more developed economies, may have limited relevance for LDCs. The latter face the direct costs of adapting these technologies to local conditions, such as a higher variance in the quality of inputs. Those with the less capital-intensive technologies may be deterred from using technologies developed in the more developed countries.

Learning-to-learn effects strengthen the latter set of conclusions. Previous lack of experience may limit the capacity of individuals in some economies to take full advantage of possibilities for productivity improvement associated with certain technological changes.

Finally, if changes in technology in the more developed countries make it increasingly difficult for those in LDCs to benefit (even with a lag) from the advances, either because they require technical skills on the part of workers which are scarce or because they require a degree of quality control in inputs which LDCs find hard to attain, then there may be a growing gap in living standards and productivity between the poorest of the LDCs and the more developed countries.[22]

5.2 Non-convexities and the Disadvantages of Being Late

As Arrow recognized in his early essay, learning-by-doing gives rise to non-convexities. These non-convexities are exacerbated by the presence of localized learning and learning-to-learn effects.

Non-convexities are important for at least two reasons. First, they imply that specialization is often advantageous. While, in the absence of non-convexities, a country might pursue a gradual process of transition from, say, labor-intensive to capital-intensive technologies, non-convexities may make this gradual approach less desirable, providing an alternative basis for a 'Big-Push' theory of development. The fact that a gradual transition is not desirable may serve as an impediment to development for the very poorest countries: in order to undertake a Big-Push, greater sacrifices in current consumption are required than these countries might be willing to make.[23]

Moreover, the sunk costs invariably associated with technological progress, whether arising from learning effects or expenditures on R&D, create an entry barrier which puts latecomers (the LDCs) at a marked disadvantage. In the presence of sunk costs, potential competition will not in general drive profits (rents on existing innovations) to zero (Stiglitz, 1988); it is certainly possible that there will be periods in which innovation rents increase, and accordingly, in which the gap in income between the innovating countries and the non-innovators may increase.

6. Concluding Remarks

6.1 A General Mathematical Formulation

There is a simple mathematical model underlying all of the formulations discussed in sections 1 to 5. Consider an economy in which individuals are characterized by some variable (say the degree of innovativeness). For simplicity, we shall assume that the variable can take on only discrete values, and for concreteness, we shall further assume it can take on only two values. The proportion of the population with characteristic i at date t is given by $x_i(t)$. Clearly, $0 \leq x_i(t) \leq 1$ and $\Sigma x_i = 1$. Thus the economy at date t is described by the vector $x(t) = \{x_1(t), x_2(t), \ldots\}$ representing the distribution of characteristics.

The economy is characterized by certain transition rules, which specify the proportion of those with characteristic i at date t who have (or whose descendants have) characteristic j at time $t+1$. These transition rules themselves may be – and in general will be – a function of the population mix at time t (and possibly at previous periods as well). Thus, we write,

$$x(t+1) = A[x(t), x(t-1), x(t-2), \ldots]x(t)$$

If A were independent of x then, under standard conditions, there would exist a unique steady-state equilibrium vector x^* satisfying

$$x^* = Ax^*$$

But the environment – here, the vectors $\{x(t), x(t,-1), \ldots\}$ – determines the nature of the transitions. A generally depends on the x's, and accordingly, there may be multiple solutions to the equation

$$x^* = A(x^*,x^*, \ldots)x^*$$

each of which can be thought of as a social equilibrium.[24]

The above description is obviously too general. We need to derive the transition rule from structural models, to explain why, and the circumstances in which, the proportion of individuals in the population with a given characteristic increases or decreases. That is precisely what the various models discussed in previous sections attempt to do.

6.2 Strategic Considerations

It should be apparent that the theories of social equilibrium we have put forth differ in a fundamental conceptual way from standard game theory, in which multiple equilibria may arise as well. In typical game theoretic models, individuals arrive at beliefs about what their rivals will do, and therefore about what is optimal for them to do, on the basis of introspection. They know the pay-offs, and the set of available strategies, and they believe that their opponents are rational. They can infer, therefore, what their rivals will do. However, some critical problems remain. For instance, there are no satisfactory theories describing the circumstances which lead to different possible Nash equilibria, or indeed, how equilibrium is attained in the presence of multiple Nash equilibria.

We would argue that most real-life situations are too complicated for individuals to feel confident, simply through introspection, about what their rivals will do. They seldom know their rivals' pay-offs, and they may not even be sure about the set of strategies available to those with whom they interact. This is particularly true in contexts where innovation is important, where actions entail thinking up something that has not been done before. But even when the pay-offs and available strategies are known ('common knowledge'), it may be difficult to infer what one's rival will do: even a simple game like chess is too complicated to 'solve.' Moreover, recent arguments by Reny (1988) and Binmore (1985) cast doubt on the underlying hypotheses of standard game theory. They have identified a variety of important situations in which the postulates of rationality and common knowledge are inconsistent.

6.3 Externalities and Multiplicity

There is an old saying that some of the best things in life are free. Only a fraction of our interactions are completely regulated by the price system. Any parent recognizes that his child learns attitudes not only from his parents but from peers, and from a wide variety of environmental influences. More than that, one picks up modes of thought and behavior. In all cultures, information is constantly exchanged among individuals; but the nature of the information exchanged may differ. In Silicon Valley in California, information about the most recent developments in computers is exchanged; on Main Street, on the other hand, it may be the latest piece of juicy gossip. Whether economically motivated or not, such interactions may have a profound effect on economic behavior and equilibrium. There are, to use the economist's traditional jargon, important externalities arising out of these social interactions. This is not to say that social interactions are not affected by economic returns: the direction of conversation – the greater talk about computers in Silicon Valley – may reflect the greater economic returns there to such information. Still, the central point that we have emphasized, the possibility of multiple equilibria, remains.

What is required for success in the development process is the transformation of a society into an innovative and adaptive culture; and what is required for that is more than the shipment of capital, the construction of oil refineries and tire factories. Indeed, some of the central roles that the government has played (for instance, in creating a large, entrenched and privileged bureaucracy attracting a significant part of the economy's pool of talent) may have served, in the long run, to suppress the development of such a culture. If this argument is correct, it has profound implications for how we should think of development strategies.

NOTES

Support from the National Science Foundation and the Hoover Institution is gratefully acknowledged.

1 Even if LDCs adopt the best practices of developed countries with a lag, according to this view, the *rates* of technological progress will be the same and differences in levels of per capita income will then be related also to the length of the lag in the diffusion of technology.
2 Both authors have had the good fortune of interacting with Carlos Díaz-Alejandro. Stiglitz's interests in development were stimulated by him, first as colleagues at Yale and later through the contact they kept up. Sah had the pleasure of discussing with Carlos Díaz-Alejandro some of the mysteries of economic history. Our emphasis on his intellectual contributions is not meant to understate his many other rich dimensions. He brought to all aspects of his life the same liveliness, humor, excitement, openness, breadth of perspective and sense of balance combined with a seriousness of purpose and a sense of commitment that he brought to his academic work.
3 The difficulty of ruling out the possibility of such multiple equilibria becomes much greater when many factor and commodity markets are considered together.
4 Though these theories did not articulate precisely how they differed from the standard Arrow–Debreu model (nor did they see the need to do so, since the point they made was perfectly clear), the central importance of the assumption of an incomplete set of markets should be clear. The users of steel would not find it profitable to construct their plants to make steel-using products in the absence of the availability of steel, while the producers of steel would not find it profitable to manufacture steel in the absence of users. Stiglitz (1987) discusses the conditions which make it likely that this kind of externality can be internalized.
5 We require $\gamma_1 - w(0) < c < \gamma_1 - w(1)$, a condition which can easily be satisfied. In these circumstances, there exists an interior equilibrium which, under most natural specifications of dynamics, is unstable.
6 Again, we can Pareto rank the equilibria. The difference between the incomes of the more able certified and uncertified is fixed; and as more individuals are certified, the wage of the uncertified decreases so that equilibria with fewer certified individuals will Pareto dominate.
7 Multiplicity of equilibria obviously arise in many other contexts as well. Diamond (1982) and Drazen (1987) have emphasized the importance of positive feedback in search models. If more employers are looking for employees, it pays workers to search more; and if more workers are searching, it may pay more employers to search.
8 That will be the case if θ is sufficiently small. If m is small, or if γ_1 is sufficiently small, then it is possible that this condition will be satisfied for all values of θ.
9 The latter is particularly important, given the possibility, noted already, of Pareto-inferior equilibria.
10 An extensive literature deals with expectation-formation processes. For alterna-

tive views on rational expectations, for instance, see Frydman and Phelps (1983).

11 Slight modifications of the model deal with cases in which the individual makes many choices each period, or in which longer term choices are entailed because, for instance, there are fixed costs associated with choices.

12 These utilities obviously vary across individuals. Also, they depend on economy-wide variables; for example, U's depend on $y(t)$. The conclusions drawn below hold if, within the relevant ranges of the parameters and for most (but not all) individuals, the reward function exhibits the property assumed in the text.

13 Some of these steady-states may be stable while others may be unstable. Sah shows that some of the sufficient conditions which guarantee stable interior steady-states are extremely mild. Explicit relationships such as (7) also provide a basis for analyzing comparative statics of steady-states with respect to changes in parameters. For previously unavailable results on such comparative statics of systems of dynamic equations, see Sah (1987b).

14 The number of individuals who are innovative acts like an atmospheric externality.

15 It is, of course, possible that diminishing returns set in. With a fixed stock of ideas, the marginal contribution of an additional innovator may diminish the gain of a number of other innovators. We are suggesting that, in many instances, this effect may be outweighed by the externality effect which is the unappropriated contribution of any innovator to the stock of available ideas.

16 This is illustrated by recent experiences in the US airline industry. In the days of airline regulation, some airlines developed organizational structures suited for dealing with the Federal bureaucracy; these thrived, and there was little room for more market-oriented airlines. Following deregulation, the latter thrived, while the former, not well suited to the competitive environment, languished.

17 Other aspects of such models, including their similarities and differences with models which have been used in various other contexts, are discussed in Sah (1988b).

18 That is, these changes are distinct from, for instance, changes in long-term choices which individuals make as a result of their beliefs or pecuniary trade-offs.

19 There are obvious dangers from excessive specialization. Specialized individuals may be less able to adapt to changes that are sufficiently far removed from their specialization, though their greater specialized knowledge may make them more able to adapt to changes that are within their sphere of specialization. The trade-offs between specialization and adaptability have not yet been adequately studied.

20 Related concerns are discussed in Lucas (1985), Romer (1986) and Sah and Stiglitz (1988).

21 Lucas has emphasized the differences in learning capacities associated with different products. He assumes limited spill-overs across national boundaries, but perfect spill-overs within a country [otherwise, as Dasgupta and Stiglitz (1988) show, there cannot exist a competitive equilibrium]. Accordingly, equilibrium will be associated with different countries specializing in different commodities. The more developed countries have the advantage of being able to choose those commodities with better learning curves. But what is important is not rates of growth in physical productivity, but in incomes; changes in relative prices may partially, or more than, offset these differences. Thus, if all individuals had unitary price elasticities for all commodities, changes in relative prices would precisely offset changes in relative productivities. See Skeath (1988).

22 To put it another way, the lag between the state of technology of the developed and the less developed countries is *endogenous*, and changes in technology have increased that lag.

23 That is, not only may multiple steady-states arise in a *descriptive* growth model, but there may be multiple steady-states in an optimal growth model. To which steady-state one converges depends on the initial conditions.

24 If the population consists of individuals of various ages, then the dynamics can be described by the fraction of those who are of age t and type i who become type j at age $t + 1$. There is thus a transition matrix for each age cohort. This approach provides a much richer description of the dynamics of the economy than an approach which simply focusses on the aggregates. See for example Sah (1987a).

REFERENCES

Arrow, K. J. 1962: The economic implications of learning by doing. *Review of Economic Studies*, 29, 155–93.

Atkinson, A. B. and Stiglitz, J. E. 1969: A new view of technological change. *Economic Journal*, 79, 573–8.

Baumol, W. J. 1986: Productivity growth, convergence and welfare: what the long-run data show. *American Economic Review*, 76, 1072–85.

Binmore, K. G. 1985: Modeling Rational Players. Mimeo, London School of Economics and University of Pennsylvania.

Dasgupta, P. and Stiglitz, J. E. 1985: Sunk Costs, Competition and Welfare. Mimeo, Princeton University.

Dasgupta, P. and Stiglitz, J. E. 1988: Learning-by-doing, market structure, and industrial and trade policies. *Oxford Economic Papers* (forthcoming).

Debreu, G. 1959: *Theory of Value*. New York: Wiley.

Diamond, P.A. 1982: Aggregate demand management in search equilibrium. *Journal of Political Economy*, 90, 881–94.

Drazen, A. 1987: Reciprocal externality models of low employment, *European Economic Review*, 31, 436–43.

Frydman, R. and Phelps, E. S. (eds.), 1983: *Individual Forecasting and Aggregate Outcomes*. Cambridge: Cambridge University Press.

Lucas, R. E. Jr. 1985: On the Mechanics of Economic Development, Marshall Lectures, Cambridge University.

Reny, P. J. 1988: Common knowledge and extensive form games. *Journal of Economic Perspectives* (forthcoming).

Romer, Paul 1986: Increasing returns and long run growth. *Journal of Political Economy*, 94, 1002–38.

Rosenstein-Rodan, P.N. 1943: Problems of industrialization of Eastern and South-Eastern Europe. *Economic Journal*, 53, 204–7.

Sah, R. K. 1985: What Affects the Level of Honesty in an Economy. Working Paper Series D, School of Organization and Management, Yale University, New Haven.

Sah, R. K. 1987a: Persistence and Pervasiveness of Corruption: New Perspectives. Paper presented at the Conference on Political Economy, The World Bank, Washington, DC, June 1987.

Sah, R. K. 1987b: Results for Economic Comparative Statics of Steady-States of Higher-Order Discrete Dynamic Systems. Working Paper, Yale University, New Haven.

Sah, R. K. 1988a: Social Osmosis and Patterns of Crime: A Dynamic Economic Analysis. Working paper, Yale University, New Haven.

Sah, R. K. 1988b: Social Osmosis and Patterns of Observed Economic Behavior: Crime, Corruption and Some Other Social Phenomena. Working paper, Yale University, New Haven.

Sah, R. K. and Stiglitz, J. E. 1988: Technological Learning, Social Learning and Technological Change. Paper presented to the World Congress of the International Economic Association, New Delhi, December 1986. Forthcoming in proceedings.

Scitovsky, T. 1976: *The Joyless Economy*, New York: Oxford University Press.

Skeath, S.E. 1988: Learning, Price Effects and Growth. Mimeo, Princeton University.

Solow, R. M. 1956: A contribution to the theory of economic growth. *Quarterly Journal of Economics*, 70, 65–94.

Starrett, D. 1976: Social institutions, imperfect information and the distribution of income. *Quarterly Journal of Economics*, 90, 216–84.

Stiglitz, J. E. 1974: Theories of discrimination and economic policy. In G. M. von Furstenberg et al. (eds.), *Patterns of Racial Discrimination*, vol. II. Lexington: Lexington Books.

Stiglitz, J. E. 1975: The theory of 'screening' education, and the distribution of income. *American Economic Review*, 283–300.

Stiglitz, J. E. 1984: Information, screening and welfare. In M. Boyer and R. Khilstrom (eds.), *Bayesian Models in Economic Theory*, Amsterdam: North–Holland, pp. 209–39.

Stiglitz, J. E. 1987: Learning to learn, localized learning and technological progress. In P. Dasgupta and P. Stoneman (eds.), *Economic Policy and Technological Performance*, Cambridge: Centre for Economic Policy Research, Cambridge University Press, pp. 125–53.

Stiglitz, J. E. 1988: Technological change, sunk costs and competition. *Brookings Papers on Economic Activity* (forthcoming).

COMMENT

Frances Stewart

Carlos had that very unusual quality of making people – even those only rather distantly connected with him – feel they were special. Since I first met him nearly 20 years ago, there has been an intermittent string of witty postcards (usually signed Lord Carlos – the English version of his signature), punctuated by occasional visits, when his rare life-giving quality added sparkle to normal humdrum existence.

He spent 1 year at Oxford where he performed a unique feat. To those who do not know Oxford let me explain that Queen Elizabeth House and Nuffield are at least as far apart as North and South, monetarist and structuralist. Locals rarely dare thread their perilous way along the Cornmarket and up St Giles. Visitors have had contacts and been welcome in both places. But only in the case of Carlos did *both* institutions feel that he truly belonged to us. Perhaps it is no accident that while in Oxford he wrote the article entitled 'Unshackled or Unhinged'.

The paper by Sah and Stiglitz fits well into Carlos' eclectic and non-confrontational mould, including non-neo-classical ideas, yet using some more 'mainstream' methodology, including maximization as an organizing concept. The paper is non-ideological in the good sense. As one would expect it is highly stimulating, full of ideas and completely lacking in empirical support. On the whole I agree with many of the ideas, and the overall conclusions. In particular:

1 that technology and innovation are historically based, and the characteristics of an innovation will depend on the context in which it is made;
2 that learning is tremendously important;
3 that dynamic and not static comparative advantage is the relevant concept;
4 that departures from resource allocation derived from static comparative advantage may be justified;
5 that there may be a case for government intervention in support of industries with strong learning potential, and in support of research and development.

These ideas are not new, but they are important. The paper, however, is disappointing in that the assumptions and the models are rather oversimplistic, while the argument is presented as if most of the literature, theoretical and empirical – with the exception of the Atkinson and Stiglitz article of 1970 – did not exist. The rich empirical literature of the 1970s on technical change and learning in developing countries, together with some theoretical developments, needs to be incorporated into the argument if such models are to add to our understanding of technical change, and especially to be relevant for policy makers.

Two areas are particularly in need of further work and more precision – those of learning and externalities.

Learning is treated by Sah and Stiglitz as an undifferentiated phenomenon, a produced commodity, the outcome of specialization and resources devoted to its production.

Empirical and theoretical work by such authors as Rosenberg (1976); Katz (1984), Lall (1981), Binswanger and Ruttan (1978) and others has shown that there is a great variety of types of learning and technical change in the course of development, including adaptation, imitation, minor and major innovations, all of which are produced by a variety of phenomena ranging from blue-collar innovation, specific in-firm R&D, purchases of outside technology from other firms, to the work of R&D institutes. The determinants of innovation have been shown to include attitudes and incentives, the market environment (including the nature and degree of competition) and the level and type of educated manpower. The accumulated level of output (the single determinant picked out by the main model presented by Sah and Stiglitz) is only one factor, and by itself not a guarantee of innovation and learning (see Bell et al., 1980).

These details might seem small-minded. After all, models must simplify reality. But the details are relevant because unless they are incorporated into the models, the wrong conclusions emerge. It follows that a model of learning, if it is to be useful for policy, must include the most important of these variables and not simply accumulated experience, or resources devoted to learning.

A second area where more careful conceptualization is needed, together with empirical investigation, is the question of how far learning is associated with externalities. In so far as learning is internal to the firm, it can be incorporated into the normal decision-making of firms. But if there is some overspill in benefits to other firms – especially of a diffuse nature as Sah and Stiglitz point out – then government intervention may be justified, in the form of subsidies or protection. There is also the question of whether, when there are external benefits from learning, these are confined to a particular industry, apply to all industries or to the economy as a whole. Again policy implications will vary. Sah and Stiglitz, in common with others, are imprecise on these issues, talking about 'diffuse externalities . . . important economies of scale associated with learning' as potential justification of government activity. One reason why the arguments of both the advocates of government intervention, and especially protection, and of the non-interventionist market supporters, are often imprecise, and sometimes incorrect, is the commonly loose reference to externalities associated with learning, with lack of the conceptual precision backed up by empirical evidence, which would provide guidance on the extent and nature of appropriate government intervention.

My final comment concerns the issue of technology choice and myopic rules. I agree with Sah and Stiglitz about the need to incorporate dynamic factors, especially learning, into technology choice. (There is also, and not just incidentally, a need to incorporate distributional factors into technology choice, which they ignore.) Whether and how dynamic factors, learning and technical change would alter technical choice will depend on the transferability of technology and price of technology transfer between firms, as well as the extent of innovation and whether it is differentially associated with alternative techniques. But the strong suggestion – which was also made by Paul Beckerman some years ago – that incorporating dynamic factors into technical choice would be likely to justify the choice of 'inappropriate' (i.e. capital-intensive) technologies is not warranted. This suggestion is based on the view that inappropriate technologies have more learning potential than appropriate technologies. Yet we now have abundant empirical evidence that appropriate technologies can realize considerable increases in productivity when attitudes favour innovation, and research and development efforts are applied specifically to them. This is illustrated, for example, by the literature on blending of new and traditional technologies, as well as by many other studies, covering many of the major industries in developing countries (see e.g. Bhalla and James, 1973; Kaplinsky, 1984; Pack, 1982).

Development economics is concerned with understanding the process of economic development, and with devising policy recommendations from this understanding. This requires – as Carlos was the first to recognize – that theory be firmly rooted in empirical reality. With a basis in the reality of developing countries, rigorous and innovative theory – of the type which Sah and Stiglitz excel in – can be exciting and useful. But without this basis, such modelling can discredit important insights and conclusions. In my view, the issues of development are too important to play games with.

REFERENCES

Bhalla, A.S. and James, D. (1973) Concepts of technological blending. *Application of New Technologies to Small Scale Activities*, Geneva: ILO.

Bell, R.M.D., Scott-Kemmis and W. Satyarakwit (1980) Learning and Technical Change in the Development of Manufacturing Industry: A Case Study of a Permanently Infant Industry. Mimeo, Science Policy Research Unit, University of Sussex.

Binswanger, H. and Ruttan, V. (1978) *Induced Innovation, Technology, Institutions and Development*. Baltimore: Johns Hopkins.

Kaplinsky, R. (1984) *Sugar Processing: The Development of a Third World Technology*. Intermediate Technology Publications.

Katz, J. (1984) Technological innovation, industrial organisation and cooperative

advantages of Latin American metal working industries In M. Fransman and K. King (eds.), *Technological Capability in the Third World*. London: Macmillan.
Lall, S. (1981) Indian technology exports and technological development. *The Annals of the American Academy of Political and Social Science*, 458.
Pack, H. (1982) Aggregate implications of factor substitution in industrial process. *Journal of Development Economics*, 11.
Rosenberg, N. (1976) *Perspectives on Technology*. Cambridge: Cambridge University Press.

Index

Indexed by Jackie McDermott